NIGER IBOS

BODY AND SPIRIT.

THIS MAN BELIEVED, AND HIS FELLOW VILLAGERS THOUGHT LIKEWISE, THAT, AFTER CERTAIN CEREMONIES, HE WAS HALF MAN AND HALF SPIRIT AND WAS TREATED ACCORDINGLY.

NIGER IBOS

A DESCRIPTION OF THE PRIMITIVE LIFE, CUSTOMS AND ANIMISTIC BELIEFS, &c., OF THE IBO PEOPLE OF NIGERIA BY ONE WHO, FOR THIRTY-FIVE YEARS, ENJOYED THE PRIVILEGE OF THEIR INTIMATE CONFIDENCE AND FRIENDSHIP

G. T. BASDEN

With 70 Illustrations and a Sketch Map
and
A new Bibliographical Note by
JOHN RALPH WILLIS

Routledge
Taylor & Francis Group
LONDON AND NEW YORK

First published **Frank Cass & Co. Ltd.**,
by arrangement with Seeley, Service & Co. Ltd.

First edition 1938
New impression with bibliographical note 1966

Published 2005 by Routledge
2 Park Square, Milton Park, Abingdon, Oxfordshire OX14 4RN
711 Third Avenue, New York, NY 10017

First issued in paperback 2014

Routledge is an imprint of the Taylor and Francis Group, an informa business

ISBN 13: 978-0-714-61633-9 (hbk)
ISBN 13: 978-0-415-76063-8 (pbk)

To
MY WIFE
*In Acknowledgement and Appreciation of all
she has done and been at Home
I dedicate this Book*

Diameter from seven to fourteen inches.

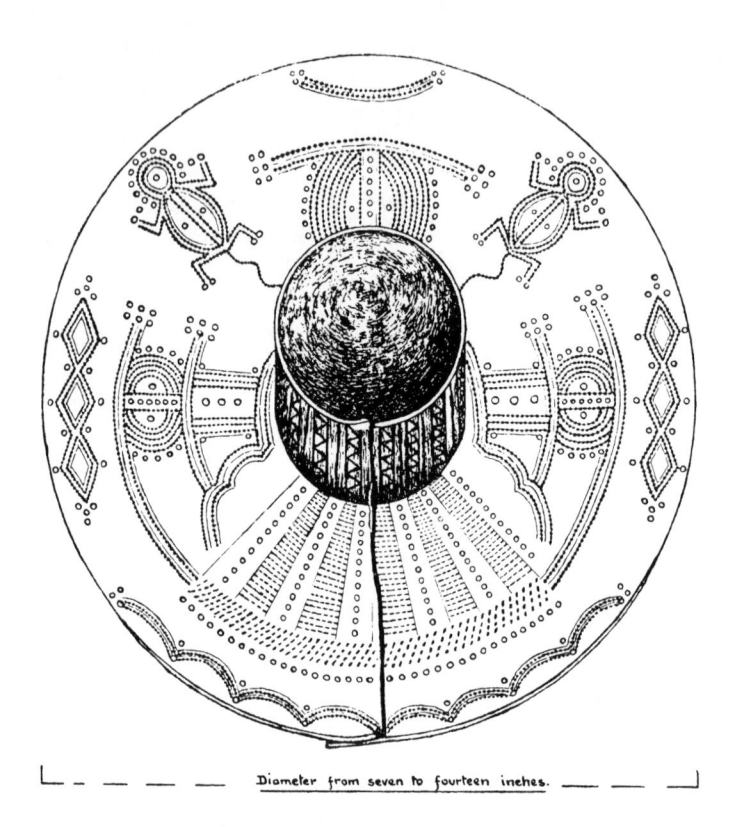

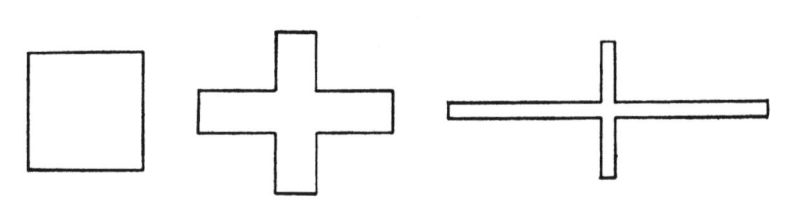

BRASS ANKLET "OGBA".
Below: The first three stages of the forging of the brass anklet.

FOREWORD

By Sir Walter Buchanan-Smith, C.M.G., M.C.

To Dr. Basden's many friends in Nigeria and elsewhere who had learnt, like myself, to appreciate the depth of his knowledge and the value of his advice, it was welcome news to hear that he was preparing this work on the lives and customs of the people of Iboland. The book now published is badly needed, and no one is better fitted than Dr. Basden to write it, for it comes to us with all the authority of one who has spent nearly forty years of faithful service in close contact with those about whom he writes and who has, moreover, gained their confidence to a degree not very usual even where so warm a friend as the Author is concerned. How great has been that confidence the book bears evidence, for it is a veritable storehouse of information, some at least of which must have involved much reluctant unlocking of doors previously regarded as permanently closed to all strangers. The result is a work which should commend itself as useful now, and which may be even more valuable to the Ibo and his friends when much that is here recorded shall have vanished into the mists of a remote past.

In a task of this nature, it is almost inevitable that an author should reach conclusions which will not commend themselves to some of his readers in their entirety. Dr. Basden has, however, avoided controversy to the best of his ability and is never dogmatic. Part, it is true, of the altered outlook of the Ibo, to which he refers, is due, no doubt, to the administrative reforms which have been in progress for the last few years. Their apparent initial success owes much, under the inspiration and guidance of a great Governor, to the patient investigations which have been carried out by the Residents and their Staffs into the structure of native government, such as it was, and native institutions in the past. It is unavoidable that some of the results of these investigations should be subjected to criticism, and no infallibility is claimed for them, but, at least, no opponent of the system established on the authority of Sir Donald Cameron can call it inelastic and, where mistakes have been made, it should not be beyond the wit of the administration to make the necessary readjustments.

FOREWORD

It is, however, pleasant to observe that even where Dr. Basden is least optimistic as to the future he has, at any rate, no doubts as to the intentions of the Administrative Officers, nor of their very real anxiety, in the difficulties that beset them, to do their best for the welfare of their people.

Much of this book is written in the present tense, but I hope that its readers will not, therefore, overlook the Author's warning that he is treating of the past, and that they will not take it for granted that the worst horrors here described are still of constant occurrence. During the last forty years, the people of whom the Author writes have been rushed through stages of development which took us many centuries to achieve, and I think that it will be generally conceded that a contemporary account of the barbarities practised in England a few hundred years ago, if at all accurate, would not make very pleasant reading.

We cannot, therefore, be too critical of the Ibo excesses in the days when they first came to our notice, and it is not their fault if their grim past is a little nearer than our own and so looms a little more terrible. It should be sufficient to remember that, with the exception of a survival here and there, which seems the more startling for its rarity, the worst days have definitely passed away, and the eyes of the Ibos are looking forward to the future and not backward. Those of us who know best this cheery, intelligent and lovable people like to believe that their place in the West Africa of the future will be very high. When that time comes, I hope and think that they will still remember the name of Dr. Basden as that of one who, in his time, worked harder than most to help them on their way.

W. BUCHANAN-SMITH.

1938

FOREWORD

By the Rt. Rev. A. C. Onyeabo

I HAVE CAREFULLY gone through these chapters and am greatly astonished with the immense amount of material that Dr. Basden has been able to collect, and the accuracy of the information obtained on many important subjects connected with the customs of our Ibo People.

Materials have been collected from different parts of the country and, what is set down, either reveals a generally prevailing principle in the practice and customs, or is a record of observation in one particular part.

Attempts have been made from time to time by enthusiastic Ibo natives to write something on the history of the country, but every effort has failed, on the ground that none was able to travel widely enough to obtain full and first-hand information. This difficulty Dr. Basden has been able to overcome and he is, himself, an indefatigable scholar.

His missionary spirit and friendly disposition have drawn him so close to the natives, that doors of guarded shrines have been thrown open to him, and information freely given of secrets which have been held sacred for ages.

To appreciate the great effort, one simply needs to study the Introduction. I am sure that every Ibo reader will be deeply grateful for what Dr. Basden has accomplished.

A. C. Onyeabo.

Ebu Owerri.

1938

FOREWORD

By the Rev. V. N. Umunna

IN THIS BOOK, the Author, who has spent over thirty-five years among the Ibos of Nigeria, gives an interesting account of the life of the people. From many points of consideration, he is qualified to undertake this task for, when he first arrived at Onitsha in 1900, and for many, many years after, he and other pioneers had to do all their work by walking from place to place and were thus enabled to come into direct contact with the people. By coming into close contact, the people took them into their confidence and regarded them as friends. This book is an attempt, on the right lines, to preserve some sound knowledge of the customs, mode of life, and religious ceremonies of the Ibos. Without such a record, many such customs and ceremonies will be lost in the limbo of forgetfulness and ignorance. As the old is fast passing away, and is giving place to the new, the book is, therefore, commendable. It is a record of personal experiences, and there is not the slightest thought to offend; the purpose of the book is clearly stated in the Introduction. The chapters and the illustrations depict the general life of the Ibos; some matters of minor importance are not made the subject of the book. His knowledge of the people was recognised by the Nigerian Government when he was appointed to take the place of the late Chief I. O. Mba as the representative of the Ibos in the Legislative Council. In this present work, he has made another fitting legacy to the Ibo People. If the rush of the petrol age will allow it, further observations into the life of the Ibos may be made, and the record of customs, perhaps, be made more complete. In the meanwhile, this book is an indispensable standard work for all who would gain an enduring knowledge of the life of the Ibos.

V. Nwora Umunna.

Awka.

1938

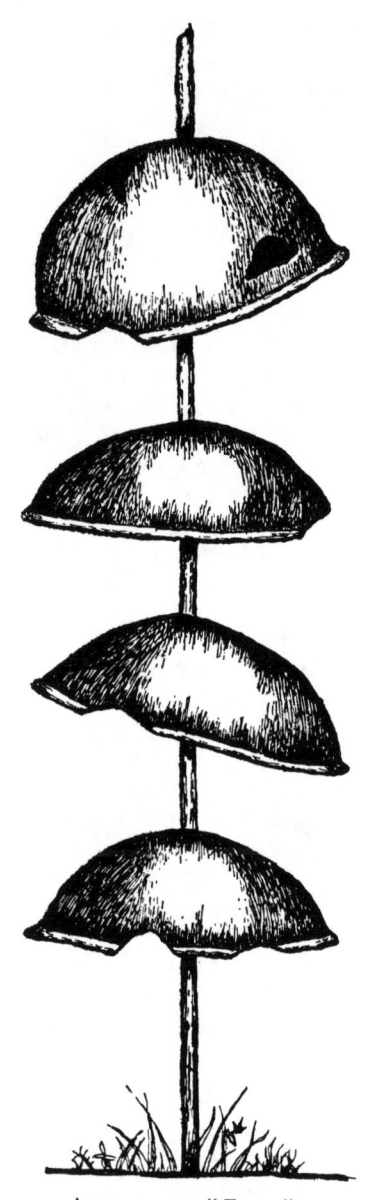

ALUSI CALLED "EKWU".

It is the god of a woman whose husband holds the "Ozo" title. Three or four shallow pots threaded on a stick fixed upright in the ground.

INTRODUCTION

THE IBO NATION ranks as one of the largest in the whole of Africa. Its numbers have been estimated as high as four, and never below three millions. These people occupy a very considerable area of the south-eastern corner of Nigeria and, of late years, their influence has extended farther afield. They are making a marked impression on the adjacent tribes, the Efiks, Ibibios and others and, also, in distant cosmopolitan centres such as Jos, Kano and even Lagos. Their readiness to travel and tenacity of purpose, especially when seeking employment, have carried many of them far beyond their native environment. When abroad, they maintain close contact, cemented and sustained by a strong tribal bond of union. Whatever the conditions, the Ibo immigrants adapt themselves to meet them, and it is not long before they make their presence felt in the localities where they settle. It has been remarked, that they make " good colonists ". This they do in a quiet, unobtrusive, but, nevertheless, effective manner. They build their own churches and schools, and support the teachers and clergy sent to minister to them. Meantime, after catering for their immediate needs, they send the bulk of their gains to their homes to be used for building better houses in preparation for their return, and to assist in schemes for the general benefit of their own village communities. They are very generous in their gifts, as well as being astute in business affairs.

Before the British Government assumed control on January 1, 1900, very little was known about the Ibo People and less still of their country.

All my attempts to trace the origin of the name " Ibo " have been unsuccessful. My most reliable informants have been able to offer no other alternative than that it is most probably an abbreviation of a longer name connected with an ancestor long since forgotten. The Rev. S. A. Crowther, writing in 1854, states that he inquired of Odiri, the son of King Akazua of Onitsha, who replied " that the people of Idah, and higher up the river (Niger), not knowing the difference, call them all Igbo, which is the name of a small town called ' Igbo Inam ' ; that their country is called ' Igbo ', but, in fact, they are all

INTRODUCTION

Elugu of Igbo or Ibo and that this (Onitsha Waterside) is the market attended by the Elugu people from the interior ".[1]

The mention of "Elugu", and the list of towns given, appears to be no more than an indication that the interior country is hilly, in the same way that the hinterland of Asaba is known locally as "Enu-Ani" (highland).

The first twenty years of the present century were palmy days for the anthropologist. Such opportunities for research work will never be forthcoming again, since there is scarcely a corner left untouched by foreign influence, and it would be difficult to find a group of people totally unacquainted with the white man. The generation that represented primitive Ibo belief, with its ancient laws and customs, has almost died out. Chiefs of the old type are being rapidly replaced by their educated sons, educated, that is, in the sense that their fathers never were nor could be. The younger generation is learning to read and write and to adopt European ideas and fashions in every detail of life, clothes, houses and pastimes. In many towns to-day will be found club and private tennis courts, football fields and many other indications of modern life. At the moment, the balance of life has been, and is being, seriously disturbed. The younger generation has shed old manners and customs freely, and somewhat hastily. They are ardently grasping at all things new and foreign. Not all, by any means, can discriminate between the wheat and the chaff. On the other hand, if treated with patience and sympathy, they will develop powers of discrimination whereby they will learn wisdom and become stabilised once more.

What I am leading up to is the fact that native law and custom has been almost completely disrupted ; indeed, as a leading Ibo man said recently, "there is no longer *any* fixed law or custom". Much is in the melting-pot ; much has perished altogether. To put the situation plainly, ancient native law and custom cannot exist side by side nor intermingle with the principles of the British Government. Considerable interest has been aroused, and much said and written of recent years, on the subject of conserving what is good in native custom. The plea is reasonable, and welcomed by every foreigner who has the well-being of the native at heart. The weakness lies in the fact that it is a wish largely devoid of substantial support. There are a number of reasons for this of which a few may be quoted.

The *real* and vital cause of its weakness is that the native, himself, is the deciding factor. He believes that he best knows what he wants, and he is unwilling for the choice to be dictated

INTRODUCTION

by the foreigner. The native asks to be left unfettered in his selection of customs in order to be free to choose those that suit his natural environment and temperament. The idealist who advocates that this or that custom should be conserved may as well save his breath for some more profitable effort. The native will not retain anything which, in his opinion, savours of the " bush " any more than the people of England will revive the antiquated customs and practices of their ancestors.

Many attempts to persuade the native to retain old ideas and customs are doomed to partial, if not total, failure. The native is suspicious, and assumes that it is a subtle way of retarding his progress, and that he is being thus advised solely because the European is jealous and does not want the African to advance. And the African is right. The only satisfactory way is for him to choose and learn for himself and, allowing him the opportunity, he will, in due time, evolve such customs as appear to him most suitable for his circumstances. What I would emphasise is, *that it is the African who is choosing*, and he will continue to do so, whatever the foreigner may say, whether he be trader, missionary, government official, educationist or anthropologist.

Again, what is not realised as it should be is that Native Law and Custom received its death-blow when the British Administration became operative in the Ibo Country. Similar comments apply to other areas in the Southern Provinces, certainly among the pagan tribes. Native Law, in its primitive form, is inextricably bound up with life and death. When the native societies apprehended that the power to take life was, henceforth, denied them, they not merely came under restraint; they virtually died. What now passes for native law and custom is but a travesty of what it was in the old days; it is but the shell; the kernel has been destroyed.

A point which is very apt to be overlooked because, either only partially grasped or, equally probably, not recognised at all, is that, before the British occupation, the government of the towns and villages rested, ultimately, with what is termed the " Maw " (spiritual forces). There might be, as at Onitsha, a King with his Prime Minister and other members of his Cabinet. These, again, were backed by the titled (Qzọ) men of the town. By virtue of the initiatory rites and ceremonies, the man admitted to this titular rank is, " *ex opere operato* ", sacrosanct; his person is no longer common; it is " holy ". These men, in session, consider questions and disputes and promulgate laws, and generally fulfil the duties of a town council. Yet, whatever opinion they arrived at on serious subjects, the final appeal was (and, as a matter of fact, still is) to the " Igaw

INTRODUCTION

Maw ". The chiefs, as semi-spiritual beings, naturally were the ones to hold consultation with the " spirits " and, so, they were the ambassadors of the gods to the common folk. Indeed, it might almost be said, that they were as gods; hence, their domineering and superior attitude towards the rank and file. The " Maw-Afia " was the final court of appeal at Onitsha, as the " Maw " and " Odo " were in other parts.

It scarcely needs to be pointed out that the conserving of a political and social authority which claims super-human sanction needs handling with extreme caution. Given fresh impetus for a " holy " order of chiefs, it is not a big step to a revival of the old " spirit " domination with its concomitant licence on the one part and fear on the other. Complications must, inevitably, ensue, to be followed, in turn, by restrictions and, thus, what may be given by one hand might have to be withdrawn by the other. The native is bewildered. What does the European really mean? The Ibo chiefs say : " We are told that the old customs are to be venerated ; that they are not to be cast aside like old clouts, yet, when we do follow them, we are brought to book for wrongdoing ! Where do we stand ? "

The downright truth is that the European finds it difficult to fathom the native mind ; he is generally ignorant of the native's mode of thinking, and he is seldom possessed of the essential spiritual element, which will equip him to unravel the intricacies of ancient native law and custom. We can write of what we actually see and hear, but cannot always follow the ramifications of the native mind. And still we presume to suggest that some customs and practices shall be retained while others should be abandoned whereas, we are on safe ground only when we say that all practices inimical to justice and the welfare of the community must be abolished. The European Administrative Officer is confronted with an extremely difficult task. He is frequently placed on the horns of a dilemma. He is called upon to decide whether sanction shall be given to some old custom which, apparently, appears harmless, or whether it shall be withheld. The men who have to fulfil these arduous tasks, and solve such complicated and, oft-times, delicate problems, deserve our sincerest sympathy. It is a tribute to their patience, and their desire to rule prudently and justly, that they do succeed, and have succeeded, so well. Having watched them for thirty-five years, I can honestly subscribe my admiration of them as a body of men whose foremost principle is the welfare of the people entrusted to their care.

By all means and ways, every possible use should be made

INTRODUCTION

of native institutions and of any framework or basis of society which can be brought into service, but the result will, quite probably, be stranger to the Ibo than to the European! I repeat, that what must not be overlooked is that the heart of native law and custom has been pierced by the impact of British authority and, when the heart ceases to beat, the limbs no longer function. To contemplate conserving native law and custom, is to concern ourselves very largely with a corpse. It will not respond as anticipated, because life has ceased to animate it. The deed is done and, unless Europeans abandon the country altogether, and so provide the opportunity for ancient law and custom to be resuscitated, it may just as well be counted as dead, for it has no future under modern conditions. Henceforth, laws will change according to circumstances, and as rapidly as the Government is able to issue legislative literature. At the same time, it must be stated that native customs are not being thoughtlessly or ruthlessly cast aside. Wherever possible, the essential elements have been, and are being, utilised with the consent of, and for the well-being of, the people in matters of Church and State as will be noted here and there in the course of this volume.

More than twenty years ago, I was asked to act as prisoner's friend in a case appearing before a District Officer. Until I went into court, I had little notion of the form it was to take. Imagine my surprise when I heard the charge: *Rex versus C.*—" You are hereby charged with intent to conceal a felony contrary to the Larceny Act of 1863 " by receiving money in compensation, heavy truly, no less than £3 10s., for a stolen fowl. The poor fellow understood not a word. Neither did I, for I was hopelessly ignorant of any such document as a Larceny Act. I sensed enough, however, to realise that the whole business was all wrong at that place and time. I managed to clear the accused on that count, but he did not escape, because the charge was changed to one of extortion or, alternatively, false pretences, and the simple soul was sentenced to six months' hard labour. I appealed and, fortunately, the judge who reviewed the case, took a reasonable view and ordered the man's release forthwith. What the accused had done was quite normal under native custom, but wrong according to the new law being imposed upon the country. The new criminal laws are English, not African, and they have little in common. We cannot, in the name of humanity and justice, return to the old ways, and it is wiser and kinder to let the ancient laws fade out of existence.

In this matter of conservation, too, we sometimes hear of

INTRODUCTION

good folk who talk of the "simple life" of the unsophisticated African. They picture him as dwelling in a sublime simplicity without anxious thought or care. Never was there a greater error than to think that a native can live a "simple" life as the expression is commonly understood. The life of the primitive native is the reverse of simple; he is tied and bound in every detail of life by inhibitions and prohibitions, tabus and laws unnumbered, known and unknown—tabus on food, movements, the daily affairs of life, from before birth until death and after. (*Vide* Chapter XI on women in a state of pregnancy as a characteristic example.) In no circumstances, and at no time, is the primitive native free from fear and superstition. He has to be continually on the watch lest he offend; his whole life is indissolubly bound up with things to remember, what to do, and what must be avoided. It is very far from being the simple life as it is conjectured by the European who has not lived in daily contact with the actual conditions.

The fact that there are nearly 115,000 pupils [2] under instruction in the Eastern Provinces of Nigeria should serve to illustrate the trend of the times. These numbers, added to the many thousands who have passed through the schools during the last twenty-five years, mean that a new generation has appeared, and it has little use for the old ways. They realise that a new administration has been introduced, and they must obey its laws. This they are prepared to do, as they have sense enough to know that progress lies along this new way. They are so engrossed with their desire to advance that they have not time for, or interest in, or patience with, the old customs and, alas, very often not even consideration for their old folk.

Time and again, I have sought enlightenment on a certain point in Ibo custom only to be met with the answer, "Nna-ayi, amarọm ncha" = "Our father, I don't know at all." These young folk go on to say that they have not assimilated the ideas and practices of their forefathers. In a few years, the old generation will have completely disappeared, and their traditions and customs will vanish with them. There are no historical documents and only the scantiest records available; hence, unless the old men and women can be induced to relate their knowledge quickly, it will be for ever lost. In any case, research work will prove much more exacting and baffling than it has been in the past. It is chiefly in order to preserve some knowledge of old customs, beliefs and practices that this book has been compiled. From what I gather, many young Ibos will welcome a record of their ancestors. They will criticise it,

INTRODUCTION

but will receive it as English schoolboys accept the accounts of their progenitors, the Ancient Britons. It is sad to relate, yet it is none the less true, that many a modern Ibo youth knows more of English History than that of his own country and people.

Collecting reliable information is not an easy task. It is apt to prove irksome and, oftentimes, disappointing. Even when one has gained the confidence of the people to the extent of being received as one of themselves, it is still a bewildering business. The old natives, though quite friendly and ready to be communicative, do not understand what is wanted, and seldom are they directly helpful. Only after much patient effort, and gleaning a little information here, and a little there, is one able to build up a knowledge of ancient Ibo custom. It is as complicated as a jigsaw puzzle—the picture becomes clear only when there is time to collect and fit together the many fragments. The business of the anthropologist is not easy under the best conditions; he is seriously handicapped when his time is limited and decidedly so when he is befogged with antecedent presumptions. A very open mind is needed—one that is prepared to note apparently trifling things, for it may be that a very small segment is just the piece wanted to complete the composition of the picture. The primitive native mind works along lines very diverse from that of the European. This is not a matter of surprise. According to one writer, " It may be the fault of fetishism itself which is the jungle of jungles; an aggregation of incoherent beliefs." [3]

A present-day investigator writes, " I study, and whatever conclusion I come to one day is reversed on the next—softly, softly is the only method, but, just now, I feel I am going so softly that I am going backward." So it must be with the foreigner who would learn some of the deeper things of the black man's mind; it cannot be otherwise. The European who is searching for knowledge of primitive law and custom is nearly as uncommon as the native who has any idea of the why or the wherefore of his beliefs or actions. The native does what seems to him to be the thing required whether he understands the reason, and whether it is palatable to him, or not; he just has to do it. Hence, it is extremely difficult to draw up a rational account of native law and custom. It is to be *felt* rather than expressed. This is particularly the case about midnight when surrounded by a company of highly excited dancers, or taking note of blood-stained fetishes. There are moments when one positively *feels* a sinister influence, though this need not necessarily interfere with one's investigations,

INTRODUCTION

especially if he is present by invitation and, therefore, enjoying a fair measure of freedom.

Some twenty years ago, I wrote somewhat as follows : " The ideas of the native are indefinite. He has no fixed thoughts. He is under the influence of an atmosphere which emanates from the family or clan. All his actions are dominated by this subliminal consciousness ; it is an infinitely more potent force in daily life than anything of a rational nature such as administrative law and order." This strange and forceful domination accounts for the unexpected outbreaks and reversions which occasionally overtake men who have received a substantial education and of whom, revulsion rather than participation would be expected. For the time being, they are carried completely out of themselves because they are under the influence of the massed clan spirit for, as it has been said, " a man's very soul is not his own in Africa ".[4]

Sufficient has been set forth to illustrate the difficulties that beset the seeker after truth when delving into the depths of the primitive mind. It only remains to say that what is related in the following pages is the result of observation spread over many years. The information presented has been checked and revised many times with the assistance of competent natives. Even so, it would be unwarrantable presumption to be positive about anything herein written which treats of actual native law and custom. Not even a native can do that. He only knows just that amount which guides or controls in his own locality. There are many variations within a radius of a few miles. There are innumerable ramifications which I have been unable to follow, and a vast amount upon which, were I directly questioned, I should have to say, " I don't know." The more one investigates, the more one realises the extreme profundity of native thought. It seems so superficial yet, actually, it is infinitely more involved than the white man's logic, and he finds it extremely difficult to interpret it satisfactorily.

Attention is drawn to the fact that the substance of this book is concerned with the Ibo People as they *were*—not as they are at the present day. Most of what is recorded deals with customs that are rapidly becoming obsolete, having been abandoned by the younger generation. Again, conditions have changed to an almost incredible extent. The government has opened up the country in a marvellous way, and travelling facilities are cheap and expeditious. Some 7,000 miles of roads have been built by the Public Works Department and the Native Administrations, and there are 1,900 miles of railway open for traffic. Greatly improved houses are being erected,

INTRODUCTION

sound buildings of brick and concrete replacing the old mud and thatched huts. Many natives possess motor-cars, while bicycles can be counted by hundreds. It is open to question whether any other tropical dependency has developed at such a rapid rate as Nigeria, and the Ibo Country shares in this progress. There is a very wide divergence between the Ibo Country of 1937 and that dealt with in the following pages. My endeavour has been to record primitive ideas and customs of the Ibo People before they are forgotten. Those who wish to know about the new Nigeria should read such books as: *History of Nigeria* (A. C. Burns) and *The Nigeria Handbook*.

Except in isolated areas, there is scarcely a town or hamlet in the Ibo Country without its Church and School. Statistics show that, in the Eastern Provinces, nearly half a million have embraced Christianity.[5] The Niger Mission of the Church Missionary Society has advanced to the extent that it has become self-governing, as well as self-supporting, and now operates independently under its own Constitution and Synod. All other Societies, Protestant and Roman Catholic, have made great strides during the last twenty years and, taken together, they are a great disintegrating force. The Government, plus the missionary and commercial bodies, have revolutionised the political, economic and religious life of the Ibo People. Modern conditions are not extensively referred to in this book; they call for separate treatment. I repeat that what is written is mainly a record of native life and customs *before* the changes brought about disruption.

Some regret may be felt that this book deals more particularly with the Ibos in the more northerly areas than with those in the southern. There have been reasons for this. One is, that circumstances have been such that I have had more opportunity for the study of the former. A more specific reason is that pure unadulterated forms are not found in the southern districts. Religion, language and customs are all tinged with outside influences, and the ideas of other tribes have been superimposed or intermingled with the ancient Ibo beliefs and practices.

A little thought will make this clear, if not convincing. We must cast our minds back a couple of centuries in order to obtain a true perspective; back to the slave-trading days. It is stated that from Bonny alone, up to 1832, no less than 16,000 slaves were exported annually. Moreover, slave-trading and slave-raiding did not cease in the interior when the Abolition of Slavery was enacted in London. Although the demand was greatly reduced owing to the cessation of exportation, slave-

INTRODUCTION

raiding continued until the beginning of the present century. The Bende Expedition of 1901-2 struck the first definite blow against the age-long custom.

What did Slavery mean to the southern areas ? They were raided from different sides ; the Aros from the east, the emissaries from Bonny and Brass and Calabar from the south. When villages were attacked many people were caught and enslaved. Always a proportion, however, managed to escape, and sought refuge in the recesses of the " bush ". From time to time, these refugees banded together and formed new villages, and each unit made its contribution to the common daily life and practice ; each added its quota to custom, religion and language. Again, since the British occupation became effective, very many ex-slaves from the Coast towns have found their way back to their original homes, bringing with them the ideas they have assimilated while in exile.

Hence, a considerable number of incorporated ideas and practices are noticeable among the Ibos of the Owerri Province. This is manifested in their dances, in the conducting of Second Burials, the erection of Mbari Houses and in various other directions. As far as I know, there are no " alusis " (gods) such as are found farther north and on the western side of the Niger. Indeed, one never sees or hears of any distinctive figures or any sort of " alusi " in the Owerri area, and in the Okigwi district there is little of any kind. Latterly, here and there, an occasional public fetish has been set up, introduced by men who have returned home after living abroad for years. This area demands independent study, inasmuch as it has characteristics of its own, which are partly Ibo and partly foreign, constituting an economy somewhat different from the remainder of Iboland.

Where, then, can ancient Ibo law and custom, religion and language be best studied ? In my opinion, the conditions are most favourable at Nri, the home of the priestly cult, and in that immediate neighbourhood. There, and at Awka, the people were left free and undisturbed from generation to generation. This applies to the eastern side of the Niger. On the western side, and including Onitsha Town, the Bini impress, in more or less degree, is apparent. Since the suzerainty of Benin was broken in 1897, its influence has naturally declined, but it was certainly clearly pronounced up to forty years ago. It is still to be observed in dress, religion, the status of kings, and in other directions, though the language seems to have been little affected.

In the following pages is recorded what I have gleaned by

INTRODUCTION

seeing and hearing. One fears that students, and especially those who are more definitely interested in Ibo law and custom, will search for some particular item and find it not even mentioned. It may have been omitted intentionally as not of any specific value. As likely as not, the omission is due to ignorance. Undoubtedly, much more information might be furnished if every detail of daily life, thought and practice were to be noted. To do this, however, would involve a prolonged visit to every village, and that, in turn, would mean a separate volume for each, inasmuch as different localities have their own methods of expressing what are, in essentials, the same ideas and practices. My endeavour has been rather to place on record what may prove of interest to the average reader, as well as being of some use to those seeking a closer knowledge of the Ibo People.

The pronunciation of native words will be puzzling to the European. The following note may prove of some assistance. The syllable " aw " is written " ǫ " in Ibo, and many words have this vowel, e.g. Ǫzǫ = Awzaw as near as can be written. Then the diphthong " gb " or " ḅ " is used as an explosive. The normal and quite reasonable way for a European, is to separate the two consonants and give each its distinct value as " Ag-bor ", " og-bu ". This is incorrect in Ibo ; the " gb " has one unbroken sound. For the foreigner, " bw " gets nearer to the idea as Abwor and obwu. Experience and practice are needed to pronounce words " native fashion ".

My sincere thanks are due to many Ibo friends, men and women, who have so readily helped me in collecting information and, particularly, to those who have scrutinised the manuscript of this book. Also, I would express my gratitude and appreciation to whose who have helped in typing and other ways, including the Editor of *West Africa* for granting permission to incorporate the essential matter of articles published on the Oracle at Ezira (p. 92) and " Pitch and Toss " (p. 352).[6]

In writing this book, I have embodied a certain amount of information, corrected, rewritten and brought up to date, that appeared nearly twenty years ago, but by far the greater part is entirely fresh material. My object in retaining any of the old subject-matter was to meet the need for an authoritative and complete book.

With sincere gratitude, I have in remembrance the many Ibo friends who admitted me to their circles and, by so doing, gave me unusual opportunities to see and hear what otherwise was forbidden to the stranger. The names bestowed on me, together with the insignia presented when they were conferred,

INTRODUCTION

are among my most treasured possessions. Perhaps the chief commendation of this book lies in the fact that what is recorded is first-hand information made possible by the intimacy I was privileged to enjoy so freely among these friendly Ibo People. I trust that no Ibo man or woman will feel hurt at anything written in this book. I should, indeed, grieve, if I thought that I had given cause for complaint. All that touches upon Ibo law and custom has been related to me by native friends. I have done no more than act as scribe after tracing the facts and placing them in order. The records of the past need not reflect upon the future. As dawn succeeds darkness, so may it be with the Ibo People. I have the greatest faith in their ability to rise and prosper ; they have the potentialities to become one of the most illustrious nations in Africa. They will soon be proud of their professional and academic records. The younger generation has sloughed the old ways with their accompanying superstitions and is reaching forth to a place in the civilised world. There is a magnificent opportunity for service among this intelligent, virile people. They possess a wonderfully patient persistence to attain any desired end, a natural astuteness born of necessity, together with a loyalty which, though often begotten by fear yet, redirected along right lines, will go far to make them a great nation. Nevertheless, they will need to preserve their balance by cultivating the spiritual side of life correspondingly with the material. They must remember that " righteousness alone exalteth a nation ". Unless a stronger spiritual influence is substituted in place of the forsaken restraints of primitive law and custom and a spurious spirit-worship, there is danger lest the last state be worse than the first.

G. T. BASDEN.

The following are the Native Titles conferred on the Author by the Ibo People of Onitsha, Ogidi and Awka:—

      OMESILINCHA = The one who entirely finishes his work.
      ǪNU-ŊEKWULU-ǪRA = The mouth that speaks on behalf of the people. = Advocate.
      OMEƵULUOKE = He who completely fulfils his task.

INTRODUCTION

NOTES TO INTRODUCTION

[1] "*Niger and Tshadda*", p. 179.
[2] Annual Report, Education Department, 1934.
[3] "*Fetish Folk of West Africa*". Milligan. Preface, p. 5.
[4] *Ibid.*, p. 40.
[5] The figures shown in the Census for 1931 are: Calabar Province, 149,489; Ogoja, 6,989; Onitsha, 65,283; Owerri, 232,798; and half Benin, 23,538—total, 478,097.
[6] Published in the issues of "*West Africa*", No. 410, Vol. VIII, December 6, 1924; No. 1002, Vol. XX, April 11, 1936.

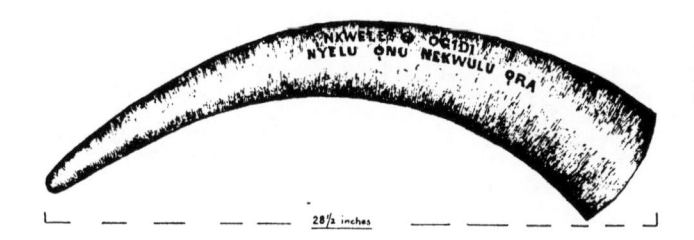

THE AUTHOR'S INSIGNIA.
Elephant tusk (horn) and staff.

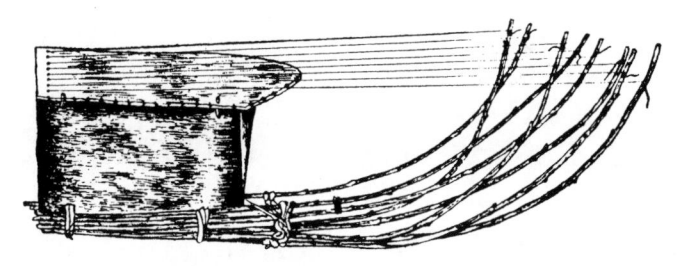

UBQ-AKWALA—STRINGED MUSICAL INSTRUMENT.

LIST OF CONTENTS

CHAP.		PAGE
I	THE HEART OF THE IBO	33
II	SACRIFICES	54
III	ORACLES	76
IV	ORACLES (*continued*)	89
V	"MBARI" HOUSES	98
VI	IBOLAND	110
VII	THE IBO PEOPLE	121
VIII	KINGS & CHIEFS	130
IX	HOME LIFE	147
X	SOCIAL ETIQUETTE	161
XI	BIRTH CUSTOMS	167
XII	CHILDHOOD	180
XIII	YOUTH TO OLD AGE—BOYS & MEN	192
XIV	YOUTH TO OLD AGE—GIRLS & WOMEN	203
XV	MARRIAGE	213
XVI	POLYGAMY & DIVORCE	228
XVII	ORU & OSU—SLAVES OF MEN AND GODS	243
XVIII	CAPITAL CRIME	259
XIX	LAND TENURE & INHERITANCE	264
XX	DEATH & BURIAL	269
XXI	SECOND BURIAL	289
XXII	PRIMITIVE LIFE	299
XXIII	CLAY, METAL & WOODWORKERS	311

LIST OF CONTENTS

CHAP.		PAGE
XXIV	WOMEN'S WORK	325
XXV	MARKETING	334
XXVI	RECREATIONS	342
XXVII	MUSIC	356
XXVIII	DAY & NIGHT CLUBS	366
XXIX	DISTURBERS OF THE PEACE	377
XXX	YAMS	389
XXXI	OIL & WINE	399
XXXII	SOME SIMILARITIES BETWEEN THE ISRAELITES & THE IBOS	411
XXXIII	FIRESIDE STORIES	424
	BIBLIOGRAPHICAL NOTE TO 1966 EDITION	439
	INDEX	451

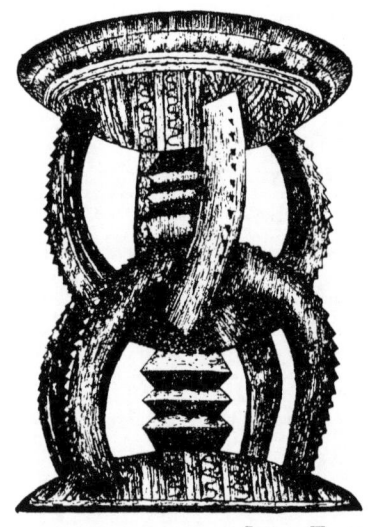

STOOL CARVED FROM SOLID BLOCK OF IROKO TIMBER AT AWKA.

LIST OF ILLUSTRATIONS

	FACE PAGE
BODY & SPIRIT . . . . . . *Frontispiece*	
SHRINES	33
MBARI HOUSE	48
Photo by kind permission of Dr. F. Rupert Snell	
"ODO" CELEBRATIONS	80
MODELLED CLAY & COLOURED FIGURES IN AN MBARI HOUSE ENCLOSURE	113
SEEN IN AN MBARI HOUSE ENCLOSURE	128
HONOUR & WORSHIP	145
FRONT WALL OF COMPOUND	160
CICATRISATION & BODY-STAINING	177
FULL DRESS	192
YOUNG MANHOOD	209
NORTHERN TYPES OF HAIRDRESSING	224
BRIDES-TO-BE	241
FULFILLING "NKPU" CUSTOMS	256
TYPES OF HAIRDRESSING SEEN IN ONITSHA	272
SECOND BURIAL	289
LIFE & DEATH	304
A YOUNG BRIDE	321
A CICATRISED WOMAN	336

LIST OF ILLUSTRATIONS

	FACING PAGE
Woodworker's Art	353
Agbọ-Maw	368
Warriors	401
On the Way to Market	416
Burdensome, but highly prized	424

LIST OF TEXT ILLUSTRATIONS

	PAGE
Brass Anklet "Ogba"	iv
Alusi called "Ekwu"	x
Author's Insignia	xxiii
Ubọ-Akwala, Stringed Musical Instrument	xxv
Stool carved from solid block of Iroko Timber	xxvi
Decorated "Okwe" Board	xxx
A poor Man's "Ikenga"	52
Bent & Rusty Iron Spear-heads	88
The Ancient "Ikolo" (Wooden Cylinder Tom-Tom)	97
The "Mbọ"	109
A New "Dug-out" Canoe ready for launching	120
Bell ("Ogenne") used by Chiefs	146
Copper Anklet	166
Operating Knives, &c.	179
Brass Tobacco Pipe, used more particularly in Western Iboland	202

LIST OF TEXT ILLUSTRATIONS

	PAGE
WOMEN'S GOD CALLED " ITE-UMU-NNE "	227
NATIVE TOOLS	242
THE ARO KNOT	263
MASK USED BY THE " MAW "	288
WOODEN COMB & SMALL IRON IMPLEMENT	310
THE " AWKA " STOOL	333
MANILLA CURRENCY USED IN PARTS OF THE IBO COUNTRY . .	341
IBO " PITCH & TOSS "	355
THE UBQ	365
MAP OF SOUTHERN NIGERIA	448 & 449

Length 26" over all; width 6¾".

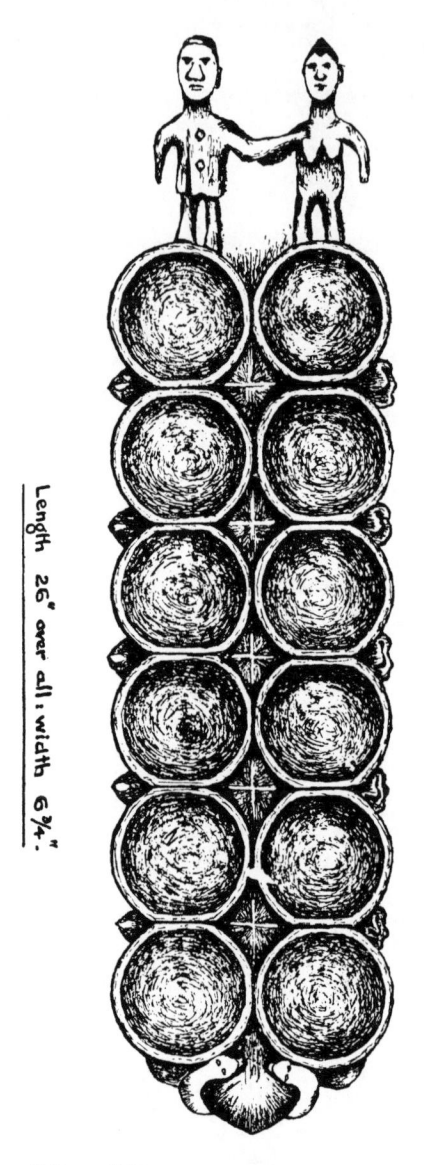

DECORATED "OKWE" BOARD AS FOUND IN BETTER-CLASS HOUSES.
The cups on this particular board are supported on the backs of ten "Atlas" like figures.

GLOSSARY OF IBO WORDS AND TERMS USED IN THIS VOLUME

Abams. Also Abikiris and Adas. Bands of mercenary soldiers who operated chiefly in the southern parts of the Ibo Country under the control of Arǫ-Chuku. Their activities were brought to an end by the destruction of the " Long-Juju " during the Bende Expedition of 1902.   115, 126, 244, 382, 384.
Ada. Eldest daughter of family or chief woman of clan.   62, 225, 271, 284, 289, 377.
Agbala. Generic name for shrine or god, especially in the Owerri area.   = The unknown god.   78, 80, 101.
Alu. Abomination ; that which is tabu. Pollution.   59, 70, 122, 181, 219, 225.
Alusi. Generic term for fetish ; ju-ju ;   44, 45, 48, 50, 54, 61, 64, 65, 66, 158, 175, 246, 262, &c.
Anasi. First, that is, legal wife = " nwayi-Isi-Chi ", the head (ruling) woman of the household.   64, 138, 229, 237.
Ani. Earth, land, ground.   In Southern Ibo = " Ala ".   122.
Chi. Generic term for " God ".   = Supreme Being. In the form of a stick stands for guardian ancestral spirit.   45, 46, 47, 59, 64, 143, 153, 276, 292, &c.
Chineke. God the Creator.   37, 46.
Chukwu. The Great God ; the Supreme Being.   = Chi-Ukwu. 37, 46, 61, 251.
Dibia. Doctor, priest, necromancer, magician.   49, 54, 102, 175, 379, &c.
Edde. Koko-yam. An edible root resembling an artichoke. Cultivated by women.   68, 149, 208, 389.
Ekwensu. The Devil. The author of all evil generally.   36, 37, 38.
Eze-Ala. Lit. : king of the land. Originally a gratuitous salutation to a wealthy man ; in recent times, in some districts, indicates a man of titular rank.   132.
Ichu-Aja. Lit. : to drive evil. Sacrifice to remove fear of the living and the dead ; to secure present and future well-being and to placate malevolent spirits.   57, 58, 59, 72.
Igǫ-Maw. To placate the spirits.   44, 56, 57, 59, 64.
Ikenga. Essentially a man's god ; the guardian of his life and property. The long horns on the carved wooden figure typify strength and courage.   44, 50, 51, 64, 153, 290, 323, &c.
Ilǫ-Maw. Most common of sacrifices. More of a festival than a proper sacrifice. Offered to retain the goodwill of the spirits, or propitiate them if offended.   56, 57, 59, 63, 64, 66, 229.

GLOSSARY OF IBO WORDS AND TERMS

Maw. Spirit and the spirit world. 60, 130, 138, 145, 281, 366, 367, 372, 375, &c.

Ndi-Chie. Ruling nobles. Administrators of affairs generally, Town councillors. 69, 123, 141, 272.

Nkpulu-chi. Generic term for memorials to deceased relatives. A single memorial is called an " Okpensi ". 46, 143, 281.

Nsọ. Holy. Set apart. Tabu, hence abomination. 56, 103, 182, 217, 225, 230.

Obi. 1. Ancestral house of the father (founder) of the village. 2. Hut belonging to the head of the family. 46, 68, 122, 153, 208.

Ogilisi. Same as " egbo ". Sacred tree planted in a new compound before building is begun. It is honoured as a god. 45, 65, 140, 147, 153, 311.

Ojji.
1. Nut shared between friends as a token of goodwill. 161.
2. Presents from one to another, particularly as acknowledgement for favours received as from tenant to landlord. 210, 216, 264, 265.

Okpensi. Memorial to the soul of an ancestor set up after the completion of the ceremonies connected with Second Burial. All Okpensis have names attached to them and thus form a register of a man's ancestors. 46, 47, 64, 266, 276, 283, 285.

Osu. Slave dedicated to the service of a local deity. 78, 151, 159, 175, 181, 243, 246, 416.

Otu. Company. This may include members of varying age as against " ọgbọ " nowadays interpreted " Age-grade ". 194, 223, 409.

Ọba. Frame on which yams are tied for storing = the yam store. 71, 156, 392, 428.

Ọfọ. Stick which becomes effective after consecration. Used with a mediating intention and as an emblem of truth. May be regarded as " God of Justice ". 51, 57, 87, 122, 132, 153, 200, 226, 251, 272, 276, 290.

Ọkpala. Heir. Eldest son or next of kin male. An uncle in the case of a minor. 46, 58, 65, 101, 121, 132, 139, 140, 142, 151, 272, 280, 292.

Ọmu. Immature palm leaves. 69, 90, 148, 153, 275, 314, 381, 408 *seq.*, 417.

Ọzọ. A title of high degree, and much coveted, conferring on the owner privileges and honour as a sacrosanct being. 122, 130, 135, 136, 137, 248, 272.

Ufie. Camwood stain. 103, 223, 271, 273, 276, 284, 330.

SHRINES.

Above: EARTHEN MOUND, PECULIARLY MOULDED. THE PINNACLES ARE TOPPED WITH HEADS OF ANIMALS AND MEN.

Middle: THE OBA OF BENIN. CHIEF "ALUSI" IN A COMPOUND SECURELY LOCKED AGAINST STRANGERS.

Below: DEITY BY ROADSIDE NEAR ASHAKA.

CHAPTER I

THE HEART OF THE IBO

WHEN CONTEMPLATING the writing of a book of this character, it is advisable to consider what is likely to prove the most satisfactory method of approaching the subject. Should the information recorded emanate from the inside and radiate outwards, or should the viewpoint be that of a spectator presenting impressions as observed from an outside detached position? In this instance, the former attitude seemed the more commendable, hence the earlier chapters are concerned with what is most vital to the Ibo. It deals with the heart that pulsates as strongly throughout the body politic, as it does in that of the individual. It is essential to understand something of what, it is true to say, constituted the controlling principle in all old Ibo tribal life.

We have been accustomed to speak of this dominating spiritual force as " religion ", but it is something much more incisive and comprehensive than what that conventional word commonly implies. The conception of " spirit " is deep and powerful, operating from within, and is not merely an outward conformity to religious observance although it includes that. It is such a prime elemental force that it might quite fairly be described as a sixth sense as much alive, and as keenly active, as the normal five. Due regard for this spiritual sense must have foremost place in the study of an animistic people, because herein is found the motive of action and the key to the solution of many problems connected with native law and custom. Without this faculty of spiritual perception, much in native thought and custom remains obscure, if not completely unintelligible.

Where, therefore, the word " religion " is used, it should be given the widest interpretation. The book begins with it, because there are names and terms mentioned here and there which call for definition. By commenting on " religion " at the outset, a much clearer idea of Ibo life and custom may be grasped from the beginning and separate explanatory notes rendered unnecessary. The list of names and definitions forming the introduction to Chapter II should also be consulted as they are in frequent use in the Ibo vocabulary.

The animistic beliefs of these people offer a topic for interesting study. They are closely interwoven with daily affairs, indeed, they are bound up in the bundle of life and are as intimately related as the fibre to the tree. It is a complicated subject, calling for close and patient observation. Its study cannot be hurried : to rush through a series of questions will inevitably lead to the compiling of a mass of conflicting and untrustworthy material. Whatever is so collected, even when obtained under seemingly favourable conditions, needs to be thoroughly sifted and probably corrected and recorrected. The European needs to develop a sense of the uncanny, otherwise his materialistic temperament will limit his perception of the spiritual ramifications of the animist. Sound conclusions are difficult to obtain and should not be expected unless protracted investigations can be undertaken. Information gleaned from one native must be checked by that obtained from many others. Even so, it would be unwise to dogmatise, for native thought is often inexpressible in words. The student must sublimate his own opinions and, to some extent, keep his pre-knowledge well in reserve. At the same time, he needs to be on his guard lest answers be given which, though specious, may prove of little value to the seeker after truth. We are inexorably faced with the question, " Can the European really fathom the depths of native thought and grasp what ' spirit ' means to him ? " The answer would be, that it is doubtful : it is too intricate and involved : it is like unravelling a tangled skein. It is a whole containing many parts jumbled together, or, again, it may be compared to capturing the morning mist with a net : one thinks he has discovered something good only to find that it has evaded him.

The native strives to excel in courtesy. Quite as likely, he may be nervous, if not actually fearful. What does the white man want to know ? Why does he ask questions ? In the former case he, in the goodness of his heart, endeavours to supply an answer that will please : in the latter he may prevaricate in his anxiety to find a way of escape from the catechism. His mind is troubled lest he commit himself. He thinks that the interrogator is prompted by an undivulged motive which, ultimately, will prove harmful to him or his people. In such circumstances, directly leading questions will be countered : either courtesy or fear will dictate incomplete or inaccurate answers, probably both. Suspicion is hard to eliminate. The most satisfactory results come from natives discussing certain aspects of the subject among themselves when they are free and forgetful of their surroundings. At such times information of an unpremeditated and unbiassed character may be gleaned.[1]

There is the further handicap that no two natives will express their beliefs identically, especially if they come from different villages. They speak from their own inner consciousness of what, to them, are vital things, but which have never been put into dogmatic form nor standardised. The beliefs have been absorbed into their beings from infancy : they have not been learned by rote, nor can the pagan native marshal them in stereotyped order. He feels rather than knows, and what he feels is very real and potent. His thoughts are his own ; suspicion is always active ; he is on the alert, hence, he considers it prudent to keep them to himself lest he inadvertently bring trouble upon himself or his family.

Before entering into further discussion, a clear distinction must be drawn between " worship " and " religion ". As the Rev. T. Cullen Young remarks concerning Animism as found in East Central Africa, " worship " connotes " religion ", and in the Ibo country, as in Central Africa, " we are dealing with something far removed from anything that the word ' religion ' can connote in the West ". It has been said a thousand times that " the African is essentially a ' *religious* ' man ", but this adjective should, in this connection, be always enclosed in inverted commas. An immense gulf separates East and West. It has to be admitted that it is correct, in a perfectly legitimate sense, to say, that when we deal with (Ibo) Animism we are within the area which, by dictionary definition, we may label " religious " ; but we are only *just* within it. A hint of the matter lies in a sentence used by Dr. Oldham and Miss Gibson, in " *The Remaking of Man in Africa* ", where they say : " The lines of division between secular and sacred that have grown up in the West (Europe) have little meaning for the African. We in the West are only trying now to heal a breach which for him has never existed." They might have made that statement even stronger. They might, instead of saying " have little meaning " have said " are quite meaningless ".[2]

Hence, in thinking of the " religious " ideas of the Ibos, we must keep in mind that we are working in a language totally different from what we are accustomed to in the West. In the Ibo country, we may speak of " religious beliefs " or call them " superstitions ". What is essential to remember is that they are deeply ingrained in the minds and lives of the people ; they are blindly accepted by the adherents. No questions are raised as to the whys and wherefores; they are part and parcel of life itself, and are given fullest allegiance and acted upon in sincere faith and loyalty.

The time has passed when the native religion was a matter of indifference to the foreigner. Undoubtedly, it could be alleged with some confidence that no great measure of sympathy was manifested towards it. The outlook has changed of recent years. Knowledge has broadened, and it is realised that there is still much to discover. The prominence now given to Anthropology and Comparative Religion has led to a more patient attitude and a genuine desire to understand native beliefs.

Disrespect is still to be found, but it is more evident among the natives themselves rather than directly from foreigners. The natives do often neglect their gods and, on occasions, go further and exhibit symptoms of actual contempt towards them. One need not travel far in the Ibo country before observing traces of this. Shrines are allowed to fall into decay and the gods left to fend for themselves. A god may be completely abandoned or destroyed at a time when feeling runs high because of trouble in the village. Either the deity was incapable of intervening, or failed to exercise his protective power. In consequence, he was denounced as an impostor; a useless encumbrance demanding sacrifices for which he gave no return. Fear might prevent the people making a deliberate onslaught as an outlet to their animosity, but they are quite willing for others to act on their behalf, and no regrets will follow the deposition of their erstwhile god. The alternative is to forsake him. The people understand what they are doing and manifest no compunction when a deity which has fallen into disrepute is brought to an ignominious end.

A circumscribed belief in a Supreme Being and a Future Life is universal among the Ibo people. They maintain that He is All Powerful and overlords all inferior spirits. His attributes include beneficence, and He grants favours to mankind in a general way. As a just God, too, He metes out punishments for wrongdoing. This is proved by happenings for which no reasons can be assigned. In these circumstances, the people believe that the Supreme Being has exercised His prerogatives as the Almighty Controller of the universe and has so acted in order to express His disapproval and to vindicate His power.

Eternally opposed to God is His arch-enemy " Ekwensu " (the Devil), whose one purpose is to frustrate the goodness of God and to disseminate evil. He is the author of all that is bad, and to him is attributed the worst ills to which man is

THE HEART OF THE IBO

subject. He, in company with innumerable associated spirits, is under the domination of God and can do no more than God condescends to permit him to do. " Ekwensu " and his subordinate spirits are at God's service at all times ; they function in order to fulfil His commands. One of the agents so employed is " Death ". He is referred to as a " Servant of God ". He is entrusted with powers on specified terms as in the case of other controlled spirits.[3]

Several names are appropriated to the Supreme Being which, more or less, assimilate the underlying ideas of some particular attribute. In the southern parts of the country He is known as " *Chineke* " (God, the Creator). In the northern parts the term " *Chukwu* " (" *Chiukwu* " = the great God) is the more common title. In some districts He is spoken of as " Olisabulu-uwa ", usually abbreviated to " Osebulu-uwa " or, in one word, " Olisa ". This conveys the meaning of the " god who fashions the world ".

Although there is a universal belief in a Supreme Being and His inveterate enemy, the Devil, the *effect* of such belief is negligible. It is purely theoretical and has no marked influence on life or character. These beings hover on the horizon of human activities and it is wise to leave them alone. When they exact tribute by means of adversity, the punishment must be submitted to as patiently as possible. The good things of life are in accordance with God's beneficent nature and are no more than may be expected of Him. In a perfunctory way, honour is due to Him for the fruits of the earth and other benefits. It is a vague perception, a faint reflection of a light which has not been quite extinguished during the course of ages. The light burns dimly : its brightness ceased to illuminate life and, to-day, the knowledge of God is, for all practical purposes, limited to an acknowledgement of His name and generally recognised attributes.

There is no symbol erected to the Supreme Being, neither is there a figure (" alusi ") to represent the Author of Evil, nor does there appear to be any trace of actual Devil Worship. " Ekwensu ", commonly translated as " The Devil ", is the most common word used for him. He is the master spirit who exercises lordship over all other agents of wickedness. Knowledge concerning him is vague and confused : it is as incoherent as that connected with the Supreme Being. All that is affirmed is that he is answerable for the evil that is in the world in a general haphazard way. As he is *not* honoured with an " Alusi ", neither is sacrifice ever made directly to appease him.

Another evil spirit has a more intimate association with

human life. This is Ogbonuke. He can be very active and the cause of infinite trouble. He is really the disgruntled spirit of a deceased companion who, because he is discontented and unhappy, manifests his vindictiveness by working mischief on his former friends. In brief, he is best described as the " Demon of Illfortune ". How much more closely he is associated with mankind is shown by the fact that an " alusi " *is* dedicated to him. Supplications are made to him with sacrificial offerings. It is believed that " Ekwensu " may also be propitiated when sacrificing to Ogbonuke. It is thought that an appeal may reach the overlord while the supplications are being made to the more familiar spirit.

It has been remarked that there is no apparent evidence which might definitely indicate devil worship. There is, however, something of a modified nature. Though " Ekwensu " is not worshipped, he is honoured in conformance with his own principles. This is found more particularly on the western side of the Niger where it is customary to devote three days in the year to placate the devil by walking in his ways as closely as possible for a time.[4] They are known as " Ekwensu's " days. All restraint is cast aside and the (pagan) folk give themselves over to unbridled licence. Sensuality and other forms of wickedness are, for the time being, accepted as the normal. Every man and woman is at liberty to indulge as freely as they please. By acting thus, they will humour the devil. Such a period of indulgence did not always end peaceably : jealousy was bound to arise in some hearts, leading to quarrels and fighting. There is more restriction in these latter days ; bloodshed has been practically suppressed and fighting reduced to an occasional minor affray ; the custom itself is gradually disappearing.

Yet the sinfulness of sin is admitted, and certain delinquencies are deemed to be contrary to the will of God. The people consider that murder, theft and adultery are heinous offences, but only really so when committed among relatives or friendly neighbours. Then they are sins in the sight of God and man. Punishment of an appropriate nature will assuredly follow the committal of such deeds. If the sinner himself escape judgement, the penalty will certainly have to be borne by his children sooner or later : the settlement may be deferred, but it will not be overlooked nor forgotton. Actual fear of retribution is not sufficiently strong to check wrongdoing. The only concern of the Ibo is to escape detection. He willingly admits that bad deeds ("Ajo ọlu") are sin, but does not refrain from committing them when conditions appear favourable. To be

THE HEART OF THE IBO

found out by his fellow-man is regarded as far more shameful than offending God. In this he is not different from the rest of mankind. Against this must be placed the fact that fear of retribution was a powerful deterrent in former days. For instance, it was an old custom for women to place small commodities, soap, breadfruit, tobacco, and such-like in a basket and leave it by the roadside under the sole guardianship of a stone which was respected as having the nature of a deity. No one would dare steal from the basket or calabash for fear of retribution.

" Those who have acquired an intimate knowledge of the mind and heart of the heathen know that it is the consequence of sin, rather than sin itself, which they would escape. There is but little real abhorrence of sin." [5]

" The African knows the difference between right and wrong ; he knows that it is wrong to lie and steal." [6]

" The African lies in self-defence, and steals in the interests of success ; but what he practises himself he condemns in others ; for he knows that it is wrong." [7]

It must be stated clearly, however, that such deeds must be performed abroad ; they are very serious crimes when committed against a fellow-townsman. If perpetrated outside the town area, when the criminal returns safely, especially if he brings back booty, he will be congratulated on his success.

Offences for the committal of which, under native law and custom, the penalty is capital punishment, are commented upon in Chapter XVIII. They, of course, constitute what are accounted the foremost crimes against individuals or the community. In addition to murder and adultery (in particular instances), the purloining of planted seed yams is, under native law, also a capital crime. Minor offences are dealt with summarily, nominally on their merits ; generally the verdict is given in favour of the highest bidder. Both parties suffer financial loss : the one who is prepared to bribe the most lavishly wins his case. Nevertheless, really evil deeds are not tolerated : they are accounted as " Ulu-ani " (defiling the land), and must be compensated for by appropriate fines or some other form of punishment. These include treason, and the breaking, removing or defiling of a man's god or property. Deceit and lying are theoretically bad, but they are so universal that they form a normal part of daily life. In any case, all are aware of this trait and no man can accuse his neighbour seeing that he, himself, is equally guilty of offence. What is a universal custom is not a peculiar characteristic, hence no one is surprised or shocked ; each denounces the other vigorously with the epithet " asi " (liar). With eyes blazing, or snake-like, peering through half-closed lids, and chin thrust forward aggressively, the Ibo instils more meaning and venom into this one word than can be conveyed by writing; he really " stings ".

A large and miscellaneous list might be made of objects which could be classed under the generic term of fetishes. They may be stones, trees, waters and, indeed, any material substance—all are believed to be capable of housing a spirit. These are not worshipped themselves : the Ibo pagan does not " bow down to wood and stone ". It is to the spirit dwelling within them that supplicatory and intercessory prayer is made. There are also animals which are accounted sacred, cows, tortoises, monkeys, snakes and, in some parts, fish ; they are held in veneration as being the servants of a god or possessing godlike properties. A sufficient reverence is held for them which is an effectual protection against harm or molestation. In a few instances only are offerings made to these emblems of divinity. They are not of a costly character ; just a matter of a few cowrie shells, a kola nut, a pinch of salt, two or three sticks of chalk, an egg or a day-old chick. As far as I have been able to ascertain, bones are *not* used as fetishes by the Ibos.[8]

Where a stream or pool is deemed to be holy, it is probably because of a belief that water is worthy of veneration ; it deserves to be so treated for the sake of its life-giving properties. Without water, life could not be sustained, a feature which appeals strongly to people living under tropical conditions. The fish of such waters have an equal share in the honour bestowed : they, too, are believed, in some mysterious way, to be the guardians of the people. They are reverenced as " Nne-ayi " (our mother) on account of their supposed protective care over the children. The fish are safe and, in some waters, manifest no fear of man. They may not be caught : except by accident they may not be harmed, nor removed from the water. Such an untoward act is esteemed a great offence and remission must be sought by sacrifice. It is effected by the offering of a white fowl. It is not killed : it is brought and released at the edge of the water and allowed to run wild. The culprit, meantime, prays for forgiveness on the plea that the offence committed was unintentional. European fishermen should be forbearing and remember this. Some have been elated with their phenomenal success not realising that the fish are guileless. A worse feature is that they cause acute distress to those who hold the fish in honour as sacred creatures.

On the other hand, in certain cases it does seem to be the

THE HEART OF THE IBO

water that is held sacred as possessing peculiar properties. For example, there is a small lake lying between Umu-Chu and Ibughubu (Awka Division), known as " Di-Awo̱ ", to which the people resort whenever they want to obtain some particular benefit. Both men and women visit the water and offer " kola ", in this case a little cooked food. While doing so, they beg for the thing wanted. They promise an offering in return should the benefit be granted. If a child be sought, and one be duly born to the suppliant, a fowl is presented or, if the petitioner be a man in affluent circumstances, a goat. The priest is called the " Osu ", he being the head of the water worship. He is not an " Osu " in the ordinary sense (*vide* Chap. XVII) as he lives in the town ; the title is merely one of convenience.

Another instance of a water god is that of " Nkpitima " as practised at Isele on the western side of the Niger. Every year a cow or goat is killed and the carcase is divided into two parts. Kola nut is thrown into the water, and one half of the carcase. To this is added a live fowl which, in due course, is allowed to escape into the bush. The other half of the carcase is eaten. This water is supposed to " give life ". Also, if a woman desire to have children, she will offer a fowl to the water that she also may have water (life). The priest gives her some clay from the bed of the stream. This she places in a pot (ububa), for which she builds a miniature shelter in her compound. Every time she cooks, she offers food to this " alusi " and, when she leaves the house, she invokes " Nkpitima " to protect it and her property ; on her return she offers kola in thanksgiving.

Over the greater part, if not over the whole of the Ibo country, the python is sacred, more especially the smaller specimens called " ekke-ntu ". These likewise are referred to as " our mother " and to injure one is a very serious offence. If a man have the misfortune to kill one accidentally, he will mourn for a year and abstain from shaving his head.

While all the Ibos hold the python in reverence and, in most places, also venerate the tortoise, yet it is not often that any substantial evidence is found to prove the practice of ophiolatry. Here and there may be found some traces of such a cult and the following account will serve as an instance.

At the town of Obusi, five miles south-east of Onitsha, there is a powerful divinity known as Ide-Milli. The founder of Obusi was a man named Adike, a native of Ojioto. When he emigrated to what is now Obusi he carried with him this specific deity. He appears to have brought only the one but, in the course of time, others have come into being until, now, there are five Ide-Millis, each with his distinctive status and functions.

THE HEART OF THE IBO

They are : 1. Ide-Milli-Ube. 2. Ide-Milli-Nkwọ. 3. Ide-Milli-Aku-Ọra. 4. Ide-Milli-Ojji. 5. Ide-Milli-Ezenta.

1. *Ide-Milli-Ube*. This deity is privileged to have the benefit of a hut and is represented by a stick. It is before this stick that a candidate receives sanction to take up the title of (Obusi) "Ọzọ". He has first to proceed to this shrine and, with the sacrifice of a fowl, make a declaration of his purpose.

The day after the conferring of the title, as a part of the celebrations, the new "Ọzọ" again visits the shrine, this time accompanied by his daughter (or the daughter of a relative). The girl places sticks of chalk alongside the Ide-Milli (stick). As she does this, she holds the hand of the man and counts seven. He is then called upon to sit upon the sticks of chalk. This he must do so lightly that not one is broken. This done, he returns home, the girls dancing and rejoicing with him until the whole populace is acquainted with the transaction. He must not, straightway, enter his own house ; instead he must repair to a bachelor's hut and reside therein for seven native weeks (28 days). At the close of this period, guns are fired to indicate that the whole ceremony is completed ; henceforth he is an "Ọzọ" titled man. If he lives for three years, that is sure proof that " Ide-Milli " found no fault in him.

A thief may also claim pardon through the favour of Ide-Milli. If his conscience trouble him, he brings a goat and ties it to one of the Ide-Milli sticks for the priest to accept and convert into a scapegoat on his behalf. A habitual thief will cease to steal after such a sacrifice because he has a profound belief that, if he revert to his former practices, Ide-Milli will destroy him for violating the sanctity of the sacrifice.

2. *Ide-Milli-Nkwọ*. He ranks second to Ide-Milli-Ube and is worshipped in general by all Obusi people. The special feature is a great feast held at the end of every eighteen years. It is the greatest festival of all ; it is called " Igbu Odunke " (you are feasting richly). This term becomes a sort of parable.

After a nine-years' interval, men sacrifice cows in honour of this deity and, after the succeeding interval of nine years, it is the women's turn ; they sacrifice goats. The feasts held on these occasions are very joyous affairs. Not only do the people don gala dress, but the animals to be sacrificed are also garlanded with cloths, necklaces and any article used for personal adornment.

As with Ide-Milli-Ube, any Obusi man taking up the title of "Ọzọ" must make the fact known to Ide-Milli-Nkwọ and, at the same time, make an offering of a fowl. The shrine of this god must be good, strong and well decorated.

To swear by Ide-Milli-Nkwo is regarded as equivalent to a legal oath.

3. *Ide-Milli-Aku-Ora.* This god is kept in a hut furnished with small pots and chalk. Formerly he served as " watchman " or " protector ". When a man (or woman) was leaving his house, he would take some of the chalk and feathers from inside " Aku-Ora's " hut and place them on a native plate (oku) and leave this on his threshold. No thief would enter a house protected by this symbol of godly power.

4. *Ide-Milli-Ojji.* Ojji is the Ibo name for the Iroko tree and so this is a combination between snake and tree. Not overmuch attention is accorded to this god. Only occasionally are yams and palm wine offered.

5. *Ide-Milli-Ezenta.* This is more of a tribal god and is identified with one part of Obusi only (Ire) : it is honoured and worshipped by that clan solely. The god is not housed ; he has to be content with small pots and chalk placed by the path leading to the Ide-Milli stream. The legend is that, formerly, Obusi had no water supply ; the people depended upon the juice of the plantain. Then a hunter appeared and created the Ide-Milli stream.

All these five gods have but one patronal head, namely, the python (Ekke). The story goes, that Ekke was travelling along the road and called at Ide-Milli's house. Later, he continued his journey, only to be killed by an Obusi man. Ide-Milli was wrathful because his visitor had been murdered. In turn, he began to kill the Obusi people. When they realised what was the cause of so many deaths, they made atonement by offering sacrifice and vowed to amend their ways. One particular promise was made that, henceforth, the snake (Ekke) should be sacrosanct. Should an Obusi person inadvertently be the cause of the death of an " Ekke ", he will incur guilt (Igba-alu), and must make atonement as for manslaughter.

In the ceremony, the man rubs his eyes with a live fowl and reports " Anya afurom ya " = he swears he did not see it or " Ntim anuro ya " = " I did not hear it ". He must refrain from shaving his head for a whole year. Further, he has to build a hut and deposit therein various articles. When complete, he calls the priest of Ide-Milli to come and accept the offerings and break down the hut. This is similar procedure to that followed in the case of one who has committed murder.

Many sacrifices have to be offered and a money payment made for the redemption of a snake-slayer. When all ceremonies have been completed, and all payments made, the pardoned man may then shave his head and resume his place among his fellow-townsmen.

Should a man meet with an accident say, due to the fall of a sacred tree, or should he be attacked by an animal devoted to a god, it is assumed that he is receiving just retribution for some crime committed. His sin has escaped detection by his fellow-men, but the god can see below the surface and does not fail to exact the penalty. If the accident prove fatal, there is no more to be said; it must be accepted that the god has executed summary vengeance on the offender. If injury result, then atonement must be made for the sin committed. Whether the man be conscious of wrongdoing does not affect the issue. That he has sinned is all too evident; what has befallen him is proof; he cannot relegate responsibility. If he was tempted to do evil, he should have resisted : if he did wrong unwittingly, innocence is no excuse, he ought to have known better.

Naturally, the household gods occupy a predominant place in the thoughts of the people. They are the ones which are intimately bound up with the affairs of the owner and his family. They have peculiar favours to bestow, and their protective qualities are for the special benefit of the folk concerned. They are jealously guarded from the attentions of intruders. A man's own private god is the only one that exercises any real influence on his life and actions. An oath sworn before it is the only one that is binding, or is of any value whatsoever. He is prepared to swear any oath before a strange " alusi ", because the doctrine of intention will exonerate him from failure to observe it : his oath being no more than mere words.

The fetish is nothing in itself, or by its own virtue. Its power depends solely upon its indwelling spirit. It is the home (shrine) of a god, not the god himself. Its value is neither more nor less than its cost when purchased. Only after consecration has the " alusi " a relative holiness, due solely to the priestly act of consecration. This ceremony is commonly performed in the house of the owner. For its observance kola nuts, yams, fowls and chalk must be provided.

Very seldom are the objects themselves called upon by name ; the petitions are invariably addressed to the spirits and this is known as " Igaw-Maw ". Occasionally, the god " Ikenga " is invoked under the title of " Ikenga Ọwa-Ọta ", that is, " he who splits the shield (of the enemy) ", hence the strongest one ; the bravest one. Occasionally it is expressed as " Ikenga Ọwa-Ọfia ". Then it refers to " Ikenga " as a great hunter. Under certain conditions this spirit-worship exercises a tremendous influence over the lives of the natives.

THE HEART OF THE IBO

Fetishes have their appointed places in every household. They are not all of equal status, though each has its own attributes and qualities : a few have only minor significance. The one that holds premier rank is the " Ikenga ". Without this god no householder would rest in peace, indeed, its absence would be considered fatal ; his family, his property and his very life would be in jeopardy. It is the first " alusi " a man acquires ; it retains its foremost place throughout his life, and shares his fate at death. It houses his guardian spirit and by the aid of that selfsame spirit he seeks prosperity for his affairs, public and private.

The Ikenga is exclusively a man's god. The owner refers to it as " my Ikenga ". He will often speak of it as his " right hand ", that is, his strength. When a man dies his " Ikenga " is split in two ; the right half is buried with him ; the left cast away.

" Ikenga " is consulted in most of the affairs of life. An example may be quoted : When a journey is about to be undertaken, oil is poured upon the head of " Ikenga " and his eyes are smeared with chalk. If the oil soak away (lit. is licked), it is an indication that the spirit has heard the petition and grants a safe journey. If the oil remain unabsorbed, doubts arise as to the wisdom of undertaking the journey. Recourse is then made to the priest who, by the use of charms, will divine the cause of the god's reluctance to grant the petition.

A safe return is acknowledged by sacrificial offerings. If, however, the journey prove unprosperous, or if sickness attack the owner, the priest affirms that the man's parents (ancestors) are unfavourably inclined ; hence more offerings are required to propitiate the parents' " Chi ".

As a sign of wellbeing, the Ibo quotes proverbially : " Ikengam kwu oto tata " = " My Ikenga stands upright to-day ". When an " Ikenga " falls it is accepted as a warning of danger.

An " Ikenga " is instantly recognised by its most distinguishing feature, namely, the horns. These are the emblems of courage and strength. The native considers the buffalo to be the bravest and most formidable of all animals, hence the symbolic use of horns often out of all proportion to the rest of the fetish. The figure is of wood, the more acceptable being made from a block of " iroko " (ojji). A full-sized one represents a man sitting upon a stool. In his left hand he holds upright a drawn sword ; in his right a head. These indicate what will happen to any antagonist. From the mouth descends the stem of a pipe stretching to the knees, on which reposes the bowl.

Cheaper examples are merely round blocks of wood, serrated or plain, and furnished with horns only. Whatever the style, the figures are all equal in religious value. Exact form to pattern is not essential; it is the indwelling spirit that matters. Generally speaking, all service rendered to " Ikenga " must be performed by the head of the family. If, for some cause, he is unable to officiate, the " Okpala " (senior next of kin male) fulfils the obligations.

It will be noted later (p. 153) that the "alusis" (gods) are accommodated in the " obi " of the compound. Besides the " Ikenga", there are the " Nkpulu-Chi " (tokens of the ancestral spirits). How many there are depends chiefly on the number the owner can recall by name, that is, recent ancestors, especially the ones in memory of those who attained to prominence during their lifetime. These " Okpensi " (or " Nkpulu-Chi ") are carefully guarded and greatly respected. New ones are consecrated as relatives die (cf. p. 281).

For a man, the " Chi " consists of a piece of wood, stripped of its bark, from ten to twelve inches long, cut from a sacred " egbo " tree. A man will never put one of these to represent a woman; on the other hand, a woman may dedicate one such " Chi " in order to show due reverence to her mother's (or daughter's) spirit. The memorial set up by a man for a female relative is in the form of a cone of clay, upon the top of which is placed the neck of a water-pot. One of these is dedicated upon the death of a mother, wife or daughter.

One stick is consecrated to " Chi ", the Supreme Being, and this is the only one to which direct sacrifice by name is occasionally offered. " Chi " seems almost to be a generic word for " god ". With a qualifying attribute it becomes a distinctive god, hence we have Chi used in conjunction with (*a*) " ukwu " = Chi-Ukwu (commonly contracted to " Chuku ") = the Great God and (*b*) Chi-Neke or Chi-Okike = God the Creator. Again, " Chi " is a sort of guardian deity, deputising for " Chi-Ukwu ". In this form every child has the right to have a " Chi " set apart for it from birth. In general, he shares his father's " Chi " until he is old enough to obtain one himself. It has no head; instead it has a rounded end and in no respect represents the human figure. Some specimens are adorned with cowrie shells.

" Chi " may be worshipped at any time. A fowl is killed and the blood sprinkled, and to " Chi " prayer is made for long life, children, forgiveness of sins and prosperity. Usually, a small dish made of clay, about the size of the palm of the hand, is placed before " Chi " from which he may take food; it is called "Qku-Iru". Also, it should be noted that a man's "Chi" is sometimes represented by a tree planted in front of his house. "Chi" is frequently referred to as "Chim" = "my god". Hence, whenever an accident happens, a man will exclaim, "Ewo! Chim" = "Alas! my god."

The native declares emphatically that there is a clear and absolute distinction between "Chi" = god and "chi" = day. Were it not for this distinction, the question might be raised as to whether there were some elements or traces of an original sun-worship. On arising, the Ibo salutes the morning with "Chi efo" that is, "day (light) has broken", and at evening time he says: "Chi ejirigo" = "the day (light) is finished". He also says: "Chi julu oyi" = "the day is cold". Again, "Chi na ubosi ana", meaning "light and day are gone". At a stretch, it might be interpreted "the *sun* and day are gone". Whether the two uses of the word spelt identically were ever connected in the remote misty past cannot be more than conjectured; certainly the present-day Ibo admits no relationship. "Chi" is one word meaning "god", and "chi" is another word meaning "day", which might be interpreted as "light" and, with a further effort, "sun"!

In some places, as at Awka, there is an annual feast, celebrated in the fifth week of the fifth month (Ibo calculation). In this, women are more prominent than men. It is a thanksgiving for past favours with prayer for future prosperity. New yams, not old, are used for this feast. The elderly women place their "Chis" in front of their houses, and invite their relatives to attend and assist in presenting gifts to them. The men take little active part, other than that the young ones adorn themselves to the best of their means. Then all move to the market-place, or other convenient open space, to witness exhibitions of wrestling, which bring the feast to a close. For proverbs concerning "Chi" see p. 437.

It is convenient here to mention one more feast, the one called "Otite", held in the month of November (onwa asa). Every man, woman, boy and girl will slay a fowl and sprinkle the blood and feathers upon his or her "Okpensi". Old men may, instead of a fowl, sacrifice a ram or goat; ordinary men take a cock; women a hen. It is, again, a service of thanksgiving combined with prayers for continued blessing.

It would be a thankless task to compile a complete list of all the miscellaneous objects which are brought under contribution to serve as repositories for spirits. There are many besides those already mentioned. Any material substance that appeals to the imagination of the native or, one might go further and say, his spiritual perception may be utilised. These objects are commonly spoken of as gods, " alusi ", " ju-ju ", or " fetishes " ; each has a proportional measure of sanctity in the eyes of the native and is treated with respect and reverence. When the owner dies, his "alusis" are placed outside the hut until it is decided by whom they shall be inherited. This is generally a matter of form, but, should any dispute arise before the next owner takes possession, a sacrifice must be made on the spot where the "alusis" had been accustomed to rest.

Charms (or fetishes) are carried in skin bags or may be placed in wooden bowls among the "alusis". When regarded as medicine only (ogwu), they are worn round the waist or neck to preserve the owner from witchcraft. They are equivalent to the lucky pig, the mascot and so forth, with which the European consoles him or herself.

In the vicinity of the kitchen, the women set up small conical lumps of clay for the installation of the gods whose functions are to protect the food from harm, notably poison. They are called " Ekwu ". The cones are smeared with chalk, but have no other distinguishing feature. There is also the " Akalogholi ", a god to prevent the spirit of death from entering a woman's hut. Not far away is the " Agwu ". (Onitsha = "Egbo" : Interior = " Ogilisi ".) This consists of a small pot embedded in the ground, encircled with fresh green sticks sunk about a foot deep in the earth. These take root and grow. The feathers from a chicken are placed in the pot together with some sticks of chalk. The business of this god is to afford protection generally, but more particularly when the owner is engaged in work, play or when fighting.

The men set up their "Agwu" in the "ilo" (courtyard) ; the women place theirs in front of their own huts. " Agwu " serves as the god of good fortune to bring increase in farm and byre but *not* to bring increase of children ; there are gods and sacrifices for that particular purpose. (*Vide* Chap. XI.)

The wife of a man holding " Ozo " title is privileged to possess a rather more elaborate form of " Ekwu ". Sticks of the sacred " egbo " tree are placed behind the kitchen and on them are threaded in inverted fashion small cooking pots, " ugbugba ". Offerings are made to this " alusi " at least once a year.

Further, it should be borne in mind that each profession has its peculiar patron god, as farming, hunting, and blacksmithing, and the richer women have their familiar spirits also to assist them in their trading ventures. The following are examples :

Ite-Umu-Nne, a distinctive woman's god dedicated to represent

MBARI HOUSE.
THE AUTHOR WITH THE PRIEST-IN-CHARGE OF THE MBARI HOUSE AT ULAKWO, JANUARY, 1935.
THE PRIEST, AS WILL BE NOTICED, IS A DWARF. (CHAPTER V.)

THE HEART OF THE IBO

her deceased mother. It is of wood hewn to have bulbous ends something like the small pestles used for grinding pepper. With it, small platters called " udu " or " okwa " are associated. This fetish is expected to protect its owner against ill-health and afford general assistance.

Akwali. This is composed mainly of cords arranged by the priest for the benefit of women who desire children. No one must know how it is bound and tied, nor what it contains. It is a woman's private possession and hangs in her own hut.

Eze Nezu. This god is peculiar to the neighbourhood of Atani, a town on the Niger, a few miles south of Onitsha. It stands for " one who can do all things ". It resembles a man in a sitting posture, modelled in clay, and richly adorned with pieces of glass, china and cloth. In his hand he grasps a spear. The figure stands beneath a shelter which is also decorated and is, usually, topped with a staff and a white flag. It is doubtful whether this is truly Ibo ; more likely it is an importation. The fact remains, that it has, around Atani, superseded almost every other form of fetish. Small chickens and kola nuts are the proper gifts to present to it. It is resorted to in any time of need. The method of sacrifice differs from normal procedure inasmuch as that *no* priest is required to act as intermediary.

Nkwu. This " alusi " is found more particularly in the Okigwi District and resembles a man. People carrying new yam will not pass it. Once a year, the priest comes out, but no one is allowed to see him. If one should transgress this law, the chief may deprive that one of all his possessions and even kill him. For three days, at the harvest season, the chief sacrifices and dances before the god. On one of the nights he sleeps in the shrine accompanied by two men who have been dedicated for the purpose.

Urai or *Urayi.* This is a household god kept in a pot with water, roots and other ingredients. One of the old men dips his hand into it and smears the liquid on a child to protect it against evil before setting forth on a journey. The " dibia " prescribes the list of ingredients which vary according to the needs of the house.

Ite Ogwu. The literal meaning of this is the medicine pot. The contents are procured from the " dibia ". Before going on a journey, a person will dip his hand into the fluid and rub it on his body to ensure protection. It is very similar to Urai, but there may be one for the whole village.

Uto. A village roadside god, a mound of clay which may be roughly fashioned to represent a man, generally provided with a shelter to protect it from the weather. Its function is to prolong life. It is rubbed with chalk and nothing black must come near it. This is quite different and distinct from Utọ described at the end of Chapter XXI.

The reader is reminded of the process whereby a material substance is converted into the habitation of a spirit. For the most part, men and women find, or convert, anything that appeals to them into a shrine. An " Ikenga " is the only one that calls for skill in manufacture and is the only one that is purchased in normal practice. There is no difficulty in buying a freshly carved specimen. It means nothing and it has no significance as a god. Its only value lies in the craftmanship of the maker, the price being in ratio to its size and the labour and skill involved. Some are small and crude, worth but a few pence ; others are large, with carving and colouring adding to their merit. Still it remains merely a piece of wood with no degree of sanctity and, apart from the workmanship, evokes no veneration. This comes only after consecration. It is believed that a duly qualified priest has power to invoke a spirit to take up residence in the " alusi ", and it is the consummation of this act which confers upon the material a relative holiness. It is henceforth the abode of a spirit. The observer unendowed with spiritual insight and sympathy will find it difficult to perceive and appreciate native thought although he is, doubtless, acquainted with very similar procedure among other and more intelligent folk. There appears to be no essential difference between the Ibo and European belief, at least the processes are allied in theory and practice.

After consecration, the owner sets up his " alusi " in a place of honour, pours out a libation of palm wine before it and offers kola ; henceforth it has the sanctity of, and receives the respect due to a god.

Sickness is often attributed to the vindictive operations of malevolent spirits. It may affect but one person, the family, or the whole community, as in the case of an epidemic of smallpox. Measures are taken to prevent " flying " sickness from entering a village and, at intervals, stipulated ceremonies are fulfilled and sacrifices offered for " driving out " sickness. Arrangements are made to propitiate the unfriendly spirits. There does not appear to be any god of sickness ; certainly, there is no emblem to represent one such as, for instance, the " God of Smallpox " in the neighbouring Yoruba country.

For the " driving out " of sickness an example may be quoted of what is done at Onitsha. Annually, there is a ceremony known as " Ọsọ Ekwulo ".[9] The people foregather in their own villages at a stated time. Each person carries a firebrand. When all are assembled, the cleansing ceremony is conducted and then, with much noise, and no little excitement, the mob moves to a prescribed spot where the firebrands are cast away. When all the quarters have fulfilled their obligations, arrangements are made for the final ceremony for driving sickness from the town. This is performed in the open space in front of the King's palace. A similar programme is followed to that carried out in the respective villages, only in a magnified fashion. When the king, the priests and the leading officials have finished their parts, the whole assembly, brandishing their torches, make their way to the river side. On arrival, they cast the burning brands into the water, crying out, as they do so, in order to drive away the demons responsible for sickness.

Although not actually a part of the religious system of the Ibos, yet closely akin to it, is the practice of divination. It is termed " Igba-afa " or " Ikpa-afa ". If a man wishes to obtain information which is beyond his powers, he consults the " dibia " skilled in the use of charms. This man, by virtue of his profession, is saluted under the title of " Agbasoaka " (able adviser) or " Okwuka-Ojelu " (one who is able to explain by divination.)

The diviner commences operations by placing an inverted tortoise shell on the ground which contains the " afa ", the medium of divination, commonly called charms. He proceeds to set up " Nkwu Agwu ", a small " Ikenga ", by whose power and authority Agbasoaka (or Okwuka-Ojelu) speaks of hidden things without fear. Alongside " Nkwu Agwu " is his " ofo " and " Udene-Agwu ", an " alusi " standing for the vulture. He also places on the ground a small water-pot known as " Udu-Arọbinagu ", the source from which the diviner receives his information. At certain times in the procedure, a drum (egede-agwu) is beaten and a rattle (ekpili) is shaken.

The charms themselves consist principally of four strings of half shells (from okwe seeds ; about the size of large walnut shells), a small bone, sometimes part of a man's collar-bone, though, more usually, a bone from a goat, and a small horn.

The diviner squats on the ground and begins to croon. Presently, he picks up the tortoise shell and shakes it and, at intervals, knocks it on the ground " Yom, yom, kpom, yom, yom, kpom, yom, kpom ", until he suddenly cries out " Arọbinagu bialu n'afa " = " Arọbinagu has entered the charm ".

The diviner calls upon the petitioner to salute " Ogwugwu ", an " alusi " that is able to impart life, and beg that no harm come to him, the petitioner, or his family. The diviner bids

THE HEART OF THE IBO

him to raise his hand skywards in order to secure long life. The man is then instructed to plant his feet firmly and repeat the words, " I have recovered my life in this world." The diviner, thereupon, scatters his charms and indicates what sacrifice is to be made by the inquirer. It is usually a white cock to be offered to the god " Ngwu " (a sacred tree).

The final shaking and subsequent scattering of the shells are now performed. All the (half) shells which fall rounded side upwards have something to communicate. With the bone, the diviner taps each shell in turn (each has its own distinctive name) then he blows on the horn and, while he blows, the shell which he has just tapped, tells him what he seeks to know. The information so collected is passed on to the man seeking counsel.

A Poor Man's " Ikenga " (p. 45).

NOTES ON CHAPTER I

[1] " A white man asks a question ; the black man thinks that courtesy bids him give the sort of answer which he believes the white man would like to get ; and so he says what he thinks would be welcome—not with the idea of deceiving, but with the idea of pleasing."—" *Savage Childhood* ", p. 127.

THE HEART OF THE IBO

[2] "*The Church Overseas*", Vol. VI, No. 23, pp. 242–3.

[3] "The African believes in a God, Who made all things—I do not know that they ever worship Him. Their worship is directed to the innumerable spirits about them who infest the air, among whom are their ancestors. The spirits are generally disposed to do them harm, but they may be placated, and their own dead may even be rendered favourable by certain ceremonies. But an incomparably greater number of spirits are always hostile and the impulse of the African worship is fear."—"*Fetish Folk of West Africa*", p. 228.

[4] The Rev. J. Taylor, in his "*Journal*", refers to the practice of the custom at Onitsha, under date of Sept. 29th, 1858.

[5] "*Fetish Folk of West Africa*", p. 256.

[6] *Ibid.*, p. 248.

[7] *Ibid.*, p. 249.

[8] "Bones, especially skulls, are valued as fetishes. It is recorded that the corpse of Dr. J. G. Batchelor, who died at Abo in 1859, was stolen for fetish purposes ; dug up and carried away."—"*Life on the Niger*", p. 34.

[9] "At Cape Coast Castle an annual custom was observed for the driving of the evil spirit ' Abonsam '. The ceremony began with the firing of guns in the houses, all the furniture was turned out of doors, and every corner was beaten with sticks, and the people screamed as loudly as possible, in order to frighten the devil. He, being driven out of the house as they imagined, they sallied forth into the streets, throwing lighted torches about, shouting, screaming, beating sticks together, rattling old pans and making the greatest possible noise to drive him out of their town into the sea."— Rev. John Martin writing in 1844. "*Tailed Headhunters of Nigeria*", p. 202.

CHAPTER II

SACRIFICES

BEFORE PROCEEDING to examine the Sacrificial System, it will serve a useful purpose if certain specific terms and expressions are made clear. The following are in common daily use :

Dibia. This, in popular language, stands for " medicine man ". Equally, it serves for " doctor " (qualified), necromancer, magician and, in some respects, priest. As noted in Chapter XI, the ranks of the " dibias " are recruited partly from new-born boys in whom the " dibia " declares he recognises features or characteristics resembling those of a deceased fellow-craftsman. A few are recruited from outside sources, while the majority are sons who inherit their fathers' profession. A son may succeed at any age from five years upwards, at first by proxy and, in due course, in actual practice.

Before a " dibia " can be initiated, he must obtain the fetish peculiar to the order, namely, the " Agwuisi ". As part of the preparation ceremony, the initiate proceeds to his mother's house and appropriates something from her " alusi ". He repeats the action on other " alusis " of the family, including that of his grandfather. Later, these relics will be used in the process of divination. At the arranged time, other " dibias " assemble for the purpose of " opening the eyes " of the novice in order that he may be endowed with power to foresee the future.

A " dibia ", by virtue of his initiation, is believed to possess invested power whereby, *ex opere operato*, he can invoke spirit into any material substance, hence into an " alusi ", the most favoured mediums being bones, teeth, a monkey's skull, and similar uncanny objects.[1] He is the accredited agent of the spirits and acts in conformance with their commands.

A " dibia " is trained by other more experienced craftsmen ; meantime, he puts forward claims to recognition on his own behalf. He differs from a " priest " and, in some respects, is greater in influence and position, inasmuch as he is acquainted with " medicine ", can foretell future events, and is in communication with the spirits.

SACRIFICES

On the other hand a " priest " is really superior in that he has the final word in respect of sacrifices and, without his intervention, pollutions cannot be removed.

There are recognised classes or orders among the " dibias " such as :

Dibia Afa. A diviner, a worker with charms whereby the spirits foretell the future and give directions for procedure in the matter of sacrifice (cf. p. 51).

Dibia Aja. His work is to perform the sacrifices in accordance with the directions given by the " Dibia Afa ".

Dibia Ogwu. He practises in medicine. There are men who combine in themselves all three offices though, on the whole, there are more " dibia ogwu " than either " dibia afa " or " dibia aja ". The doctors are numerous, some being " specialists ", practising for the treatment of one kind of sickness only.

Priests are known by the following terms : *Onye-Nchu-Aja* or *Onye-Igbu-Aja*. One who offers sacrifices. He may be a " dibia " also, or a sacrificing priest only.

Ora-Mili = Rain-maker. He is called to produce rain, or cause it to be withheld. His most important medium is a stone, frequently a piece of meteorite, which is thought to have an affinity with water. With it " medicine " and fire are associated. It is to be noted that the practice of the art coincides pretty closely to the wet and dry seasons !

The necessity to propitiate the powers that operate outside the sphere of human control is a dominant feature in Ibo life. To appease these spirits the people resort to sacrifice. Fear is the driving force ; the sacrifices do not spring from any inherent desire to give, nor from any spontaneous love to render honour or worship. Sacrifices furnish the only way of escape from the evil designs and activities of malignant spirits. Failure to perform propitiatory sacrifices would make life unendurable : every department would labour under imminent threat of possible disaster. Every adult man must fulfil his obligations on behalf of himself and his family (if he has one), but his liabilities do not cease there. He must contribute towards the public sacrifices also in the interests of, and for the benefit of, his fellow-villagers. It cannot be foretold to what extent, or in what manner, the spirits may manifest their displeasure ; the ramifications are many and widespread ; hence it behoves the community to take precautionary measures against unknown dangers.

This is much more the case when adverse conditions disturb the people. The thought to bear in mind is that voluntary sacrifice is not common ; force of circumstances, and the dread

SACRIFICES

of retribution, are the moving factors as a general rule. It is the " dibia's " duty to call the people to sacrifice as occasion demands, either at appointed seasons, or for particular needs, and he announces the type of sacrifice to be offered. As the god's executive, as well as the religious leader, he acts on behalf of both god and man.

The observer should bestow careful attention when investigating the system. In a general way, all offerings may be listed under the generic term "sacrifice", whereas, there are elements which distinguish one form from another. Outwardly, they appear to be alike, but the underlying principles, both in their purpose, and in their method of offering, are different. To obtain a clear perspective, discrimination is called for, indeed, it is essential to attain to a certain degree of native-mindness. The real difficulty lies in cultivating a faculty wherewith to perceive the difference between a propitiatory sacrifice and what may be regarded as a festival to placate the spirits.

The motive behind the services to the " Igo-Maw " (strange spirits) corresponds somewhat with the " Burnt Offering " of the Israelites. The underlying principle is derived from the word " Igo-agugo " = to deny. The offerings are presented with an element of protestation. The petitioner asserts that he has done no known wrong ; he has not trespassed against the law of the land, or against the community, then *why* has this evil befallen him ? If, however, by any chance he has sinned inadvertently, he now makes this sacrifice as an atonement for these unknown misdeeds.

As it is all so uncertain, the food brought before the " Igo-Maw " is left untouched ; it is " nso " (holy). There can be no sharing in a feast where there are no happy mutual associations. Almost in despair, because he does not know *why* he is troubled with sorrow, ill health, or whatever form the visitation takes, he leaves the sacrifice at the altar ; he cannot partake of it.

A man who knows perfectly well that he is guilty of wrong-doing will, on no account, venture to make sacrifice to the " Igo-Maw ". He would be in mortal dread lest the spirit should take summary vengeance on his hypocrisy.

The services to the " Ilo-Maw " (familiar spirits) have some similarity to the " Peace Offerings " of the Israelites. They are propitiatory sacrifices which, having proved acceptable, bring about a sense of reconciliation. Hence, the act of sacrifice, which has established peace between god and man is followed by rejoicing and feasting.

The distinction between sacrifices " proper " and " peace

SACRIFICES

offerings " is amplified by the fact that " Igọ-Maw " may be celebrated by every man, rich and poor alike, as its observance need cost little, while offering to the " Ilọ-Maw " is arbitrarily restricted to the family (*not* the individual) which is able to afford the accompanying feast. The more generous the feast, the more ingratiating it is to both the quick and the dead.

There seems to be a dim distinction between the spirits, some appearing to be more familiar than others. This is demonstrated by the fact that the offering of sacrifice is deemed to be essential only to those spirits which reside or operate outside the pale of human ken and control. The animist's life is permeated with the thought of their sinister power. All he can comprehend is that there are devastating forces at work in the world about him. He believes that, in some mysterious manner, these spirits can, and do, execute vengeance upon unprotected men. He may be unable to trace any definite reason for their antagonism, nevertheless, he is forced to conclude that punishment is meted out for some sin committed. Whether of omission or commission he may be unable to state : all he can do is to accept the verdict and meekly submit to whatever falls to his lot. In his distress, he appeals to the " dibia " and, either by his own endeavours, or by the services of the " dibia ", he seeks a way of forgiveness by offering appropriate sacrifices in order to " drive away evil " (" ichu aja "), or to " drive out the devil " ("ichu Ogbonuke"). For this latter, a dog or a fowl is killed and left lying in the street, or outside the village, as an offering to the evil one.[2]

No " alusi " is ever used for the observance of " Ichu-aja ". The only semblance to one is the " ọfọ ", sometimes referred to as the " God of Justice ". The symbol is a stick cut from the " ọfọ " tree which becomes effective after consecration. All Ibo men, and a great many women, possess an " ọfọ ".

Whenever sacrifice is to be offered, the " ọfọ " stick is an essential. It is held in the hand and serves two purposes ; first, " ọfọ " is regarded as a mediator between the spirits of this and the underworld and, secondly, on it a man swears innocency of wrongdoing against others.

The holder taps the ground with it to summon the attention of the ancestral spirits whose assistance he desires, the number of beats corresponding to the names he can call to remembrance at the time.

" Ọfọ " is also used when oaths are sworn. The majority of disputes are settled by swearing an oath, especially in the case of ownership of land. An oath so sworn before reputable witnesses generally establishes a claim. For the purpose of swear-

SACRIFICES

ing, " ọfọ " is applied to the mouth, thus signifying that the word spoken is true. Literally speaking, the man " swallows " ọfọ and then holds it on high and calls upon heaven to witness to his fidelity. " Ọfọ " is then placed in a bag with the words, " If all that I have said be proved false, then let ' ọfọ ' kill me."

As a mediator between man and the spirit world, " ọfọ " is carried while travelling in order to ensure safety ; it is used during the time of sacrifice to supplement the prayer for forgiveness of sin, preservation and for victory in time of battle.[3]

" Ọfọ " is also used in the ceremony of " Igọ-Maw " (p. 56).

To return for a moment to " Ichu-aja ", the offering consists of a selection of the following : food, strips of cloth, a gin bottle, a lizard, a chicken or a kid, and other things up to a bull or, in the past, a human being, according to the instructions of the " dibia ", and as the circumstances demand. A man may be his own sacrificing priest on occasions. When, however, the " dibia " so directs, the " di-ọkpala " alone can act.

The main objects of " Ichu-aja " are :
  (a) to remove fear of the living and the dead ;
  (b) to secure present and future well-being ;
  (c) to appease malevolent spirits.

The immediate results are hope, peace of mind and expectations of blessings to come.

Note may be made of other occasions when " Ichu-aja " is observed. The most common occur when a member of the community dies from a noxious complaint which rouses feelings of repulsion, such as leprosy or smallpox ; in the case of self-inflicted death, or when a man dies during the time of mourning for his wife, or a woman for her husband. The bodies of such are not buried in the ordinary manner : they are carried out and deposited in the " ajọ-ọfia " (bad bush). For this sacrifice, not much preparation is required. It is a small affair, the offering demands no more space than a wooden platter, or a makeshift one, cut from a banana (tree) stem, or a fragment of dried gourd (calabash), or merely a plaited palm-leaf dish. The offering is carefully laid at the junction where three or more paths intersect at a spot outside the confines of the village and, usually, adjacent to a path leading to a burial ground. The place selected is known as " Abu-itọ " and is near the spot where the disgruntled spirit is supposed to have his dwelling.

The person carrying the offering is enjoined to maintain strict silence while passing along the road ; not even a salutation is permissible. It is hardly necessary to exercise caution, because an oncoming traveller is usually quick to notice the presence of

SACRIFICES

the platter and incontinently gives way to the bearer. He will do this from fear rather than from feelings of respect, hence there is little likelihood of the bearer being accosted by the other person. Some guidance in direction comes from the fact that the spirit is alleged to be residing at an indicated spot. The presentation of the sacrifice is deemed sufficient to mollify his feelings and to induce him to cease from troubling the living.

Another occasion for " Ichu-aja " is prior to crossing water. Its observance is a guarantee of a safe passage. For removing pollution (alu), the custom is, where possible, to employ a Nri priest. Generally speaking, the person most concerned acts on his own behalf though, even so, he must consult the " dibia " in order to be sure of right procedure.

It is advisable to recall attention to the fact that the Ibo sacrifices for two main reasons. First, because of the pinch of adversity in some form or another. In common with other folk, the sense of sin and evil at work in the world drives a man to seek help from an outside power whom he believes to be his guardian spirit. The insufficiency of man, and his consequent inability to walk uprightly, is recognised by the Ibo. This is really why sacrifices are offered. The terms " Igọ-Maw " (" to propitiate the spirits ") and " Ilọ-Maw " (" to placate (feast) the spirits ") have deep significance for the Ibo. This underlying meaning must always be present in the mind of the student if he is to approach the study of Ibo sacrifice and ceremonial sympathetically.

We note that " Ichu-aja " is offered to malevolent spirits only ; there is no form of direct sacrifice to the Supreme Being. Annually—in July—when food is scarcer than at any other time of the year, a feast is held in honour of " Chi ", and this is known as " Aja-Chi " ; but, though the word for sacrifice is used, it is a loose way of using it. The procedure is on similar lines to any other feast to the " Ilọ-Maw ". It is not a " proper " sacrifice, rather it is a service of penitence for sin. The people show their contrition by wearing ordinary or, more customary, old clothes ; they do not dress in their best as for other festivals. This " Chi " is not to be confused with " Chukwu ", the Supreme Being.

Igbu Aja. This is the highest form of sacrifice known to the Ibo and is national in character, both as regards repentance and reform. It is never offered by an individual or a family, but by the whole quarter and, maybe, the whole town. On the average it takes place about once a year. There may be other occasions, such as when there seems to be an abnormal sequence of deaths among children, or a succession of births of

SACRIFICES

twins; when crops are not up to standard; when an epidemic makes its appearance (oya nefe efe = sickness that is transferable = infectious), or when there has been a violation of tabu regulations.

For the actual sacrifice, two goats, herbs, roots and other offerings are provided in accordance with instructions from the " dibia " who, by the by, for this ceremony, must be a stranger hired to come from another town to minister on behalf of the afflicted community. The preliminaries consist in much gesticulating and shouting, which continue until the real ceremony is taken in hand. Some of the victims are slain and burnt; then a bundle is bound up containing portions of the sacrificial offerings. In this sacrifice nothing may be eaten; not even by the priest. The bundle is placed upon a man or woman, who starts on a perambulation of the town followed by the " dibia " and the whole assembly. When the circuit has been completed, the " dibia " rushes about shouting and the followers imitate him.

All then move off to a spot situated at some distance from the village where the remaining rites are performed. The idea is that " aja " has gone round absorbing all impurities, iniquities and abominations. The first goat having been slain as an atoning sacrifice, the second goat is now loaded with all the reproach and stigma as the sin-bearer; its face is turned towards the " bush " and it is driven away and allowed to run wild; in brief, it is the " scapegoat ". At some of the riverside towns offerings of goats and human beings were also offered to the waters.

Sacrifice, in consequence of pollution, is called " Ikpu-alu " = " to drive out abomination "; it may be on behalf of an individual or for the township. The following are some instances for which " Ikpu-alu " is necessary for purification purposes :

1. A man having carnal knowledge of his mother, sister, or another of his father's wives.
2. A man committing adultery with his brother's wife, or the wife of a member with whom there is blood relationship.
3. Major misdeeds against Native Law and Custom.
4. A man committing suicide by hanging.
5. A man fighting with a " maw ". (*Vide* p. 375.)
6. A man having sexual intercourse with an animal.
7. The birth of twins.
8. A child cutting its upper before its lower teeth.
9. Abnormal presentation in delivery.

These are examples; there are other offences which demand

SACRIFICES

purification ceremonies; a complete list would absorb considerable space.

The " dibia " dictates the appropriate sacrifice and, when provided, gathers all who are involved in the pollution, whether a family or the whole village community. The carcase of the animal sacrificed is divided into pieces and the offender's name mentioned before the " alusi " brought along for the purpose. The culprit confesses his sin before the " alusi " and his body is smeared with ashes. This constitutes the outward sign of repentance. Absolution is pronounced, and the assembled folk declare to the " alusi " that they are satisfied, and the forgiven sinner resumes association with his friends from whom, because of the abomination committed, he has been estranged.

The custom of " Ikpu-alu " is followed in a generally non-specific fashion. A village is cleansed by a fowl being dragged through the streets.

Some sacrifices are ordered by the " dibia " for definite purposes such as for the healing of sickness. The underlying idea is to propitiate the malevolent spirits whom the sufferer has, consciously or unconsciously, offended.

Some are offered as thanksgivings for requests granted, such as restoration to health or calamity averted. The " dibia " decides what is to be offered and he consumes most of the sacrifice. The other people present eat any remnants he leaves, while the blood and bones are reserved for the " alusi ".

For some sacrifices, the animal or fowl must be white. Such may be offered to " *Chukwu* ", the Supreme Being, whom no man can see owing to his eyes being unable to pierce the blinding rays of the sun. Because the sun is white, it is thought that the Great God will accept no other than a white sacrifice.

In a case of sickness, if the " dibia " ordain a black goat as an offering, it is taken as an indication that the patient will not recover; if a white sacrifice be ordered, then the omen is hopeful. Sacrifices connected with water spirits are always white. (*Vide* p. 40.) When a sheep or fowl is thus offered, the head only is given to the " alusi "; when a goat or cow is sacrificed the skull is given.

For cases of " breaking ju-ju ", that is, for removing an oath previously sworn, a distinct breed of fowl must be used. It is of speckled hue, dark brown and white, and its feathers are ruffled; they do not lie flat as the feathers of an ordinary chicken. It is known as " Okuku Ayiliya ".

A house or compound is deemed unclean after:
1. The delivery of a child.
2. Menstruation.

SACRIFICES

3. Prior to the celebration of a festival. In this case, the purification ceremonies must be performed whether there has, or has not, been pollution.
4. A bed is unclean ceremonially if a woman pass urine upon it or, indeed, wherever she sleeps.

For case 4, a similar ceremony is observed as for " Isa ifi " (*vide* p. 225), except that the woman concerned takes the fowl first and presses it on the spot where the pollution has taken place pleading, as she does so, for forgiveness, and protesting that she is innocent of any intention to transgress ; that the sin was committed unconsciously. After this confession, the " ada " (chief woman) completes the ceremony as for " Isa ifi ".

5. A woman crying in the house is regarded as polluting it. The cleansing ceremony is performed by the " ada ". She impales a snail shell on a stick and passes round the premises touching the walls with it.

Purification must always be performed after menstruation. This is little more than ceremonial washing. The woman must first wash herself *outside* the compound walls after dark, using a water-pot reserved solely for the purpose. It is a round pot with a wide mouth called " oku aru ", meaning the one vessel used for cleansing after menstruation. Next day, she may proceed to the stream, but is forbidden to enter the water straightway. She stands on the bank apart from other people present. Another woman brings a pot of water to her and she washes her body thoroughly. This completed, she may enter the water as a cleansed woman ; and (if married) resume cooking for her husband and others in the compound.

The purification of a house or compound is the responsibility of the " ada " or chief woman. Everything is cleared out of the house. The necessary sacrifices are provided, and the priest sprinkles blood on every article that has been defiled saying, as he does so, " Alu pua " (" pollution depart "). Next, he ceremonially touches every person with the sacrifice and, after bathing, they are clean once more. The articles are then cleansed and returned to the house. Henceforth, the pollution, whatever it is, is no more mentioned. All the expenses are borne by the " ada ". Occasionally, she takes a snail and, passing round, touches the articles with it, or she may do likewise with a chicken and some pepper. After use, these cleansing mediums are cast away.

The pollutions which call for ceremonial cleansing of a house or compound are very much the same as " Ikpu-alu " for the village. They are, chiefly, the birth of twins ; abnormal pres-

SACRIFICES

entation at the time of delivery; death of the mother in childbirth; child cutting upper teeth first; known and acknowledged sins of immorality; infectious diseases; the death of a husband.

Ilǫ-Maw. This is the most common of all forms of sacrifice. The term " sacrifice " is hardly applicable in this case and can only be used in a broad sense; actually, it is more of the nature of a festival or a " peace-offering ". It is associated with feasting, rather than with the idea of atonement for trespass committed. It is, on the one side, an expression of good fellowship and, on the other, a means of placating the spirits of the nether world in order that all may rejoice simultaneously. The gifts signify goodwill towards those who are alive and towards those who have passed beyond this present world : it marks the allayment of suspicion for the time being. Deceased relatives are, by this feast, refreshed and cajoled into good humour. Thus they are induced to manifest favour, especially towards any who are sick or suffering under the hand of adversity. With the assistance of their good services there is much better prospect of recovery.

When a feast to the " Ilǫ-Maw " is observed, the procedure is as follows. Before describing it, attention must be called to the fact that, for the most part, sickness is not attributed to natural causes. Instead, it is believed that ill health, for which no visible reason can be assigned, is the result of witchcraft, or that it springs from the activities of spirits who have, in some unknown way, been offended and who display their wrath by inflicting sickness. One of the leading members of the family approaches a " dibia " and relates his story. The " dibia " inquires into the circumstances, the kind of sickness, how and when it began, and so forth. He thus obtains all the information available and derives some foundation upon which to base his diagnosis. He is then in a position to proceed with his own professional part in the business. He does this by divination. The upshot is that, as a general rule, blame is attached to some person, very frequently a woman. Clandestine infidelity is assumed to be a cause of sickness, including rheumatism and other ailments which have no connection with sexual intercourse. Too often, the allegation cannot be denied and, though the woman cannot understand " how " it has come about, yet, being unable to refute the charge, it is taken for granted that her sin is the cause of the sickness. Her one and only chance to prove herself innocent of deliberate evil intention was to pass successfully through a trial by ordeal. This consisted of swallowing the contents of the poison cup. (Ǫrachi

SACRIFICES

= sasswood.) A woman who was unfortunate enough to be condemned to this form of trial died, forthwith, unless there was found a way of escape. Not often, however, was a woman rich enough to negotiate successfully with the administrator of the cup. He was most probably quite amenable to a monetary compromise. If made sufficiently attractive he might be persuaded to omit the poison altogether or, failing that, add a potent emetic which would cause the drinker to vomit before the poison could take effect.

The nature of the sickness and other circumstances involved decide the type of sacrifice to be offered. It may be of serious importance in which case sacrifice to the "Igo-Maw" is the more likely to be prescribed. In the majority of cases a feast to the "Ilo-Maw" is advised. Arrangements for the latter present little difficulty, and there is no reason for prolonged delay. The "alusis" are brought into the open compound and ranged according to significance. The "Ikenga" occupies the place of honour in the centre : on either side are the symbols of lesser importance, the "Okpensis" representing the ancestors, "Chi" (the guardian spirit) and the remainder of the "alusis" (if any) in due order. When all are arranged, a little water is poured over them wherewith the spirits "wash their hands" prior to partaking of the food provided. The next item is the presentation of kola nuts as a token of friendship. Then follows a gift of pounded yam, previously dipped in the palm-oil relish, a small portion being placed on the head of each "alusi". Each wife contributes her portion to the food cooked, that of "Anasi", the head wife, being accepted first. This ceremonial offering of the food being completed, it is assumed that the spirits are satisfied, that is, they have absorbed the spiritual essence of the food. Thereupon, a child is invited to collect the food from the heads of the "alusis". It carries the food away and shares it with other children. The drink offering is then made by pouring a little palm wine (or gin) over the "alusis" in turn, similarly to the way the food was offered. Finally, more water is sprinkled in order that the spirits may comply with the custom of washing the hands after partaking of a meal.

On one occasion, I was a guest of a chief and had the good fortune to be a spectator throughout the ceremony of an offering to the "Ilo-Maw". He was an old man, the victim of rheumatism. He was anxious to trace the cause of his pains and discover the means to cure them. So far, in spite of many sacrifices offered and the use of medicine, he had experienced no relief. Finally, the "dibia" had pronounced that one

SACRIFICES

of the younger wives was the author of her husband's sickness.

A space was swept clean at the base of the sacred " ogilisi " tree. Here the " alusis " were deposited as previously described. Then followed an exciting chase after a hen which, when caught, was tied by the leg to another tree with a cord of sufficient length for the fowl to be " waved " freely over the assembled " alusis ".

When these preliminaries were completed, the sick man's elder brother (Ọkpala) placed a low stool before the " alusis " and took his seat upon it. Until this moment there was no indication that a religious ceremony was in progress, with the exception of the display of the " alusis ". People moved about freely and there was no diminution of noisy conversation. The " Ọkpala " assumed an utterly indifferent attitude towards the surroundings, being completely absorbed by the task before him. He began his address to the spirits and, immediately, the assembled company became profoundly silent. The old man spoke eloquently : it was a really fine oratorical effort and no one could have failed to be impressed. He began in a subdued voice as if he were conscious of his nearness to the spirit world and was rather afraid for himself. Gradually, he became carried away and his prayers and entreaties increased in force and passion until they resounded throughout the compound. Meanwhile, he was swaying from side to side and his whole body became convulsed with the intensity of his emotions. He appealed to the ancestral and other spirits to be gracious, to send relief to the sufferer, and to bring the author of the sickness to judgement.

The oration came to a conclusion and the " Ọkpala " rose from the stool preparatory to departure. Before leaving, he transferred the remaining duties to a younger brother. He took hold of the man's right hand and placed it upon the central " alusi " and, thereby, delegated his priestly powers. In profound silence and with great dignity the old " Ọkpala " withdrew from the compound.

What to me was even more interesting was the subsequent procedure. After the departure of the old " Ọkpala ", all the wives of the sick chief came forward and stood before the " alusis ". Each wife, in turn, picked up the fowl and " waved " it over the " alusis ", at the same time calling upon the spirits to testify to her innocence of being the cause of the sickness. The spirits, who could discern and judge the inmost thoughts, would, doubtless, establish her integrity in the presence of the assembled witnesses, indeed, let the gods do to her,

SACRIFICES

and more also, were she guilty of lying or wrongdoing. This procedure was followed by all the wives with the exception of the one upon whom suspicion had fallen. She stepped to the front, but, instead of taking the fowl into her hands, she addressed the company and sought to vindicate herself. In place of the formula " let my life be as the life of this fowl if I am guilty ", she could do no more than make a general declaration of innocence. On the other hand, if she should be proved guilty, let it be known that her offence had been unintentional ; she had neither wished nor planned to bring suffering upon her husband. Confession is not infrequently made by a woman labouring under the impression that she is the unwitting cause of her husband's illness. If she has committed adultery (ifi) she has forfeited her claim to be blameless, she and others about her believe that she must surely be guilty. The effect on the man is clearly apparent and, no other satisfactory cause of the sickness being observable, the sinning wife cannot escape the responsibility.

Her declaration having been listened to in stony silence, the priest forthwith presented the fowl to the " alusis " with invocations beseeching the spirits to accept the atoning sacrifice. In his left hand he held the bird by its wings ; with his right he seized a matchet. With this he sawed lightly across its throat in order that the blood should fall in drops rather than flow too freely. The " alusis " were sprinkled one by one until the blood was exhausted. Before the blood could dry, small tufts of feathers were plucked from the breast of the fowl and stuck on the " alusis " by means of the blood, the wretched bird, meantime, being alive and slowly bleeding to death. When, at last, the blood ceased to flow, the fowl was thrown aside. The blood alone avails for remission of sin : the carcase, drained of its life-giving force, is no longer of sacrificial value.

The fowl was snatched up immediately by one of the young men who, forthwith, began to pluck it. While he was performing this task, another fellow was kindling a fire. Into this the bird was thrust to singe off the remaining feathers. It was then hacked to pieces and the bits grabbed by the men around. These were fixed on skewers (sticks) and grilled more or less. Actually, they were little more than scorched and blackened with smoke, mostly the latter. After this pretext at cooking, the pieces were again divided, so that about a score of men had a small share each. The women present did not partake of the flesh : they are not permitted to eat of sacrificial food of this nature. (*Vide* p. 68.)

" Ilǫ-Maw " is observed as a public function on certain ap-

SACRIFICES

pointed days of the year of which the chief are as stated below. All other occasions are irregular ; they are contingent upon disturbances of normal conditions.
1. *Aja-Chi*. The sacrifice to one's chief guardian spirit, commonly spoken of as a " god ". " Chi " is, however, not to be confused with Chukwu, the Supreme Being. (*Vide* pp. 37 and 46.)
2. *Umatọ* :
    Preliminary to :
3. *Iwa-ji*. The feast of new yam ; lit. the breaking of the yam = Harvest Thanksgiving. Fowls are offered in sacrifice, and the people pray for renewed life as they eat the new yam.
4. *Ikelle-be-ji*. A feast in which the yam is cut into chunks and eaten unmashed.
5. *Osisi-ite*. A sort of cooks' festival ; a feast to the spirits who protect the cooking utensils and the food from poison.
6. *Ife-afia*, or *Afia-ji-ọku*. A harvest festival connected with the yam field. An offering to the spirits of the field, with special reference to the presiding deity of the yam crop. The fowls offered must be carried to the farm and slain there, the blood being sprinkled on a few choice yams. When the ceremony is completed, everything is taken home ; the yams are laid up before the " alusis ", together with all the farming implements. The fowls are eaten at the subsequent feast. The whole community shares in this harvest home thanksgiving.[4]

The meaning and significance of the " Ife " or " Afia-ji-ọku " is, perhaps, worth mentioning. The idea behind " Afia " seems to indicate exertion, industry, to strive after, hence to trade ; " ji ", to lay hold of, and " ọku ", riches. Thus, the full meaning is : " Industry or trade brings wealth." And in past days, food, that is yam, largely constituted wealth, and so the feast became essentially connected with yams.

The feast is celebrated once a year and is observed at a sacred spot. It is held in the sixth month after planting and, in some parts, is observed on an Nkwọ day only. It is held when the first new yams are available ; yams, the seed of which were planted in the first month of the year, in order to be ready in time for " Afia-ji-ọku ", whereas the main crop is planted in the second month. In the ceremony, blessing is sought of the yam spirit. Kola nut is produced and, standing in front of the " alusi ", the petitioner repeats : " Eat this kola and help the yams in the small farms that, if the rain be too much they may

SACRIFICES

not drown and, if the sun be too strong, he may not cause them to wither."

The sacrificial offerings vary a little in different localities. The gift may consist of kola nut and a fowl, together with "ogilisi" and new yams, these last being boiled. Sometimes, the thick skin, together with kola nut and young palm leaves are offered. The petitioner says : " See this fowl which I have brought you ! " " Afia-ji-oku ne okuku m'wetalu ka m'nye i." The throat of the fowl is slit across and the blood sprinkled. The carcase is given to the children wherewith to make soup. He, the petitioner, goes on to say : " If I plant yam as small as this, when I dig it up may it be as long as this ", indicating with his hands and arms the sizes he has in mind. He prays that fever may not trouble him or his people and that all things may prosper in his hand.

That night a feast is held, of which men only partake as they are responsible for the growing of the yam ; in any case, women do not eat food that has been offered to a spirit. A month later, the people begin to dig up their yams.

On the western (Asaba) side of the Niger, the " Ife-ji-oku " is rather a subject of fear. Neither a menstruating nor a pregnant woman may enter the farm. She must invoke the aid of a friend to dig her yams for her. A mother must wait until three months have elapsed after the birth of her child.

At Awka, a man performs the ceremonies on his farm on Nkwo day only. After the sacrifice is made, he places small pieces of yam or fresh yam shoots into a long basket. After that, new yams may be eaten by all, old and young. They respond : " Afia-ji-oku, you have done well to lead us so far ; lead us on to full ingathering ; thank you for all good things up to this time ; lead us in the days to come."

Afia-ji-oku-nwayi. (Edde = koko-yam.) There is no definite " alusi " for this. The ceremonies are performed in front of the spirit (iru-maw) in the " obi " (house). Edde is cooked and, when ready, the woman calls her husband. He addresses " Afia-ji-oku-nwayi " : " Make this woman's edde to be big like this (doubling his fists to indicate the size suggested) ; keep her in health and prosper her and her children that, next year, she may be strong to come and give you more food. Do not allow sickness to visit this house."

It will be convenient to mention here one or two other festivals which have their place in Ibo life, although distinctly local.

Ofalla. Until recently, this feast was confined to Onitsha as far as the eastern side of the Niger is concerned. It has now

SACRIFICES

been introduced into one or two other places. On the western side, the feast which corresponds to " Ofalla " is known as " Ine ". It follows immediately after the " Iwa-ji " and its origin has connection with the yam festival. It is the occasion of the annual appearing of the King in public.[5] According to old practice, two months prior to this event, the chiefs (Ndichie) visited surrounding towns until they found a girl suitable for sacrifice. She had to be between fifteen and twenty years of age, good-looking and of light colour. With their purchase, the chiefs returned home. Their prize was placed in restricted quarters, otherwise she was cared for very well.

Then came the day for the great sacrifice " Iru-Ani " (lit. face of, i.e. to worship the land). The girl was adorned richly and placed on a seat before the King's Palace. In due course, the King came out and paraded before his people. Then the chief priest appeared, grotesquely covered with feathers and cowrie shells, with minor priests in attendance. The priest proceeded to inquire of the King what was to be done in respect of the annual sacrifice for cleansing the town from sin? The priest presented an animal which the King rejected and, in its stead, substituted the girl, at the same time tossing a stick into her lap. Others followed his lead and cried out, " We are going to send you to the spirit world and you must request the spirits to send us good things." Straightway, the victim was thrown to the ground, bound with ropes and young palm leaves (*vide* omu, p. 408) and dragged round the town. As this was in progress, the crowd pelted her with sticks and stones and called upon her " to take away the sin from our town ". Eventually, she was dragged to the river bank, a distance of nearly two miles, and pushed from the rock into the swollen stream, the Niger being at that season in full flood.

My old friend, Archdeacon D. C. Crowther, related to me that, once when the ceremony was in progress, he sought to effect a rescue of a stricken girl, but arrived on the scene too late to save her life.

Writing on February 27th, 1858, the Rev. J. Taylor, the first missionary settled amongst the Ibos at Onitsha, records a case of human sacrifice witnessed by himself and an agent of the factory (trade depot). " The victim was ' a poor young woman '. Her hands were tied behind her back, with her legs fastened together with a rope, decorated with young palm leaves. In this position she was drawn, with her face to the earth, from the King's house to the river, a distance of two miles. . . . The young woman was dying, through the suffo-

SACRIFICES

cation of dust and sand in the streets. The motley groups who attended her premature funeral cried, as they drew along the unfortunate creature, victimised for the sins of the land, ' Alu ! alu ! alu ! ' that is, Abomination, or that which defiles. This alarm was given to notify to the passers-by to screen themselves from witnessing the scene. The sacrifice was to take away the iniquities of the land. The woman was dragged along in a merciless manner and finally cast into the river. A man was killed too as a sacrifice for the sins of the King." [6]

Under the heading of " Tabus on quitting the House ", we read : " The King of Onitsha does not step out of his house into the town unless a human sacrifice is made to propitiate the gods : on this account he never goes out beyond the precincts of his premises. Indeed, we are told that he may not quit his palace under pain of death or of giving up one or more slaves to be executed in his presence. As the wealth of the country is measured in slaves, the King takes good care not to infringe the law. Yet, once a year, at the Feast of Yams, the King is allowed, and even required by custom, to dance before his people outside the high mud wall of the palace." [7] While it is true the King did not, by royal custom, step outside the walls of his palace and, normally, never seemed to manifest an inclination to do so, yet, if he had suspicions that underhand work and plottings were on foot, he did not hesitate to make surreptitious visits to the town—in the dead of night—in order to glean information.

The sacrifice completed, and all pollution duly carried away from the land (town), the " Ọfalla " rejoicings could now be observed. Warriors, known and acclaimed for their prowess, went in procession (more or less) headed by their respective Ndi-chies to make obeisance to the King. It was at this time that candidates for the rank of warrior were approved, hence it was a sort of New Year Honours Festival ! The rest of the time was given up to feasting and drinking, music and dancing, until strength and supplies were exhausted, a real old carousal to the last drop !

" Ọfalla " is still observed in a restricted form. Cows are substituted for the human sacrifices, and the ceremonies generally have lost much of their significance ; there is a vast difference between present-day ceremonies and the original observances. The age-old custom of the King living in seclusion throughout the year, except for the one occasion when he appeared before his subjects at the annual festival of the " Ọfalla ", collapsed soon after the British occupation of the country. After the installation as " Obi " of Samuel Okosi in

SACRIFICES

1901, he abandoned all ideas of seclusion and moved about as freely as any of his subjects ; another instance of disintegration of ancient law and custom.

In these modern days, it is nothing more than a fête with dancing, music, feasting and general manifestations of pleasure and enjoyment, with congratulations for the year past and good wishes for the year to come.

Mgbobo. This is a feast carried out by girls at Onitsha. They cook food and, at evening time, place it before the gate of the compound and sit beside it. Presently, they take some of the pounded yam and throw it away, repeating, as they do so, " We have sacrificed." Afterwards they eat all they want of the food and take the remainder to their rooms.

Aro-Ichu-Aja, sometimes known as " *Igu-Aro* " = counting of the year. The celebration of this feast is held late in December or early in January. The easiest way to explain this is " the god of good fortune ". In many ways it corresponds to the old ideas of the Maypole in Europe. A goat and fowls are offered in sacrifice with special petitions for blessings on farm and home during the ensuing year.

Nothing can be planted prior to the celebration of the feast. On the day it is observed no unnecessary noise is allowed. There must be no splitting of firewood, or beating of palm-nuts, as it is a day of peace. On the eve of the day appointed for the " Aro " festival, the folk resort to the stream for ceremonial washing, thus signifying that they are starting the new year purified from the sins of the year that is past. The women prepare a special meal of which the important ingredient is smoked fish known as " Ngbakulu ".

On the day of observance, the men rise early and collect young sticks from the " ese " tree. This wood is largely used for making the frame upon which the yams are tied (the " oba "). The sticks are cut into small pieces and has the significance of " that which settles all quarrels ". After he has cut the sticks into pieces, the man places them near the entrance of his house. He then breaks a cocoanut and places the fragments with the pieces of stick.

During the late afternoon and evening, there is much firing of guns. The feast follows, the women bringing what they have prepared while, on this occasion, the owner of the house roasts the yams close to the spot where the sticks have been deposited. After all have partaken, more gun-firing follows, until the headman of the village sounds his horn to proclaim that the feast is at an end.

The elder folk then retire to the house, while the boys and

SACRIFICES

girls collect the sticks and pieces of cocoanut and run round the compound shouting as they run :

    Umu-Arọ gbafelu kwọnu.
    Umu-Arọ gbafelu kwọnu.
= Sins (lit. children) of the year run away.

A little later the horn is heard again and the voices of the men respond :

    Welu kwọnu ebenebene.
    Welu kwọnu ebenebene.
= Take ye, be quiet and depart.

 The boys and girls, thereupon, leave the compound and go into the streets of the village, or the neighbouring " bush ", and throw away the pieces of stick and cocoanut, or they may deposit them in the bed of a stream, whence they are swept away by the next freshet, thus signifying the " mystical washing away of sin ". After the fulfilment of the ceremony, planting may be begun.

 Some reference must be made to a custom which is now defunct, but which, in days prior to the advent of the British Government, had a definite place in the religious and social economy of the Ibo people. This tribe was not alone in practising the custom of human sacrifice—other tribes around them were equally addicted to it.[8] The taking of human life did not, in every instance, bear the true idea of sacrifice for sin. The term is generally used to comprehend all cases where ceremonies were considered to be incomplete without the shedding of human blood. Understanding is necessary to discern the distinction between " proper " sacrifice and a social custom carried to its extremity : the underlying principles were not always identical, as will be pointed out in due course.

 Using the term in its broad sense, human sacrifice was a generally accepted custom among the Ibos. There was a widespread and deeply rooted belief that, in some way, this was more than ordinarily efficacious ; at least, it could be affirmed, that it was the highest type of sacrifice. In the offering of a fellow-being, the native attained to the zenith of his standard of values.

 The chief distinguishing feature is to be sought in the reason for the sacrifice. Where it was made as an atonement for sin, it followed the usual procedure for " Ichu-aja ". In other cases, the victims were provided to furnish a retinue to accompany a leading man into the spirit world, and they were killed

SACRIFICES

during the course of the funeral obsequies. These latter are more particularly discussed in a later chapter (XXI).

Human beings were offered in sacrifice for specific reasons, some of them on regular occasions, more often they were governed by some untoward circumstance. The community shared fully in the responsibility; it was not customary for individuals to undertake such an important task. The call to sacrifice sprang from some disturbing element which it was feared was threatening the village, or to pray for a visitation to be removed. Whether in the form of a hostile attack from outside, the outbreak of an epidemic, or some equally disastrous catastrophe, it was believed that sacrifice was the only essential means to obtain relief. Forces beyond the control of the people were at work, and these must needs be countered by appropriate sacrifices in order that the wrath of the gods might be appeased. It was an anxious time for the priests : it was their business to diagnose the cause of the trouble and point out a way of escape, that is, to arrange for the lifting of the anger of the spirits.

Animals were used in the majority of cases ; it was only when the offering of these failed to bring about a cessation of the trouble that the people felt that the only course left open to them was to offer a human being ; it was the final appeal : beyond that they could not go. Such a victim had to be sought from outside ; it was tabu to make use of a fellow-villager. Normally, it was a slave purchased from another town. Whether man or woman, he or she must be young and strong, and of attractive appearance. When it *had* to be done, it was considered essential that the victim should be one well fitted for the great task in hand. He must inspire confidence as the one chosen to bear the sins of the people. This sin-bearer was spoken of as " onye-uma ". It is difficult to render into English the word " uma ", but the underlying idea is exactly that of Deuteronomy xxi. 23 : " He that is hanged is accursed of God." The man was to die an ignominious death—he himself becoming an abomination—a cursed thing. Indeed the ceremony itself is termed " ikpu-alu " (to carry away abomination). He was the sin-bearer. The arms and legs of the man were tied, and he was then bound to an " egbo " tree ; the head man stepped forward and solemnly transferred first his own sins, then the sins of his household and, finally, the sins of the community to the head of the sacrifice. The trespass-transfer being fulfilled, the man was loosed from the tree (his legs and arms remaining bound) and a rope was attached to his ankles and, forthwith, he was dragged round the town by two slaves

SACRIFICES

appointed for the task. The whole populace treated the wretched creature as an accursed thing; he was reviled, spat upon, kicked, stoned; dust was thrown upon him, and in every form imaginable he was despitefully treated and denounced as an abomination. The slaves continued to drag him through the streets until life was extinct, and then the corpse was taken back to the King's quarters and cast away in the spot reserved for the bodies of human sacrifices. The victims were not buried; they would have been left to rot, except for the fact that the corpses were stolen during the succeeding night by the friends of the official executioners, who were not members of that community. The bodies were taken away to the native town of these officials and were there eaten. In towns adjacent to the river, the corpses were sometimes cast into the stream.

Occasionally, instead of dragging the man through the streets after the ceremony at the " egbo " tree, he was placed upright in a hole and buried alive, his head being left above the ground. Here he was subject to all manner of abuse and ill-treatment, the sufferings of the unhappy creature evoking gross abuse without a thought of pity. The corpse was left in this state, the memorial of an accursed thing to every one who passed that way.

Again, the form of death might be different. After the initial ceremonies, the man, bound hand and foot as above, was laid on the ground, covered with grass and wood and burned to death.

The most horrible of all deaths was when the sacrifice was crucified and left bound to the tree. The tortures he was compelled to endure can scarcely be conceived. During the initial stages, it might not mean extreme suffering, but death was slow in coming. A young virile man would naturally linger long. Meantime, he had to endure unspeakable and unmitigated agonies from heat, hunger, thirst and maddening attacks by ants. Knowing West Africa, and the capabilities of the native for inflicting torture, the thought of such a death makes one shudder.

What is here recorded is no matter of report. The information has been collected on the spot from competent witnesses. In respect of human sacrifices, one of my informants was a man who had himself actually been selected as a victim. He was bound to the sacred tree and all preparations made for observing the last rites. The ceremony of transferring the sins to his head was about to be performed when, through the unremitting exertions of a friend, he was released, and another died in

SACRIFICES

his stead, he himself being witness of the tortures and sufferings of his substitute.⁹

NOTES TO CHAPTER II

¹ The underlying beliefs and methods of the Ibo " dibia " are no more grotesque or unscientific than some that are practised and accepted by many religious folk in Europe and elsewhere.

² " The hostility of spirits other than ancestors is appeased in various ways . . . arbitrary restraints and prohibitions are imposed. The commonest prohibition is that of some particular food."—" *Fetish Folk of West Africa* ", p. 236.

³ Further information in respect of the " ọfọ " holder will be found in Chapter VIII.

⁴ " Among the Kagoro of N. Nigeria a fowl is killed when the corn is ripening, a hole is dug in the centre of the farm and the blood of the fowl, and the leaves of certain trees are put into it, but the flesh is eaten when the corn is ready for harvesting. After the corn has been stored in the granary, another fowl is killed, and the blood is smeared on the outside, the flesh being eaten."—" *Tailed Headhunters of Nigeria* ", p. 207.

⁵ Crowther relates that, in his day (1857-9) " the King does not step out of his house into the town, unless a human sacrifice is made to propitiate the gods : on this account, he never goes out beyond the precincts of his own premises."—" *Niger Expedition* ", p. 433.

⁶ " *Niger Expedition* ", *1857-1859*, by Crowther and Taylor, pp. 343-5.

⁷ " *Golden Bough* ", Frazer, p. 200.

⁸ " Among the Jukum, Igbira and other tribes in Northern Nigeria the immolation of slaves was a regular feature. The victim was especially chosen for his strength and beauty and, during the interval before the sacrifice, he was the most privileged man in the community. Nothing was denied him. He was given the finest clothes and food, and could have sexual relations with any woman in the town. He was the bearer of countless private messages to the spirits of the dead. Among the Yoruba, the social lust for human blood reached the highest point, and the Igbede priest of Owa told me that he had sacrificed as many as ten human victims on a single day."—" *Northern Tribes of Nigeria* ", Vol. II, p. 40.

" Among the Fang the offering of human sacrifice to placate the spirits is not customary. . . . But among the more highly organised tribes of Calabar and the Niger . . . multitudes have been offered in sacrifice to appease the hostility of the spirits : and they would still be offered but for the presence of foreign governments."—" *Fetish Folk of West Africa* ", p. 236.

⁹ " The justice of vicarious atonement is not incredible to the African because he already has the idea."—" *Fetish Folk of West Africa* ", p. 255.

CHAPTER III

ORACLES

THIS CHAPTER IS written during a period of transition. The activities of several of these oracles have been suppressed by Government orders, although the belief in their efficacy has not altogether disappeared. Some, if not all, operate still under greatly restricted conditions, hence, present and past tenses are used, because frequently both apply. For the most part, what is written is concerned with the past.

Scattered here and there throughout the Ibo country, more particularly on the eastern side of the Niger, are certain local deities alleged to possess supernatural powers. They are mainly consulted for purposes of divination. They are not connected in the ordinary sense with the religious system, nor can they be included under the category of secret societies. To a limited extent, they partake of the nature of both and, yet, are quite separate and distinct ; their functions are more accurately defined as judicial. They are the instruments for settling disputes and for refuting charges of witchcraft. When reconciliation cannot be effected and feelings run strongly, an appeal is made to the oracle whose verdict is final.

Though deception formed a great part of the procedure, it was either not realised by the litigants, or they ignored that feature, because they were convinced that the issue was right and in accordance with justice. The deities were shrouded in so much mystery that fear of retribution swamped any suspicion of deceit. It is not easy sometimes to sense the measure of gullibility on the part of the people. Undoubtedly, they were profoundly moved when under the influence of the oracular powers. At the same time, it is understandable, because of the uncanny nature of some of the ceremonies. For the owners, the local deities were a source of no little profit. Strangers betrayed their guilelessness by resorting to them, and submitted to the judgements without demur. An appeal to such a deity was, in most instances, pretty much on a par with trial by ordeal. Moreover, it was a costly business, all the parties concerned being equally mulcted of the resources at their disposal.

The paths leading to the thickets wherein the oracles were

ORACLES

concealed were kept under strict observation and intruders were rigorously denied approach. The regulations which governed the procedure were equally stringent and to divulge any of the secrets met with quick and drastic reprisal. By means of this rigidly enforced secrecy, the atmosphere of mystery was maintained at a high pressure, and was a great factor in fostering the profound conviction that the oracle did possess the powers claimed on its behalf. Outsiders knew nothing of its inner workings : they could only judge by results and there was no uncertainty about them. The reports spread abroad by the agents of the god inspired such abject fear that all doubt of the efficacy of the oracle was dispelled. A god with the attributes ascribed to him was so awe-provoking that no one would dare to question his authority. The simplicity manifested seems incredible ; only those who have had experience of its effects can realise something of its power. I count myself fortunate in having been privileged to live in close proximity to some of these shrines, and to have had opportunities to investigate on the spot facts connected with them. Also I have been able to discuss the procedure with actual participators in the operations.

The following is an account of the divining oracle which was a great institution at Awka until it was broken by the Government. It is a revised edition of a description originally written over twenty years ago. It is included here to make the chapter on this subject complete.[1]

The town is large and straggling, typical of the district. From time immemorial it has been famous, partly because of its skilful blacksmiths (who travel throughout the length and breadth of the land plying their trade) and, perhaps, even more so, on account of the prestige accruing to it as the home of a famous oracle, reputed to be endowed with marvellous gifts of divination. Strangers were conducted thither from all parts of the country in order that they might hold consultations with the deity. The Awka blacksmiths made it as much their business to advertise their oracle as to carry on their normal trade. Both honour and profit were to be gained in this way, and the Awka man was always ready to act on behalf of an applicant.

Locally, the deity was known as the " Agbala ". The name is somewhat difficult to explain. It may mean a " woman " ; such an one as is mentioned in Acts xvi. 16 as endowed with a " spirit of divination ". A more convenient term perhaps is " oracle ". How this " Agbala " came into existence is a matter of conjecture based upon legend. She was, however, declared to be a daughter of the great oracle, known as the

ORACLES

" Chukwu of the Aros ", commonly called the " Long Ju-ju ", the destruction of which was one of the objectives of the military expedition of 1902. One peculiarity was that, though " Agbala " is feminine, and is the daughter of " Igwe-ka-Ani " yet, in the ceremonies, she was always addressed as "Father ", and the masculine pronoun was used.[2]

According to local tradition there are three great deities, 1, Igwe-ka-Ani, 2, Agbala, and 3, Ebulu-Okpa-Bia. The first name indicates a " King who is higher (greater) than the land ", and Agbala is his daughter. Ebulu-Okpa-Bia may be interpreted as the " one who receives you graciously and fills your basket " ; in other words, " a kind and generous benefactor ". For an account of " Igwe-ka-Ani " see p. 91.

Of these three, Agbala took first rank throughout the upper part of the Ibo country. She was proclaimed as *the god*, the creator of all things, a discerner of the secrets of men, the judge of poisoners, the revealer of witchcraft, the omnipotent one, the forgiver of sins, and the dispenser of blessings of every kind, including the gift of children.

The old shrine of the Agbala was situated at Ezi-Awka and to the people of this village was entrusted the guardianship thereof. Their huts were built right up to the edge of the sacred precincts on the two sides that give access to the shrine, and strict watch was maintained against trespassers. The path leading to the shrine was narrow and tortuous ; suddenly, it opened out into a spacious square in the centre of which were the remains of a rude hut sheltering a huge and somewhat dilapidated tom-tom (ikolo). There were ruins of small " alusi " houses in other parts of the square and, at times, there were folk in residence who had been devoted to the deity (Ndi-osu, *vide* Chap. XVII).

The ancient tom-tom was some six feet in length and about three in diameter. One end was shouldered off and shaped to represent the head and neck of a man, the other end was similarly carved with a woman's head. On one side, the drum was ornamented with six faces, three at each end, carved in high relief. On the far side of the square, an opening in the dense bush gave access to a narrow defile. The track through this glade was rough, and overhanging trees cast deep shadows, shrouding the path in semi-darkness. The path descended for some seventy yards, where further progress was barred by a wall. Entrance was gained through a narrow aperture, and only the chief actors in the drama might pass through it. Beyond the wall, the light was still more subdued ; the bush being denser. It was altogether more gloomy and

ORACLES

uncanny until, at the end of another fifteen yards, the path broadened out into a leafy bower. In the centre stood two sacred trees. Turning sharply to the right, and passing on a few paces, a narrow opening between high banks became visible. This was the entrance to an artificial winding alley ending in a cul-de-sac. At the foot of the latter, a log was stretched across the track. This was the sanctuary, the actual abode of the deity.

The above is a brief description of the shrine and its approaches as noted by the stranger. There was, however, a secret entrance by means of which communications could be maintained between those impersonating the Agbala and her attendants, and those who were conducting affairs in the square above, or in the lane leading to the barrier.

We now turn our attention to the mode of operations. As previously observed, no stranger was permitted to enter the sacred precincts, except under the leadership of a duly authorised guide, and after being closely blindfolded in order to prevent him from making observations. We must also continue to bear in mind that every Awka man, while practising his ordinary profession in any part of the country, was prepared to conduct parties to consult the Agbala. This leader was expected to collect at the actual place of dispute all possible information concerning the case prior to starting for Awka. He must leave no stone unturned in eliciting facts about the parties themselves, the grounds of the accusations, the circumstances and the resources of those involved. He, thus, returned home well posted with details whereby the oracle had little difficulty in pronouncing a verdict which was quite startling to the litigants, inasmuch as it showed an intimate knowledge of affairs.

Fees, directly, and in the shape of presents, together with the killing of goats and fowls in honour of the leader, must be forthcoming from the very beginning of the transaction. When matters were ripe, the interested parties made the journey to Awka, some coming very long distances. On arrival, they were billeted in the houses of the conductor and his personal friends and, from this time, the victims were gradually but surely fleeced of their money. The wife of the conductor had the right to shave the hair of the strangers and, in payment, received a piece of cloth from each. Each had to purchase a fowl and many yams; these were offered as the first sacrifice, and were afterwards consumed at a semi-sacrificial family feast. A present and about £10 in cash were demanded as first fees on behalf of the Agbala, the same being quietly pocketed by the leader. Whilst waiting, the last details of the case were gleaned, and the prospects fluctuated *pro rata*, according to the presents distributed. Considerable delay, sometimes extending to months, might ensue in this manner before the favourable day arrived for presenting themselves before the Agbala. This, with sublime coincidence, invariably happened when funds showed signs of failing. The formal arrangements were now made, and an appointment fixed. The parties were led along the winding tracks into the square, where the preliminary formalities were observed and the first sacrifices offered. Having complied with the regulations, preparations were made for the settlement of the case. The plaintiffs and defendants were securely blindfolded and led to the opening in the glade leading down to the shrine; here they were turned round and forced to walk backwards until the barrier was reached, the gateway of which had been covered with a hanging cloth. The parties waited at this spot; no stranger might enter the " kamanu ", the secret dwelling-place of the oracle, under any pretext.

Presently, the leader commenced to cry out : " O ! Agbala-Awka, hear us ! O ! Igwe-Ani, hear us ! Prove by thy power which of these people is guilty (who is a poisoner, or an extortioner, or guilty of the sin of witchcraft). Thou that revealest all secrets, hear us ! Thou that killest and rewardest with life, hear us ! O ! Igwe-Ani, hear us ! "

After a brief interval, the voice of the " Son of Agbala " was heard begging that the god would take heed to the appeal of the strangers, " O ! my father, awake ! Awake, and hearken to the petitions of those who come from afar to prove thee. Arise ! and show that thou art the discerner of all hearts."

Suddenly, and apparently from the very bowels of the earth, a sepulchral voice was heard, causing utter consternation and terror to the strangers present. It was the voice of Agbala replying to the request : " E-e-e-e-dum-e-nwam e-nwam." " O ! yes, my son." " I have the power of life and death. He who proves me sees me with eyes. I am the beginning and the end."

As this oration concluded, there was a great commotion and Osu-Agbala, the servant of the oracle, burst forth from the bush. His person was liberally adorned with eagle feathers and in his hands were short sticks with which he laid about him vigorously, beating the petitioners until they made it worth his while to desist. He declared that Agbala was angry at being awakened, and must be appeased with money and gifts. The demand was backed up by the oracle himself, who, forthwith, commanded the strangers " to advance no further lest they

"ODO" CELEBRATIONS.

VILLAGE DISPLAY IN CONNECTION WITH "ODO," A GREAT INSTITUTION IN THE NSUKKA DIVISION. THERE IS KEEN RIVALRY BETWEEN VILLAGES AND MUCH GUN-FIRING.

be swallowed up in the great water" (which does not exist!).

The deity having been conciliated, the parties were ordered to state the case. They strove earnestly, each endeavouring to vindicate himself by declaring his innocence of all crime from the day of his birth. May the god do so to him and more also if he had been the cause of any man's death, whether by the sword or by poison; may he suffer if he be guilty of the sin of witchcraft or of extortion. He had been accused falsely and now appealed to Agbala for righteous judgement.

It was at this stage that the impersonator of the deity needed to have his wits about him. He had to be on the alert to detect the signals which would enable him to declare, without mistake, which was guilty and which was innocent; any error in this respect would be fatal. In reality, the verdict had long been a settled question, but care had to be exercised lest the reputation of the god be jeopardised. The first man selected for judgement was practically certain to be proclaimed innocent. He was bidden to rise from the ground where he had been crouching behind the barrier wall, and to listen as Agbala pronounced judgement declaring him innocent of crime. His honour was vindicated and blessings were heaped upon his head. Before, however, these could operate in his favour, he had to give thankofferings to the righteous god in the shape of three or four cows or a couple of slaves. An eagle's feather was presented to him as a badge of innocence, together with "medicine" which he was enjoined to store carefully in his own house on reaching home. It was a preparation absolutely to be trusted as a safeguard against every form of evil, natural and spiritual. The happy man was led back to the open square above and, immediately the bandage was removed from his eyes, he rushed about dancing and shouting, "Agbala nyelum ugo-ugo-ugo (Agbala has given me the eagle's feather)." Such an one had abundant cause for rejoicing. On his return to his own town, he was fêted and honoured as one who had triumphantly emerged from the greatest of all ordeals. He gladly paid all amounts demanded. These were handed to the man who had managed his case so successfully, and who gave a solemn assurance to use them for the benefit of the deity!

There might be others likewise declared innocent and the programme duly repeated. Eventually, however, the turn of a guilty one was bound to come. The preliminaries were similar to those followed in the case of the innocent. The man, hearing his name announced, was inspired by hope, he having heard the favourable verdict given to his predecessors, and he humbly offered his salutations to the deity. The answer immediately and unmistakably disillusioned him. With vehement and angry tones, the Agbala taunted him as an evil-doer, or, it may be, accused him directly of being a poisoner, or of some other crime. Every protestation of innocence was contemptuously rejected, and the poor wretch had no alternative other than to grovel on the ground and plead for mercy. The god retorted that there was no escape from the trap in which he was now caught, except by the payment of three cows as a fine, and he urged the condemned man to hurry and bring these. The man eagerly consented and rose to obey the injunction, whereupon, as he stood up, a noose was dexterously thrown round his neck and he was violently jerked and hauled over the wall, thus falling into the fatal clutches of the god. If, after this ordeal, he were not already dead, he might be resuscitated in order to be sold as a slave or, if Agbala signified that blood alone would satisfy him, the victim was killed forthwith.

The executioner was the only regularly appointed official attached to the deity. His sole occupation was the slaying of those appointed to die. He might not travel, nor could he plant a farm ; he must let nothing interfere with his business, and he had to be ready at any time for his ghastly work. All corpses were hurled into the valley sloping away from the lower edge of the shrine ; they were afterwards collected and disposed of in accordance with the usual custom prevailing in a cannibal country.

There were cases in which the Agbala was consulted for the purpose of obtaining some personal benefit entirely distinct from criminal trials. The blessing of the god was sought in order that sons might be born to the suppliant, of course, on receipt of adequate compensation. A not uncommon practice was for a man to beseech Agbala to deliver him from the hands of his enemies by bringing death and destruction upon them. One of the attributes of the deity was the faculty of exercising his deadly powers over persons at a distance, hence the appeal to him. This could be done privately, the unsuspecting enemy being in total ignorance of the designs upon his life. The unfortunate one was mentioned by name and, at the conclusion of the sacrifices and payments, Agbala ordered a piece of iron to be driven into the tree as if the man in question were being actually executed on the spot. Some of these irons were roughly shaped staples, some had chisel edges, others were spear-heads. Green leaves were sometimes rolled up containing " medicine ", and the spike driven through the bundle. On one occasion, I went into the grove shortly after a cere-

ORACLES

monial function. There was a bundle of fresh leaves held in position by the usual piece of iron which, on being extracted, and the bundle unrolled, was found to contain the head of a small snake spitted through the gullet with a short piece of wood.

No one man was consecrated to the priesthood of the deity. It was entirely a matter of mutual arrangement, and any Awka man could impersonate the god and fulfil all the functions connected with the ceremonies. The conductor of the suppliants undertook the management of the business from beginning to end, and he appointed his acquaintances to act as the Agbala, Osu-Agbala and other assistants. These together constituted themselves into a limited company for dispensing divinations, a concern which paid a handsome dividend to its shareholders; the chairman, that is, the director of the party, naturally absorbing the major share of the proceeds.

Apart from the fact that all strangers were blindfolded before entering the sacred precincts, the profoundest source of deception was the peculiar voice of the Agbala and its votaries. This was disguised to sound as if issuing from the nether regions; moreover, the note was taken up on all sides so that the location of the deity could not be easily traced. The voices came first from the front, then from behind and, finally, from all round, until the strangers were hopelessly bewildered. There were three sets of voices; that of the Agbala himself, that of his special attendant, Osu-Agbala, and those of the chorus, the Umu-Chuku, the children of the god.

The change from the natural voice was wrought by means of small clay pots, specially manufactured for the purpose, called " mbọ ". They were four inches in diameter, with wide necks, and a little hole was punched through the bottom of each. One of these pots was fixed over the mouth of each man assisting in the ceremony. The effect of shouting into the pot may be better understood by the reader if he will try the experiment of speaking loudly into a tumbler held over his mouth. The sepulchral voice of the Agbala was effected by his placing his head in a hole of a tree which stood in the centre of the glade. The hole was level with the ground, and the voice sounded as if issuing from the depths of the earth.

Of how many lives were " eaten " (lit.) by the Agbala-Awka, it would be risky to quote an estimate. One of the facts proved by experience is that trustworthy figures are not forthcoming from natives living in primitive conditions; concrete numbers are unlucky, and " many, many " is all that they will state. One of the most well-informed men of Awka told me that the lives so sacrificed were incalculable; and there is substantial authority for believing that, on occasions, as many as thirty persons perished in a single day. The policy of frequent executions was zealously upheld lest the idea should spread abroad that the power of the Agbala was waning. It was a sure method of instilling fear into strangers and, at the same time, maintaining the dignity of the oracle. If the pieces of iron embedded in the sacred trees may be taken as an indication, then there can be no question but that many hundreds of people lost their lives as a result of appeal to the Agbala. When I first saw the trees they were, from ground-level to eight feet above, thickly studded with spikes. The trees were black with the marks of the irons driven into them.

The Agbala was a source of huge profit to the town, and the people of Awka suffered heavy pecuniary loss when, in 1905, a military expedition gave the oracle its death-blow. The prestige of the deity, however, was not entirely broken, and recourse continued to be had to his oracular powers, though the ancient practices were no longer retained. The rendezvous of the god was changed and, further, it was clearly recognised that he could no longer demand the life of people brought before him for judgement, nor condemn them to be sold. The old-time ceremonies were followed as closely as possible, with fines as substitutes for the former sentences of capital punishment and slavery. Fear of Government reprisals has also been generally inculcated into the native mind, and the number of those prepared to risk the consequences of perpetuating the profitable deception has been so reduced until, to-day, Agbala may be counted as dead. Under British rule, and in no small measure owing to the influence of Christian Missions in Awka and the neighbourhood, the fate of the Agbala has been sealed. His reputation, his very existence, and all that appertained to him have ceased to be. The final blow fell in 1921 when two sons of a leading chief were publicly hanged in Amikwo Village for the murder of a man who was brought before Agbala. The execution of these men made such an impression that " Agbala-Awka " and " Rabba, Agulu ", a somewhat similar institution, both collapsed. Yet, even so, should the Government relax its vigilance, attempts would be made to revive and restore the prestige of the oracle. There are still people who are in favour of the deity, and who would like to retrieve their proprietary rights in him, had they reason to think they could do so with impunity.

The " Agbala " of Enu-Ugwu deserves notice. This was a proscribed oracle after the Onitsha Hinterland Expedition, but

ORACLES

there have been, of recent years, attempts to resuscitate its activities.

The oracle is located at a quarter called Urunnebo of Enu-Ugwu. This town lies between Nǫfia and Agukwu (Nri). In olden days the people of Urunnebo were ordinary traders who prosecuted their business as far as the Agbaja district, the main articles of trade being iron bars, gin and salt.

At last, came one, by name " Akpu-Nwa-Eze-Nri ", who ventured yet further, and entered the Nkanu country. He enlarged on his trading operations by combining with them the profession of a doctor and, in the latter capacity, gained a considerable reputation.

He returned home with the gains in money and livestock which he had collected from the Nkanu people, his obvious success creating no little excitement at Urunnebo. When making preparations to repeat his venture, one of his relatives named Dilibe asked that he might accompany him. To this Akpu-Nwa-Eze-Nri gladly agreed, as he felt the need of assistance in his expanding practice.

But first, Dilibe said, he must acquaint his father-in-law with his projected movements in accordance with custom. This was " Alum Mba-Ǫnu " of Umu-di-Awka (a village of Awka). The request was easy to fulfil, and they both went to see Alum Mba-Ǫnu as they passed on their way to Nkanu.

Alum Mba-Ǫnu discussed the situation with them and then made the brilliant suggestion that Akpu-Nwa-Eze-Nri should continue to reside at Urunnebo and let the sick folk come to him rather than he go to them. However, on this occasion, the pair continued their journey and Akpu-Nwa-Eze-Nri greatly enhanced his medical reputation. Before finally leaving Nkanu, he notified his clientele that, in future, sick folk, if they wished for his treatment, must be brought to his residence.

Upon Akpu-Nwa-Eze-Nri's return, the Urunnebo people perceived that the medical profession was far more profitable than common trading, and asked for a share in the business. He agreed, on one condition, namely, that he should be regarded as the " Head " of the town. He built a consulting-room (hut), and to his fellow-townsmen he allotted the task of shepherding the patients.

This seems to have gone on for some time without particular incident and, probably, might have continued so to do had not Alum Mba-Ǫnu come to visit his son-in-law. He, at once, interested himself and, after watching the procedure, tendered further advice. This was to the effect that Akpu-Nwa-Eze-Nri and Dilibe were acting foolishly in allowing the patients to observe the proceedings. He suggested that they should follow him home and he would give them an insight how to do things properly.

They, thereupon, accompanied Alum Mba-Onu to Awka and he, in due course, conducted them to a dense grove, where, he affirmed, medicine and knowledge were dispensed to visitors. This was the Agbala (Ayanwu) previously described.

When the two doctors returned home, they counselled the people to select a site covered with thick bush and there build a hut with the purpose of concealing operations from the public. Further, the new centre must be known as " Agbala-Nri ". Hence, this institution was founded ostensibly for the treatment of sick people, but, in due time, was changed to something of a much more sinister character. Akpu-Nwa-Eze-Nri and his confederates continued to attract the people from Nkanu and Agbaja, and became even more influential in proportion as their operations became more secretive. Indeed, it was not long before the Nkanu and Agbaja peoples began to regard the Urunnebo men as superhuman, even to the extent of speaking of them as the " Children of God ". This arose from the fact that the Urunnebo people seemed to possess to a marked degree a spirit of divination ; certainly, they had a very uncanny knowledge of the affairs, possessions and relatives of the people who came to consult them. So it went on, and a report spread that God was at Urunnebo and people who wanted his help in order to rid themselves of any objectionable persons from their midst should apply to his sons and they, the sons, would see to it that such persons were removed.

All this suited the Urunnebos admirably, and they made a compact with the Nkanus and Agbajas. The venue of operations was laid out afresh, paths diverted and other changes

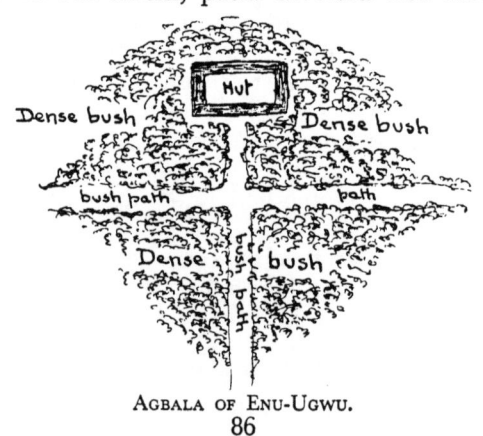

AGBALA OF ENU-UGWU.

made. Henceforth, the practice observed was that, when an unfortunate individual was brought into the presence of the oracle, the men of Urunnebo concealed themselves in the dense thicket on the left side of the hut. One member of the fraternity was inside to act the rôle of god. To aid him in the deception, he used a clay pot, an " ọfọ " stick and some " ekpili " (these are seeds, the shells of which dancers tie round their legs ; the impersonator used them in the form of a rattle).

The procedure very closely resembled that of the Agbala of Awka. The victim was made to walk backwards to the shrine. When all was ready, the impersonator placed the pot over his mouth and roared out the words, " Anyone approaching Agbala should fear, because god knew all about him, and had knowledge of his sins as well as of all his affairs." This was generally substantiated from information gleaned by the emissaries of the Agbala.

When the wretched man heard the sepulchral voice he was stricken with fear ; then to be told things concerning his distant home, and deeds committed far away, added consternation to his fear. He was ready to promise everything if only his life might be spared, or medicine supplied to meet his necessity. If it had been prearranged that he was to disappear then, at the propitious moment, the men concealed to the left of the Agbala rushed upon the man and secured him. He was conveyed to Nimo to be killed and eaten, the people of that town being more frankly cannibalistic than those of Enu-Ugwu ! Apparently, a price was fixed for the victim, although it is stated that it was rather small, usually equivalent to about forty or fifty shillings in cowries. The essential stipulation was, that the Agbala-Nri faculty had to be assured that the man had actually been killed. For this it was considered sufficient proof if a finger, or some other noticeable part of the body, was supplied as a guarantee that the sentence had been fulfilled. Without such proof peace would be broken, and the Urunnebo people would take the matter into their own hands.

In the case of one seeking merely advice or medicine, the amount he was to pay was duly stipulated. The applicant was escorted back to his home and the amount in money and goods collected, brought to Urunnebo and disbursed.

Thus, the Urunnebo people acted as keepers of the Agbala-Nri oracle until the Expedition led to its disruption and subsequent prohibition. This sort of craft, however, dies slowly, and there have been surreptitious attempts to revive operations for the purpose of " giving counsel " or " to make medicine ". On occasions, it has been given another name in the hope of

ORACLES

diverting suspicion. It has sometimes been referred to as "Agbala Ngenne", but that is a misnomer. More recently, it was spoken of as "Obassi", a distinctly foreign name altogether, and apparently used as a blind to divert attention from the real thing.

NOTES TO CHAPTER III

[1] "*Among the Ibos of Nigeria*", Chap. XXIII, "In the shadow of death".

[2] See also p. 101 for another interpretation of Agbala.

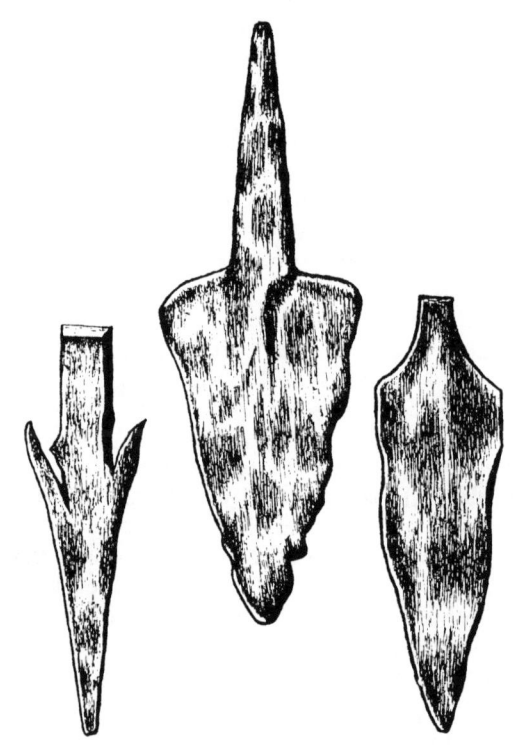

BENT AND RUSTY IRON SPEAR-HEADS TAKEN FROM THE SACRED TREE OF THE ORIGINAL AGBALA AT AWKA (p. 82).

CHAPTER IV

ORACLES (2)

TO THE NORTH OF Enugu, stretching from the railway westwards, and all over that section of the Nsukka District, the god, or oracle, or spirit (for it is a mixture of all these and more) called " Odo " exercises a very powerful influence.

The headquarters of " Odo " are at Eha Iheyi, a part of Eha Amufu and, consequently, the Eha Iheyis claim precedence in all affairs connected with the deity. Actually, each family throughout the countryside has its own " Odo " shrine and there is a communal one to serve for each township.

The dominance of " Odo " is a very potent force in the lives of the people of this area, and the influence operates at all times, in spite of the fact that " Odo " is only visible at intervals of two years. " Odo " makes his appearance on the first day of alternate years. The Eha Iheyis lead off and, after four or five days, others follow. This is the time of many sacrifices of horses, cows, goats and fowls, accompanied by a vast expenditure of gunpowder.

The current belief is that " Odo " dwells underground ; that, at these intervals of two years, he rises and, after his manifestation, he returns once more to earth. The origin of this belief arose from circumstances connected with strangers. It is related that these came to consult " Odo ", and the Eha people were in a quandary as to how they could maintain the atmosphere of mystery. They decided to dig a pit and cover it with grass and branches. Inside, a man dressed to represent " Odo " was concealed. While the strangers were peering about, " Odo " suddenly appeared, he having ascended from the pit by means of the ladder provided. At once, he began to beat everyone within reach with the staff specially prepared for the purpose. He appears to have inspired the strangers thoroughly with a belief in his reality. The effort having proved successful, this method of inculcating mystery has been in vogue ever since.

In a sense, it partakes of the nature of a secret society. Novitiates must be youths about fifteen years of age. When

ORACLES

these are accepted as candidates, they are sworn to secrecy. The old penalty for revealing any part of the mysteries to a non-member or to a woman was death. Further, if any of such a culprit's family intervened on his behalf, or interfered with the judgement of " Odo ", the properties of the whole family were confiscated.

Naturally, there are rules to be observed of which the following are some :—

During the time that " Odo " is abroad, any woman walking about after sundown must cry out as she proceeds " Ogbanidu " to indicate that she is on the road. Strangers (ndiobodo), being non-members, must do likewise. The cries serve as signals to " Odo ", who slips into hiding until the woman or stranger has passed. This practice is followed for six months from the date of the first manifestation of " Odo ".

If, by any unfortunate chance, a woman (or a non-member) should see " Odo " undressed, that one must be put to death. She has seen too much !

A man having donned the " Odo " garb must take care lest he stumble or fall down, because this is a sure omen that death will shortly overtake him. Nor must he become afraid and run away at some sudden contretemps, for that also is a portent of death.

Women or non-members are forbidden to enter the " bush " set apart for " Odo's " use. In this secret place the young palm leaves (omu, see p. 408) are prepared and essential " medicine " concocted.

For the six months that " Odo " is abroad no other drum may be beaten save Odabata and Igede. The reason why these are allowed is because they are the drums used in connection with Second Burials in these parts.

Before British occupation of the country, human sacrifices were always an essential part of the ceremonies at the beginning and ending of the visitation of " Odo ".

At the end of the six months, " Odo " returns to his underground dwelling-place. On the day appointed for his disappearance, not only the women and non-members, but even the cattle and goats must remain indoors. Further, it is a time of mourning and, among other business, all the old gear used in connection with " Odo " must be cast away and destroyed. The men, and especially the young ones, will dress up in all manner of fetish apparel or, in many cases, without any covering at all.

A man noted for his strength is called upon to fulfil the duties of the last day. He wears a sword on his right side and an axe on his left. As he moves about, chickens are hung upon him and also " medicine ". He marches along in advance, with a priest following him. The remainder of the men, armed with matchets, parade the town in the wake of the two leaders and, eventually, turn into the bush where " Odo " disappears not to be seen again for some eighteen months. Care must be taken by the followers :—

It is fatal for one of them to get ahead of " Odo ", or for his shadow to fall upon him.

Any man found guilty of betraying " Odo ", or any of the secrets associated with him, must be handed over to justice by his father or, failing him, by his nearest male relative.

The influence of " Odo " cannot adequately be estimated by the foreigner. It pervades everything in the life of the native, and its presence is a very serious factor to be reckoned with in the Nsukka area.

Igwe-Ka-Ala (*Igwe-Ka-Ani* of the Northern Districts) is located at Umunoha, about twelve miles north of Owerri Town. In the neighbourhood, the name is commonly abbreviated to " Igwe " (sky) and, in that area, he is regarded as second in importance to " Chukwu " of the Aros. Resort is had to this oracle for the purpose of divination.

As at Awka and Enu-Ugwu (Nri), the residence of " Igwe-Ka-Ala " is in the midst of a dense thicket. Footpaths lead to this concealed centre from different directions, each being used by different quarters of Umunoha, the villagers exercising their own prerogatives to conduct clients seeking counsel of the oracle. The men of Umunoha travel widely and one of their chief items of business is to advertise the attributes of their oracle and to offer assistance to intending applicants.

Occasionally, a man will resort to " Chukwu " at Aro only to meet with disappointment. With a hope of better success he appeals to " Igwe-Ka-Ala ". Should the stewards of " Igwe " discover that the applicant has previously visited Aro, he will receive a frigid reception and be chided for expecting better treatment from " Igwe-Ka-Ala " than what was meted out to him by " Chukwu ". The only course open to him in these circumstances is to pay exorbitant fees in order to escape a worse fate.

" Igwe-Ka-Ala " speaks to each consultant in his own language but, as at Awka and Enu-Ugwu, the voice is disguised by the use of a pot placed over the mouth. This was, however, at the conclusion of the ceremonies ; all previous transactions were conducted in a language not understood by strangers, the initiated (owners) alone could interpret the mysterious utterances of " Igwe ".

In former days, the secrets of " Igwe-Ka-Ala " were jealously guarded and the penalty for divulging them was death. Government realised the fraudulent and inimical character of this institution and caused the bush to be cleared, and this struck a devastating blow to the traditional activities of the oracle. Since, the bush has grown again, and recourse to " Igwe-Ka-Ala " has been revived. Nowadays, however, he does nothing more serious than dispense advice ; his power over life and death has been effectually destroyed. In addition to the salutary results of Government intervention, the spread of Christianity and Education have also made an appreciable impression in the neighbourhood. As one of the prominent members of the " Igwe-Ka-Ala " fraternity remarked : " The Church has dealt a death-blow to our oracle ; we cannot any longer induce clients to appeal to ' Igwe ' as we were accustomed to do before missionary work was established in this country." What remains to-day is but a reflection of former days.

Ezira lies some twenty miles south of Awka and, beyond the claim of owning a Water Deity, has nothing to distinguish it from any other Ibo town. As proprietor of this god it is well known over a wide area, even as far as the Niger Delta country.

The name of the god is " Onyilli Ora " and means " The one who surpasses all " (both in power and knowledge). Whatever any god can, or cannot, do, " Onyilli Ora " is able to do more is the idea conveyed by the name. He has two subordinates (children), namely, " Omelichibe ". He, as elder son (okpala), of his father the king, reigns. The second son is " Ezemenyiba ".[1]

The approach to " Onyilli Ora " must be through the mediation of these two sons in the order given. Suppliants never got beyond them, inasmuch as Mgbafo, the priestess, alone could look upon the face of " Onyilli Ora " and live.

This woman Mgbafo was a noted character. Over a wide area she was known as " Mgbafo-Ezira ". Her influence was so great that the authorities had to place her in custody more than once. She was alleged to be an inspirer of serious trouble in the Nsukka District in 1924.

Certain men acted as agents to advertise the powers of " Onyilli Ora " and to introduce clients. These agents conducted the applicants to Ezira and, there, handed them over to other men who relieved them of the prescribed fees. All the

ORACLES

agents were members of Mgbafọ's family, and the fees were distributed proportionately in order of precedence.

Prior to the regime of Mgbafọ, " Ọnyilli Ọra's " sole function was to pass on communications from deceased relatives. (*Vide* p. 296.) This was so all the days of Nwọgọ, Mgbafọ's elder sister, the former priestess ; Mgbafọ extended the business widely.

In former days, when a person died and the cause of death was not obviously apparent, relatives sought enlightenment through the medium of " Ọnyilli Ọra ". No definite amount was fixed as a uniform fee, but payment was demanded in money and fowls for the necessary sacrifices. The introductory arrangements having been completed, the clients were led to the sanctuary of " Omelichibe " and " Ezemenyiba ". Before the face of these gods oblations were made and sacrifices offered, and the requests of the suppliants stated. As they were uncertain as to the cause of the death of their father or brother, they prayed the god to relieve their minds on the subject. And an answer certainly came ; there was no doubt of that. What they did not know was that, as men well versed in the business have admitted, a medium was concealed between the masses of roots of the huge trees who was an expert in assuming the voice of a dying person. The answer came in faltering tones stating that he had grown very old and the time had arrived for him to be gathered to his fathers ; in other words, they were assured that his death was quite natural. Or, it might be, there was a vindictive note and the impression was conveyed to the anxious listeners that their loved one had come to an untimely end, either through witchcraft, or the machinations of some enemy. In either case, the inquirers were convinced and returned home in peace, or with a firm determination to avenge the death of their unfortunate kinsman.

Mgbafọ widened the range of benefits to be obtained from " Ọnyilli Ọra's " counsel. Consultants came from many parts, some of them with seemingly trifling requests. The nature of the appeal did not worry Mgbafọ and her confrères so long as the fees were forthcoming. Of the common reasons for seeking the aid of " Ọnyilli Ọra " the following are examples :—

When either a person or a town received more than ordinary attention from thieves, representatives went to Ezira to seek a remedy. Mgbafọ sought advice from " Ọnyilli Ọra " and duly supplied " medicine " which, she assured her customers, would effectually remove the trouble by the simple process of causing the death of the thieves.

When farms were being overrun by wild animals, or even

ORACLES

guinea-fowls, " medicine " was sought to drive these away, or to destroy them. When hawks were taking too great a toll from the young chickens, the same programme was followed.

A really serious reason was when one town considered it had received sufficient provocation to break the peace with another. Resort was had to " Onyilli Ora " to deal with the situation without risk to themselves. The fees, of course, were in proportion to the services rendered. On the completion of the case before the shrine of " Omelichibe ", Mgbafo consulted " Onyilli Ora " and then handed to the parties a small earthen pot. This possessed no other virtue than that it had once been filled with water from the sacred pool, which had been allowed to evaporate. This pot had to be carried to the enemy town and there smashed in some public place.

The effect of this would be that many of the enemy would forthwith die. In due time, the people of the estranged town would conclude that so many deaths could only be the work of unseen powers, and earnest efforts would be set on foot to remove the cause. Negotiations would be opened up with the town, known by this time to be at enmity with them, with a view to settling the quarrel.

Envoys were appointed and terms of peace dictated. When these were satisfactorily arranged, gifts of fowls, goats and other eatables had to be provided for the purpose of sacrifice and for presents to the people of the offended town. The gifts had to be presented with the customary etiquette, namely, each article must be taken into the hands of the donor and he would breathe on it. This indicated that a genuine agreement was sought, and in order to make peace with the land.

The ceremonies consisted of a series of sacrifices, the blood being sprinkled over the adjacent ground. The sacrifices and other eatables were then consumed by the representatives of the town which had laid the " medicine " (the men of the enemy town might not eat of the things they provided), and anything left over was carried home by them.

As the sacrifices were being offered, the envoys seeking peace had to swear an oath that they would abide by the terms of the treaty and give a guarantee that there should be no further cause for complaint. If, after this, the original town should behave contrarily, any of its people eating anything whatsoever obtained from the town seeking peace must die. In other words, the destroying powers would turn and wreak vengeance on the breakers of the pot themselves.

Some account of a visit to " Onyilli Ora " may now be given. The traveller passes through Ezira along the winding paths of the town in a westward direction, the last village being Ubaha, the quarter which owns the " bush " wherein the god has his dwelling. On the way, several " alusis " are passed. The first is a very ancient one and is in ruins ; the roof and sides have collapsed, leaving two or three of the carved figures standing forlornly at different angles. These were once the best carved figures of any hereabouts, but they have been allowed to fall into decay. This is typical of the pagan Ibo. In Europe, age generally conduces to veneration and veneration instils care, but in this pagan country the people are apt to neglect their gods.

Some distance further another shrine is seen named " Okpala-Uwa-Oma ". This consists of four figures—two male and two female—under a single plank as a canopy. They are provided with heads and trunks highly coloured in black, white, yellow and red, but possess no legs. We pass on another quarter of a mile and meet with a similar set of figures by the wayside.

A little beyond this is the grove where " Omelichibe " and " Ezemenyiba " are accommodated. Strangers never pass this spot. It is here that applicants, seeking counsel of " Onyilli Ora ", state their cases and receive their answers. " Ezemenyiba " consists of a row of sixteen carved figures—in two sets of eight—similar to the fours described above. Close by is the great shrine. It is situated between the gnarled roots of an enormous cotton (bombax) tree and is furnished with a pair of curious old carved figures, unadorned with any colouring or other embellishment. One has no difficulty in realising the ease with which the medium could hide himself in close proximity to the shrine and make his voice distinctly audible to the suppliants.

But " Onyilli Ora " dwells a mile beyond this grove. The path leads across country until we are midway between Ezira and Umu-Okpulukpu. Here it descends, and the casual traveller would notice nothing to cause him to think he was near the abode of the god. The sign is a stick and just a common mushroom-shaped ant-hill a foot high. Looking carefully to the right at this point, a faint track is discernible, and this leads to the shrine of " Onyilli Ora ". Along this path, once a year, Mgbafo, having laid aside all earthly covering, was conducted by her appointed attendant in order that she might render homage and offer sacrifices. My guide led me by an indirect route ; it had the advantage of crossing the stream by a crazy bridge. That is a doubtful benefit, inasmuch as it entails passing through dense jungle in order to reach the desired spot. Hands and knees suffered considerably from thorns.

ORACLES

There is no path whatsoever; it is sheer forcing a way through the thick undergrowth. When returning, we followed the direct route and, except for the fording of the stream, found it easy travelling.

The final approach is through dense bush with the track almost invisible. Perpetual shade exists, but, here and there, the leaves are dappled with sun spots when the sun is directly overhead. It was deadly quiet on the occasion of my visit, not a leaf stirring, and no sound of bird or other sign of life. Expectations naturally run high at such a moment, and the issue is anticipated with some excitement. And then we arrived. What a disillusion! " Onyilli Ora " is nothing more than a slimy, stagnant pool wherein live a few catfish. It is just a mudhole from forty to fifty yards in length and from four to six feet in width, its deepest part being about two feet. It is overhung by trees and so remains in shade. It has nothing to raise it above the dignity of a slimy ditch. Its reputation has been built up entirely on the fact of its mysterious situation.

No stranger was permitted to visit this pool. Instead, reports were carried abroad gulling people with stories of the wonderful powers of " Onyilli Ora ". People were silent at the mere mention of his name. Even had some plucked up courage to attempt to visit the sanctuary they were told that, at the approach of strangers, daylight was immediately changed into total darkness in the vicinity of the shrine. Moreover, an intruder looking upon the face of " Onyilli Ora " must certainly die. Such fear was instilled into the minds of people living beyond the confines of Ezira, that it came to pass that Mgbafo, as the priestess of the god who surpassed all others in power, came to be regarded with almost equal veneration as the god himself. This was the secret of her influence, and accounts for its extraordinary power in different parts of the country. She was believed in implicitly, and she practised the vocation of priestess so long and effectively that, in all probability she deceived herself, and came to believe that she was possessed of the god-like attributes claimed by her master, " Onyilli Ora ".

There are other oracles of similar character in different parts of the Ibo country, e.g. there is one at Obunka, situated on the southern border of the Awka Division. It's votaries operated between and beneath the roots of a huge tree standing in the midst of thick bush. This, like some of the others mentioned, was quiescent for several years, but, of late, has been reorganised and, at the time of writing, it is alleged that considerable business is being transacted.

ORACLES

At one time, the most prominent of all these oracular deities namely, " Chukwu " of Aro, exercised a notorious influence throughout the land. Its power was broken by the Bende Expedition in 1902 and it has never recovered as far as I am aware. Its chief feature was the stream into which the blood of victims was made to flow. I hesitate to write of this, because I have no first-hand acquaintance with the shrine, or the ceremonies connected therewith. From reports, one is inclined to assume that the practices observed at other oracles were largely based on those in use at Aro-Chukwu.

NOTE TO CHAPTER IV

[1] The name " Omelichibe " is derived from : (*a*) Omeli = He overcame and, therefore, is to reign (ichibe) ; (*b*) Omelu = He was made, therefore let him reign. The meaning of " Ezemenyiba " = the king who can do more than any other since his father, being greater than all, so also the son surpasses all others.

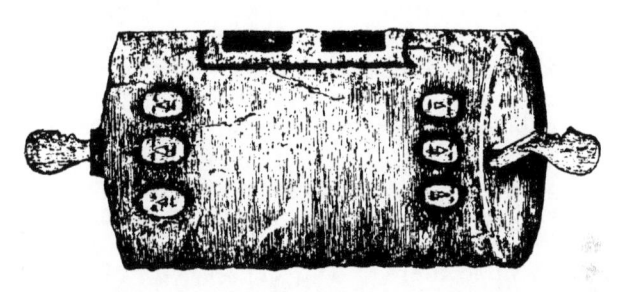

The Ancient "Ikolo" (Wooden Cylinder Tom-tom) which stood in the Square leading to the Agbala at Awka (pp. 78, 359).
Body of tom-tom is about six feet in length by three feet in diameter.

CHAPTER V

"MBARI" HOUSES

WHAT ARE KNOWN AS "Mbari" houses are curious and interesting both from an artistic and an ethical standpoint. They are distinctly local and are confined entirely to a part of the Owerri Division. I would go further, and venture to suggest that they are not Ibo in origin. The ideas underlying them, that is, those that render homage to "Ala" are, to some extent, similar to the use of "ọmumu" among other Ibos. (*Vide* p. 167.) The houses, with their many and varied embellishments, are novel features which have been imported, like so many other ideas and customs in the Owerri Province. (*Vide* Introduction.) In addition to the artistic skill displayed, they are of interest in other respects. In the course of my travels, I have visited a score or more " Mbari " houses and seen them in all stages of development, from the early beginnings behind the stout high fences to the crumbling remains of the last vestiges of ruin. Up to the time of writing, I know of no other European who has been admitted within the secret enclosure prior to the usual public opening of an " Mbari " house.

These " Mbari " houses are jealously guarded during the months of preparation ; even fellow-townsmen and relatives of the workers are forbidden entrance. I have been fortunate, and have had opportunities to inspect several " Mbari " houses while in the making.

The specific purpose for which an " Mbari " house is erected is fulfilled on the opening day. Immediately the prescribed sacrifices have been completed, the compound is given no further attention. The public are free to wander about at leisure. Nothing is maintained or repaired and, within three or four months, the figures and buildings fall to pieces. The sacrifices are the essential elements ; the material features are of no further use. They have served their purpose, short-lived though it is, and are allowed to perish forthwith.

I have personally known a number of professional craftsmen ; also some priests ; and they have talked with me freely and frankly, especially the craftsmen, as we have sat and chatted together at informal gatherings. They have been foremost in the talking while my part has been mainly to listen and make notes. Then, we have met again and criticised the notes, revising and amplifying them as required. My aim has been rather to set down what the Ibo people themselves think and practise in connection with the " Mbari " houses ; what they mean to them, and why they build them. With the facts and beliefs available, experts in anthropology and its allied sciences may be able to offer some suggestions concerning them and, possibly, trace probable sources of origin.

The first ostensible purpose of an " Mbari " house is to render worship to the god in whose honour it is erected : the second, and the real motive, is to pray for prosperity and, especially, offspring. In most cases, this god (or rather goddess) is " Ala ". Now " Ala " is the word for land or earth and, therefore, the name may, presumably, imply " Earth-goddess ". This arises probably (although the primitive accepts beliefs without argument) from the basic idea that, as the earth brings forth its fruits in due season, so " Ala " is the goddess of increase in all departments of life ; at home and in the field.

" Ala " is invariably the central figure in an " Mbari " house although, in some places, others have a position that is equal and, possibly, superior to her, e.g. " Ota-Miri " and " Opurogu ". It seems that though " Ala " is the central figure to whom special homage is offered, yet she is *not* responsible for the real incentive which governs the erection of an " Mbari " house.

" Ala " is reputed to be the mother of " Ota-Miri " and " *he* " is the dominating authority. Besides her son, " Ala " had two daughters : Ekwunoche and Ula-Mu-Kwa-Oche. The latter is the goddess of a tributary flowing into the Ota-Miri.

Ota-Miri had for wife, Nwanyei, and these had three sons : Opurogu, Amadi-Oha (The Thunderer) and Ogba-Egbe (The Gun-firer).

All these are notable names, and they have great weight in the part of the country which lies between Oguta and Ahoada and, more particularly, within a twenty-mile radius of Ebu (Owerri). The names are unknown in other parts of the Ibo country.

Formerly, " Mbari " houses were erected at fairly frequent intervals, say from three to six years, by each town under the sway of " Ota-Miri " or " Ekwunoche ". For some years, there had been a tendency to allow the custom to lapse as, with so many others, the result of European occupation of the country. Recently, there has been a revival, but this will

"MBARI" HOUSES

probably be short-lived. People will not be so ready to subscribe to the building funds as their fathers were.

The erection of an " Mbari " house is prompted by local circumstances. A report begins to circulate that deaths have been rather too frequent and measures should be taken to check this evil. Following old-time precedent, the chiefs consult the " dibia ". He advises the building of an " Mbari " house, assuring the people that this work of merit will placate the gods and win favours from them ; the lives of the old will be preserved and new life (in the form of children) will be bestowed.

The next move is to consult the priest of " Ota-Miri ". He it is who will, in consultation with the heads of families, make the necessary arrangements in respect of the site, workmen and other details.

Before going further, something more must be said concerning " Ota-Miri " and the others mentioned in addition to " Ala ".

" *Ota-Miri.*" This deity dwells in a big " bush " at Okohia (Ili-Amogo), a village of Ihi-Agwa, a few miles south-west of Owerri. This town claims to be the " *Head* " of " Ota-Miri." [This claim cannot be sustained. There is no doubt that Ebu is the " *Head* " of the Confederation. At this place is found the source of the Ota-Miri stream, and the priests of that town naturally hold a predominant position in all affairs connected with " Ota-Miri," including " Mbari " ceremonies.] People around may not plant their farms until Ihi-Agwa has consulted " Agbala " ; and they, the Ihi-Agwas, are the first to begin planting. On the day this work is begun, roads are cleaned and crowds repair to Ihi-Agwa for a drinking carousal (oṅuṅu).

" Ota-Miri " owns all the waters that are called by his name. These waters rise at Ebu and flow in the neighbourhood of Nekede. Hence, it may be inferred that " Ota-Miri " is the " Water God ", even as " Ala " is the " Earth-goddess ".

" Ala " and " Nwanyei ", the wife of " Ota-Miri ", also have their dwelling-place at Okohia, but they are not imprisoned there as " Ota-Miri " is : they are at liberty to roam and, moreover, " Nwanyei " has other resting-places, one of which is at Nkwo-Ukwu, Ihi-Agwa. Both " Ala " and " Nwanyei " can move freely to and from Okohia as they please.

Opurogu, the eldest son of " Ota-Miri ", lives in the waters which are known by the god's own personal name, Ota-Miri. In some cases, it is the priest of " Opurogu " who issues the command to build an " Mbari " house, as, for example, at Ihi-Agwa and Nekede. The present (1935) priest is blind, a man named " Ihe-Anacho-Anorue ". Where he holds sway, all the business is done in his name and by his authority.

"MBARI" HOUSES

Amadi-Qha. (" Onitsha Ibo = Egbe-Enuigwe " or = " Akpala ".) The second son of " Qta-Miri " and " Nwanyei ". He is the god of " Thunder ". He always has a foremost place in an " Mbari " enclosure, but, though prominent, is not the chief figure. At Ihi-Agwa and Nekede " Opurogu " holds the premier position, and " Amadi-Qha " is present as the servant, or messenger of his elder brother. " Opurogu ", being the " Okpala ", must have his younger brother to serve as his assistant.

Ogba-Egbe. The effigy of " Ogba-Egbe ", third son of " Ota-Miri " and " Nwanyei ", is identified by his gun. Probably he is the most feared of the whole family ; certainly he appears to exercise a salutary influence on dishonest persons. If one man cheat another by short payment, should a suspicion of the fact be aroused, he is warned to make full recompense quickly otherwise " Ogba-Egbe " will surely lay him by the heels. If a person steal from a basket in the market, " Ogba-Egbe " will follow him (or her), and exact punishment, because that one has spoiled " Ogba-Egbe's " market. It is related that a fowl was stolen from a village of Ihi-Agwa which was under the spiritual care of " Ogba-Egbe ". Because of this theft, all the people of the village died, except one lad who ran away !

Ekwunoche, daughter of " Ala ", is the goddess of the waters at Umu-Ekwune. She has a distinguished position in the " Mbari " houses in that town and neighbourhood.

Ula-Mu-Kwa-Oche, is the second daughter of " Ala " and ranks after her sister.

The generic term for all big shrines in these parts is " Agbala " (cf. Chap. III). This really has reference to " the unknown god " (cf. Acts xvi). The dominant idea at the back of this name is a personality (one or more) who is infinitely beyond and superior to all human ken and knowledge. He cannot be consulted or worshipped directly ; the only way of approach is through the mediation of " Agbala ".

Certain places possess the prerogative of having " Ota-Miri " as the chief figure in the " Mbari " house, while others are not allowed this privilege ; they have to be content with " Ala ", " Opurogu " or " Amadi-Qha ". Sacrifices are made to them all simultaneously at the time an " Mbari " house is first declared open. On subsequent occasions, such as when trouble, sickness or any other adversity inflicts an individual, on receiving directions from the " dibia ", he (or she) will sacrifice either to " Ala ", " Opurogu ", " Nwanyei " or " Amadi-Qha " specifically.

Apart from these individual figures, all others in an " Mbari "

"MBARI" HOUSES

enclosure are purely incidental : they stand on a par with the statues and other decorations outside and inside public buildings in Europe. There is very keen emulation in respect of "Mbari" houses; towns vieing with one another in their attempts to stage the best show.

After the edict has been published that an "Mbari" house is to be erected, the necessary funds are collected from the whole township. A site is selected within reasonable distance of the priest's quarters, the ground is cleared of bush, and a stout close fence, six to seven feet in height, is constructed to prevent the public from observing the work while in progress.

The next procedure is the selection of workers, for which task the priest enlists the help of the "dibia", an instance where two men fulfil distinctive offices (cf. p. 55). Together, at night, they pass through the town, calling at the different compounds. One by one the head of each house is called out, and the priest names this person or that of his household saying that "Ala" or "Opurogu" or "Ota-Miri" is calling him or her to work. The first to be chosen are a son and daughter of the priest himself; the others are chosen in due order until the number is complete. After selection, a chalk mark is made on the wall at the entrance to the compound. For one person called, a perpendicular stroke is made ; for a second, an additional mark is scored horizontally across the first. Not more than two can be taken from any one compound at the original selection. The sexes are of equal numbers and may reach a total of as many as one hundred though, usually, they are rather less; everything depends on the size of the "Mbari" house contemplated. Theoretically, there is no age limit; actually, those selected are between the ages of twelve and thirty-five. Nor does the fact of being married or single affect the choice. If so called, husband must leave wife, or wife husband. Some may resent the call, yet feel they have no option as they have been selected to work for the god. Occasionally, one will visit the "dibia" to inquire whether "Ota-Miri" or "Opurogu" is really calling him and, it maybe, a change effected ; such a change, when desired and paid for, can be arranged, though it is a rare occurrence.

Throughout the time the chosen ones (ndi-mgbe) are employed on the work of the "Mbari" house, they are not at liberty to plant or trade ; they are forbidden to engage in anything likely to distract them from their labours within the enclosure. The service may be for one or two years ; whatever the length, the workers must be supported by their responsible relatives.

"MBARI" HOUSES

During the months they are engaged in fulfilling this service, they may wear nothing but " alapa " (obi-akwa = loincloth), and they must smear their bodies with " ufie " (camwood dye) ; they are forbidden to wear any sewn garment. Once work has commenced, they must not venture abroad even to procure food ; they must wait until the messengers bring the supplies, however much their patience be tried.

At first, all live together in a house specially built for them in the priest's compound. Here they stay for a full month, male and female together. During this period, they must rigidly abstain from sex relationships ; for they are " nsǫ " (holy).

After this month of sanctity, they transfer to huts built in the " Mbari " precincts. On the occasion of their entering the enclosure, a man will hand over a woman from his compound to the care of a man of another and that man, in his turn, will do likewise, that is, temporary alliances will be effected. If a wife has been chosen, and her husband is very fond of her, he will pay well in order to be allowed to spend his nights within the enclosure and so keep guard over her. It is usually too difficult for a man to maintain this practice and, in any case, the woman has no lack of opportunities to go astray. A period spent in an " Mbari " compound often leads to a complete separation between husband and wife and the breaking of engagements. On the other hand, many engagements are contracted between men and women during the months they are living together in such close proximity. Then, again, some of these women, when they are freed from service, become harlots ; they have become so accustomed to promiscuous habits that they follow them when they resume their liberty abroad.

One of the first tasks of the " ndi-mgbe " is to raise a prolonged platform or washstand to contain as many basins as possible. At the base, on each side, parallel with the platform, trenches are dug to carry off waste water. All wash at the same time, the men standing on one side, and the women facing them from the opposite side of the improvised stand.

Once the enclosure receives them, all restrictions disappear in respect of sex relationships. It falls out that all women conceive who are capable of doing so, and they thank " Agbala " for honouring their services by giving them children. The only stipulation is, that a man and woman having sexual relationship are forbidden to work the day following : it is so ruled whatever the nature of their particular work. It is hardly necessary to state, that there are many days when no work whatever is done; all are out of action and rest at ease. When, however, an order is given that work is to be done on the morrow and a man, knowing of this order, deliberately cohabits with a woman, he will be fined a fowl, because he knew the next day was appointed for work and he should have abstained. There are no fixed times for labour or rest; on occasions, there are holidays of a week's duration; indeed, the whole programme is haphazard.

During her time of menstruation, a woman must abide by custom as closely as circumstances permit. She withdraws to a hut in a secluded corner of the enclosure. When again free, she purifies herself by washings and a sacrifice of eggs. She thereupon resumes her place in the community.

Though the "ndi-mgbe" are theoretically confined to the enclosure, they can go outside under cover of darkness: on no account may they venture forth in daylight. On occasions, they engage in spells of strenuous labour, when they work on day and night shifts. Night work consists in going forth to procure "ọzu", = ant-hill clay. Should a man hear a company of clay collectors approaching, he must hide himself, otherwise, if he be caught, he will pay a goat as forfeit; it will be the man's own fault as the clay collectors make no secret that they are abroad, an "ọgene" (bell) being beaten as they travel; hence an outsider has ample warning to steer clear of the party.

The "ndi-mgbe" have ways of increasing their supplies. They artfully cut one or two tunnels beneath the fence in secluded spots. Any fowls or goats that stray through from the outside are promptly seized, and regarded as the lawful property of the servants of "Agbala"! Should, however, the intruder be a dog or a sheep, it is promptly ejected, for dog is tabu, while the sheep is the daughter of a god, and it must not be molested. Here and there, as at Ikeni, mutton is not eaten, because it is alleged that a sheep once gave birth to a man-child, and from him has descended the present inhabitants of the town, hence, mutton must not be eaten there: it is tabu.

During the operations on the "Mbari" buildings, should a man quarrel with his (temporary) wife he must forfeit a fowl as penalty; if they fight and draw blood, the reparation sacrifice is a goat. Likewise, if any others fight and draw blood, there is a similar penalty to pay.

The "ndi-mgbe" may not sleep outside the "Mbari" precincts till the whole work is completed; not even in their parents' houses, except in a case of sickness or death in the

"MBARI" HOUSES

family. On such an occasion, a visit to the home is permitted. On returning, a fowl must be sacrificed and purification ceremonies observed.

Should one of the " ndi-mgbe " die while operations are in progress, his body will be removed and buried by his relatives. Meantime, the enclosure is deserted ; the workers scatter, and fear prevents them from returning for a month or more. Even so, they will not resume life in the enclosure until appropriate sacrifices have been made whereby assurance is restored.

Should a priest of " Ota-Miri ", or of one of the other gods (save " Opurogu ") die while the " Mbari " house is under construction, the whole business is abandoned. The building of another house will be in abeyance until entirely fresh arrangements have been made. Such a priest will be buried under the floor of his house. A priest of " Opurogu " is never interred ; his corpse is carried away and deposited in the " bad bush ".

These men and women perform all the plain and straightforward tasks in the preparation of the " Mbari " house. They collect and puddle the " ozu " (clay). Under a director, they construct walls and do other general work. The modelling is done, and the figures are set up, by professional artists ; men hired solely for the purpose. These craftsmen are not to be found in every town ; rather, certain towns are more or less noted for their skilled workmen.

A framework of light wood and cane is lashed together according to the model contemplated, and upon this is pressed the plastic clay, each limb or figure gradually being moulded into shape. These cane contraptions are very flimsy and the stranger, on seeing them, would not connect them with any practical purpose. However, the clay is built up around the sticks and moulded and rubbed until it becomes beautifully smooth and polished. The final effort is to decorate the figures, man, beast, bird or creature of the imagination, with colours, dead white and pink from chalks, black from old long-buried ashes and, nowadays, ultramarine from washing blue, and magenta from permanganate of potash ; also brown and yellow ochres from stone and wood.

Before the advent of Europeans into this part of Nigeria, the figures set up in an " Mbari " compound represented typical scenes from village life, nearly always on an exaggerated scale, the hunter, perhaps, being the most noticeable. I refer here to the extra and incidental figures as distinct from the representations of " Ala, Ota-Miri, Amadi-Oha " and the other gods for whose honour and worship the whole conception of an " Mbari " house is planned.

"MBARI" HOUSES

All the scenes represented are quite subordinate to the main theme, which is to offer sacrifice in order to persuade the gods to grant favours in the way of new life in home and farm. With this purpose in mind, here and there in the " Mbari " enclosure are to be seen crude illustrations of the history of life from the act of procreation, birth scenes, and other intimate episodes of daily existence.

In the primitive days, these representations were simply and naïvely realistic and, in some cases, highly and even grossly exaggerated. With the advent of the foreigner, increased facilities for travelling, and the demand for labour, many natives have been attracted to the coast towns. There they have learned many things ; some of them not for their good. To-day, there is to be seen in the " Mbari " compounds reflected expressions of these new concepts. The war provided a theme, and in a number of " Mbari " compounds there are representations of British and German gunboats in action. Modern life is depicted by models of the administrative officer, the banker, with his safe and keys, the judge presiding at the assizes with prisoner, police and council all complete, the teacher before his class, the priest and his congregation, or a church wedding scene. In one of the latest I visited, the large compound was linked up all round with a telephone system, with operators at work in the different sections. Motor-cycles, cars and locomotives have their places according to the fancy of the artists or, rather according to what is of predominant interest at the moment ; in fact, the whole " Mbari " compound is redolent with strikingly real and vivid illustrations of life as seen and interpreted by the native. Though the work is crude, yet there is extraordinary reality in the attitude and poise of the figures, and the observer is immediately struck with this. There is no mistaking the intention of the artist ; the caricatures are instinct with " aliveness ". And, with these new figurative conceptions of modern activity, come also new ideas of obscenity. What has been thought by some to be modern expressions of ancient ideas and beliefs are neither more nor less than crude tangible replicas of indecent photographs, or modelled reproductions of seaport and smokeroom stories as gleaned by steward boys and others. These have been transmitted to their friends in the interior during holiday seasons and, in due course, visibly expressed in some of the modelled figures in the " Mbari " compounds. I have personally questioned numbers of professional artists and, without a single exception, they have replied that they have received their latest ideas from pictures, or stories related to them.

"MBARI" HOUSES

The whole conception of an " Mbari " is based on the continuity of life. In the first place, there are the sacrifices to the Earth-goddess (" Ala "), Water (Ota-Miri), and their relatives. The episodes depicted and, in certain cases emphasised, do their work. As the crowds of men and women throng the new " Mbari " enclosure, they comment upon the art and skill of the artists and, also, upon the topics. The obscene subjects invoke outbursts of ribald laughter, the more unexpected and grotesque the elaborations, the more excited the people grow. The result is the rousing of passions, the ultimate result of which is the birth of children and this, of course, is forthwith placed to the credit of " Agbala ", who signifies his acceptance of the worship and honour given to him (by the building of the " Mbari " house) by granting the gift of children.

We must not forget to take note of one other figure usually to be found in an " Mbari " compound, namely, " Okpangu " = Ozo-di-mba = Chimpanzee.

" Okpangu ", as modelled, is a grotesque creature, a caricature of nightmare conception. He is a short stumpy figure, coal black, white eyes, and as ugly a devil as it is humanly possible to imagine. Some parts of his body are studded with long thorns (an inch or more in length) as thickly as a well-stocked pin-cushion. In his hands he holds several black balls of the size of an orange ; these represent the fruit of the creeper called " Ngu ". " Okpangu " is reputed to hurl these hard fruit-pods at folk who pass through the forest. He is feared by men and women alike. In the case of the latter, there are more reasons for fear, inasmuch as it is believed that this forest demon is liable to seize a lone woman and force her to submit to him. There is also a further belief that he is always on the prowl to catch feeble-minded folk for the release of whom he demands a ransom. So strong is the superstition that, if some simple fellow happens to be out of sight for a few days, it is at once assumed that he has been kidnapped by " Okpangu ".

Occasionally, a female " Okpangu " is installed. She is bigger than the male, and more repulsive in appearance. She may have a house (shelter) for her sole occupation, whereas the male has to be content with an odd corner, or unoccupied spot under the eave of one of the other houses.

In every " Mbari " compound, the sacred python is represented, sometimes in long undulating form, in other cases coiled. The reasons given for the presence of the reptile are because :

1. It is " nso " (sacred) to all Ibos.

"MBARI" HOUSES

2. Pythons dwell in Akohia and are regarded as the children of " Qta-Miri ". They may neither be killed nor molested.

Should a large one show signs of becoming a nuisance, he will be removed from the area. A number of men approach the reptile. The leading man pins its head to the ground with a forked stick while the rest rush forward and seize the body. It is a ticklish business, for these pythons are immensely strong. Having secured a firm grip, the wriggling procession moves off to the stream. On arrival, they cast the python into the waters of his parent, Qta-Miri.

All the back walls and pillars of " Mbari " houses are decorated with bright outstanding colours rubbed on in a series of curves, squares and triangles. The whole makes a very good jazz effect, and demonstrates the artistic gifts of the craftsmen.

In addition to the blatantly realistic representations of life, there are illustrations of unnatural practices, some based on declared accomplishment, some imagined, some semi-legendary and some entirely legendary. We find present, occasionally, a figure half woman and half beast (mermaid idea). This illustrates the Ibo belief that a " spirit " may have the characteristics of both man and beast. Other incidents must be left out of a book. In certain cases, the representations serve as an epithet (and are depicted with that intent) of contempt against a people of a neighbouring town such as " they give their virgins to dogs ", or they form a means of reproach, by alleging that these deeds are practised by the people of such and such a place.

The cost in cash for an " Mbari " house is stated to be between £6 and £12, according to its size, and the number and style of the figures modelled. The fees for the hired and professional craftsmen are independent of, and additional to, the daily maintenance. The village contingent of workers are not paid any wages. It is pretty generally reckoned and, no doubt with sound reason, that the priest who arranges for the erection of the " Mbari " house collects probably four or five times the amount required, and so gathers in a generous commission to compensate him for his share in the responsibility of erecting it. The amount stated above does not include the expenses in connection with the sacrifices ; these are separate altogether, and may amount to considerably more than the money expended on the " Mbari " house itself. An " Mbari " compound recently erected at Owerri (town) was stated on a notice-board to have cost £205. This great expense was

"MBARI" HOUSES

chiefly due to the fact that the houses were roofed with corrugated iron, a novel and modern innovation.

In the neighbourhood of Ngwo, Nsude and Agbaja Ọwa in the Udi Division, at intervals, the people construct quaint circular pyramids. Clay is used for the purpose. The bases are about sixty feet in circumference and two to three feet in height. Then another section is laid about forty-five feet in circumference and so on until the pinnacle is reached. They are erected to the honour of " Ala " and to indicate ownership of land.

Two rows of five are built parallel to one another which means that " Ala " gives children with the right hand and the left. The god (or goddess) dwells in the pinnacle and, thus, is in a position to detect any person committing evil. Such a person will be caught by the god and secured with shackles ; these are represented by small sticks inserted in the clay near the tops of the pyramids.

The " Mbọ ".
Small pot fixed over the mouth wherewith the " Umu-Chuku " disguised their voices.

CHAPTER VI

IBOLAND

THE FOREGOING record illustrating the compelling force that " spiritual " domination exercises upon Ibo thought and practice, naturally leads to a desire for a closer acquaintance with the country and the people.

Iboland lies astride the lower reaches of the River Niger, immediately north of the Delta. The West African Protectorate known as Nigeria, of which the Ibo country forms a considerable part is, of course, named after the great river. The name *Niger* comes from the Greek word *Nigir*. Hence, it will be seen that it does not mean " black " as if the word were derived from the Latin adjective. Above Lokoja, the river is known as the Quorra which, being interpreted, means " white " ! On the lower reaches, the natives speak of it as the " Big Water ". The addition of the word " salt " serves to distinguish the sea from the river among the Ibo people.

The following summary, culled from the narrative of Captain Allen's " *Expedition to the Niger, 1841*," will be sufficient for the purposes of this book :

" The Greeks, in the time of Ptolemy, had extensive information of countries south of the Desert. Herodotus states that two large rivers traversed the Sudan, the *Gir* and the *Nigir* : that the latter is the *Joliba* of Park cannot admit of a doubt." [1]

The Arabs, and especially Ibn Batuta in 1353, and Leo Africanus in his work (1556), speak of the great river as the Niger.

In 1778, an association was formed for promoting the discovery of the interior parts of Africa. " An opinion had long obtained that the Niger flowed to the westward, instead of, as Herodotus had asserted, to the eastward : it was thought to be a branch of the Nile."

On July 21st, 1796, Mungo Park arrived at Sego and saw " the majestic river, (which the natives called ' *Joliba* '), as broad as the Thames at Westminster, and flowing slowly to the eastward ".

Park embarked on the Niger again on November 19th, 1805. Details of this voyage were not known for a long time. When

IBOLAND

the report arrived, it stated that there was an "unexpected change in the direction of the Niger from an easterly course to one nearly south".

In 1830, the brothers Richard [2] and John Lander traced the river from Boussa to Brass and thus removed all doubts concerning its course.

Another expedition was despatched in 1832 with Richard Lander as chief adviser. The launching of this venture was practically a personal effort on the part of Macgregor Laird, a prominent marine engineer and merchant of Liverpool. Attempts to stimulate interest in the exploration of the Niger in those days met with scanty encouragement. Laird, however, was an enthusiast, and proved it by becoming himself a member of the band. The expedition arrived at the mouth of the Niger in August 1832, and carried on operations until February 1834. Three ascents of the river were made under very arduous conditions. During the third attempt Richard Lander was wounded by hostile natives at a spot near Aboh. He died shortly afterwards at Fernando Po. It was an unfortunate undertaking altogether for only nine of the forty-eight men, who originally comprised the expedition, returned home to relate the story of their adventures.

Not the least interesting fact of this expedition is that the "*Alburkah*", the smaller of the two vessels employed, was the first iron vessel to be sent to sea. Her dimensions were: Length, 70 feet; Beam, 13 feet; Depth, $6\frac{1}{2}$ feet; Engine, 16 h.p.[3]

For some years, the subject of Niger exploration was discreetly avoided. Meanwhile, the Slave Trade had been abolished by Act of Parliament. One result was that the countries from which slaves had been exported came more prominently under public notice and the future of Africa and its peoples became a topic for serious discussion, particularly among those who had been mainly instrumental in bringing slavery to an end in the British Possessions. Sir Thomas Fowell Buxton, who had taken a distinguished part in the struggle, turned his attention to West Africa with the idea of fostering legitimate trade as a substitute for the prohibited traffic in human beings. Among other activities, he was largely responsible for the inauguration and planning of the Expedition of 1841.

At Sierra Leone, two missionaries were invited to join the expedition, one the Rev. J. F. Schön, a brilliant linguist. He had studied a number of West African dialects, including Ibo, with the assistance of slaves who had been rescued by British warships and landed at Freetown. The second was a native of

IBOLAND

the Yoruba country, himself a rescued slave, Samuel Adjai Crowther, then a schoolmaster, but, later, to be known as the first Black Bishop.

The expedition arrived at the mouth of the Niger in the middle of the wet season, August 1841. Almost immediately, sickness attacked the party and one after another died, until 49 of the 145 members who had sailed from England under such auspicious conditions paid toll to the treacherous climate.

It was a very expensive undertaking, involving great loss financially in addition to the lives sacrificed, and nothing of substantial value was achieved in spite of the heroic services of officers and men.

Mr. John Laird, of Birkenhead, built three steamers of iron expressly for this expedition, the " *Albert* " and " *Wilberforce* " of 457 tons each, and the " *Soudan* " of 249 tons. Each of the two larger had " two engines of 35 h.p. and bunkers to contain coals for fifteen days of twelve hours' steaming. The ' *Soudan* ' had one engine of 35 h.p. and coals for ten days of twelve hours ".[4]

So long as the results of this ill-fated venture remained poignant in the memories of the English public it was useless to contemplate fresh enterprise : the set-back had been so drastic that any scheme would have met with prompt rejection. Nevertheless, in the minds of a few and, notably, Macgregor Laird, there was an unshaken belief that, ultimately, success would reward their efforts. He, in particular, refused to abandon hope until he had exhausted every means of testing his faith.

Hence, it came about that, in 1854, he succeeded in despatching the " *Pleiad* " to try, once again, to open the Niger to trade. It was intended that the vessel should be commanded by Mr. Beecroft who, as British Consul, had a personal knowledge of the river. When, however, the " *Pleiad* " arrived at Fernando Po to embark Mr. Beecroft, it was met with the sad news that he had died. The charge of the expedition, therefore, fell upon the second-in-command, Dr. W. B. Baikie, R.N., a man whose name is still held in remembrance on the Niger. Under his skill and care, the first prosperous voyage was completed. The " *Pleiad* " steamed up the Niger and also explored its great tributary, the Benue, nearly as far east as Yola.

In the early days, vessels followed the course of the Nun River. At the end of last century, this had become so silted up that the way of approach had to be changed and shipping has since entered the Niger by way of the River Forcados. Until comparatively recently, this Forcados River route was the normal

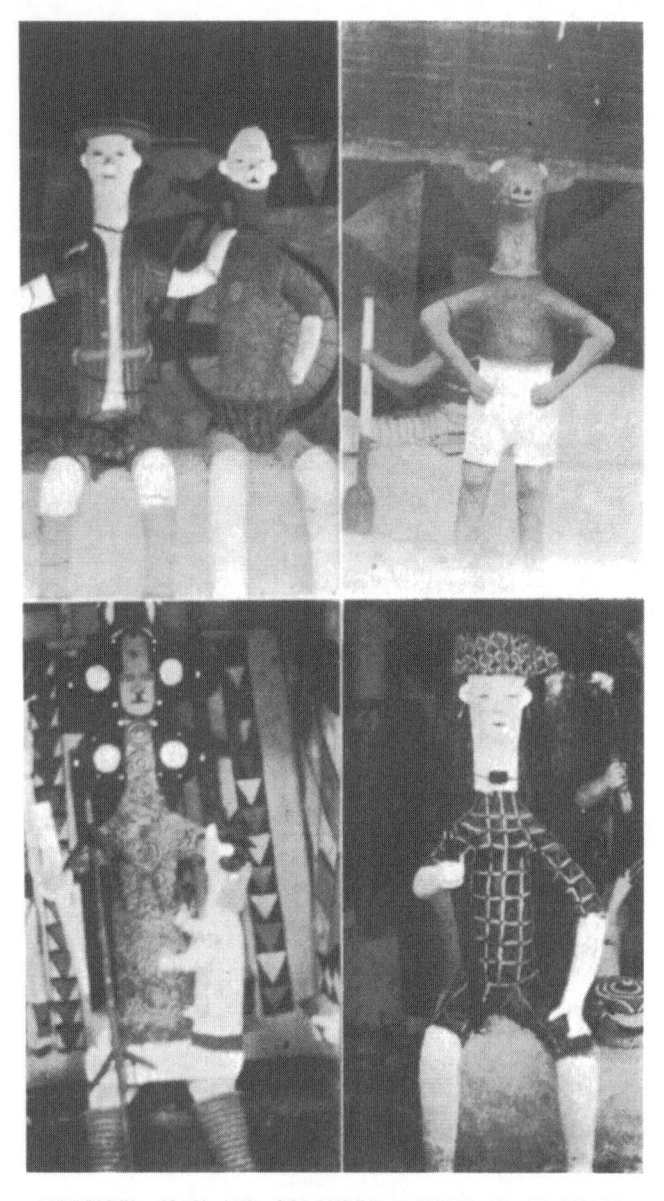

MODELLED CLAY AND COLOURED FIGURES IN AN MBARI
HOUSE ENCLOSURE.

Top left : AN OFFICIAL AND HIS WIFE.
Top right : MAN WITH A SHEEP'S HEAD.
Bottom left : THE EARTH-GODDESS "ALA," THE CENTRAL FIGURE IN ALL MBARI HOUSES AND IN WHOSE HONOUR THE HOUSE IS ERECTED.
Bottom right : A CHIEF'S WIFE. NOTE EAR-RINGS AND AGGRY BEAD ON NECKLACE.

IBOLAND

one for travellers. Since the completion of the North Eastern Railway from Port Harcourt, and the extensions of the Western Railway from Lagos, plus the construction of good roads and the general introduction of petrol-driven vehicles, the river has largely been forsaken by passengers. River transport has its compensations, but it is very slow in comparison with the railroad and the motor-car or lorry.

From Burutu, the seaport and the Headquarters of the United Africa Company, earlier known as the Royal Niger Company, Chartered and Limited, to Gana-Gana, the waters are tidal, and they are not affected by the annual rise and fall of the river. Innumerable channels intersect the area traversed, for this is the lower section of the delta of the great river. The prospect offers little more than an immense vista of mangrove swamp.[5]

Nothing other than water and trees is to be seen and the unchanging aspect soon becomes deadly monotonous. No habitations are visible and the only signs of human life are the men and women paddling their tiny canoes close alongside the tree-fringed edges of the swamp.

This dreary outlook extends for nearly two-thirds of the distance between the sea and Onitsha. After passing Aboh, the banks of the river begin to shape themselves. Villages also appear and, altogether, the scenery is more attractive. The huts stand close to the water's edge, for the river is the highway for these people ; a large part of their lives must be spent in their canoes. Those commonly seen are small, though large ones are possessed by some of the chief men, indeed, some are commodious enough to accommodate fifty people, or two or three tons of cargo ![6]

The Niger Delta extends northwards nearly as far as Aboh. Here the many channels converge into one stream and it justly deserves its title of the " Lordly Niger ". From July to the end of October, it is a magnificent sheet of water with a swirling current, sinister and brown owing to its muddy content.[7] From November onwards, sand-banks begin to thrust up their heads, causing the channel to contract and become sinuous, and making navigation complicated and tedious.

Up to this point, the country is inhabited by the Jekri and Ijaw tribes. From Aboh, the Ibo people come into prominence. At the same time, the general aspect of the country changes. Swamp gives place to rising ground and the river is definitely bounded by banks. The foliage has changed also ; the mangroves have disappeared, their place being taken by trees of many varieties. Some are very fine specimens, notably the bombax (silk cotton), the iroko (sometimes called African oak or teak), mahogany and palms.

From Aboh to Onitsha is a run of about forty miles. For many years Onitsha served the Ibo country for all purposes. Modern developments of the country have led to changes and, though still important, its status has been reduced. The main reasons for this have been the construction of the North Eastern Railway, the founding of new townships and improvements of old ones. As an instance of the former we may quote Enugu, now the Headquarters of the Government of the Southern Provinces of Nigeria.

The trading depot on the left bank of the Niger, commonly termed the " Water-side " (Onitsha), was originally called " Laird's Port ", after the name of the man who was the first to establish a trading factory at this place.[8]

It would appear to have been rather a precarious venture for, at that time, it is related that the Onitshas were at enmity with the surrounding towns and were shut up by themselves. " People came from the interior, but it was not safe for the Onitshas to visit the towns with which they were at variance, nor pass through them to the interior. They were, for example, at war with Ogidi, the people of which place had planted a cocoanut and sworn that, until the tree grew, bore fruit, and it was eaten, their quarrel with Onitsha should not be settled. They were also on war-like terms with Aboh, and had been from the time of Obi Ossai who swore that as long as there was a son of his living, he would be at variance with Onitsha. Nor was there friendship between Onitsha and Asaba. Till the Factory and the Mission Station were established, Onitsha was entirely shut up and dared not visit the Waterside, except in a large armed body ; and on market days, unless nearly all the male inhabitants turned out armed, to guard their wives, no one would venture. The establishment of the Factory and Mission Centre did useful work in persuading the people to respect their properties as neutral ground for the reception of all parties on equal terms." [9]

When I first arrived (1900), foreign influences had not appreciably affected Onitsha. Very largely, the people and the country were as they had been for generations. The Royal Niger Company (now operating as the United Africa Company) had a small depot at the " Waterside " some two miles west of the native township. The District Headquarters of the Company were at Abutshi Wharf, a short distance lower down the river, while the Courts of Justice and the Administrative Buildings were at Asaba on the opposite bank. At Onitsha,

IBOLAND

the Nkissi stream flows into the Niger, and the adjacent hillside was covered with a coffee plantation. This has been removed and the site occupied by Government buildings.

It was difficult to obtain trustworthy information concerning the interior. Before leaving London, I had endeavoured to secure maps, but, beyond a survey of the river, there was little else procurable. No Europeans had penetrated far into the Ibo country and native reports were scanty. The names " Abam " [10] and " Nri " were mentioned. They had elements of interest for two reasons. " Abam " stood for bands of mercenaries employed and controlled by the chiefs of Aro-Chuku, while " Nri " is the home town of a priestly cult whose particular services are connected with the coronation of kings and purification ceremonies. These priests travel widely and, because of their reports, their home-town was engrossed upon the maps in what was, otherwise, a blank space.

All is now vastly changed : the maps, to-day, are thickly studded with names and the boundaries of the various tribes have been delineated, among them those of the Ibo people. The country occupied by this tribe covers a considerable area of the Eastern Provinces and extends across the Niger into the Benin Province, as far as Agbor, half-way between Asaba and Benin. As stated in the Introduction, their numbers are computed to be between three and four millions, or about half the population of the Southern Provinces of Nigeria (latest Census 1931).

By means of the former slave-raiding activities, many Ibos became domiciled in the neighbourhood of Bonny. Their attachment to their language, strengthened by their sturdiness of character, has caused " Bonny Ibo " often to displace the dialect of the aborigines of that part of the country. The Ibo country has marked characteristics. In the lower sections, swamp conditions prevail over thousands of acres. In this region, there is not only a heavy rainfall : there is the additional feature that the water does not drain away freely. This cannot take place until the dry season returns and the sandy soil ceases to be waterlogged. The land is heavily wooded, with dense undergrowth. The vast quantities of water and the rank vegetation, sweltering in tropical heat, produce an atmosphere saturated with moisture.

Above the Delta, the land remains uniformly flat for many miles. In bygone ages, the Atlantic flowed where now are villages and farms. The soil is still alluvial and stands but a few feet above high-water level. In the neighbourhood of the railway line as it proceeds northwards from Aba, in the Bendi

IBOLAND

District, quaint little hills thrust up their heads. One has the impression of a mass of candy ; it looks as if the country in this part had boiled and suddenly cooled, leaving little conical hillocks. Farther north still, higher hills appear on the left side of the railway, stretching from Okigwi past Awgu, Enugu, and Nsukka over the borders of the Southern Provinces and forming the eastern watershed of the Niger. Here, there are hills attaining to a height of nearly 2,000 feet, and the whole aspect is a delightful change from the low-lying swamps of the littoral.

The vegetation has also changed ; the densely wooded country has given place to an orchard-like appearance with scrub and intervening patches of moorland. Where clumps of trees are seen they indicate, as a rule, the thickets, conserved for protective purposes, in which the villages lie concealed.[11]

Along the Niger valley, the soil is sandy and of reddish or grey colour. There are stretches where no stone is to be found ; any required for building or road construction has to be brought from a distance. This sandy soil is of inferior quality for agricultural purposes and the returns, in proportion to the labour expended, are oftentimes disappointing. This type of land is easily turned, a contrast to that of the hilly country to the east where laterite abounds. Breaking up land of this nature is a slow and laborious business, especially as the gravel is compounded with sticky clay and packs down into a hard mass. From it the natives obtain very fair results.

There is not much naturally exposed ground. Whatever else fails, there are sure to be weeds and grass, giant elephant grass (achalla), jungle grass (ikpo), reminding Europeans of a cornfield, and much in demand when ripe for thatching. There is also a species of spear grass, called " atta ", which spreads rapidly, for the smallest section of root is capable of propagating itself. A few inches below the surface of the ground, the roots spread laterally and weave themselves into a thick, tangled mass. To clear ground carrying a crop of " atta " grass is a tiresome task, demanding great patience and persistent labour. It corresponds to English couch grass in greatly exaggerated form.

It is quite different on the western side of the Niger. There, open spaces are the exception rather than the rule. There is abundance of forest, which is also a factor in conserving the fertility of the soil. The dense undergrowth prevents the rain from scouring away the good material, and the great quantities of decaying leaves serve as a dressing. There is seldom a scarcity of home-grown food, for nature is truly bountiful in this part of the Ibo country. To provide sites for villages, and

IBOLAND

land for agriculture, clearings are made in the forest. There used to be a ruthless and indiscriminate destruction of valuable timber, chiefly by firing, when clearings were made. This evil is now being restricted to reasonable proportions by the active intervention of the Forestry Department of the Government.

People travelling to a tropical country generally anticipate finding flowers of many species, hues and foliage. They are apt to be disappointed with the comparatively meagre results in the Ibo country, for flowers are not in profusion. There are numbers of beautiful flowering creepers, shrubs, and trees. In the undergrowth, lilies predominate in most parts. With the exception of the " gloriosa superba ", with its multi-coloured flowers, the lilies are almost all of pure white, some with trumpet-shaped blooms : others of spider-edged variety. Palm trees are everywhere, though much more conspicuous in the vicinity of villages. The oil palms (Elœis Guineensis) are really features of the landscape in certain areas. There are also localities chiefly, though not necessarily so, in the precincts of water, where the Raphia Vinifera palms flourish. From these great quantities of palm wine are extracted by tapping. Cocoanut palms are confined to the villages ; they stand dotted about between the huts. The natives have an infinite variety of uses for palm trees and their products ; every part being utilised for some purpose.[12]

As regards big game, there is no comparison between the Ibo country and, say, Eastern and Central Africa, and the same also applies to small game. There has been, since the introduction of firearms, an unrestricted slaughter of bird and beast until they have been reduced almost to vanishing-point. One may travel hundreds of miles and only occasionally see a few monkeys or a scared deer. In the course of covering 100,000 miles, I doubt if more than half a dozen wild animals have crossed my path. There *are* animals, leopards, bush-cow and others, but to find them entails time and arduous hunting. Elephants were not uncommon in the past : it is rare to hear of one at the present day. The Ibos have a partiality for ivory and the massive " horns " (elephant tusks bored for sounding as horns) carried by chiefs as part of their insignia of rank, attest that elephants were, at one time, a regular feature in the upper parts of the country. This lack of game is, perhaps, chiefly due to the general use of firearms : it is also influenced by the density of the population, particularly in the southern districts. There is little country where wild animals can roam undisturbed, e.g. in the Onitsha Province it is computed that there are over 300 people to the square mile. Of course, this density is not universal : in the northern districts, and on the western side of the Niger, the hunter's prospects are certainly brighter.

The climate can be comprehensively summed up in the two seasons, the wet and the dry, and, on the whole, they function with little variation in their regularity. What changes there are from this annual rotation are of a spasmodic character and mainly consist of what are sometimes termed " the Little Dries " and the Harmattan (Ugulu). The wet season normally sets in about the end of March, or early in April, and is ushered in by a series of violent tornadoes, wind, rain, lightning and thunder between them producing awe-inspiring sensations. Not infrequently, they are responsible for damage to life and property. The wind, at times, attains to hurricane force, while the rain brings to mind the story of the Deluge. The lightning flashes in all directions simultaneously, the thunder is constant, with intermittent crashes resembling the close proximity of high-powered artillery. Happily, the tornadoes soon blow themselves out, leaving the rain to bring the storm to an end. A huge rainfall is annually registered.[13] Between the tornado season and the regular wet season, there is a short period in May and June when the weather is fair, with brilliant sunshine alternating with occasional heavy showers. This is the time of the so-called " Little Dries ".

The wet season draws to an end in the manner in which it began, except that the tornadoes are less violent in character. This is in November. At the close of this month, rain ceases and no more than an odd shower or two need be anticipated until the next wet season falls due. Meantime, round about Christmas and from that date onwards to, perhaps, the middle of February, the " harmattan " may be expected. This peculiar wind is not regular in its behaviour. Some years it may last no longer than two or three days ; in others it may continue for as long as six weeks. The natives assert that a strong prolonged harmattan, though distinctly uncomfortable to human beings, is beneficial, particularly to the palm trees. This, no doubt, is because the excessive dryness has a similar effect as frost by providing a period of rest for the vegetation.

The " harmattan " shows signs of its approach by the sky becoming overcast with heavy clouds and the rumbling of thunder. This may continue for two or three days with some drizzle. Then, abruptly, the unusual coolness of the atmosphere indicates that it has arrived. The natives feel the cold intensely and bring out their warmest coverings and also make fires wherewith to warm themselves. As long as it lasts, the air is permeated with grey dust as finely ground as flour. A smoke-

IBOLAND

like haze obscures the rays of the sun. The powder-like dust settles everywhere, penetrating drawers and boxes, food and raiment. Eyes, nose and lips are affected by the excessive dryness. Leather curls up, book bindings crack; woodwork shrinks or splits. The climatic conditions are in complete contrast from the remainder of the year, the dryness after the usual humid conditions being very marked. It is unpleasant, or the reverse, according to one's own reaction to the complete change.[14]

Apart from the climate with its usually humid heat, tropical downpours and awe-inspiring tornadoes, there is one other irritant which cannot be altogether avoided by the resident in the Ibo country, namely the insect pest. There are creatures innumerable of all sizes and descriptions, but all equally pernicious. Several varieties of mosquitoes attack viciously, more particularly after nightfall, some the carriers of virulent germs productive of malaria and yellow fever. In some parts, sand-flies are a real plague, attacking uncovered parts of the body throughout the day. It is difficult to believe that such infinitesimal mites can be responsible for so much inflammation. Besides these, there are winged insects of many species to be avoided, especially the tsetse and mangrove flies. The so-called " sweat-fly " is another nasty little insect. Nor must the ants be overlooked; they certainly will not fail to make their presence known. There are literally armies of these. As scavengers, they serve a useful purpose and probably the white ants (termites) act as a substitute for worms in turning the soil, but they are very destructive unless care be taken to protect devourable property.

In spite of all these drawbacks the Ibo country has many attractive qualities. The average European, provided he has the gift to adapt himself to the conditions, need not be unduly worried at the prospect of residence in it. On the contrary, there are endless compensations, and there is much that is enjoyable. The morning and evening hours are very pleasant : the gorgeous sunsets are a joy to behold, the moon riding in her glory above the shimmering river, the lightning tracing bewildering patterns across the sky, and the star-spangled velvet of the tropical night, are features which cannot be equalled in our northern latitudes.

NOTES TO CHAPTER VI

[1] " *Expedition to the Niger, 1841* ", (Captain Allen), Vol. I, pp. 6 and 8.
[2] First Royal Medallist of the Royal Geographical Society.

IBOLAND

[3] "*Expedition into the Interior of Africa*", Laird and Oldfield, Vol. I, pp. 6 and 311; also "*Expedition to the Niger, 1841*", Vol. I, p. 19.

[4] "*Expedition to the Niger, 1841*", Vol. I, pp. 26, 27, 30.

[5] "Mangrove, Rizophora mangle of Linnæus (Rizophora racemosa). This tree, like the banian of the East Indies, is propagated by shoots thrown out from the upper branches; these descend, take root, and become the parent trees, throwing out leaves, branches, and shoots in their turn. Hence, a whole forest of mangrove trees are intimately connected with each other and are thus so firmly rooted as to resist the most rapid tides and most impetuous current. They grow in wet places, and are generally covered with large quantities of oysters, here called mangrove oysters. They render creeks unhealthy by retaining the mud and ooze and other putrefying substances among their tangled roots; they also render them dangerous, by affording a secure retreat to alligators (crocodiles). The wood of this tree is extremely hard, and much used by the natives for building houses, as it is not so easily destroyed by the termites (white ants) as other kinds of timber."—Winterbottom.

[6] William Cole (1859) tells of one—Prince Akia—whose canoe was "propelled by fifty athletic paddlers".—"*Life on the Niger*", p. 5.

[7] Dr. Oldfield states early in 1834: "From absolute measurement with a line, I found that the difference in the level of the water in the course of the year was nearly sixty feet."—"*Expedition into the Interior of Africa*", Laird and Oldfield, Vol. II, p. 276.

"By the mark ordered to be made by Captain Trotter at Idda, the river was found to have fallen thirty feet, i.e. up to the date of measurement."—"*Expedition to the Niger, 1841*", Vol. II, p. 347.

[8] "*Life on the Niger*", p. 72.

[9] "*Niger Expedition, 1857–1859*", Crowther and Taylor, pp. 428–9.

[10] *Vide* p. 384.

[11] "For the greater security of smaller towns a bush or thicket called 'Igo-ile' (home forest) is kept about half to one mile from the town. This forms a safe ambush for defence and hiding places in defeat. The tall trees are sometimes used as Watch-towers to observe the movements of the enemy. Except in times of profound peace it is penal to cut trees in the home forest."—"*History of the Yorubas*", p. 91.

[12] *Vide* Chap. XXXI.

[13] Asaba 53, Enugu 69, Owerri 98, Opobo 141 inches respectively, culminating with 356 at Debundscha in Cameroon.

[14] The average temperature is round about 80° (minimum 64°, maximum 96°). On occasions when the "harmattan" is blowing, the early morning temperature may fall as low as a few degrees below 60.

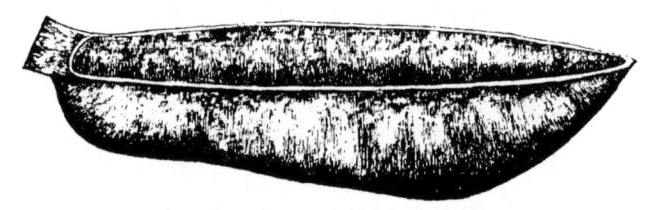

A New "Dug-out" Canoe ready for Launching (pp. 113, 350).

CHAPTER VII
THE IBO PEOPLE

IN THE IBO COUNTRY lying on the left bank of the Niger, society is largely based on patriarchal lines. Every town and, incidentally, every clan and family is an independent unit. There is little trace of any combination, or even co-operation between town and town. Although speaking the same language, and in times of peace intermarrying with one another, the nearest neighbours may still be regarded as strangers.

Communal life, within limits, is a potent factor in the life of the people. The impact of Western ideas is responsible for disrupting this. Under the old system, every person knew the " Head " to whom he or she was attached, and they realised their mutual allegiance and responsibility. Hence, there were, in past days, no homeless vagrants in Iboland, the family being responsible for the less fortunate relatives. The " Di Ǫkpala " (head) looked after the family and its common interests and properties, though he did not, in any wise, claim personal ownership of the properties or the fetishes of individual members.

With the exception of the King of Onitsha, there are no kings on the eastern side of the Niger. The Ibo proverb runs, " Ibo enwerǫ eze " = " the Ibo has no king ". The solitary instance owes its origin to Benin. History affirms that the Ǫba (King) of Benin demanded tribute of the people of one, Chima. These people, if not directly subject to Benin, were under its suzerainty. Whether this was a new imposition on the part of the Ǫba is not noted. What is stated is that the attempt to force tribute led to war and, eventually, the retreat eastward of Chima's people. Another assertion is that the mother of the Ǫba, by name Asije, strayed over the boundary into Chima's territory in search of firewood. She was caught and beaten. This led to war and Chima and his people had to flee. After Chima's death, his successor was unable to withstand the pressure from Benin and moved as far as the Niger. A section of the people, under Oreze, founded Onitsha, and another section, under Ekensu, sailed down the river and founded Aboh.

Oreze expelled the people of Oze who owned the land now occupied by the Onitshas. The Ozes are greatly reduced in numbers; only a few families remain, and they are settled on the right bank of the Nkissi stream, about four miles east of their former territory. Sufficient evidence can be adduced to prove that the connection between Onitsha and Benin was not completely severed until this century, e.g. the Onitsha people were accustomed to wear the white cloth woven on the western side of the river. The most important relic of allegiance to Benin is the venerated " Ofo " brought by the refugees to Onitsha. It is alleged that this was the insignia of authority granted by the Oba to Chima before the war between the two. This iron " Ofo " is still in existence, though the last two kings have not enjoyed the benefit of its authority. The eldest son of the former king, Anazonwa (who died in 1900) retained, and, at the time of writing, still has possession of, the ancient " Ofo " of his forefathers.

It makes for better understanding if the distinctive attributes and functions of the following men be borne in mind when studying Ibo Society.

" *Onye-isi-Ani*," sometimes " Eze-Ani " = the Head (lit. King) of the land. The land " Ani " ranks as a god and the Onye-Isi acts on his behalf. Such a man must be town-born ; a stranger cannot be nominated for the position. Normally, it is the eldest male representative of the first family to settle on the site. Where it becomes necessary to make an appointment it is done by divination. The villagers gather together and the " dibia " seeks guidance by the use of charms. Sometimes a man will claim that " Ani " has appeared to him in a dream. In such case, it is probable that the " dibia " will forthwith affirm that " Ani " wishes him (the man) to superintend his worship.

It is at the house of the Onye-isi-Ani that meetings take place preliminary to any business of importance. His insignia consists of five or six ankle strings similar to those worn by men of " Ozo " title, but rather thicker. He is entitled to carry an " ogbanchi " (staff of office). The fact of his being the " Onye-isi-Ani " gives him equivalent rank with " Ozo ", but he cannot in any way share the monetary or other benefits ; he has the outward respect only. Whatever he declares to be " alu " (abomination) is, perforce, tabu. Besides the " Onye-isi-Ani " for each clan, there is one who represents the whole combined town. He is the eldest male descendant of the man who founded the first village. He maintains the ancestral " obi " (house of the father of all), and here must be performed the first sacrifices. By virtue of his office, he ranks highly in

THE IBO PEOPLE

the eyes of the people. On the other hand, he may quite possibly be a man of no substance, power, or status.

It is the business of the " Onye-isi-Ani " to make sacrifice to the land (" Nmeya-Ani " = to sacrifice to the earth = to worship the land).

" Onye-isi-Obodo " = The oldest man in the community.

" Onye-isi-Emume " = The senior man of those holding title, dating from the time when the title was assumed, not seniority in age.

" Onye-eze-Okwu " = A good speaker ; a sort of village orator. Sometimes there is a man known as " Onye-nekwuluora " (" one who speaks for the people " = advocate).

" Onye-isi-Ogbu " or " Onye-isi-Akpu " = The leader in war and in any big business. This needs explanation. A man who succeeds in killing an enemy in war or, what is counted as an equivalent, a leopard or a buffalo, plants a young " akpu " (silk cotton = bombax) tree to mark the great feat. This accounts for the presence of many of these huge trees in some towns, sometimes planted with a certain amount of regularity. In some towns, annual festivals to commemorate their prowess are observed called " Igba (ilo) Ekwensu " (Parading in honour of the Devil) at which none other than the " akpu " planters is allowed to participate. No woman or child is allowed to appear in the streets while the " Ndi-isi-Akpu " are parading, as it is thought that the Devil might, himself, appear suddenly on the scene, making it unsafe for women and children.

" Ndi-Chie (Ani) " = The Elders = the rulers of the land, the administrators of the general affairs of the community. No one particular chief has individual power, though a man with an " Ozo " title is respected (or feared) more than a commoner. His wife and son also possess greater freedom of action than ordinary folk. This is solely because of his being in a position by wealth or influence to exact his demands ; it is not due to any inherent or recognised right to exercise authority over and above his fellows.

The physique of the natives is affected to some extent by the productive capacities of the locality in which they dwell. Where the soil is of inferior quality, the people are inclined to be thin and scraggy. The staple food, generally speaking, is yam. This contains a fair proportion of starch, and where yam is freely eaten there is a tendency to stoutness. Where the people have to augment the food supply with maize, cassava and beans, they are not so well-favoured. There is not the need to supplement on the western side of the Niger where the yam supply is abundant. On the whole, the Ibos are of good

THE IBO PEOPLE

physique and compare very favourably with other African tribes. Real famine conditions are quite unknown; nature is lavish in providing the great majority of the Ibo people with a fairly adequate supply of grown food. There is not a sufficient supply of meat to allow a completely satisfactory diet. To a certain extent, this deficiency might be met were the Ibos not opposed to the use of milk from their own cattle.

There are many fine specimens of physical development, though men are not often seen such as one described by Cole. He states that "on the river (Niger) side where food is plentiful, men grow to full size. It is recorded that Ajie, the usurper king of Aboh, was six feet ten inches in height and weighed fourteen stone."[1] This stature, though not the weight, would, however, be as exceptional as a man of similar height in England.

There are divers degrees of colour. Many Ibos are truly as black as the proverbial coal : others are almost as light-skinned as the natives of Southern Europe, while a few are distinctly reddish. The folk who stand out obtrusively are the albinos, their pale skins being markedly prominent among their dark-coloured or black neighbours. Though not exactly welcomed, they are accepted on an equal footing with other folk and there are no tabus connected with them. They are free to enjoy similar rights and liberties; any sense of inferiority would probably be traced to their own personal complexes. Certainly their appearance is rather repulsive. They are termed "Any-ali", sometimes, loosely, "ndi ocha" (white people). The unprejudiced way in which they are accepted by their Ibo brethren is in complete contrast to the treatment meted out to albinos by some tribes. For instance, the Fang tribe regard them with abhorrence. Some of the Niger Delta tribes frankly repudiated them and, not infrequently, destroyed them. The neighbouring Yorubas allow them to live; they are claimed by the king as his prerogative.

Quite a number of the older folk have piebald patches on their skins, more particularly upon the hands and feet. The patches are irregular in size and shape and are white or pinkish white in colour. These eccentricities normally appear some time after full growth, generally speaking from middle age onwards. Only one certain case (and one other so reputed) have I seen of a child born with white patches on the skin. The natives affirm that these discolorations are hereditary. They may be absent at birth and in the early stages of life, yet, in due time, they will manifest themselves. Certain families seem peculiarly addicted to this characteristic, hence it is assumed that they are inherited.

THE IBO PEOPLE

In their primitive state, the Ibos were not acquainted with any method of brewing intoxicating liquor. They never made use of corn or bananas for manufacturing beer or spirit. Their favourite drink was, and is still, palm wine. This they extract from the trees, the common oil palm or the Ngwọ (Raphia Vinifera), the former being the stronger of the two. It is harmless when fresh ; left for a time, fermentation sets in by natural processes. After fermentation has begun, if indulged in too freely, the result will be a fuddled state if not actual intoxication. Comparatively few of the old men could be designated drunkards. In any case, it is not a common weakness and the Ibos generally can be classed as a sober people. Market days, festivals, and during burial ceremonies, are the times when the effects of drinking are most evident. On occasions, the bouts may be prolonged, with the inevitable consequences that might be expected. Even so, the effects are probably as much due to the enormous quantities imbibed as to the amount of actual alcohol consumed.

It is the imported liquor that has given cause for comment.[2] The introduction of spirits on the coast is a practice centuries old, but it should always be remembered that it is a foreign feature. Its importation is not the best way to conserve native customs ! Lately, the natives of Southern Nigeria have learned how to distil spirit from palm wine. To do this, they rig up primitive stills from petrol-tins and metal or bamboo tubes. The knowledge of the process is spreading and, being established, it will be exceedingly difficult to control, let alone eradicate. It is questionable whether the severe penalties imposed by recent legislation will be an effectual restraining influence. The chief obstacle in compelling obedience to the new laws is the difficulty of locating stills concealed in the bush. There is the further factor, that the natives feel that the prohibition of distilling is an act of interference with their rights. They contend that, as they have discovered methods of manufacture, they ought to be allowed to make use of their knowledge and enjoy the benefits thereof. They argue that, if the white man maintains that spirit-drinking is beneficial, then its production should be encouraged and that, if importation is permitted, surely it is only reasonable that the black man should be granted similar favours. This, of course, is not the whole story : it is stated merely as a matter of fact and to explain the situation. It is advisable to be acquainted with native opinion.

Prior to the present century, the Ibos had little intercourse with the outside world. Apart from half a dozen factories on the banks of the Niger, serving as depots for trade, there was little contact with the country people. No attempt had been made to establish trading centres in the interior. Protestant and Roman Catholic Missions had been operating for some years, but their agents had not penetrated to any appreciable extent, and the Ibo country was practically unknown territory. The most experienced men had no more than fragmentary knowledge. For one thing, the average life of the white man was short in those days, and travelling was a formidable task. The natives were almost as ignorant, because they were too frightened to venture far from their homes. Fear dominated them and was an effectual barrier to travelling. This was aggravated by the rumours that filtered through from time to time. From the east came stories of the atrocities perpetrated by the notorious Abams ; [3] from the west came reports of the raiding activities of the Ekumeku Society.[4]

There was genuine reason for these fears. The reputation of the interior was certainly unwholesome and it was founded on fact. The fate that befell unfortunate strangers was well known. Savage practices were rife, including cannibalism and human sacrifices. For the latter, the occasions were chiefly in connection with the deaths of notable persons, though these were by no means the only occasions. To-day (1937), there is standing at Onitsha a tree used in former days for crucifixions. Nails are still in position, mementoes of the past, now so embedded in the overgrowing wood that they are not noticed unless attention be drawn to them.

Before going further, it should be stated that cannibalism does not appear to have been a custom universal throughout the Ibo country. Onitsha, for instance, claims that it never conformed to the practice and this contention is supported by the fact that there is no trace of it on the western (Enu-Ani) side of the Niger, whence the Onitshas came.

It was quite different in the eastern interior. There was no doubt about the cannibalistic propensities of the people in that part, and early missionaries and officials were not without evidence of the practice ; indeed, at times, attention was drawn to the fact in no uncertain manner. The people usually refrained from boasting on the subject of eating human flesh but, now and then, they were not so reticent. After one of the little wars, the people of one of the villages involved complained bitterly of their ill fortune ; they had not succeeded in capturing as many victims as their opponents and declared that there could be no genuine reconciliation until a further contribution had been made to their fleshpots !

THE IBO PEOPLE

One of my native friends had a rather gruesome experience. As a small boy he lived with his brothers. One night they were away from home till a late hour and the lad fell asleep. Suddenly, he was roused and saw the arm of a man being cooked, the elder brothers' share of the evening spoils!

In another case, a sturdy youth who had been a couple of years in our service disappeared. He had recently changed to other employment and one of his first duties was to carry messages. He departed, and was never seen again. We were left in no doubt concerning his fate; he had been enticed into a compound, under pretence of being supplied with refreshment, and had been murdered and disposed of in accordance with ancient accepted custom.

The general practice was to eat all captives taken in war, though it was not limited to this. The only binding restriction was that the victim must be a foreigner; it was forbidden to eat a member of one's own community. A slave might be purchased wherewith to make a feast and, in some parts, corpses were received from agents, or stolen from other village burial grounds. In my earlier days in the country, I was requested on several occasions to appeal to the authorities in order that the purloining of recently buried bodies might be suppressed.

A chief who, later, became a great friend of mine, managed to obtain possession of one of his enemies. He had long waited for revenge and, at last, the opportunity came. He derived great satisfaction by first lopping off the ears and nose of his victim and, then, completing the operation by flaying him alive. The carcase was eaten: the skin was utilised to provide a " royal " drum for the compound.

The question may be asked, " What are the reasons for cannibalism ? " No completely satisfactory answer can be given. Undoubtedly, there has always been a genuine meat hunger in the Ibo country where flesh food is scarce. There is also a belief that, in some mysterious way, the partaking of human flesh imparts courage and strength. One old man assured me that his son would be greatly benefited by the addition of human flesh to his diet. It is asserted that human flesh is particularly nutritious and causes the bodies of the consumers to grow strong and lusty. It is reputed to be the " best of all meat ". Further, it formed a subject for derision and boasting against an enemy, " Beware, lest we eat you ! " [5]

In some parts of the Ibo country, men only were permitted to partake of human flesh: in other places, the sexes shared alike. I have been acquainted with many erstwhile cannibals and have not noticed any difference between them and other folk in the ordinary affairs of life. It goes without saying, that they have abandoned old habits and they do not care to be reminded of the past. Although inclined to be reticent on the subject generally, one has gleaned that among the choicest titbits were the knuckles. Confirming this, Seabrook writes : " I asked what parts of the meat were considered the best ? He (Firehelmet) replied that, for solid meat, the loin cuts, the ribs and rump steak were the best. The liver, heart and brains were titbits, but tasted identically the same as those of other animals. Firehelmet interpolated that, as a matter of personal choice, the palm of the hand was the most tender and delicious morsel of all." [6]

While fear was the dominating cause in restraining the natives from moving far from their own village precincts to this must be added the difficulties to be surmounted in actual travelling. Apart from the fact that there was nothing worthy of the name of a road, there was no method of transport other than by means of carriers. Some attempts were made to introduce horses and donkeys from the north only to be met with disappointment, as the animals quickly succumbed to disease transmitted by tsetse flies. Had these efforts met with better fortune, the employment of horses would have resulted in only partial success, because the tracks through the forest and over streams were unsuitable for animals. The tracks were tortuous and narrow, being no more than mere paths worn by the feet. Obstacles abounded, fallen trees over which the traveller had to clamber, deep gullies, streams had to be forded and rivers crossed by bridges of primitive type, often no more than a single treetrunk. Incidentally, a wet, uneven and well-worn tree-trunk does not afford good foothold for a man ; it is entirely useless for a horse. The crossing of one of the larger rivers was an arduous task, taking half an hour or more to negotiate. When traversing forest country, the pedestrian must, perforce, watch his steps, for innumerable roots protrude, ready to trip up the unwary. Frequently, swarms of black ants covered the path and procedure was of the hop, skip and jump variety. Nothing scares an animal more than a swarm of ants : instinct justly gives it cause for fear. Two or three ants attach themselves to a foot and begin to sting. Not having hands to dislodge them, the animal puts down its nose to brush them away and immediately more ants attack. The poor beast, in its distress, rubs its nose on the ground only to have still more ants to worry it. Unless it can escape quickly, it will suffer intensely. Where it cannot escape, it will surely die and be speedily devoured. There will be a mass attack on eyes, ears, nostrils and mouth

IN AN MBARI HOUSE ENCLOSURE.
Top left : CLAY CORNER PILLAR WITH WOMAN'S FIGURE IN BAS-RELIEF.
Top right : FREAK MONKEY.
Bottom left : CARICATURE OF A HORSE.
Bottom right : THE IBO CONCEPTION OF A EUROPEAN COUPLE DANCING.

THE IBO PEOPLE

and, sooner or later, the stricken beast will, after excruciating agony, succumb to the savage onslaught.

Until the advent of petrol-driven vehicles and the subsequent construction of roads for their use, all travelling had to be done on foot and loads transported on the heads of carriers. Because of the inherent fear in the minds of men, the carrier problem was no simple one. Usually it meant engaging a fresh party every few miles. Even so, there was always the liability of a sudden panic. Loads would be incontinently dropped, and away bolted the frightened carriers. On the whole, however, the men were very good, and travelling by foot, though arduous at times, had many compensations. Trekking alongside the natives was slow, but one gained an intimate knowledge of the country and people. (This is largely lost under modern conditions.) By day, there were countless opportunities to become acquainted with native thought : at eventide, one was regaled with many interesting folklore stories.

NOTES TO CHAPTER VII

[1] " *Life on the Niger* ", William Cole, p. 31.

[2] Strong drink has been a snare to the native ever since contact was established with Europeans. Dr. Oldfield tells of a woman in 1832. " This old hag drank six and a half glasses of rum that were given to her undiluted and, as she swallowed each one, began to caper and dance in the fandango style, throwing herself into the most indecent postures and contortions possible."—" *Expedition into the Interior of Africa* ", Laird and Oldfield, Vol. I, p. 328.

Of the Mpongwe, Milligan writes : " The native is constitutionally incapable of being a moderate drinker. And, besides, drunkenness is not disgraceful. I have seen little children intoxicated. I have known parents getting their own children to drink to intoxication for their own amusement."—" *Fetish Folk of West Africa* ", p. 47.

[3] *Vide* Chap. XXIX.

[4] *Ibid.*

[5] Milligan writing of the Fang states : " I doubt whether the Fang eat any but their enemies—captives taken in war. And their chronic meat hunger is not the only reason for eating their enemies. It is done as an insult to the enemy, the most deadly insult that can be offered, or, at least, until the other side has eaten one of the enemy. But the practice of cannibalism in war is intimately related to fetishism. It is believed that, after eating one of the enemy, the latter can do them no harm. Their bullets will glance harmlessly off their bodies, or will even go through them without hurting, if, indeed, they hit them at all. Cannibalism affords them the strongest possible fetish protection."—" *Fetish Folk of West Africa* ", p. 118.

[6] " *Jungle Tales* ", W. Seabrook, p. 151.

CHAPTER VIII

KINGS & CHIEFS

PRIDE IS ONE OF THE outstanding traits of the Ibos ; indeed, in some cases, there are obvious signs of a superiority complex. This is expressed by men in their striving for titular rank, and their arrogance when they have attained to it. This arrogance is not of an offensive type as a rule ; rather it is of a naïve simplicity, taken seriously by the native ; a source of amusement to the foreigner. All too frequently, the dress and surroundings do not bear the impress of pomp and ceremony. Equally, this attitude may arise from the opinion of the foreigner who naturally considers his viewpoint the superior one. To be really sympathetic, he must cast his mind back to his ancestors of a thousand years ago.

The wives are affected also, because they advance in social status automatically with their husbands.

The titles vary greatly in different parts of the country. The controlling factors are : birthright and money, particularly the latter, for titles must be paid for ; they are not free gifts bestowed as honours for service rendered to the community. Occasionally, there has been a tendency to foster the principle that no man should hold office in the body politic unless he were of the rank of " Ozo ". This policy is very largely, if not entirely, due to the attitude of the native adherents of the system who clamour for a titled man to represent their interests in the local clan courts and in transactions with Government. Further, the statement must be qualified, because " Ozo " is confined to a very circumscribed area ; it really only applies to Onitsha, Awka and a few adjacent towns. Generally speaking, under native law and custom, the government of a village was entrusted to companies or societies such as " Otu-Iwofu ", " Ochokwu ", " Akpali " and " Otu-Ofolo ". Each company acted in turn, always in co-operation with the " Maw ", a secret society maintained in every town, having for its basis association with the spirit world. Without the service of the " Maw ", practically nothing could be done. The influence, and very existence, of the " Ozo " title has

KINGS & CHIEFS

been sustained chiefly by the official support given to it, invoked by the appeals of the village folk.

A king is saluted with the title of "Eze", "Igwe" or "Obi". The term "Igwe" may have some affinity with a remote idea that the king was a semi-divine being, the word also being associated with the "sky". The position and power of a king to-day is very different from what it was formerly. On the eastern side of the Niger, with the exception of Onitsha, there are no kings in the real sense of the word. That of Onitsha is solely due to its original connection with Benin. There are, it is true, two or three more places where the title is assumed, though not in a single instance does it confer the right to rule. It depends upon the character of the man how much honour and respect are paid to him.

On the western side, practically, if not quite all the towns are more or less subject to an "Obi". He holds a superior position as the acknowledged "head", and resides in a "palace". Under British control, he has not the autocratic powers of his ancestors. The conquest of Benin in 1897 led to a general collapse of Overami's despotic rule and, when he was deposed, the power of the tributary kings greatly declined. Prior to the conquest, the authority of Benin was paramount, and in all important affairs these tributary kings had to obtain sanction of the Oba before undertaking any important business. Homage and service are rendered by the people subject (more or less) to the king. The natives on the western side have a passionate regard for the ancient title and ceremonial etiquette though, when it comes to practical politics, it all too frequently amounts to little more than a courtesy title. Under the ægis of the Government in its laudable efforts to conserve what is useful in native institutions, in order to build up a system of government based upon ancient local custom, the kingship is receiving sympathetic support, and successors to the title are now installed with ceremonial dignity suitable to the occasion.

A call on one of the kings in the early days demanded a considerable amount of time. The programme could not be expedited. There were compensations during the waiting time, because there was generally something of interest to observe.

The king's custom was to keep his visitors waiting as long as he deemed it consonant with the dignity of his exalted position, governed, to some extent, by the rank and status of the visitor. When he did, at length, appear, and had seated himself upon his chair of state, his officers, in order of seniority, came forward singly to make their salutations. It was all done in royal fashion in accordance with the procedure at each court. On the king's part, it was an act of condescension, especially when the caller had no business to discuss, but was merely making a courtesy call.

Normally, the practice here outlined was reserved for strangers : generally speaking, a king's own subjects have fairly free access to his majesty. As a rule, people pass in and out of the palace without much restraint. On coming into the presence, the common mode of salutation is to prostrate and touch the ground with the forehead, at the same time repeating " Eze ", " Igwe " or " Obi ", whichever word is customary in that particular area.

In the Owerri and Okigwi Districts, of recent years, there has appeared a new class of men who style themselves " Eze-alas ". The compound word " Eze-ala " (king of the land) came more particularly into prominence just prior to the introduction of direct taxation (1928). About that time, the word was appropriated to an entirely new use, and " Eze-ala " was converted from a mere salutation into an institution. Apparently, many men who claimed to be keepers of " Ofo " appropriated to themselves this pseudo-title.

Now, no interior Ibo would agree that the holding of " Ofo " entitles a man to assume the powers of a ruler, or even of a minor chief. The maxim holds good, as a general principle, throughout the Ibo country east of the Niger, namely : " Ibo enwero eze " (" The Ibos have no king "). It is very seldom indeed, that the guardian of " Ofo " is a man of any prominence in the village. Where chiefs are recognised, they hold their positions quite independently ; very, very rarely are chief and " Ofo " holder combined in the same person. The guardian of " Ofo " is really the " Isi-Maw " (head of the spirit worship), or " Di-Okpala " (family or clan priest), and he has no status in the community beyond that which is attached to the sacrificial office. The " Ofo " holder is frequently poor and insignificant, and no more respect is paid to him as a man than he can command by his own personality. The only time honour is shown is when he is performing an act of sacrifice ; then it is the office that is respected, not the man. It should be noticed, also, that women who are priestesses hold " Ofo " in virtue of their office.

Before 1928, the " Eze-alas ", generally speaking, were men who had managed to elbow their way to the front and, either by sheer personality, or monetary methods, had made themselves prominent in the affairs of the community. The earlier ones were of mixed origins, ex-court messengers, stewards and others who boasted of some experience of European ways.

Taking full advantage of their " superior " knowledge, as compared with their unsophisticated compatriots, to say nothing of their arrogance, these men styled themselves " Eze-alas " ; à la John Smith who expects to have his letters addressed : John Smith Esq.

When the Government assumed control of the country, these men were thrust forward as the representatives of the people on the assumption that they were versed in European methods, and would best know how to assist the inexperienced village folk. But this use of the unwarranted title of " Eze-ala " by unauthorised men only lasted for a time. The deception was exposed, and in no place is such a man now recognised unless with the full support and approval of the people.

In old days, on the eastern side of the Niger, rulers were unknown : cf. the proverb. In times of emergency, a dominating character automatically came to the front, and the people accepted him as leader until the trouble ceased. He then reverted to his former position in common with other citizens. Nor were any hereditary rights attached to the erstwhile leadership ; the basic principle of no ruling families in Iboland remained inviolate. Where such prerogatives are beginning to appear, they are the fruit of modern innovations ; they are really contraventions of native law and custom. Where there is an established system of titular orders, the status of each holder is determined by the degree to which he has attained, plus the date on which the title was conferred. That is, precedence is governed not by age, but by seniority in taking the title. It is a democratic country, hence titular rank is open to all men who can claim freedom by birthright. In some towns, and especially on the western side, a fairly large proportion of the men qualify for one or more degrees, if only to escape manual labour. In other parts, the expense is too great, consequently a lesser number present themselves as candidates. Where the taking of a title is a costly affair, only a few entered the higher orders in former times. Latterly, the demand increased, because many young men became wage-earners and by work, and other means, managed to collect the fee money. One tendency has been to open the doors of the orders widely, and to accept any applicant who was willing to pay. The financial gain for a time was gratifying to the old chiefs, but the money so obtained did not compensate for the serious loss of dignity and respect for the titles. The sale of honours degrades them to a monetary level, and ends by producing an indifferent attitude towards them and their holders.

The members advance in rank by grades, beginning, of

course, with the lowest. The candidate is allowed to pay the initiation fees on demand, or he may pay by instalments. If he adopt the latter course, he cannot enjoy the benefits of the title until the final instalment has been handed over—he is a candidate-in-the-making.

There is no central authority under which the titular system functions. Each town has its own traditional titles and compiles its own regulations for the control of them. To produce a comprehensive list would be a long and arduous task which, when completed, would be of no practical value. The number of grades vary : some towns have as many as ten, whereas others have no more than three. The initiation fees also differ widely in amount. Sometimes, it costs several hundred pounds ; in other cases the fees can be reckoned in shillings. A richer locality naturally is better equipped to demand higher fees ; a poor district must, perforce, accept lower ones. Should any question arise, the decisive factor is traditional practice.

The rules are not uniform in the matter of succession. Certain of the more inferior titles pass by inheritance to the eldest son. This is not so with the higher titles ; they die with the owner as will be noted in due course. It is not essential for the candidate to be present in person at the installing ceremonies : the title can be conferred by proxy. If the father be alive, and be of accepted titular rank, he can make all the arrangements for the initiation of his absent son. The fact that the fees have been paid, and the rites observed, entitles the son to carry the insignia and to receive the associated salutation of his rank, a token of respect which the holder jealously expects from his acquaintances.

Since the time arrived when the sons could venture forth and become wealthier than their fathers, the number of candidates for titles has increased considerably. It has not only affected the sons, but the fathers also, because a son under old regulations (but not under new) must always remain at least one degree below his father. To proceed himself, he must first arrange for his father to advance a step further. Apart from the sense of respect due to the elder, the council would not entertain an application which was liable to disparage the precedence of the father in the order.

It has already been noted that the qualifications necessary are first freedom by birthright and, secondly, the ability to pay the stipulated fees. There is not likely to be any question concerning their origin ; that is not considered to be any responsibility of the council governing the order. Rather, it might be, that a candidate who shows ability to " make " money would be commended for his astuteness : certainly his reputation would not suffer. Everybody is well aware that, without recourse to collecting " extras ", the great majority of applicants could not produce the fees.

In former days, a much-coveted honour was the title of " Ogbu-madu " (man-killer). It mattered not *how* the unfortunate man was slain ; the essential thing was to be in possession of his head. A captured stranger provided an easy way to fulfil the conditions. This method was particularly favoured by any chief who was desirous to promote his son. The captive was securely bound and the son, who might be a small lad, was bidden to cut off the man's head. It was a gruesome business, yet the lad was immensely elated with the task, and was spurred on by the encouraging shouts of the crowd. It was an achievement which brought pride to the father and honour to the son. To be saluted as " Ogbu-madu " was, indeed, a great distinction however unworthily the title might be won.[1]

For the general bestowal of titular honours, the following examples may be quoted. They constitute the governing rules and regulations at Awka. The list is somewhat longer than in the great majority of towns and they are also the most costly. A perusal of the list will show that, in olden days, not many men could afford to ascend through the grades. Nowadays, some candidates pass through the grades in quick succession and are titled men at a much earlier age than their less wealthy fathers could ever be.

1. Titles may be conferred upon any free-born man ; an alien is also eligible, provided he be a resident in the town at the time of his election. Should he depart, he appoints a receiver to collect his share of the entrance fees.
2. The fees received are distributed between the members of the respective orders. Sometimes the senior members receive an additional small sum.
3. The Ozo title dies with its holder. Other titles may be inherited. The order of precedence in the degrees or titles are as follows : They begin with Amanwulu, the first degree, and proceed by regular grades to Fu, the highest title.
    1. Amanwulu.
    2. Chi.
    3. Aja-Ama ⎫
       Ife-Ji-Oku ⎬ These three are usually taken together.
       Amawanli ⎭

4. Aghalija.
5. Ekwu.
6. Ọzọ subdivided into Ọzọ-Unọ and Nukwu Ọzọ.
7. Fu or Aja-Chi. Sometimes spoken of as Pu, F and P being interchangeable in this locality.

The following notes give more detailed information :

1. *Amanwulu.* To obtain this title, fees amounting to about £10 must be paid in cash and kind. The insignia consists of one cord, specially made for the purpose, fastened around the waist, and several round the ankles, the former being discarded on the fulfilment of all the ceremonies. The staff is a whittled stick of " osaga " or " okeakpa " wood. The benefits accruing are a share in the entrance fees of new candidates ; the right to wear a loincloth or other clothing. Until this title had been taken, it was formerly not permissible for a man to wear a garment ; he had to be satisfied with a piece of cord and a narrow strip of cloth passed between the legs, looped through the string at front and back. This rule is now obsolete, save in unopened districts ; men wear what they choose, irrespective of old-time obligations. Usually this title is sought in quite early youth.

2. *Chi.* This degree entails an outlay of at least £20. It is a distinct advance upon " Amanwulu ". The recipient is authorised to carry an iron staff, about five feet in length, embellished with a three-inch brass binding at the top. He also carries a small horn (elephant tusk) whereby he proclaims his rank. He chooses a new name for himself, and receives a share of investiture fees.

3. (*i*) *Aja-Ama.* (*ii*) *Ife-Ji-Ọku.* (*iii*) *Amawanli.* These three minor orders are not counted of much importance save for the fact that they are stepping-stones to the higher degrees. They are taken simultaneously, the three involving an expenditure of about £10 to £12. There is no special insignia and the only benefit is the usual share of profits.

4. *Aghalija.* At this stage, the titles become more select, owing to the greatly increased cost. The entrance fees for this order are between £50 and £90. The amount depends to some extent on the past actions of the candidate. Should he, in some way, have roused the ill-will of one or more of the existing members, he must seek reconciliation and this involves a payment of about £10 to each one who can substantiate a complaint.

The order is divided into ten sections ; each receives one-tenth of the entrance fee for distribution among its members individually. The candidate also supplies sufficient cows to allow one for each party and, on account of this, a member of

KINGS & CHIEFS

the order is occasionally saluted as " Ogbu-Efi " (he who has killed a cow for making title), though he has no sanctioned right to the use of this salutation. Sometimes, more cows are provided than are wanted for sacrifice and feasting; in such cases they are turned loose and, henceforth, are free to roam, and are no man's property. They often become semi-wild and, frequently, are a nuisance, especially when they stray amongst the young corn.

The insignia of the order are an iron staff, five feet long, forked at the top end, spear-pointed at the bottom, with brass bindings at the top, bottom and centre, and chased anklets of burnished copper from four to six inches in depth. The holder is privileged to carry a full-sized tusk and a goat-skin bag, to use a chief's carved stool, and to carry a skin, usually a goat's, upon which to sit. He has the further benefit of being buried in a coffin (mgbo ojji), within the precincts of his house, and to have a cow sacrificed at his funeral. (*Vide* p. 272.)

In this order, a son is granted a share of the profits on account of a deceased father, hence it follows that some men holding the "Aghalija" title take two shares when profits are distributed, namely, his own and his father's. On attaining to this title, the candidate may add three new names to those he already possesses.

In the great majority of cases, men rest content when they have reached this grade, only few make a serious attempt to advance further; they have reached quite an honourable position in the community.

5. *Ekwu*. The fee for this title is about £15. This sum includes the expense of providing goats and a liberal supply of palm wine. It has no special benefits other than the usual share in the profits. It is really the stepping-stone to the most important of all; it is never taken except by men proceeding to the title of " Ozo ".

6. *Ozo*. This is divided into " Ozo-Uno " and " Nukwu Ozo ", the idea being that the candidate is recognised as an Ozo chief by those of his family first (hence the addition of the word " Uno " = house), and then passes on to the full title, " Nukwu " (great = complete).

It is the most expensive of all titles. The cost cannot be stated precisely. The lowest estimate is £120, of which some two-thirds must be in cash, and the remainder in kind. The first £25 is paid to the members of the candidate's own " umunna ", that is, to those who can claim any sort of kinship with him. The next payment—perhaps, £40 in cash and £20 in kind—is handed to the " Ozos " of the particular quarter in which the candidate resides. Other payments to the remaining " Ozọs " of the whole town follow. In addition, there are many expenses in connection with drummers, dancers and all the paraphernalia associated with the conferring of this title. Whenever possible, a horse must be slain as part of the ceremony. The condition of the poor brute matters not, so long as it is not actually dead. Sometimes, the animals are in such a decrepit condition that they have to be carried to the place of sacrifice. The important thing is that the candidate for the title must let out its life-blood. The killing of the horse confers the courtesy title of " Otigbu-Anyinya " and, henceforth, he is saluted by that name, " the one who has killed a horse ". Horses used to be very difficult to procure, and more difficult to keep alive, owing to the devastating effects of the tsetse fly ; this accounts for the special honour attached to the killing of a horse.

The first part of the concluding ceremonies is performed at night, followed by a rather protracted series of purifications. The newly-made " Ozọ " must not appear in public for two months. He may not sleep in his own compound ; indeed, his feet must not come under the roof of a house. Usually, he is accommodated in a friend's compound, where a small booth is erected for his benefit. Should it rain heavily, he may sit under the eave of his friend's house, with the stipulation that he keeps his feet outside. During these months he is smeared with chalk from head to foot.

The whitening of the body has its root principle in the idea of resurrection from the dead. To become a member of a titled society, a man passes through sacrificial ceremonies whereby he enters into " Maw ", that is, the realm of the spirit world. Thus he metaphorically dies. After the purifications are completed, he emerges as a resurrected being, hence the white body. From this time, he is respected as a semi-spiritual being and, as such, is sacrosanct. (*Vide* p. 145.) During the two months he is undergoing ceremonial purification, he must see none but his own immediate relatives and keep to his first wife (" anasi ") only.

All these preliminaries being fulfilled, he prepares to parade the town. It is a time of great rejoicing. A new bell, called the " ogenne ", is carried before him and solemnly beaten to announce the approach of the new member. This bell is made of beaten iron and is about three feet in length ; it is oval in shape with flattened edges and tapers from the mouth up to the handle ; the note is a deep-sounding one. While at the market-place, or other open space where crowds forgather, the new " Onye-Ozọ " publicly embraces his wife and eldest son.[2]

KINGS & CHIEFS

The insignia of the order are : an iron staff with a coronet of twisted iron. In the centre there is a series of six or eight pieces of iron similarly twisted, bellying out on the shank of the spear. At intervals, the shaft is bound with brass. Around the ankles are bound cords stained red with " ufie " (camwood). A huge tusk forms part of the regalia, also a stool of a pattern formerly jealously restricted to the use of members of the " Ozo " order.

The benefits and privileges that accrue to members of the order are :

Complete exemption from manual labour.

Immunity from bodily assault.

He has the right to inflict punishment on any man who tampers with his wives.

He sits upon the council which exercises jurisdiction in civil and criminal cases in the town and which regulates customs, promulgates laws, &c.

He is publicly saluted with the title of " Ogbu-Efi " (cow-killer) or " Otigbu-Anyinya " (horse-killer) according to whether his great sacrifice has been a cow or a horse.

He is entitled to service (Ife-nru) from his subordinate folk, and to a part of any animal killed in the chase.

A further sign of importance is that the holders of some titles eat before darkness falls.

In the presence of non-members, he takes the lead at any function, and breaks the kola nut prior to its general distribution.

At the time of sacrifice, a titled man takes the first share, he having precedence over all commoners.

He has the right to sit upon a throne (" ukpo "), and to carry a goat-skin upon which to sit when abroad.

Only a titled man can officiate before the " Iru Maw ". A non-titled man may inherit the " Okpala-ship ". As he cannot perform the service to " Iru Maw ", he transfers the sacrificial duties to the nearest male relative holding title.

And last, though not least, he receives his share of entrance and other fees paid into the treasury of the order.

There are certain general rules controlling the affairs of the order of which the more important only need be mentioned.

1. The " Ozo " title can be taken by no man prior to the decease of his father. (This rule has been quite discarded—another sign of the disintegrating forces of the times.)
2. On assuming the title, the holder takes four additional names.

3. An "Ozo" man committing theft is liable to be expelled from active membership of the order.
4. It is not permissible for an "Ozo" man to sit upon the bare ground; he must use either a stool or an untanned skin.
5. He is forbidden to cross water. (This rule has also been abolished under the new conditions of life in Iboland.)
6. Should necessity arise for the arrest of an "Ozo" holder, it is contrary to etiquette for him to be handcuffed or tied in any manner.
7. A wife can pay for a title on behalf of her husband, but she herself, in common with all other women, is ineligible for election. A wife, however, is granted accompanying rights and privileges. She takes a new name corresponding to the one adopted by her husband on taking the title, and she wears distinctive cords around her ankles equivalent to those worn by him.
8. The title is not hereditary. Indeed, on the death of an "Ozo" titled man, there is a ceremony whereby the conferring ritual is reversed—literally undone. When a man's spirit arrives in the next world, if he be questioned as to whether he has a title, he will be able to prove that he is free ("chira"), as the title cannot be taken to "Ani Maw" (Spirit land).

Before a man holding "Ozo" title is buried, the ankle cords must be removed; to leave them would be an abomination. Before the cords are cut, a cock is sacrificed, this being the corresponding sacrifice made at the title-conferring ceremony. All "Ozo" members must be present, and the "Okpala" performs the ceremony. The sacrifice is made before the "alusi" in whose honour the title was taken; the cock is for the withdrawal of the "alo". Afterwards, a goat is sacrificed to "Ogilisi". (*Vide* p. 272.)

There is one other point in connection with the "Ozo" order which, incidentally, sheds an interesting light upon the priesthood. It becomes apparent when deciding the question of precedence among the members. This is controlled chiefly by the man who is technically known as the "Okpala". He is the recognised head of the family who, in virtue of his position, is also the priest of the clan. There are three grades actually:

1. The "Okpala" of the family or household.
2. The "Okpala" of the clan. This is confined to the descendants of one family.
3. The "Okpala" of the town generally. This is held by the head of each clan in turn.

KINGS & CHIEFS

Now an " Okpala " by birth, who is also a member of the " Ozo " order, always takes precedence of an " Ozo " who has not that distinction. An " Okpala " can only be one by birth, but an " Ozo " man, who does not possess that qualification, may act as deputy for a proper (minor) " Okpala ", or he may act in his own right in exceptional circumstances, such as the confession of adultery.

7. *Fu* or *Pu*. This is the last of the orders in vogue in the town of Awka. It is taken up on very rare occasions. The costs amount to about £30. No one but an " Ozo " can enter the order and, from a material point of view, there is no gain other than, very occasionally, a participation in the entrance fees. In this instance, the share is a small one, inasmuch as the relatives of the deceased holders of the title receive the share which the dead " Ndi Fu " would receive were they still alive, the number of sharers being, consequently, greatly in excess of the living holders of the title.

The distinctive salutation is " Ogbuzulu ", conveying the idea that all killings have been completed.

Of all these titles, the only one that really counts is the " Ozo ". In past days, this order was undoubtedly a great power in the land. The members exercised a widespread influence, and they administered all the affairs of the community. They were treated with the utmost respect on the one hand, and were feared on the other. They had the power of life and death, and were the accredited despots of the town.

At Onitsha, after attaining to the grade of " Ozo ", the next step is into the ranks of the " Ndi-Chie ". The advance is not automatic ; candidates are accepted only as vacancies occur in this order. There are three degrees among the " Ndi-Chie ". Beginning at the lowest and ascending to the highest there are : 1. Ndi-Chie-Okwaraza. 2. Ndi-Chie-Okwa. 3. Ndi-Chie-Ume or Ndi-Chie-Ukpo. (These two names are synonymous for the same rank. The terms indicate the king's personal councillors. " Ume " has the sense of " in camera " and " Ukpo " that of sharing the throne.) This third and highest grade is limited to six members and they comprise the Council of State. The regular way of making appointments to this honourable position is by the king sitting in Council. To fill a vacancy in one of the first four seats a man holding the rank of " Ogene " or " Owele " may be raised and, in turn, his place be filled by a new member drawn from the " Ndi-Chies ", or he may be a completely new man chosen directly from those holding the " Ozo " title.

The order of precedence of the "Ndi-Chie-Ume" is:
1. Onowu = Prime Minister. He acts as proxy for the king in emergencies.
2. Ajie.
3. Odu.
4. Onya.
5. Ogene.
6. Owele.

" The king's throne is a raised bank of mud in the verandah, about four feet long, two feet wide, and two feet high, from the level of the floor. On this is spread an old ragged mat, and a dirty white calico. A similar cloth is spread on the walls against the king's back, stretching from the top of the walls to that spread on the mat on the throne. This is a sign of royalty, and prerogative of the king, which no one in the country is to imitate. Strangers are not allowed a mat, stool, or any kind of seat in the king's palace. The king has established this custom with an oath. Strangers must either stand, or sit on the bare red ground in the court while before his majesty."

As regards the chiefs, everyone " upon entering the room must stoop, and address each of them by the title he bears. Each one must occupy a separate seat : a bench may be twelve feet long, but as soon as Onowo or Ajie has made towards it, it must be quitted by all its previous occupiers in honour of him. On this account, each one carries his sheep or goat skin about with him, and sometimes a stool." (*Vide* "*Niger Expedition*", pp. 432-4.)

At Ogiddi, Erulu ranks next highest to the king.

On the western side of the Niger, men taking the title of " Ichi-Maw " are free from public work. As the fees [3] are low in that neighbourhood, the majority are able to claim exemption. In former days, when there was a call for labour, these men always escaped their share and, consequently, the unfortunate men who were not members had to perform more than their fair proportion.

Under primitive native law and custom, the title of " Ozo " was not taken by any man other than the one upon whom the office of " Di-Okpala " devolved. In some cases, the whole family would rally round and collect the money for the expenses. At Onitsha, in olden times, a candidate for the title had to be a man known for his integrity and sound judgement and, equally necessary, a man of tact and in favour with his people.

Unfortunately, the order has degenerated of recent years. In some cases, the holders of the title are young men who inspire no feelings of respect and who detract from, rather than add to, its dignity. These men, working as clerks, interpreters, carpenters and so forth, seized the opportunity of making money which presented itself simultaneously with the opening up of the country and, earning (or otherwise collecting) money quickly, immediately offered themselves as candidates for the " Ozo " order. The old men, tempted by the fees, received the young aspirants into membership. They reaped a monetary benefit ; their original investment turned out more profitable than they had anticipated. But this avaricious procedure led to the degradation of the order. To make matters worse, and what gave impetus to the breaking down of the system during the money-making years of the present century, the fees soared up fivefold, and greed led to disrepute, and all right to exercise any control over the affairs of the community was forfeited. The mere possession of an " Ozo " title will never again automatically endow a man with political authority. All power in this respect is now under the control and supervision of the European Officials who closely watch affairs in the interests of integrity and right government.

The above was written over twenty years ago. In the interval, the " Ozo " title has continued to depreciate in favour for several reasons.

1. " Ozo " is confined to free-born men, yet there are many slave-born in Iboland. Slavery is not, of course, tolerated or recognised by the British Constitution, whereas the native adheres rigidly to the division in social affairs. Are these slave-born men never to have an opportunity to rise to position solely because of accident of birth ? If " Ozo " is to be the " *sine qua non* " of a ruling order, then in a democratic country is should be open to all men alike.

The alleged reason why a slave cannot be accepted as a candidate for a title is because he has no future life. When he dies, he is dead—extinguished—body and soul—and his name is blotted out of the book of remembrance. No " Chi " is placed on his behalf with the ancestral " Nkpulu-Chi ". Hence, when the priest or " Okpala " is calling over the names of ancestors prior to sacrifice, the slave has no place ; he has not even a name and so can neither confer a benefit nor hear a petition. (*Vide* pp. 275–81.)

2. Young educated men are maintaining, in increasing numbers, that money can be far more wisely spent than by using it to purchase a title which has little to commend it in these modern days other than a salutation. A substantial house is preferable to such an abstract thing as a title. It is being

realised that when an " Ozo " titled man dies, his rights and privileges perish with him. Sons now prefer to inherit real estate!

3. The initial expenses lead, in many instances, to permanent financial strain. Many have impoverished themselves and their families in raising the installation fees. Where this occurs, the children and other dependents suffer. Men are foolish enough to contract loans wherewith to embark on the enterprise and, consequently, are never free from the incubus of debt. Whatever accrues from the share of fees from initiates is insufficient to meet the interest on the loans ; indeed, some of the " Ozo " holders are practically paupers. This, of course, applies to those towns where the taking of " Ozo " is an expensive undertaking and, more particularly, to Onitsha, Awka, and two or three towns near the latter. In some areas, as at Nando, Awba and Nobi, the expenses are insignificant, ranging from 25s. to £3.

4. The idea that the taking of " Ozo " may be counted as an investment is, at the present time, founded on unsound financial principles. The returns are few and far between ; the best do not show an average return of £2 per annum and, outside Onitsha, the average annual sum is not more than 10s. and, even so, it is frequently offered in kind, and that " kind " of a sort of which the man has already a good supply himself.

5. A great drawback to the fee-paying system is that it debars some of the best men, because of the difficulty in raising the fees, and they are too prudent to contract loans.

6. Another weakness, and one which is obviously detrimental to the title, is that it can be pawned or sold outright—e.g. at Awka, a man may owe money ; a woman can come along and *buy* his " Ozo " title. She cannot be admitted to the order, but she can dispose of it to any man she favours. At Nobi, a man who has no son will take up an extra share by getting a title conferred on a selected tree. Then, when there is a man upon whom he wishes to bestow a benefit, he can arrange for the transfer of the title from the tree to him.

In some places, young men take up " Ozo " at the time they marry and settle down to citizenship. This means that a large proportion of the men attain to titular rank. It need hardly be stated that this is where the fees are low as at Awba, Nobi, Nando, &c. Even small boys are accepted for the title on payment of fees by their elders.

7. Civilisation militates against the system, and tends to break it down. In former days, only a " titled " man could be the spokesman at a gathering ; to-day, the educated man is thrust forward, irrespective of title.

HONOUR AND WORSHIP.

Above: A CHIEF BLOWING HIS HORN (ELEPHANT TUSK), PART OF THE REGALIA ATTACHED TO TITULAR RANK. (PAGES 137-358.)
Below: A PYTHON (EKKE), REGARDED AS SACRED BY THE IBOS. (PAGE 41.)

8. The licence to intimidate has been removed by good government. Formerly a " titled " man could bully a non-privileged one ; he could pour scorn and ridicule upon him as a nobody. He did this with impunity, because no one was allowed to retaliate. If a commoner should be so imprudent as to take the law into his own hands, and throw a titled man to the ground, he would be punished severely. This former semi-sanctity of person no longer avails for the titled man ; he takes his place alongside the rest of his fellows.

Attempts have been made to revive the " Ozo " order, and suggestions have come from outside and inside whereby Christians as well as pagans may be accepted as members. The old members are willing to grant concessions, and to be content with a cash payment alone in return for the conferment of the title. But the omission of the essential idolatrous rites and ceremonies would, to all intents and purposes, destroy the whole foundation upon which " Ozo " is based. An Ibo will scoff at the notion that an " Ozo " title, bereft of its accompanying sacrificial rites, can be valid. The whole essence of the system is bound up with the initiatory sacrifices. Men admitted to the order, by the ceremonies enacted, become, " *ex opere operato* ", " holy ". To the common people they stand for the " Maw " ; indeed, " Maw " is the " *fons et origo* " of the whole organisation ; hence, a new member is saluted " Ikpa-Maw " (Onitsha) or " Isa-Maw " (Interior). He is thus acknowledged as having entered into " Maw " during the process of passing through the initiation ceremonies.

The order, in its primitive form, is based on authority over life and death. To understand its power, as it operated under its ancient unrestricted régime, one needs to sense the native mind as it was before the coming of the white man. Then there was liberty to exercise the full unfettered rites and ceremonies ; and " Ozo ", in co-operation with the " Maw ", really did have power to impose and fulfil its enactments, even unto death. Under British authority, those powers no longer exist ; the shell alone remains ; the kernel has been destroyed. A bolstering up of " Ozo " would be a reversion to old conditions and would, inevitably, lead to attempts to revive the power of the " Maw ". This is the main reason why the old men want it recognised and supported whereas, to the enlightened man, it is a retrograde step. For it to be possible for a man to become " sacrosanct ", in return for a money payment, is in itself absurd. To foster a belief that the holding of an " Ozo " title is a necessary qualification before a man can aspire to a position of authority in the clan, does not commend itself. It would be giving sanction and support to a close union of vested interests. The best men will remain outside that union, barred either by fees or, more decisively, by refusing to comply with conditions that are essential for valid membership, but are contrary to Christian principles.

NOTES TO CHAPTER VIII

[1] " The acquisition of an enemy's head is the young man's passport to manhood. Until he has attained this distinction his social status is no better than that of a girl, and no girl would consent to marry him. But when he has won his trophy, and can prove that it was obtained in the manner prescribed by custom, he can take his place in the ranks of the warriors, and his prowess is celebrated by a public feast."—" *Northern Tribes of Nigeria* ", Vol. II, p. 49.

[2] See also p. 42 for procedure at Obusi.

[3] The fees in 1858 amounted to " about 15 goats, 200 fowls, 100,000 cowries, a large quantity of yams, accompanied with a large supply of palm wine ".—" *Niger Expedition* ", p. 433.

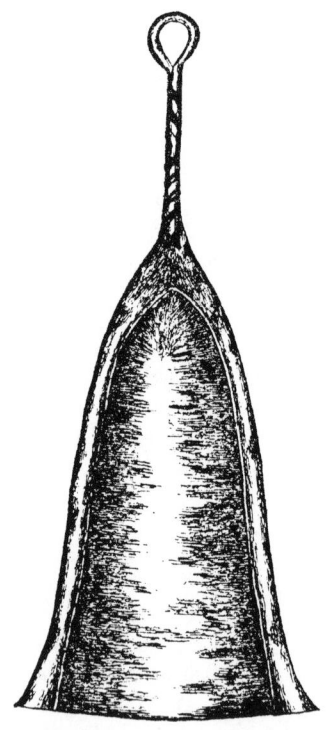

BELL (" OGENNE ") USED BY CHIEFS (p. 138).
From two to three feet in length, made from two sheets of thin iron, oval mouthed.

CHAPTER IX

HOME LIFE

To the casual observer, who refrains from probing too closely, life in an Ibo village appears very attractive. There is a simplicity which is enhanced by natural surroundings. No straight streets, or ugly rows of houses obtrude themselves; each hut is a separate entity. It may be large or small, but it enjoys the privilege of being independent of its neighbours. Many dwellings have their own compounds (courtyards) walled off and private or, again, a compound may contain a miniature village. Previous to the disintegrating effects of foreign influence, there was nothing other than what had been customary for untold generations.

The huts are constructed of local materials and built by the people themselves; they do not have to resort to outside craftsmen. The owners look to nature for the supply of most of their requirements and, as stated later (Chap. XIX), contend that every man has a right, not only to air and water, but also to plots of land whereon he can erect a dwelling and grow his food.

Graceful palms and giant trees spread their branches overhead providing refreshing shade from the tropical sun and adding beauty to the scene. It is worth while to notice some of the trees which stand either within or around the compounds, because some are planted for specific purposes: they are not chance bounties of nature. Certain specimens are always present of which the chief are:

The " *Ogilisi* " [1] (Eastern side) or " *Egbo* " (Western side) will be referred to again in some chapters of this book. It is planted before a man begins to build a house and is an object for worship while building operations are in progress and during occupation. Honour due unto a god is given to it. (*Vide* p. 311.)

The " *Abuba* ". A large tree honoured in some localities. " Kola ", that is, a meal offering, is made to it every morning before the owner breaks his own fast.

The " *Agwugwu* "—usually planted near the " Egbo ". Sacrifices are offered to it under guidance of the " dibia "

HOME LIFE

when trouble arises. It is also used when investigating cases of theft.

The "*Ojji*" (Iroko) (Pandanus) is venerated mainly on account of its size, though the real and underlying reason is to be found in animistic beliefs of the Ibo people. This tree and the "Ngwu" must not be felled by the people of certain towns, though outsiders are at liberty to do so. They are sacred to the town deities. There is a man's heart in the tree and, when the tree falls, the heart dies and, with it, the heart of the man. Also, when fighting occurs, the tree-spirits protect the men from the bullets of the enemy. After the fighting is over, a feast is made in honour of the tree and a live chicken is tied to it.

If a man wish to climb the sacred tree to cut branches, it is girdled with a string fence and each of the elders of the owning family has to tie a live chicken to it. When the man descends, a cock is offered to the tree. The older people also take eggs and break them on the tree, first touching their own breasts with them. At the same time, they pray that the heart may not leave the tree because of the trespass of lopping the branches. If an Iroko tree fall, the owners receive the branches; the trunk is the perquisite of the "Isi-alusi" (the head priest of the tree-spirit).

At the entrances to villages and compounds a screen or festoon of young palm leaves (omu) (*vide* p. 408) and "medicine" is hung to prevent the entrance of sickness. It is a sad story when the screens fail to keep away an epidemic of smallpox and similar visitations.

Every man exercises his own judgement in choosing a site for his house with the one stipulation that he does not actually impinge upon the rights of his fellow-villagers. There is no building authority to whom he must submit plans and specifications: he is at liberty to adopt any style that appeals to him. Nor are there any by-laws to which he must conform; the Ibo is free to act pretty much as he chooses. He may even encroach upon paths already in existence. The ultimate result is seen in the winding paths which thread their way between the walls. The pedestrian is continually turning corners; straight paths (more or less) occur only when running alongside a compound wall in many villages. This applies more especially to the eastern districts; on the western side, there are some really fine streets, straight and wide, and shaded with forest trees. Moreover, these are regularly swept and kept free from litter,[2] albeit the debris is swept no further than the edge of the bush parallel to the road.

The farms are generally at some distance from the villages,

HOME LIFE

though the women utilise every bit of spare ground between the huts for the cultivation of koko-yam (edde). Water is sometimes near at hand : often it is not ; in fact a supply does not enter seriously into the calculations when selecting sites for villages. Convenience of situation, or restrictions governing land available for settlement, are the main considerations. Some of the villages are as much as five miles or more from a stream. To augment the supply, or rather to have water nearer, catchpits are dug to store rainwater. These are sunk either in the compound itself, or at a suitable spot in the vicinity. Channels (of a sort) conduct the surface water to the pits. Where the people are a little more fastidious, a small clay rampart, a few inches in height, is placed round the edge of the pit. An entrance hole is cut in which is inserted a bundle of fine twigs to serve as a strainer. Abundance of water is available throughout the rainy season whereas, in the dry, the supply not only shrinks, but, being stagnant, it becomes very foul and coated with slime. This is more the case on the western side of the Niger than on the eastern.[3]

The foreigner is pleasantly surprised on his first sweeping glance at an Ibo village. It is when he begins to investigate that his opinion changes ; he meets with sudden shocks to eyes and nose ! The houses are clean, the compounds well swept, and little fault can be found with them. The disturbing element lies in the fact that all refuse is dumped too near to the huts. The Ibo has no conception of the rules of health and can scarcely be accused either of neglect, or of violating them. What he does is done in ignorance. Fortunately, the sun helps to remedy the evil, otherwise the conditions would be wellnigh intolerable.

Though there is no intelligent acquaintance with the subject as a science, yet there are unwritten regulations concerning sanitation. Land must on no account be used for latrine purposes where yams are growing, because yams are " Ife-ji-oku ", that is, tantamount to sacred. Where " edde " or cassava is planted, there is no restriction. On the other hand, land planted with small crops such as pepper, okwulu, (okru) spinach and such-like must not be fouled. These small crops have a feast of their own at harvest-time called " Itube-onu akuku " ; hence they must not be polluted. Generally speaking, any spot may be used for nature's needs provided it is not too near a house or compound. Women take cover ; men are usually not so considerate. One has seen public latrines constructed in the form of large styes in which pigs wallow and feed on indescribable filth.[4]

HOME LIFE

While neither thought nor care is exercised in respect of town planning, yet there is a distinct division into communities. The towns are not cramped for room; they straggle over wide areas. Some extend no more than a quarter of a mile from one end to the other, whereas, there may be a mile or more between the boundaries of larger ones. For example, a distance of four miles along the modern high road separates the western from the eastern border of the town of Awka. This is unusual, it is true, nevertheless all Ibo towns are widespread in character. It is only in new cosmopolitan towns which have sprung up under modern conditions that overcrowding is found. This evil is being controlled or combated by the authorities as circumstances permit.

It may be noted that many Ibo place-names are capable of translation. They are, in such cases, founded on personal names of ancestors, or were adopted because of some feature of the locality or, again, as a record of the circumstances which led to the founding of the town. There is first the original settlement with its foundation name. Later, sons or grandsons find they require more room for their families and they move a little further afield and establish new settlements, distinguishing them from the ancestral home by adding a qualifying adjective.

The first outer " quarter ", as these communities are nowadays termed, is usually called " Azu " (back = the following after) to distinguish it from the parent town. As the population increases, further emigrations take place and new villages come into existence. These have prefixes to mark them such as " Umu " or " Aro " (children), " Ifite ", " Ama " (street), " Ezi ", " Enu " (high) or " Ugwu " (for hilly situations) and so forth. Each new village becomes fully established with its own headman, yet, though becoming a separate colony, all the quarters together constitute a township.

There is no lack of open spaces. These are called " ilos ". They are reserved, for the most part, because they are respected as the property of the local god. They serve as market-places, play-grounds, public meeting centres, and for festivals. They are excellent for all these purposes, particularly those that are shaded by massive trees. All gatherings of importance, social, political and religious are held in these " ilos " and, at times, they are centres of animation and, maybe, no little excitement. Some are furnished with galleries constructed of whole trunks of suitably sized trees, or large branches fixed in forked uprights at each end. The seats rise in tiers and provide good accommodation for spectators watching a wrestling or other display. The " ilo " corresponds to the old English village green.

HOME LIFE

The Headman used to be an autocratic person. He was accorded the honour and respect due to a patriarch. He was the arbitrator in all matters, public and domestic, affecting the family which comprised the whole village community. He could act independently, but it was more customary for him to act in association with other men and also the older women when women's affairs were under consideration. As " Di-Okpala " (firstborn son), he also fulfilled sacrificial duties for the benefit of the family and judged marital misdemeanours.[5]

The Ibo Calendar is divided into thirteen lunar months of twenty-eight days each or seven weeks. The four days comprising the Ibo week (Izu-nta) are named " Ekke ", " Oye " (" Olie "), " Afọ " and " Nkwọ ". Two four-day periods make " izu-ukwu " (big week).

The markets bear the names of the days on which they are held. The market-places formerly contained no buildings other than fetish houses with, perhaps, one or two small huts occupied by " *Osus* " (men and women devoted to the service of the god).[6, 7]

The village shrines are protected from wind and weather by small sheds. Formerly, they were thatched ; nowadays many have galvanised-iron roofs. Some stand in the open square, visible to passers by ; others are enclosed within a courtyard similarly to house compounds. Where there is an appointed priest in charge, the gods are ministered to with care ; in the majority of cases little attention is bestowed upon them so long as affairs are normal. While conditions remain favourable, there will be no more than occasional sacrifices. An outbreak of sickness or some other form of trouble, will prompt a revival of devotion. Repairs to the shrine are undertaken forthwith and, for the time being, there is a display of religious zeal and activity. Sacrifices are offered and, once more, the god is appeased. This service rendered, apathy again settles on the community and remains undisturbed until a fresh demand is made when the programme is repeated. This is a mere statement of fact expressed without sentiment or prejudice.

Except in the extreme northerly parts of the Ibo country, the huts are always of rectangular shape. Nearer the boundary line, the round pattern is adopted, after the fashion of their northern neighbours. The poorer folk must, perforce, be satisfied with unpretentious huts while the better class prefer houses enclosed within what are commonly termed " compounds ". This means that an area, large or small according to the needs or circumstances of the owner, is completely surrounded by a wall from five to ten feet in height. Greater precautionary measures seem to be advisable in certain neighbourhoods as compared with others; hence the higher walls. The walls are protected against rain by palm-leaf mat shelters, or layers of butt ends of large palm fronds. The front wall may be decorated in modelled relief, or with mural designs in colour laid on in orthodox jazz or Surrealist interpretations of art!

The entrance is a small aperture, fitted with a door which can be secured inside by means of a bar passed between shackles fixed in the posts. The door turns on two butts, one at the top inserted in a hole in the lintel and the other at the bottom, in a similar hole in the threshold. These serve as substitutes for hinges and fulfil their purpose very well.

Just inside the door is a fair-sized water-pot. It contains " medicine ". Standing in the pot is a bundle of twigs, the equivalent of a " bunch of hyssop ". The " medicine " is always ready for application. Those using it, lift the bunch of twigs and brush or shake it over the lower parts of the legs and across the feet. The sprinkling with this prototype " holy water " is believed to guard against evil on the one hand and to give assurance of good intentions on the other.

The first thing to notice on entering a compound is the shrine of the guardian god. It is always crude in form, usually little more than a mound of clay. Four corner sticks support a light framework on which are tied a few palm-leaf mats. The little shed does not provide much protection to a god who presumably has important functions to fulfil!

Over the greater part of the Ibo country, the compound walls serve no purpose other than for protection. In certain areas, the interior sides are utilised as back walls for apartments; sleeping quarters and store rooms. The floors of these are elevated some two feet above ground-level. Without this precaution they would be constantly flooded during the wet season. The rain pours off the roofs from the four sides into the open courtyard and the water may be a foot in depth while a heavy storm is in progress. Most of this drains away through a hole in the wall leaving the courtyard sodden with water and inches deep in mud and slime.

The conditions are much better where the compound walls are not used in this manner. The apartments are much less congested and, consequently, have superior facilities for light and ventilation. Except in pits and potholes, water drains away rapidly and the sun quickly dries the ground. The huts are distributed around the master's own sanctum although, frequently, he has a separate enclosure for himself, a smaller

HOME LIFE

compound within the greater. The owner's hut (obi) stands by itself, and is the hub of the little universe. In it, he spends most of his time when at home. It contains his gods, his treasures, weapons and implements, and herein he receives his visitors.

It is an oblong building with, as a rule, rounded ends and a steeply pitched roof, the eaves stretching down to within three feet of the ground. The guardian god, " Ikenga ", occupies the place of honour on the back wall surrounded by his " Ọfọ ", " Chi " and other emblems of his faith.[8] From the rafters quaint objects hang suspended including fringes of dried palm leaves (ọmu), calabashes, skulls of animals killed in sacrifice and other items.[9] In former days, the collection was often embellished with human skulls as well as those of beasts. On the floor is a fire which burns continuously, day and night, with the end of a long log acting as an enduring ember. The smoke passes via the roof and acts as a preservative for the thatch. Insects avoid it, but it is no deterrent to rats, indeed, by the noises they make, they revel in the thick covering of grass. The floor is of beaten clay ; occasionally such a floor is reinforced by being studded with palm-nuts or the hard nuts of a fruit known as " Nkpulu-ogwu-olo ".

Near the " obi " stands the " egbo " (" ogilisi ") tree already referred to on page 147. In the religious life of the family it corresponds to the sacrificial grove of the ancients.

Should a skull or wooden platter be observed outside a house, it is an indication that it is vacant, and no one has the right to enter. Should any person do so, and steal therefrom, he is expected to die within two or three days. The skull is sometimes used for administering an oath and is then called " Idoiyi ". There is not much furniture in an " obi " ; what there is is of almost nondescript character ; it is easier to describe it as " junk ", though the owner thinks differently ! A number of calabashes, a matchet, a hoe and, if the man's occupation be other than simple farming, there are the tools of his trade. In some districts chairs (agada) are present. These are ingeniously made from triple pronged boughs. The straight section forms a back rest and the three prongs the legs. These " agadas " are quite picturesque as well as serviceable. The more common practice is for chiefs to bring their own chairs (a small boy or girl accompanying each man to carry the chair). The imported folding garden pattern, or a cheap deck-chair, usually called a " stretcher ", are nowadays much in favour. These have superseded deer and goat skins spread on the clay seat that runs along the side of the " obi "

The father of the family sleeps on a couch at one end of the " obi ". The wives have separate huts where they sleep with their children : the young men have their own little apartments detached from the others.[10] It will be seen that a compound may contain a number of huts and accommodate a little community. Inside the rooms there may be couches, though these are not counted essentials, more often than not no beds are provided. There is not much floor space and beds occupy too much room. The general practice is to spread mats upon which to sleep. One habit may be noted. Before spreading the mat, the floor is always carefully swept : it almost amounts to a ritual.

A mat is used whether the sleeper uses a couch or lies on the floor ; there is always a dividing partition, slight though it is, between the body and mother earth. A few of the more intelligent older folk might state a reason for this observance, but it is a custom so ingrained from infancy that the great majority spread the mat oblivious of its significance. When probed to its source, it will be found that it is tabu to lie on the bare ground if it can possibly be avoided. It is thought that, in some way, contact with the ground pollutes it. Certainly, sexual relations must not be perpetrated without the presence of an intervening mat. That would be deemed an abomination.

Couches are made of palm fronds (offolo) or clay : nowadays, wooden bedsteads are coming rapidly into favour. The clay couches are more uncommon. Where they are adopted, it is not unusual for them to be hollowed out under the platform. Within the arch thus formed, fire can be placed to give warmth to the sleeper. When a notable man dies, the corpse may be stretched on such a couch and dried. By this means, the body can be preserved indefinitely, in other words, until such time as arrangements are made for the proper fulfilment of the burial ceremonies.

In some badly infected areas, mosquito-proof houses are built specially for sleeping quarters. The roof consists of very thick thatch which rests solidly on the walls. There are no windows and the one small door is made to fit closely. At bedtime, the family, accompanied by fowls, goats and dogs, retire to this apartment and stay there until dawn appears. It must be dreadfully stuffy for, in barring out mosquitoes, every breath of air is also excluded. Yet it is the only way to have a moment's peace after nightfall in some districts.

The majority of compounds are provided with tiny shelters to serve as kitchens. These are necessary in wet weather, otherwise a couple of stones or cones of clay placed near a wall is all that is required to make a cooking range. A person of some means might purchase a little tripod from a local blacksmith. This is made of hoop iron. A circular band, in which the pot rests, is supported on three or four legs. Whether a tripod be used or stones placed against a wall, firewood can easily be inserted beneath the pot, which is the essential thing. The iron " negro " pots sold at the trading factories are very convenient for use in the open compound as they are fitted with legs and the bigger ones have handles also. The home-made pots are of clay. (*Vide* Chap. XXIV.)

One or two pots are sufficient for the average household. It is another matter when preparations have to be made for a feast. For the family and its friends an extra pot or two, with more improvised ranges, are all that is required. For communal festivals, the women adjourn to the " ilo " where the feast is to be observed. A trench is dug in a straight line about six inches wide and deep. At intervals of say, four feet, cross-sections are cut. The cooking-pots are placed over the four corners where the sections meet and the firewood inserted in the trenches on all four sides. By this method, cooking facilities can be supplemented as circumstances demand.

No household is complete without a pestle and mortar for the pounding of yam. These utensils are hewn from solid blocks of " iroko " timber and are heavy, cumbersome articles. The mortars vary from one to two feet in diameter and from a few inches to a foot or more in depth. The pestle is about two and a half feet in length and may be either shaped, or a plain piece of round wood.

A strong knife is essential for stripping the rind from the yam, because it is thick and, when dry, almost as tough as the bark of a tree. After peeling, the yam is split into pieces and boiled. To ascertain whether it is cooked sufficiently, the pieces are pricked with a sharply pointed stick in the manner that an English cook uses a fork or skewer to test potatoes.

When cooked, the yam is placed in the mortar and pounded until it resembles a mass of dough. To the casual and inexperienced observer, this operation does not suggest much difficulty beyond the labour involved ; actually, the manipulation of the pestle demands considerable skill. The pestle must occasionally be dipped in water, otherwise the sticky mass will adhere to it and the result will be unsatisfactory ; indeed, it is probable that the yam will be pulled out of the mortar and come to grief on the floor, thus rendering it unfit for use. In such case, the owner of the house will give vent to his annoyance ; yams are not to be wasted by careless cooks ! The

HOME LIFE

master personally controls the yam-stack (ǫba) and hands out the daily supply. Only in exceptional circumstances are other persons permitted to enter the " ǫba ".

For the average household, two cooking-pots, a small and a larger, will meet the need. With these, the chief meal of the day can be prepared. This meal is eaten at eventide and, if up to the Ibo's quantity-estimate, he will not concern himself unduly over food until the evening of the following day. What he eats during the daytime, he regards as mere snacks (elevenses), unworthy to be classed as meals. A piece of yam, or a cob of green maize, roasted in the embers, will satisfy him.[11] The larger pot is used for cooking yam, the smaller one for a decoction commonly called " soup " (ofe). The chief ingredients are palm oil, herbs and a small quantity of smoke-cured fish. This simmers for a long time and the food is certainly well cooked as well as highly flavoured. Generous contributions of raw pepper convert the soup into literal " hot-pot ". Such free use of pepper is made that the substance of the pot itself becomes permeated. Water boiled in a pot in regular service for cooking soup is pungent with the heat and flavour of pepper.

A certain amount of unconscious ritual is observed preparatory to partaking of a proper meal, namely the washing of the hands. A bowl of water is passed round and the hands, particularly the right, are dipped into it. By far the more general practice is for each diner to take a huge mouthful of water and squirt it over the hands. Primarily, this is a sanitary precaution, since the fingers are the natural substitutes for spoons and forks. But the washing may also have a sacrificial significance, because, after it, it is usual to offer a small portion of food to the gods as an acknowledgement of their favour, and a little drink is poured on the ground as a libation, thus constituting a symbolical meat and drink offering preliminary to partaking of the meal.

The diners squat around the pot containing the relish (ofe). Before each is a platter containing a round mass of pounded yam (nni-ji) about half the size of a football. From this, a lump the size of an egg is pinched off with the fingers. After being thoroughly squeezed and rolled, it is dipped into the soup and then swallowed. Time is not wasted by mastication : apparently chewing would be a work of supererogation. The yam is soft and well oiled, hence the pill slips down the throat with an almost effortless gulp. The partakers of the meal observe the code of table etiquette. There is no thrusting forward of the hand in haste ; a diner always manifests a readiness

HOME LIFE

to give preference to his neighbour when dipping his yam into the soup.

The master of the house partakes of his meals in his own apartment. Each wife takes her turn to cook his food and to wait upon him in domestic affairs.[12] For drinking, he uses his own private calabash. This he jealously guards, never allowing it out of his personal control. No one must be tempted by an opportunity to administer poison in his cup.

In certain places, as at Obinọfia (Udi Division) a tom-tom (ufie) is beaten throughout the time the chief is partaking of food. The reason is to let the town-folk know that the chief is eating. He must not be disturbed by visitors, nor must his name be uttered during the time, lest he stop eating and never eat again. (*Vide* p. 197, par. 2.) [13]

The Ibo is not an epicure. He is not worried by vitamin problems, nor does he concern himself very much about the wholesomeness or otherwise of the food that comes to his plate. Not willingly, but by force of circumstances, he is largely limited to a vegetarian diet. For his stock-pot, he has not many opportunities to exercise a preference : he has chiefly to rely on smoked fish and not much of that in interior districts. There is the consolation that a little of this goes a long way ; it has distinct and pungent properties ! He delights in flesh food on the rare occasions that it is forthcoming. This consists of goat-mutton, beef, or the meat from wild animals. The carcases are hacked in pieces through skin and bones. No scrap is wasted ; all becomes food, even the entrails. The blood of animals slaughtered is saved and allowed to solidify. It is then treated similarly to liver.[14]

It matters not whether the beast be old or young, fresh or partially decomposed : the only part to be discarded is the gall-bladder, the contents of which are deemed to be poisonous, that of some animals being considered more deadly than others. The flesh of any creature may be eaten unless prohibited by tabu. It includes dogs, rats, snakes and indeed, every specimen of beast, bird or fish. Except in cases where tabu limitations are in force, the only universally omitted item from the pagan Ibo's menu is the sacred python (ekke). Those who have forsaken their ancestral faith are not punctilious, and python flesh is equally acceptable with that of other creatures. When a snake is killed, the tail is severed near the extremity and buried with the head. It is believed to be furnished with a deadly sting and so must be deposited in a safe place.

A particular dainty to the Ibo is the locust. These creatures are uncertain in their habits. I first saw a swarm in 1901 or

HOME LIFE

1902 and then there was an interval of thirty years before I saw more. Whenever a swarm appears, the women and children turn out in crowds to collect stocks of the insects. Immense numbers are caught and parched, in due time to be consumed with great enjoyment. To give an idea of the favour in which locusts are held, it is alleged that a certain chief packed a few hundreds in paper and took the parcel to the Post Office for despatch to his son then at school in England. He could not understand the action of the officials in declining to accept the parcel which, by this time, was somewhat odoriferous. He was distinctly annoyed and disappointed that he could not forward such a delectable contribution to his son's tuck-box!

Another item highly acceptable to many Ibos is the male white ant (termites). At certain seasons of the year, these swarm and come out of their holes in millions. They fly a few feet in the air, and then come to earth, and soon afterwards shed their wings. The children catch the insects as they emerge while, in many parts, wicker cages (something like eel-traps) are fixed over the holes and great quantities are caught by this method. The insects are lightly parched before they are eaten. When exposed for sale in the markets they look like small heaps of miniature shrimps.

It will be conceded that the range of flesh food, though strictly limited in quantity, is, nevertheless, comprehensive in character. From the human being to the tiny insect, a choice is offered of a broad and varied selection—when available.[15]

We have set forth what the Ibo may eat; there are things which he is forbidden to use. There are tabus in respect of food which apply in certain places, and also under certain conditions (cf. prenatal prohibitions, Chap. XI). The tabus vary in different localities; the following will serve as examples.

At Adazzi (Awka Division) it is tabu to eat cocoanuts, while at Awka men are not allowed to eat snails, whereas women and children may. The python and the tortoise are generally regarded as sacred and are never molested by the pagan Ibo.[16] The tortoise may be connected with an "alusi" as at Achi (Alusi-Achi-Hi). This "alusi" has no image; it is represented by stones. Frequently, these are set up by the roadside. Men and women passing along, particularly the women, touch the stones with their feet, praying for a safe and prosperous journey. At Achina, it is tabu to partake of dog flesh which is very unusual. The reason given is that it is supposed to induce sickness. Yet dogs are used for sacrifices to "Ezeokolo", the deity residing in the "Oye" market. Tradition says that, in ancient time, at a gathering of the people, a dog

HOME LIFE

entered the assembly. Because of its behaviour, the men consulted the " ọfọ " and the dog was elevated to be a special sacrifice to " Eze-okolo ". The story was supported by showing me a woman who had partaken of dog's flesh and it was alleged that she had contracted leprosy as a result. I examined the woman, but could find no trace of the disease. She admitted having suffered from some skin trouble which had disappeared under treatment. All the same, she was treated as an outcast, because she had transgressed the ruling of the town. Should a dog be killed, or die a natural death, the carcase is passed on to people of another town who are not under the obligation to abstain from eating dog flesh.

The eating of the vulture (udene) is forbidden in most places. One reason given is that the people placed food for the use of the local god and a vulture flew down and ate it. A man was angry at this and retaliated by killing the vulture. Shortly afterwards, he died. His relatives consulted the " dibia " to ascertain the reason for his death and the reply was, that it was because the man had killed the " osu " (slave) of the deity. Since then, the people have not killed or eaten the flesh of a vulture and it must not be interfered with when consuming food offered to the god.

At other places, the flesh of the vulture was not prohibited and it was not despised as food. That gruesome habit operates no longer, because the killing of these useful scavengers is wisely forbidden by law.

Before concluding this chapter, mention should be made of two elements which never cease to operate, and which are apt to disturb the serenity of primitive folk. Fear of poison and witchcraft dominates the minds of all. Its presence is constant, though it varies in degree according to the prevailing conditions. In times of peace and prosperity it is kept in subjection, but, in the days of adversity, it is a distressing factor and sadly affects the life of the people.

NOTES TO CHAPTER IX

[1] " I believe the scientific name for this is Newboldia laevis."—Seem.

[2] " The streets of the (Yoruba) town simply follow the old lines of the footpaths to the farms."—" *History of the Yorubas* ", p. 92.

[3] " It does not appear that any care is ever taken to choose the site of a town, as the neighbourhood of large streams."—*Ibid.*, p. 92.

" Wells are sunk by individuals to supply drinking water. The streams that may be flowing through a town are fouled beyond degree, and are by no means fit for drinking purposes."—*Ibid.*, p. 92.

[4] " The system of sanitary arrangements is the most primitive imaginable.

HOME LIFE

A spot is selected as a dustheap for the disposal of all sorts of refuse and, at intervals, fire is set to the pile of rubbish. Here and there are groves, the neighbourhood of which is unsavoury from the disposal of sewage."—" *History of the Yorubas* ", p. 92.

[5] " Every chief is responsible for the quarter in which he resides."—*Ibid.*, p. 92.

[6] *Vide* Chap. XVII.

[7] " Market squares, as a rule, mark out the frontage of a chief or distinguished man. It is planted all over with shady trees for sellers and loungers of an evening. The central market also contains the principal fetish house of the town."—" *History of the Yorubas* ", p. 91.

[8] The generic term in Ibo for any god, fetish, idol, ju-ju is " alusi ", either used singly or collectively. The more important of these " alusi " are generally referred to under their specific names as " Ikenga ", " Chi ", &c., but, even these may be included loosely under " alusi ".

[9] Writing of the Kagoro of N. Nigeria, Tremearne says : " Skulls of men and also of the hartebeeste, antelope and monkey, are strung on a piece of native rope and hung up on the outside walls under the thatch to advertise the family's prowess, and being passed on as family trophies."—" *Tailed Headhunters of Nigeria* ", p. 136.

[10] As among the Kagoro of N. Nigeria and the Yorubas.—" *Tailed Headhunters of Nigeria* ", pp. 131 and 142.

[11] The Fang have no regular time for eating ; and when they have begun to eat there is no regular time for stopping. The quantity of food is the only limit. On a long journey they can go without food a very long time, far surpassing the endurance of a white man. And they are often compelled to travel with empty stomachs from their habit of eating all their food the first day.—"*Fetish Folk of West Africa,*" p. 117.

[12] " The men (Kafirs) eat first by themselves and give what is left over to the women . . . In Gazaland a man eats with his wife, even out of the same dish, until the birth of the first child. He never eats with his wife after that."—" *Savage Childhood* ", p. 95.

" The Bachame Chief was accustomed to eat in private ; his food was cooked by his favourite wife . . . the reasons assigned for eating in secret are : (1) The Chief is a divine being and is not, therefore, supposed to eat at all, and (2) the ritual secures protection from witchcraft and poisoning."—" *Tribal Studies in N. Nigeria* ", Vol. I, p. 45.

[13] Among the Ewe-speaking people " the common belief is that the indwelling spirit leaves the body and returns to it through the mouth : hence, should it have gone out, it behoves a man to be careful about opening his mouth lest a homeless spirit should take advantage of an opportunity and enter the body. This, it appears, is considered most likely to take place while the man is eating. Precautions are therefore adopted to guard against these dangers."—" *Golden Bough* ", p. 195.

[14] " The pagans of Northern Nigeria also consume the blood but cook it with the fat of the stomach and eat it hot. The Hausa practice is much the same as that of the Ibos."—" *Tailed Headhunters of Nigeria* ", p. 245.

[15] For specific examples of flesh diet, see p. 54, " *Among the Ibos of Nigeria* ".

[16] See also note on Ophiolatry, p. 41 *seq.*

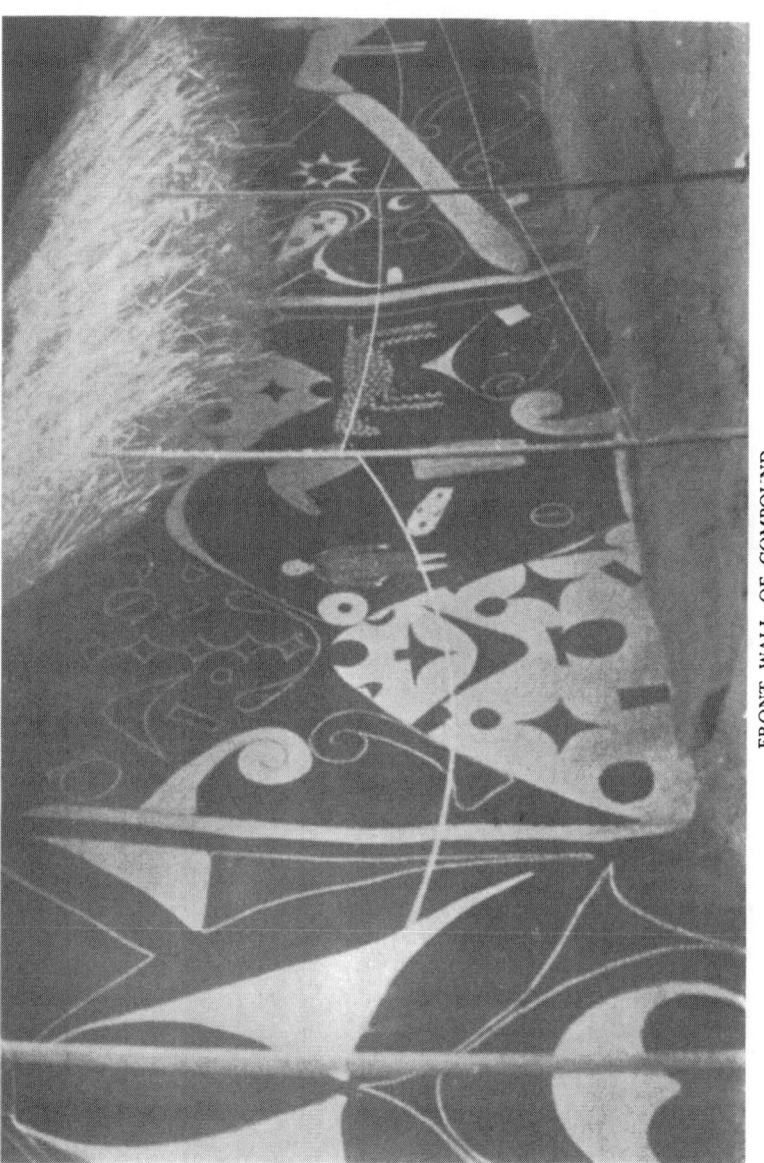

FRONT WALL OF COMPOUND.

DESIGNS IN WHITE, YELLOW AND RED WASHED ON A BLACK BACKGROUND. (PAGE 317.)

CHAPTER X

SOCIAL ETIQUETTE

THE IBO CONFORMS to rules of conduct, and it is useful to have some acquaintance with them in order to be familiar with the proper procedure in certain circumstances. It helps considerably, for instance, to place a visitor at ease, if he knows what is likely to happen, and what is expected of him. The code is not exactly catalogued; it is no more tangible than manners are systematised among civilised races, yet the appropriate customs are well known, in fact they are part and parcel of daily life. The well-conducted Ibo is as clearly recognised as the cultured man in any other country. Proper behaviour is instilled rather than taught; it develops from childhood, and becomes part of his subliminal consciousness. Old people seldom fail to conform to the traditional conventions; the younger generation is becoming less particular, a trait which brings displeasure to their elders. This tendency to laxity is to be deplored, and supplies another indication of the changes brought about by foreign contacts. Progress is blamed unjustly for effects of which it is not actually the cause. There is too great a readiness to shed old customs for the mere sake of new fashions.

The ancient custom of sharing the kola nut is a typical instance.[1] This was always observed when a visitor called at a house, whether a humble one or a palace. If the owner was too poor, or for some other reason was unable to offer the nut, he would always apologise for the seeming lack of courtesy. He would make the visitor feel that he was genuinely sorry for his inability to fulfil the time-honoured custom. The welcome is not complete without the sharing of the nut. When circumstances prevent fulfilment, the owner apologises for the omission with the words " enwerọm ojji " (I have no kola). He means that there has been no intentional slight, but that he is unable to do the proper thing.

After many salutations, which chiefly consist of a repetition of the word " Nnua " or " Ndo-o " or " Ndewo " (all meaning welcome), according to the expression used in different areas, the kola nut is brought forth on a dish or saucer or, what is more correct, on a wooden platter (really a small box fitted

SOCIAL ETIQUETTE

with a cover) prepared and kept for the sole purpose of presenting kola nut.

In the dish are one or more nuts. The owner first receives it from the slave attendant or one of his wives. He takes a nut and puts it to his lips, thus signifying that it is about to be offered in good faith. This symbolic action proves him to be free from malice. The dish is, thereupon, passed to the visitor. It is etiquette to remove all the nuts from the platter, and then to split one or more according to the number of people present. This is his (the visitor's) special privilege. When the nut is turned bottom upwards, the natural lines of division are visible. The two thumb-nails are pressed into the cracks, and a smart jerk splits the nut into sections. If the company be small, there will be sufficient portions : if they will not go round the party, these sections are broken into smaller fragments. The visitor now presents the dish to the owner, who acknowledges the gesture by a wave of the hand, indicating that the visitor should first partake. He takes the first piece : the remainder is passed to each member in turn in order of seniority or precedence. Women may partake, though they seldom do so ; in any case their turn comes after that of the men.

The kola nut (and, indeed, any gift) should always be accepted with the right hand : to use the left is disrespectful, if not an actual offence. A stranger committing such a misdemeanour would be forgiven ; it would simply betray his ignorance. The use of the right hand signifies fellowship, and the sharing of the nut is a token of goodwill. Those who share the nut, seal thereby a bond of friendship which, so long as normal conditions prevail, is not likely to be broken. It would, however, be unwise to place too great a reliance on the custom in the belief that it is an unbreakable bond. It would not hold good should differences arise. It is a friendly gesture at the time of sharing, but has not the binding significance of the sharing of salt among the Arabs.

After partaking of the kola nut, the business of the interview (if any) is discussed. When that is completed, gifts are presented to the visitor. He duly acknowledges these and, later, reciprocates the action by sending equivalent presents. The visitor should be prepared for surprises and be ready to smile his thanks even though, inwardly, he may be somewhat repelled. So much depends upon the nature and quality of the gift and the actions when presenting it. Good and obviously wholesome presents such as fowls and yam may be welcome. Eggs should always be under suspicion. One has seen the servant slip his hand beneath a sitting hen and ruthlessly rob her

SOCIAL ETIQUETTE

of her eggs and, a few minutes later, these very eggs are ceremoniously handed to the visitor. Again, a gift of meat may be thoroughly licked in the presence of the visitor before being offered to him. A preliminary of this nature must not be thought offensive; rather, it is a special token of goodwill. The experienced visitor knows that, what seems to be repulsive, is a genuine proof that the meat is free from poison : it is licked as a personal guarantee that all is well.[2]

The Ibos are a friendly people. In former times, no man or woman would pass another without exchanging greetings. Strangers are content with the common salutation : those with the merest pretence of acquaintanceship will inquire concerning the health of the home-folk. To refrain from greeting is to advertise oneself as a morose person who exhibits his lack of breeding by the unfriendly omission. The only occasion with which I am acquainted when a salutation is neither given nor received is during a period of mourning, or when bearing offerings to the spirits of the dead. (*Vide* p. 58.)

This salutation business is apt to be carried too far at times. Whether on the road, or in the house, the greetings are often protracted unto boredom, although intended to be, and are, genuine expressions of goodwill. The idea seems to be that the more said, the more friendly spirit is manifested ; according to the pleasure of the occasion, so is the " welcome " proclaimed. The word for welcome is repeated again and again.[3] It corresponds to the old English practice of wishing one a " good-day ".

There is little variety in the salutations. The morning greeting is " iputago-ula ? " (have you come out of sleep ?). This serves up to midday. After that, the word " ula " (sleep) is omitted, and it then becomes equivalent to " is all well with you ? "

A person engaged in work provides an exception to this general rule. Instead of the common greeting, it is the fashion to say " dalu-ọlu ", that is, a word of thanks for the work being done. Similarly to the common salutation, this expression is reiterated, though abbreviated to the single word " dalu " (thanks). If the work be rather above the ordinary, further commendation is added ; the workman is rewarded with an appropriate remark as an indication of approval such as " imeka " or " iluka " (you do well).

To attract another person, the right hand is used. Beckoning is done in the opposite way to the English fashion, that is, the palm is turned downwards and the hand moved as if drawing something towards you. On the contrary, if a man wishes

SOCIAL ETIQUETTE

to signify ill-feeling towards another, he clenches his fist with the exception of the thumb. This he maintains in a stiff upright position. Shaking the fist in this fashion towards another person is equivalent to cursing him or her.

Should one come near a spot where one or more people are partaking of a meal, Ibo courtesy demands that that one should be straightway invited to share the food. At the same time, it is not expected that the new-comer will accept the invitation : it is generally a conventional act, denoting friendship. Only on rare occasions would there be an active response. The customary answer is " thank you, but I have eaten ".

The sexes maintain a fairly rigid independence, each following its own traditional customs. Except in unusual circumstances, neither intrudes on the established rights and privileges of the other. Both have their own associations, spheres of work, recreations and so forth. Each is concerned with its own affairs, intermingling with those of the other, it is true, yet quite separate and distinct. At public meetings, men sit together, and the women by themselves. Apart from any other reason, this arrangement avoids any infringement of the convention which rules that it is an offence for a man to step over the feet of a seated woman.

On the way to market or farm or, indeed, whenever walking for a specific purpose, single file is maintained, even if going but a short distance. This follows ancient custom, born of necessity, owing to the primitive narrow bush and forest tracks. This practice remains unchanged at the moment, even where wide roads have been constructed. Like other institutions, there are indications in the larger (new) communities that this processional custom is being modified ; the younger generation is not trammelled with the fears of the old, and naturally fall into line with the improved conditions.

A man accompanying his womenfolk rarely carried a load himself. This is right when properly understood. It is a survival of the primitive law of necessity whereby the man, armed and unhampered by any burden, took up his position at the rear of the procession. His business was to shepherd his flock and be on the alert to defend it. In former days, his task was an important and often hazardous one. Foreigners are sometimes inclined to charge him with being ungallant and lazy, whereas he is following an ancient custom and fulfilling what, at one time, was a great responsibility. He had to be free in order to be able to move and act immediately danger appeared.

When friends meet, they greet each other with the salutation already noticed, and then proceed to inquire after each other's

SOCIAL ETIQUETTE

health and their respective households. They do not enter into intimate details; to do so might seem to manifest too great an interest in particular persons. It is safe to inquire about, or send salutations to, the " ndi-be-i ". The whole household is comprehended in this term (those of your house), and no suspicion of an ulterior motive is roused.

The physical expression of pleasure when men meet each other is not by a hand-clasp. It is expressed with the fingers only. The forefinger of the one is pressed rigidly on the forefinger of the friend. Each man withdraws his finger sharply, which produces a crisp explosive sound on the principle of the familiar snap of the finger and thumb. The most demonstrative form of welcome is to embrace with the right arm and clasp breast to breast (" ti-obi "). It does not include kissing: it is equivalent to that token of affection. Practically all women demonstrate their feelings to their women friends in this fashion: only men who have a right to the privilege may " ti-obi " a woman.

Normally, the Ibo is loathe to say a final good-bye: he always contemplates and wishes a safe return. This is signified in the word " nagbo " (" to go and come "). In that word is implied the hope that the departing friend will, sooner or later, return, however long he may be absent, and however distant he may be travelling. The definite farewell " nodumma " (rest (sit) well) is more for casual acquaintances: between real friends it is expressed with great reluctance.

NOTES TO CHAPTER X

[1] " Kola (Cola or Sterculia acuminata and macrocarpa). Tree twenty to thirty feet in height, both indigenous and cultivated in most parts of West Africa between 5° S. and 10° N. Lat. It thrives on all soils, and is found at all heights, from sea-level to three thousand feet and more. The nuts, which are bitter in taste, are highly esteemed by the natives. In England, they are worked up with cocoa and other food products. To the Mohammedan of West Africa the kola nut supplies the place of coffee. For satisfying the cravings of hunger and for sustaining properties it is deemed equal to the dried dates of the Bedouin. The roots are favoured as ' chew sticks ' for cleaning the teeth and sweetening the breath. The nuts grow in pods, and vary in size from one to two inches in diameter. Each nut has three or four natural divisions enabling it to be split easily. In colour it ranges from white to red. Kola nuts enter into the daily life of all West African Mohammedans and constitute almost a language. Offers of marriage, refusals and acceptances, declarations of war, and countless other transactions are arranged by means of the number and colour of kola nuts strung together (or otherwise) and sent by one party to another. The first act of friendship and hospitality is a present of white nuts, and before commencing any discussion on any subject, the sharing of the kola nut as an

SOCIAL ETIQUETTE

act of friendship is a necessity. The export of kola nuts is a very flourishing trade, and they are in great demand throughout all the countries of the Soudan as far as Khartoum. The value increases according to the distance they have to be carried until they cost from sixty to one hundred times their original value."—Modified extract from "*British Nigeria*", Mockler-Ferryman, p. 317. See also "*Flora Nigritianna*".

[2] Dr. Baikie, when entertaining Tshukuma and his retinue at lunch at Aboh in 1854, says, " a large meat-pie was on the table, which I divided among all present, tasting, according to custom, a little bit from each of the plates before offering them to our guests. This has been rendered customary by attempts at poisoning having been frequent. A slave always tastes a cup before presenting it to his master."—"*Baikie's Exploring Voyage*", p. 47.

[3] Onitsha " Nnua " ; Interior " Ndewo " ; Asaba side " Ndo-o ".

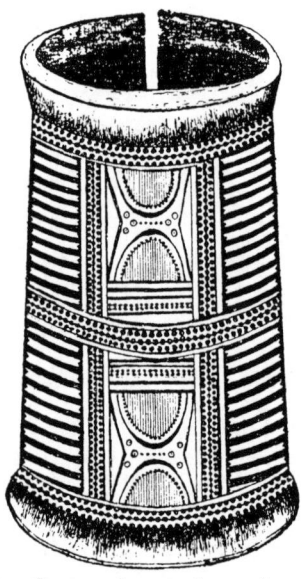

COPPER ANKLET (p. 137).
Worn by chiefs and richer men of certain districts.

CHAPTER XI

BIRTH CUSTOMS

"Omumu" is the goddess whose aid is invoked to secure the gift of children and several shrines will be found in the Ibo village. The name is sometimes lengthened into " Ekwu- " or " Akwali-Omumu ". It is a conical mound of earth decorated with small earthen pots (oku), embedded mouth outwards. The priest performs the initiatory rites for the installation of a new " Omumu ". He kills and buries a goat at the selected site and over this builds up the mound. A feast follows to celebrate the event, the blood, bones and feathers of the sacrificial offerings being devoted to the spirit of the new " Omumu ".

Grown-up girls of the village do not partake of the offerings on the ground that, should any children be born as the result of the service they, the children, will be claimed by outsiders. This means that, as the girls are likely to marry men of another village (though, maybe, a village belonging to the same town), they should not associate too closely with the " Omumu " of their native village. Young married women, brought as brides from other places, and all men (strangers forbidden), may partake of the feast. Each woman interested in the " Omumu " ceremonies provides a cock. The birds are killed, and the blood sprinkled, the priest, as he does this, invoking the blessing of the village ancestors, as many being called upon by name as can be remembered. The women then prepare the feast. During the course of it, the priest places the legs and heads of the fowls on the " Omumu " and, again, calls upon the ancestors. Small children are then invited to take these sacrificial gifts and consume them. A husband partaking in the ceremony will call upon his own immediate ancestors by name.

At the close of the feast, all dance to a sort of chant : " Zoto nzoto ayi azolu nwa na okpa " = " We have danced (shuffled or trodden) a child out of our feet." [1]

A woman desirous of bearing a child resorts to " Omumu " and, with sacrifices, beseeches the goddess to grant her the favour. Should the prayer be answered, appropriate thanksgivings are brought ; for a boy, a cock ; for a girl, a hen. The blood of the sacrifice is sprinkled and, by means of it, the feathers are plastered on the " Omumu ". The carcase of the sacrifice is then cooked and eaten.

BIRTH CUSTOMS

Besides the village "Omumu", a woman, on marriage, makes a small one for herself, composed of three sticks fixed in the ground just inside the compound. This becomes her special " alusi ", and she sacrifices to it whenever she feels so inclined *after* sundown. She does this to ensure her bearing children. If conception occur within a reasonable time after marriage, a woman will not bother to set up a private " Omumu " ! No male member of the household has any lot or part in connection with this personally owned " Omumu " ; it is entirely the woman's own affair.

If, by any chance, the woman pollute herself, the head woman of the village brings a sacrifice and performs the cleansing ceremonies, and thus makes atonement. The same process is followed for the cleansing of the village " Omumu " whenever pollution occurs.

I have not met with a single example of phallic worship during the whole of my thirty-five years in the Ibo country. I have not even heard it mentioned, or anything that had any resemblance to it. That may be due to lack of enterprise on my part. At the same time, if there be such a worship, it must be very infrequent and unobtrusive, because, whenever travelling, except on rare occasions, I stayed in the villages and had fair opportunities to make observations by day and night.

The " Omumu ", from its shape and location, may sometimes have been confused with a phallic pillar, but the native does not interpret it as such ; in fact they deny any knowledge of phallic worship. Here and there, some pillars do answer in appearance to the characteristic of " phallic ". They are rare, and I have seen them but on one or two occasions. They are round obelisks about eight feet high. It was evident that they had not been served for some considerable period, as they were green with moss, and the worse for wind and weather. I can trace no material wherewith to justify an attempt to write on phallic worship. My most reliable informants state that they have no knowledge whatever of such a worship in the Ibo country.

Any account of Child Life in the Ibo country would be incomplete without first noticing some of the curious ideas pertaining to the ante-natal stage. The pregnant woman seems to have a fair number of regulations to remember—not so much what she must do, but, rather, what she must not do.

There is quite a list of prohibitions ; they vary in different districts, and are general all over the Ibo country.

During the months of pregnancy, the prospective mother

BIRTH CUSTOMS

must not eat snails (ejuna). Should she do so, the eyes and nose of her child will stream with water, and it will dribble. This rule, however, is often disregarded.

Individuals sometimes bear little irregular patches of lighter colour on their skins. The native doctor declares that these patches prove that the mother ate snails during the months that she was pregnant; she violated the prescribed prohibition. Such persons, in their turn, must regard snails as tabu.

She must not eat the flesh of the " nchi " (a rodent). This animal has a peculiar habit of running forward and stopping suddenly. If a pregnant woman eat of the flesh, when the time of her delivery arrives, the child will come forward and then slip back. Delivery will be checked, and the danger to both mother and child thereby increased. Should there have been an infringement of this rule, when the time of delivery draws near, the woman is given a piece of " nchi " meat to eat, or a bone of the animal to suck. This is supposed to be an antidote against the effects of the sin committed.

She must not eat bananas. Should she infringe this ruling, her child will be weak and pale (anæmic).

A pregnant woman is barred from eating plantain. This fruit, when peeled, shows a line extending its whole length. To partake of this fruit will result in a line (orowa) appearing on the child's head: a depression from the front to the back. The banana and plantain prohibitions are met with only here and there, and do not seem to be widespread.

For the first three or four months after conception a woman must not eat the native pumpkin (ubogulu). If she transgress in this, her child will have pimples (obe) on its body, similar to the protuberances covering the skin of the pumpkin.

Here and there, the restriction on the eating of pumpkin is governed by the place of growth. Pumpkins grown in the village gardens may not be eaten, while those grown in the farms are allowed. The reason alleged is that those grown in the town may be used for the administration of poison by malicious neighbours. In one place it is stated that, if a woman partook of pumpkin grown in the village, the child would be poisoned and die in the womb.

The " Ukpa " nut is forbidden to a prospective mother. This is a nut somewhat similar in taste to a chestnut. It grows in a four-cornered pod, and is boiled before eating. To eat this during pregnancy would mean lumps on the child's body, as in the case of eating pumpkin or, according to some women, and more usual, the effect is the same as that caused by eating snails.

She is warned against eating " Ukwa " (breadfruit) and the

"ube" (a fruit resembling a dark purple plum). The eating of these would cause the child to be inflicted with small boils (obo).

Again, she must not eat "Egwusi" (the seed of the "ogili", a species of gourd), an ingredient much in favour in the preparation of palm-oil stew. Should she partake of this, her child will suffer from sore mouth, set up by the gastric condition of the stomach. The resulting sickness is known as "Abubuọnu" (foul mouth).

And the succulent pig-meat must not be touched. The breaking of this prohibition will cause the child to breathe stertorously as one snoring. Another informant states that the rule is made because of the richness of pig-meat. It is liable to bring on a bilious attack, and violent vomiting may induce abortion.

The pregnant woman must not eat "thick meat", e.g. salt beef. The eating of this will cause the navel to thicken, and the piece of umbilical cord, left after the main part has been severed, will remain attached for a long time.

A woman is prohibited from eating the flesh of an animal killed while it is in young.

On the other hand, if the prospective mother consume eggs, the result on the child will be umbilical hernia (otubo), a condition which excites pleasurable satisfaction. It is much liked for its ornamental (*sic*) appearance. The child will be saluted "Ọnwelu akpu otubo, ọ maka nma". "He has a magnificent navel"!

Contrariwise, some say that women and girls must not eat eggs at all, because to do so will prevent conception. This applies only in certain places and is not general.

The above are some of the restrictions in respect to food; there are doubtless many others, ruled for their own particular reasons. We pass on to notice some of the anxieties of daily life which press upon the pregnant woman.

She must not look upon any "ju-ju", or any creature with an ugly face, such as a monkey. If she should have the misfortune to do so, the baby will resemble what she has seen. Nor must she see her reflection in liquid palm oil; should she do so, miscarriage is liable to result![2]

It is tabu for a pregnant woman to cross a line of travelling ants. Should she do so, the umbilical cord will encircle the child and strangle it. When she meets a stream of ants, she must take a branch, and sweep a passage clear for her feet, or she may try to outflank the swarm. At the same time, she will slap her thigh. If she find she cannot get round them, and yet they are not too many, she may be able to clear a passage by scattering them with her foot. Some say that for a preg-

BIRTH CUSTOMS

nant woman to cross a line of ants will mean that her child will suffer from fits of trembling and be of a nervous temperament.

Hot water must not be used during the early months of pregnancy on the ground that overheating of the body has a tendency to induce miscarriage. For the same reason less pepper and palm oil must be used than at normal times.

A pregnant woman must not enter a place where a child has been recently born—say two Ibo weeks. To infringe this rule is to invite miscarriage ; the idea being that the smell would upset and drive out her child prematurely.

Again, she is advised not to sleep during the day, and she is provided with work to keep her busy in order to safeguard her from becoming drowsy. It is thought that too much sleep is weakening for a prospective mother. She needs exercise to stimulate circulation of the blood and prevent her from becoming sluggish ; hence, she must be kept occupied. On the other hand, she must not be burdened with strenuous work during the heat of the day. In the early stages of pregnancy she must not walk too much in the sun otherwise " she will melt ", in other words, the child will evaporate away !

During the first four months of pregnancy, a woman should not carry loads, and a pregnant woman must not rub (te-uno) a high wall. Also, she must be restrained from fighting. To engage in fighting shows contempt for life, a sort of " don't-care-whether-the-child-dies-or-not " attitude. Hence, for a pregnant woman to fight will lead to family trouble in addition to any physical injury she may suffer.

A woman who has a husband alive is forbidden to spin cotton. This is the tradition and practice, but no reason is forthcoming for it.[3]

When the signs of her approaching delivery begin to manifest themselves, the woman's headcloth must be untied and her hair, if in plaits, must be loosened and, if wearing necklaces, they must be removed. If this be not done, the child will be bound and held captive in the womb.

At about the eighth month, the prospective mother will seek medicine from the doctor. This consists of a mixture of chalk (nzu) and a stimulant to make her " light and strong " (ogwu-ufe-aru). Also medicine is sometimes taken to prevent Elephantiasis (Nsi-ulu-enyi).

Many women eat clay (ulo) ; but they do this at any time and not only when pregnant. They nibble off a fragment and swallow it at intervals during the day. They say they like the taste ; it is very similar to a man who chews tobacco. It becomes a habit, as snuff-taking, and it is said to make a woman feel " light ", also that it is an antidote against heartburn and vomiting. Men object to the practice, and a husband will throw away any clay he finds in the possession of his wife.

The birth must take place outside ; it is abomination for delivery to take place inside the house. After the birth, the woman lives in a small booth alongside the walls of the house ; constructed for the purpose of sheltering her and her new-born babe. At the end of her time of separation (seven Ibo weeks or twenty-eight days), she is considered clean again.[4] Then everything belonging to the booth, the materials thereof, and any mats, cloths and, indeed, everything used during these weeks, all is collected, carried off, and cast away into the " bad bush ".

Nothing is in readiness for the newly born babe. The mother has not worried herself during the months of waiting. She continues to perform her daily tasks oblivious of the ordeal awaiting her, nor does she give a thought towards any preparation for it or the infant. Conception is just a phase in normal life, and no more notice is taken of it than of any other natural function. When the hour for her delivery arrives, the woman, having given no thought to the prospect, is not unfrequently caught unawares. She may be at the market, at a meeting, or at fieldwork, or even by the wayside. In such circumstances, as can be imagined, help may be difficult to obtain. One has known a woman to fend for herself at such a time. This, of course, is not contemplated. A pregnant woman does, as a general rule, arrange beforehand for a midwife to attend and, when confinement takes place at home, this woman is called in to do her part. In addition to the midwife, one or more other old women are present to render assistance : the young mother's mother is always present if her attendance can possibly be arranged. Many women make it a practice to reside at their daughters' houses during the later months of pregnancy in order to be at hand to give assistance when needed.

For a case of protracted labour a " dibia " (doctor) may be called to assist. He may resort to medicine, or manipulation, or both. A hook instrument called an " Nkọ " is used by some practitioners.

To aid difficult delivery, the hook is inserted at the lower part of the vagina and the tissue is pulled back. If this does not produce the desired result, the stretched skin is slit in a downward direction. It is assumed that hindrance to delivery can be at the base only.

To induce delivery by medicine, the leaves of a plant called " Anakalla " or " Aguba na k'ochie " (lit. old man's razor) are taken, and a decoction made which the patient drinks. It is

BIRTH CUSTOMS

a small herb with a fibrous root; the leaves are long and resemble those of a peach or nectarine tree. Twenty or thirty leaves are soaked for a few minutes in half a pint or so of water, and then squeezed through the hands. The result is a green-coloured mucilage of the consistency of castor oil.

In the case of a miscarriage, up to say five months' pregnancy, the fœtus is placed in a clay pot and thrown away. If of a longer period, say, from six to nine months, the dead babe is carried on the palms of the hands, laid in the burial ground and covered with grass. A seven-months' child is expected to live; an eight-months' child is expected to die. No reason was advanced for this belief.

The newly born babe has no other nourishment than a little water for the first two or three days of its life. Custom forbids the mother from suckling it at this early stage; instead, one of the old grandmothers or the midwife acts as proxy which is not exactly hygienic, nor is it of much more nutritive value than a rubber teat.

It is alleged that the first milk is unfit for consumption or, as the women say, it is " bitter ". It is argued that it is unwise for the mother to suckle her child until this has been drawn off. The women have ways of testing the milk by its reaction to leaves or ants. A small quantity is extracted from the breast by pressure and allowed to fall upon the leaf of a koko-yam (edde). If the leaf turns brown, that is, " ọbuluna akwukwọ ajanwu (maọbu nlonwu) ", which, being interpreted, means, " if the leaf shows signs of withering ", then the milk is condemned. For the ant test, the species known as " Agbisi " is selected as the agent. Some milk is expressed into a broken sherd and placed on the ground. If the ants refuse to drink it, or if they partake of it and die, the milk is stigmatised as poisonous. On the contrary, if they drink it freely, and no disastrous results follow, it is accepted as a proof of its wholesomeness.

To obtain full soft breasts, recourse is had sometimes to massage with saliva saturated with the juice of a chewing stick or palm kernel. To develop the nipples, some women chew palm kernels, then they hold the nipple firmly and rub it vigorously with the chewed fibre, especially at the time the child is born.

Some mothers manipulate the nipples of little girls from the time of birth, pressing them inwards periodically until they are almost inverted. The idea is that this will cause the breasts to spread widely and be very full.

To remove the remains of the umbilical cord, the juice of the banana-skin is used. It is heated and applied drop by drop

BIRTH CUSTOMS

on the spot three times a day. When the cord comes away, warm palm oil (warmed in a sherd called " Eju ") is applied with a feather, and the cord itself is taken and placed between the fronds of a young palm tree called " Nkwu ana ". The first hair of the child is similarly treated. At the birth of a first child, a palm tree is planted and given this name " Nkwu ana ". The tree belongs to that particular child ; the practice is not followed for children born subsequently.

There are no swaddling clothes for the newly born Ibo baby. In the tropics this is not such a serious matter ; in any case there is always a fire burning on the floor, and over-ventilation is not a feature of native huts ! The babe receives its first rude shock from the unsympathetic world when it is soused in cold water immediately after birth.

Sleeping accommodation for the babe is a share of the mother's couch. The Ibo mother thinks this is the proper place for her offspring. To suggest a cot would raise doubts of the woman's affection towards her child : it would be equivalent to treating the child as an object of little, or of no more importance than a common utensil.

Both boys and girls are given two or more names. The privilege of naming a child (" igu-afa ") is generally the prerogative of the older relatives. The ceremony is observed with feasting and general rejoicing. In due course comes the actual bestowal of the names. The first is easy, because it is merely a combination of the word child (nwa) with the name of the day on which it was born. Thus we have " Nwa-Afọ ", the child (boy) of Afọ Day ; or " Nwa-Okọnkwọ ", the male child of Nkwọ Day. For a girl " mgbọ " is used instead of " nwa ". The succeeding name (or names) is suggested by some real or fancied peculiarity, or a certain resemblance to a deceased relative.[5, 6] Again, circumstances, or prevailing conditions of the time, may suggest an appropriate name whereby the unusual happenings are kept in remembrance. Some of the names sound rather strangely to European ears, for it should be remembered that all names are capable of translation. Quite a number include the name of the Supreme Being as " Chukuka ", " Okechuku " and " Nwa-Chuku ", and many have " Ọnwu " (death) associated in their names, " Ọnwudiwe ", " Ọnwuka " and " Ọnwubalili ". The great majority, however, have to be content to be known by their first name, hence, before the advent of foreigners, there were literally scores of " Okoyes ", " Okekes ", " Okọnkwọs ", and " Okafọs " (the " nwa " omitted when adolescence was reached) among the males, and " Mgbafọs " and other combinations of " Mgbọ " among the womenfolk.

BIRTH CUSTOMS

In addition to the giving of names of ancestors, some names are influenced by circumstances. For example, a couple who have waited several years for a child will name it " Ogwalu Onyekwe " (He who is told (of it) will not believe ! that is, the birth of a child after all these years is almost incredible), or " Ife-yi-nwa " (There is nothing like a child).

Accompanying the ceremony of " Igu-afa ", there is a feast called " Ima- (or Iputa-) n'omugwo " = to look after a woman after delivery, or the word " Iputa-asa " may be used = to come out after seven weeks. The father and mother of the child make feasts for men and women respectively. The guests are expected to give presents ; particular friends will bring a basket of yams and a pot of palm wine. The gifts correspond generally with what the father and mother themselves offered to the self-same friends when they were celebrating the birth of a child. It is a time of great rejoicing and feasting, and large quantities of palm wine are consumed on these occasions.

" Ima-n'omugwo " is followed by " Ife-afia " (to walk round the market). For this, the mother adorns herself in her best, and places on her head, front to back, the fat (flay) of a goat, as in the Nkpu ceremonies. (*Vide* p. 224.) The skin of the goat is laid across her shoulders and back. This indicates that the birth ceremonies have been completed. The mother parades the market-place ; other women follow her in procession and present her with gifts, voicing, as they do so, the praises of the husband who has done so honourably by his wife.

Occasionally, there is a rite which corresponds to a form of dedication. It is associated with the ceremony of " naming the child ", and is restricted solely to boys, more especially those who are destined to become " dibias " (medicine men). This is definitely the case when, after inspection, a " dibia " is persuaded that the infant manifests some trait or resemblance to a deceased " dibia ". It is thought that the boy is a reincarnation of the dead man, hence he will, naturally, resume his former profession. The boy remains with his parents until he is about eight years of age, and will then enter the service of the " dibia " who, as it were, has established his claim to the child. He thus begins his initiation into the mysteries of the medical cult at a very early age.

Children born within the precincts of an " alusi " shrine are, in consequence, claimed by the priest for service to the god. Such a birth may occur when the mother is brought to delivery suddenly, and is unable to reach home in time for the event. The infant becomes automatically the property of the god and, henceforth, is known as an " Osu ". (*Vide* Chap. XVII.)

This cannot be accepted as a " dedication " in the proper sense of the term : it is mere accident of birth, but the effect is the same.

Both boys and girls have to submit to the rite of circumcision. The operation is performed, normally, between the fourth and eighth day after birth, but, if the child be weak, it may be postponed for a time. This rule applies chiefly on the eastern side of the Niger. On the western, circumcision is generally delayed until the age of puberty.[7] Certainly this is so in the case of girls : they are left untouched until preparing for marriage ; indeed, circumcision can almost be regarded as an associated rite with the marriage ceremonies. As far as can be ascertained there is, nowadays, no religious significance connected with the operation.

On the western side, there is a strict professional union among the women circumcisers. They have a special badge of office, a small brass, paddle-shaped token, attached to a necklace, or hanging on a piece of cord from the waist. Very often the little razor hangs alongside the badge. The rules of the company are close and strict.

On the eastern side, there is no such union, nor is there an outward badge to indicate that a man or a woman is skilled in the art. Both men and women are equally free to perform the operation on this side of the Niger.

" The practice of circumcision most probably was brought from Egypt or Ethiopia. Herodotus states that its origin, among both Egyptians and Ethiopians, may be traced to the most remote antiquity. It seems to have been in use long before the arrival of Joseph into Egypt or the Exodus of Moses ! "[8]

" The rite of circumcision is universally practised and rigidly regarded, but nobody knows why. It has the Authority of Custom."[9]

The operation on girls is usually performed by women, though many men do it also. Whether for boy or girl, the mother (or another woman) sits on the ground, holding the child between her knees with the feet towards the operator. Sometimes a small hole is scooped out in the ground and the child placed in it. Again, in some parts, e.g. the Enugu District, the operator smears his own and the child's face with " edo " wood stain (like yellow ochre in appearance) as a ceremonial preparation, and " medicine " is placed in a small basket (okpulu) to ensure success. A crude razor of triangular shape is used for the operation, the " Aguba " or " Ikpu-kpe ".

In the case of a girl, the operator (Onwene or Omenka) picks up the clitoris (agama) firmly between finger and thumb, and cuts it right out at the base. With deft movements, the cut-

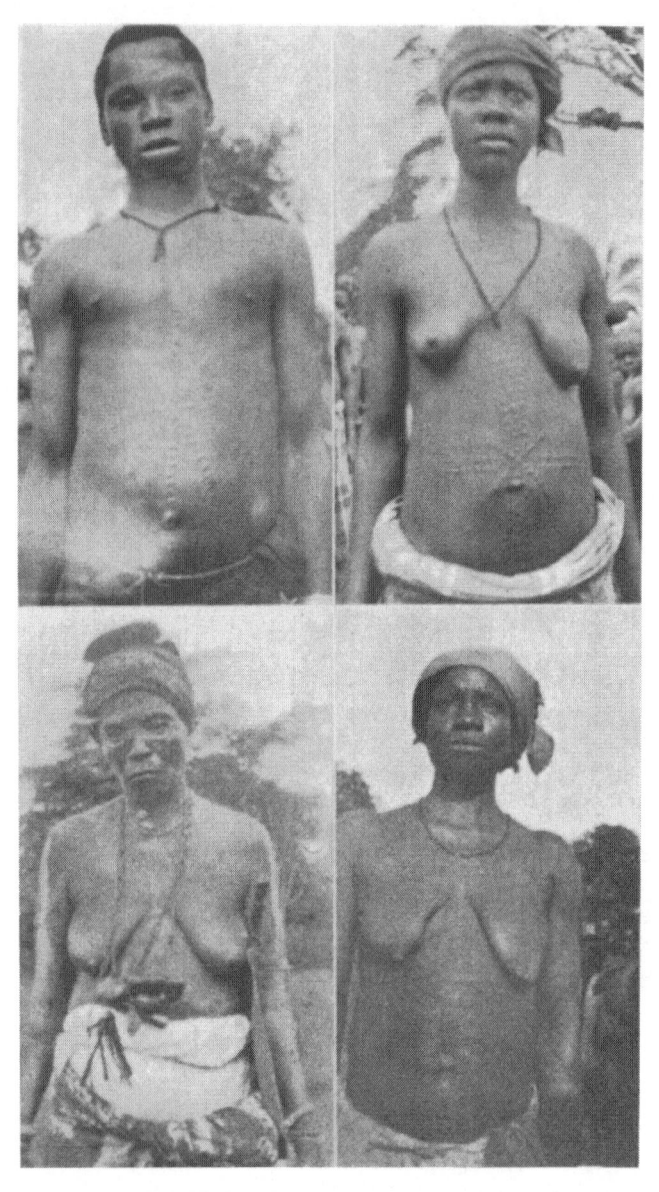

CICATRIZATION AND BODY STAINING.

Top right and left: PATTERNS FORMED OF "MBUBU"—RAISED SCARS (PAGES 176-331.)
Bottom right: STAINING WITH "ULI" SUPERIMPOSED OVER CICATRIZED "MBUBU." (PAGE 330.)
Bottom left: THIS OLD WOMAN WAS PRESIDENT OF THE UNION OF PROFESSIONAL "CUTTERS" AT UMUNEDE. HER UNION BADGE AND RAZORS HANG AT HER WAIST. SHE GAVE THEM TO THE AUTHOR. (PAGE 179.)

BIRTH CUSTOMS

ting is continued down each side of the organ, thus removing clitoris and labia minor in a single piece. A skilful " Onwene " performs an exceedingly neat operation. In addition to the above, the small piece of stretched skin at the base of the organ is slit down as far as the thick tissue. During the operation, warm water is made to fall, drop by drop, as a substitute for swabbing.

After the operation, native soap mixed with oil, or with the juice of the Agbiligba leaf, or the juice of a piece of Anwilinwa stick is applied to the wound. The Agbiligba juice is said to be " hot ", that is, it has styptic properties, while the juice of Anwilinwa is like liquid rubber.

Next, a small pad is made of either a certain kind of grass, or with " uli-nkwu ", the downy substance found around the base of palm fronds, where they join the trunk of the tree. This soft substance is saturated with oil. The pad is inserted between the parts and remains there until the first urine is passed, after which it is expected that bleeding has ceased and, therefore, it is no longer necessary.

After the operation, it is the business of the mother to attend to the child. A mixture is made of kernel oil and mother's milk, or a concoction is made of " odo " leaf, ufie (camwood dye), chalk and oil. With this, she anoints the parts for about seven days. While so anointing, she gently rubs them together to prevent the two sides adhering. At the lower part, she inserts her little finger and presses downwards once or twice a day until the wound is healed. The slight enlargement of the opening which results is thought by the natives to be helpful when the babe, in its turn, comes to the time of delivering a child. Finally, banana and " Isikala " leaves are applied to finish the healing process.

It is a bad custom. Not unfrequently, the parts do adhere, and the operator has to be called in again to reopen the aperture ; sometimes on more than one occasion. The operation designated as " repairs after circumcision " is well known at the hospitals in these latter days.

Meek, in his " *Northern Tribes of Nigeria* ", Vol. II, p. 91, says : " Female circumcision, or the removal of the clitoris (and labia minor), is practised among some tribes. No explanation of the rite is given, but it is believed to be an aid to chastity."

On the other hand, Seabrook, in " *Jungle Ways* ", p. 55, states : " Ethnologists have denounced this custom of female circumcision, asserting (on hearsay) that, in the operation among the West Coast people, the clitoris is excised, which seems a fine example of learned ethnographic nonsense. The operation consists solely of excising the surplus folds inside the lips of the vagina, a measure, which had become ritual, but must certainly have had as its basic purpose common-sense facility for cleanliness, just as in the case of male circumcision."

Still, the ethnologists happen to be right, and Seabrook's assertion finds no support, certainly none in the Ibo country.

The operation on a child of a few days old is simple ; it is quite another thing when a girl is full grown. It is extremely painful, yet is submitted to with a mixture of willingness and reluctance, the latter because of the anticipated suffering. The girl *knows* that it is an ancient custom accepted in infallible good faith. To avoid the pain would only mean probable death (as the people think) when her time for delivery arrives. And what constitutes a greater incentive is that she knows no man will marry her unless she has submitted to the ordeal ; he would not risk his dowry money on one who had neglected to conform to an institution believed in and practised for untold generations.

This is the ancient and present pagan practice. Female circumcision is prohibited by regulation to members of the Church in the Diocese on the Niger. It is interesting to note that this prohibition was enacted by the native members independently of the Europeans. For some fifteen years, one or two missionaries made it their business to impart instruction on the subject as opportunities presented themselves. Eventually, it led to discussions in local committees and, from them, to District Church Councils. One after another passed resolutions deprecating the custom until, finally, a Joint Board representing all the Councils drew up a regulation to prohibit the practice among Church members.

The remarkable feature has been the very few cases calling for disciplinary action since the rule came into operation. This is, without doubt, due to the fact that the people themselves were responsible for it. It is a gratifying instance where patient teaching has been rewarded with mutual satisfaction to both teachers and taught.

Similar remarks might be written of other customs, e.g. the " Iwa Ji " (p. 67) has been converted into a Christian Harvest Festival, and a further cheering aspect of this is that many pagans attend these special services in order to share in the general thanksgiving for the fruits of the earth. In like manner the " naming of the child " (" Igu-afa ", p. 174) and the " coming out of a woman after childbirth " (" Ima-n'omugwo ", p. 175) are now celebrated after the Christian manner.

There is good ground for hope that, gradually, public opinion and common sense will lead to the abolition of female circumcision among all sections of the community.

BIRTH CUSTOMS

NOTES TO CHAPTER XI

[1] Zoto nzoto = rubbing feet like wiping them on a doormat.

[2] Cf. the neighbouring Ijaw custom. If a pregnant woman meets an attractive man or woman she will beg that one to pass round her with the idea of influencing the child to be similarly fine, but she will flee at the sight of an ugly person.

[3] " Among the Ainos of Saghalien a pregnant woman must not spin or twist ropes for two months before delivery, because they think that if she did so the child's guts might be entangled like a thread."—Frazer's " *Golden Bough* ", p. 20.

[4] Cf. Leviticus xii.

[5] See also pp. 54, 175, 285.

[6] " The pagan tribes of Northern Nigeria believe that a ghost may transmigrate into the body of a descendant born after the ancestor's death. Such a thing is common as it is proved by the likeness of children to their parents or grandparents."—" *Tailed Headhunters of Nigeria* ", p. 173.

The neighbouring Yorubas hold the same belief; deceased parents are born again into the family of their surviving children.

[7] With the sole exception of Onitsha Town. Girls are never circumcised there; it stands quite unique in this. Towns related to it on the western side practise the rite, yet Onitsha is free from it.

[8] " *Expedition to the Niger, 1841* ", Vol. II, p. 399.

[9] " *Fetish Folk of West Africa* ", p. 273.

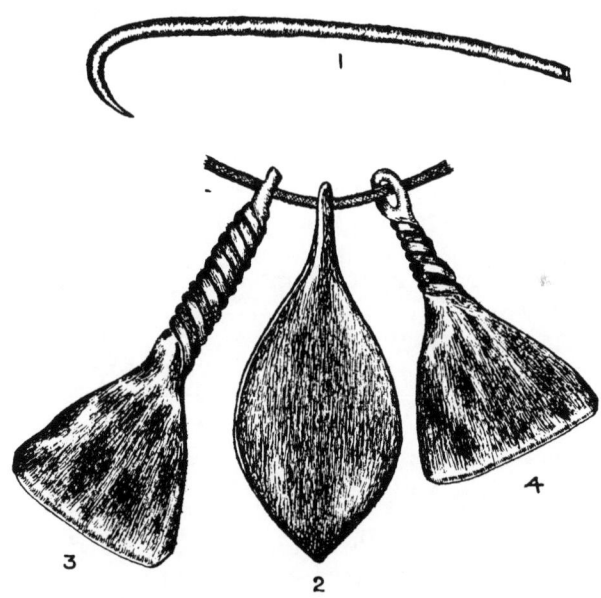

1. Nko. Iron wire hook used occasionally for midwifery cases (p. 172).
2. Brass token of membership of union of women circumcisers.
3 and 4. " Aguba " or " Ikpu-kpe "—iron operating knives (p. 176).

The token and knives were given to the author by the senior woman of the union at Umunede.

CHAPTER XII

CHILDHOOD

THE EARLY DAYS OF the Ibo child are beset by hazards due to deeply rooted customs, general ignorance of the first principles of Infant Welfare, and gross superstition. The mortality of children under the age of twelve months is colossal. One competent medical authority, with many years of experience to support his judgement, places the lowest figure as 200 per 1,000. In some parts of Nigeria it was as high as 900 per 1,000.[1] Yaws (Framboesia), craw-craw (Pustular or Nodular Dermatitis) and other diseases work havoc upon the children, while every one is a victim of intestinal parasites. The risks are so many that it is a matter of surprise that any children survive. What thousands must be born to maintain the population, and in the Ibo country there is a density to the square mile probably in excess of any other part of Africa, save Egypt and the large cities. Nature is prolific in the matter of children, as it is prodigal in other realms, and it needs to be in order that the natives may continue at all. In addition to the dangers to infant life which arise from tropical diseases and conditions, and from ignorance, there are others which are the outcome of deliberate intention to destroy, prompted by fear and superstitious beliefs.

A child conceived before " Ama-izizi ", that is, the public intimation (generally by the parents) that a girl has passed her first menstruation, is cast away. It is termed " Ime-ogbi "—a dumb conception. A child born before the mother has resumed her menstrual periods after a previous birth, is destroyed; this applies to some parts of the country only, not everywhere.[2]

When a woman dies in childbirth, the baby, whether alive or dead, is buried with her.

In many districts, if the infant fails to cry vigorously at birth, it will not be taken into the house; indeed, it forfeits its life, the omission being considered an evil omen.

A child born with six toes or fingers, as a general rule, is abandoned; to be born feet first is equally disastrous. A child that is weak, or a cripple, or for some other reason cannot move about on its feet by the time it has reached the age of two or

CHILDHOOD

three years, is regarded as "alu" (abomination) and is destroyed, or sold to become an "osu" (*vide* p. 246), or as a sacrifice (cf. p. 164).

Certain children, though considered unsatisfactory, escape the penalty of being cast away, e.g. a child that walks before cutting its lower teeth. An attempt is made to remedy matters by cutting away the gum to expose the growing teeth. Again, two children of different parents, who feed from one mother, are regarded similarly as twins; this is tabu, and restitution must be made with cleansing sacrifices. Whatever chance of surviving there might, or might not, be for the children referred to in the preceding paragraphs, there was no doubt about the fate of twins (ejima) under old Ibo law and custom; it was incumbent that they should be destroyed without delay. At the same time, reproaches were heaped upon the stricken mother for being the author of such a forbidden issue.

It is sometimes alleged that this aversion to twins is rooted in the belief that it is contrary to human nature. The order for mankind is to propagate by means of single births; there must be a difference between the human species and brute creation. To function as an animal is to degrade humanity; a mother of twins is brought down to the level of a common beast. She has fallen from her position and, in doing so, has brought disgrace upon herself and her household. She is, in consequence, thrust outside the pale, and is entitled to no more respect than is given to the animals of the field. This is the reason why the children are cast away immediately after birth, and their mother subjected to abuse and persecution.

Such a mother has no way of escape, nor any defence to make. She has broken the law of humanity and must pay the penalty. The facts are patent. All she can do is to submit, and dumbly wonder why this calamity has befallen her; the joy of motherhood is turned to the ashes of bitterness.

Her attitude towards her offspring is as scornful as that of her relatives, and she refuses even to look at them. Despair smothers every spark of affection. Finally, she will make no effort to suckle them. Only where brought under close and constant supervision (where such has become operative), can she be persuaded or forced to feed them. Disgrace falls upon the family, because of the sin of the mother (or father), at least, it is so affirmed by the native priest. The transgression may be in neglecting to offer sacrifice, or failing to fulfil the ceremonies and rites of "Second Burial", or omitting to perform some function on behalf of a relative who has died or, again, it may be the punishment for some crime committed and unconfessed, particularly murder. The visitation of twins is a sort of detective agency bringing past crimes to light.

We may note here that the birth of a deformed, crippled, or otherwise abnormal child is likewise considered to be the result of evil doing on the part of the father or mother. Concealed crime will, in due course, bring its own punishment, if not upon the parents, certainly upon the children.

Another explanation of the cause of twin births sometimes given is that it is the result of sexual intimacy between the woman and a spirit man during sleep ; the spirit is, thus, the father of the additional child. Evidence of this idea among the Ibos is very meagre and unconvincing.

Whatever may be the accepted cause, the fact remains that the unwanted children must be removed from the village without delay ; they are " nsǫ " (abominations), and to allow them to remain would be to court disaster. Fear and disgust urge the speedy disposal of these accursed things from the sight of gods and men. An old water-pot is brought, and into this the living infants are crammed without pity or a spark of gentleness. A few leaves, or a handful of cocoanut fibre, is thrust in to cover them, and then the pot is carried away and deposited in the " bad bush ".

This revulsion against the birth of twins is widespread in Africa. It is found among the natives of Bukara Island in the south-east corner of Lake Victoria Nyanza. They follow a custom very similar to that of the Ibos. Twins, and babies born feet first, are not wanted. " The babies are placed in pots and deposited in the bush. The mother must undergo a ceremonial purification, but is not considered free until she has vindicated her reputation by giving birth to a normally-placed single child." [3]

Speaking of Kaffir customs, Dudley Kidd says : " A native thinks that twins are scarcely human ; he thinks that they are more animal than human, and that the bearing of twins is a thing entirely out of the ordinary course of nature. In olden days one of the twins was always put to death and frequently both. It is natural, as it was thought, for dogs or pigs to have twin offspring in a litter, but for human beings it is disgraceful. A woman who has twins is taunted with belonging to a disgraceful family and, in olden days, if she gave birth to twins a second time, she was killed as a monstrosity." [4]

After such a calamity as the birth of twins, the procedure for removing the pollution is as follows : At the end of seven Ibo weeks (28 days), an Nri priest is summoned to the house. He kills a sheep in sacrifice in the courtyard, and performs the

CHILDHOOD

necessary ceremonies for cleansing the house and compound (Ikpu alu) = driving out of abomination.

In some parts, the mother is driven away, and she will be rejected by her husband. Round about Onitsha, the woman, after purification, may return to her husband.

Contrast this attitude with that of the Yoruba people who are neighbours of the Ibos. With them " no condition is invested with an air of greater importance, or has a halo of deeper mystery about it, than that of twin births. Twins in Yoruba are almost credited with extra human powers." [5]

The treatment meted out to twins, drastic as it is, does not necessarily cause their immediate death ; some live for many hours. One reason for this is that the umbilical cord is not severed ; a certain amount of vitality is, no doubt, retained owing to the child still being attached to the placenta. In one case with which I had to deal, the children had been cast away for at least sixteen hours. When the pot was broken, one child was found to be dead from injuries either (and probably) deliberately inflicted, or because of the ruthless manner in which it had been crushed into the pot. The other, and uppermost, had fared better ; it was unhurt and, under supervision at a Medical Mission, it thrived and, in due time, grew up to robust manhood.

The custom is cruel and inhuman, but the pagan is not his own master. He lives under the stress of fear, believing sincerely that to allow the children to live would be acting in direct antagonism to the gods. By all the laws which, hitherto, have governed his existence, twins are forbidden and, when any are born, the only avenue of escape from the wrath of the gods is to remove them from sight as quickly as possible. Their continued existence would provoke the anger of the malignant spirits, and disaster would fall not only upon the family, but also upon the whole village. He is not so much to be blamed ; rather he is to be pitied, for he knows no alternative. The practice is now condemned by law, but the native does not find it easy to accept the new legislation. The mind and attitude towards this subject need to be changed, which, in its turn, will produce a public opinion that will not tolerate such atrocities. Happily, it can be confidently affirmed that, though the fear caused by the birth of twins still holds sway, in most parts of the Ibo country there is a growing tendency on the part of the people to bring the custom to an end.

In South Africa, now that British rule has spread, " the killing of twins is forbidden, though it is a custom that is extremely difficult to put down, for the matter is kept profoundly secret

CHILDHOOD

—when possible even from neighbouring natives and much more so from white men ".[6] These words might have been written in connection with the Ibo country, inasmuch as they express the situation exactly.

Given that the child has managed to escape the danger of its earliest days, there are still perils for it to face. The first and greatest comes at the teething stage. The cutting of the first tooth is of supreme importance, for it is the deciding factor whether the child shall live or die forthwith. The parents are greatly concerned at this season, and watch anxiously for its appearance. The lower gum is the centre of interest for, should the first tooth break through there, it means life to the child, and general thanksgiving on the part of the parents and friends. On the contrary, should it pierce the top gum, the omen is bad, and the child's fate is sealed. Very commonly, though not in every case, such an unfortunate child was treated similarly to twins; it was thrust into a water-pot, and cast away into the " bad bush ", there to suffer unmitigated torture from hunger, thirst, and, most terrible of all, merciless attacks of ants, until death brought release.

Some children who are unfortunate enough to cut the upper teeth first may escape being killed. The people of some towns pass on such children to Nri (Agukwu). There, the children are nourished until they are old enough to be of service. Boys are sold to outsiders who are told the histories of the youngsters. Many used to be bought by the people of Aro-Chuku for sacrifices; others were sold at Uburu for sacrifices at the water god " Akaja ". Prominent chiefs strove to make " big " sacrifices, and would buy five or more of these tainted children wherewith to make the requisite offerings when " making title ". Henceforth, such chiefs would be saluted " Ogbu-ise ", or " Ogbu-isa ", that is, the killer of five (or seven). Girls were treated similarly, but many were retained by the people of Nri for the sake of begetting children by them.

The aversion to children who cut their upper teeth first is based on the belief that such children will be dominated by a wicked disposition, and prove hateful to gods and men. The parents and elders consider that, if such children are allowed to live in their midst, they, themselves, will perish. Cutting the upper teeth first is acting contrary to the laws of nature.

Children dying *before* cutting their teeth are thrown away; they are not buried.

It is a source of wonder that the infants are not injured when lifted from the ground, for the whole weight of the body is borne by a single little arm, no support whatever is given to relieve the strain. The forearm is grasped by the adult, and the child is swung up into its place. One shudders at the thought that dislocation of the shoulder must be the inevitable result, yet no apparent harm follows, nor does the infant, as a rule, manifest any signs of discomfort, indeed, it seems to understand instinctively what is being done and hangs limply. The absence of struggling, no doubt, largely eliminates the danger of injury.

The value of massage and limb stretching is taken for granted by Ibo mothers. After bathing in warm water, the flesh of the baby is rubbed and squeezed, arms and legs are pulled out to their full length, and the joints exercised. Attention is then given to the head and, to a moderate extent, the skull is shaped, though there does not appear to be any standard of style ; it is haphazard, the conforming to habit, rather than purposeful. If the reason is to modify the shape, the measure of success is too insignificant to make a noticeable difference in feature. Water is poured into the baby's mouth and nostrils. Some mothers hold the baby upside down by the ankles and shake it, in order to distribute the water to all parts of the body ! Another fairly common custom is to toss the baby up and down after meals as a form of exercise. Some of the older ones find amusement by grasping small children by the ankles and swinging them round in circles ; this is done more with boys than with girls ; also boys are tossed, the idea being to expel fear and inculcate courage. One of the objects of half-choking the baby by pouring water into its nostrils is to prepare it for the first sensation when learning to swim. This, of course, applies to riverside villages only.

Before proceeding further, it may be of interest, and certainly informative, if I quote from records made by Sister Mary Elms who, during the course of her twenty-five years of service, had special facilities (and privileges) to observe the methods followed by Ibo mothers in the treatment of their newly born babies :

" The mother sits upon a low seat with her apparatus handy. This consists of a small pot containing liquid in which a certain herb has been stewed, and a bundle of fibre obtained from a native loofah. She places the baby upon its back in her lap, and applies the concoction internally and externally. For the internal application, the left hand is placed funnel-wise at the corner of the child's mouth, with the little finger pressing on the nostrils. It is thus forced to keep its mouth open in order to breathe. The liquid is then allowed to trickle through the curved hand into the mouth and, thence, down the throat, the poor baby, meanwhile, protesting as vigorously as its restricted opportunities will permit, and appearing to be in imminent danger of suffocation.

"The child having been allowed to swallow the dose, the loofah is now dipped into the liquid and strenuously applied to the body ; the bones of the skull are pressed together, and the spine and limbs are massaged in a more or less methodical manner.

"The ablutions completed, the mother blows into the eyes, nostrils, mouth and ears with a force one would think must produce paralysis of the brain. Finally, streaming wet, the babe is put down to rest, sometimes on a banana-leaf beside the fire, sometimes on a piece of cloth, and often on the bare floor with nothing but a rough pad beneath its head. This treatment, Spartan though it may be, is nevertheless beneficial, for the children thrive under it, and in cases where European and Ibo methods have been practised simultaneously on two infants, the greater success of the native system has been clearly demonstrated."

The Ibo mother is at a disadvantage when sickness overtakes her baby, even though it be but an ailment common to children, and which would readily yield to proper treatment. All too frequently, nothing whatever is done ; the mother, if not actually apathetic, simply resigns herself to the situation ; the baby pines and dies.

If advice is sought, an old woman, or a native doctor is consulted, who either directs the mother what measures to take or, more generally, prescribes a sacrifice, or concocts a medicine, very probably both. Some of the remedies advised are novel and, again, I quote from Sister Elms' report. The following was the treatment prescribed in the case of a wasting infant. "Seven ants cut in halves, mixed with proportions of red pepper, chalk, red ochre and palm oil ; this preparation to be well rubbed into the body, when the tiny insect infecting the skin will come out in the semblance of small white hairs. It must be stated as a simple fact, neither for nor against native medicines, that very beneficial results have followed this treatment. After a few applications, the child has visibly fattened, whether from the effect of the remedy, or of the massage, cannot be confidently asserted."

The claims of motherhood bring no respite from the daily round of duties whether they be at home, at the farm, or at the market. The great difference is that the woman is now handicapped by the care of her baby. A better-equipped mother carries her child on her back by means of a strip of cloth.

CHILDHOOD

This is the fashion where suitable cloth is available, and the woman has the money to purchase it. In the interior parts, especially on the eastern side of the Niger, until recently, such cloth was not forthcoming. When about to start on a journey, she takes a piece of cloth about a fathom in length and from thirty to thirty-six inches in width. This she holds in her left hand. She now bends well forward. With her right hand she grasps the baby, as previously described, and with a dextrous turn swings it across the lower part of her back; here it lies with arms and legs spreadeagled. The strip of cloth is cast over the child, enfolding it completely with the exception of the head. It is then pulled tightly round the woman's body and made secure by rolling the top edges downwards.

A mother carrying a child in this fashion has the unrestricted use of her hands; her movements are slowed down, but are not otherwise greatly impeded. She can, and does fulfil many and various duties with her child strapped upon her back. The feelings of the baby are not on record! It appears to be distinctly uncomfortable, if not actually in danger. There seems to be no serious cause for apprehension, however, for accidents very rarely happen. The little head bobs and sways when the mother walks, or flops this way and that according to the attitudes she assumes. The fact that the baby's nose is in close proximity to the sweaty back of the mother for long periods is not considered; hygiene is not yet a practised science among the Ibos.

The method above described is adopted for longer distances. About the compound, where there is not the same need, a simpler style of carrying the baby is followed. It is placed astride the hip, the infant assuming a semi-recumbent attitude, its body leaning back on the arm of the mother, or clinging to her body with one hand. In this position it is usually suckled. When a woman wishes to be entirely free, she places her child in the care of a boy or girl at home. Where possible, a boy is chosen for a baby-boy, and a girl for a baby-girl. Regularity of feeding is not a strong feature among Ibo mothers. Consequently, when a woman does leave the baby at home, she is apt to forget all about it for the time being. The nurse has no great difficulty at first: it is when hunger asserts itself that the trouble begins. When the baby cries, water is administered. Every time the baby opens its mouth to give vent to its feelings, the nurse promptly pours in water, this treatment being repeated, as occasion demands, until the mother returns and resumes her maternal duties.

Some of the nurses have a novel way of keeping their small

CHILDHOOD

charges in good humour. They squat on the ground, on the clay-floored verandah of a house for preference, with the baby lying alongside them. On inspection, small holes may be perceived in the floor. The nurses procure stems of grass about a foot long. These are from grass which bears a fluffy flowering head. When the fluff is stripped off, a rough surface is left. The grass stem, rough head downwards, is inserted into the hole in the floor as far as it will go, and then twirled round slowly. On withdrawing the stem, there are generally one or two lively ants clinging to it. These are pulled off and dropped into the baby's mouth, to be swallowed with sounds of gurgling satisfaction.

The feeding of infants raises no problems for the parents to solve. The only milk obtainable comes from the mothers. As soon as the children are capable of swallowing more solid food, they are given small pieces of boiled yam, bananas, and any other titbits that happen to be at hand. Mothers continue to suckle their children until they (the children) show no further inclination for it. This is tantamount to saying that there is no definite process of weaning. Actually, weaning takes place between the second and third year, and is practically voluntary on the part of the child. The only exception is when the mother again becomes pregnant: then she will discontinue the suckling. In this connection, the custom must not be overlooked which rules that it is repugnant for a woman to bear a child until an interval of about thirty months has elapsed after the birth of the previous one, if still alive.[7]

Many of the children that are well able to run about trot to their mothers as they sit about the house or compound, grab hold of a breast, suck vigorously for a few minutes, as they feel disposed, and then resume their play, the mothers, meanwhile, remaining totally unconcerned.

Great affection abounds, normally, between parents and their offspring. There are, admittedly, many things which are cruel and inhuman, but this is not because of lack of love. The cause for this paradoxical treatment lies in the ancient beliefs: they are compelled by their creed to act as they do. The tiny children are very attractive in appearance. When in sound health, their chubby faces pucker up with smiles and their large brown eyes are like forest pools. At this early stage, the characteristic features of the negro race are not very pronounced: taken altogether, they are charming little creatures. It is only dirt and neglect that spoil the picture. The Ibo is not alone in that!

Children are the pride of their parents: a man with a host

CHILDHOOD

about his compound is accounted wealthy and fortunate. The ties of affection between full brothers and sisters, and between children of one father but different mothers (the Ibos being polygamists), are very strong. Family law and tradition demand that help must be given to a brother or sister in distress, regardless of the origin of the trouble, whether domestic, financial, or otherwise. This can be carried to the extreme and become the incipient cause to give way to temptation, e.g. when a son or brother is induced to loan funds, because he is in a position where he can handle money of which he is only the custodian. A man thinks it a perfectly justifiable action to " borrow " money in order to assist one of his people in time of stress ; if he be not of that opinion, his relations will bring pressure to bear, and it is extremely difficult to resist family demands. It is the personal conscience competing against tribal law : a test of character which the European is not called upon to endure and, not knowing, cannot understand or sympathise when perhaps a hitherto trusted employee suddenly defaults. Under English law he is guilty of dishonesty : to the native, the man had no choice : he could not go against the will of the family, plainly spoken or, equally probably, unexpressed and, withal, the more suggestive, and the more fearful to contemplate.

One of the most pleasing characteristics of the Ibos is the bond of affection between mother and son. This bond may be strained, but it is never severed. The son, on occasions, may be unkind to his mother, possibly neglectful, but such conduct would always bring condemnation upon him : it would be utterly contrary to Ibo tradition. Seldom, indeed, does a son treat his mother with anything other than honour and respect. In his affections, she holds the premier place, and to her he turns as being the most trustworthy receiver of his confidence. His first thought in times of danger is for his mother : she ranks before wife and children, because she alone is irreplaceable.[8]

When the child is no longer dependent on its mother for sustenance, it soon finds its place among the other children of the village. The older folk worry little about them so long as they are not too mischievous. In between the hours of play, the little tots perform the lighter household tasks and, at a very early age, obtain an insight into domestic affairs. In the home-life there is little discipline, that is as the European understands the term : the Ibo has a different idea on the subject ! The Rev. Samuel Crowther noticed this in 1859 when he wrote : " The Ibos seldom punish their children ; hence they have

CHILDHOOD

their own way, and are very self-willed." [9] Self-expression has a fairly free field ! The children meet with little restraint and, as a rule, one has to be exceptionally aggravating, not merely naughty, before chastisement is administered. The only thing inculcated is traditional native law and custom, which includes respect for their elders. This is not taught in class, or by rote : it is absorbed by contact with their fellows. Other than obedience to the laws of the village, there is little check upon their activities. The introduction of schools in recent years has brought another element into the lives of some children. Pupils are being taught, under the new conditions, to bring their natural impulses under control : character training being one of the essential subjects of the Nigerian (Government) school curriculum.

Soon after the infant stage is passed, boys and girls cease to play together. The sexes have their own companies (*vide* p. 194) with their respective recreations and occupations. On the whole, the boys enjoy more liberty, because they are, for the most part, free from domestic tasks. The girls start their apprenticeship to household work at about the age of four. They do not rebel at this : indeed, they fall into line almost as if impelled by instinct ; they seem to realise from the first that the main business of a woman's life is to minister to her male folk.

The children's playgrounds are the compounds and the streets (ilos) and these serve the purpose very well. In most villages, the " ilos " are long stretches of sand, scoured clean during the rainy season, dirty in the dry. The scouring and the passage of many feet produce a deposit of sand several inches in depth. The sand is soft ; it is wiser not to raise the question of its sanitariness. Suffice to say, that the children enjoy the benefit of it, free from the dangers of vehicular traffic, and protected from the sun by the shade of surrounding trees. Until the advent of the European, the children ran about untrammelled with coverings. The new conditions have instilled a complex of self-consciousness which did not exist in former times, and the naïve simplicity has been displaced. The use of coverings for these little children may be another sign of progress, with a capital " P ", but——

NOTES TO CHAPTER XII

[1] The reader should be warned against attaching too much reliance on these figures. In one issue of *West Africa* (Jan. 9, 1937) a doctor of forty years' experience is reported to have said that " the teaching of simple hygiene had reduced infant mortality in one area from sixty to ten per

cent ". A few pages earlier, a striking account of a lecture by Dr. R. R. Kuczynski, a famous statistician, challenges effectively the published figures. At the present stage, statistics are not trustworthy: they cannot be yet. Among other items, he affirms that " with an infant mortality of fifty per cent, a population was bound to die out in a few decades ". With such imperfect data, it is manifestly unwise to make definite statements; it is prudent to go no further than agree that infant mortality stands at a high figure.

[2] For further information concerning children that are tabu see under Capital Crime, Chap. XVIII.
[3] H. Lyndhurst Duke, " *Cornhill Magazine* ", June 1920, p. 710.
[4] " *Savage Childhood* ", p. 45 ; " *Fetish Folk of West Africa* ", p. 32.
[5] " *History of the Yorubas* ", p. 80.
[6] " *Savage Childhood* ", p. 45.
[7] In Ibo three years of twelve lunar months each.
[8] " A man loves his brothers and his friends at least as much as he loves his wife ; his children he loves far more and his mother he loves most of all. Indeed, his love for his mother is the deepest emotion of his heart and his best moral quality."—" *Fetish Folk of West Africa* ", p. 132.
[9] *Niger Expedition* ", p. 431.

CHAPTER XIII

YOUTH TO OLD AGE — BOYS & MEN

PARENTAGE MEANS much to a man or woman in the Ibo country. Society is democratic, and the poor man has equal rights with the rich although, as in other countries, he may find it difficult to maintain them when contending with his wealthier fellow-man. While it is true to say that Society is based on democratic principles, it must be noted that there is a clearly cut division between " free " and " slave " born. Under the British Constitution this distinction is not acknowledged ; slavery is not countenanced in any form, but the accident of being of slave descent is still a powerful element in the lives of the people. The following remarks are concerned with men who enjoy the rights and privileges conferred by virtue of free-birth. This freedom is the open door to all opportunities in life. Because of it, a youth enjoys the full benefits of tribal law and custom. In normal daily life, free and slave born mingle together unconcernedly, and little difference is observable on the surface ; in actual fact, the superiority of freedom is constant and always effective in operation.

Environment also plays its part. Different towns favour different professions with correspondingly different standards of living. The great majority of men are engaged in agriculture (so called) : a lesser number are traders, while those dwelling near the large rivers are fishermen, as well as agriculturists. Craftsmen are comparatively few and those chiefly blacksmiths. Hence, birthplace is associated with birthright. This may be illustrated by the following : The men of Nkwerre are practically all traders and, incidentally, money-lenders. Awka men are blacksmiths almost to a man. Those of Nri exercise priestly functions, especially in connection with the initiation of chiefs and those taking up titles ; also they officiate in the purification sacrifices for the removal of pollution from persons, houses and land. Other men are famed for their skill as cicatrisers, and some travel considerable distances in order to fulfil commissions. They cut the " ichi " or tribal marks on the faces of boys in towns where this is customary, and scarify the

FULL DRESS.

Above: HAPPY IN THE POSSESSION OF A FULL SET OF "NJA"—BRASS SPIRAL LEG RINGS. HAIR DRESSED FOR "NKPU" CELEBRATIONS. (PAGES 206-223.)
Below: BLACKSMITH FIXING "NJA" ON THE LEG OF A GIRL.

bodies of women. This art seems to be chiefly confined to men on the eastern side of the Niger, whereas, on the western, women are also experts.[1]

Before the introduction of foreign ideas and practices, it was the custom for a lad to follow in the footsteps of his father. Under the old conditions, apprenticeship began at an early age. As a child, he accompanied his father to the farm, or on trading expeditions, and rendered such assistance as his strength and knowledge permitted. On attaining to young manhood, it was instilled into him, not so much by word as by force of circumstances, that he must earn money if he had any aspiration towards a worthy position in life ; without money for fees he could make no advance. In certain areas, a man was not allowed to wear as much as a loincloth until he had been initiated into the first degree of titular rank and, in some places, title-taking is a costly business. The son of a wealthy father had better prospects. For his own dignity's sake, as much as for the benefit of his son, such a father might subscribe the money wherewith to pay the expenses connected with the initiation into one or more of the lower orders. In the majority of cases, the young man has no alternative other than to depend upon his own ability and exertions.

It goes without saying, that some professions are more lucrative than others and, where this is so, the problem of raising degree fees is not too difficult. For those practising fishing or agriculture, the saving of money is a harder task. At the same time, where these occupations are paramount, the expenses attached to the titular rank are relatively lower.

During the earlier stages of life, work, as a rule, does not press too heavily upon a lad ; he has fairly abundant opportunities for leisure and recreation. There are periods when work ceases entirely, and the youth is free from all demands. Provided he enjoys sound health, life is one long holiday. He will, however, find it difficult to avoid certain diseases in addition to the common ailments to which children are prone. Yaws (Framboesia) and " craw-craw " (Pustular Dermatitis) cause acute suffering. Yaws, and its allied diseases, produce nauseating eruptions, repulsive to the sight and painful to endure. The old folk believe there is no escape from these loathsome complaints, and that it is better to endure them in childhood. They allege that, if the affliction is delayed till later in life, the suffering is intensified. Some parents innoculate their children in order that they may be through with the disease while they are still young. Others believe that the eruptions are a preventive against other ailments, and assert that the freedom from yaws means, at a subsequent stage, trouble with the legs and feet.[2]

Boys, while still quite young, as well as youths, mingle quite freely with the old men : to all outward appearance there scarcely seems to be any consciousness of age in general affairs. At the same time, there are regular age-grades or, as they are called, " Otu " or " Ogbo. The " Otu " comprises men (or women) who are of about the same age. In modern terms, the " Ogbo " is referred to as " age-grade ". Each grade is a distinct entity, and the members of it discuss questions and act in conformity together. The " Otus " and " Ogbos " have a recognised status in the social and political economy. The influence of an " Ogbo " is determined by its seniority, whence the usefulness of the interpretation " age-grade ".

The friendships made in boyhood's days remain unbroken throughout life, and form a fine feature in Ibo relationships. Friendship, thus formed, continues unimpaired after marriage, for the wife does not supplant the friend of many years' standing. As regards the women-folk, the only one the Ibo man clings to fervently is his mother. The ways of women are different from those of men and they are not allowed, nor expected, to share overmuch in the affairs of men. The lives of the sexes run alongside one another, touching and crossing each other at irregular intervals. Under modern conditions, this detachment is passing out of fashion ; wives are becoming fitting companions for their husbands, especially where education has been on more or less parallel lines.

Seldom can a lad complain of being overworked ; indeed, he is more often at play than at work. This is certainly the case up to the age of twelve or fifteen. After that, he is strong enough to take his fair share in the field and other work ; also he has become moderately expert in the use of tools and implements. Simultaneously, he is gaining experience of the world and, almost as soon as he becomes man-conscious, he takes his place and part in the affairs of the village.

It is sometimes asserted that the native works only when some form of pressure is brought to bear on him, for example, he must labour to produce a food supply for himself and his dependents.[3]

This is only partially true. Work depends upon the seasons. There is a time for planting and a time for ingathering. The agriculturist is compelled to remain idle during the dry season. It would then be sheer waste of time and effort to attempt fieldwork. To some extent, the fishermen has to confine his main labours to the season ; he cannot do much during the heavy

YOUTH TO OLD AGE—BOYS & MEN

floods. Those who are craftsmen work all the year round though, at places like Awka, the blacksmiths return home for the dry season and give themselves over to pleasure and enjoyment.

Formerly, the great majority of the men were content to look upon the dry season solely as a period of rest. For some four months practically no work was done. Towards the end of the season, supplies of ripe grass must be collected wherewith to repair the roofs. This is done just prior to the bush fires which rage sporadically over the country at this time of the year. After the fires, the countryside presents a blackened, desolate appearance for a time, otherwise no great harm seems to result. During the dry season, life is a holiday: the old men meander around, gossip and, at intervals, play at their favourite game " Okwe ". The young men amuse themselves as inclination prompts them. Sacrificial and other feasts, accompanied by the consumption of copious supplies of palm wine, provide interludes in what, to the European, seems rather a monotonous existence.

There were not many thrills and, under old conditions, when time began to drag, the young men became restive and sought relief from the monotony. One common form of supplying an outlet for superfluous energy was to initiate a small war. This not only provided physical relief; it also opened up possibilities of profit and, maybe, one or more captives, a welcome event in the areas addicted to cannibalism. It was simple enough to start a miniature war of this kind; a pretext for a quarrel with a neighbouring village was all that was necessary. Once the game was started, the remainder of the dry season was given up to raiding and skirmishing, each side generally concluding with equal success. No very serious results ensued: excitement formed the chief inducement for the sport. It was *not* inter-tribal warfare. There was neither much slaughter, nor any great destruction of property. These village contests bore no resemblance to the devastating raids of the Abams. (*Vide* Chap. XXIX.)

The first rain storms brought an end to fighting for that year. Both sides automatically closed down in order to be free for the more important business, namely the production of food. Hoes and matchets were substituted for weapons. Food they must have; fighting of the nature described was little more than a pastime.

At the other end of the year, that is towards the close of the wet season, clay-puddling constitutes the " extra " work for those who plan to erect houses. By making use of the latter rains, the carrying of water to the pits is obviated. This may be a troublesome business if the puddling be postponed to a later date, and there are parts of the country where it is practically impossible, except in the wet season, owing to the non-existence of rivers or springs of water. Clay puddling or, as it is more commonly termed " mud-treading ", is confined to the men : women do not engage in it.

A boy lives in his mother's hut until he is old enough to build quarters for himself. Then he builds a small hut where he sleeps, stores his treasures, and receives his friends. When he is ready to marry, the general procedure is to inaugurate a new compound. Once that is established, beyond occasional repairs and the annual fieldwork, he has little cause to exert himself. When he does additional work, it is mainly in order to raise initiation fees for a title. To enhance his social status, he endeavours to add to the number of his wives, and to advance to higher grades of titular honours. He cannot do either, without finding ways to make money : for these purposes he must work.

On reaching manhood's estate, every free-born youth automatically enters upon the privileges and duties of citizenship, and bears his share in all that appertains to the well-being of the village. He is called upon to contribute to the public festivals and sacrificial obligations, and to pay his quota towards any expenses incurred by the town. As required, he must render personal service in war and peace ; also he must give support to the head of his house, and to the king or paramount chief where there is one. The demand may be for money to assist the chief in his desire to take up a higher title, or a contribution towards the expenses of building a more dignified dwelling, or to give his services in fieldwork. Custom rules that every fourth day should be at the disposal of the head of the family or clan.

Men who are traders, or who practise a specific craft, spend several months of each year in the districts where they find it profitable to operate. They return home, some for three or four months, others for a shorter period. Of late years, it has become a custom to spend the Christmas and New Year season at their homes. The holiday is devoted very largely to feasting and entertaining. Palm wine and, nowadays, foreign liquors are much more in evidence than at other seasons of the year.

The old folk continue to favour the product of the country, the superior young men like to flaunt their supplies of bottled beer and spirits. The men have extraordinary capacities, and

YOUTH TO OLD AGE—BOYS & MEN

seem able to drink unthinkable quantities and yet, in the Ibo country, drunkenness is seldom a public spectacle. One of the most noticeable features is the serious manner in which drinking is conducted, particularly in the early stages. The arrangements appear to be governed by a determined purpose to drain all the vessels at a steady rate of round upon round until all the liquor is consumed. The men squat about with the pots and demijohns in the centre. There is little conversation : no more than an occasional remark or passing joke, nor are there any signs of revelry at this earlier stage : all are intent on the one purpose of drinking. No man willingly leaves the party until the wine-pots are empty : it is considered bad form, or folly, to forfeit one's chance to share the drink. One of the younger men has charge of the supply, and he fills and refills the horn or calabash of each man in order of seniority.[4] It can scarcely be termed " drinking ". There is no tasting, no smacking of the lips in appreciation of the flavour ; the liquor flows in an unbroken stream as easily as water down a drain-pipe. This is the practice with freshly drawn palm wine. As fermentation increases (by the simple process of allowing the wine to stand), it becomes too much like vinegar to be palatable. Though it is seldom declined, it is not popular as a drink, and only moderate quantities of strongly fermented wine are consumed. It must be repeated that, in spite of what is stated here, the Ibos, on the whole, can genuinely be described as sober people. (*Vide* p. 125.)

In some places, when the chief starts to drink, the other folk assembled must clap their hands and continue to do so until he puts down his calabash. This custom is observed only when drinking palm wine—not for any other liquid—and is done as a mark of respect. Probably this is a relic of the days when the chief was regarded as a semi-divine being ; certainly the palm-wine libation made by pouring out a little on to the ground before starting to drink has a sacramental significance.[5]

Mirrors not being in common use, personal appearance does not cause the Ibo much concern. What he lacks in that respect, he endeavours to rectify by the use of all the finery he can muster. The men are much more vain and conceited than the women, chiefly, no doubt, because the women, under old conditions, had few opportunities to express themselves. For young men, especially the dancers and athletes, the fashion is to wear circlets of ivory just below the knees and on the biceps. Rich old men burden their arms with a number of loosely fitting ivory bracelets, whereas those used by young men fit tightly. Prominent men on the western side of the Niger wear six-inch sections of huge elephant tusks as anklets similar to those worn by the aristocratic women of Onitsha. On the eastern side, rich men show a preference for anklets of chased copper, necklaces of elephants' " eye-brows " (" akia ")—really whiskers or tail hairs—and " aggry " beads threaded on a cord are greatly esteemed. These beads are called " aka " and are said to be cut from stone found more particularly in the neighbourhood of *Uzai*, situated between Ifon and Ọwọ, north of Benin City.[6]

The displays of ornaments and apparel (so called for convenience) at public functions and festivals provide a picturesque and often amusing spectacle. The question of suitability is not considered ; to attract attention is the great objective. Once again, be it noted that the Ibos are not different in their natural passions from other races, including the civilised, for these likewise are not free from eccentricities, and are every wit as much slaves to fashion as the unsophisticated folk of Africa. So much depends on the whim of the season and the opportunities to conform to it.

It is difficult to decide under which department of life dentistry should be included ! Here we will confine the subject to mutilation. It was a very common practice to remove, chip or file the front teeth ; some of it was merely customary, some the outcome of vanity, some, perhaps, of more sinister significance. The removal of the two top front teeth was the fashion mostly favoured. It did not make for beauty, though tastes differ in that respect. One is inclined to think that it affected not only the appearance, but also it may have had some influence on pronunciation.

The people of Onitsha and the Asaba Hinterland make full use of the letter " f " ; the Ibos to the south-east substitute " h " for it. It needs no great stretch of imagination to presume that people who had lost their top front teeth would have considerable difficulty in articulating " f " and, consequently, it changed to " h " with a nasal intonation.

Many, while retaining their full set of teeth, had them chipped or filed. The former consisted of drilling between the teeth of the upper jaw, thus widening the interstices into roundish holes. The top row of teeth was thus loopholed. This atrocity was, apparently, favoured solely for its pleasing appearance ! Finally, there were others whose front teeth, top and bottom, were filed to points resembling those of a saw. It has been suggested that such filing was an indication of cannibalistic tendencies. It might have been ; personally, I attach little importance to the theory as far as the Ibos are concerned. They maintain that all they ever had in mind was personal beauty!

I have not been able to trace a connection between this custom of teeth mutilation and the practice of Totemism—with the Ibo it is purely a question of vanity. On the Zambesi, the teeth are filed with a view, it is said, " to make the person like the totem of the clan in appearance. It would be natural for clans whose totem is the crocodile to file the front teeth." [7]

Nature is lavish in her gifts in the Ibo country, and the Ibo man living his primitive life had little cause to extend himself; his needs were fairly easily supplied. They could be summed up in a dwelling-place, a few tools and his agricultural implements. The heat of the tropics eliminates actual necessity of body coverings though, in the wet season, and at night, it is cold enough to make a blanket desirable. When he wore a garment at all, it was for adornment rather than because of utility. It mattered not of what character it was either in texture, shape, colour or material. The only essential was that it should somehow hang on his limbs. His household effects consisted of a few fowls, a pariah dog for scavenging purposes, and some goats, if possible. In some districts, a rather better type of mongrel was kept and trained for hunting. The most coveted of all his possessions was a gun, and no Ibo would be content without one. Wives, and particularly children, he also desired, for these established his social position, and they largely fulfilled his idea of wealth. Money had its value for him and consisted of cowrie shells, brass rods and, in the southern districts, manillas.[8] His personal and household treasures were varied, and often nondescript in character, consisting, in some cases, of lengths of iron chain, stoneware demijohns (generally foul) and ancient iron cannons, these last being in great demand when fulfilling ceremonies connected with " Second Burial " ! (*Vide* p. 290.) Here and there were some good specimens of toby-jugs,[9] lustre ware, willow pattern and other plates and dishes : also bottles cast in the form of monkeys, some of glass, and others made of a species of white ware. These glass and ware goods were highly esteemed, because they were not common articles to be found in the markets ; very many of them came to grief during the journey up-country from Bonny and Calabar. Many of those that still exist are imperfect owing to the custom that, when the owner died, fragments were broken off in sympathy with the life which had been severed by death.

Customs and manners are undergoing rapid changes and not always for the better. Before the impact of Western influence, old people were held in the highest respect by the young, and their word was law. They were able to maintain their rights, because they were able to enforce obedience, should there be any inclination on the part of the young to fail in complying with the due acknowledgement of their superiority. Yet, this did not mean much, for some fathers, as everywhere, failed to restrain their sons in their behaviour; in fact, discipline, *per se*, was not an outstanding characteristic. Sons were rarely corrected, other than by word of mouth, after they had reached the adult stage, and not much prior to that, even when a sound thrashing was more in accordance with their deserts. This lack of discipline had its roots in a sense of fear of after effects. To offend a son, especially the eldest, created a dread lest he should neglect to fulfil the last rites at the old man's death. The thought that a man would not be given a fitting farewell as he passed into the underworld was sufficiently powerful to restrain him from incurring the displeasure of his son : he was reluctant to do anything likely to hurt his feelings. To ensure his own salvation was more important than correcting his son's misdeeds.[10]

Occasionally a father will take strong measures. He will swear on " Ọfọ " to the effect that his son is wilful, disobedient and obstinate, and will disown him as an unworthy and contemptuous encumbrance.

In another place (p. 180), reference has been made to the high rate of mortality among infants. As children grow to adolescence, this tendency is naturally checked. At the same time, there does seem to be an abnormally heavy death-rate among the young people. They succumb chiefly to what they commonly call " iba ". The usual translation of this term by the people is " yellow fever ", but it should really be " pneumonia ". Natives living in the tropics are susceptible to chest complaints, especially during the rainy season when sudden chills are easily contracted. Those who do survive these early dangers are of a sturdy type, and many of the Ibo men and women pass to good old age. One frequently met men reputed to be of ninety years of age and upwards.

At public festivals, the old men always put in an appearance. For the time being, they strive to forget their years. It is one of their prerogatives to start the dancing, and they exert themselves to their utmost power in order to make a brave show. With uncertain steps they pirouette before the assembled crowds. It would be rather ridiculous, but for the seriousness under which they labour. Flourishing their staves and waving their arms, they make valiant attempts to appear young again,

YOUTH TO OLD AGE—BOYS & MEN

and to demonstrate their prowess; they seek to impress upon the public that they are still to be reckoned with as lively members of the community. What they cannot manage physically, they endeavour to cover by assuming fierce expressions. It would be exhilarating if the tendency to laugh could be restrained. Altogether, the performance on these occasions is rather pathetic.

Then comes the end. The time arrives when the old man finds he can no longer play even this part: life largely ceases to interest him. He eats and sleeps, and does little else. Whatever his life has been; whatever part he has played in peace or war, or in the chase, he gradually sinks into oblivion. Until almost the end, he relates the stories of the past and his share in them. Of the old men there is not found one who has not witnessed strange scenes, including bloodshed in many forms; they themselves have, doubtless, shared in many deeds of violence. The old man's dying wish is to be favoured with a worthy burial in order that he may share the benefits awarded to his ancestors. He must enter the spirit world in a manner whereby no shame shall overtake him when he joins his former boon companions. He covets in death similar honours to those he enjoyed in his lifetime. The more lavish the burial rites observed on his behalf, the more confident is he of a fitting reception into the underworld of spirits.

NOTES TO CHAPTER XIII

[1] " The scarifier is an important person, though he has not the exclusive right to operate upon everyone. The office is practically hereditary (as among the Ibos) for no man would teach the secrets of his art to any but his own son or nephew."—" *Tailed Headhunters of Nigeria* ", p. 112.

[2] Happily a remedy for the foul sores has been discovered and literally, thousands flock to the doctors in order to receive injections to cure yaws and allied diseases. Perhaps, it is not unreasonable to hope that they may be stamped out completely in the course of a few years.

[3] It has been said, and there is truth in the statement, that " the African is idle not so much because he hates work, but rather because he is unambitious and the victim of a habit of content. He will not work like the white man because, unlike the white man, he can be supremely content in idleness. But offer him something that he really desires or deems worth while, and he will work amazingly."—" *Fetish Folk of West Africa* ", p. 126.

This might well have been written of the Ibo man. However, of recent years, he has awakened to the fact that there are many things he desires and deems worth while, both material benefits (or luxuries) and education, good houses and other amenities.

[4] At Onitsha the one drinking vessel passes round the assembly. In the interior each man carries his own calabash. He never trusts it in the hands of another, ever having in mind the fear of poison.

[5] " A chief will commonly ring a bell at each draught of beer which he

YOUTH TO OLD AGE—BOYS & MEN

swallows and at the same moment a lad stationed in front of him brandishes a spear to keep at bay the spirits which might try to sneak into the old chief's body by the same road as the beer."—" *Golden Bough* ", p. 199.

⁶ Aggry (or Aggri) beads. " A cylindrical, light-coloured bead, exactly the same as some of those exhibited in the British Museum, taken from Egyptian Sarcophagi. These are much appreciated. The Kru people say these are very old, and that their ancestors found them growing a long way off in the bush, but there can be little doubt they were obtained when their possessors inhabited the mountain district to the North and trafficked with other tribes who had commercial dealings with the Egyptians."—" *Expedition to the Niger, 1841* ", Vol. I, p. 121.

⁷ " *Savage Childhood* ", p. 91.

⁸ *Vide* p. 338 for note on manillas.

⁹ These toby-jugs, and other pieces of old pottery, are of different manufacture. Some are of Staffordshire ware, others Rockingham and, again, others are of French make, decorated with " fleur-de-lis ". Of a pair of the last, one was found on the border of the Ibo-Benin district; its fellow was collected from a town many miles up the Benue River, some three hundred miles distant one from the other.

¹⁰ " The animistic notions of the soul, being easily wounded, forbid all attempts to exercise an educative influence on the child . . . sons are expected to offer worship to their parents after death. In the Indian Archipelago parents are honoured only after their death, because then their souls are dangerous."—" *Living Forces of the Gospel* ", p. 123.

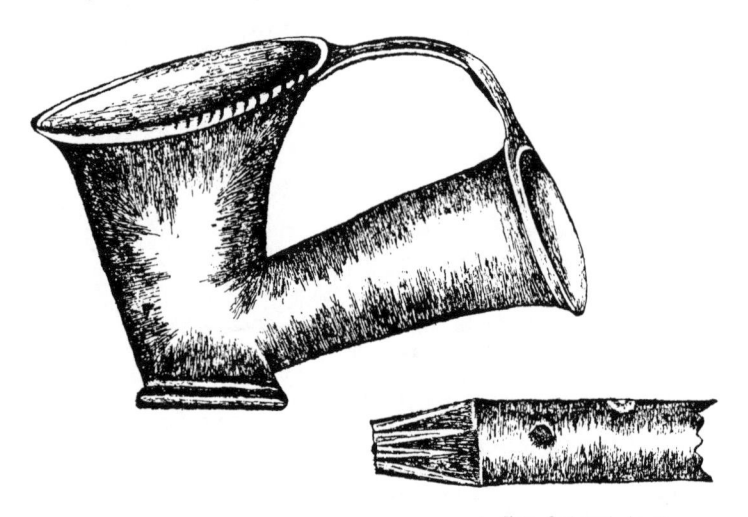

L— Stem 5–6 feet in length.

BRASS TOBACCO PIPE, USED MORE PARTICULARLY IN WESTERN IBOLAND.

Clay pipes of similar shape are more common. The stem is from five to six feet in length. The wood used has a soft core, which is fairly easily extracted, thus making a tube. The base of the pipe stands on the floor and the pipe passes round the circle, each man, in turn, taking one long draw and emitting a colossal " puff " of smoke. Shredded leaf tobacco is inserted in the bowl and a piece of red-hot charcoal placed upon the top.

CHAPTER XIV

YOUTH TO OLD AGE — GIRLS & WOMEN

WHEN WRITING ABOUT the women of the country, it must be emphasised that what follows describes their lives as they were under the old conditions. The changes that have appeared during the present century are more striking among the women than among the men. There is much more freedom than there used to be, and the women are moving with the times. The lot of a slave-born girl is becoming easier, though she has not yet the full privileges of the daughter of free-born parents. Freedom of birth still figures strongly in the Ibo social world. This is manifested most of all in marriage customs, because a free-born youth will not consent to engage a girl of slave descent. Accident of birth may place a girl at a great disadvantage. But under whatever conditions they were born, bond or free, the women in past generations had to bear more than their fair share of the burdens of life. They accepted the situation philosophically : it had always been so, and why should they raise objections ? Rather, they took it all for granted, and, on the whole, contrived to be satisfied.

From the age of four or five years, girls begin to share in domestic duties. They learn their tasks naturally, assimilating them almost as unconsciously as they eat and sleep. While still mere infants, they are given the care of the younger children. They also begin to balance articles on their heads. Equipped with a tiny water-pot, they accompany the older girls to the stream to bring home the daily water supply. They help, too, in other ways, sweeping the huts and compounds, rubbing the walls and floors, collecting firewood and cooking. The Ibo girl is quite an adept at household chores at a very early age.

The water supply takes precedence of all other tasks in an Ibo household ; it is the first thing to be done and, at break of dawn, strings of girls and women wend their way to the stream or spring. The supply, as already stated (p. 149), may be near or distant : in the latter case, two hours or more may be absorbed in fetching a pot of water. When this is so, there is naturally a tendency to use water sparingly and the huts do not, in consequence, receive so much attention : they are rubbed less often, and not so thoroughly. There is no such hindrance to sweeping : brushes and besom brooms can be purchased cheaply, or made from locally grown materials. When the house and compound have been tidied, young girls are at liberty for practically the remainder of the day. The older girls and the women, having completed their domestic duties, pack their baskets and set forth for the market. There is a market somewhere within reach every day of the week, and no woman willingly forfeits her chance of visiting it. It is the one place of entertainment for the women. Apart from buying and selling, it is the centre of all the news and gossip. (*Vide* Chap. XXV.) Girls soon want to accompany their mothers on the daily expeditions, and, as soon as they are old enough, they begin operations on their own account. It is the men's business to provide the staple food of the family, that is, yam. The women are expected to find the other necessaries, such as smoked fish, palm oil, peppers, ocru and other commodities. Some of these they garner from the gardens : the rest they purchase at the markets.

Prior to the opening up of the country, women manifested very little interest in personal apparel ; there was little inducement for them to do so. There was no such thing as a manufactured garment in the country-side, and not one had knowledge of sewing, or had even seen a needle. Strips of homewoven cotton were all that were available and, in some parts, these were scarce. Nowadays, it is easy to purchase (foreign) material and, where there are traders, and in practically every village market, ready-made garments are now exposed for sale. At the time of writing, the cost of sewing the material to make a dress is sixpence in the bigger markets (Onitsha), and as low as one penny in smaller places, e.g. Ogwashi-Uku.

The chief reason why women went naked, or with no more than a scanty cloth, was because the men had a rooted objection against their women-folk being covered, and legislated against their wearing cloth. It was contended that this prohibition acted as a deterrent to misbehaviour : nature has its own way of betraying acts of indiscretion, and it was held that misdemeanours could be quickly detected so long as the women remained uncovered. In certain districts the women, young and old, rich and poor, married and single, passed their whole lives in a state of nudity. Even to-day, though they wear a shred of material as a loincloth when abroad, they shed it on entering the home compound, and especially at evening time. It is forbidden for them to cook for their husbands girded with cloth. Where the elements of civilisation have penetrated, the injunctions of the old men against the use of cloth by women have been thrust aside : the girls defy the old men and their impositions, and now do as they please as regards dress.

This law of prohibition did not apply on the western side of the Niger. The custom in that vicinity is to wear a loincloth and a larger loose cloth swathed round the body. Most of the women use a fair-sized cloth which they wrap round them, covering the whole person from the chest to below the knees. White cloth is invariably used on this side of the river. It is rather coarse in texture, strong and durable, woven from cotton grown in the farms. It is usually ornamented with a pattern approximating to drawn thread-work.

At the first sign of menstruation, a girl places a slender cotton cord round her waist. This suffices until she is reckoned to be a full-grown woman—say sixteen years of age. When that time arrives, she discards the cord, and substitutes a girdle of stronger material, the most common being a circlet of coiled brass wire known as " ọna idide " (brass worm). This, in its turn, gives place to a string of black round beads, or flat discs, of a particular pattern and termed " nkpulu-ife ". This must not be removed while a woman's husband is alive, except during purification ceremonies, and to do it then is considered a matter of doubtful propriety.

The " state of nudity " is not so dreadful as it sounds, for " the dark skin . . . seems to prevent any impression of nakedness. No one who has seen a white man bathing alongside a black man can for a moment help feeling that the natural colour of the skin is dark, and that the white man has a bleached skin which must therefore be covered up in sheer decency." [1] Moreover, times have changed and, except in remote back areas, this state of nudity is a thing of the past. Fashions have been completely revolutionised under modern conditions.

The disregard formerly shown in respect of clothing did not include a complete indifference towards all forms of personal adornment. Women and girls always showed a fondness for trinkets, though some of these are more appropriately described as afflictions, for the wearing of them was not only burdensome ; it was also painful. Fashions varied ; ear and hair ornaments were (and are) very popular, while others were peculiar to certain districts. In one part, huge plate-like brass anklets found most favour. These were forged out of solid brass bars by the Awka blacksmiths. They not only manufactured them : they attached them to the owner's legs, and a smith was usually needed to remove them. Once in position, the proud, but deluded, wearer could no longer walk, stand or lie in a natural position. In size, they varied from seven to fourteen inches in diameter. When walking, one leg had to be swung widely outwards in a semicircle, partly in order to swing the weight ; more particularly, to prevent tripping over the anklet on the other foot. To watch a number of women wearing these " ogba ", as they moved along in procession, was an entertainment. The brass was highly burnished, and flashed brightly as it caught the rays of the sun. Young girls were fitted with the smaller-sized samples. When they were fully grown, these small anklets were removed and the large ones substituted. When lying on a bed, a woman had to lie with her feet extended beyond the end in order that the anklet could hang over the edge, otherwise her feet would be raised to an uncomfortable position. These " ogba " were grotesque, also very cumbrous, being of several pounds weight, yet the rapidity with which the women walked was extraordinary : more wonderful was it to see them run. Equally astonishing was the manner in which they avoided striking one anklet against the other.

Spiral rings made of quarter-inch brass wire are the fashion for leg wear over a wide area. They are still in great favour, while the large anklets (ogba) have disappeared from the scene. The rings are built up from what are colloquially known as " brass rods ", which were, at one time, used freely as currency. The rings are graduated in size. The bottom one fits fairly close to the ankle. Above that, each ring is slightly larger than the one beneath it until, by the time the top one is reached, it is about seven inches across. Blacksmiths weld the rods together, each rod being about two feet long. They then bend the whole length into a long coil of loops of a uniform diameter of about six inches. This size allows sufficient play for the rings to be slipped comfortably over the foot. The girl, when being fitted, squats on the ground facing the smith. He adjusts the ankle ring first and builds upwards from that. He uses his bare fingers for shaping them, except when manipulating the welded joints. For these, he makes use of a stout pair of pliers. Care is necessary in bending the welded parts, otherwise they will break asunder, hence the judicious use of pliers.

A complete set of spirals, locally known as " nja ", contains many feet of solid wire, and is a heavy encumbrance. The number of rings worn by a girl depends on her size. Up to a certain age, they must not extend above the knee ; for bigger girls, the rings are continued several inches higher, almost to the top of the thigh. Unlike the " ogba " which remained on the ankles year in and year out, the " nja " is never worn after marriage. Again, they are only worn at certain seasons, and then but for a limited period during the dry (and festive) season. The spirals are daily scoured with water, sand and leaves until they are polished to a brightness that would satisfy the strictest old-time admiral.

At Onitsha, and on the western side of the Niger, ivory is preferred to brass or copper, both by men and woman. Ivory is costly, and the anklets and bracelets made of this material are highly prized. Many are very old, having come to their present owners as heirlooms. They are worn by few woman and are associated with the aristocracy. The anklets ("odu") are formed of sections of the largest elephant tusks. They vary in depth ; the usual size being about six inches, and from two to three inches in thickness. Some of the bracelets are large and clumsy and hang loosely on the arms ; they correspond to what are commonly termed bangles.

Fixing the anklets is a protracted and painful business. It demands patient massage of the foot with oil and much pressure, and the foot has to bear all the strain. Once they are fixed they remain, in normal circumstances, undisturbed until death overtakes the owner. Many were not removed at death ; they were carried into the grave. They may be removed for either of the following reasons : One, if a woman behaves in such a manner that she incurs her husband's just displeasure, he will deprive his wife of her ivories in order to disgrace and degrade her. The second reason is when there is a long and serious illness. Then they may be taken off in order to afford relief to the patient. It may be noted that, during a period of mourning, some women cover their ivories with black cloth or leaves as an emblem of grief.[2]

Girls at Awka, at the time they are passing through the " Nkpu " ceremonies preliminary to marriage, borrow ivory bracelets as a part of their " make-up ". They are granted the loan of these for the occasion, and no longer. The bracelets are not lifelong treasures as are the " odu ". A woman who is entitled to wear a pair of ivory anklets may be poor, but she would never dishonour herself by selling them ; they are regarded as beyond price, and money, even where greatly needed, will not tempt the genuine aristocrat. The anklets are of great weight, and pride demands a heavy price from the wearers. In order to prevent sores caused by chafing, the women bandage their ankles with rags. This also applies to the brass anklets (ogba) and spirals (" nja "). Without these precautionary measures the flesh would be lacerated to the bone.

It goes without saying, that the above are not the only articles of adornment. Necklaces are worn by a great number of women, especially those made of hairs abstracted from the tails of elephants. (*Vide* p. 198.) Hand-wrought iron hairpins are prized by women wherever they are purchasable ; notably in neighbourhoods where the male members of the community are chiefly engaged in smith's work.

As a rule, an Ibo woman is not blessed with an abundance of this world's goods. There are instances of women becoming rich, but they are the kind who prefer an independent life, and are able to dominate the situation ; they are not of the average type. A few women occupy very influential positions, and by force of character and sheer ability have become wealthy. For the ordinary woman, the only property that can definitely be classed as her own are her market equipment, her cooking utensils and her water-pot, together with small odds and ends that she has accumulated and the koko-yam (edde) which she cultivates in her garden plot. She has the use of other articles, and shares in the purchases she brings back from the market. At her death, her eldest son inherits her personal belongings : they cannot be appropriated by her husband. A wife is expected to contribute her share in providing for the needs of the family, as indicated earlier in the chapter. A husband shows his appreciation of her services by giving her a present occasionally : usually a piece of cloth.

A wife does not share the hut of her husband. He has his own apartment (obi) while she, and her children, occupy separate quarters. She may share his bed, but not his hearth ; she goes in fear of her husband's gods ; she may not serve nor handle them. She enjoys no religious privileges beyond the attention she bestows on her own particular gods, consisting mostly of cones of clay and such-like humble materials. These are located either in the hut, but more usually near the place where she cooks the food. Her great objective in life is to retain the good favour of her husband, for on his goodwill her own happiness depends. If he become disgruntled, her lot will not be an enviable one.

The great majority of Ibo men are peasant farmers, which means that they are primitive agriculturists. The women-folk always share in the fieldwork, though they are not often called upon to fulfil the most arduous tasks. Their part comes chiefly after the first month of the rainy season. From that time until about a month before harvest, regular and frequent weeding must be done, and this task is usually left to the women-folk. Fieldwork, in addition to domestic duties and marketing, fill the days fairly well. This does not necessarily mean that the women are overworked : there is seldom severe pressure either

YOUNG MANHOOD.
A GROUP OF "IKOLOBIA" (ATHLETES). THEY ARE EXPERT DANCERS AND WRESTLERS.

YOUTH TO OLD AGE—GIRLS & WOMEN

on strength or time. The daily duties are of a routine character, and there is little need for rush or bustle. To foreigners, it appears to be humdrum and monotonous, whereas, Ibo women remain bright and cheerful, largely because it is their nature to be so : they are inured to the conditions, and experience has taught them to meet life philosophically, thus securing a fair measure of contentment.

When children are brought under instruction, girls exhibit equal mental ability with boys up to the age of ten or eleven. After that age, the girls show a tendency to fall behind the boys. This tendency will be lessened in the future as they are allowed to enjoy the same favourable conditions granted to boys. Hitherto, domestic duties have claimed their attention, and intellectual progress has been retarded. The prejudice against the education of girls is steadily dwindling, and the number attending classes is increasing rapidly. The old restrictions will not operate again : a new generation is taking charge. How much happier the educated women will be remains to be proved ; certain it is, that they will not be content with the old simple ways of life, nor will they be so willing to fulfil the daily round of marketing, house- and fieldwork. This seems to be the inevitable issue of modern progress everywhere, and is not peculiar to young Ibo womanhood.

Previous to the introduction of education, the women were practically all on one intellectual level : it could scarcely be otherwise. What they lacked in education was to some extent balanced by their general good humour and cheerful dispositions, supplemented by a keen sense of wit. In the mass, the old women patiently accept their lot and exhibit no active desire for change. They consort with others of their own sex : they cannot help this as the men keep to themselves. Many a woman, however, has at least one male friend with whom she maintains an intimate relationship independently of her husband.

They used always (and the majority do so still) to travel in companies to fetch water and, especially, when going to and coming from market. They do not walk in groups or pairs, but in single file. The reasons for this are that most of the paths are narrow foot tracks unsuitable for walking abreast, and because there is safety in numbers. The old custom prevails even on the modern roads where there is ample space, and there is no longer cause for fear.

Each village has its women's committee or club which legislates for the women independently of the men. It cannot be ignored or lightly treated, and in judging cases where both men and women are implicated, the chiefs must make requests of the Committee to express an opinion and, when advisable, tender a suggestion of procedure in order that an acceptable settlement may result. The club is comprised of influential women and, within its limits, it wields considerable power, more particularly in women's affairs and market control. The president of the club is installed with regal ceremony, for the rites include a symbolic crowning performed by an Nri priest on similar lines to the coronation ceremonies observed when installing a king. After this ceremony, the president is known and saluted as "Omu" (queen). It is merely a courtesy title, for the "Omu" is never the wife of a king. (See also p. 335.)

In this custom also changes have been introduced. The crown is no longer of the traditional fashion: sad to state, quite probably a man's hat becomes the crown of office. The fact that a hat is worn constitutes in itself a mark of distinction between the "Omu" and other women. Formerly, it was forbidden for a common woman to wear a hat. The "Omu" is assisted in her duties by a limited number of other women who take precedence according to status and seniority. On the western side of the Niger, a place is specially reserved in the market for the "Omu". Here she sits in state upon a royal stool; she is saluted as a queen, and "ojji" (gifts) are presented to her as tokens of respect. Her appearance does not enhance her beauty: the old felt hat, probably of billy-cock pattern, and tilted sideways on her head, and the heavy chalk rings round her eyes, are apt to induce a smile rather than inspire deference due to majesty.[3]

The clubs are governed by their own rules and regulations. Occasionally the customs in force are peculiar. In one instance observed, the women were dressed as men. They wore men's hats, and some had coats. Their breasts were bound close to their bodies by cross-over straps and each woman brandished a cutlass. They looked a fearsome crowd. This procedure seemed contrary to general custom which dictates that a woman should not degrade herself by wearing man's apparel. (*Vide* p. 415.)

Except in a few places where some of the young men allow their hair to grow long, and bind the strands into grotesque plaits, hairdressing is almost exclusively a characteristic of the female sex. The style for prospective brides is described in Chapter XV. As regards hairdressing in general, there are many examples, each designated by its specific name; different districts evolve their own fashions. There is a subtle meaning attached to hair: it is valued for its attractive qualities, hence the great pains taken to anoint and dress it. At opportune moments, it is displayed ostentatiously to court attention. It is dressed with care only at one season during the life of a primitive woman. Young girls are not greatly interested in the matter : the older women find it too much trouble. With the former, self-consciousness has not developed while, with the latter, vanity has ceased to function ; also the cares of life restrain overdue attention to personal foibles of this character. Soon after marriage, the women abandon elaborate hairdressing, and revert to the natural woolly-headed condition. At intervals, they either crop it closely, or shave it off completely.

It is the girls of marriageable age who spend so much time and care over their hair. Many hours are spent in combing, pulling and anointing it. Combing produces a gollywog effect, the hair standing out in a stiff mass : it must be plaited to conform to fashion. The ways in which this is done are many and diverse. Sometimes, the head is decorated with stiff tails : sometimes, the plaits are looped and intertwined and so forth. The most common practice is for girls to dress each other's hair in turn ; a much more satisfactory result is obtained when the operator can see what she is doing. First comes the combing, and a strenuous business that appears to be. The hair is stiff and wiry, and the wooden combs have a great strain put upon them. When the head has passed through this process, a few hairs are separated from the mass at a time. These are stretched to their full extent, and are plaited in a threefold strand. The majority are content with variations of the many rat-tailed effect. Others prefer the plaits to be plastered tightly on the head. For this style, the hair is reinforced with a mixture of oil and clay, or powdered charcoal. Others, again, favour a crown covered with puffs. For this, a larger quantity is gathered into the hands. The section near the head is fluffed and the ends fixed with short plaits.

In addition to the plaiting, there are scores of patterns wrought by clipping and shaving. These need to be illustrated rather than described.

African women have sometimes been termed "burden-bearers". Like many other general statements there is an element of truth in this remark, but, as far as Ibo women are concerned, it does not apply more than for the majority of the women in the world. It is true that they have their daily tasks, and frequently carry heavy loads on their heads. This is the method commonly adopted : indeed they know of no other. When the hair has received special dressing as described above, the basket is balanced on the shoulder. A king's wife always

YOUTH TO OLD AGE—GIRLS & WOMEN

adopts this practice, because she is forbidden to carry a load on her head, whether her hair be dressed or undressed; it would be "*infra dig*" for her to follow the custom of ordinary women.

The use of the head for carrying articles of different sizes, shapes and weight, from a couple of ounces to loads of sixty pounds and upwards, fosters poise, and the young folk grow up straight and graceful. The faculty of balance is highly developed, and this reacts to some degree and helps to produce an upright carriage. This uprightness is further promoted by the custom of sleeping on hard flat surfaces, usually the ground itself, with the head on a level with the feet, except when the forearm serves as a pillow.

The middle-age spread manifests itself before its proper time with most Ibo women. It becomes prominent rather suddenly about the thirtieth year. Instead of being sprightly, they are inclined to become fat and comfortable looking; they have reached the stage of complacency. From the age of thirty onwards, little change is to be observed until the hair begins to change from black to white. Old age follows its natural course and the evening of life sets in. The lot of the average old women is very much on a par with that of the old men, only that the women potter about the hut more than the men. The weight of years may press heavily upon them, but they retain the affection of the younger generation until the very end of their days.

NOTES TO CHAPTER XIV

[1] "*Savage Childhood*", p. 29.

[2] Dr. Baikie states that at Aboh the value of a pair of these anklets was equal to the price of three slaves. He further states that the ivory ornaments were never removed and were buried with their owners.—Baikie's "*Exploring Voyage*", p. 49.

[3] "To complete his (Chief Ajie of Aboh) make-up, his eyes were tastefully set off with a chalk outline."—"*Life in the Niger*", p. 9.

CHAPTER XV

MARRIAGE

BEFORE EMBARKING upon this subject, it will be appropriate to state that, as far as I am aware, there are no Initiatory Rites and Ceremonies connected with either Ibo youths or maidens of the character and nature of those met with in East and Central Africa. The fact that circumcision is usually performed soon after birth, and that life in all its aspects is an open book to every boy and girl, would appear to obviate the necessity for further instruction. There are certainly no " camps " or secret meeting-places reserved for initiatory purposes. They would be superfluous, and time spent on sex questions would be largely wasted. By the time young people have arrived at the stage of puberty, they have learned all they can learn from their daily contacts with life, certainly as much as their own folk are capable of teaching them.

" Inu-nwunye " (marriage) has a foremost place in Ibo social economy. It looms upon the horizon of every maid and youth as an indispensable function to be fulfilled with as little delay as possible after reaching the age of puberty. The idea of a celibate life finds no favour whatsoever: to the Ibo it is rank foolishness, as well as being utterly contrary to the laws of nature. Except in peculiar cases, as are noted later (p. 226), men and women, and particularly the latter, are scorned and mocked if they remain unmarried. A childless woman is regarded as a sort of monstrosity; indeed, it is not unknown that, when such a woman dies, in order to express the contempt in which she is held, her abdomen is slit across prior to her burial. She has failed to fulfil her function in life, and this mutilation of the corpse is the token of her failure; her name is blotted out for ever.

This is probably true of all African tribes. Of the Fang (Gaboon) it is said: " The marriage relation dominates all customs, and is the foundation of the whole social structure. With the African, love is not so closely linked with sex as among Western races. Friendship is deemed nobler than romantic love. This, of course, is due to the inequality of the sexes; a woman is not regarded as fit for companionship with men ".[1]

MARRIAGE

Innocency, in the accepted sense, is not a strong feature. It is not an uncommon custom for boys and girls to cohabit as a " game ". At the first symptom of menstruation, however, the girls stop " playing " and, on the whole, restrain themselves until they are betrothed. The customs vary in different localities ; likewise, some parents are more strict than others, and keep their girls under sound control, holding it a matter for pride to be able to proclaim their daughter's chastity when a suitor asks for her in marriage. In due time proof is provided by the use of a cloth as in the case of an Israelitish maid (Deut. xxii. 17). If a girl prove to be unchaste, besides words spoken, there will be a curtailment of gifts to the parents and other " in-laws ".

The word " love " according to the European interpretation is not found in the Ibo vocabulary. As Warneck says : " Animistic heathenism is the negation of LOVE. God is Love and, where in the wanderings of centuries God has been lost, love is also lost." [2] The nearest approach to the idea of love is " ifu-n'anya " (" to look in the eye ") in a favourable manner. The verb " to hate " is constantly in use, and there is an expression " to look " which implies the reverse of love.[3]

In former days, love may, or may not, have been a feature in Ibo courtship. At a later stage, a substitute for it may have developed, consisting of a certain amount of affection or favour bestowed by the husband upon his wife and *vice versa*. Generally speaking, according to the old social economy, after marriage the woman is ranked with the other property of the husband with a proportionate value attached. " The man prizes his wife because he expects descendants from her, and because he has bought a valuable slave." [4] At the same time, he secures the best one within the power of his choice ! Further, the statement is not wholly true. What is generally forgotten is that it is not merely a man taking to himself a wife. It is more than that ; it is the bringing in of another person into the family. She is something more than a wife ; henceforth she is a member of the clan, and has her rightful place and share in all things pertaining to it.

In former days, girls rarely manifested antagonism to a proposed marriage. Under the process of emancipation, born of modern conditions, this submissive attitude is being superseded by a spirit which demands liberty in the choice of a mate. Hence, occasions arise when a girl stubbornly refuses to accept the suitor asking for her in spite of entreaty or threats. In such case, any expenses incurred by the man must be refunded by the guardian of the girl. If possible, he, the guardian, will

MARRIAGE

postpone action until another suitor comes forward to relieve him of the financial responsibility.

Degrees of affinity are very rigid with the Ibos. Any exceptions are not by marriage, but by right of succession. A son inherits all his deceased father's wives, or a brother takes those of a deceased brother, where there is no heir, or if the heir be a minor. This method is referred to as " Nwunye nkuchi " (= a wife taken in another's stead ; an inherited wife). In proper marriage, consanguinity up to eight or ten generations is " nsọ " (forbidden). The mixing of bloods is known by the term " Ugwa ".

Yet, at Idah, Dr. Oldfield remarks : " I was conducted by Abboka to Amagdohby, the King's sister, who was also his head wife." [5] He makes no comment whether this was the practice of the common people, or was the sole prerogative of the Royal Family of Idah, in which case it would appear to be either an imported custom, or one surviving from ancient Egyptian associations.

The people of Idah and the Ibos are neighbours, and have had more or less intercourse for generations, yet this sort of union would be regarded with intolerable horror by the latter.

Rich parents often select a wife (or wives) for a son while he is still a boy, he, probably, having no knowledge whatever of the transaction. Meantime, children are being born, and the foundation of a family laid on his behalf. This method of acquiring a wife is known as " Nwunye nwa-madu ". It is a way of displaying well-to-do parentage (cf. " nwa-madu " = freeborn).

Normally, a young man has something to say in the matter of choosing a wife, although it frequently happens that a father will select and calmly tell his son, " This is the girl I have chosen for you." Where a man acts entirely on his own behalf, it is spoken of as " Nwunye aka-ya " (the wife of his own free choice).

When the man acts independently, the procedure in the early stages is not much different from that in civilised countries. He may be stirred by an impulse to marry and act with set purpose to find a wife, or he may be suddenly moved to the same end by meeting a girl whose attractiveness specially appeals to him. If she be a stranger, he forthwith makes inquiries concerning her parents, whether she is engaged or still unappropriated, her capabilities in trade and domestic affairs, her character; whether she be of amiable disposition, industrious and so forth.

Once the man is satisfied on these points, he consults his parents or a familiar friend, and arranges with one of them to

MARRIAGE

approach the guardian of the girl; it is contrary to Ibo etiquette for him to make the first advances himself. This man, the " Onye-ukọ ", (intermediator in dowry transactions), visits the home of the girl bearing a pot of palm wine as a gift (" ojji "). The acceptance of the present is an indication that the visitor is welcomed. The subject which brings him to the house, probably as well known to the guardian as to himself, is on this occasion scrupulously left out of the conversation. Other visits follow; more gifts are presented until, eventually, all the prospective " in-laws " have been mollified. The question of a possible betrothal is not broached until all these preliminaries have been fulfilled. When it is put to the guardian, profound surprise is simulated; the proposal comes as a shock! This is all part of the business, for after protesting at length that the idea is repugnant, the man (or woman) proceeds to detail the sterling qualities of the girl. In due time, the situation clears and then, and probably not till then, is the girl herself consulted. The proposal is put before her and this provides the first opportunity to refuse the man seeking her in marriage. If she raise no objection, which is the case as a rule, the next item is to settle the amount to be paid as dowry (bride-price).[6] This involves prolonged bargaining and possibly strong contention on both sides, but, like the rest of the business, is eventually settled to the satisfaction of all.

Formerly, the bride-price was reckoned in cows, goats and cowries. Any presents given are additional, and quite irrespective of it. Nowadays, the figure is fixed on an English cash basis. Moreover, the price is steadily rising. The social rank, age and personal qualities of the girl are all assessed, and to these must, in these days, be added the costs of training and education if any have been incurred. If, for some reason, there should be a demand for restitution, all will be claimed (and upheld) in the bill presented to the parent or guardian. Only in the last remaining backward parts of Iboland do the old customs prevail. The bride-price is becoming a heavy burden under the new conditions. A prospective bridegroom may be faced with costs amounting to £100 or more, according to the social standing of the girl, her personal charms and qualifications, whereas, in the olden days, the price varied from the equivalent of a few shillings to a few pounds.

In certain places, it is easy to secure a wife cheaply. For example, at Ibuzọ (near Asaba), there is a custom whereby, if a man snips off a tiny wisp of hair from a girl's head, she automatically becomes bound to him for life; she cannot marry another man in regular and accepted fashion. If she

MARRIAGE

should respond to the attentions of another man, the pair are driven from the town and are " nso " ; trespassers against tabu regulations.

All preliminary arrangements having been satisfactorily settled, a time is fixed for the celebration of the dowry sacrifice (Aja-nwa-ada). Until this sacrifice is completed, the father (or guardian) may not make use of any of the money paid. Palm wine and chalk are provided, together with a calabash (oba). These are placed in a basket (ukpa ekwele) and this is laid on the head of the newly betrothed girl. The parties enter the house-yard, where a hole is dug, and a pole set up on which the basket is to be hung when emptied. The father lifts the basket from the head of the girl, and waves it with a circular motion four times round her head. This signifies that all impurities have been removed, and the father is able confidently to proclaim " Achugom adam aja " (" I have performed the sacrifice for my daughter "). A feast follows the ceremony.

No man who has not performed " Aja-nwa-ada " can share in the feast, though a man who has no daughter may qualify by being given a part in the making of the sacrifice for a friend's daughter. This practice of " Aja-nwa-ada " is not universal ; it applies in certain areas only.

The dowry consists of :
(i) " Ntutu "—small gifts such as mats, cloths, spoons and trinkets, chiefly for the relatives of the girl.
(ii) " Ego-nwayi " or " Ego-nwunye " arranged on set terms (iru onu nwayi). If the engagement be made when the girl is young, the " ntutu " may accumulate until it exceeds the " Ego-nwayi ".
(iii) " Isi-ego "—presents of money from one penny upwards given to the girl.
(iv) " Ego-iza-oku "—gifts given to the girl on her first visit to the intended husband's house. She may accept the gift without demur or comment. If, however, she dislikes the man, she will return the gift after she arrives back home. To return the gift, or reject the " Isi-ego ", is her great chance to refuse the man as a husband if she does not want him. Retainment of the gifts implies acceptance of the man as a suitor.

If a girl break the engagement, the " Ntutu ", the " Ego-nwayi " and the " Isi-ego " have to be refunded to the man. The repayment is spoken of as " Isi-ngo " or " Ngo-nwayi ".

It is within the bounds of possibility that, within the next few years, dowry, as such, will be abandoned. Young people will be inclined to act on their own initiative and responsibility, and will choose mates for themselves, with less and less consideration for the opinions and customs of their forefathers. Indeed, the abolition of dowry will probably become a necessity for economic reasons. Young men find it extremely difficult to raise the ever-increasing prices now demanded, and they must either postpone marriage until well advanced in years, or contract loans. Grave evils arise from the latter course, for a man may be burdened by the incubus of debts incurred in connection with his marriage which will cripple him financially throughout his life. Such debts invariably lead to unhappiness and mutual recriminations between husband and wife, and may also be instigatory to dishonesty. On the other hand, girls will not wait an indefinite period. Faced with almost insurmountable obstacles, the young people are much more readily disposed to cohabit without marriage.

But the abolition, or rigid curtailment of dowry, must come from within Ibo society itself. Legislation would be fatal : that has been proved, e.g. " The dowry paid for a wife among the Mpongwe is forty dollars. Among the uncivilised Fang, it is several times this amount, although the Fang are very poor in comparison. The Mpongwe dowry was reduced by the French Government as a step in the direction of its abolishment, for it was nothing more than a purchase price. But the result of this forced reduction has been demoralisation rather than civilisation. Until the African attains the moral sentiment that makes the marriage bond sacred, it is better that there should be the bond of outright purchase and ownership rather than no marriage at all. The early missionaries made no church laws against the dowry, but they preached the equality of woman and the higher idea of marriage ; and as the Christians became imbued with this sentiment, they themselves abolished the dowry within their own society. But they did it at the instance of a moral sentiment which made marriage more secure than ever. The inward preceded the outward change." [7]

Very rarely is the whole of the dowry money paid in one instalment ; as a matter of fact, the girl as a rule has not attained to marriageable age. The common practice is to spread the payments over months and even years, indeed, right up to the very day on which the man takes his wife permanently to his own house. This is in accordance with the Ibo distinctive ideal. The money is an " earnest " of something to come. It contemplates an " engagement " ; it is not a downright purchase as for a slave.

The use of the word " permanently " implies that the girl has paid " temporary " visits to her betrothed husband's home

MARRIAGE

as, indeed, she has. Nowadays, a girl is said to be " engaged ", and the term covers the period between the payment of the first instalment of the bride-price and the last, that is, the day when the marriage contract is fulfilled. Under Ibo law and custom, the girl is technically the man's wife from the moment the first payment is accepted by the parent or guardian ; a prototype of the hire-purchase system of England and America!

The periodical visits paid by a girl to the home of her affianced husband are more or less systematised and are technically known as " uri ". The first visit is made after the settlement of the betrothal, that is, after the initial instalment of the bride-price has been accepted by the guardian. It follows about sixteen days later. This provides an opportunity for the girl to become acquainted with the members of the family into which, in due time, she herself will be admitted a member. The man's relatives, in their turn, will be able to judge the qualities of their new " in-law ". On this first occasion, she stays four Ibo weeks (sixteen days). There will be words of welcome, but there will also be a fair salting of criticism. There will be comments upon her looks, her figure, her behaviour and general character. On the practical side, opinions will be expressed concerning her capabilities in cooking and other items of housecraft. The native is not reserved or punctilious when pronouncing a verdict in such circumstances. The girl is to become a member of the household and, naturally, the relatives are curious, and want to have some assurance that, in their judgement, she is up to standard, and likely to prove a worthy addition to the clan.

The number of succeeding visits depends on the age of the girl at the time of the betrothal. If of marriageable age, or approaching to it, they will be few. If she be young, as a great number are when affianced, she will make periodical visits staying, as a general, but not binding, rule about two weeks at a time. During the course of the visits she may, or may not, cohabit with her affianced husband ; in the eyes of the people they are legally man and wife. For the most part this is what actually happens, although some parents are strict and will not consent to this. They take steps whereby the girl is safeguarded, holding it a matter of honour to return her to her parents as she came from them. Old custom ruled that the girl must not be touched by the affianced husband while spending her days of " uri " at his home. It was " alu " (abomination) to cohabit with the intended husband, or any other man, before the performance of " Ama-izizi " or the " Ine mgbe " as it is called in some parts. (*Vide* p. 180.) This old custom, how-

MARRIAGE

ever, is not so closely observed as it used to be and, among young people, morals, instead of being fairly rigid as they once were, have become lax under the new conditions. A girl, however, is not supposed to have intimate relations with any man prior to the first occasion of " uri ". After that is over, she is more or less free to select her own friends, and frequently does so. Should a child be born in the waiting time before the formal marriage ceremony, it is the property of her betrothed husband.

At Onitsha, the " uri " visit is usually once a year about harvest time, but the general practice in the Ibo country appears to be two native weeks per month. Theoretically, sexual relationships are restricted to the " uri " periods. In actual fact, the couple, once they are betrothed, follow very much their own inclinations as circumstances permit until the first sign of menstruation, when the girl will reject the attentions of the man until the " Ama-izizi " ceremonies have been fulfilled. This, again, is theoretical! Should a child be born before the ceremonies have been fulfilled, in some places it would be " nso " (tabu) and be destroyed forthwith, while in other parts, it would be accepted without demur. (*Vide* p. 180.)

On very rare occasions, it is found that, if the intended husband of a girl die, instead of being taken over by the next of kin, which is the common procedure, she remains at home unmarried for life. Should she bear a child it is " nso " (forbidden) and cast away, the same practice being observed if more children follow.

Again, in some localities, when a betrothed girl becomes pregnant by a man other than her fiancé, this man brings two goats and gives them to the intended husband, and the child becomes his by right of redemption as well as by fatherhood. The mother nurses the child until it is about four years old, and then the actual father takes it. Failing the payment of the goats, the intended husband is on the *qui vive* for an opportunity to kidnap the child. If successful, he sells it. The much more common practice, however, is for the intended husband to take the child as his own, and his claim will be supported.

There is no fixed period between betrothal and actual marriage. The time is governed on the man's part by his circumstances. On the girl's side, age is the important factor. The man may make the first advances by intimating to the parents that he is desirous of completing the contract with them, and taking the girl to his house. If, however, he seems reluctant to move in the matter, and postpones action beyond a reasonable period, then both the girl and her parents become restive.

MARRIAGE

The latter want their money : the former grows tired of waiting, and she is open to ridicule and scandalmongering from her neighbours, who begin to impute reasons why she is left unclaimed. Whatever be the moving cause, the interested parties now consult together and fix a date for the marriage. Relatives and friends gather together, and celebrate the occasion with feasting and drinking—the amount being governed by the money the bridegroom has at his disposal, whether his own or borrowed. Whatever else he may provide, he must not fail to arrange for a plentiful supply of palm wine—this is virtually an essential to a truly native marriage. During the course of the feast, the final instalment of the bride-price is paid to the guardian, the whole assembly acting as witnesses to the transaction. This last payment, duly attested, puts the seal on the contract. That which, up to this moment, has been the man's possession only by virtue of his " earnest " money, now becomes his own in fact by the fulfilment of the whole of his obligations, in other words, the payment of the final instalment constitutes the marriage.

Preparatory to departing to her new home, relatives and friends present gifts to the bride. These mostly take the form of domestic utensils, money and, where the parents are able to do so, they add a couple of goats and a few chickens. In former days, a wealthy man might also donate one or two slaves to act as his daughter's personal servants. Throughout the marriage feast, the bride and bridegroom sit demurely side by side looking rather the picture of misery than happy beings. It is not considered good form to show any signs of joy, indeed, it is proper for the bride to manifest signs of grief because of leaving her old home. Presently, the bridegroom leaves alone for his house : the bride waits until darkness falls and then, with great reluctance, she is induced or dragged by her girl companions to her new home. It should be noted that, in some parts of the Ibo country, there is no marriage feast : the girl goes to her husband's house forthwith after the first instalment of the bride-price is paid. In such cases the feasting is deferred until the first child is born.

The reader might be left with the impression that the Marriage Customs of the Ibos are little more than cut-and-dried business transactions carried through in accordance with a stereotyped formula. While it is true that the more important affairs are negotiated by others, very frequently by the older folk, yet the young people have their own ways of adding romance to life. Neither sex lacks initiative or resource in its desire to display its fine points with the object of drawing

MARRIAGE

attention of the one sex to the other. Herein the Ibo are not different from other races : all that is needed is to note how this is done.

Attention centres first, naturally, on physical attractiveness. Very little manufactured material used to be at the disposal of the Ibo youth or maiden. Until foreign cloth and foreign fashions invaded the country, the young people had very meagre wardrobes : their chief and practically only asset was just themselves. On the eastern side of the Niger, the girls went totally unclothed until they were married. They supplemented nature's gifts by anointing their bodies with oil : not smeared on heavily : but sufficiently to impart a gloss to their brown or black skins and giving them the appearance of velvet. On the western side of the river, the conditions were not quite so crude : a piece of native cloth, however small, was used. Those days are past as far as lack of covering is concerned.

Particular attention is given to the hair, for the girls consider this has a peculiar attraction to the male sex. It is burnished with oil and, at the proper time, is dressed in elaborate style. (*Vide* p. 211.) The body itself is painted with cleverly drawn free-hand designs in deep black, or by the more effective method of cicatrisation. Around the waist there may be a string of beads, or a rolled fragment of cloth studded with tiny brass bells. On the legs of richer girls are coils of brass wire or heavy brass anklets.[8] The toilet is completed with ivory bracelets where these can be borrowed. To these are added what is most effective of all, namely, the arts and graces of the girl herself. Most of the girls are quite capable of making full use of these. Further details relating to the freehand designs and the ornaments are mentioned in Chapter XXIV.

Young men rely even more on their physical attractions. Those who make a special feature of display are usually finely developed specimens of young manhood. They wear no more than a tightly rolled piece of cloth known as an " ogodo ", and ivory circlets above the biceps and between the knees and upper part of the calves of the legs. The hair is plaited into thin tails which give an impression of fierceness rather than add to beauty of appearance. Some districts are particularly addicted to this feature. They also paint their bodies similarly to the women, but not to the same extent.

Both sexes are equally vain, and vie with each other to attract attention. Both, at times, resort to measures which do not always reflect a modest mind ; the actions of the girls being often more patently blatant than those of the men.

MARRIAGE

It can be generally accepted that girls are married at about the age of sixteen years. Actually, there is no trustworthy record, and no great consideration is given to the question of age. All the girls belonging to a specified " otu " or " ogbo " (age-grade) generally marry about the same time : they are all accepted as equally fit, whereas it does not follow that all have reached mature development. A. may be fully grown and can, with reason, be reckoned as of marriageable age, while B. may be more backward, yet the fact that both are of the same " otu " gives simultaneous sanction to the marriage of both. In any case, the first signs of menstruation finally settle the question : that removes all doubt should any exist. The reason for the young age of brides is, of course, the desire to profit as much as possible by their marriages, both in receiving the " dowry money " on the part of the guardian and, on the husband's part, to make the utmost of the child-bearing years.

In the districts with which I am most familiar, all the girls of marriageable age go into " nkpu " together. This is a peculiar custom, the object of which is to proclaim the fact that these girls will be shortly entering the marriage state. Considerable preparations are made for the observance of this ceremony. Six months prior to going into " nkpu ", the girls take up their quarters in separate apartments. They must not venture out into the open during daylight, though they do not hesitate to wander forth after dark ! They do no work whatever during this period, and are provided with abundance of food. Their only occupation at this time is the preparation of camwood dye wherewith to stain their bodies red. Poorer girls have to reduce the time for this fattening process to four months, as they cannot be spared so long from work, nor can the parents afford the bounteous supplies of food for the longer period. Some of the girls become grossly fat, and all exhibit signs of over-feeding. When on parade, they receive honour in proportion to their size, and the fatter they are, the more gratified are their prospective husbands.

The final festivities are spread over some seven days. The less fortunate girls must be content with little more than an extra plaiting of the hair and a plentiful use of camwood stain ; those in more affluent circumstances make a grander display. They wear no clothes whatever, other than the ropes of tightly twisted cloth already mentioned, or threaded cowrie shells. One or more tiny brass bells are fastened to the cloth or cowrie-shell waist-band. Rings of brass adorn the legs, graduated in size from the ankles to just above the knees. (*Vide* p. 206.)

MARRIAGE

The coiffure is a very elaborate affair, and requires great patience and skill to arrange. The hair is saturated with a mixture of clay, powdered charcoal and palm-oil, until it becomes a sticky mass. It is then moulded into a shape resembling the central crest of a fireman's helmet. The central ridge comes well over the middle of the forehead and extends backwards into the nape of the neck. Below the main erection, and on either side, delicate patterns are traced with tiny plaits of hair, curled into small coils plastered down flatly to the head. Finally, the high centre has its sides embellished with mother of pearl or bits of brass; the pieces (about the size of shillings) being sewn in with hair. The tufted end of a cow's tail, mounted on a leather handle, is carried, together with one or two small mirrors, set in handled frames carved specially for the purpose.

Maids of honour attend upon the " nkpu " girls throughout the round of festivities and these also are smeared with camwood dye, the fashion being to use as much paint as possible, from the crown of the head to the feet. In cases where the girl's parents can afford it, or where the affianced husband is a man of means, a goat is slain on the first day of the carnival. This mark of affluence is advertised by the kidney fat of the goat being laid on the head of the prospective bride and fastened securely thereon with finely drawn strands of fibre. The mass of fat is spread completely over the high central decorated portion of the hair and remains there until the ceremonies are concluded, it having, in the intervening days, suffered very severely from exposure, which is a mild way of expressing its condition !

The parades generally take place in the late afternoon. When the bride-to-be is ready, she sallies forth into the street. She may join company with other girls observing the " nkpu " custom and, together, wander through the town attended by their maids, or she may elect to parade alone. The attendants carry large fans wherewith to refresh their ladies after the bouts of dancing in which they indulge. Dancing is an exhausting business, and the " nkpu " girl does not spare herself in her efforts to win the applause of the spectators. If she succeed in pleasing them, the basket or calabash, placed at her feet for the purpose, receives a contribution of cowries or cash from the bystanders as a token of their pleasure and good wishes.

Cicatrisation is an essential to marriage in many parts of the Ibo country. The bride-elect must submit to this operation before the day fixed for the final ceremony. This consists of scarifying the front part of the body, generally in the form of a

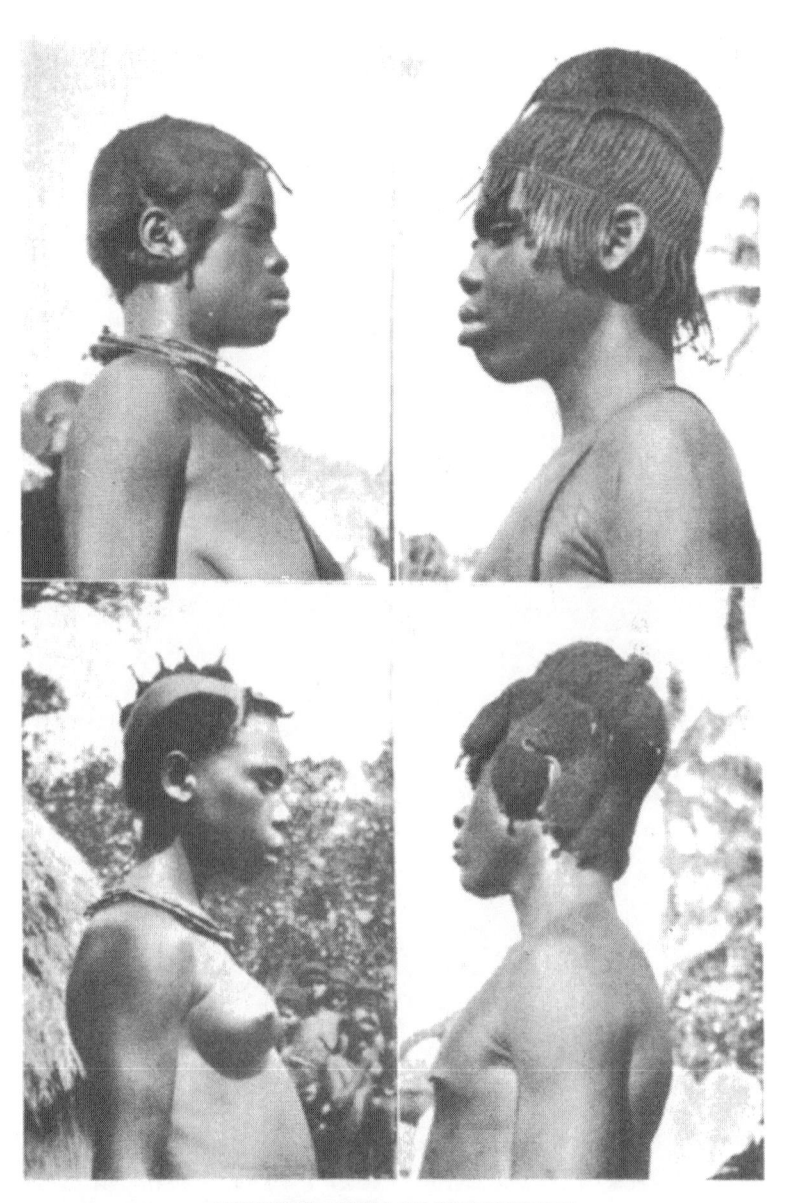

NORTHERN TYPES OF HAIRDRESSING.

HAIRDRESSING IS A STRONG FEATURE. YOUTHS PLAIT IT TO ENHANCE THEIR ATHLETIC APPEARANCE. YOUNG WOMEN DRESS IT TO ADVERTISE THEIR BEAUTY AND INCREASE THEIR ATTRACTIVENESS. (PAGES 210-222.)

MARRIAGE

cross, made with triple lines of " mbubu " or " ebubu " (small raised lumps = keloids). The fashion varies in different districts. It is the custom in some parts to cover the whole front of the body with an intricate pattern having the appearance of crochet-work and, in due course, the design is continued over the shoulder-blades at the back. On the western side of the Niger, from Umunede to Benin, a series of parallel lines are the mode, running diagonally from the centre of the abdomen. Also the cuts are superficial as compared with the incisions on the eastern side.

A similar procedure is found among the Kagoro of Northern Nigeria. " When a girl reaches the marriageable age, the chest and back will be scarified in two parallel sets of long lines of short cuts running from the breasts to join the pattern already on the stomach, and from the shoulder-blades to the small of the back." [9]

The neighbouring Munshis favour another style of cicatrisation for girls. Using the navel as a centre, the pattern is worked in very pronounced outstanding circles until the whole abdomen is covered. Scarification of the body, therefore, can be accepted as a proof that a woman is already married or is preparing to enter that state. For conception to occur before cicatrisation is a disgrace (" alu ") according to native custom. Actually, it is not adhered to strictly, and it often falls out that the girl is hardly through the " nkpu " celebrations before she becomes a mother. In some districts, the scarifying is done at different intervals, a part before conception, and a part after pregnancy occurs.

It might be thought that there was not much left for the grown-up Ibo girl to learn concerning the facts of life, for little attempt is made to cloak them. Nevertheless, it is considered desirable, if not necessary, for her to receive instruction on matters relating to the married state. She must appear before a council of older women who supplement her knowledge and, more particularly, interpret to her the rules which regulate the lives of the married women of the community. She will learn what things are forbidden (" nso̱ "), and the penalties which will ensue should she be found guilty of infringing one or more of them.

The final custom to be observed in connection with marriage takes place after the bride has settled at her husband's house. It is in the form of a confession and is known as " Isa-ifi ". At this ceremony, the " Umu-ada " (female relatives of the husband,) demand the names of any men, other than her husband, with whom she has had sexual relations since the day

MARRIAGE

she was affianced. Her bare word is not acceptable: she must swear an oath when making her declaration to attest the truth of her statement. The family " Ofo " is produced, and she takes her stand before it. Then she takes a chicken in her hands, and waves it before the " Ofo ", making her confession as she does so. The fowl is forthwith killed, and the blood sprinkled upon the " Ofo " in token of expiation, and to seal the acceptance of her confession.

The " Umu-ada " having thus been satisfied, the husband will also be content as far as his wife is concerned. His wife may have divulged the names of certain men. His business is now to seek reparation from them. Until they make amends, peace between him and them cannot be established. The rupture is soon repaired: all that is necessary is to offer the prescribed sacrifices, and pay the assessed damages neither of which, as a rule, make any excessive demand upon the resources of the accused. Complete reconciliation is restored by sharing the kola nut and palm wine provided for the occasion. (*Vide* p. 233 for Adultery Fines.)

A childless marriage is a source of grievous disappointment and, sooner or later, leads to serious trouble between man and wife. Neither knows which of the two is to blame for the misfortune; hence, each accuses the other. Should the wife feel that her husband is to blame for her non-conception, she is at liberty to cohabit with another man in order to prove her contention. The husband will raise no objection. If a child results from the alliance, he will be satisfied, because it will be his by right of ownership. That he is not himself the father will not affect possession: the child is born to his wife, and that is the argument that counts.

At the beginning of this chapter reference was made to the fact that there were a few peculiar instances where men and women remain unmarried. This is the case where eunuchs are members of a royal establishment. It is rather rare, indeed, probably no longer applies. It was confined to king's households on the western side of the Niger.

In the same neighbourhood, and in some of the eastern districts, one or more daughters were withheld from marriage. These remained domiciled at home and were placed at the disposal of their father's guests. As an example, in one town, where there is a family of five or more children, should the last child be a girl she would not be given in marriage. She continues to reside at home. No reproach falls upon a woman in such circumstances; although she has no husband, she is not likely to be stigmatised as childless, because it is probable that

MARRIAGE

she will become the mother of as many children as any married woman, the fruit of the liaisons between herself and her father's guests, or by other men with whom she cohabits.

NOTES TO CHAPTER XV

[1] "*Fetish Folk of West Africa*", p. 132.
[2] "*Living Forces of the Gospel*", p. 122.
[3] *Vide* p. 68, "*Among the Ibos of Nigeria*".
[4] "A wife is bought with a price and is part of a man's wealth. A man's wealth is always reckoned by the number of his wives."—"*Fetish Folk of West Africa*", p. 133.
[5] "*Expedition into the Interior of Africa*", Laird and Oldfield, Vol. II, p. 187.
[6] The term "dowry" is to be interpreted throughout in accordance with West African usage, namely, as money paid by the prospective husband for his wife. Bride-price has been suggested, but the Ibo terms it "iche oji nne na nna" (to present gifts to mother and father). "Earnest money" is the more correct interpretation (cf. Ephes. i, 14).
[7] "*Fetish Folk of West Africa*", pp. 52–3.
[8] These anklets are now gone completely out of fashion. *Vide* pp. 205 and 319.
[9] "*Tailed Headhunters of Nigeria*", p. 112.

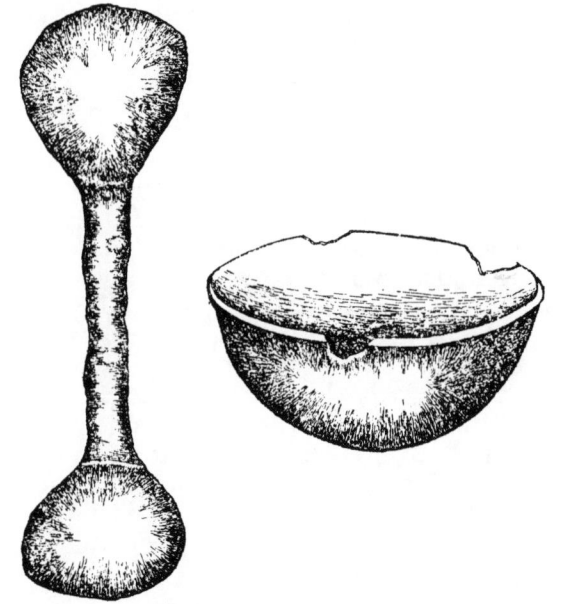

WOMEN'S GOD CALLED "ITE-UMU-NNE" (p. 48).
About eight inches in length with bulbous ends. Pot about six inches in diameter.

CHAPTER XVI

POLYGAMY & DIVORCE

POLYGAMY IS A subject that is honeycombed with pitfalls; a slippery path even to the wary. Anything written is open to criticism, because its problems, complications and ramifications are so manifold. With the exercise of extreme caution, one is still liable to misjudge, or to fail to discern the true aspects of this widely spread and deeply rooted institution. The European mind, owing to its different training and outlook, does not function on the same lines as the mind of the African and, consequently, thought and patience are needed to appreciate the native point of view. As, however, Polygamy is intimately bound up with the lives of the Ibo people, the subject cannot be omitted altogether. Some reference must be made to it in order to understand the implications of relative customs. The problem is to write so guardedly that, as far as possible, opinions on its merits or demerits may be suppressed, and only the facts of the system stated as they are seen in operation in Ibo Society.

One feature frequently left out of the calculations is that the custom is supported nearly as much by the women as by the men; it is by no means a one-sided affair with the advantage on the side of the men-folk as sometimes implied. Indeed, it is not uncommon to find that women are stout protagonists of the practice. To the pagan Ibo, a plurality of wives is a laudable ambition and, given the opportunity, he will add to the number up to the time that old age causes him to lose interest in life. A man who is able to multiply his wives rises automatically in the social scale. They largely constitute his working capital. Every fresh outlay for the provision of an additional wife is looked upon as a shrewd investment. For these reasons alone, on the lowest level as they are, polygamy to the primitive Ibo, is a worthy institution.

A clear distinction needs to be affirmed between a wife and an additional woman taken into the house. To all intents and purposes both are wives, and they are commonly called so; the casual observer would notice no difference. In actual fact, under native law and custom, the first woman the man marries

POLYGAMY & DIVORCE

alone enjoys the privileges which belong to a legal wife. This does not mean that the other women have no rights ; they have, but they are in all respects secondary to those of the first wife. She alone of the number is qualified to be called " Anasi " or " Nwayi-isi-chi " (Headwife = wife approved by the family god) and, in virtue thereof, claims, and is given, a measure of respect greatly superior to that accorded to the other women of the household. Further, because of her standing as legal wife, she wields a much greater influence than any of the others in the management of family affairs. When her husband assumes a new title, she shares in the honour. As he adds another title cord to the number round his ankle, so " Anasi " must tie a similar cord around hers. Neglect to comply with this rule leads to friction between husband and wife ; she is charged with compromising his dignity. In all public and social functions she only is openly acknowledged and embraced by her husband, and she alone of his wives shares in the congratulations showered upon him. The other wives have no such privileges ; they share in the rejoicing, but not in the honours.

The " Anasi " is a privileged person at the celebration of feasts to the " Ilọ-Maw " (spirit worship). Her position as *the* wife is clearly distinguished by the fact that the first food offered at the feast must be prepared by her. Only after this has been accepted can gifts be received from the other wives. The two presentations are quite separate, the second being inferior in degree to the first.

In the women's apartments, " Anasi " fulfils the duties of priestess of the gods called " Ekwu " (small cones of clay). It is her personal privilege to minister to these, and no subsidiary wife may presume to impinge upon her prerogative.

So long as she remains a member of the household, that is, unless for some reason she has forfeited her position, " Anasi " is the foremost figure among the women-folk of the compound. She holds a very strong position from which she is not likely to be deposed, except for some very special reason. She may not always be in prime favour with her husband, but she *is* what she is by right of being his first wife. Normally, she assumes undisputed control over all the other women.[1]

One wife does not constitute a harem ; she is but the foundation of one. Polygamy begins when a second woman is added to the establishment. In tracing the course of this action, it is possible to gain an inkling of the mentality of the two sexes. The husband, provided he has the means, may act on his own initiative, prompted by his own natural impulses. On the other hand, he may be persuaded so to act by his wife; hence, the taking of a second wife may be an individualistic or a mutually co-operative act. The change in domestic policy is generally mooted soon after the first child is born to the couple, because this is responsible for a readjustment in the conjugal relationships between husband and wife. According to Ibo custom, they are expected to refrain from sexual intercourse, because it is " nso " (tabu) for a woman to bear a subsequent child until the former one is no longer dependent on its mother for nourishment. Roughly, there is an interval of about three years.[2,3] This prescribed interval has sound reasons for its support. It is maintained that a woman needs prolonged rest after giving birth to a child; she must be allowed time to recuperate thoroughly, both for her own sake and, particularly, for the sake of the next child she may be called upon to bear. Its chances in life must not be jeopardised: risks must not be taken. It must be remembered in this connection, that there is no system of artificial feeding, and no woman should be expected to nourish more than one child at a time. No relief being forthcoming for the mother, it is wiser to avoid the possibility of another child appearing on the scene. It may seem strange that the milk of the cows and goats is not utilised. As a matter of fact, the former are so few in number that they would not supply much milk even if it were acceptable—which it is not—for the Ibo has an inveterate objection to the use of the milk of animals. People dwelling near medical centres are beginning to realise the possibilities of artificial feeding, and a few are resorting to it for motherless children. Strangely enough, the Ibo revels in *tinned* milk, whereas he shudders at the thought of milk fresh from the cow.[4]

It, therefore, comes to this. Husband and wife practise abstinence for a couple of years; at least, they are supposed to abstain. It does not call for much imagination to form some idea of the difficulties created by this impasse. To solve the problem, the husband seeks a second wife. In doing so, he evokes no resentment on the part of the first, indeed, as stated above, she probably has a share in securing one or, instead, a wife will, in some cases, arrange for the service of a harlot during the period of waiting.

So much from the man's point of view. What is the case for the woman? To be the one and only wife is humiliating. It is a sure indication that her husband is a poor man. She would rather be the mistress controlling a number of other women than be a person of no importance. Also, instead of being alone, she prefers to have companions about her; in any case, there will be others with whom to share the household chores. The wife of a polygamous husband stands to gain considerably. She has more honour and respect from the community, freedom from loneliness and domestic helpers at her beck and call.[5]

Taking the country as a whole, the number of wives in a polygamous household is from three to five. The doubtful privilege is, of course, denied to many men. Owing to lack of means, they must remain monogamists, not from choice, but because of circumstances which are beyond their control. On the other hand, rich men can, and do, indulge pretty much as they please. The kings of former days were notorious for the size of their harems, the number of women often running into three figures.[6] What may be conceded is that both sexes support polygamy, because of the benefits which each, from its own point of view, derives from it.

A question that might be raised is what is the proportion between the numbers of adult men and women? Must it be taken for granted that, in order for polygamy to be practised, there must be an excess of women over men? As a matter of fact, in some areas, the females appear to be less, and in no part of the Ibo country is there a proportion greater than 25 per cent. The figures available are, however, " based on guesses and estimates . . . in the present state of statistical knowledge ".[7] In the absence of trustworthy evidence, it would be unwise to express an opinion whether more girls are born than boys. When visiting the compounds and markets, females do seem to preponderate, and that is as far as one dare venture to state.[8] It is commonly held that young men are called upon to meet greater risks in life and, consequently, their numbers fall below those of the girls. This was just possibly the case formerly when intertribal warfare accounted for a few lives : at the present day, there are no more dangers for men than for women. In any case, polygamy stands independently of population statistics.

It is sometimes argued that, were monogamy the rule, a large number of women would be husbandless. As far as the available figures show this is dubious reasoning *per se* ; the sexes balance out fairly evenly. No doubt, it is this thought at the back of their minds, namely, that unless polygamy be practised, many women would perforce have no chance to marry, that they, the women, are such strong supporters of the institution. The Ibo woman shrinks from the prospect of being husbandless : she knows only too well the disgrace that is attached to that unfortunate condition. Such a woman is mocked and ridiculed, especially by other women, while her own instincts are outraged, causing her to suffer acutely both mentally and physically. Not even in death would her failure be forgiven. (*Vide* p. 213.) The men object to monogamy on very similar grounds. The idea of women remaining celibate is scoffed at: it is unnatural: it is a wicked interference with the normal functions of a woman's life. The instinct to procreate is a very strong factor; it is *the* great reason put forward by the Ibo people for the support of polygamy.

The course of daily life does not always run smoothly. When quarrels occur in the household of an Ibo man, especially if he be the cause of the upset, he is liable to find himself in a humiliating position. The chief duty of a married woman is to cook for her husband. If, in a fit of anger, she refuses to prepare food, she will bring retribution upon herself, but her punishment is tempered by the thought that her husband does not altogether escape discomfort; he is left to fend for his meal. Probably, he will make shift for himself, knowing that he will be ridiculed by his friends and neighbours if he apply to them for help.[9]

In circumstances of this nature, polygamy provides a remedy. It enables the man to be independent of the tantrums of a disgruntled wife. When one fails, another will minister to his needs. The same thing happens when sickness prostrates a wife: also during the periodical seasons when she is forbidden to cook for her husband. Hence, it comes about that a man may argue very plausibly in favour of the multiplication of wives for, by it, he is assured of a cook, and this is of paramount importance to a native. One wife may be at variance, or physically unfit, but another will serve him equally well.

There is an aspect of polygamy which is not always obvious on the surface, yet it needs to be emphasised for it is the cause of much infidelity. This is the inflation of dowries of recent years, one of the serious innovations consequent upon the impact of European influence. It arises from the introduction of money and what money does. The man of means can marry as many women as he will, and girls consistently manifest a preference for well-to-do men, whereas the poor man is seriously handicapped. He may have to wait years before he can save the bride-price demanded and, even so, his choice will be limited. This is further aggravated by the tendency on the part of parents and guardians to seize the opportunity of making money by raising the price. The outcome of all this is that wealthy men often accumulate more than their fair share of women, while the less fortunate men are the more handicapped.

POLYGAMY & DIVORCE

Another innovation is the practice which has insinuated itself whereby guardians present girls to men in influential positions in order to gain favour. No dowry is asked in such a case; they are " gifts ". An intimation that it would be more correct to call them " bribes " is indignantly resented ! Whatever they are termed, the fact remains that the donors expect to receive compensatory benefits in return for the " gifts " !

The inflation of dowries, and this custom of presenting girls in anticipation of favours in lieu of dowry, are real evils. Young virile men are often held back from marriage. The girls on their part, while welcoming the idea of marrying men of affluence, soon become disillusioned. Discontent ensues; they find themselves little more than playthings, and the men soon tire of their new toys. The result is that the young wives seek satisfaction elsewhere. Sometimes this is merely tolerated; more often it is definitely condoned with the idea of procreating children. At other times, this promiscuous intercourse between wives and outside men is systematised, certainly encouraged, for the sake of monetary gain. A charge is made and fines for adultery inflicted. Some courts became notorious for this practice. But, like other abuses, the misuse of the Courts in order that men might profit by adultery fines, has been checked. In these days, success in a case of this type only slips through by accident, that is, if it should happen to escape the notice of the supervising officer. When such an action comes under his review, it meets with the treatment it deserves, and is promptly quashed or justly assessed.

With reference to adultery, it has always been fairly common, but it has increased of late years owing to the relaxation of punishment; it is no longer possible to inflict the old penalties. Usually it was a fine, but it could be a death penalty. One remembers cases where extreme measures were carried into effect. In one instance, the guilty woman and her paramour were bound together back to back, placed upright in a hole, and buried alive. Another example was where the injured husband took his unfaithful wife to the farm, and there bound her to a crudely made cross, X-shaped. Not content with crucifixion, he added to her agonies by kindling fire beneath her outstretched body. Such punishment was allowed by native law and custom, though it was of extremely rare occurrence. The generally accepted method of reparation was a fine proportionate in amount to the status of the aggrieved husband. Adultery with one of the wives of a man of high titular rank was reckoned as a great sin (" ome alu "—to do abomination). The fine varied, of course, in different localities. The following is typical. One she goat, the " ewu-ani ", which stood as " the goat of reparation " or, as it might be termed, " ewu-eneni " = the goat of contempt (lit. despising). In addition to the goat, seven " akwas " of cowries (*vide* p. 338) a quantity of yams, a cock and a hen, and eight kola nuts had to be paid.

For the abomination called " ugwa ", that is, miscegenation or, more particularly, when a man commits adultery with the wife of a relative, if the husband be of humble position, the fine is two small fowls, but, in most cases, the fine is heavier, say, one goat, one bag of cowries, a fowl and some kola nuts. In this case purification sacrifices are necessary.

Adultery with a woman of another town is not regarded as a serious offence. Should, however, the guilty man be charged, he must comply with the prescribed sacrifices, and pay the dues in force in that town. In the case of a man committing adultery with the wife of a fellow-villager, it is open for the family of the offender to beg the aggrieved family to forgive the sinner. It may be settled by the gift of a fowl and, in such case, the aggrieved family take witnesses to prove that " as we have accepted this small gift and have forgiven ; so, likewise, remember that, should a similar offence be committed by one of our men, we shall, in our turn, be let off with a similar small fine ". Often the proceedings dwindle to a mere farce, and there is no punishment for adultery on either side. As an example, it is said that, if an Achalla man commit adultery with the wife of an Awka man, no punishment is inflicted or demanded, and *vice versa*, whether the woman be the wife of a titled man or of a commoner.

Polygamy has been an institution so long in the Ibo country that it has become part and parcel of the social economy. When the Nigerian Government assumed authority, it found polygamy deeply entrenched, and did not interfere with it. Marriage under native law and custom is valid, and it is still the general practice.

In due season, the Government legislated on marriage and brought an ordinance into being, not so much with the idea of introducing changes, but rather to regularise marriages between people who wanted something more satisfactory than marriage by customary law. In any case, it had to legislate for the Colony of Lagos, and it included the Protectorate under its ægis. This means that there are two sets of laws in operation in the Ibo country. Under native law, there is no restriction as to the number of women a man may marry. Also, when a man wants to divorce a woman, no serious problems are involved. Government law technically restricts a man's choice to one, while divorce proceedings are (rightly) very difficult to negotiate.

What, then, is the situation of a man who marries under the Government Ordinance and, later, wishes to take unto himself another wife? All he needs to do, as conditions are at present, is to marry the new wife under native law. He is not likely to meet with any serious opposition and, if questioned, will probably reply that she is not a wife but a concubine. Thus, he is able to use both systems without bringing penalties upon himself.

It might be argued that, by marrying an additional wife, a man lays himself open to a charge of bigamy, and he certainly would do so were he to marry a second wife under Government regulations while the first was still living. When he takes another wife by means of native law no charge is preferred. This does not apply where pagan women are concerned, for, as already noted, she is not likely to resent the bringing in of another wife: also it is very improbable that she would be married other than by native law. On the other hand, an enlightened woman, married under the Ordinance, might reasonably object to the introduction of another woman into the household. She will either have to endure the humiliation, as numbers do, or forsake her husband. The Divorce Court is open to her, but for all practical purposes there might be no Court in existence, because the expense of carrying her plea through it is too heavy for her to undertake.

The same conditions apply for a man married under the Ordinance who wishes to divorce an unfaithful or deserting wife: he is handicapped by the financial obligations. The conditions are, however, worse for a woman because it is not only a question of losing a husband: she also forfeits her home and, in most cases, it works out that she loses her children. Unless she is capable of maintaining herself, she is in danger of being left in sore straits. She has to sacrifice all, and must face the fact that she will, in all probability, have to remain without a husband for the remainder of her days. Nor will she receive much sympathy in the present state of public opinion. Not much imagination is required to understand why a woman hesitates before embarking on a petition for divorce through the medium of the Supreme Court even if she be able to surmount the preliminary difficulty of providing the legal expenses.

The subject needs to be studied in perspective in order to form some opinion of the total effect of polygamy on the individual and on the community. As regards the latter, what bearing has it upon numbers? The chief reason advanced by the people is that it is to ensure the procreation of children to its full limit. It sounds plausible, but the results from observed households do not tally with reasonable expectations. Many children are, indeed, born: at the same time, infant mortality is unduly high. Is polygamy responsible for constitutionally weak children? Some comparisons made between polygamous and monogamous households seem to suggest this. Whatever the cause, there are not the numbers there ought to be according to the number of women.[10]

In substantiation of this, the following examples are quoted, drawn from personally counted numbers in the homes of polygamous acquaintances where the conditions were favourable for gleaning information without arousing suspicion. One old chief had nine wives at his beck and call: the only child alive was a daughter. Another had twenty wives with one boy between them and a few girls. C. had several wives: no son, and the daughters averaged one to each wife. D. had three wives and one child. E. had five wives and three children. F's compound seemed full of women, yet there were no more than three sons and these were no credit to him or the community, indeed, the eldest became unendurable and was expelled from the village.

A false impression must not be conveyed by these statements. When visiting some compounds, one is struck by the number of children present. What needs to be computed is the average number per wife. If this is assumed to be at the rate of three or four apiece, then the number of children would be much greater. The next thing to ascertain is who is the father of those that are seen, for, in many instances, the husband is not the man, although the children call him " father ". Many young wives would not become pregnant if they did not find paramours outside the compound. The husbands do not object as a rule; indeed, they often give surreptitious hints to encourage collusion when a particularly good-looking young man happens to be in the neighbourhood.

When discussing this subject, it has to be admitted that many unpleasant social evils are rife in monogamous countries. They cannot be refuted, nor explained away. At the same time, they are not an integral element of the social system. They may be more or less condoned as necessary evils by some, but are, nevertheless, regarded with shame, and are generally deplored. The efforts of legislators, doctors and social workers testify to this.

POLYGAMY & DIVORCE

There is an aspect of polygamy which does not always receive the attention it should, and that is jealousy between the women. While it is true that additional wives are often brought into the compound with the consent, and possibly at the instigation, of the first wife (" Anasi "), yet feelings cannot always be held in check. A jealous wife may be so roused that she may become a source of danger. Antagonism may be quiescent as long as the husband treats all his wives impartially; should he show signs of favouritism, trouble speedily ensues. Further, it is impossible to prevent quarrelling, and women who have no sense of restraint often develop fiendish proclivities. The outcome is frequently devastating : probably leading to wounding by snatched-up implements, teeth or nails. All polygamists acknowledge that the outbursts of strife among the women are serious defects in the system.

It not infrequently happens that conditions become so bad, and jealousy is so acute, that the only safe procedure is for a mother to send her son away from the compound; she is afraid of the machinations of the other wives, fearing that her son is in danger of being poisoned. This is especially the case with the heir. Naturally, the heirship is coveted, and each mother is jealous for her son's sake. If an opportunity present itself to remove a rival, the temptation may prove too strong for her. It is wise policy to lodge the heir at a safe distance.

Polygamy abounds in intricate and baffling problems and needs to be contemplated with great care. The two extreme schools of thought are not likely to meet with widespread success. The first says : " It is a custom dating from time immemorial. It has been good enough for past generations of Africans, why, then, advocate changes? " The logical, and often expressed, opinion of this school is that the native should be kept in his place; changes are not welcomed. This policy usually has its origin in a desire to retain the native as the main source of cheap labour. The second school condemns polygamy with a sweeping gesture as unchristian, and tolerates no argument on the subject. This is hardness personified; lacking in sympathy and understanding.

There is a third element, initiated and fostered by native men. They argue that polygamy cannot be wrong as it is not condemned *per se* in the Bible. They base their contentions chiefly on the example of King David. He is stated to have been " a man after God's own heart " (1 Sam. xiii. 14), and yet he multiplied the number of his wives. Needless to say, the men who argue in this strain are of the class who have married, for the most part, as Christians and, later, have yielded to the temptation of taking more than one wife. It is difficult to refrain from regarding such men as knaves. They ignore the fact that these words were spoken of David *before* he became a polygamist and also Psalm li. More specifically, they want sanction for this particular indulgence. In this one respect only are they desirous or willing to follow David's example. It is only when convenient to their own inclinations that they advocate Old Testament practices. In every other department of life these men grasp and follow the most modern ideas of which they are capable, and look askance at suggestions to retain many of the good old native customs. Those who argue thus are not worthy of sympathy ; they have not the backbone to stand for their earlier and expressed obligations. They sometimes contend that, though they made their vows, they did so with reservations. That is their affair ; the point is that they put forward David's action only and solely when it happens to be convenient to their desires.

There are serious and diverse problems from whatever angle the subject is viewed, social, economic and religious. Wholesale pronouncements will avail little of substantial value. The African cannot, even if he would, continue to live in the manner of his fathers. The impact of civilisation is pressing heavily upon him from every side, and changes are daily forced upon him. His marriage customs are being affected equally with others ; there is no escape from this under the new conditions imposed.

We are confronted with the old trouble, namely, trying to force the pace. Contact between European and African is a settled fact ; it is also disturbing. Customs must inevitably rearrange themselves to meet the altered circumstances. Time is needed for readjustment with respect to polygamy as for other customs. Every thoughtful student of affairs is prepared to admit that there are many evils inherent in the system ; the polygamists themselves freely confess as much. What has to be realised is that reforms must come slowly. A general introduction of monogamy suddenly would completely disorganise the social and economic life of the country ; there would be absolute chaos and confusion. Native agriculturists depend almost entirely on their wives and families for manual labour ; the peasant farmer would be sadly crippled without his wageless staff of workers. Vast numbers of women would be cast adrift, homeless and penniless. Increased illegitimacy must be another natural result. The pagan Ibo woman's constant yearning is for a home and children of her own. She will strive to secure the latter, though she be deprived of the former ;

so long as polygamy exists she can have both. All elements of shame and dishonour (if there are any) are, thereby, avoided, and she prefers the protection of a husband's name, though she be no more than a subsidiary wife. Hence, proposals to eradicate the system suddenly would meet with strenuous opposition from both men and women alike.

That there are so many practising monogamy is due solely to the work of Christian Missions. The enlightened Ibo admits the evils of polygamy. He contends, however, that it is not so bad as the prostitution which is now spreading abroad. Harlotry, as a profession, was unknown in the Ibo country prior to the impact of Western influences.

Gradually, public opinion will probably come to the conclusion that monogamy is the better system for the body politic, especially as the Government legislation concerning property and inheritance becomes operative over the whole country. The more the people are educated, the higher the standard of life will become. As in civilised countries, the tendency will be to prefer quality to quantity. Men and women will wish to give their children the best education they can afford. The family of a monogamous couple will have better chances than a horde of children all claiming paternal benefits from one and the same harassed man.

Divorce under native law and custom is a much simpler proposition than that which pertains under the Marriage Ordinance. This is only to be expected, the new laws are for enlightened people who have advanced beyond the primitive customs of their forefathers.

Under native law, divorce is literally " the driving out of a wife " (" Ichupu-nwunye "). This involves no protracted litigation and finance has no place in it. It is no more than ordering the woman to quit the compound. The husband may have genuine reason for his action : on the other hand, the excuse may be a flimsy one amounting to little more than mere caprice. Among the unsophisticated folk, divorce is not a prominent feature in the community : when it is put into operation, it is crude, maybe brutal, but certainly simple and definite.

A woman can demand divorce if she can state good reasons in support of her claim. She will find it difficult, for the husband holds the stronger position, inasmuch as he has paid a bride-price for her and, in that sense, she is his purchased possession.

All that a man has to do in order to make divorce effective

is to order his wife to depart or, if she shows reluctance to obey, to drive her out. As she leaves the compound, he hurls her cooking-pot after her, together with one or two other of her personal belongings. This action is symbolical; it demonstrates complete renunciation; in plain language it constitutes divorce, and receives the support of native law and custom. The articles thrown after her are the only possessions she is permitted to take with her. She forfeits, if she has given reasonable cause for the treatment meted to her, all other property. The result is the same if she has given no just cause. In that case, the fact of her being driven out means unfair deprivation. Other than her market basket and her pots, it is assumed that she owns nothing more, not even her children: all are the property of her husband, including herself. If she is nursing an infant she will take it with her. In due time it will be claimed by the husband and must be returned to him.

The woman is free henceforth and left to her own resources, both as regards where she lives and the manner of her life: the husband is not further interested in her, except that he retains his right to receive the dowry price should another man seek her in marriage.

Occasionally, a woman takes the initiative. Because of ill-treatment, or for some other reason for dissatisfaction, a woman of strong character will leave her husband and return to her people. In such case, it is left to the husband to make the next move. He can, if he so desire, demand her restoration. Before this request is granted he must first state his case before the "in-laws". Should it be proved that the husband has given genuine cause of offence, he must offer "nmari", that is compensation to regain her good will. The husband, however, may not wish to see her again, in which case the dowry money, plus any additional expenses incurred, must be refunded.[11] He is not likely to recover his money from the parents; they do not pay in such a case. He has to wait until another man appears who is prepared to marry his ex-wife. A woman may deliberately retard a proposal from another man in order "to tease" her former husband, though this practice is not often followed.

To state it briefly, a woman obtains divorce by running away from her husband; a man by driving his wife out of the house.

This reads as if divorce were a simple and easy matter depending chiefly on the caprice of either the man or the woman. Actually, it may be a cause of much bickering and quarrelling, for it must be remembered that it is not only the man and woman who are affected, but the whole family. The woman

BRIDES-TO-BE.

GIRLS DRESSED FOR FINAL OBSERVANCE OF "NKPU" CEREMONIES PREPARATORY TO MARRIAGE. (PAGE 223.)

POLYGAMY & DIVORCE

has, by marriage into it, become a member of the clan; she is something more than the wife of one of its members, hence many others are implicated in addition to the couple particularly concerned.

Annulment of marriage is permissible in certain circumstances. If a husband prove to be impotent, the woman is free to leave him. In such a case, if the couple be fond of each other and choose to continue life together, a meeting of relatives is called, and the situation stated in their presence. Arrangements are, thereupon, made whereby a male friend acts as sponsor for the defaulting husband. Again, a husband who contracts leprosy may not cohabit with his wife unless she herself is also a leper. If she is free from the disease, another man is requisitioned to serve as proxy for her husband.

NOTES TO CHAPTER XVI

[1] The same practice is found among the Kagoro: " The first wife is the chief, and she looks after the others. She can, apparently, punish them for disobedience by slapping or by other ways, and they are not allowed to retaliate."—" *Tailed Headhunters of Nigeria* ", p. 235.

" A source of injustice, in the case of polygamy, is the influence of the head wife."—" *Fetish Folk of West Africa* ", p. 136.

[2] " Children are not weaned until the age of two or three years. During this period of lactation the husband and wife observe continence in regard to each other. But he has other wives and this continence imposes no restraint on him."—" *Fetish Folk of West Africa* ", p. 138.

[3] Cf. the customs of the Kafirs. " A woman lives in isolation from her husband while she is suckling her child, a process which may last several years. Her isolation from her husband is thought to be essential. If she neglected this custom, she would be troubled with sterility. . . . This incubation period usually lasts for three years at the longest."—" *Savage Childhood* ", p. 82.

[4] " A similar idea prevails among the pagans of Northern Nigeria who never milk cattle in spite of their proximity to the Hausawa and Fulani who regularly milk their cattle."—" *Tailed Headhunters of Nigeria* ", p. 78.

[5] " The wife of a monogamist is a ' nobody ' and, besides, has an unusual amount of work to do."—" *Fetish Folk of West Africa* ", p. 138.

[6] " Dr. Oldfield states that when he visited Idah in 1833, the number of wives attached to the Attah (King) exceeded two thousand."—" *Expedition into the Interior of Africa* ", Vol. II, p. 190.

[7] " *Census of the Southern Provinces, Nigeria, 1931* ", pp. 6–9.

[8] A fact also recorded by Captain William Allen, " *Expedition to the Niger, 1841* ", Vol. I, p. 177.

[9] " She owns the garden and her husband is dependent upon her for his food. If she runs away she leaves him much the poorer . . . and then, he is mortally afraid of her tongue, her chief resource; and well he may be; for in an outburst of passion it is the tongue of a fiend."—" *Fetish Folk of West Africa* ", p. 137.

[10] Macgregor Laird quotes a case: " An elderly chief died, leaving 15 wives and no children."—" *Expedition into the Interior of Africa* ", Vol. I,

POLYGAMY & DIVORCE

p. 225. Cf. table prepared by Dr. McWilliam, " *Expedition to the Niger, 1841* ", Vol. I, p. 247.

[11] The custom varies somewhat in different parts of the Ibo country. In the southern districts a woman is considered to have fulfilled all obligations, pecuniary and otherwise, as soon as there are two of her children running about the house. If the husband gives her cause for complaint he is liable to lose her; she is at liberty to forsake him and go to another man, in which case the original husband has no means of redress.

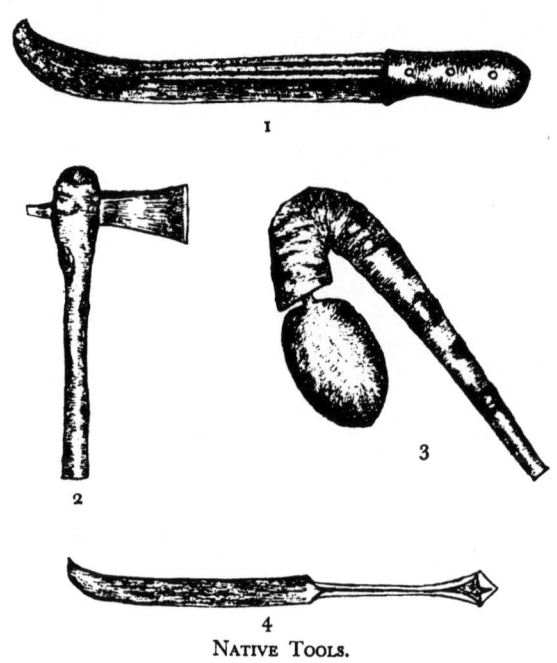

NATIVE TOOLS.
1. Machette (foreign made).
2. Axe.
3. Hoe.
4. Knife for peeling yam. (Note typical folding for handle.)

CHAPTER XVII

ORU & OSU—SLAVES OF MEN & GODS

UNTIL THE ADVENT of the British, slavery was rampant among the Ibos. In earlier days, great numbers of these people were transported to America and the West Indies, and traces of their language and customs still survive among the negroes in these countries. Many Sierra Leonians are descendants of Ibo stock. The first settled foreigner at Onitsha was a missionary, the son of Ibo parents, originally slaves who, after rescue, were landed at Freetown. The suppression of the overseas traffic did not lead to the cessation of slavery in the interior; it continued to exist until the operations became more and more restricted. Under the rigorous methods now in force, the day cannot be far distant when the sporadic cases of kidnapping will be abandoned. Child-stealing will cease to be a profitable institution; the Police will see to that!

At the same time, the stigma remains. There may be no open manifestations of slavery, yet, underneath, the old ideas still persist. To-day, many of the civilised, educated men will not share " kola " with a man of slave descent though, in other respects, he be a friend and an equal, or even superior in wealth and employment. In some areas, it is not permissible for slaves to be buried in the same cemetery where free-born folk are laid to rest, nor will free-born parents allow their children to attend school in company with children of slave-born parents. It will probably be a long time before all traces of slavery disappear from the minds of the people. Even if a man redeem himself he does not, thereby, get rid of the stigma; he has merely emancipated himself. His fellow-townsmen may extend a superficial recognition of his changed status, but they do not appreciably alter their attitude towards him. Except for his own satisfaction, he might just as well save his money. Under the new conditions, a master can no longer force allegiance and service from his slave, since, under British Law, the institution is no longer tolerated.

The law cannot do more; it is for public opinion to act. Until the conscience of the people functions, the distinctions between slave and free-born will be maintained, curtailed, it is true, but nevertheless ever present. In this respect, the Christian element has failed miserably and, to its shame, it has done little to obliterate the inequalities, or to purge out, once for all, the stain of slavery. Until there is a willing spirit to accept all men on equal terms in the social economy, including, notably, intermarriage, the evil will continue as in the past, and be a constant rebuke to, and negation of, Christian principles. This change of attitude cannot be achieved by legislation; it must be the work of conscience creating a sound public opinion.

There are distinct differences between the customs of the Ibos and those of their neighbours in the Niger Delta. In the case of the latter, slavery led to the formation of what are termed " Houses ". A " House " may contain anything up to three hundred people or more, all rendering allegiance to the " Head " (father). This form is not found among the Ibos.

Prior to the establishment of British control, four methods were employed whereby the supply of slaves was augmented, namely, war, kidnapping, purchase, and what is locally termed " pawning ". Greater profits accrued to the first two methods, but the undertaking of them involved risk to life and limb. The third was a mere question of buying and selling, or a slave could be utilised towards the settlement of a debt. A pawn was one who was handed over to a fellow-townsman as security for a loan. To all intents and purposes such a one was no better situated than an ordinary slave. The only difference was that redemption was possible; it was, however, rarely attainable.

Little tribal wars were of frequent occurrence; raids were made on neighbouring towns almost as a matter of course. Captives taken were devoted to serve as human sacrifices,[1] sold into slavery, or eaten at cannibal feasts. Some towns feeling unequal to the struggle, sought the assistance of outside co-operation, and engaged professional soldiers for the purpose. These demanded certain perquisites; they claimed the major portion of the booty taken, including the captives, as part payment for services rendered. Of these mercenaries, the most dreaded were the Abams and Abikiris who operated in the southern parts of the Ibo country. Their methods were drastic in the extreme, and bore no comparison with those adopted by the men of towns that quarrelled and fought without resort to aid from foreign sources.

At one time, kidnapping was notorious. No town or village escaped the attentions of the thieves who made a speciality of child-stealing. When conditions were favourable, they did not hesitate to seize adults, but that was a different proposition from stealing children. The evil has, by no means, ceased, in spite of the vigorous exertions of the Police and the heavy penalties prescribed for those convicted of the crime. Likewise, the fear of kidnappers is still potent throughout the countryside, and it will be a long time before it disappears. It is so deeply embedded that it will continue to exert itself long after the criminals have been suppressed. Travellers in lonely places were in danger of being seized by thieves lying in ambush. To avoid risk of being kidnapped, the only safe plan was to travel in companies. Even so, a sharp look out had to be maintained, and to straggle was to court trouble. Further, the travellers needed to be equipped with weapons. The display of these might act as a deterrent to the kidnappers; they would hesitate to attack fearing that their attempts to steal might be frustrated with damage to themselves. It should be noted that, in olden times, this system of kidnapping was normally restricted to towns at enmity with one another.

The most favoured, but not the only method of stealing children, was by burglary. A house containing children was watched. On a night when the parents or guardians were occupied elsewhere for a time, the thieves stealthily entered the hut, or, if necessary, forced an entrance, and carried off the children. Some of the kidnappers were bold and reckless, and would enter a hut even when adults were present. If these were asleep, the thieves might carry out their objective without waking them. On the other hand, they might be roused, in which case murder was added to the crime. The thieves would not risk the possibility of witnesses to their evil deeds: every precaution was taken to prevent identification. I remember a case where the eldest girl, too big to be carried easily and quickly through the bush, feigned sleep while kidnappers killed her father and mother, and then departed with her brothers and sisters.

The hours selected for these night raids were when the children were soundly asleep. They were seized and gagged before they were really awake, thrust into bags, or smothered in a cloth. They had no chance to raise an alarm: they probably were too frightened to cry even if they had been left free to do so. Having stifled the possibility of the children raising cries of alarm, each burglar seized his bundle and made off with all speed. The number of children kidnapped in this manner was large. All over the country are men and women who have not the remotest idea where they were born, or have but vague recollections of their early surroundings. They can, perhaps, remember being kidnapped, but have not sufficient knowledge to help them further. Occasionally, faint memories survive and, of recent years, one, here and there, has been able to trace his or her parental home and renew contact with their relatives. The usual practice was (and is) to sell the kidnapped children to serve as common slaves, or for dedication to local deities. Naturally, it paid the procurers to offer their captives in as sound a condition as possible. That, indeed, was essential for disposing of them as ordinary slaves, but was not so necessary in the case of slaves devoted to the service of an " alusi ". As a matter of fact, some of the children were handled roughly. Some of those attached to town shrines had suffered such maltreatment that they were permanently disabled. In certain cases, it was asserted that the injuries had been deliberately inflicted with the object of frustrating any attempt to escape, but the evidence for this is unreliable. Some foundation for the statement is found in the law that prohibited consecrated persons from wandering beyond the precincts of the shrines. These dedicated people are spoken of as " *Ndi-osu* ".

This leads us to examine the " Osu " System, an integral part of Ibo religious practice. The word " Osu " means a " slave ", but one distinct from an ordinary slave (oru) by the fact that he is the property of a god ; in plain language " a living sacrifice ". Once devoted to a god, there is practically no prospect of such a slave regaining freedom, and, formerly, his movements were restricted to the precincts of the shrine to which he was attached. Redemption is possible, but of extremely rare occurrence ; even then the fact is remembered against the one redeemed.

In most towns of the Ibo country there are public deities. They are of many types, crude figures of human beings of wood or clay, or merely mounds of earth or, again, no more than pieces of timber set upright in the ground. They are sheltered under small thatched roofs. The latest idea is to abandon grass or palm-leaf thatch in favour of corrugated iron ! It is customary to offer sacrifices to these deities when invoking blessing on the community, or seeking relief in times of distress. Further, it might fall to the lot of a man to do something specially, either acting upon a not-to-be-neglected hint from the native priest, or in order to satisfy his own conscience, or when wanting some particular benefit. Whatever the motive, the man seeks an offering. His feelings are mixed ; on the one hand, fear urges him to act ; on the other, he exercises his wits to secure a sacrifice on the most economical terms. In former days, his main idea was to purchase a boy or girl

ORU & OSU

cheaply, present his gift to the deity, and thus fulfil his obligation. In some cases, the only thought that worried the man was that his "sacrifice" should live for a year, because, should the victim die before twelve months had expired, he would have to provide a substitute, and so incur the expense a second time. This rule was not universal; in certain towns all obligations were fulfilled immediately the sacrifice was accepted by the priest on behalf of the deity. A human being was not always demanded; instead, a sheep or a cow, or even a fowl, was sufficient, but whatever was offered, immediately it was accepted, it automatically became sacrosanct.

There was one other way by which the number of " osus " was augmented. A man or woman, labouring under the impression that he or she was in danger, could flee to the shrine and claim protection. In return for benefits of sanctuary, such an one forfeited liberty and became an " osu ", the property of the deity. In some areas, terms could be stipulated. A person might claim sanctuary on condition that he or she might be redeemed by the exchange of a cow or something of an acceptable value. If, however, the person demanded safety for life, the choice was irrevocable; such an one could under no circumstances be redeemed.

All persons and animals so dedicated are sacred and inviolate. Anyone injuring an " osu " exposes himself to serious trouble and, should death ensue, the guilty person must provide a substitute and, in addition, make fitting recompense for the misdeed, whether committed accidentally or with criminal intention.

The animals naturally stray in search of food, browsing about the countryside at will, and frequently wandering far away from the villages to which they are attached. They are always recognised and left unmolested; certainly no pagan Ibo would venture to injure or slay one. The animals (and formerly human " osus ") are marked by a small slit cut in the lobe of the ear; in the case of a fowl the foot is cut. The human " osus " do not, as a rule, wander far, living as they do within the precints of the " alusi " shrine. Often they sleep under its eaves; in other cases they erect tiny booths adjacent to the shrine. In such conditions, many of the " osu " people, especially the elderly ones, pass a miserable existence.

Generally, the deity to which they are attached is the presiding god of the market. The " ndi-osu " roam about, and are not restrained from collecting small pickings from the goods offered for sale. Also, when walking behind people carrying baskets, they may abstract what they can clutch with their fingers, and remain immune from retribution. The owner may, perhaps, be angry, but he can do no more than vent his wrath in abuse. If he should, in the heat of the moment, flog an " osu " to the extent of drawing blood, the result is great commotion, and the sinner will be required to bring an appropriate sacrifice wherewith to make atonement for injuring the slave who, in such circumstances, represents the god.

There must, of course, have been a time when there were only one or two living victims devoted to a deity of this character. It is possible for one to remain the sole devotee though, normally, others are forthcoming to share in the service of the god. There may come by purchase, or as offerings, two or three women and a man or two and, once the sexes are mixed, children naturally follow. All children born under " osu " conditions are, " *ipso facto* ", slaves of the god. Again, a free man having intercourse with an " osu " girl automatically becomes an " osu ".

When a young child is brought for presentation to a god, the first " osu " man or woman to set eyes upon it claims the child by right and assumes ownership forthwith. It thus becomes a slave in a double sense, namely, firstly of the god, secondly, and in a far more pronounced fashion, the slave of the man or woman who has claimed the right of possession by virtue of first sight.

The history of some of these deities stretches back to immemorial times and, during the years, by natural increase and by additional offerings, the numbers have grown to such an extent that they are sufficient to form communities of their own. Where this is the case, there is, outwardly, nothing to assist the ordinary observer to distinguish between these sacred slaves and the free-born people of the town. They build huts to meet the family needs, cultivate farms, marry and bear children. A man may even aspire to honours ; indeed, within certain limits, it is open to him to pass through the various titular degrees to " Ozọ " itself, the highest and most coveted of all. Where these conditions prevail, the measure of comfort depends, as in other sections of the community, chiefly on the man's own efforts, always with the proviso, that he *is* the slave of the god, and his liberties are strictly encompassed. Outside the " osu " village, his privileges are nil ; he is regarded as a slave by all free-born folk, and his social status fixed accordingly. Any titles he may have acquired are recognised by his fellow " osu " villagers only ; not by the freemen.

It has been noted that it is a rare thing for an " osu " to be redeemed ; the risk is too great, and it may turn out a profitless speculation. In the first place, there is the menace arising from offending the god; he may resent the loss of his slave. In the second, the redeemer is liable to lose what he has purchased. To quote an example: I was acquainted with a man who "fell in love" with an "osu" girl, so much so, that in order to avoid becoming an "osu" himself, he redeemed her prior to marrying her. All went well for a couple of years; then there was a quarrel. The woman, in her rage, rushed back to the hut of the god and claimed sanctuary. The man lost his wife and had no means of redress. Hence, the inducement to redeem an "osu" is not very potent, and its rarity is understandable.

Where there are a considerable number of "osu" people, the problems of daily life are fairly easily solved, for each will help the other in building, farming and in any other rôle required. Where there are only one or two, the situation is very different. They cannot build huts and, as often as not, have to depend on the charity of the villagers, a very precarious means of livelihood. Some of the folk will give scraps more or less cheerfully in the belief that they are rendering service to the god. Others give grudgingly, and solely because they fear his vengeance. Thus, it comes about, that the "osu", in some cases, is apt to be neglected and suffers accordingly.

The duties of the "ndi-osu" consist of cleaning the compound of the god which, as a rule, is the market-place. They must cut the bush and grass, and keep the precincts tidy; they are permitted to farm the land assigned to the god and they, alone, may eat of the fruits thereof.

When sacrifices are brought, such as goats or fowls, the priest, after shedding the blood of atonement, takes a portion of the flesh for his own use; a share is given to the one presenting the offering and the remainder, that is the offal, is passed on to the "osus".

It is of importance to observe that the practice of purchasing or kidnapping human victims for dedication to town deities has ceased officially in the Ibo country. The British Government prohibits such practices; animals only now are used. It is equally important for Government to be alive to the fact that many chiefs and other prominent men find means to retain, or increase, a retinue of slaves by clever manipulation of the "osu" and "pawning" systems.

It has been suggested that this Osu System is an institution going back not more than three or four generations and that, at its initiation, the "osu" held an honourable position until the slave trade brought it into degradation, and caused it to degenerate to its present unhappy condition.

ORU & OSU

These assertions are confined to the Owerri area; one does not hear of them in the more northerly districts. One report states that the cult was founded in the neighbourhood of Okigwi in the following circumstances. A chief was killed in war and his people sought revenge upon his rival. Not finding a way to accomplish this, resort was had to the Oracle (" Long Ju-Ju ") at Aro-Chuku. The advice given was that sacrifices prescribed by the Oracle must be executed on the grave of the dead chief. In order, however, to make them acceptable to " Chuku ", and to be really effective, they must be performed by an Aro = " Son of Chuku ".

There seemed to be some delay in securing the services of an Aro (man) and, either because of this failure, or to expedite matters, it is alleged that " Chuku " gave sanction for a non-Aro to officiate. The only stipulation in respect of the man to be appointed was that he must not be a native of the town. So a man was chosen as directed, who acted as substitute for the unobtainable Aro. He, it is stated, was, thereupon, given the name " Osu ", with authority to act as proxy for an Aro priest. He was to be venerated with the honour and respect due to an Aro. He was also to act as mediator between the people and " Chuku ".

Another assertion is very similar in form, but is more definitely expressed. It springs from the town of Uratta near Owerri.

The following diagram sets out the issues more clearly :

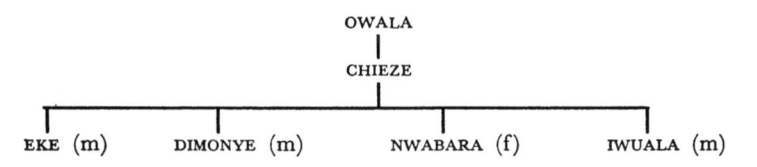

```
                    OWALA
                      |
                    CHIEZE
                      |
    ┌────────────┬────┴───────┬────────────┐
  EKE (m)    DIMONYE (m)  NWABARA (f)   IWUALA (m)
```

It appears that Chieze entered into conflict with Ndumoha, the founder of the village of Umunaho, a part of Uratta, and one of Chieze's relatives was killed. Chieze sought to retaliate, and made several unsuccessful attempts to avenge his loss.

He then appealed to the Oracle at Aro-Chuku and was directed to perform certain sacrifices through Okitankwo, the goddess of the spring of that name. Owing to the nearness of the other belligerent village, Chieze consecrated his own son, Iwuala, to act as substitute for an Aro priest calling him " Osu " (said to stand for " pro-Aro "). He did this for fear lest his intentions should become known to the enemy while waiting for an Aro man to be brought. Iwuala, under his new name,

"Osu", performed the sacrifices. Chieze went to war again and succeeded in killing two men of the opposing village. By virtue of his consecration, Iwuala usurped to himself authority to mediate whenever the Umunaho folk were in need of priestly assistance. The position proved lucrative, and he was soon in affluent circumstances and a prominent person in the community.

His new office did not sever his connection with the other members of his family. When his sister, Nwabara, was married, the dowry was paid to him. He seems, further, to have managed to succeed to his father's property and position, and became the founder of Umu-Iwala-Chieze village. To this day, the descendants of Iwuala hold the Ofo of Owala, one of the ancestors of Uratta. The eldest male descendant of Iwuala, living at Umu-Iwala-Chieze, is the priest of the god "Umune", and of the goddess of the farm land (Ala-Ubi), officiating both for the "osus" and the "non-osus" of the descendants of Owala.

These first "osus" appear to have enjoyed many privileges, and ere long became subjects of envy. The example began to be copied elsewhere, one of the first places being Ngwoma, where there is said to be the largest number of "ndi-osu" at the present day. The office being lucrative, volunteers came forward for appointments as "osus".

There were many obligations attached to the office. An "osu", under the original constitution, must be of an upright character, and live an orderly pious life acceptable to the god whom he served. Any infringements or failures would bring disaster upon his head. There were no restrictions on his movements; he was at full liberty to move at will, protected from violence by virtue of his office.

As related above, it would appear that, in the beginning, the "osus" were privileged folk enjoying honours and benefits compatible with their claims as the servants of "Chuku". Whether or no this was the case, for very many years they have been living under quite different conditions. Whatever truth there may be in the traditions, they are of local authorship. Going back not more than two generations, there is doubt whether "Chuku" of Aro fame exercised any influence whatever over the greater part of the Ibo country, apart from his powers as a divining oracle. Spiritual domination in those days emanated from Nri *not* Aro-Chuku, and it is difficult to give much credence to the statements, though, for the sake of many friends who are members of the "Osu" confraternity, one would like to think of their forefathers as men respected

ORU & OSU

and honoured by virtue of their office. One fears, however, that the desire to give the cult the benefit of bygone pre-eminence, or even equality, has very little to support it. The wish to rehabilitate those who are under the " osu " ban seems rather to be uppermost in the arguments used above. One cannot overlook the fact that very many " osus " were devoted to the " alusi " when little children, who could not possibly be thought of as sacrificing priests. Another fact should be noticed, namely, that the " osu " seems to have no place on the western side of the Niger. It is widely spread on the eastern side, with special prominence in the Owerri and Okigwi Districts.

There is a small area where certain " osus " seem to enjoy privileges similar to those stated to have originally belonged to the priests in the Owerri and Okigwi Districts. This is situated in the north-east corner of the Nsukka Division on the extreme border of the Ibo country. A god named " Adolo " holds sway in this part. His priest is held in great respect and he, the priest, exercises considerable influence and authority. It is a lucrative post by virtue of the many sacrifices presented to the god and there is no doubt that, prior to his activities being curbed by Government, it was common to offer children as human sacrifices to " Adolo ". All children so dedicated were, of course, " osu ". The chief point of interest in this case is that the priest is called " Osu ", and that he has maintained his authority. Further, that it is a profitable profession, so much so, that there is no lack of candidates, especially from among the younger sons of chiefs who are willing to become " osus " with a view to becoming agents for " Adolo ". The prospective returns are sufficiently attractive to induce young men to take any risks involved.

This instance of the predominance of " Osu " practice appears to be an isolated one. It may probably be accounted for by failure to distinguish between the priest and the sacrifices presented to the god. The priest may be loosely termed " Osu " as the one at the water " Di-Awo " near Umuchu (p. 41), while the offerings, particularly the human ones, are the real " osus ".

The system became bound up with the Slave Trade and, while some victims were sold as slaves (" iru " = plural for " oru ") others were devoted to the local gods. Gradually, whatever respect there may have been towards them decreased, and finally disappeared, though, to this day, to injure one may prove a serious offence. The essential change was from a recognised and accepted servant of " Chuku " to that of a living sacrifice, compelled to live outside the compound of the master who presented him to the deity. There may be reasons for this. Fear of malice may have prompted segregation or, again, by refraining from association, liability to injure an " osu " was avoided. It were better for the ordinary man to keep apart from the " osus " lest he fall into trouble. For the same reasons marriage between a free-born and an " osu " appeared unwise, involving too many risks.

The impact of European influences, especially the freedom of body proclaimed by the Government on the one hand, and liberty of mind preached by the Missions on the other, have put the whole " Osu System " into the melting-pot. Large numbers of the younger folk are breaking away from their former environment; they have entered the schools, and have gone on to secure positions as teachers, clerks and other kinds of employment. To the ordinary observer, they are not distinguishable from free-born folk, but, in the community, they are still a class by themselves. Of course, this distinction must go; it cannot long survive among an educated and enlightened people. It is for public opinion to rise up and destroy the system root and branch as an anachronism no longer tolerable in a free country.

After this long digression on the " Osu System ", we come to the third method for recruiting the supply of slaves, namely, by purchase. This scarcely calls for discussion. In most towns of any importance, and boasting a reputable market, slaves formed part of the regular merchandise.

There remains to be discussed the fourth method whereby slaves are procured. It is locally termed " pawning ", and that nomenclature fairly accurately describes the system. Actually, the pawn is a bond or a security for a loan. When a man is in need of money for some specific purpose, and he can find no other way to meet the demand, he resorts to the custom of pawning. Such a man is at liberty to pawn his children, his younger brothers or sisters, or his own person. The Ibo manifests no compunction in contracting debts and, consequently, money-lenders thrive. Borrowing amounts almost to a curse among these people.

There are no stated rules governing repayments of money borrowed. Excessive usury is charged, and the creditor makes spasmodic attempts to collect this, but the repayment of the principal is usually postponed indefinitely.[2]

The debtor is generally left undisturbed for years or, what is more likely, until the creditor himself is in need. At such time, the claim must be met somehow, either by cash paid down, or by confiscation of property. Thus, it is no unusual thing for a man to be confronted suddenly with a demand on account of a debt contracted years previously, or, it may be, in respect of money borrowed by his father or grandfather. If he cannot pay what is demanded, nor raise a new loan, he resorts to pawning. Those who are handed over as securities virtually become slaves; henceforth, they are at the disposal of the money-lender until the loan is refunded, plus accrued interest. And it is almost true to say that "once a pawn, always a pawn", for, although redemption is possible its achievement is extremely rare, indeed, almost unknown. The fate that befalls the pawn is not only his to bear: it applies also to any children he may beget during the time he is subject to the conditions that govern the life of a pawn: automatically, a pawn's children are born to that estate.

One aggravating fact is that a child's liberty may be forfeited in exchange for a very small loan. For a couple of pounds a man may be plunged into servitude for as many years, while a child may find no way of escape and remain unredeemed for life. One typical case investigated revealed that a man had given his son as security for a loan of fifty shillings value. Ten years later the youth was still a pawn!

For the most part, a pawn submits resignedly to the system, and puts forth no effort to regain his liberty. He seldom has the necessary initiative and, where that is forthcoming, he still needs outside assistance. His sole chance of success lies in the intervention of a friend. Redemption can be wrought by patient care and waiting if a friend will act on his behalf. It can be done by the friend presenting a she-goat to the pawn. The money accruing from sales of the kids is allowed to accumulate until there is sufficient to meet the claims of the creditor. All that can be said in favour of this hypothetical arrangement is that it is possible; it is very rarely put into execution, and the longer action is delayed, the less probability is there of the pawn being released from this form of slavery.

Another injustice lies in the fact that a debt so contracted is not extinguished by the death of a pawn. The money-lender enters a fresh claim, and demands a substitute to replace the one lost by death. It matters not how many years a man has served; the redemption price has not been paid and, until that is handed over, there can be no cancellation of the debt.

When discussing the system with a native, he argues that a pawn is not a slave, because it is open for a pawn to regain his freedom at any time. In that sense there is a difference, but so long as he remains a pawn his status and treatment

ORU & OSU

varies little from that of an ordinary slave. There is one saving clause and that is, that a pawn cannot be sold while a slave may be.[3] This pawning system is, like many other customs of the Ibos, of ancient lineage. It is of a type that possesses no qualifications to recommend its conservation. It is doomed to disappear, because of the many injustices attached to its practice. If legislation does not succeed in crushing it root and branch, it will continue until public opinion exerts itself and abolishes the anachronism.

Pawns who have given fair service, should be immediately freed from further obligations, and in no case should the contract be heritable; indeed, the pernicious system should be prohibited in its entirety. In certain areas, it has reached notorious proportions and some well-to-do men have, by its use, secured a considerable number of wageless workers; in plain language, slaves. Sometimes, the issue is not so far reaching. For example, one has known a chief to secure all the labour he needed for his extensive farm work by arranging to pay the tax for numbers of men of the village, on condition that they repaid him by working without wages for the farming season, that is, for some six months. Six months' labour to be given in return for three or four shillings! In this case, however, the man concludes the bargain himself; there is no one else involved, and it is not a debt of any importance. Only during a time of economic depression would such an agreement be contemplated.

In past days, a slave (as distinct from a pawn) was reckoned as of no more value than his equivalent in money. He was entirely at the disposal of his owner, even to life itself. He had no privileges beyond those extended to him by the goodwill of his master. Should that goodwill be of small extent, or absent, the slave was in rather a distressful position. So much depended upon the attitude of the owner. Many slaves, if not altogether happy, were considerately treated, and lived in fair comfort compared with the lot of slaves in some countries, and accumulated a certain amount of property. The master was not unaware of his need to keep on terms with his slaves for opportunities abounded for them to retaliate if treated badly. The slave often administered food and drink, and no great skill or cunning was required to introduce some virulent poison with one or the other, hence a master had need to be careful for his own health's sake.

A slave had certain compensations which somewhat ameliorated his condition. On one day per week, he was at liberty to do pretty well as he wished. He had his own hut, his plot of ground for tilling, and every fourth day he could devote to his private schemes—within limits. When he wished to marry, he applied to his master who, if favourable, as he usually was, made arrangements to fulfil the request. The most common course was for the master to hand over a female slave as a mate for the man. In such case, no dowry price was offered or expected; the man had his woman, the owner was satisfied, regarding it, bluntly, as a breeding contract. In due course, it would be a source of profit, for all children born to the couple became, automatically, his property. The result was similar when the master purchased a female slave in order to provide a mate for his man slave. Occasionally, two owners would enter into a compact whereby one would supply a woman from his establishment to be a companion to the man slave of the other house. The contract stipulated that, in compensation for the loss of the services of the woman, each alternate child born of the union must be transferred to the woman's original owner.

It scarcely needs stating that the advance of his master's interests was expected to be the slave's chief concern. In addition to the demands upon his physical strength, it was his duty, where possible, to assist financially towards any project undertaken by his owner. This was more particularly the case when a new house or compound was in course of construction, or funds were needed to pay instalment fees for a more advanced title; also for funeral and sacrificial ceremonies. Such demands had to be accepted without complaint or demur. Resentment there might sometimes be, but the wise slave refrained from giving expression to his feelings in public, while to manifest signs of insubordination meant severe chastisement; possibly death to the offender.

The thought might arise, " Why was it more slaves did not run away from their owners ? " There were a number of reasons. The country is covered with dense " bush ", and a man would rather have a poor home than be a homeless fugitive. The runaway was in jeopardy of being kidnapped by other men, and he might find himself in worse plight than that from which he had fled. What deterred most was lack of enterprise, emphasised by the devastating fear of recapture and restoration to an angry owner. The treatment meted out to an absconding slave was barbarous in the extreme. He was bound and beaten, half-starved, and many were brutally mutilated. The prospect of the fearful consequences, if recaptured, was such, that the average slave was afraid to attempt flight. Some did succeed, and managed to find sanctuary at Calabar and other coast towns.

FULFILLING "NKPU" CUSTOMS.

GIRLS OBSERVING CEREMONIES PREPARATORY TO MARRIAGE. (PAGE 223.)

ORU & OSU

Escapes, however, were rare events. The great majority of slaves accepted their conditions philosophically. They mingled with the rest of the villagers and, except that they *were* slaves, and were barred from the privileges of the free folk, they passed their days in fair contentment. Master and slave were frequently the closest of friends, the latter becoming the confidential companion of the former, trusted with affairs which could be successfully negotiated only by a faithful, trustworthy servant.

Before the spirit of liberty began to assert itself in the country, that is, before the freedom of all men proclaimed by the British Government and fostered by Missions and education became effective, the possibility of freedom roused little enthusiasm, indeed, a suggestion that liberty was attainable, if desired, was more likely to be received with scorn than with pleasure. On one occasion I discoursed at length on " Liberty " and its benefits to a young man with whom I was closely acquainted. He listened attentively to all I had to say and then quietly remarked, " What has N. done to me that I should seek my liberty ? I never knew my parents. I do not know where I was born. All the love and affection that I have ever experienced have come from N. He has been father and mother to me ; he has clothed, fed and educated me. Why should I forsake my benefactor and, by so acting, repudiate all that he has done for me ? Why ! he is my father ! " It should be added that slaves who are born and domiciled in a household were not sold except under pressure of extreme necessity, and then the sale was to a fellow townsman if at all possible.[4]

The outlook is rapidly changing, and the attitude of that young man is different to-day from what it was five-and-twenty years ago. Under the old conditions, emancipation was beset with difficulties for both slaves and owners. A poor old man might be infinitely better off as a slave than as a freeman wanted by nobody. Wherever he went, he would be treated as an outcast. This strong feeling of repugnance against a person of slave descent is still rampant, and the day is not yet when the emancipated slave of the old type can enjoy freedom.[5]

The young people of slave descent will fare better. There are opportunities for them to attend mission and other schools. Education up to a useful standard, backed by practical training, will place the slave on equal terms with free-born artisans and labourers. There appears to be no valid reason against his making fair progress. But, among his own people, he will still be a slave, for, with them, a slave is always a slave. He may

ORU & OSU

attain to a well-to-do position and in all respects prove himself a worthy citizen, nevertheless, the stigma remains. If at no other time this distinction was apparent yet it would emerge when he wished to marry, or presumed to submit his name as a candidate for titular rank. He is, at present, barred from marriage with a free-born girl, and will not be accepted as a candidate for a title.

There were some good points connected with Domestic Slavery. The old-time slave was always sure of board and lodging. The master had certain responsibilities towards his slave, as the slave had obligations towards his master. That, at least, prevented vagrancy in the land, with all its associated social and economic problems.

Slavery, in any form and under any pseudonym, is unsound in principle, and all types have been abolished by law. The system outwardly is practically ended, except in very remote parts, and where clever rogues are snaring ignorant victims by means of the " Osu " and " Pawning " Systems. With the increasing spread of education and civilisation, plus improved transport facilities, slavery as an institution will pass away. It only remains for the Christian public to act in accordance with its profession and the stigma, as well as the institution, will vanish into the limbo of forgotten things.

NOTES TO CHAPTER XVII

[1] In the neighbouring district of Idah, Dr. Oldfield, writing in 1833, states : " On a mound at the southern end of the Queen's apartment was a pile of fifteen human skulls, eight of which were evidently quite fresh. The King is in the habit of thus butchering three or four slaves every week."—" *Expedition into the Interior of Africa* ", Vol. II, p. 190.

[2] When a money-lender makes use of a Native Court to enforce his demands, the European officer who reviews the case will not sanction an exorbitant rate of interest ; the figure is changed to a fair and just amount.

[3] " A similar custom prevails among the Kagoro of N. Nigeria where the pawn is compelled to remain with the creditor for four years, and farm his land and work for him generally. After that, supposing that he had not previously escaped, he would be free, and the debt would be extinguished. The pawn would be kindly treated, and not sold if of the same tribe."—" *Tailed Headhunters of Nigeria* ", p. 121.

[4] " Among the Mpongwe Domestic Slavery is rarely attended with the usual horrors of alien enslavement. They are serfs rather than slaves. Until the advent of the white slaver, they were rarely sold or exchanged. They were sometimes taken for debt and sometimes stolen from other tribes."—" *Fetish Folk of West Africa* ", p. 32.

[5] " Many former slaves have chosen to maintain the old relationship—somewhat modified—rather than accept full freedom and be left without friends, family or possessions ; a peculiar misfortune for those who have never had an opportunity to acquire a habit of independence."—*Ibid.*, p. 32.

CHAPTER XVIII

CAPITAL CRIME

THIS TITLE IS USED in its widest and most literal aspect and includes Murder, Infanticide and the slaying of birds and animals.

MURDER

Generally speaking, under ancient native law, capital punishment was always meted out to the murderer. There is a saying " O gbulu ǫchu adeli olo ", which means that a " murderer does not go unpunished ".

It may be noted in passing that the introduction of English Criminal Law is very perplexing to the Ibo mind. That a man, known to be a murderer, should be pronounced " not guilty " and set at liberty, because of insufficient evidence, or some other technicality, is beyond the Ibo's understanding, and appears to him to be absurd. With the Ibos, there is one law, and one only, for the murderer, and that is hanging.

There are at least four classes of murder. The Ibo has no difficulty in distinguishing between them, or in deciding upon the established procedure for trying the case. They are classified as follows :

1. QCHU QGHUM = accidental or unpremeditated murder ; otherwise manslaughter.

The manslayer is notified and given opportunity to flee the town. He must remain in exile for three years. After that interval he may return, if he so desire, and will be received on payment of compensation to the relatives of the man slain, at a rate to be fixed. If the victim happen to be a pregnant woman, compensation must be paid in respect of two lives. It was a common practice for the accused's family to hand over a girl as a substitute (Nkechi) for the person slain, thereby providing means to balance the loss.

2. UNPROVED CASES (Ibu Qchu).

When a man pleaded " not guilty " of murder, it was customary to establish his innocence by means of trial by ordeal.

CAPITAL CRIME

The dead person was washed, and the water was collected as it ran off the corpse. A relative took a sip of this water to demonstrate that no poison had been mixed with it ; then the accused person swallowed a mouthful. The gods, thereupon, decided the issue. If the man should outlive the stipulated period (generally twelve months) and, as far as one can see, there was no special reason why he should die other than by sheer auto-suggestion, then he would, at a specified time, appear in the market-place and declare in public that the gods had proved his innocence.

3. DEATH AS A RESULT OF FIGHTING.

In a fight between relatives, or people of the same town, guns were forbidden, while matchets, spears, bows and arrows, staves and such-like weapons were permitted. At the same time, it was not permissible to use them indiscriminately ; there must be no fatal wounding. It might be, however, that in spite of warnings and conventions, a man was hurt to such an extent that he died from his ill-treatment. In such case, his opponent was informed, and notice sent to the people of his village. The whole population of the village fled to another town and their property was confiscated by the relatives of the deceased. The huts were burned, walls broken down and trees felled. Henceforth, the land was " Umu-Ochu " land (children of murder). It remained untilled and desolate for at least three years, after which the offending villagers paid compensation and were granted leave to return. The case was considered as finally settled. If the manslayer wished to save his village, he could do so by hanging himself immediately on hearing of the death of the man he had wounded. To secure a full measure of vengeance, and to satisfy jealousy, sometimes a prominent man was named as the culprit instead of the actual man ; thus the accident might be used to provide the opportunity to remove a man against whom a grudge was held.

Another point to be noted is what is termed " Egbue ebelu isi " that is " killing and cutting off the head ". In tribal wars, it was often customary to make a treaty between the towns concerned whereby it was agreed that, in the event of a man being killed, he must not be decapitated. To cut off the head would be equivalent to swearing eternal enmity, the one town against the other. Hence, we find the retort in a dispute, " Mu na-i adigo na egbue ebelu isi ? " " Have you and I come to the stage to kill and cut off the head ? " in other words, " Are we such enemies to one another that we cannot forgive and forget ? "

CAPITAL CRIME

4. DELIBERATE OR WILFUL MURDER.

Should a man wilfully slay a member of his own village, the houses and property of the whole family are destroyed. If he had not already run away, he was expected to hang himself. Should he delay action, he was prompted to do so by having a suitable rope handed to him. This was the honourable custom, acknowledged by all proper-spirited citizens. Occasionally, a murderer might be coward enough to run away from the village. Usually he was not pursued, nor was any demand made for his extradition. In such case, he must remain in exile until all bitter feeling towards him had died down, which was generally a matter of from three to seven years according to the place and custom. In some places the exile was for life.

Should any of the dead man's relatives see the murderer return to the village, they had the right to kill him at sight. He was " onye-ochu " (murderer). On the other hand, after the stipulated period spent in exile, negotiations might be opened up whereby he was, in due course, allowed to return to his village and resume his life among his old companions. He must fulfil the appropriate sacrifices, and make restitution as prescribed. Even though the man escaped into exile, or ran to sanctuary, the whole family property was destroyed and forbidden to be used by anyone ; there was no avoiding that part of the penalty.

DEATH OF NOTORIOUS EVIL-DOERS

This includes such as were unruly and who refused to submit to the protests of relatives, or who acted in such a manner that they placed the family or village in jeopardy ; in other words, were a menace to the community. Driven to desperation, the relatives quietly arranged with the people of another town to rid them of the nuisance. Under some pretext, the man was induced to pass along a selected path until a spot was reached where his executioners were lying in ambush. Nowadays, the manslayers would be charged with murder and, if declared guilty, would suffer accordingly. In old days, natives regarded the crime as justifiable homicide ; they were doing nothing more than getting rid of a menace to the well-being of the community, with the same underlying idea as clearing away an insanitary nuisance.

While on the subject of killing, it may be of interest to note some of the laws pertaining to domestic creatures which happen to infringe tabu prohibitions in some form or another.

CAPITAL CRIME

Capital punishment follows for instance :
A hen hatching but one chick.
A dog or sow bearing but one offspring instead of a litter.
A goat that climbs on to the roof of a house.
A hen laying an egg in the night.
A fowl that flies over a corpse.
A crowing hen or cock that lays eggs (*sic*).
A cock crowing at midnight.
A dog that eats kola nut, or a piece of human hair.
An animal procreating one of another species.

INFANTICIDE

More has been said of the liability of children to die violent deaths in Chapter XII. It may be helpful to tabulate some of the causes which lead to infanticide. Any abnormality in child-bearing is " alu ", that is, abomination to most Ibo people. The old practice was to kill the child immediately after birth, or to cast it away or, in some neighbourhoods, to pass it on to the people of Nri. The following are some instances where death followed birth without delay :

Nwa-okpi. This indicates conception before the accepted age of maturity, and it refers to a child born before the girl-mother has fulfilled the customary ceremonies preliminary to child-bearing. The actual ceremonies vary more or less in different neighbourhoods. Such tabu-breaking children are quietly put out of the way.

Nwa-aghom, which means a child born before a previous brother or sister has been weaned—say an interval of two years. A child conceived before the resumption of menstruation is always cast away. No blame is attached to the parents for destroying such a child ; it cannot be allowed to interfere with the progress of its predecessor.

Nwa-azu-nkpa. A child born during the period of its mother's mourning the death of her husband. A child so born, or conceived, is cast away or passed on to Nri.

Nso-nwa-ejero-ije. If a mother has a menstrual period along the time she is expecting another child, while the previous one is unable to walk, although it may have been weaned, the new baby is justified, but the one born before it is handed over to Nri. Also sacrifices are offered for the purification of the compound.

Umu-nabo or *Ejima.* Twins. Placed in a water-pot and deposited in the " bush ", or otherwise destroyed.

Iji-okpa-puta. Footling or breech presentation. An abomi-

CAPITAL CRIME

nation involving the death of the child whether the mother survives or not; in the great majority of cases she does not.

Ifilifi. That is, when a child is born in a bag of membranes. It is destroyed.

Ipu-eze-n'afọ. A child being born with teeth—the penalty is the same as for—

Nwa-eze-enu, cutting the upper teeth first.

Ime-ogbi = a dumb conception. That is, conception before the ceremony of "Ama-izizi" has been fulfilled. (*Vide* p. 180.)

THE ARO KNOT.
Wrought from manilla metal. Held in great honour by the heads of the Aro-Chuku people.

CHAPTER XIX

LAND TENURE & INHERITANCE

IT CAN GENERALLY be accepted that, under native law, it is not customary to alienate land from the family, and the head acts as trustee of the property.[1] This statement is, indeed, general, for exceptions are numerous. Permission is freely given to tenants to cultivate land or to build upon it, but the " Head " can always lay claim to proprietary rights. The occupier is seldom disturbed so long as he is prepared to acknowledge the ground landlord. Rent is not usually demanded, the tenancy being confirmed by the offering and acceptance of " ojji " at the time permission to occupy the land is granted, and on more or less regular occasions subsequently.[2]

This system of granting permission to occupy land, nowadays termed " Kola Tenantship ", is an interesting subject and worthy of study. An important fact that must be kept clearly in mind is that this system, in its original form, did *not* contemplate the allocation of land to any person other than a member of the clan or village ; normally, it was a relative, certainly someone well known. The advent of foreigners never entered into the calculations and, again, each village was self-contained. In such circumstances, land was allocated to friends only, men and women over whom the owners and village elders had competent control.

The coming of Pax Britannica, with the resulting cessation of tribal warfare and the opening up of the country, has brought about fundamental changes, especially in modern cosmopolitan centres. Large numbers of strangers have appeared of recent years and their settlement has led to complications, with the result that the original idea of " Kola Tenantship " has been thrown completely out of gear.

There were (or are) three forms of " Kola Tenantship " :
1. When a man applied for permission to occupy a piece of land solely for agricultural purposes.
2. When a man applied for a plot on which to erect a building.
3. A man may donate a plot to his daughter as a marriage portion. Really this amounts to a gift to his son-in-law.

LAND TENURE & INHERITANCE

Such a plot remains in the occupation of the new family practically for all time. Yet there is one condition, namely, the donor (or his descendants) must be recognised. The acknowledgement of landlordship is made by presents given at festival seasons consisting of a gown, cap, cloth, tobacco and such-like. Also, and this constitutes a stronger bond, the landlord continues to offer the annual sacrifice.

When land was sought for agricultural purposes, it was clearly understood that no trees of a permanent character such as palms, bread-fruit and similar long-enduring trees could be planted. Farming meant the planting of yams and other yearly crops, and nothing more. In this case, the landlord acted alone, and his word was sufficient sanction to, and for, an applicant to cultivate a plot of land. Some small " kola " (Ife-nru-ana) was given when the harvest was gathered in return for the favour granted, and as acknowledgement of the landlord's rightful ownership. It still remained the landlord's duty and prerogative, and this is very important to remember, to make the annual sacrifice to the land (Ikpuba-ani = to establish the land). The tenant could not, and still cannot, in any wise, or under any conditions, perform this.

The normal practice is for the " Ife-nru-ana " (" kola " or " ojji ") to be offered to the landlord annually by the tenant. This consists of small presents including a pot of palm wine, some yams or cooked food and any other small gift. This service must be rendered at the time the landlord is preparing to make the yearly sacrifice.

In the case where permission is sought to erect a house, that is to take up a more or less permanent tenancy, the " titled " men of the families of both the contracting parties must attend as witnesses when the agreement is made. There may be only one payment of " kola ", but, even if there be one only, and no annual acknowledgement made, the landlord must carry through the ceremonies of sacrifice. The tenant might fail in duty and courtesy, still the landlord maintains his claim by virtue of his right to offer the customary sacrifice.

After the terms are arranged, and " kola " offered and accepted, the tenant cannot be evicted merely at the whim or prejudice of the landlord. He cannot be disturbed except :

1. He leaves the land voluntarily.
2. He commits some abomination whereby he forfeits his tenancy : that is, some offence against the land or society, or in some way violates native law and custom.
3. He may be called upon to make sacrifice to remove some

pollution. If he cannot, or will not, fulfil the obligation, he is deprived of his right of tenure and is, forthwith, evicted.

The question of sub-letting by the " kola tenant " is not so clearly defined. It is generally conceded that a " kola tenant " can sub-let after first obtaining sanction from the owner ; also that, when agricultural land is sub-let, the owner is entitled to a tribute of yams from the tenant and also from the sub-tenant. It is customary for the tenant, when about to sub-let, to give fresh " kola " of a value settled between himself and the landlord, but solely and entirely as an act of courtesy ; the tenant is not forced to do so ; nor can the landlord automatically claim it. And this is just where native custom has been disrupted. As pointed out earlier, such sub-letting was never contemplated and, consequently, no provision made to regulate it in Native Law. It was (and still is, generally speaking) repugnant to the Ibo mind " to make trade ", that is, to regard the land as a source of profit. This old-established principle has been vitiated of recent years owing to the development of the country. The land, in the Ibo economy, is for the people and stands on an equality with air and water. God gave all freely, and every man and woman is entitled to the use of them without price.

The question of transfer from one site to another does not appear to present the difficulties met with in East and Central Africa where the souls of the ancestors are bound up with the land itself. It is obviously impossible to transport, for example, a sacred grove. A better site and other inducements might be offered to stimulate a proposed transfer. These benefits would not, however, compensate for being deprived of the " souls " ; they cannot be transplanted ; it involves a complete break-up of sacred traditions.

Such beliefs do not bind the Ibo. Although, in sacrificing, and in other circumstances, he may call upon as many ancestors as he can remember by name, and though he entertains a certain reverence for the abode of his forefathers, referring to it as " Ani-Ezi ", yet he can, and does, rise up and depart without allowing the thoughts of the souls of his ancestors to intrude upon or impede his plans.

The Ibo has the benefit of being able to transport the souls of his ancestors whensoever and wheresoever he removes his habitation. He carries the " Okpensis " of his ancestors, and so has the souls always at hand. The souls are not in any tree, grove or particular plot of land ; they are in the " Okpensis ".[3] (*Vide* p. 284.)

LAND TENURE & INHERITANCE

These ancestors do not appear to exercise overdue influence on land tenure. On the contrary, an Ibo man (or family) can, if he be so disposed, donate or sell land known as " Ukwu ". Usually, by old custom, it was limited to transfers between members of the family; this, however, no longer applies. An Ibo man would not lightly, or merely and solely for monetary gain, sell land known as " Ukwu " or " Okpuno ". At the same time he has the *right* to do what he likes with his own property.

When the land is retained, it is not necessarily for fear of offending ancestors, though fear of displeasing them may have some influence (in any case, should it be considered a transgression, it can be remedied by appropriate sacrifice): it is kept as a memorial with very similar ideas to old family entails and traditions in England. In actual practice, it amounts to little more than sentimental attachment to the old ancestral home.

Another reason is that the Ibo man likes to have some land in reserve. While he himself has moved off the ancestral plot, he thinks that his sons may want land in days to come, and so he may keep the " Ukwu " land in trust for them.

In regard to testing ownership, the quickest and most certain procedure before civilisation came was to bring forward the man who had the authority, that is, the recognised right to make sacrifice (iru ani). In former times, no one other than the rightful claimant would ever dare to fake a sacrifice. Nowadays, the sophisticated man will attempt anything, though even he will hesitate unless he be assured that he is likely to be backed by influence. It can be generally accepted that the man who arranges for the sacrifice (Ikpuba-ani) to be performed at the original settlement and, after that, annually, is the owner of the land in question.

There are one or two other points to bear in mind in connection with the land question. Under the primitive Ibo system, land could be definitely transferred from one owner to another either as a gift or by purchase; also land could be seized in lieu of debt, or confiscated for some infringement of law and custom. The point to be established is that, although it is customary to speak of land as being " communal ", yet there is, in the Ibo country, a definite personal ownership carrying the right of transfer. Outright purchase was the practice before the Government introduced the present land laws, one of the finest efforts ever made to safeguard the rights of a subject people and to promote the prosperity of the country.

Personal property descends to the eldest son as heir or, failing

LAND TENURE & INHERITANCE

a son, to the eldest brother or male relative. Should any dispute arise about inheritance (ilu-ogu), it will be decided at the time the Second Burial rites are performed. (*Vide* p. 289.)

The heir takes over all the properties, including wives. He may keep them all; usually he disposes of some to other men for the sake of the dowry money. If the women are old, they remain quietly as members of the compound under the new owner and are rarely disturbed.

It is true that a wife has her own rights theoretically; they are generally overridden, however, by her husband or the inheritor, both with regard to herself and her children. Herein, the Ibo differs from his northerly neighbour, the Igarra. At Idda, the succession to the kingship is hereditary in the female line, the eldest son of the sister succeeding.[4] I know of but one part in the Ibo country where matrilineal succession is the accepted order and that is among the Ohafia towns (a little north of Aro-Chuku). It is strange to meet with this apparently isolated example.

The heir not only succeeds to his father's property; with it, he inherits his father's liabilities and, also, any which may have come down from his grandfather or even earlier ancestors. The settling of ancient debts, perhaps three generations old, is a very intricate business, and the new owner may find himself in an undesirable and, possibly, critical position owing to his being suddenly confronted with a debt contracted by his grandfather, the repayment of which has not become easier by lapse of time.

In the old days the debt was paid in kind; nowadays, it is expected that the refund will be made in cash, a vastly different proposition.

NOTES TO CHAPTER XIX

[1] " It is a curious fact, that land is possessed by inheritance in the Ibo country; and the right of alienation is not in the power of the king, nor in that of an individual member, unless by consent of all the leading members of the family owning the land. Although no sale of land is proposed, yet, before any portion is given away, it must be with their united consent, for which suitable presents may be given, in acknowledgement of the transfer."
—" *Niger Expedition* ", p. 432.

[2] " Ojji " = the word for a small gift such as a fowl. " Kola " is frequently used with a similar meaning.

[3] Onitsha word is " Okposi ".

[4] " *Expedition to the Niger, 1841* ", Vol. I, p. 325. Also *vide* pp. 215, 418.

CHAPTER XX
DEATH & BURIAL

THERE ARE THREE phases connected with death and burial which stand out with distinctive prominence. First, there is death itself, "Onwu". The second phase is what may be termed "First Burial" ("Ikposo-ozu"—Onitsha or "Mgbasu-ozu"—Interior). It may be a simple matter of rolling the corpse in a grass mat, carrying it forth and disposing of it, or it may be complicated with symbolical rites, in proportion to the rank and social status of the deceased. The third phase is commonly known as "Second Burial". If done soon after death, it is termed "Ozu-ndu"; if after a longer interval, it is called "Ikwa-ozu-ndu" or "Ikwa-ozu-okponku". This last is very important; indeed, a very serious business for, without it, there can be no rest for the spirit which has, as it were, slipped its moorings. The disembodied spirit is doomed to ceaseless wandering to and fro until the ceremonies are completed whereby it may enter its final resting-place and be at peace.

The Ibo is somewhat of a fatalist. This is, perhaps, more obvious during illness than in other circumstances. If a patient get a notion into his head that his complaint is of a serious nature, it is more than probable that he will yield to despair and cease to struggle towards recovery; he is suffering from what has proved a fatal illness in the case of others: why contend against fate? So it often comes about that a patient dies for no other reason than he has not the will-power to live: to die is the appropriate thing to do!

The provision of food and shelter is not dependent on daily employment and the native has plenty of time wherein to indulge his inherent weakness for yielding to minor ailments. A small ache or pain will put him out of action, and he sits about the picture of misery. The natives are submissive patients; they will swallow any medicine prescribed, however nauseous it may be, and tolerate any treatment, however drastic. At the same time, instructions are by no means respected unless they happen, by chance, to coincide with the inclinations, e.g. unless carefully watched, a patient will partake of a hearty meal shortly after the performance of a serious abdominal operation. He feels hungry, and food ought to be eaten by a hungry man ! To be restricted in diet is likely to make the patient believe that he is too ill to recover, so he just dies !

Although the family cannot do much medically to relieve pain and suffering, yet there is no lack of sympathy. As the patient lies on his rude couch in the dark room, probably entirely windowless, friends and neighbours are free to enter the chamber. All, with one accord, repeat the single word " ndo ", " ndo ", which conveys a deep sense of " sorry, sorry ".

Meanwhile, the sick man is drawing near to his end. In the average home, the members of the family gather round. They do not display much emotion at this stage. All remain quietly watching : there is no eating or drinking, but some of the women-folk may quietly sob. There is probably little difference in actual essentials between the death scenes in an Ibo home from those in a peasant household in other parts of the world.

It is when the moment of death arrives that the tumult begins. There is an outburst of wailing, the women particularly giving full vent to their grief. Sometimes a wife or mother will rush from the hut heedless of direction, waving her arms, and beating her breast as she bewails her loss at the top of her voice. Such an one will wander aimlessly for hours, crying the same words, until she becomes an automaton. Eventually, after possibly being out all night, she struggles back to her hut, physically and mentally exhausted. This is not, however, the common practice. Usually, the stricken woman is surrounded by her friends and induced or, failing that, forced to sit down. This is done to safeguard her, for often a woman, bereaved of husband or child, will work herself into a state of frenzy and she cannot be trusted to go forth alone lest she do injury to herself, or even commit suicide while temporarily insane. For a time, there is great confusion and noise, all wailing in unison, and then the casual visitors withdraw, leaving the family to mourn their loss undisturbed.

It is quite a different matter when a " titled " or other notable man passes away. In this case, the assembled folk refrain from wailing immediately after death has taken place, because the news must not be published abroad until the other " titled " men, the " in-laws " and the relatives have been notified. Word is despatched to these to the effect that the relative (or friend) has entered " ofe " (a small back room). This is equiva-

DEATH & BURIAL

lent to saying that the man has died. The next day, visitors will arrive bringing presents of money, cloth, drinks, brass rods, hats, eagle ("ugo") feathers and other gifts befitting the occasion.

The following description of death and burial customs pertains rather to the Awka District; they are not universal in the Ibo country. Each neighbourhood has its own peculiar adaptations.

The corpse first receives attention. A long stockinet hat ("okpu nwa-agbala"),[1] somewhat resembling a maltster's, is placed on the head, while eagle feathers and the scarlet feathers of a bird called "aghu-nme" are laid along each side of the face. The body is then rubbed lavishly with camwood dye ("ufie"). This is done for "dressing", and corresponds to the anointing of the Easterns. The eyes are marked round with chalk rings, giving the effect of a huge pair of white spectacles. All this follows the exact usage as on the day of his taking title. Their use now, as then, indicate that all sacrifices have been completed.

The next ceremony can take place only after sunrise, for when the sun is "up" is the right and proper time for a man's spirit to take its flight. When the sun's rays are shining from directly overhead, a palm-frond ("igu") is spread along the ground; the idea of this is that, by placing the leaf between the corpse and the ground, pollution of the land may be avoided. The body is now brought out on a (grass) mat and laid lengthwise on the palm-frond. It is covered with another mat and cloth, with the exception of the face which is left exposed to view.

A strong man now takes a cock, grasps with each hand the upper and lower jaws and splits the beak back to the neck. The flowing blood is made to drip on to the eyes of the corpse in sufficient quantity for sticking feathers plucked from the cock. In a corner of the yard, a male goat ("mpi") is killed. In this case, blood must not be shed and, for the killing, the goat is seized by the legs and bashed on the ground until it is dead.

Two "adas" (daughters) are then commanded to bring two small pots of water. They stand, one on the right and the other on the left of the corpse. They dip their hands into the water and make passes over the face and continue right down the body to the feet. This is repeated until it has been done four times. Camwood dye is next taken and a fourfold passing over the face and body is made similarly to that done with the water. Then follows a fourfold passing with razors ("aguba"). The whole constitutes the symbolical form of: 1. Washing;

2. Anointing; 3. Shaving and, all combined, ceremonial cleansing. The first two are in general practice; the third is omitted in some parts.

A hen is now produced and, with it, "Alọ" and "Ọfọ". The former is the oldest-fashioned insignia of office—a spear-headed wand about five feet in length. The shaft is of wood; the spear-head and butt are of iron. The "Ọfọ" is taken from the deceased's own "Ọfọ" tree. The dead man's "ọkpala" (eldest son, or brother if the son be a minor) takes the "Alọ" and the "Ọfọ" and waves them down the length of the corpse after the manner of the women who have previously functioned. When "Alọ" and "Ọfọ" are thus used in burial rites, they signify that all title obligations have been consummated.

This use of the "Alọ" and "Ọfọ" is found at Awka and is probably a local practice. In most other places they are placed outside the house near the "ogbu-chi" tree and blood sprinkled upon them.

Meantime, a grave is being prepared in the middle of the floor of the small room called "ofe". (The room is also known as "unọ-nga". This word is translated and used for "prison", and is so called because, formerly, captives were kept in this room.) The food of an "Ọzọ" titled man used to be cooked in the "ofe". Some "Ọzọ" men prepare their own graves ready for their burial, meanwhile filling in the holes with sand, which can be quickly scooped out when the grave is wanted. Four long and two short slabs of wood are arranged to serve as a coffin ("mgbọ-ojji"), but they are not nailed or otherwise fixed together. The bottom is laid flat and the two sides and ends wedged into position. Then a quantity of cloth is placed on the bottom plank and the corpse laid upon it, while the fourth long slab becomes the coffin lid. As soon as this work is completed, great lamentations break forth which continue until the grave has been filled in. Only men who have the titles of "Ọzọ", "Ekwu" or "Aghalija" are permitted to have the benefit of "mgbọ-ojji". In places where the "Ọzọ" and other titles mentioned do not exist, the privilege of the use of "mgbọ-ojji" is confined to the "Ndi-chie" = the ruling elders. On the eastern side of the Niger, ordinary men have nothing more than mats and leaves, with as much cloth as relatives and friends can afford, or are willing to provide.

The corpse having been buried, an old ram ("ebuna") is sacrificed and the blood sprinkled on a tree called "Ogbu-chi".[2,3] There are usually a number of "ogbu" (? cassytha) trees in the compound; the one selected is the one specially

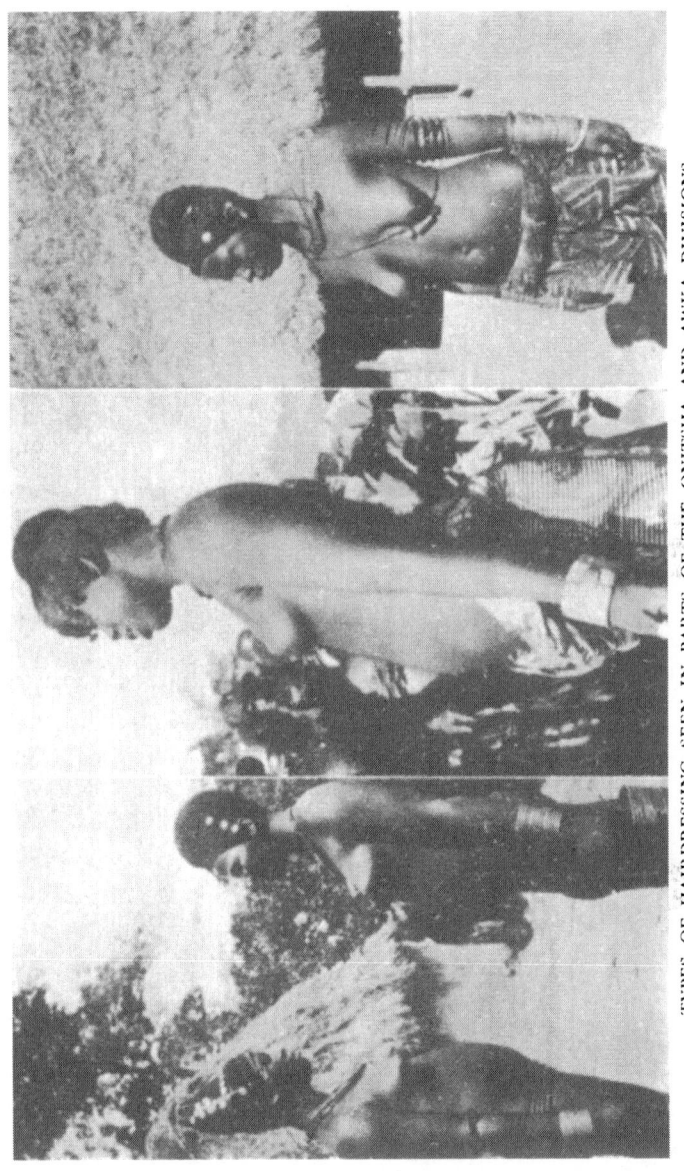

TYPES OF HAIRDRESSING SEEN IN PARTS OF THE ONITSHA AND AWKA DIVISIONS.

planted for worship. After the sprinkling, camwood dye is smeared on the tree.

All the above being completed, as evening falls, the drum ("ikolo") is beaten to notify all and sundry that the burial will be on the morrow. If any man has not heard previously to this notice, he hears now the message proclaimed by the drum. Crowds flock to the scene next day. The ram is observed hanging ready prepared for the ensuing ceremonies. It is cut up, cooked and eaten by the men; the women do not partake. Again, this is the practice in a few localities only. The family, that is, sons and brothers, is expected to supply liberal quantities of drink with the exception of water! In modern days, in addition to palm wine, there will be whisky, beer, lemonade and such varieties of drink as may be purchasable. All who have heard the drum, and to whom a message has been sent, will bring gifts of cloth and other appropriate articles.

Considerable quantities of cloth ("ikpu-akwa") are buried with the dead, especially with rich folk. This giving of cloth has significance. The reasons given are :—

1. The belief that the departed are still alive in the underworld and, therefore, will be in need of cloth.
2. As a token of respect and friendship; it becomes a last present to the deceased.
3. As a sign of sympathy with the relatives bereaved.
4. In the majority of cases, though not always (as at Onitsha where the custom is unknown), it is accepted as a settlement of any debt owing to the deceased or the person conducting the burial.
5. If no debts are outstanding, sufficient cloth is set on one side for interment purposes; the remainder is sold and the money applied towards the payment of the funeral expenses.

The whole of the time is occupied with drinking and dancing. For the latter, not only local folk take part; in addition, companies of dancers are engaged from other towns. It is accounted a mark of respect and affection to bring a party to dance at a friend's funeral. The carousal brings the ceremonies to a conclusion for the time being; further activities are postponed until the celebration of "Second Burial".

For a commoner, the proceedings, as would be expected, are much less lavish in character. Still, a certain amount of ritual is customary. While the newly made widow and other closely related women are wailing, other women attend to the corpse. Similar procedure is followed as in the case of a titled man, but in a very much modified form. It amounts to washing the corpse and smearing it with camwood dye, the shaving of the head and chalking the eyes. The body is clothed in the finest garments from the deceased's wardrobe and, in the case of a man, the corpse is placed on a stool in a sitting posture, reclining against the wall of the chamber.

For a woman the same procedure is followed, except that she must be placed on the ground; very occasionally a sitting posture is adopted. Usually, she is laid flat, the idea being that, as it is not customary for a woman to sit upon a stool in life, she should not be placed in a false position in death. Some of her dishes, the " oba " or " abuba " (calabash) and small pot (" oku ") are placed outside at a short distance from the house, together with her sleeping-mat, the pots all first being broken. These are for her use in the unseen world. In due course the fragments are collected and thrown away.

There is another form of procedure which may be noted. At Obusi, for example, upon the death of a person, the first thing to be done is to tie the two big toes together and the two thumbs. For a titled man a small he-goat (" ewu-onwu " = " the goat of the dead ") is provided. At Onitsha, it is termed " ewu-izuzu ". All the other titled men must be present at the slaying of the goat, the actual killing being performed by a priest qualified to offer the sacrifice known as " Akpaja " (= bag of sacrifice). The dead man's staff of office (" Otulukpa okala ") is carried to " Ide-Milli-Ube's " house and there deposited. (*Vide* p. 42.)

For a commoner, the above procedure follows as closely as circumstances permit. Wherever possible, a goat will be provided, in this case called " ewu-igba-mme " = " the goat which sheds blood ". It is killed at the spot where the dead man had been accustomed to sit or bathe; sometimes two goats are killed, one at each place. The carcase is divided according to custom: one leg to the king, one leg to the folk of the dead man's village, the drummers receive a share, and the remainder is taken by the relatives present.

In some districts, more particularly, where gin is a common article on sale, the corpse is liberally sprinkled with the spirit. This has no symbolical significance; it is alleged that it is done solely for the sake of the aroma, that, no doubt, being preferable to the odour of the corpse!

The corpse, having been duly " dressed ", the emblems of the man's life and work are placed before it. His chief implements and tools, his gun and bag, or some part of his fishing gear, according to his profession. A poor man has little else to distinguish him while, for a man of wealth, a bowl filled with cowries or cash will be added to the collection. The placing of these articles is symbolical; they represent the equipment that the man will need in the underworld, the tools to enable him to prosecute his occupation, and the money wherewith the rich man will be able to maintain his proper dignity. This lying in state extends over a day or so, thus providing an opportunity for relatives and friends to visit the hut and pay their last respects to the dead. At the close of this period, young men come forward to bear the corpse to its last resting-place.

In some places, the mat on which the patient died is used as a shroud. This is generally one named " Upette ". Where Hausa-made mats are obtainable, as in the neighbourhood of Onitsha, a choice is made of one termed " Afika ", or one called " Nkpala ", or a mat made of rushes named " Ute-amilli ". For better-class men, the " Ute Ekwelle " is used. This is made of palm-tree fibre cord. After shrouding the corpse in the mat, the young men carry it to the burial ground and bury it in a shallow grave. The body is laid upon its back; no thought is given as to position, that is, whether it faces east, west or in any other direction.

Before digging the grave, a bunch of young palm-leaves (" omu ") is taken. A young man beats the ground with these, crying, as he does so, " Let the old dead body depart because a new (dead) body has come." " Ochie ozu gbana na ozu ofu abia." Should old bones be disturbed, they will be carried and thrown away. On the other hand, if more or less recently buried bones are unearthed, they are reinterred decently in another grave. When the burial is finished, more " omu " are deposited on the top of the grave. The closing words said over the grave are : " Sokwu onye bulu-i " (" follow and fight (kill) the one who killed you "), or " Imalu onye bulu-i iso ya " (" You know the one who has killed you; follow him "). On the grave of a woman, a small pot (" oku ") alone is placed. This is the customary course for a normal death and burial. There are, of course, many variations, almost every village having some custom peculiar to itself.

Whether the death and burial ceremonies be more or less depend upon three main conditions, birth, status and cause of death. The demise of a slave entails but little labour and no expense whatsoever. Such an one is simply shrouded in his bed mat and carried away. He may be buried; more likely he will be dumped in the bush and abandoned without ceremony or burial. It is a pauper's funeral for which no man is held responsible. As a slave he is entitled to no better treatment. In life he was a person of no substance or position, and he has no right to expect anything different in the world beyond.[4]

On the other hand, this will not do for a free-born. He may be poor, nevertheless, he is entitled to the privilege of a freeman's funeral rites. The relatives must do their utmost to provide a worthy burial even though it may entail running into debt. For a chief or a wealthy man, the arrangements must be proportionately lavish. His funeral must correspond with the circumstances of his life. When fowls are killed in sacrifice, and the " Alo " and the " Ofo " are displayed in the funeral ceremonies, they indicate that all rites have been consummated. The cause of death also plays an important part in the question of burial. The bodies of those who die from noxious diseases are disposed of hurriedly. Lepers, and those who die from smallpox, or some cause which cannot be accounted for satisfactorily, are quickly removed. Lepers are wound in their sleeping-mats and, like those who die of smallpox, are not placed in a grave ; they are deposited in the " ajo-ofia " (bad bush) very often, indeed, before they are dead.

It is abomination for a dropsical person to die in the house. Death by dropsy is the due result of evil-doing, such as administering poison ; the culprit has escaped human detection, but has not escaped punishment at the hands of the gods. People dying as the result of accident ; women dying in childbirth ; lunatics, suicides and those who have been murdered, drowned or burned are considered as having come to their untimely ends by " Onwu Ekwensu ", that is, by the instrumentality of the Devil. None of these may be rubbed with " ufie ", and they must be disposed of without delay. Should, by chance, any rubbing be done for one of these, it is done with " edo ", a brilliant yellow stain obtained from wood prepared in the same manner as camwood dye. They must be buried outside the confines of the town as befits those whose death is of the Devil. In the case of a suicide, it is essential, too, that the culprit's house be ceremonially purified.

The corpse of a man or woman who dies during the period of mourning for wife or husband is treated similarly. The privilege of " Second Burial " is denied to all who die " Onwu Ekwensu ", nor is a " Chi " or " Okpensi " set up for them or the slave ; they are for ever blotted out of the book of remembrance.

In the hinterland of Asaba, the grave is marked by the figure of a man pricked out with cowrie shells.

DEATH & BURIAL

Normally, the heir succeeds to the property and household affairs go on much as heretofore. Occasionally, the whole compound is forsaken. This is done, not out of respect for the dead, but because the surviving members of the family have come to the conclusion that it is located on an unlucky site. Deaths (or other calamities) have been rather too frequent, and it is deemed advisable to try another and healthier neighbourhood.

The humid heat of this tropical country is an effective bar against delay in burying corpses. A period of twenty-four hours is the utmost limit in normal circumstances; usually there is much less time between death and burial. The exceptions to this practice are in respect of men of high position, chiefs and kings. When one of these dies, the corpse is preserved pending fitting arrangements for an honourable funeral. In the case of a king, the first thing to be done after death is to decapitate the body. After that, the most common plan is to dry the corpse by means of slow fire. It is placed on a clay couch. This is hollowed out and fire placed in the recess. The heat evaporates the juices, leaving the body a shrivelled mummy, which can be kept more or less indefinitely.

When burial is delayed in order to secure time to arrange for proper pomp and ceremony, the publication of death is postponed until the preparations are complete. The interval may be a week, a month, or a year, or even more, according to the status of the dead man and the resources at the disposal of the family. The death of King Anazonwa of Onitsha was not publicly announced until a full year after his decease. The fact that he had died could not be concealed all that time, but it was not openly mentioned. Rumours were whispered and heads shaken, but it would have amounted almost to treason to proclaim that the king was dead. True, it was, that he had not been seen for weeks. This did not signify much, because by ancient royal law and custom, he was virtually a prisoner confined to the palace compound. He was not a common person; as a semi-divine being he did not appear in public, except once a year at the Ofalla Festival. (*Vide* p. 68.)

The interval between death and its public notification sometimes depended upon the situation of the successor to the throne. On the western side of the Niger, when a king dies, the news is not announced until the heir is present in the royal compound. It is the custom for the heir to live elsewhere so long as his father is alive. Usually, he resides with another king who undertakes to train the young man in the duties and responsibilities required of him when he, in his turn, becomes king. In

DEATH & BURIAL

any case, it is wise policy to place him at a safe distance from his home compound.[5] The practice of waiting before publishing the news of the death of the king is based on the principle that the throne is never vacant. When the heir is present, ready to assume his position, the death is announced: "The king is dead; long live the king."

To die and be buried in a strange land is utterly repugnant to the Ibo. If at all possible, burial must take place at home. The spirit can never find rest in alien surroundings, hence every effort is made to transport the corpse to its old home. It is no uncommon sight to see a couple of men hurrying along the path bearing a roughly made stretcher. It is not necessary to be told that they are conveying a corpse, the pungent reek of putrefying flesh is all too evident! This is particularly the case when distance, or some other reason, causes a delay in transporting the body. Some will even go to the length of exhuming the corpse after it has been in the ground several days rather than suffer it to remain in exile. The wish of every Ibo man and woman is to rest among the souls of their ancestors, and it is a very real and poignant hope.

The preparations for transport are simple. A couple of bush poles, with a strip of cloth tied between them, serve as a stretcher. The corpse is shrouded in cloth and the sleeping-mat bound about it. Men always act as bearers unless the prevailing conditions render the task unsafe. Should there be trouble in the neighbourhood, women undertake the duty. A safe passage for them is granted on condition that they belong to the same village as the deceased. Where men would run the risk of capture women are, in these circumstances, allowed to pass in safety. If conditions render it impracticable to convey the complete dead body, it is decapitated, and the head only is taken to the old home.

Mourning is more of a characteristic of the women-folk. Men do break down, and some wail bitterly, but it is more usual for them to control their emotions. They generally sit in stolid silence, and manifest their grief by their pathetic expression and demeanour rather than by vocal effort. Custom rules that a man bereaved of his wife shall mourn his loss for seven weeks (28 days). This is the period of intensive mourning during which he is expected to restrict his activities to the compound enclosure. A newly made widow, as earlier noted, gives way to unbridled grief.

After the initial outburst, which may last for several hours, she cries loudly for about half an hour for four or five days, beginning each day just before daybreak. At the end of this period, she moves from her deceased husband's house to a small hut in another part of the compound. While dwelling in this hut, she wears no clothes unless perhaps a rag; she must sit on a block of wood ("ugbo-ukpa") and nowhere else; instead of a sleeping-mat, a banana-leaf must suffice. No man is allowed to see or to speak to her for three native weeks. She may not pass in or out of the main entrance to the compound; a specially made opening through the wall is made for her. Should she go out through this prepared opening, it is tabu for her to be seen; should this happen, it will be necessary to offer sacrifice to make amends. For seven native weeks she neither works nor cooks; her sole occupation is to sit in the hut, mourning for her dead. She is prohibited from washing her body or combing her hair. In her hand she holds a stick wherewith to drive away the spirit of her husband. (See p. 291 also.)

The rest of the household remains in mourning for three native weeks (12 days). Throughout this period, there is no washing of person or clothing. At the conclusion of the lamentations, and after the burial ceremonies have been fulfilled, both widowers and widows shave their heads as a symbol of grief and bereavement.[6] A woman also breaks her necklaces and, if the wife of a titled man, she will sever the ankle cords. (*Vide* p. 229.) The breaking of necklaces and ankle cords symbolises that all connection with the former husband is ended. Instead, a cotton thread necklace will be worn indicating to all that the woman is a widow. (*Vide* p. 291.)

The period of mourning is by no means a time of undisturbed retreat. People pass in and out of the compound almost incessantly in order to condole with the bereaved family. For a month the conditions resemble a wake in character. The visitors express their sympathy on the one hand, while companies of dancers and musicians strive valiantly to divert the attention of the mourners and thus save them from brooding too deeply over their loss. At these funeral wakes, great quantities of food and palm wine are consumed. The intention is good; it is the expression of a friendly desire to relieve the mourners of some of the sorrow and stress caused by the death of their loved one.

Occasionally, when passing through a village, signs are visible which indicate that death has, more or less, recently visited a compound. The signs consist of fragments of cloth. One end is fixed to a cross stick, the other and free end is tapered roughly to a point (pennon). The flag hangs suspended from the top of a long pole. Another custom is to run a stick through the sleeves of a shirt—scarecrow fashion—and suspend it on a pole. By these signs the passer-by knows that death has claimed the owners.

The Ibo is an animist and his belief in the spirit world is profound. It has its bearing on every detail of the life that now is and of that which is to come. To him the unseen world is a reality : he is conscious of its nearness always. He knows that the end of this life will come in due course, and his one anxiety is that he may be granted a worthy entrance into the land of spirits when the call comes. He realises that the funeral rites and ceremonies he covets are dependent upon the goodwill of his family and especially upon his eldest son, or the " Okpala ". Normally, the son would also be the " Okpala ". If the son be a minor, his uncle will fulfil the duties of the " Okpala " on his, the son's behalf. It is sound policy to retain the affection of the male relatives ; it is a sort of insurance premium wherewith to secure the benefits of a good funeral. It is worth while, because on that service depends very largely the reception the departed will meet with as he makes his entry into the life beyond the grave.

In earlier days it used to be related that, in certain parts, it was not unknown for a woman to make arrangements whereby she secured, some time before she died, the consolation of the prospect of a worthy burial. The thought that everything was in order for the attainment of this desired end brought great relief, but it also had its more sinister aspect. The woman had to complete her plans while still capable of doing her part ; they could not be postponed too long, that is, until her activities were curtailed by old age. Moreover, by that time, she might find herself impoverished and unable to raise funds. With these thoughts in mind, she consulted with her son, or some male friend, and planned the programme for her funeral. He undertook to fulfil her wishes ; she, on her part, compensating him for his trouble, and defraying the calculated cost. When all was settled to her satisfaction, she was content, and signified that she was now ready to die. Generally speaking, the time of waiting was not long—a draught of poison either self-administered, or by the assistance of another person, brought her quietly to her grave. All arrangements for this emergency having been previously ordered, there was no hindrance to the fulfilment of the old woman's wishes. The " Second Burial " rites on her behalf could be conducted without undue delay. This is the substance of statements made thirty years ago, but proof to substantiate it is not now forthcoming. At the time, it was stated in all seriousness as being a custom among some of the Ibo people living in the Aguleri-Nando area. Just possibly it might have been an imported idea from the Igarra country.

A similar comment applies to statements concerning another custom somewhat alike in character. These affirm that it was by no means unknown for a poor family to sell their old people, especially decrepit women unable to fend for themselves. Very little money could be obtained by the sale of a poor old creature. It was stated that she was only wanted for the sake of her carcase; she was of no use for work, but would serve to satisfy meat hunger. What accrued from the sale was supposed to be devoted to defray the expenses of a " Second Burial ". Somehow, this altruistic consummation does not tally very satisfactorily with the original deed ! If sales of old folk were made as reported, and one knows of no reason to doubt the truth of the statement, it is hard to believe that the proceeds were given towards funeral expenses. A part might have been for fear that the spirit of the old woman would rise and trouble the family ; largely, it would seem to be a matter of out of sight, out of mind.

The hurried disposal of corpses has been mentioned earlier. Burial must follow shortly after death and, consequently, there is not time to make arrangements for the proper celebration of the rites and ceremonies ; these must be postponed to a subsequent date. The intrigue lies in the connection between this world and the next, the relationship of body, soul and spirit. The difference between soul and spirit is somewhat difficult to elucidate. In Ibo, there are three words which have reference to the spiritual, " Nkpulu-obi ", " Nkpulu-chi " and " Maw ".

" *Nkpulu-obi* " may be used to indicate the virtue which we have in mind when we speak of a man possessed of a strong spirit, one which inculcates courage, endurance, or, in modern speech, " sportsmanship ".

" *Nkpulu-chi*." These are the memorials set up to house the souls of departed relatives. It is before them that appeals are made to the ancestors when they are called upon by name. It is interesting to note that one, if not the chief reason, why a slave is not allowed to take title is that no " nkpulu-chi " can be set up for him. His name is not remembered ; after death he is no more than a dead dog, in plain language, a slave is not credited with a soul.

" *Maw* " has reference to the spirit world in general, including activities by its agents, yet it is associated with living people also. When something strikingly unusual happens, when we should say " I was dumbfounded ", the Ibo will say " Maw-m efepu ", " My spirit flew away." It is thought that the

DEATH & BURIAL

"Nkpulu-obi" is the residence of the "Maw". When the "Maw" goes out at death, the "Nkpulu-obi" is deprived of its life-giving force. The spirit ("maw") departs; the tabernacle ("nkpulu-obi"), being deserted, perishes.

Belief in the spirit life is deeply rooted and, with it, there is a profound conviction of the existence of a future state. This belief exercises a strong influence in creating fear and superstition, but it does not act very forcibly as an incentive to regard the present life as probationary, preparatory to the life to come. The idea, however, is not altogether absent, as witnessed by the expression, "ikpe di na maw" = "judgement is in the spirit-world".

The belief in a future life is further manifested when speaking of death. The Ibo interprets death as temporary separation. So far is this the case that, when a man dies, he is said to "have gone home", or "gone to the land of the spirits". It is not regarded as a final farewell; it is all part of a wider plan. Men and women come, they stay for a while, they go, they fulfil some purpose in their day and generation, and then they pass on to the beyond and, later, reappear again in this world and so complete the cycle. This is the way a succession of mankind is maintained on the earth! There may be broken links, if not actual gaps in the chain, as when the reborn babe fails to live long enough to fulfil any function in life. The Ibo solves this problem by stating that, though a child may die, and thus fail in its task, yet the lapse may be only a chance misfortune. The loss may be made good on the next occasion, as it is believed that there is no reason why the same child should not be reincarnated and offered another lease of life.

It is to be noted that the term "going home" is never used when speaking of the death of a child. There is an element of uncertainty about a child's life and death. Its death may, perhaps, be no more than a misadventure and, at its next incarnation, it may be more fortunate. On the other hand, all doubt disappears when two or more children of the same mother die one after the other. The first two of such children are given an ordinary burial. Should a third, and subsequent ones, die, then it is taken as clear evidence that the child can not, or will not, live in this present world. It is either unlucky or obstinate. Whatever the reason, it does not conform to the natural conditions of life, and the quicker it is put out of action the better for all concerned. It is assumed that it is the self-same child appearing again and again in successive births. Having failed to profit by the chances vouchsafed to it, the reasonable course is to put an end to its contrariness and foolish

DEATH & BURIAL

vagaries by blotting it out of existence. Such a child is termed " ogbanje " = " the same child making repeated appearances " or, perhaps, more widely, " nwa-ume-omumu ".[7] When such a child dies, the corpse is marked, and petition made that it may not return. On the birth of a subsequent child, search is made for traces of the marks.

The method of destruction of " nwa-ume-omumu " varies according to locality. In some parts, the corpse is carried beyond the village boundary and burned; in others, it is dismembered prior to burning. The ashes are usually scattered to the four winds; sometimes they are placed in a pot. In some parts the corpse is dropped beneath a waterfall; in others the body is suspended from a tree, where it is left to rot, the spirit rotting with it.

The night on which the infant corpse is removed, the mother is led from the house in order that, should the child's spirit return, it will not find her. If there should not be actual removal from the compound, she is advised to change from her customary sleeping-quarters.

With the neighbouring Yorubas, where a woman has lost several children in infancy, the deaths are attributed to the supposition that they belong to a certain class of children called " Abiku " (born to die). These are supposed to belong to a fraternity of demons living in the woods, especially about and within large iroko trees, and each of them coming into the world would have arranged beforehand the precise time he will return to his company. Means are, therefore, adopted to thwart the plans of these infants in order that they may stay.[8]

When men have run their course on earth, they return to their master, the Supreme Being, and live with him in the spirit world. In this connection, some concentration of thought is essential in order to perceive what the Ibo really does believe. There are three distinct spirits or, as it is maintained, it is the one and self-same spirit with a threefold manifestation. When a man dies his spirit departs into the unknown. At the same time, he is also present in the vicinity of the hut. Eventually, the spirit enters into a stick called the " Okpensi ". There is an order of procession. The " spirit " does not enter " Okpensi " immediately after death; that cannot happen until the ceremony of " Second Burial " has been performed. Up to that time, the spirit haunts this present world, wandering at will in the dwellings, compounds and farms, and taking an unremitting interest in the affairs of the individual, the family and, indeed, the whole community with which it was associated in life. It even shares in the eating and drinking; the spirits are always invited to partake, especially in the eating of the kola nut.

Again, until " Second Burial " is completed, no food can be offered to the homeless spirit inside the hut or compound. Instead, women place some food in a palm-leaf dish (" eluaka ") and deposit it at a forked pathway. (*Vide* p. 58.) Meanwhile, the spirit will be complaining that he cannot enter his house, because he has not been welcomed. The fulfilment of " Second Burial " ceremonies enables him to take up his residence in " Okpensi ". This is a piece of ogilisi wood, from six to eighteen inches in length with a roughly carved head at each end. It may be wood taken from any ogilisi tree, or it may be a ready-made one purchased in the market. The " Okpensi ", now the abode of the spirit, is deposited in the deceased man's house with the other " nkpulu-chi " and, thus, is in a position to see and hear all. He reports the results of his observations to the spirits dwelling in the underworld. Offerings are regularly made to the spirit in the following manner. First, there must be the customary washing of hands, followed by the offering of kola nut; the ceremony cannot begin without this. Then the supplicant holds a fowl in both hands and, standing before the " Okpensi " says, " Look, my father, you see this fowl (goat or cow) and you see these my children, and you know all about us. Please see that no harm befalls us, and deliver us from the evil designs of wicked spirits and guard us well." The throat of the fowl is then cut, the blood drips upon " Okpensi " and, with it, some of the feathers are stuck on. This is the blood of redemption for the man and his family.

In the case of sudden death, or where the fatal illness has been of short duration and, especially in the case of a normal young person, whose flesh is in sound condition at the time of death, the corpse is marked with " uli " (dark-blue dye). This is to register the fact that the deceased was not really due to die. He (or it may be she) has died, it is true, yet still looks as fresh as in life. People will cry, " Get up ! " " Why are you lying there? ", and will fall upon the corpse and weep. This " uli " marking advertises untimely death.

A daughter (" ada "), being a native of one village married to a man living in another, ought not to be buried in her husband's village and, except in rare instances, will not be buried there. The corpse is smeared with camwood dye. After the staining, it is wrapped in cloth and the whole bound up in grass mats. Notification is sent to the woman's native village

DEATH & BURIAL

and her people requested to convey the body home. Before, however, the corpse is touched, the woman's children must pay the bearers. They must offer a goat (cow for a rich woman), fowls and money ("Igba ọta"). This payment is termed "Ewu-ichọ"; occasionally, it is known as "Egba-ite-ofe" (soup payment). It is a symbolical restoration of the soup-pot, as a token of remembrance that the mother was accustomed to cook for them.

This coming to carry the body is referred to as a "strong" business, because the bearers will refuse to remove the corpse until they have scrounged the last possible contribution. On the other side, the children are begging them to be content and depart. Each party strives to out-bargain the other until, at last, a settlement is reached. For the family, acting in desperation, to suggest burying their mother forthwith themselves, would lead to very serious trouble. This is the general practice; as in most customs, there are exceptions.

For a very aged woman, the remembrance of her native village being so distant, this rule for burial may be overlooked, and her sons will bury their mother in the old woman's own house or compound.

Again, if a woman and husband make agreement beforehand, she can be buried at her husband's village. Also, a rich son can arrange for his mother to be buried at home by negotiation with the relatives living at her birthplace, and paying stipulated fees for the concession.

It is said that a woman has two spirits only and not three as in the case of a man. At death, one departs into the unknown, the other remains near at hand.

The disembodied spirit wanders around as in the case of a man. In a similar way, small offerings are placed on "ọmu" platters. Then the time arrives when the husband or son will perform "Second Burial". Immediately these ceremonies are fulfilled, her spirit is at liberty to enter both her old homes, her husband's and her father's. As in the case of a man, her spirit comes finally to rest in her "Okpensi". In due time, she may be reincarnated through her daughter, daughter-in-law, or through one of the close female relatives at the old home. Such a (supposed) rebirth is a source of great rejoicing; "See how my wife (or child) loves me; she has returned to me." If the reincarnation take place at the old home, and though it be agreed that she has verily returned, the husband cannot claim the girl babe from the father. It might be argued that, as he had once paid dowry for her, he has a legitimate right to her possession on her return to earth! This is not so; she belongs to the household in which she is reincarnated. The " Okpensi " is honoured with renewed praise for doing so well in helping to bring back the lost one. At the same time, the belief is held that the spirit is still in the " ani-maw " (land of the spirits) and so " Okpensi " continues to receive appropriate regard and respect.

This reincarnation is, more or less, subject to the good behaviour of the spirits in the " ani-maw ". Should they be so unfortunate as to rouse the ire of their master, they are in danger of being banished to " amanri maw na madu ", an intermediate state between this material world and the spirit world. The term indicates that such spirits have no place of abode, they are thenceforth wanderers, lost souls. There, for ever, they pass a miserable restless existence without hope in their spirit life, and prohibited from being reborn into this world. Such god-forsaken spirits are ever on the look out for opportunities to inflict death. For example, one may cause a man to fall down when at work at the top of a palm tree. Such a spirit may snatch away children. People declare that they can be seen and that they visit graves, unearth the bones and burn them.

Belief in reincarnation is universal among the Ibos. It is the rightful heritage of every free-born person, and it is the person's own fault if the benefit be lost. The heritage can be forfeited as the result of bad behaviour in the nether world. On the contrary, provided his conduct meets with approval, when the appointed hour arrives, he will be reincarnated and take his place once more in this present world. He will live his life as in former existences, and at the end of the course be called back to the spirit world. So the cycle of living and dying slowly revolves *ad infinitum*.

This reincarnation is limited to rebirths in human form ; never in any other body. There is, however, a definite belief in metamorphosis. It is confidently affirmed that certain people possess the faculty to transform themselves at will into animals. The most common form is to change into a crocodile or a buffalo. For instance, at Onitsha, on the bank of the Niger, there are men and women who are reputed to be able to transmogrify themselves into the forms of these creatures. In a case where a woman was badly bitten by a crocodile, it was affirmed that she had been attacked by another woman operating under the guise of the reptile.

About 11.30 one night, after an evening spent with friends living half a mile away, I walked down the hill to my quarters. Being young and inexperienced, not to say foolish, I declined

DEATH & BURIAL

the offer of a lantern. Hence, I noticed nothing as I passed over the road. Early next morning, I had reason to retrace my steps and, greatly to my surprise, came upon the spoor of a herd of buffaloes, less than fifty yards distant from my compound. I next interviewed the watchman who calmly informed me that, within five minutes of my passing the spot the night before, a herd had crossed the road. I inquired of him, " Seeing you have a gun, why did you not shoot one ? " He was horrified at the notion and regarded me with genuine astonishment. Did I not know that they were not buffaloes of the ordinary bush type : they were Onitsha men ! The men had changed themselves into the form of buffaloes for the time being. After a few hours roaming the countryside, they were, when they crossed the road near my house, on their way home. The watchman proceeded to prove his contention by relating that, on one occasion, a friend of his had shot a buffalo during the night. The next day, a man challenged him. This man confronted the hunter with a bullet. To his great concern, he instantly recognised it as the one he had used when he fired at the buffalo. The human-buffalo demanded an explanation. Why had the hunter, who professed to be a friend, made the attempt upon his life ? This is related here simply in order to record the Ibo's belief in metamorphosis ; it seemed convenient to insert a note here following upon the subject of reincarnation.

NOTES TO CHAPTER XX

[1] Woollen garments produce heat, and heat leads to irritation and scratching—" agbala " is the name of a shrub, the seed-pods of which on contact with the skin, set up intense irritation.

[2] Ogbu-chi or Ogilisi or Ogirisi. Formerly, when a big chief died, three human beings at least were killed ; one as an offering to the deceased's " Ikenga ", one at the " Onu-uno ", i.e. at the Ogilisi tree (" Ogbu-chi "), and the third where the man used to wash his body. In modern days cows are substituted. Cf. " *Among the Ibos of Nigeria* ", p. 122.

[3] At Onitsha, the ram is not killed except, and solely, where the deceased was famed as a man or leopard-slayer.

[4] " Oru fulu ka eji mbazu eni ibe ya onelo na onwu ewelu ogu we nie ya ? " " The slave who sees that another slave is buried with a stick, does he think that, when he dies, he will be buried with a hoe ? " = he will be lucky if someone scratches a hole with a stick (such as is used for uprooting yams) in which to bury him.

[5] See also p. 237 for other reasons why the heir is sent away from home.

[6] The Kafirs, in times of mourning, either shave off the hair entirely or leave it undressed or uncombed. Among the Mpongwe the men shave their heads.—" *Savage Childhood* ", p. 93 ; " *Fetish Folk of West Africa* ", p. 152.

DEATH & BURIAL

[7] "Onye-ume-ọmumu" is the term for a woman whose children do not survive long after birth.

[8] "*History of the Yorubas*," pp. 84-5.

"Very similar ideas and practices prevail on the Gold Coast around Accra, *vide* p. 173."—"*Tailed Headhunters of Nigeria*", quoting from the Rev. John Martin of Accra.

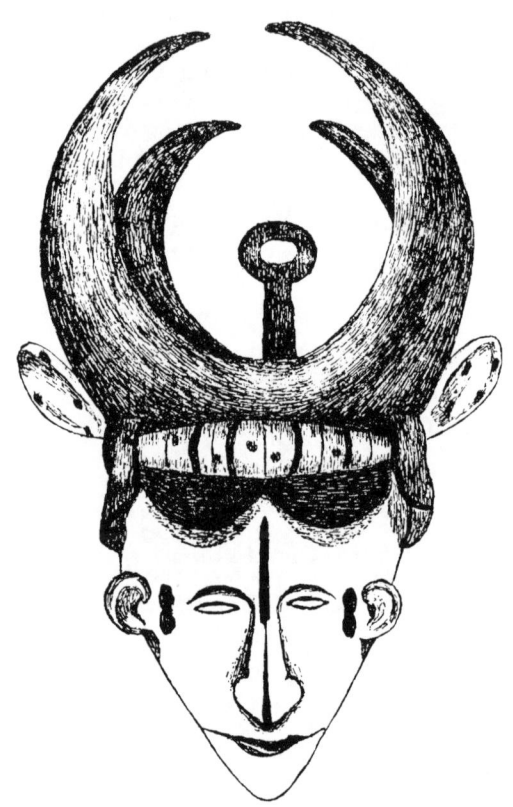

MASK USED BY THE "MAW".

SECOND BURIAL.

Left: CURIOUS MOUNDS ERECTED IN HONOUR OF "ALA," THE EARTH GODDESS. (PAGE 109.)
Middle: OLD IRON CANNONS USED AT SECOND BURIAL CELEBRATIONS.
Right: MEN COVERED WITH BLOOD AND FEATHERS SIGNIFYING THAT THEY HAVE PROTECTED THEMSELVES BY PROPITIATORY SACRIFICES.

CHAPTER XXI
SECOND BURIAL

REFERENCE HAS BEEN made on a number of occasions to what is commonly designated " Second Burial ". The words " Second Burial " are not translations from the Ibo : they are an adaptation which illustrates the logical meaning of the custom. To all intents and purposes, there are two burials. The real body is buried soon after death takes place, before arrangements can be made for a satisfactory funeral. When these are completed, the second burial takes place, on this occasion by proxy. There are two expressions in use by the people in connection with the celebration of this ceremony. Those on the western side call it " ini-ozu " (to bury the dead) ; those on the eastern side refer to it as " ikwa-ozu " (to mourn ; lit. to cry for the dead). We have also the terms " ozu-okponku " (dry corpse) as compared with " ozu-ndu " (fresh corpse), this latter having reference to the first and real burial. The original burial is accompanied by great lamentations, but with little or no ritual. For this second ceremony the programme is reversed. It is a time of feasting rather than of mourning whereby the departed is given a hearty send-off on his journey into the realms of the spirit.

A day is appointed for the festival. In some parts " Oye " is selected for a man and " Nkwo " for a woman (the second and fourth days of the Ibo week). This rule is by no means universal to all the country, any convenient day of the week may be chosen. A generous allowance of food must be provided and copious supplies of palm wine. Cocoanut is also an essential item for this festival. The eating of this at a funeral has a symbolical significance, it is associated specially with mourning. If the deceased had proved himself a valiant man in war or the chase, a ram is slaughtered as a mark of distinction. It must be killed by a brother warrior and only warriors are permitted to partake of its flesh. The deceased's old comrades are expected to organise a great hunt in his honour. Whatsoever is killed is consecrated, and eaten as a memorial feast.

On the first day, the " Umu-ada " (first-born women) visit

SECOND BURIAL

the bereaved house to express sympathy and to keep vigil ("iche abani"). For this purpose, they dress as elaborately as circumstances permit. It resembles feasting rather than mourning, inasmuch as they dance and sing and generally make a great noise. They process round the town and, by this means, placate the spirit of the dead man.

Due notice must be given of the coming celebration. The evening before the appointed day, guns are fired to intimate to the friends and neighbours that the ceremonies will be duly observed on the morrow. By the same token, the spirit of the dead man is also notified of the coming proceedings in order that he may rejoice simultaneously with his relatives, and that he may be fully cognisant of his dispatch to join his brother spirits. An equally cogent reason is to drive away any vindictive spirits that may be loitering in the vicinity of the house of the deceased.

A wicker-work dummy ("igbudu") is constructed of a size corresponding to that of the deceased, the corpse having been measured with a line immediately after death. This is first covered with a grass mat and then with cloth. Thus enshrouded, it serves as a substitute for the body. The "igbudu" is placed in the man's hut or compound in a position where it can be viewed by the assembled folk. Two "alusi", namely, the "Ikenga" and the "Ofo", are set up before the "igbudu" and these are sprinkled with the blood of the sacrifices. At the conclusion of the ceremonies, the man's "Ikenga" is cut to pieces with a matchet and his "Ofo" hung up as a memorial. The flesh of the animals is consumed by those partaking in the rites.

At Onitsha, the practice is, that the night following the ceremonies, the "igbudu" is buried in the same grave as the corpse. This last act is performed by the same company of "umu-ilo" (children of the street) who buried the real body. This work of supererogation seems to be confined to Onitsha; it certainly is not general.

Having been accorded honourable burial the spirit is, henceforth, at peace.[1]

As previously noted, custom forbids a widow from leaving her deceased husband's compound during the period of mourning, nor can a widow remarry until all the rites in connection with the "Second Burial" have been fulfilled.

If a woman be pregnant at the time of her husband's death, the ceremonies may be expedited in order that delivery may come *after* "Second Burial". A child born *before* "Second Burial" has been completed must be cast away, and cleansing

SECOND BURIAL

sacrifices undertaken to remove the pollution which has accrued.

A widow places a thread ("owulu") round her neck not only as a sign of widowhood; rather, it is to signify that she has not made "ani" (see below). Should she die with this "owulu" still on her neck, no people of the village will touch the corpse; men must be hired from another town to bury her. The reason for this repugnance may arise from a belief that a woman dying shortly after her husband is, thereby, proved to be guilty of causing his death.

Should a widow become pregnant while still wearing "owulu", or before the days of mourning are fulfilled, she must go elsewhere for the birth of her child. In due time, after making the proper sacrifice for removing pollution from the land, usually performed by a priest from Nri, she may return home again but *without* the child. It is cast away or, if near enough, passed on to the people of Nri. To free a widow from her obligations, and sanction the removal of the "owulu", the following custom must be observed, namely, "Nme-ani", that is, "to make (worship) the land." Briefly the ceremony is as follows, with small variations according to locality.

It is performed in the compound of the "Onye-isi", otherwise "Eze-ani" (*vide* p. 122) and nowhere else. The Ogilisi tree (Face of Ani) fixes the site; the sacrifices are in proportion to the seriousness of the case, or the pollution to be cleansed. When a man desires to make sacrifice on behalf of a widow, he takes a single kola nut to the "Eze-ani" and gives notice of his intention. The "Eze-ani", thereupon, appoints a day. On the day fixed, the man brings a fowl and more kola. The "Eze-ani" presses the breast of the man and woman with the fowl and also with a ram. This ram is the property of the "Eze-ani" and is kept for the purpose. It is used in lieu of one which should be brought by the suppliant; rams are too scarce for indiscriminate slaughter and so, in this case, it is not sacrificed; it is retained by the "Eze-ani". In virtue thereof, the applicant brings its value in cash, as if he had actually provided it. This is the ceremony for releasing a widow from the ties of her deceased husband; she is now at liberty to sever the "owulu" necklace, and substitute another of beads or other finery. She may now marry again; until this ceremony is performed, no man will consider her as a possible wife.

"Second Burials" are costly affairs. The very poorest will spend their all, and often heavy debts are incurred in the effort to give the best possible "send-off" to a relative. Some idea of this lavish expenditure may be gathered from an instance of which I made some notes. Displayed among the funeral trophies were the skulls of 21 cows, 11 of pigs, and 10 of goats. The prices at the time were : cows £5 apiece, pigs £2, and goats 10*s*.[2] In addition to these animals provided for sacrificial feasting, many cases of gin (then 15*s*. per case) and a vast supply of palm wine, yams and other provisions were consumed. That funeral must have cost, at the lowest estimate, £150, and it would probably be nearer the mark to fix the figure at £200. Of course, such expenses could be incurred only by a rich family, though every family will spend to its utmost capacity in order to fulfil properly the rites of " Second Burial ".

The women have certain functions at that part of " Second Burial " known as " Itu-ani ". This is performed on the day of the ceremony, and must be done while the " igbudu " is still in position in the hut or compound. The " Ǫkpala " (or priest) says the prayer and offers the sacrifice. Without these the ceremony could not proceed. Beneath the " igbudu " is the deceased's " alusi " called " Chi " and, alongside this, are placed the special offerings brought for the occasion by the women of the house. The first-born son (" Ǫkpala ") places a piece of white cloth upon the " Chi ". The cloth having been consecrated, it is removed by the " isi-ada " (chief woman) of the clan or village, who proceeds to tear it into strips for distribution among the dead man's daughters. The strips are girded round the waists of these women and indicate to the public that the final ceremonies for the glorification of their father's spirit have been duly performed.

When a king was buried, or during the ceremonies of " Second Burial " on behalf of a chief, it was customary to put to death one or more slaves " ndi iji kwa ozu " (those held (as victims) for (use) at burials). In the case of a king there was no need for " Second Burial " celebrations. There was ample time between his death and its public announcement wherein to make preparations for his funeral. All the ceremonies were included in the one celebration.

Something must be said about the " ndi iji kwa ozu ". Under normal conditions they were ordinary slaves. When their master died, it was their duty and, some would argue, their privilege, to accompany him into the unseen. It would be a disgrace to allow the master to arrive in the spirit world unattended by a retinue of servants. The slaves who were killed as part of the burial celebrations are often included under the term " human sacrifices ". Only in a loose way is this

SECOND BURIAL

true, for there is really a sharp distinction. Human sacrifices were offered with the definite purpose of making atonement for sins known and unknown. The " ndi iji kwa ozu " were *not* in any sense sacrificial victims ; they were killed solely in order to accompany their master as he entered the great beyond.

The number of slaves doomed to render this last service was not a fixed one. Certain personal attendants were always the first to be selected ; they could not be dispensed with. After them, the number was largely dependent upon the status and/or the financial resources of the family.

The grave was a commodious one, and around it assembled the spectators, the officiating priests and their assistants. The first slave to be brought forward was a young fellow round about fifteen years of age, who would continue service to his master as personal attendant and messenger. He carried his master's bag slung from his shoulder. During the owner's lifetime, it did not leave his possession, he would not entrust it to others. The bag is formed from the skin of a small species of goat or, very often, that taken from a small animal with spotted fur. The head is severed, and the skin flayed off without further cutting, thus making a long bag. On the day of the funeral, the personal cup (small gourd) and snuff container are placed in the bag ; also some kola nuts and a little food. The personal attendant being now in readiness, the next task was to place two young men at the bottom of the grave. They were very roughly handled, including the breaking of their legs, thus rendering them helpless and possibly unconscious. Half-dead, they were placed in position, and it was required of the attendant to lie between the two. The corpse, in the case of a king, or the " igbudu " of a " Second Burial ", was laid lengthwise on the bodies wholly covering the attendant and overlapping on to the bodies of the other two on either side. The grave, thereupon, was filled in, the three men being buried alive.[3]

The remainder of the retinue to accompany a king's spirit into the underworld were killed by, or under the direction of, the public executioner. It can hardly be designated otherwise than murder. The first victim was conducted to the main door of the house where he was bound hand and foot and his throat slit across. The next man was led to the entrance to the compound near the spot known as " obubu madu " (place of killing men). He also was bound hand and foot, but his blood was not shed. Instead, he was laid on his back with his neck resting on a log of wood. Another piece was then placed above so that the man's neck was between the two. Then men stood, and jumped, on the ends on either side and, by their weight, the poor fellow was throttled (" nfi-bu " : killed by tying). Another man was taken to the sacred " egbo " tree in the midst of the compound. Decapitation was the fate meted out to him. More were slaughtered at other places, e.g. before and upon certain " alusi " which were brought out and arranged under the " egbo " trees. None of the bodies was buried ; they were deposited in the " ajǫ-ǫfia " (bad bush) where outcasts, lepers, suicides and other undesirable corpses were thrown, including the bodies of human sacrifices.

It is related that, " at the decease of Obi, King of Aboh, as many as forty slaves were killed, these being specially purchased for the purpose, domestic slaves never being so treated. . . . Graves of the chiefs are large pits into which are first thrown a number of dead slaves, then the body of the departed and, lastly, more slaves." [4]

William Cole states that, on the death of King Azaka (Uzǫka) also of Aboh, " the pleasant task of headsman is bestowed upon the son and heir, who will, to his own shame and satisfaction, behead, and otherwise torture, some forty individuals. The ' modus operandi ' is as follows : Each doomed wretch is bound, and goaded on to dance and, while the assembly are loud in their praises of the dance, a number of torches are held on high to gleam in the midnight, and the butcher advances and, with swoop after swoop, severs the heads of his victims. This over, the burial demands attention." [5]

In the Asaba hinterland, the custom for the burial of leading men was to place them in a huge coffin constructed of roughly hewn planks (" mgbǫ-ojji "). The grave was deep and wide, and the bottom was lined with from one to three, or even more, human victims. The cumbersome coffin was raised as high as the bearers could lift it over the open grave, and then allowed to drop with a sickening thud upon the wretched creatures below.

At Onitsha, Asaba and other towns on the banks of the Lower Niger, some later customs have been incorporated from the Igarra people. Among them is the " Maw-ozu-olu ", a ceremony which is observed only in connection with the " Second Burial " of a man who was of titular rank and had attained to the age and status which conferred on him the right of creating one new " Maw-afia ". For such a man the rites extended over several days. The ceremony of " Ozu-olu " begins on the day following the burial of the " igbudu ". The signal for this is the appearance twice a day (morning and evening) of the " Maw-afia " (spirits of the Olu people).[6] There

SECOND BURIAL

is much noise from the beating of the drums (" egwu-olu ") and the shouts of the people. Eventually, the proceedings end with a drinking carousal. The number of the " maw-afia " is determined by the number of the " umunna ", that is, the heads of the different families constituting the clan, each head being required to supply one " maw-afia ". These curiously clad figures, needless to say, are men disguised in grotesque garments which completely envelop their bodies. Between their teeth they hold an " okpili " (= " igwe ", p. 368), with which they disguise their speech. The excited spectators are fully persuaded that these figures are, indeed, re-embodied spirits, visitors from the underworld. During the first four days, there is little variation in the programme. Then follows the formal visit to the grave of the deceased. When this takes place, the excitement is intense, all the relatives loudly shouting, " Welcome, welcome to our father." Suddenly, firearms are discharged and the " maw-afia " appear escorting the " spirit " of the dead man from his house, beneath the floor of which his body lies buried. The " spirit " walks slowly with tottering uncertain steps, muttering, as he moves, in a feeble voice, his speech also being disguised by the use of an " okpili ". The weakness is due to his enforced imprisonment in the grave ; time and nourishment are required for him to renew his strength ! Meanwhile, the escorting " maw-afia " are dusting away the earth-stains from the garments of the " spirit ". Amid profound expressions of joy on the part of the assembled relatives, the " spirit " slowly totters round ; on this first day for a short time only. His strength is soon exhausted. This being so, he returns to his house and disappears. On the fifth day, the " spirit " appears again, on this occasion without the " maw-afia " escort. They are no longer needed as the " spirit " has, by this time, recovered his strength. He is able to walk freely and speak clearly. He mingles with his kinsfolk, comforting and exhorting them, especially his wives and children. At the conclusion of the tour he returns to his house and sits, as he used to do, upon the " ukpo " (throne), while his attendants fan him vigorously as they did in his lifetime. His daughters bring presents of palm wine and cowries and, to manifest his pleasure and gratitude, he fixes a day, through the good offices of the men present, on which he will make a special visit to the women-folk of the village. Once more he retires and disappears.

On the day arranged, he parades the village speaking words of encouragement and counsel and, in return, receives many presents. Having fulfilled all the duties of a good, and kind-

SECOND BURIAL

hearted benefactor, the well-satisfied " spirit " departs to his own place and is no more seen.

For men of secondary status, the celebration of " Ozu-olu " is reduced to two or three days, with proportionately less ceremonial and appearances.

After " Second Burial " some departed spirits come to rest at Ezira. This is a town lying some twenty-five to thirty miles south of Awka. It is considered by many people of the surrounding country to be the gate of heaven. If anyone wish to know the mind of a deceased relative upon any particular matter, he may be put into communication with the spirit of the departed. It can all be arranged for him for a consideration, which varies in amount according to circumstances, the equivalent of £12 being the price paid on some occasions. Direct communication is not advisable; there must be a medium, otherwise the spirit from the unseen world may exercise such an influence over the inquirer that, ere long, he himself will be dragged down to the nether regions! Hence, all conversations with departed friends are carried on indirectly, that is, through a third person. Many years ago, before the country was opened up, after a visit to Ezira, I was asked eagerly to describe the place. Was it very beautiful? Did it appear to be like heaven? and many similar questions. (*Vide* p. 92.)

At Nsude, in the Udi Division, there is a powerful " deity " by name " Uto ". He is declared to be a god of war. His interests are watched over by the village of Umu-Okpala. The services connected with Uto are controlled by the priest attached to him. The man is chosen by the casting of lots (" Afa " = charm, p. 51). When selected, he must abandon his own dwelling and live in that housing the " deity ", known as " Nkoro Uto ". He must not leave its precincts on " Ekke " and " Afo " days, because they are the days appointed for the offering of sacrifices. He is forbidden to sleep in any other house, nor must he accept an invitation to eat anywhere else lest he should, haply, eat food that had been stolen.

In connection with " Uto " there are ten platforms erected, according to the number of villages. These consist of four corner-posts, about six feet above ground-level, on which cross-sticks are placed. In olden days, these platforms were used to display the heads of enemies killed in war.

At the present time, they are used for other purposes. When a man has been accused of some wrongdoing he is called upon to swear by " Uto ". Should he die soon after swearing, his body will not be buried; it will be deposited upon the platform attached to his village. It stands well outside the confines

SECOND BURIAL

of the village, but all the people know to which one it belongs. If two relatives die in this manner within a short interval of one another, the second corpse will be superimposed upon the first. This was the case with one which I closely examined. It is very likely to occur when a whole family is accused and called upon to swear.

The corpses are wrapped in remnants of cloth which soon rot by the action of wind and weather. Meanwhile, carrion birds are busy, but after a few days the sun has dried and shrivelled the remainder of the flesh and the pungent and putrid odours have evaporated. Sooner or later, the platform collapses and the bones fall and litter the ground beneath.

When a man dies in these circumstances, the members of his family must pay stipulated fees to " Uto's " representative in order to redeem his property; otherwise all is confiscated by " Uto ".

" Uto " is also a place of sanctuary to which a man or woman may resort in times of danger. Should a woman seek the benefit of sanctuary, and carry with her what is known as " Big Ofo ", this being borne on her head, she remains the property of " Uto " for life. (Cf. " Osu ", Chap. XVII.) Should she bear a child while under his protection, it will also be appropriated by " Uto ". If she merely seek temporary refuge, and does not carry the " Ofo ", she remains in sanctuary until the trouble has been settled. After that is accomplished she is at liberty to return home.

Included in the property of " Uto " are certain dedicated cattle. These are unmolested by the people and, when one dies, it is claimed by the " Umu-Uto " (children of " Uto "). They are really " Osu " (Chap. XVII).

A male child born in any village of Nsude is carried to the dwelling-place of " Uto ". Offerings are brought of a fowl or a ram, together with palm wine and " ighu " (a species of cassava). As part of the ensuing ceremonies, a seven-mouthed pot is placed on the infant's head as a symbolical guarantee of protection against accident and the dangers of war.

The above notes on " Uto " are recorded here more particularly to illustrate the method of disposal of the corpse of a person who dies under his (reputed) influence.

NOTES TO CHAPTER XXI

[1] " Pagan tribes in N. Nigeria hold similar beliefs. They think that the spirits of the dead will find no rest unless honoured in burial in the proper fashion. They imagine that the ghosts will work evil on the living unless propitiated."—" *Tailed Headhunters of Nigeria* ", p. 190.

SECOND BURIAL

[2] Prices have changed greatly of recent years. At the time of writing (1935) they are round about a third of the above.

[3] "The custom with the Aragga of Northern Nigeria is to bury the corpse of a chief together with the favourite wife, child and three attendants who have been killed for the purpose; also the chief's horse and one half of his clothes and other possessions."—"*Tailed Headhunters of Nigeria*", p. 187.

[4] Baikie's "*Exploring Voyage*", p. 315.

[5] "*Life in the Niger*", pp. 23-4.

[6] All spirits (maws) are supposed to rise from the ground. Before the advent of the British Government " Maw-afia " was the highest and ultimate authority in the town. It was the final court in judging affairs. For example, a man alleged to be guilty of some serious crime was first tried by the " Ndi-Chie ". They, however, could not pass sentence until, and unless, " Maw-afia " pronounced the man guilty. It was " Maw-afia " also which denounced witches and expelled them from the town, or compelled them to drink of the poison cup (orachi).

CHAPTER XXII

PRIMITIVE LIFE

THE PRIMITIVE Ibo was an easy-going soul. Life was seldom a strenuous business. There was no particular reason why it should be so as long as the country remained free from contacts with the outside world. The materialistic and practically minded foreigner was inclined to scoff at the native's conception of work. As a matter of fact, the Ibo is not lacking in latent faculties waiting to be developed, and he is endowed physically to cope with any amount of manual labour. His chief fault is lack of persistence, especially when things do not respond to his expectations. His patience, under old conditions, was seldom tested, and he has to learn that, without it, success will not come. He is apt to become weary of his task, and is too ready to abandon any project that demands endurance. During the last twenty years, however, there have been very marked changes in this respect. The advent of machinery, especially motors, bicycles and sewing-machines, has led to a marked increase of patience and mechanical knowledge. The Ibos, like other natives, have proved themselves fair pupils.

It has been stated that " the African recognises only the dignity of idleness and deems it the true badge of superiority; work is not so obnoxious to his laziness as it is to his self-respect. It is the brand of inferiority. It is not *exertion* that he hates; he exerts himself in war and hunting. It is when work assumes the form of *servitude* that it offends him!" [1]

This, undoubtedly, was true of the Ibo a generation ago, but it no longer applies. The Ibo *is* proving himself a worker, probably above most of the other tribes in West Africa, and is moving farther and farther afield in his quest for employment. He is now to be found all over Nigeria and is proving himself an enterprising workman.

Tremearne remarks: " The native will not work unless there is a great necessity, but when he has put his shoulder to the wheel, he does it with all his might. But there must be a necessity, either hunger, or else superior force must be present to make him toil." [2] Again, it has to be affirmed that the Ibo now *seeks work* and, ere long, he will supplant the white man in many occupations. He has yet much to learn, but the progress made in one generation has been noteworthy.

What is here written is to place on record the manner of life that prevailed before the impact of western influences, and what still applies in the remoter parts of the Ibo country. The material needs of the native did not press heavily, nor is the enervating climate conducive to excessive exertion. The absence of pressure on the one hand, and the lack of energy on the other, combined to foster a leisurely disposed temperament. There was no call for initiative, nor demand for strength of purpose. The needs of life were, on the whole, easily satisfied. The farms supplied practically all the food. Cooking- and water-pots, a few implements, and some grass mats, pretty well completed the list of necessary property. Whatever accrued beyond these counted as "extras". The majority never troubled themselves further. Here and there, a few were more ambitious and collected treasures of sorts. (*Vide* p. 199.) These were accumulated chiefly by those who had other means than farming in making money, such as slave-dealers. Scarcely any grew more foodstuff than was required for their households. There was not much sale for farm produce, in any case, and it was not customary to till more land than would suffice for this purpose.

The sole inducement to work was to provide food and shelter. Naturally, the former ranked first, for the native hates the thought of being limited in food. He gathered his supplies from the farm and the chase and, in the neighbourhood of the large waters, he caught fish. (The fish of many of the smaller streams are sacred.) The soil in some districts is of poor quality, but, on the whole, the people had no great difficulty in raising crops of yam, maize and beans. The women add to the stock by cultivating koko-yam (edde) in the little plots around the huts. Fairly large quantities of cassava are now grown. To this list may be added ground nuts (*Arachis Hypogea*), ocru, gourds and other small crops. Fishing and hunting are confined to men, but only a small number are professional hunters or fishermen.

A more or less adequate supply of yams is the chief concern of the Ibo. Without the cultivation of this staple vegetable, the country would be short of food. Its production is locally known as "farming". This is a misnomer: the native is an agriculturist and in no sense a farmer. He has no interest in cattle, or other live stock, beyond what he may profit by the sale of a goat, dog or fowl occasionally. All animals fend for themselves and breed unrestrictedly, the more the better, irrespective of quality. There are not many cattle: What there are are mostly " osu ", that is, dedicated to local deities. (*Vide* Chap. XVII.) They are of a pygmy breed and are apparently immune from tsetse fly diseases. A valiant attempt to introduce a better strain of cattle was made by the Government on the Akpaka Estate, Onitsha, in the year 1905. An English bull was imported with the idea of cross-breeding with local cows. Unfortunately, it soon died in spite of every care to safeguard it from tsetse fly. A further effort was made with West Indian and Canary Island beasts. The results were again disastrous and the experiment was given up in despair, a sad ending to a well-planned and expensive endeavour to improve the local stock of cattle.

The implements employed in tilling are two, the matchet and the hoe, the former an imported crude cutlass used for clearing grass and scrub, and the latter for turning the soil. Both are of the simplest pattern, though eminently suitable for the primitive type of fieldwork. On the western side of the Niger, the blade of the hoe is less than half the size of the one favoured on the eastern side. The blade of the larger is almost equal in size to that of an English spade. The blades are manufactured from bar iron purchased at the trading canteens. The farmers fix them into elbow-shaped handles hacked from a forked branch of a tree. When in operation, the action is similar to that of a carpenter wielding an adze.

Around Maku, in the Awgu Division, the country is hilly, consisting largely of laterite, and is full of boulders and stones. The adze-shaped hoe is quite unsuitable in such country; the edge of the soft iron blade doubles up. Instead, the natives use an extraordinary implement resembling an eight-feet-long punting pole. It has a heavy wood shaft shod with iron, shaped like a cold chisel, two inches wide at its cutting edge. The hoe is grasped by both hands, raised two feet and is brought down vertically. It penetrates an inch or two at each stroke. It is then thrust away from the operator and the ground is levered up and broken. It is a very slow, tedious method of turning the soil.

The hoe is superior to the spade for the work it has to do. A good workman can turn the soil much more rapidly than an English gardener using a spade. It is also better fitted for the task. A new hoe is equipped with a pointed edge which enables the workman to drive it into the earth with a single downward sweep: a sharp pull forwards brings the soil into position. If in a hurry, a native can drive his hoe at the rate

PRIMITIVE LIFE

of fifty or sixty strokes per minute. He only needs to use his arms: his body and legs remain rigid. He manipulates his tool as freely as a chicken picking up corn!

Except in certain areas, as in the countryside around Enugu, where it was extremely dangerous in former days to venture beyond the boundaries of the village, farms are located outside the towns, sometimes several miles distant. Some men do not mind the daily tramp to and fro: others find it more convenient to build little booths for accommodation during the farming season. These not only save the daily journeys; they enable the owners to be always at hand ready to guard their farms against thieves. This is particularly advisable early in the season to prevent seed yams being unearthed and stolen, and at the end, when the yams are ready for lifting. The yam supply, being so important, it is more specifically dealt with in Chapter XXX.

FISHING

In a country where meat is very scarce and unattainable by the great majority of the people, smoke-cured fish serves as a substitute. The supply of locally caught fish is inadequate to meet the demand, and immense quantities of dried stock fish (more usually and appropriately dubbed " stink-fish ") are imported.[3] It is an essential ingredient to palm-oil relish (soup, so called). The men engaged in fishing practise different methods, employing nets, hooks and traps.

Netting is the most common method on the Niger, the patterns being adapted to meet the changes of the seasons. During the floods, nets operated from towers and canoes are used; in the dry season, seine nets are employed. The two former are novel to the foreigner.

Fishing towers (ikwum) may be observed on the banks of the river along the reaches above the tidal waters. They are constructed of stout poles standing some thirty feet above ground-level, strengthened by cross-pieces lashed on at intervals: these cross-pieces also serve as ladders. The towers are erected towards the close of the hot season when the water is at its lowest depth. A straight row of stakes is driven into the dry river-bed extending forty or fifty feet from the bank. On the lee side of these stakes, a shallow wicker net is attached measuring about ten feet long by six or eight feet in width. At the land end of the row, on the river-bank, the tower is built. At the top of the tower a platform of sticks is placed surmounted by a rough thatch to give some protection to the fisherman. Fishing

PRIMITIVE LIFE

begins from August onwards when the river is in flood. The fisherman takes up his position on the platform. It is rather cramped, being only about four feet square, or even less than that, but he manages to maintain a small fire when so disposed. At intervals, he hauls the net to the surface by means of a long rope made of pliant creeper cane which stretches from his perch to the outside beam of the net.

When fish are in the net, they are easily seen. If the man be working single-handed, he ties the rope to one of the struts, clambers down the tower, and along the row of stakes, to collect the catch. Not infrequently, two men work together, the one to haul the net, the other to gather the fish and, during the intervals, cure them over a smoke fire.

The balanced canoe style of fishing calls for dexterity and skill. It can only be practised in fairly quiet waters, where there is not much drift. Two men are essential. The net, made of finely woven cane, is of shallow depth : in length it corresponds to the straight side of the dug-out, and is some six feet in width. It is lashed to the gunwale in such a manner that when the canoe is on an even keel the outer beam is just awash. When moving from place to place, it is raised clear of the water.

On arrival at the fishing ground, the two men stand upright, one at each end of the canoe. Each man grasps a length of cane rope attached to the two outer corners of the net. This they let slip through their hands until the net has sunk as far as they dare let it sink without capsizing the craft. The men exercise great control in distributing their weight. After a few minutes, they proceed to haul the net to the surface. This they accomplish by standing on the free side of the canoe and leaning backwards, at the same time hauling in the rope hand over hand. The fish caught by this method are of a small species called " ellem " ; they resemble whitebait. The net is much too shallow, and the business of raising it far too slow, to bring any success with bigger and quick-moving fish.

The old locally made seine nets are very heavy and crude ; they are arbitrarily limited in length owing to the weight of the cane and native woven cordage. On the lower reaches of the Niger, these are being supplanted by imported cotton nets. In use, the net is carried out into the water and stretched parallel with a sand-bank, as a rule not beyond moderate wading depth. The ends are, thereupon, hauled ashore, and the net slowly and tediously warped home.

The only fishing undertaken by women is for prawns. Masses of twigs plaited together into balls some two feet in diameter are baited and placed under the banks of streams, and prawns attracted by the bait become entangled in the twigs.

Young urchins on the Anambara Creek use what appear to be the most unlikely method of catching small fry. They weave closely woven wicker boat-shaped baskets. These are about a foot in depth, and the sides curl slightly inwards at the upper edges; they are from three to four feet in length. Carrying these in their hands, they wade out a couple of yards into the water, generally in groups of half a dozen or more. There is no finesse about the business: instead the boys splash about freely. When up to their waists in the water, they place their baskets before them, press on them with their hands, and then step into them. Standing thus in the nets, they strike the water vigorously with sticks, reaching out at arm's length and drawing the sticks towards them. For a few minutes they continue this, and then stepping out of the nets raise them to the surface. Strange as it may seem, they do succeed in catching small fish.

Fish trapping has neither risk, skill nor sportsmanship attached to it. It is practised on lake-sides, seldom in running streams. The traps are enclosures built of stakes placed upright in the water bound closely together, a sort of palisade affair. They stretch out a few feet in semicircular or oblong formation. An opening is left for fish to enter. It does not appear to be a very profitable pursuit!

A simpler and, for small fish, a more successful trap, is one called "iko". This word also means a "cup" and the net probably is so named because of its resemblance, when ready for setting, to an elongated cup. Stalks of stout grass, or finely split cane, are used in the manufacture of these. The strips are laid parallel and fixed loosely, but firmly, together, tatty fashion. The sides are then brought together and lashed, so making a circular light framework. One end is pulled together with a draw-string, thus making a pointed nose. The traps are placed in fish runs with the open end facing upstream, being more frequently employed where the water is receding after the floods. Once the fish enter the trap, they can neither advance nor retire. The owner has no more to do than collect his traps, release the draw-string and bag his catch.

Quantities of steel fish-hooks are now imported into the country. This has brought about a great increase in hook-and-line fishing. The old native hook was a crude affair, useful only for big fish capable of swallowing a large bait. With the small foreign hooks available, boys fish with, or with-

LIFE AND DEATH.

Left: VISITORS, FORTIFIED BY DUTY SACRIFICES, TAKING PART IN SECOND BURIAL RITES. (PAGE 273.)
Middle: A FEARSOME-LOOKING "MAW" (RE-EMBODIED SPIRIT) ON PARADE. (PAGE 368.)
Right: A PLATFORM AT NSUDE CONNECTED WITH THE DEITY "UTO." (PAGE 296.) TWO CORPSES ARE ON THE PLATFORM AND SKULLS BENEATH.

out rods. The men still resort to the old customary method of fixing a length of line either to a tree-stump or to a calabash. In tributary waters, like the Anambara Creek, lines of carafe-shaped air-tight calabashes may always be observed floating on the surface. Fish caught in this manner are drowned. The fisherman needs only to pay occasional visits to his lines, gather in any fish that have swallowed the hook, and reset his lines.

Poisoning is another way of obtaining supplies of fish. Still water is the most suitable for this, though not essential. In the past, many fish have succumbed to this unsportsmanlike system. The Ibos make use of the flowers and leaves of a plant they call " iwelle ", probably of the genus leguminosæ (*Tephrosis Toxicaria*). The leaves are bruised before being cast upon the water. The anæsthetic effect stupefies the fish, and quantities are soon helplessly floating belly upwards needing only to be lifted from the water.

Away from the main river (Niger) and the larger tributaries, the greatest number of fish are caught during the dry season. The heavy rains cause great floods, and the fish retreat into the small water-courses. All these have become connected with the main stream by a labyrinth of channels. These inland waters attract the fish, because they are the habitat of immense numbers of grubs and insects and other forms of fish food. As the waters recede during the dry season, the fish are penned up in the pools. In many cases this comes about from natural causes. In many others, it is effected by natives blocking the outlets with barricades. Whichever it is, there is no way of escape for the fish. They are easily taken either by means of poisoning, or by chains of people wading through the water who seize the fish as they are driven to the edges of the pools.

Nothing has been mentioned in the foregoing paragraphs concerning the fish, because the chief purpose of this book is to place on record old Ibo customs ; it is not a fisherman's manual. Suffice to state that there are many varieties from the tiny " ellem " referred to earlier, to the giant Niger perch weighing up to 100 lb. and more. Nearly all are good table fish.

Though not a fish, yet because it has certain affinities, it will be appropriate to notice the Manatee.[4] This curious mammal is found in some of the waters of the Ibo country. Similar methods are adopted for capturing it as for trapping fish : hence the pursuit of it may conveniently be discussed under fishing. The body of the beast, at first sight, is greyish, but the thick inner skin is dark brown. Its size, when full grown, is ten feet; occasionally, it is said to be even more than that. In the districts with which I am acquainted, it is caught in traps (nkwu). They are constructed of stakes driven into the bed of the stream in the neighbourhood of the feeding grounds. The beast swims through the gap in the stockade, and is despatched with spears and knives.

It is forbidden for women to look upon a dead manatee until the tail and flappers have been removed. The meat is esteemed a luxury. The thick hide from the back is cut into half-inch square strips tapering gradually from the top to the bottom. These make useful switches, whether left uncut or when split half-way up into two or three thongs. The switches dry a middle brown colour, with a certain degree of transparency. This transparency is emphasised by polishing, and the final appearance reminds one of amber. The natives state that the flesh of the under part is soft (? fat) and compare it with the creamy substance of a cocoanut. This under part is cooked similarly to pork, that is, the skin is left intact, and is consumed with the flesh.

The natives regard the manatee as rather an uncanny beast. They allege that the animal has a habit of tickling a man under the ribs should he be discovered floundering in deep water. The man, unable to resist the desire to laugh, opens his mouth and drowns.[5]

HUNTING

In the north-eastern districts of the Ibo country, which are much more open than the other parts, the hunters sally forth in companies. They are always accompanied by trained dogs. These are provided with tough hide collars, studded with spikes, to protect them when attacked by savage beasts. Over the rest of the country, hunters usually work single-handed and do not employ dogs. Real hunters are few in number, though every man declares that his chief reason for owning a gun is to shoot game! Until recently, the guns were of the old-fashioned flint striker type. Modern weapons are now much in demand. Before a man can own a gun of precision, a licence must be obtained. This is issued only on condition that the Government Authority is satisfied that the applicant is of trustworthy character and understands the responsibilities attached to the privilege. For the ancient guns, common black powder is used. The slugs are locally made from bar iron, or are fragments of broken pots; these latter are colloquially known as "pot-leg". As can be imagined, these

PRIMITIVE LIFE

missiles are liable to inflict gaping lacerated wounds. These guns are not classed " arms of precision " : they are just " firearms ". For success, the hunter has to depend very largely on his wits and his stalking skill. He must approach his quarry very closely in order to have a fair chance to bring it down.

The equipment carried advertises a man as a hunter. It consists of his gun and a skin bag slung over the shoulder. In the bag he carries his supplies of powder and slugs. The old long-barrelled gun is fired by means of flint and striker. To protect the exposed sparking powder from moisture, a large cowl of raw hide is fitted as a shield. On the western side of the Niger, a piece of chimpanzee skin is the most favoured. The flints are of English production imported from East Anglia. Altogether, the gun is rather a fearsome weapon ; it is likewise dangerous to handle when fired, inasmuch as the heavy charge of powder is liable to burst the barrel, much to the discomfiture of the hunter. To reinforce the section near the trigger, it is bound with stout cord. The mass of cordage soon becomes as black and as shiny as pitch, the effect of congealed blood and rubbing. As each bird or animal is killed, the blood is smeared on this corded section, a symbolical gift to the gun in gratitude for the success achieved, and as an act of thanksgiving to the hunter's god.

When in pursuit of game, the hunter is burdened with nothing other than his gun and bag. His only garment, using that term for want of a more appropriate one, is a slight strip of cloth around the loins, passed between the legs. He has to penetrate dense bush and clothing is unsuitable for this. Successful stalking is a slow and tiring business. To attain to any measure of proficiency as a hunter, a man must learn the habits of wild creatures. Some men become very expert, and can imitate the cries of animals and birds to a remarkable degree.

The Ibo country is by no means a hunter's paradise : animals are few and far between. Because of his knowledge of the craft, the native meets with more success than the European. He develops an instinct which stands him in good stead when in search of game. He has no cause to hurry, and is hardened to the conditions. All the same, not much falls to the gun of the average hunter. Occasionally a buck, bush-cow, or leopard is shot. The men do not care to tackle leopards : it is too risky. They are more often caught in traps. This is understandable for if the one discharge fails to kill, or effectively maim the animal, the hunter is in great danger of a severe mauling even if he does not meet with a worse fate.

Leopard traps are built of stout timbers, and are generally of oblong shape. Most are fitted with a door which falls and blocks the entrance when the suspending rope is released. Some are equipped with a heavy log which falls upon the animal and pins it to the ground, probably fracturing its skull or spine. In the former case, the leopard prowls around inside the cage until the hunter takes advantage of the interstices of the palisade to insert his gun or spear, and, in this safe position, slays the unfortunate captive. By whatever method it is killed, great honour is accorded to the man who accomplishes the deed. The only pelts preserved are those of the leopard and the buck : the meat of all is a welcome addition to the larder.

Equal honour is meted out to the man who kills a leopard as that accorded to one who slays a man. It is regarded as a great feat worthy of high praise. When the hunter returns home, he is received with shouts of applause. He removes the tail and the pads : they are his special trophies. The body of the beast is then carried to the compound of the chief of the village who ceremoniously waves it before his gods, while congratulations to the hunter are symbolically sealed by the presentation to him of a chicken. When these formal rites have been completed, a miniature circus procession parades the streets. The dead animal, slung by the feet to a pole, is carried by two men. Alongside, struts the hero of the day waving the tail in demonstration of his prowess. He is applauded and saluted as the " Leopard Killer ". At the conclusion of the parade, the carcase is skinned and hewn in pieces. One leg is the perquisite of the chief ; of the remainder, the hunter takes what he requires for his own use and distributes portions to his friends. From a monetary point of view, the fangs and claws are the most profitable, these being highly prized as trinkets. They are especially liked for display on necklaces. The same remark applies to the tusks taken from wild pigs.

At Onitsha, the man who kills a leopard parades around the town for a period of twenty-eight days (oge isa), singing lustily praises of his own prowess. At the end of that period, he makes a feast for his fellow-hunters. He is then enrolled as a member of the " ogbu " (slayers). The complete carcase is given to the king as a token of homage. Here the leopard is classed as " anu ife nru " (animal of homage or service).

I can call to mind but one instance of an elephant being killed in the Ibo country during the present century. It was brought down in a thickly wooded valley some ten miles east of Awka. Traces of elephants are to be found in the Anam District after the floods have subsided, their spoor being con-

PRIMITIVE LIFE

spicuous in the soft soil. In the forest country lying parallel with the Niger from Asaba (western side) northwards, there were elephants up to the end of the last century. In the autumn of 1900, while travelling through this area, an old hunter joined our party. He carried the ear of an elephant which he had killed. It was a trophy of the chase of which he was excusably proud, and its presence in his hand always elicited respect and honour wherever we went. As already noted (p. 198), the tusks and tail hairs of the elephant are greatly valued by the people.

No hunter will set forth on an expedition without first pleading with, and sacrificing to, the god whose sole business is to assist him in his enterprise. He prays for deliverance from all dangers and for good success. On his return home, he again sacrifices, and returns thanks for favours received. All skulls of animals slain are preserved and displayed in the hunter's personal hut (obi). They are trophies of which he is as proud as the European who decorates his walls with mounted heads. When sitting quietly with his friends, the hunter tells his stories of the chase. Most Ibos possess the gift of oratory: this, with fair faculties of imagination, enables him to relate thrilling yarns of adventure.

Finally, in the olden days, there was the hunter whose prey was his fellow-man. When working alone, he followed his regular stalking methods. The more common practice, however, was to go forth in companies and either ambush some unfortunate wretch, or surround him and prevent his escape. The man-killer was given a great ovation on his return, and the ceremonies were similar to those observed in the case of the successful leopard hunter described above. Instead of a tail being carried by the man-killer, he bore an arm or a leg in his hands. As the procession passed through the streets, the hunter was applauded and fêted by his friends and neighbours.[6]

This man-killing, however, was restricted to men of enemy towns; it was not practised against the folk of friendly villages. It was not uncommon too, that, after peace was restored, reparations were made to compensate for any killings that had taken place while the towns were at enmity one with the other.

NOTES TO CHAPTER XXII

[1] "*Fetish Folk of West Africa*", p. 275.
[2] "*Tailed Headhunters of Nigeria*", pp. 198–9.
[3] 15,493,800 lb. imported in 1934. *Vide* "*Trade Report*", p. 80.
[4] "Manatus senegalensis, or sea-cow, of the Sirenian family, an air-

PRIMITIVE LIFE

breathing and vegetarian animal. It has no teeth in the front of the jaws, but has a good set of grinders. It is a slow, sluggish creature and quite unhappy out of the water. It prefers quiet shallow water. It has but one calf at a time, and this the mother is said to hold under her fore-flipper, the teats being situated just behind the armpits."—" *Wild Beasts of the World*", Frank Finn.

[5] Since the above was written, a very informative account of the Manatee and the methods of capturing it, with many other details, has appeared in the " *Nigerian Field* ", Vol. VI, No. 1, January, 1937, p. 23, contributed by Mr. F. J. Woods.

[6] A youth of the Kagoro (N. Nigeria) was not supposed to have attained to the full dignity of manhood until he had killed someone. The general idea was that " no Kagoro male was allowed to marry until this most desirable feat had been performed. When a man had been lucky enough to procure a head, he naturally did not like to hide his good deed and, on the return of the hero to his house, his whole body was smeared with red earth, and he was carried in procession on the back of a friend, the women of the quarter meanwhile dancing, waving their hands before him, and singing his praises."—" *Tailed Headhunters of Nigeria* ", pp. 113-14 and 152.

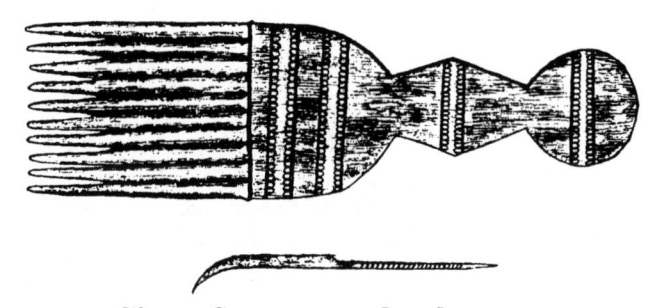

WOODEN COMB AND SMALL IRON IMPLEMENT.
Used in the Awka District for inscribing freehand designs for body markings.

CHAPTER XXIII
CLAY, METAL & WOODWORKERS

INDUSTRIALISM HAS not yet invaded the Ibo country, and long may it be preserved from its ugly associations. The people practise certain crafts and, considering the fewness of the tools, their crudeness, and the absence of training, the work executed is creditable. Modern developments are bringing changes, and the number of skilled journeymen is increasing. This chapter is not concerned with them : it is written to describe old Ibo craftsmanship. Naturally, the earliest exhibition of this is in the home where the ideas and artistic gifts of both men and women have freest scope. Local traditions play their part, sometimes so plainly that designs and workmanship are as well known as if stamped with a trade-mark. The quality of the materials ranges from good to very poor, though the same type is used throughout the country.

Before a man starts building in a new compound, he plants a live stick of the " ogilisi " tree to grow in front of the house that is to be. This is called " Ani-ezi " and represents the owner's deceased father. Once a quarter, or oftener if so directed by the priest, " Ani-ezi " must be mollified with a small feast ; in plain words he must be " fed " ! " Ani-ezi " comes further into notice from the fact, that when a robbery is perpetrated in the village, the people assemble before him and swear in turn saying : " If I am guilty, may ' Ani-ezi ' slay me." It may be a man trembles ; if so, he is immediately proclaimed guilty, and must suffer accordingly. His property is seized, including his wife, and a heavy fine imposed. Usually, the confiscated properties are taken over by the community ; in some places the " ndi dibia " appropriate and share them among themselves.

In the middle of the compound, a live stick of the sacred " egbo " tree is set for growth. This is frequently called " Chukwu " (God), and is essentially the property of the owner of the house who regularly worships and offers sacrifice to it. (*Vide* p. 147.)

All old men understand house building, and most men take charge of the erection of their own house. A few, such as the blacksmiths of Awka, employ outsiders to do the work for them. When a man plans to build a house, he relies on the co-operation of his relatives and friends. That is a good feature; it brings out the better qualities of their nature, especially in the willingness shown to help each other. No wages are paid, but the workers are mollified with supplies of food and drink.

The walls are of clay either built up in the mass, or held in place by a wooden framework. In some regions, this is the common wattle-and-daub system. In the northern parts, the clay is of a rich brown colour. In certain areas laterite predominates. Both these combine well. In the southern districts, and in some areas of the country west of the Niger, the clay is of very poor quality and is either of a yellowish or grey colour. Also, on the western side, some small single-roomed huts are constructed of logs placed upright in the ground, packed closely side by side, without any filling of the intervening spaces : they do not lack ventilation !

For the best houses, puddled clay is used. To build a house of this type, puddling begins towards the end of the rains. Having selected the site, preparations are made to provide a supply of clay. A hole is dug as near as possible to the house that is to be. A foot or two beneath the top loam, the workmen expose the clay subsoil. One or more channels are cut around the hole to conduct surface water into the pit. Meanwhile, the clay is broken up into clods in readiness for the rain. Immediately after rain has fallen, young men enter the pit and puddle the desiccated clay with their feet by simple up-and-down treading, or mashing it sideways with one foot at a time. This latter motion ensures a smooth mixture. It is an exhausting task, because the clay is heavy and sticky. If there be too much water, more clay is hewn from the sides of the pit; equally probable, more water must be added. The essential thing is to be sure that the clay is of a proper consistency. When thoroughly puddled, it is thrown out into a heap. At the close of the day's work, the mass is protected from rain and sun by a covering of banana-leaves or grass. Puddling is continued at intervals until a sufficient quantity is ready to meet probable requirements. The clay, when thrown from the pit, is too saturated for immediate use : it must be left for a time in order that the superfluous water may drain from it. It is ready when it has dried to the consistency of stiff putty.

Building operations commence soon after the rains cease. There is little preliminary organisation of the workers ; each

CLAY, METAL & WOODWORKERS

man and boy is quickly appointed to his particular task, some to cut the clay into lumps, boys to carry these to the site, some to excavate the foundations, and others to act as builders. No measurements are made worthy of the name. It does not signify whether the lines are exactly straight, or the angles mathematically true. The important object is to erect some outside walls and, maybe, some partitions inside the building. Often, a more ambitious man fails to complete the work, because he has miscalculated the cost. In such case, it has to be left until circumstances improve. If resumption of the work be too long delayed, the walls suffer from rain.

As a rule, the walls do not exceed a height of eight feet, generally they are rather less, hence the foundations need not be deeper than a foot. The thickness is from ten to twelve inches. This is sufficient, as the walls have no weight to bear : they do not support the roof.

Boys bring the lumps of clay to the builder. These are rather less in size than a football. The man takes the lump into his two hands and flops it down with force. He proceeds to ram it thoroughly with his fists, and finishes the operation by pinching off any clay that bulges at the sides. Finally, he screeds the sides with his fingers. The clay is laid in courses. Only a limited height can be laid at one time : no more must be added, otherwise the wet clay will slide down by its own weight. From twelve to fifteen inches constitutes an average course. The clay must, thereupon, be given time to harden before the next course is laid. The walls of a small house may take some weeks to build if the weather happens to be unfavourable. Normally, a second course may be added in from seven to ten days. After the water has dried out, but before the clay has set too hard, the walls are dressed with a sharp cutlass ; usually a well-worn one, the point being slightly bent outwards from the wall-face being trimmed. At this period, too, all cracks should be filled, and the wall well rubbed down with clay water. Large cracks always occur during the drying process when " upa ", the best clay, is used. To mitigate serious cracking it is advisable to mix a proportion of sand with the raw clay.

There is a much more expeditious, and much less expensive, method of building walls. This is the untreated dry earth type known as " egwe ". (Cf. p. 386.) They are not, of course, of similar strength and substance as those constructed of puddled clay ; nevertheless, they serve their purpose very well. The workman stands with his back to the wall that is to be, and moves along in a more or less straight line throwing back the soil between his feet. He repeats the operation on

CLAY, METAL & WOODWORKERS

the reverse side, thus throwing up a long mound of earth with a sort of gutter running down each side. This mound of loosened earth he pounds with his feet. He adds more and more soil until the wall is a couple of feet in height. Then he proceeds to tamp it with a wooden beater. First, he fills his mouth with water which he squirts in a fine spray over the soil, repeating this action until a fair-sized patch is damped down. Next, he takes the wooden patter and beats the earth vigorously. The moistened surface responds, and the result is similar in effect to that of patting butter.

The base of an " egwe " wall must be fairly broad, at least two feet and generally more. As the height is increased, the thickness decreases until, by the time a height of five feet is reached, it has tapered to a width of six inches. A wall of this type can be cast up very quickly. With good workmen, one day is sufficient for twenty to thirty feet of wall. When well beaten and, later, well rubbed with clay water, such a wall is quite sound for average-sized huts and for compound surrounds. They will stand for years if given fair protection from heavy rain. The worst feature, when used for houses, is their non-resistance to rats and other vermin.

The construction of the roof is a less strenuous business. The neighbouring " bush " supplies materials for posts, wall-plates, and rafters. These may be of ordinary wood, palm tree or bamboo. The framework of a house roof is frequently placed in position before beginning to build the walls. In such case, the four corner-posts set the boundaries and lines for the walls. It is also a useful asset after building has started, because, if thatched as well, it gives protection to the clay walls should rain fall in the intervals between the laying of the courses. Many Ibos are rather partial to the use of cocoanut and another species of palm tree (ubili) for posts and wall-plates where they are available. Much bamboo is also used, especially for rafters. Where a heavy thatch of grass is to form the roof, stout poles are utilised as rafters packed closely side by side, the whole being supported on sturdy posts and wall-plates varying from six inches to a foot in diameter. The underside of a thatch of this type is finished off with fine examples of plaited cord (palm fibre), a native form of macramé work. Often the rafters are of large palm fronds (ọfọlọ) ; likewise the laths to which palm-leaf mats are attached. The whole framework is lashed together with " tie-tie " (ekwe) ; a creeper cane either used whole, or split according to the strain it has to bear. The palm-leaf mats are tied to the laths with fine " tie-tie ", but more often with young palm leaves (ọmu) prepared for the purpose by being rapidly passed to and fro through fire. (Cf. p. 408 *seq*.)

The most satisfactory and enduring material for thatching is grass; and, in some areas, nothing else is used. In other parts, palm-leaf mats are the general fashion. These " akanya " or " atani " are fixed to the laths similarly to slates or tiles. A grass thatch will remain sound for several years; the palm-leaf mats do not last for more than one or two, though they serve for a longer period when they are saturated with smoke. On the western side of the Niger, these materials are less frequently seen; instead, the leaves of the " uma " tree are used. These are the most common. Actually, " igbodo " leaves are preferred, but they are not found in the same abundance as the " uma ". The leaves are fastened to the laths by their stalks. They are picturesque in appearance when newly tied: but soon become untidy and, at all times, leak pretty freely. As they become dry, they shrivel and crumble, leaving many holes. Over the ridge piece, and down the corners of hipped roofs, layers of grass are bound. These make the joins watertight, and help to keep in place the rest of the thatch, saving it from being lifted by the wind. A leaf thatch must be steeply pitched, otherwise it will be little better than a colander!

A roof composed of these materials, each part being held in position by means of supple " tie-tie ", is essentially suitable for a country where tornadoes blow with hurricane force at certain seasons of the year. The springiness relieves the strain when the pressure of the wind is great, and is particularly adapted to resist the sudden gusts. On the other hand, the palm and other leaf thatches suffer damage from the storms. It is advisable not to be too ambitious as to size. The length is not so important as the width for, unless the roof is very well strutted, it will sag when the heavy downpours of rain fall upon it and, when it sags, it soon perishes and is no longer weatherproof. Again, all thatched roofs, and more particularly those composed of leaf mats, need unremitting attention; replacement of broken mats is constantly necessary in order to maintain the roof in sound condition. Smoke is a protection; it preserves the thatch from rot and from boring insects, thus rendering it more serviceable.

In the earlier years of British occupation, Europeans residing in the interior were accustomed to dwell in houses built with clay walls and thatch roofs of the type described. Many reached the stage when they preferred them to houses built of more substantial materials, especially when they included the use of corrugated iron. A native-built residence may be a

CLAY, METAL & WOODWORKERS

very comfortable abode, and can be made very attractive and picturesque.[1] They have, it must be admitted, disadvantages as already indicated. The absence of fires deprive the thatch of the beneficial effects of smoke ; also creeping things, insects, rats and bats make their homes in it. In order to avoid over exposure to wind, sun and rain, the roofs are low. The resulting shade affords welcome relief after hours spent in the glare of the sunlight, but low dark rooms may react on the temperament of the average European, causing him to be moody, if not actually depressed.

The roofing mats, " akanya " or " atani ", or, as they are more commonly called, " bamboo mats ", are made from the leaves of the " ngwo̱ " palm (*Raphia Vinifera*). The upper side of the leaf has a brilliant glossy green surface, well adapted to throw off water ; the under side is a flat sage green. The leaves are from two to three feet in length, and a couple of inches wide at the butt ends. Two strips of palm-frond bark, varying from two to four feet in length, are laid parallel to each other on the ground about five inches apart. The leaves are attached to the strips, first by folding over the butt end inwards so that the glossy side will be uppermost when the mat is finished. The folded piece is carried over a couple of inches beyond the second strip. It is fixed by a single splinter stitch just behind the top strip, and by stitches above and below the lower strip. The next leaf attached slightly overlaps the previously fixed one, and so on until the end of the two strips is reached. Although the mats have a superficial area of a foot in depth, multiplied by the length, they will not prove satisfactory if laid more than four inches apart. They are fastened to the laths by tying in two or more places as required.

It might be thought that a native house has little to attract the artistic eye ; the impression may have been formed that it is rather a drab affair. This is undoubtedly the case with the great majority of houses, but there are many scattered about the country which demonstrate the Ibo's sense of decoration. This is illustrated by coloured drawings, carving and clay modelling. Here and there are to be seen good interpretations of the skill of both men and women.

Much of the carving is of the " chip " pattern. Instead of a long sun-baked clay front wall to the compound, men of means manifest a partiality for a series of carved panels. These are of " ojji " (iroko) wood. The natives possessed no saws in former days, and planks were hewn from solid logs with their clumsy axes. Most of the timber was wasted ! The front door is placed in the centre, the remainder of the panels are fixtures.

CLAY, METAL & WOODWORKERS

The door moves by means of two butts, one each at the top and bottom corners of one side. These butts fit into holes to correspond, one in the lintel, the other in the threshold. This makeshift for hinges is crude, nevertheless, it serves its purpose fairly efficiently. A drawbar secures the door on the inside : occasionally a few links of chain act as a handle on the outside.

The walls themselves provide plenty of scope for clay modelling. The fashion is to trace designs in curves and straight lines : outlines of creatures, real and imaginary, are not so common. Only occasionally are ordinary houses and compounds possessed of full figure models, that is, standing by themselves independently of the walls of the house. The bas-relief designs are first cut with a sharply pointed matchet. The lines are then moulded with the fingers and, finally, they are smoothed and polished by rubbing with clay water.

Some very good work is done on sculptural lines. A mass of clay is beaten into a solid compact block and the figure is carved from it. Again, such work is finished off by means of the fingers and rubbing. There are specimens of this plastic art which are extraordinarily good : they would earn commendation at any exhibition.

Clay modelling seems to be peculiar to the men : on the other hand, women are mainly responsible for wall painting. (*Vide* Chap. XXIV.) Besides the wash colour drawings on front walls, other marks are often noticeable. They may be plainly drawn chalk lines, or they may be roughly sketched representations of human beings or, again, spread-eagled crocodiles and other weird creatures. In no single instance, after repeated inquiries, has an answer in the affirmative been vouchsafed that these drawings have any significance attached to them. Some of the marks are merely the handiwork of children who happen to find a piece of chalk ! On either side of the doorway, blots and splashes of dirty grey colour are quite commonly seen. These *do* have significance ; they are the stains left by " medicine " daubed on the walls. They represent the Ibo idea of the " bunch of hyssop ", or the sprinkling of " holy water ". Other marks bearing an interpretation are those made by the priest when summoning " Mbari " workers to service. (*Vide* p. 102.)

Just inside the main entrance to the compound is a large pot containing the sacred water, commonly called " ọgwu " (medicine). Standing in the pot is a small bundle of twigs. Each visitor to the compound (not members of the household or near-by friends and neighbours) lifts the bunch of twigs and brushes them across his legs and feet. The " medicine " is also splashed on the outside wall as a sacrificial rite ; it is a symbolical way of invoking protection from dangers spiritual and physical.

There are some towns which practically monopolise certain specialised professions. For example, Awka, Nkwerre and a few other places manufacture nearly all the metal work produced in the Ibo country. Apart from the agriculturist, the blacksmiths have more scope for their activities than any other craftsmen. It was a sound money-making business before so much foreign ironmongery was imported. It is still a good profession, for farming implements are always in demand. The trade is controlled by the councils of the smiths in the different villages. No man may go forth to practise until sanction has been granted by the council under whose auspices he serves. Ceremonies have to be observed and areas assigned to those who are authorised to work as journeymen in different parts of the country. These men travel widely, not only in the Ibo country, but in the regions beyond its borders as far as Calabar, Bonny, Warri and even farther afield. They generally leave home about March or April, and remain away till November at the earliest : many do not return till just before Christmas. They take a holiday during the dry season as the farmers do.

Considering the few tools they possess, and the inadequacy of their plant, these blacksmiths produce wrought-iron work of very fair quality. The workshop is quickly erected wherever they make their temporary quarters. Four light corner-poles, standing about four feet above ground-level, support a light framework, which is thatched with a few leaf mats. The anvil is a piece of round iron fixed firmly upright in a block of wood. This, in turn, is buried with the top of it level with the floor, thus securing rigidity. The hammer is a similar piece of round iron, about a foot long, two inches in diameter, with one end tapered down to form a handle. No coal is available : charcoal is used instead. This is prepared from a shrub called " icheku " or " araba " : hence the word for charcoal is also " icheku ". This makes a good furnace under draught from the primitive bellows. These consist of a skin bag to the top of which two light sticks are strongly bound. The smith's boy pumps air by quick up-and-down movements by each hand rising and falling alternately. The outfit is completed with a clay nozzle attached at one end to the bag, the other, and

CLAY, METAL & WOODWORKERS

tapered end, extends to the centre of the fire. It is a simple affair, nevertheless, it is capable of generating intense heat.

The smith is always accompanied by a boy whose chief occupation is to manipulate the bellows. Whilst squatting on the ground fulfilling this task, he has facilities for watching his master at work. In due time, he gathers knowledge of the craft, and starts to manufacture small articles himself from pieces of scrap metal. A favourite initial attempt is to learn how to convert a piece of brass into finely drawn wire. Having mastered this, he proceeds to fashion the wire into chains. At one time, these were purchased by young men to wear as ornaments round their legs, from the ankle upwards. These have now gone entirely out of favour. It was a custom which could well be dispensed with, inasmuch as the chains were bound round the legs so tightly that they could not fail to interfere with the circulation of the blood.

The massive brass anklets which once were fashionable in certain towns (mentioned on p. 205) deserve some description of their manufacture. They take a comparatively long time to forge, and care is needed, otherwise the brass will crack. Each anklet is manufactured from one piece of brass. To render the metal malleable, it is heated almost to melting-point, and then allowed to cool. This softening process is repeated until the brass is ready for hammering into shape. The piece of bar brass is, at the start, oblong. The smith hammers this along each side and gradually brings it to a four right-angled shape. He continues to beat out the four flanges until they are less than one-eighth of an inch in thickness. By that time, the horizontal flanges of a full-sized anklet are some six inches in width, while the vertical ones are about three inches above and below. The two ends are then brought together with a slight overlap. This completes the forging process. The smith next demonstrates his artistic gifts by chasing fanciful patterns on the surfaces which are clearly exposed to view when fitted on the ankle. These consist of straight and curved lines, sometimes following a definite scheme, at other times amplified by spread-eagled frogs and various other figures. The designs are pricked out with a punch. Finally, the upper parts are burnished to a highly polished surface. So long as these anklets were in favour, the manufacture of them was fairly profitable. At the beginning of this century, the people who prized them were prepared to pay up to 15s. per pair ; a high price in those days. Later, foreigners came along and some paid as much as £3 for a pair to be treasured among their African curios. Recently, I have purchased specimens at 3s. per pair !

They are rarely seen nowadays; hardly ever in the hands of curio vendors: they can only be purchased occasionally from blacksmiths who have a pair left in stock, or who have been employed to remove them from the ankles of women who have decided to dispense with them. To-day, they are relics of a bygone fashion. The demand for the anklets having ceased, the smiths no longer manufacture them.

It is interesting to watch an Ibo blacksmith at his work, and to note the dexterity with which he handles the rude tools he has evolved for his task. A little knowledge of the craft adds to the entertainment. When travelling through an area previously unvisited by a European, I had the opportunity of making the acquaintance of a smith which, as it turned out, had a wider result than I anticipated. Watching the smith, I noticed how much he was handicapped by his having to maintain a firm grasp of his tongs throughout the time his metal was heating in the fire. I made a link for him whereby it was an easy matter to fix the grip and his hand was left free. It was a very ordinary arrangement, only it had never penetrated the mind of the native. To indicate his pleasure, the smith forthwith made a bangle from a piece of scrap iron. This he duly chased with a punch and then presented it to me. He proceeded to forge some needles. They would not meet with approval from a tailor, and still less from a seamstress, yet, they represented skilful craftsmanship considering the tools. It would be more fitting to class them with stout carpet needles! Long before the demonstration came to an end, a considerable crowd of people had assembled about the little smithy. One was able to inculcate a friendly spirit where, previously, it had been somewhat doubtful.

A capable smith finds no particular difficulty in constructing a gun of the old flintlock type with the exception of the barrel. He could forge a barrel of a sort, but he knows quite well that his labour would be wasted. He has no knowledge of tempering. He realises that bar iron, his only material, is not strong enough to stand the strain of exploding gunpowder. What he does manufacture in the way of gun equipment serves its purpose satisfactorily. He makes taps and dies from old cutlasses, or other scraps of superior metal he is able to collect. The native blacksmith is certainly a good jobber. The gun stock he hews out of a solid block of wood. When fitted, he may reasonably be proud of his handiwork.

Until legislation was introduced which restricted the importation of percussion caps, the smiths had an outlet for their skill in converting flintlock into cap guns. The gun which

A YOUNG BRIDE.
GIRLS ARE GENERALLY MARRIED AT ABOUT THE AGE OF SIXTEEN YEARS.

could be discharged by means of a percussion cap was, for the native, a distinct advance, inasmuch as the risk of a missfire was lessened. The hunter could not always be sure that his touch powder was dry enough to explode! This profitable occupation has, like the making of the brass anklets, disappeared from the activities of the Ibo blacksmith.

The manufacture of hoes is the main business of the majority of the smiths, followed next in quantity by axe-heads. There are examples of more artistic merit such as the staves which form part of the insignia of titled men. For the minor degrees these are little more than plain shafts, spear pointed. The higher degrees entitle the holders to use staves of more elaborate pattern either of iron or brass, or in combination. Some of the twisted iron effects on these are neatly executed. The smiths also forge door furniture, chains, hair ornaments for women, brass and copper anklets and so forth.

Metal casting is not practised by the Ibos; there is nothing that corresponds with the brass foundries at Benin City, which is no farther than forty miles from the western boundary of the Ibo country. The art of casting did not spread outside Benin. It is, however, not absolutely unknown, because, very occasionally, cast-brass tobacco pipes are seen. These are probably the outcome of a smith's hobby rather than a regular practice.

The evidences of smelting have not, as far as I am aware, been investigated. In the hill country of the Udi Division there are quantities of hæmatite ore. Loose stones are coated with run iron. Whether these are traces of one-time smelting operations, I am unable to state. The fact that the stones are broken into small fragments, and the shape of some of the mounds, may support the suggestion that iron was formerly smelted in this part of the country.

The Ibo blacksmiths appear to have anticipated the Trade Union Movement. In former days, the rules and regulations governing the craft were rigidly enforced. They still operate, although recourse to force and fighting in order to maintain the rights and privileges is no longer tolerated. On the whole, the members respect the instructions issued by their councils, but there is much more freedom in these days, and the impositions do not weigh heavily on the members, nor is jealousy so rabid as it used to be. Compliance with the general principles of the institutions, as they apply in the different towns, is all that is now demanded.

This freedom from arbitrary restrictions is a reflection of the changes wrought by new conditions. What has affected the blacksmith's profession most is the vastly increased importation of foreign ironmongery. Large quantities of cheap hardware goods are now on sale in the markets. Bolts, hinges, locks and other useful articles can be purchased where, before, the people had to depend upon the local smiths for their supplies. The foreign article is cheaper, and much more convenient for its purpose. It saves time, money and material. An example will suffice. Planks are now cut by saws instead of being hewn from baulks, thus eliminating the excessive waste of labour and timber necessitated by the old system.

These inevitable changes are leading to the introduction of fresh methods to meet the contingencies of modern requirements. A few of the more enterprising native blacksmiths are rising to new heights of craftsmanship. Some fine specimens of wrought-iron work are now being manufactured, such as entrance gates and garden chairs. Sewing-machine stands, complete with treadles and belt wheels, are now on sale or order. A person buys a hand machine, and the smith fits it with a treadle at a big saving of cost when compared with the shop price of the complete article. This illustrates the way trade will develop as the smiths are able to seize the opportunities, and profit by catering as far as possible to meet the new conditions.

In the Ibo country, missions founded the first schools of carpentry in the eighteen-nineties. Before that time, the woodworkers were not so numerous as the blacksmiths. To-day, the positions are reversed. In the old days, the woodworkers had not much scope: their main efforts were devoted to the production of slab doors and panels, plain or chip-carved, as noted earlier in the chapter. They, similarly to the blacksmiths, were equipped with a meagre outfit of tools, an axe, a matchet, and one or two small home-made wood chisels. With these they manufactured stools, small kola boxes, chests, " alusi " figures, masks and, here and there, more ambitious specimens of carved work.

Some of the stools are massive affairs hewn out of blocks of timber. Top and bottom match in size. Between may be a collection of supports ornamented with birds or curved columns of intricate pattern. Other stools are of slight build with seats shaped like a large slice of melon. The stools which are most in favour are made of " iroko " or mahogany. These also are cut from solid blocks. The seat is round and slightly hollowed to fit the figure. It stands on a single pedestal which divides into three or four feet at the base. The central column and the feet are neatly chip carved. These stools are attractive in appearance, and are sturdy, yet graceful. They are more commonly known as " Awka " stools. Formerly, only one family appears to have held the right to manufacture stools of this pattern. Then there was not a great demand for them, because only chiefs and notable people were permitted to use them. Europeans, nowadays, buy most of the stools produced.

The " alusis " chiefly consist of the god " Ikenga ". Every house has one or more of these. In a few places, there are wooden figures, mostly in human shape, varying in size from that of a large doll to the height of a man. Much more often the female figure is displayed. Some of the owners of these make exorbitant demands from what may be termed their " parishioners " extorting, by threats of retribution, money payments. Then, most of the Native Courts are equipped with out-size examples of the " Ikenga " god. The chiefs think that no court would be properly furnished without one of these, although they attach little importance to them for serious use. They serve no more real purpose than a statue of " Justice " in an English building, being more symbolical than useful. The average native will swear anything on such an " Ikenga " since, whatever he professes, it would not bind him ; his oath only has a salutary effect when sworn on, or before, his own personal god. For the foreigner, the interest lies rather in the demonstration of the woodworker's skill. A court god generally displays a figure sitting on a stool. He holds a drawn sword vertically in his right hand, with the victim's head in his left. The whole figure is highly coloured with black, white, purple and yellow stains when first installed. These fade within a few months. The faded colours, the hangings of dirty strips of cloth, dust and dirt soon give the " alusi " a disreputable appearance. It has not much to recommend it, and nobody takes the trouble even to give a " brush-up " to the god that ostensibly rules the court.

A single block of wood is also used for the manufacture of a mask of which there are many different forms. Many of these are used in dancing displays, but the great majority are the monopoly of the " maws ". (*Vide* p. 368.) The wood for these is taken from " aron " and " egbo " trees : it is soft, easily worked, and as easily broken, some of it not much more substantial than pith. They are of great variety : some are face masks only, others completely cover the head ; some are wonderfully ornate, with carved birds and animals, plumes and pieces of mirror glass which flash in the sun. Many of this pattern rise in tiers, sometimes three or four of them, and tower up two or three feet above the head of the wearer. Others, again, are carved to represent nightmare beasts, with huge fangs and glaring eye spaces, fearful-looking caricatures, so carved in order to inspire awe, and to frighten especially the women-folk. But that old fear is almost dispelled now and, in many parts, the use of masks has become a source of amusement. What is of real interest are the examples of the handicraft of the makers : also that many of the masks have white faces. The underlying principle for this custom is a fundamental primitive conception of a resurrection, hence, all re-embodied spirits appear with white faces. A further item to note is that the masks do not reflect negro features ; the faces as carved are of Egyptian type. The nose is long, straight and narrow ; there is no hint of the broad flat nostrils ; it is, indeed, quite different from the negro nose in every respect. Likewise the teeth : they are shown as smaller than those of an average child, while the mouth is also small with scarcely any lip at all.

On the western side of the Niger, in the interior parts between Asaba and Benin, the roofs of the reception compounds and the palaces of the kings were, up to recent times, supported by carved pillars, and many of the doors were embellished with figures carved in bas-relief. The men who worked these were endowed with considerable artistic taste and skill, and it is a pity that their work is no longer in request. Concrete is a sound building material, especially in a country plagued with white ants, but it is rather sad to see the old specimens of carved wooden posts being rooted out and concrete pillars substituted for them. Utility has displaced the picturesque, a change to be regretted.

NOTE TO CHAPTER XXIII

[1] Tremearne says : " In many ways such a house (i.e. an improved native hut) is preferable to a bungalow, for the native makes but little noise when moving about and the mud is cooler than wood, but insects find a more congenial habitation in a hut and the earthen floor and walls are very hard to keep clean."—" *Tailed Headhunters of Nigeria* ", p. 142.

CHAPTER XXIV

WOMEN'S WORK

THE CRAFTSMEN described in the previous chapter have their counterpart among the women. It is fitting that a short account of their activities should be given, for there are articles which only women manufacture; men have no share in their production.

The first examples that may be quoted are the spinning of cotton and weaving the thread into cloth. The quality *and* the quantity manufactured correspond to the different localities. In the Niger Delta region some fairly intricate coloured patterns are woven into the cloth itself. On the western side of the Niger, scarcely any of the cloth is dyed, and the workmanship is quite different in fashion from that of the Delta. The Northern Ibo produced little cloth: it was not much in demand!

Cotton is grown in a haphazard manner throughout the Ibo country. It would not be quite accurate to state that it is cultivated; it is planted, it grows, and in due season it is harvested. Comparatively few women are interested in it. After collecting the ripe pods, the cotton is ginned by fingering and threshing with a strip of cane stretched between the ends of a bent stick, that is, a bow. After ginning, it is spun on a spindle. A pinch of cotton is pulled from the mass and the end attached to the spindle. Then more cotton is drawn, leaving a thread of fluff about two feet in length. The spindle is set spinning by a sharp twist between finger and thumb. The women are very expert in this trick and cause the spindle to revolve so rapidly that it appears to be stationary. Much patience is required to spin a moderately sized ball of thread. The consoling feature is that a woman can carry her outfit in her hand. She is thus able to engage in spinning at any free moment similarly to women who find spare-time employment by knitting. Often a woman continues to spin as she walks about the village, for spinning on the roads in the Ibo country is not " tabu " as it was in ancient Italy. There is no similar idea that " the twirling of the spindle might, by sympathetic magic, cause the corn stalks to twirl and spoil the crops ".[1]

This primitive method of spinning does not produce fine

thread. What is wound up is coarse, but it has the virtue of being strong and durable. The looms are as simple as the ginning and spinning apparatus. All looms are similar in type and construction, some being capable of producing better results than others. The strips of cloth woven on the smaller looms are from nine to twelve inches wide ; better looms allow for a greater width. On the eastern side of the Niger, dyes are extensively used, those predominating being saxe and dark blue and brown. In some cases, the thread is dyed before weaving and the pattern is woven into the cloth, whether it is fanciful or merely plain stripes. In other cases, the cloth, as a whole, is dyed after the weaving. Certain neighbourhoods manifest great partiality for a pattern of squares, three inches by three inches, divided diagonally into blue and white triangles.

Weaving does not appear to be an attractive occupation. The loom is generally set up in an odd corner amid dismal surroundings. Further, it takes a long time to weave a fair-sized piece of cloth and, when finished, it has not a pleasing appearance. The locally manufactured article cannot, on any grounds, compete with imported cloth either in quality, pattern, or price. Hence, spinning and weaving are among the declining industries in their present forms. The young people will not yield the time, nor have they the patience required for these occupations. What is a more potent factor is that the demand for native cloth has almost vanished. The people naturally prefer the attractive and varied foreign goods which are on sale in every village to-day. Enormous quantities of cheap material are annually imported into the country. This is yet one more instance of the old being displaced by the new. In the large towns, the demand for imported dress material is expanding, and the native cloth is not only going out of fashion ; it is being squeezed out of the market altogether.[2]

Against this, it is cheering to know that the demand for native-made mats has increased of recent years. With the better facilities for travelling, there is wider scope for marketing these useful articles. The mats vary in material, in pattern, and in the different districts. The following examples will serve to illustrate the industry which is practically, if not entirely, confined to women. We begin with what is locally termed the " Asaba " mat, the simplest of all the plaited work both as regards material and manufacture. This type of mat comes chiefly from the western side of the Niger as the name indicates. The material used is sun-dried pith from palm fronds, cut into thin strips. These are placed parallel on the ground, and are then tied together with coloured fibre at intervals a few inches apart. When finished, the mats are from six to seven feet long and four feet wide. They will not fold without cracking, though folding does not break them. They are sought chiefly for use as bed mats, ceilings and screens and, for these purposes, they are particularly useful. Another kind of bed and floor mat, even more common than the " Asaba " mat, is produced by plaiting the leaves of water flags (akamala). These are as thin as stout brown paper and an inch (average) in width. The plaiting of these calls for little skill and mats are quickly made ; also they are very cheap.

The manufacture of baskets is a more difficult class of work. Some are made from the leaves of the " ubili " palm. These are also about an inch in width. It does not take long to weave a basket with this material, but some skill is required to bring it to an even shape and, more particularly, to make a cover to fit it.

Trays and shallow baskets are made of thinly split cane (ekwe), while the strongest are woven from " atta " (spear grass). Several spikes of grass are bound together by whipping into a single strand. Baskets made by this process are very strong. This grass is also woven into mat form and then worked up into bags. Many of these are made very attractive by the use of dyed strands.

Fresh green palm leaves furnish a fibre almost as fine as spun silk. The leaf is bent backwards, broken and then pulled back gently, thus separating the fibre from the leaf substance. It is the finest texture of fibre used for weaving. From it, material is woven about half a yard in width. It can be obtained either in its natural colour or with dyed stripes. This fine material (" uko ") is produced on the western side of the Niger. Only chiefs can use it, and they only on certain days as a semi-sacrificial vestment. Strips of the cloth are joined together, making a piece large enough to fulfil its purpose. It is thrown over the shoulder, toga fashion, and is very effective with its fringed ends. It is expensive to buy. Women manufacture it, but they are not permitted to wear it, except when mourning for a husband.

One other example of fine weaving may be mentioned and this, again, comes from the western side. Beneath the bark of young branches of the " ufa " tree a species of down is found. This is gathered and spun similarly to cotton. The material woven from this silky thread is the native interpretation of " fine linen ". It is not often seen, since only a few people can afford to purchase it. The premium thus put upon it adds to

WOMEN'S WORK

the high appreciation held for it. The expense incurred in acquiring a piece is compensated for by its unusual durability.

Women manufacture most, if not all, of the locally made earthenware. Some of it is of fair quality, and some specimens exhibit a measure of artistic ability. For the most part, the industry is concerned with the supply of household utensils, chiefly cooking and water-pots. The majority are of plain pattern, but some are of good design and workmanship. They are all made of puddled clay. Water-pots are, naturally, the most common, and these used to be in great demand. Kerosene and petrol tins are, nowadays, preferred as they are lighter, more easily cleaned, and are of more substantial material. Likewise, for cooking, the natives, where they are able, purchase the iron negro pots from the traders. These are not easily broken, nor do they become permeated with essences from the ingredients as do the clay pots. The average size of a water-pot is from fifteen to eighteen inches in height and from twelve to fifteen in diameter. In some districts huge pots are made for storage purposes. They are far too large and heavy for carrying water, but are useful for storing corn and for steeping raw cassava.

Smaller pots are made in the form of decanters. These are wanted chiefly for palm wine. When new, the original drab colour is frequently relieved by the addition of black and white stains, and very often with modelled decorative work. The white, however, soon disappears after the pots come into use. This is only chalk smeared on. The black remains because it is burned on and so is permanent. Certain places are noted for their all-black glazed earthenware, while others specialise in fine terra-cotta work, the interiors of the bowls being especially well rubbed and polished.

One of the most symmetrical examples of pottery is the musical instrument called "udu". (*Vide* p. 357.) This is very similar in appearance to an ordinary water-pot, only that it has a longer neck and an extra hole in the shoulder. It is frequently decorated with lines and knobs. The lines are scored while the clay is still moist with a pronged scriber cut from a thin piece of wood or, more often, the butt end of a palm frond. This comb-like instrument is drawn deftly across the clay, thus producing a series of parallel lines straight or curved according to the mind of the artist. A good "udu" reveals considerable skill and idea of design on the part of the potter.

WOMEN'S WORK

No wheel is used for shaping the vessels. Instead, the women rotate the clay in the hollow of the neck of a broken pot which they revolve as required, hence the symmetry achieved is almost exclusively a result of clever handwork. The mass of clay is gradually worked up to shape by deft movements of the fingers and finally rubbed smooth as the pot is slowly turned. When a quantity of pots have been prepared, arrangements are made for the baking. There is nothing comparable to an oven; the women make shift with a crude kiln type of firing. Dry grass and branches are spread on the ground and on this a layer of pots is placed. These are covered with more fuel, then a second layer of pots and so on until the kiln is complete. The type of fuel used burns fiercely from the moment of firing, and the erection soon settles down to a smouldering heap. The ashes retain great heat for some hours. By the time they have cooled the pots are ready for the market.

Water-pots manufactured by this method are easily broken. The clay itself is less than a quarter of an inch in thickness. This, together with the violent and rapid baking, causes the clay to be as brittle as an egg-shell; not infrequently, they collapse under their own weight when being lifted. On the whole, however, they give good service and, if reasonable care be taken, they will last for years.

By the way the people behave, there would seem to be something uncanny about the breaking of a water-pot. As stated, these sometimes collapse from their own inherent weakness. Occasionally, the carriers drop one and it smashes to fragments. Accidents of this nature happen more particularly when going to and fro for the household water supply. When it does occur, it is the signal for an outburst of violent distress. Shrieks and wails rend the air and, for a time, the owner is inconsolable. In the stillness of early morning, a sudden tornado of shrieks is somewhat startling. The shock is but momentary: there is no need for agitation; the cause is only a pitcher broken by the wayside. I am not aware of any specific reason why there should be such an exhibition of grief at the breaking of a water-pot. It is probably the active expression of an old tradition of which the underlying principle has been forgotten.

The custom of the Ancient Britons of staining the body with woad has its counterpart among the Ibos. Both men and women are addicted to the practice of painting. Formerly, the men conformed to the fashion equally as much as the women, and this is still the case in less enlightened areas. The styles and patterns are diverse. The staining in some cases is no more than a mass smearing from head to foot, or in large daubs, with canary yellow ochre or red camwood dye. In other instances, and more frequently, clever designs are drawn by means of " uli " stain, which dries black. The yellow stain in some cases is connected with sickness; the red (" ufie ") is associated with marriage, while the black (" uli ") is entirely for personal vanity. Old people occasionally resort to " ufie " on account of its alleged medicinal properties.

The custom of painting with " uli " alone needs comment. The " beauty parlour " is generally a convenient spot in the home compound, but, if so inclined, the girls perform this part of their toilet under the shade of the trees in the village street. The common method of applying the " uli " is with a pointed stick. In the Awka neighbourhood, the blacksmiths forge a small iron instrument for the purpose. It is thin and curved, enabling the artist to pull long sweeping strokes; it approximates to the long-haired brush of the sign-writer. With this little tool, clean-edged strokes and curves can be drawn with precision. The designs possess merit, and they are known by specific names in the different localities. The lady who is being painted must lie still in order to give the artist a fair chance. This, and the soothing effect of the instrument moving lightly over the body, often lulls the girl to sleep.

Three kinds of " uli " are used. The most common is " Uli Oba ". It is the juice from a fruit with a hard corrugated shell about the size of a large orange. Then comes " Uli Nkpulu ". This is a species of bean the seeds of which are mashed; the juice constitutes " Uli Nkpulu ". Finally, there is " Uli Ogalo ". This has a yellow flower. To obtain the dye, the root of the plant is scraped and pounded, and the juice constitutes the dye.

For the purpose in hand, a fruit-pod of " uli oba " is cut in half and squeezed. The stick, or iron instrument, is dipped in the juice and applied to the skin. At this stage, it is dark green in colour and the markings are faint. After a few hours they change to deep black. The stain retains its freshness for about a week, and then gradually fades. Some specimens of the freehand designs are very intricate, consisting of circles and triangles in regular, but involved sequence. When the face is covered with black markings, the effect is curious and rather disconcerting to the foreigner. It is much more so when the subject is an albino. Then the black superimposed on the pinkish-brown skin is distinctly weird, not to say startling!

WOMEN'S WORK

There is another form of body staining which I believe is done with emulsion extracted from a species of ant. It is "combed" on to the skin in a series of lines and sweeping curves. The lines are much less pronounced than those produced by "uli", though quite distinct. They are not so noticeable, because they approximate in tint with the skin.

There are several styles of tattooing or scarifying. In certain circumstances, the operation is a form of tribal marking; in the majority of cases, it is for personal gratification. The latter appeals more to women, whereas the tribal marking ("ichi") is much more the prerogative of men. Cicatrisation of the body is, in many parts, connected with marriage. In certain areas, a girl submits to the ordeal about the time she experiences her first period. Only a part of the body is scarified on this occasion; the remainder is completed later, usually after conception. Men are generally content with "ichi" marks, though some follow the fashion of women and are marked with "mbubu" (keloids).

To obtain the desired effect, a solution of chalk is smeared over the body and the design is roughly sketched in with charcoal. This is most commonly in the form of lines intersected with a cross, with small circles, about the size of a shilling, in the angle spaces.

The blade of the instrument is triangular shaped, with the cutting edge along the base. It is crude, but a keen edge is obtained by honing on a stone. The corners of the "ughelle" or "uche" (razor) is pricked into the flesh and a series of slits about a quarter of an inch in length are opened. The edge is lifted with the razor and a small wad of cotton, or palm-leaf down, is pressed into the aperture. When wads have been inserted in all the slits, a mixture of palm oil and charcoal or, more usually, soot from the bottom of a cooking-pot, is rubbed into the wounds. On several days subsequently, more soot is rubbed in, after which the cuts are allowed to heal. The final result is a crochet-like design of black keloids which stand out more or less conspicuously on the skin. The plugging process is not always adopted. Instead, the cuts are saturated with the black mixture only. In such cases, the "mbubu" will be proportionately reduced in size and intensity and sometimes are only discernible at close quarters.[3] Men occasionally have their necks scarified. These seem to prefer extra large keloids. To secure this desired result, the cuts are aggravated by additional rubbing so that, when they eventually heal, they stand out very distinctly.

Scarifying in order to imprint tribal marks ("ichi") is

limited to the free-born males of areas where it is a time-honoured institution. It should be noted that face and body marking is confined to Northern and Western Ibos. Those living in the southern parts do not practise it. Boys are expected to conform to this painful and disfiguring custom between the ages of eight and fourteen years. They seldom manifest unwillingness to undergo the operation, because to carry the marks is regarded as an honour : it is the badge of the clan. The manner of the scarifying varies according to the prescribed forms of the different districts. On the western side of the Niger, they consist of three or four vertical scars beneath the eyes. These are referred to as " egbugbu ". It is a primitive type of tattooing rather than the scarifying operation for the production of " mbubu " and " ichi " keloids. The " egbugbu " are tattooed on the faces of infants when they are one month old ; the body marks are not incised until the age of puberty. In this part of the country women are the chief exponents of the art. (*Vide* pp. 176 and 192.)

For proper " ichi ", the whole of the upper part of the face is scarred, right across the forehead, over the temples, and including the eyelids. The flesh is slit and laid back, producing a series of rough-edged ridges. Men from towns called " Umudi-Awka " and Nneni, are engaged to cut the " ichi ", indeed, these practically monopolise the profession on the eastern side of the Niger. The " ichi " custom prevails more particularly at Nri and the near neighbourhood. It is just possible that it originated as a distinguishing feature of the priestly cult.

The same type of razor is used for cutting " ichi " as for the " mbubu ", but the procedure is different. Instead of a wad being inserted in the cavity, the flesh is turned back with the thumb-nail as far as possible without tearing the flesh. While pressed back, soot from the kitchen roof is smeared on the raw wound. Any tendency for the cuts to close up too quickly is checked by repeating the pressing-back process for a few days. Those who submit to the ordeal are called upon to suffer greatly, and, for all they endure, they are rewarded with permanent disfigurement of the upper part of the face. So long as they remain among their own kith and kin they are content : they bear on their persons the insignia of their clan.

This chapter is really concerned with the industries under the control of women, whereas the " ichi " operation is performed by men. These comments on tribal markings are included here because the custom is associated with other forms of scarifying. The same applies also to tattooing. The medium of tattooing is lampblack. The subject to be imprinted is

WOMEN'S WORK

sketched upon the skin, usually that of the arm, and the artist pricks out the design with a pin.

Scarifying and tattooing are going out of fashion. Many of the young men, once so proud of their " ichi " marks, would gladly be relieved of them. They find that these disfiguring marks are disadvantages when they travel beyond the confines of their home towns. The facilities for travelling have induced many to venture abroad, and the wider outlook has led them to revise their opinion about " ichi ". For example, the scarred man discovers that, in other districts, the marks are regarded with abhorrence (nsǫ = abomination). An Onitsha woman, for instance, will not sit upon the same form with a man so disfigured ! Some go further, and manifest their repugnance by refusing to shake hands with such a man. What is a matter of pride, when among his own clansmen, becomes a reproach, because of the ridicule and contempt which is meted out to him in other parts of the country. This treatment is bound to react. It is discussed during visits to the old home. It cannot be long before the ancient institution entirely disappears from the customs of the Ibo people.

NOTES TO CHAPTER XXIV

[1] " *The Golden Bough* ", p. 20.

[2] " In 1934 the quantity of imported cloth was 68,298, 992 sq. yds. valued at £1,304,860. In 1932 the quantity imported reached the huge total of 117,423,582 sq. yds. valued at £2,559,788."—" *Government Trade Report for the year 1934* ".

[3] Among the Kagoro of Northern Nigeria " for scarification, the incisions are painted with grease mixed with soot from the bottom of the cooking pots ".—" *Tailed Headhunters of Nigeria* ", p. 113.

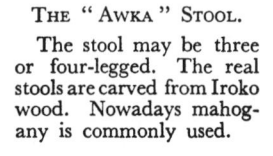

THE " AWKA " STOOL.

The stool may be three or four-legged. The real stools are carved from Iroko wood. Nowadays mahogany is commonly used.

CHAPTER XXV

MARKETING

UNTIL RECENTLY, all the business of buying and selling was transacted in the open. The idea of a shop or a room allocated definitely for the sale of commodities had not been entertained. It is different now. Shops, and stalls in the markets, are becoming popular, and the Ibos are responding keenly to the attractions and advantages of the new fashion. It has led, among other innovations, to great numbers of young men " setting up in trade " for themselves, where, before, they had no interest in buying or selling. Now, they proudly advertise the fact that they are " traders " by profession.

Seldom, in the old days, did men concern themselves with market affairs; they were regarded as pertaining to women rather than to men. The goods offered for sale were mostly connected with the domestic side of the household, and the wives were chiefly responsible for this. A man who purchased foodstuff was generally one who had no women-folk to minister to his needs. Here and there, a man might assist by carrying a load to market, but it was not a common practice.

The smallest village has its market-place (" afia "), while large towns have several. Where there are distinct quarters, each will have its market. Usually, the appointed days do not clash, each quarter holding its market on its own fixed day of the Ibo week. The name of the day, in the majority of cases, supplies the name for the market. The names are " Ekke ", " Oye " (" Olie "), " Afo ", and " Nkwo ". In certain places, for " Ekke " and " Nkwo ", instead of every fourth day, the market is held every eighth day. Where this is the rule, it is indicated by the names being changed to " Ekke-nta " and " Nkwo-uku ". As an exceptional, and possibly sole, instance, there is an interval of sixteen days between the " Kwulu-oto " (= standing upright) market at Ubulu.

With women so much in the forefront, it naturally follows that they have most to say when market affairs are under discussion; indeed, very largely, the markets are under their control. This quickly becomes apparent when any dispute

MARKETING

arises, or there is a failure to observe some particular law relating to the market. To such an extent do women dominate the situation, that it could be said with a fair measure of truth that " trade in the Ibo country was in the hands of the women ". I say " was " instead of " is ", because customs are changing. Men are entering into trade more freely, metal coinage has come into general circulation, and always-open shops have made it more convenient for many purchases. Again, the young generation of women is not so keen on marketing as their mothers and grandmothers were ; they prefer to earn and spend or, if married, to use money supplied by their husbands.

This latter remark applies only to the more advanced towns. In the interior, it is still the practice of the women to spend a portion of each day at the market. A woman will visit the market if she can, whether she wants to buy or sell, or not, because it is the one sphere of entertainment in the ordinary life of the village. There she will meet her friends ; there she can learn the latest news, and share in the gossip of the hour. To be deprived of this privilege is a hardship. The women have ample time to fulfil their household duties before the market opens. Some markets appeal more strongly than others. Again, some women have reasons for favouring certain markets, which may be ten or more miles distant from their homes. In such cases, most of the day is spent in walking to and fro, and but an hour or two can be spent in trading. Where the village is small, the market may not open till sunset. It would seem hardly worth while to begin operations at that hour. Usually, there is very little on sale, but the women like to congregate together and make small purchases, and, more especially, to enjoy an hour's association with their friends.

The government of these interior markets is managed by a number of privileged women who dictate the rules and regulations that apply to the particular market. All questions that arise are referred to this committee. One of their number is chosen as president of the council or, as she is acknowledged, the " Omu " (queen).[1] This council prescribes the rate of cowrie exchange, what markets shall be associated with them, and it exercises its authority in other directions as demands arise. Also, it decrees what articles are forbidden entrance to the market under tabu law, if any. A prohibition of this nature is largely influenced by the patron " alusi " of the market. This ruling is not often brought into operation, but the council has the right to act when they feel justified.

Many of the markets have rows of shelters which afford a

MARKETING

modicum of shelter from the sun. They are very flimsy structures of light framework and a few palm-leaf mats. They are, as a rule, utterly useless as a protection against rain. Some of the markets have not even this amount of shelter, all the goods being exposed to the weather. The only erection of a more substantial character is the shrine of the patron deity. Where tom-toms are a particular feature, a scrappy roof covers the " ikolo " (wood cylinder shaped drum). Again, in those parts where there are men and women devoted to the god (" ndi-osu ", *vide* Chap. XVII) small huts stand in the precincts of the shrine. These old conditions are changing, and use is being made of stalls instead of spreading the goods on the ground. This applies more especially to small articles of merchandise like reels of cotton, matches, soap and other items which are easily packed in boxes ; also cloth. This is the line of business introduced chiefly by young men. In the bigger markets, definite plots are allotted to specific merchandise ; for example, those who are selling cloth, yams, palm oil, meat and other commodities are all in their respective quarters. The sections are known as " odu ". For a member of one " odu " to leave his or her place and attempt to occupy a pitch in another " odu " is a serious offence. In the smaller markets this does not apply.

Other than where this " odu " system is customary, there is not much evidence of order. The usual practice is for the first arrivals to select their pitches where and as they please. They dump their wares on the ground before them and leave late-comers to squeeze themselves in where they can. These do not ask for much space ; so long as a woman can find sufficient room to wriggle down with her basket she will, somehow, manage. It comes about, that very little space is left for the buyers to move round, and it is necessary to pick one's way carefully when perambulating a native market. The crowds meander round slowly, inspecting the wares that are displayed. Some of these are placed in shallow wicker baskets, some on banana leaves, whilst most are spread on the bare ground. The goods are left to advertise themselves ; there is no attempt on the part of the vendors to advocate their qualities. On the whole, the women sit mutely as if they had no interest whatever in the business, and wait for a prospective customer to make the first advance. The methods of enterprising salesmanship are only just beginning to manifest themselves in the Ibo country. Usually, it is possible to wander throughout a market without a suggestion of being pressed to buy.

Purchases are made in terms of the local currency. Formerly,

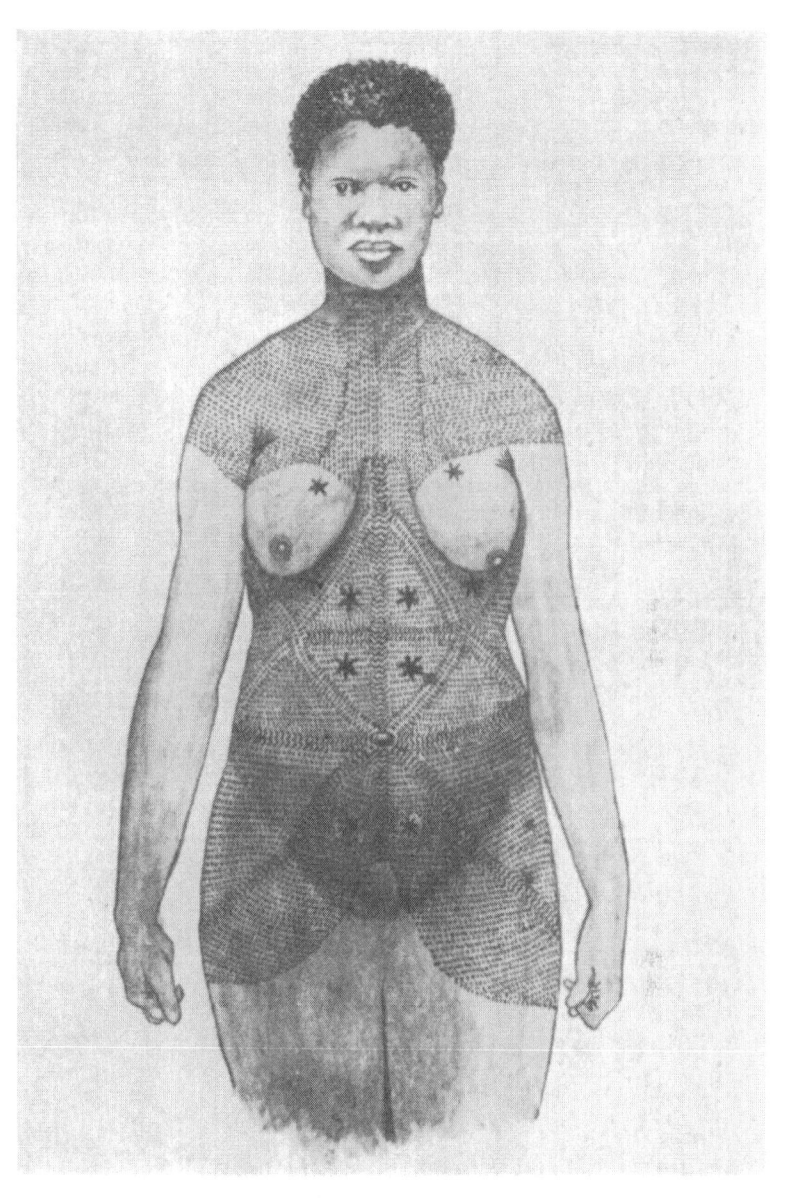

AN ARTIST'S EFFORT WITH RAZOR AND LAMP-BLACK
A CICATRIZED WOMAN.

THE DESIGN, AS SKETCHED, IS SLIGHTLY OUT OF PERSPECTIVE TO ILLUSTRATE CLEARLY THE LINES AS THEY FOLLOW THE BODY CURVES. THE PATTERN IS CONTINUED OVER THE SHOULDERS, &c. THE LOWER PART IS CUT BEFORE MARRIAGE: THE UPPER PART AFTER THE BIRTH OF THE FIRST CHILD. EACH OPERATION IS PERFORMED AT ONE SITTING AT A COST OF ABOUT HALF A CROWN.

MARKETING

it was, for the most part, reckoned in cowries, brass rods, or manillas, according to the area in which the market is located. In the more sophisticated markets, West African coinage is superseding these clumsier methods. There is no direct bartering of goods in exchange for other goods. Each transaction is conducted separately and finally. A may sell to B and, later, B may buy from A, each, in turn, bargaining on a currency ratio. The bargaining itself is a wordy contest, and very few articles change hands without a prolonged bout of haggling.[2] The Ibo is an inveterate bargain-hunter. Only in exceptional circumstances, such as severe trade depression, is a deal completed unless both buyer and seller are satisfied with the terms.

The initial figure quoted as a price of any article is always considerably in excess of the one the vendor will eventually be content to accept. *Per contra*, the first offer on the part of the prospective buyer is well below the sum he or she will ultimately pay. Occasionally, the two will come to mutually acceptable terms fairly quickly ; usually, a liberal allowance of time and patience is absorbed. It would not be quite correct to say that either was wasted, because there has been a certain amount of satisfaction, and marketing is the only common source of pleasure in an otherwise monotonous daily round.

The seasons and the prevailing conditions affect market prices. Towards the end of the year, that is, during the weeks following the harvest, yams are plentiful and at their cheapest. From March to June they are much dearer. The sale of palm oil is governed by the demand from the commercial companies. The fluctuation of prices for this raw product is a very disturbing element. The untaught native does not understand the vagaries of world markets and, when there is a slump, he is puzzled, not to say disgruntled, when he cannot sell his oil, or can only dispose of it at a low price. In turn, the producer has less money to spend, and that means that all prices depreciate proportionately. Since the beginning of this century, the cost of food has more than doubled. At the same time, there is a much wider variety of imported foodstuffs on sale.

Prior to the introduction of an authorised monetary system, different local currencies formed the mediums of exchange. In the more southern and eastern districts, manillas are used ; formerly brass rods were also currency. In the northern and western parts, cowries have been for generations the most popular form of currency. In the northern parts, the manilla is not current, and the brass rods are wanted solely for the sake

MARKETING

of being converted into " nja " (leg rings for girls, *vide* p. 206). Manillas are horse-shoe-shaped tokens used in exchange. They are composed of an alloy of brass and iron. Formerly, copper was used instead of brass. They probably originated as bracelets introduced by the Portuguese. Mary Kingsley speaks of the manilla as " a bracelet in a state of sinking into a mere conventional token. An alloy of copper and pewter manufactured at Birmingham and Nantes." At Onitsha, and on the western side of the river, the large cowrie shells are used whereas, in the eastern hinterland, the small type only are acceptable, these smaller being reckoned at double the value of the larger.

In cowries the table of the value is:

6 Nkpulu (= single shells)	=	1 Ekpette (or " isi ego ")
12 ,,	=	Ego nabọ (or Ekpette nabọ)
18 ,,	=	Ego n'atọ

and so on.

10 Ekpette	=	ofu Ukwu (or Ekpette ili)
20 ,,	=	Ukwu nabọ
30 ,,	=	Ukwu n'atọ

and so on.

20 Ukwu	=	Ofu Akwa
20 Akwa	=	Ofu Akpa (bag) [3] (calculated as a man's load).

The value of the cowrie is not stable, nor is that of the manilla. The quotations are liable to frequent changes according to the state of trade. The fluctuation is small at any specific period; it is considerable when compared over long intervals. There is, for example, 100 per cent. difference between the value to-day and that of forty years ago. The cowrie has appreciated greatly; it has doubled in value. The use of the shells has not been interfered with, although their importation was prohibited long ago. They continue to hold first favour with the people; indeed, the person purchasing by means of cowries fares much better in the interior than the one offering cash.

Although the importation of cowries ceased many years ago,

MARKETING

great quantities still remain in circulation. Fresh supplies being no longer forthcoming may account for their appreciation in value. Early this century, thirty " ukwus ", or more, were exchanged for a shilling. Later, the number dropped to about fifteen. In times of trade depression, the price decreased heavily, e.g. during the slump of 1932–3, the exchange rate soared to forty " ukwus " to the shilling. Recently, there has been a recovery, and they are gradually appreciating again as a result of the more favourable conditions.

I am not sufficiently acquainted with the history of the cowrie to offer any suggestion as to how and why the cowrie gained its position and popularity as a medium of exchange. Cowrie shells appear to be in use over a large part of tropical Africa, and the Ibo country shares in the widespread distribution. Up to a few years ago, it was possible to see large heaps of shells in the houses of the wealthier men ; they could be measured by the bushel. A clean shell is whitish and light brown in colour. The back and lip edges are crumpled. A hole is usually broken through the crown. This enables the shell to be threaded on a string, though this was seldom done in practice. Occasionally, other species of shells, bearing a close resemblance to the true cowries, are found mingled with the mass. A native counting shells will not fail to notice a spurious shell and, as he counts, he deftly flicks the intruder to one side. A single cowrie shell is of the merest trifle in value, yet one is never wantonly wasted. An odd shell, dropped on the pathway, if noticed, is gathered up by the next person following. The women, especially, are quick to observe a stray shell. She may be hampered with a load upon her head, and find it inconvenient to stoop. Instead, she picks up the shell with her toes and, thence, transfers it to her hand.[4]

In the area lying between Awka and Enugu, a novel currency was discovered. Equally strange was the fact that cowries had no place in business transactions ; they were not in service in the markets. This unique currency is formed of tiny pieces of thin flat iron, half an inch in length, with one end barbed, resembling a miniature arrow-head. These " umumu ", as they are called, have the advantage of being very compact as compared with cowries, but are easily lost. The value works out in cash terms at about forty-five to a penny. At Awka, itself, the value of one " umumu " stands at two cowries, that is, it is double the value. The higher currency in this neighbourhood was brass rods, which carried a cash value of roughly sixpence each. Awka men, in former days, used the " umumu " extensively for the purchase of slaves from the people of Umu-Mba. It must have been a tedious business counting a few thousands of these tiny scraps of iron.

It was customary for the chiefs of Awka to carry some of these " umumu " about their person. A man holding an " Ozo " title would not be without a small supply. They were used with sacrificial intention whenever the chief partook of food in another man's house. Again, some form part of the special offering when purification ceremonies are in progress. Those that are used for this purpose pass out of circulation : they are collected, bound up in leaves, and the bundle cast away into the bush.

The standard metal and paper currency introduced by the Government has brought great relief. It has provided a convenient medium of exchange in place of the troublesome cowrie shell and manilla. It has facilities far in excess of these old-time currencies. Nevertheless, the native has a great regard for the cowrie, partly for conservative reasons, but, more particularly, because it is so useful for small purchases. The lowest value of the metal coinage is the " tenth " of a penny, which is about equal to nine or eighteen cowries according to the kind in circulation. But many small items are purchased for less than half that value, such as a little salt, snacks of food in the market, and other odds and ends. Hence, the cowrie will continue to retain favour so long as it is available.

In times of prosperity, when money accumulates above and beyond what is required for daily use, the surplus is buried for safety. Metal coinage lends itself to this practice, whereas the old forms of currency were ill adapted for the purpose. There was no other way to store cowries than to place them in a room made as secure as possible. In evidence given before the Liquor Traffic Commission (1909) mention was made of an alleged custom of purchasing gin to hold as treasure. This might have been the case in some parts ; it most certainly was not so in the Ibo country. In earlier days, stacks of bottles stood in the compounds of prominent men, but they were all empty ! They were not counted as treasure ; they were no more than trophies recording past carousals.

NOTES TO CHAPTER XXV

[1] For further details of the " Omu ", *vide* p. 210.

[2] Crowther states that " even in common transactions, as buying and selling, they get so warm at a little difference or misunderstanding in settling the price between them, that I often imagined they were going to give blows ; but they soon settle it, and all is calm and friendly again."— " *Niger Expedition* ", p. 430.

MARKETING

[3] "Mr. C. Wakeham, purser of the *Wilberforce*, found, after a careful and tedious inquiry, that about 400 cowries weigh about one pound avoirdupois, and that an imperial pint measure will contain, on an average, about 500 cowries when compact and the top levelled."—"*Expedition to the Niger, 1841*", Vol. I, p. 460.

[4] "Kafir women show similar dexterity in picking up small articles with their toes."—"*Savage Childhood*", p. 214.

MANILLA.
Currency used in southern parts of the Ibo country.

CHAPTER XXVI

RECREATIONS

THE IBO, IN HIS primitive days, did not allow himself to be overwhelmed with the problems of life. His chief objective was to enjoy himself as much as possible. On occasions, he asserted himself, and he had his own opinions of his personal importance. At bottom, he is a humorist. He shares with his Negro brethren the ability to smile and rise above his troubles and, God knows, the Negro has had to endure more than a full measure of sorrow and suffering. When he seeks entertainment, the Ibo enters into it wholeheartedly; he lets nothing interfere with the pleasure of the moment.

The pastimes of the children have been mentioned briefly in Chapter XII. Here, we will digress a little on the recreations of the older folk. These may be individualistic or communal. Thus, a man finds entertainment when rambling about the countryside with his gun. Then, there are dances. This, too, may be an entirely personal affair, each participant being unconcerned with the movements of others, or it may be as a member of a troupe. These, with a limited amount of wrestling and swimming, practically sum up the physical recreations of the people. Naturally, these pastimes belong mostly to men, though women are equally partial to dancing, and girls·living by the riverside become expert in the water.

If there is one thing an Ibo covets more than another, it is a gun. In former days, scarcely a man rested until he was in possession of one of these fearsome weapons. The use of the spear and bow and arrow for warlike purposes, or in the chase, must have gone out of fashion many years ago. Except on occasions, as noted below, men do not patronise the bow and arrow now; archery is a pastime pertaining to boys who are not old enough to be trusted with a gun. The bows are simple affairs made by the boys themselves, and are seldom more than three feet between the tips and, generally, rather less than that. The string is a thin strip of bamboo or cane bark. The arrows match the bows, and are made of light cane with a few flight feathers inserted at the butt ends. They are not shod, hence have no barbed point. Instead, a series of notches is cut in order to give them some small hold when they pierce.

The boys practise with these on birds and, more especially, the lizards that dart about the compounds. They are about as successful as the average English boy who stalks birds with a catapult! There is more fun and excitement in the competitions which they organise among themselves. Each member contributes a stipulated number of cowrie shells to the pool which constitutes the prize for the winner of the shoot. Another way is for the winner to collect all the shot arrows after each bout. The prize then goes to the lad who holds most arrows at the end of the match. The target is a piece of the stalk of a koko-yam leaf, or a fragment cut from the stem of a banana tree. This is thrown forward about five paces, and the throw serves as the signal for all to shoot. The first marksman to pierce the target is the winner of the bout. There is no time limit to the competitions; the boys continue to shoot round after round until they are tired of the game.

Better and stronger bows and arrows are sometimes made with which the more expert men demonstrate their skill. Under match conditions, arrows are shot over a range of fifty or sixty yards. These men also understand the art of feathering an arrow so that it can be made to fall perpendicularly.

Something has already been said about the gun of the hunter (p. 307). Men who make no pretence of real hunting retain their old weapons. They are relics of days when little wars were of frequent occurrence. As they can no longer be used for this purpose, they are regarded as a sort of insurance against burglary. It is alleged that a robber will not enter the house of an armed man. What the guns are mostly used for to-day is to make noise at festivals and funerals, gun-firing being counted an essential feature of these assemblies. Great quantities of black powder are blown away at these functions.

There can be no question that dancing, in one form or another, is by far the most popular and widely practised of all recreations among the Ibos. Its fascination lays hold of the youngest, and it retains its grip until old age. One has watched a baby of less than a year old held with tiny feet on the ground being dandled to the jingle of the band and, close alongside, a hoary-headed old dame shuffling round, keeping time and rhythm with feet scarcely capable of being raised off the ground. Unable longer to dance, she shuffles, with eyes

RECREATIONS

sparkling with renewed animation. The dances vary in character according to the fashions of different towns; also as regards the performers. There are dances for boys, for girls, for men, for women and for mixed companies, the last being associated chiefly with public festivals and sacrificial and funeral ceremonies.

The dances which are connected with festivals are free and open. All are permitted to share in them, assured that no comments will be forthcoming in respect of the quality of the dancing. Men and women have unrestricted liberty to express their emotions as they please. It is very different with the dances that are performed by trained troupes. These are difficult to execute, and a long course of preparation is required for their proper fulfilment. Locality plays a great part in these. In the southern areas (Owerri District), as noted in the Introduction, the people do not really dance; they amble round in circles as closely together as they can pack. The best examples of " *set* " dances are found in the north-eastern parts of the country. Some towns are specially noted for their performances. Men and women spend almost all their free time learning new movements; they become obsessed with the pastime. The most famous dancers are found in a corner just to the north of Awka, the people of Achalla, Nando and adjacent towns, rivalling with one another to produce the best companies of skilled artistes. The members of a troupe performing in public are limited in number, for only those are admitted who prove themselves adepts. For the great majority of these set dances men only are admitted as members of the troupe. A much fewer number are performed by women only. Very occasionally, girls who show exceptional ability, and prove it by learning the steps of the dances, are permitted to attach themselves to a troupe of young men. They execute the figures and movements exactly as their male friends. It must be remembered that each dances independently and separately, though all conform to the one programme. This mingling of the sexes in set dances is not often seen. The custom only prevails in certain areas.

A long course of training is essential to learn the movements for they are intricate, and muscular power must be developed; also perfect timing has to be acquired. As the dancers train for their share in the programme, so also must the musicians learn their parts since they set the time and rhythm. At first sight, the stranger would scarcely credit the fact that the so-called instruments could be capable of being termed a band! They are certainly primitive, but they serve their purpose with complete satisfaction to the native members of the company.

RECREATIONS

The instruments include drums ("igba"). The notes produced by one of these are varied by fingering, and by beating on different sections of the surface. The wind instruments are reeds. These are generally about six inches long and correspond to a whistle pipe. The notes are shrill and highly pitched. Carafe-shaped pumpkin gourds (the pumpkins are allowed to ripen, then the seeds and fleshy parts are scooped out leaving a hard shell). These calabashes ("oyo") have flounces of cowrie shells attached to them. The musician holds one of these in each hand and shakes them alternately with great precision. Another instrument is the "udu", a description of which will be found on pp. 328 and 357.

The band takes up its position under the shade of a tree at a convenient spot well clear of the space reserved for the dancers. No definite signs of organisation are apparent; the dancers wander about nonchalantly. Then one of the bandsmen sounds a few desultory notes to announce that all is ready to begin. The other instrumentalists join him, and this is the signal for the dancers to fall into line. These arrange themselves under the direction of a leader. In the early stages, the leader stands in the centre, but soon begins to dodge in and out between the dancers. The initial movements are slow swaying steps. After a short period, for the sensing of the rhythm, the complicated movements begin and, gradually, the dancers work up to full pitch. The concentration becomes more and more intense until the performers are intoxicated by the effect. The speed increases, and the excitement and fascination also increase. Meanwhile, the spectators are, for the most part, silent, intently absorbed in watching. Twisting, turning and leaping, the performers go through a series of acrobatics which are bewildering to watch, and which entail very great physical strain. This goes on until the dance reaches its climax, when all the performers are at the highest pitch of their powers. Then, the signal is given and the dance ceases abruptly, the men remaining absolutely rigid in their last pose. For an instant there is profound silence, followed by rounds of applause. The effect of the sudden cessation of music and movement is startling and no words will convey the impression adequately; it must be experienced to realise the sensations of such a moment. The dancers themselves stand panting, while sweat runs from their bodies in streams.

These dances, as indicated, impose severe strain on the performers. A specific example is the one known as "ubo-ogazi" (the guinea-fowl dance). A good troupe finds frequent opportunities to display its powers. Great muscular development is necessary, because the movements are not only complicated, they are also extraordinarily difficult to execute. Muscles that are not usually highly developed are brought into use. The dance involves a prolonged series of body contortions carried through at high speed. In order to attain proficiency, the men undergo long training. This is necessary, otherwise the body would not respond to the strain. Absolute uniformity of movement is expected of the dancers. To this, and similar forms of dancing must be ascribed the fine development of abdominal and back muscles of so many of the young men. Some of the movements are expressive of free and graceful motion, while a feature of others is their rigid or staccato action. The muscles are tensed and joints stiffened. Whatever the form, the movements are sure and precise, manifesting complete control of the muscles. This is particularly noticeable where the dancers wear rattles on their legs. These consist of ripe pods, cut in halves, and strung loosely on string. Circlets of these are attached to both legs, one set around the ankles and another just below the knees. During a display, these rattles are shaken, sometimes one leg at a time, sometimes both together. They rattle, or are silent, in perfect unison, again a matter of perfect muscle control.

At certain seasons, these professional dancers fulfil engagements for which they receive fees. In addition, those who employ them must provide liberal supplies of food and drink. For entertainments, the programme can be varied by inviting dancers from different towns each of which is noted for its own particular exhibition of the art.

There is no similarity between the dances performed by the trained troupes and those associated with festivals where every person present is at liberty to take part. At these dances there are no stereotyped movements which can only be mastered by persistent training. Dancing, perhaps, is hardly the word to describe what is really the physical expression of pleasure and, at times, religious emotion. Dancing, on these occasions, assumes the form of sinuous glidings, with arms waving, and hands turning in sympathetic unison with the body.

There is a rigid etiquette to be observed in all these public dances. It is forbidden for a man to attempt to dance with a woman and *vice versa*. There are no partners; the men and women never dance in couples, each person remains a separate entity, and acts entirely independently of all others present. Even to disturb another dancer is an offence.[1] As the dance proceeds, the tension gradually increases until many of those taking part become oblivious of their surroundings; they are mazed in their abandonment. A fixed stare settles on their eyes. They do not appear to be conscious of fatigue ; they continue to glide about for long periods at a stretch. In the dancing at these public festivals this hypnotic effect is the result of emotion. In the set dances, described earlier, it is a common practice for some of the chief performers to be drugged in order to stimulate their activities. The effect is sometimes dangerous since, occasionally, one or more will run amok and, unless quickly controlled, will create trouble. For the time being, he looks and actually is mad. It is some time before such an one becomes normal again. The drug stimulates men to exert themselves abnormally. Under its influence they are capable of feats beyond anything they would attempt to do under natural conditions.

Mention has been made of rigid staccato movements. A further note should be made of dances where the feet are not raised off the ground ; all progression is made by a sort of wriggling motion. In this way a company of twenty or thirty men will slither round in a large circle and then reverse the movement backwards, retaining their positions and keeping to the line of the circle whether going forwards or backwards. A single exponent will squat upon his haunches and spin round at great speed, something like a huge water-beetle. To me it has always appeared to be a most remarkable feat. These dances seem only to be performed at night, at least I have not seen them earlier than eleven o'clock ; they are usually carried out in concealed glades on moonlight nights between eleven o'clock until a short time before dawn. Again, one has seen girls shaking their bodies while hands and feet are moving independently. As they wriggle, the strings of tiny brass bells fastened round their waists are made to jingle in time with the syncopated music of the band.

The subject of native dancing is one on which a whole volume might be written. It grips the spectator as well as the active participant. The instinct for dancing is highly developed in every native. Probably it is the most ancient and most natural way of expressing physical emotion ; it certainly has very great fascination for the Ibo.

A popular and widespread pastime among Ibo young men and boys is wrestling. Practically all boys learn something of the sport and engage in it in a rough-and-tumble way. From among these experts will emerge some who, in due time, become local champions. These, as opportunity serves, will be matched with the leading exponents from other villages. At certain seasons of the year many contests are held. Sometimes they are associated with semi-religious gatherings as at the " annual " festival at Awka (p. 47). It is a purely amateur sport and no prizes are to be won ; the only reward is the applause of the spectators. The loser usually takes defeat in an unsportsmanlike manner. The Ibo young men who come under school discipline are now learning what is meant by the sporting spirit. Rather than face defeat and possible ridicule, most men decline to wrestle after marriage. Abstaining from competition is discreet policy for men who are peculiarly susceptible to the taunting word.

The absence of a real sporting spirit manifests itself when a bout of wrestling is in progress. The Ibo is not gifted with the grace of endurance, and is inclined to cease from struggling should he find it difficult to make headway quickly. A competitor may, as far as can be judged, be holding his own fairly well, and then will suddenly release his grip and walk from the ring. When asked the reason for his action, he makes the excuse that he felt he could not succeed and, therefore, it was useless to continue to struggle since he could not win. This is but a personal characteristic ; the majority of the contests are fought out to the end, and some thrilling bouts are witnessed. Hands, legs and head are all brought into service and as the wrestlers shove and pull the head does its full share. The style is most easily described as " free " ! The tactics are not all of uniform character, and the most exciting displays are those between competitors from different villages. In such contests, the wrestlers are able to demonstrate the particular styles of rival champions.

The wrestlers have their own methods of fitting themselves for a contest. Of recent years, they have taken to the use of lucky charms. When this custom came into favour, another innovation came with it, namely, the swearing of oaths which would be more accurately described as doing service before an " alusi ". The charms must be concealed in the " ọgọdọ " (a piece of tightly rolled cloth passed around the waist and between the legs), the sole bit of covering on an otherwise naked body. In addition, " medicine " is applied externally and another kind is drunk. The external mixture is to handicap the opponent by causing him to weaken on coming into contact with it. The medicine which is swallowed is a species of drug for stimulating the powers of the wrestler similar to that used by certain dancers as mentioned earlier in the chapter.

RECREATIONS

The wrestlers enter the ring from the midst of their personal supporters. They advance to the centre and smack their right hands together in the approved manner. Then, they retire backwards to the edge of the ring. The contest now begins in earnest. The men approach stealthily, each trying to out-manœuvre the other. They double down until their knuckles touch the ground, with heads well up and eye to eye. The impression, at this stage, is that of a pair of freak animals stalking one another. Finally, they meet, and the struggle becomes grim. Much feinting and dodging ensues, interspersed with vigorous slapping of faces and bodies. These actions are allowable and in order ; they do not inflict much damage, rather, the stinging blows stimulate the tempers of the combatants and make them the more eager for the fray. They become more active and agile, darting this way and that, watching warily for the moment to come to grips. These tactics may be short or prolonged according to the comparative qualifications of the men. Sometimes the bout ends quickly by one man darting in, seizing a leg and, with a dexterous jerk, throwing his opponent off his balance. If they enter into a clinch, a stiff bout of wrestling usually follows in which strength and endurance are required in addition to skill. As the struggle develops, the crowd gives vent to its feelings and shouts itself hoarse. The wrestlers pant and strain until, at last, either one man is pressed backwards on the ground, or both relax their hold and the battle is drawn. A well-fought match has many thrilling moments, and the excitement of the supporters of the respective champions rises to full pitch.

The one regulation that must be observed in a wrestling match is that there must be no common fighting, nor may use be made of teeth and nails. Use of these leads to disqualification. Other than abiding by this rule, the competitors are at liberty to take full advantage of any tricks they know. They keep, more or less, to the ring space, but often surge beyond its limits, the crowd giving way before them. They do not, however, as a rule, trespass much in this direction.

People, whose dwellings stand on the banks of the Niger, or its larger tributaries, are so familiar with the water that it is almost their natural element. From their earliest days, they have been accustomed to it, and swim almost as freely as they walk. Whether the river be in flood, or at its lowest and quietest level, they plunge in fearlessly. Moreover, they can remain

RECREATIONS

under water for considerable periods. To them, it is all part of everyday life. The exciting moments come when a steamer happens to pass the village. As soon as it appears in sight, the boys and girls rush to the waterside, spring into their little "dug-out" canoes, and paddle forth to meet it. They are on the look out for tins and bottles. These are valued by people in a country where white ants and other pests plague them. Immediately some of these are thrown overboard, the children tumble out of the canoes and race for the prizes. Some are already in the water swimming directly in the steamer's course in anticipation of possible trophies. One fears for the safety of these lest they should be overwhelmed. Such anxiety, however, is wasted, for, as the steamer seems about to swamp them, the children neatly fend themselves off with their hands along the length of the steamer and then disappear in the swirl and foam of the stern wheels. A few moments later, they emerge again some twenty or thirty yards astern. Meanwhile, the canoes drift downstream. The boys and girls, with lusty, trudgeon strokes, soon overtake them. Catching hold of the stern with one hand, they jerk the frail craft backwards and forwards until the water is evacuated. Then they clamber in again, shouting and laughing with the enjoyment of the game. It has given them a few minutes' entertainment in an otherwise rather dull existence. These pleasant episodes are much less frequent since the opening of the railways. Passengers on river steamers are few and far between as compared with the days prior to the building of the roads and railways. The native crews of the steamers have not the bottles and tins at their disposal and, if they had, would not throw them overboard.

The most widespread of all games in the Ibo country is the one known as "Okwe". The word is derived from the name of a tree, the fruit of which supplies the seeds used as counters in the game. They resemble grey marbles in size and appearance. It is a game well known all over West Africa, and probably everywhere among the black races of the Continent.[2] All the people are familiar with it, and the majority are experts. Men, women, boys and girls find pleasure in playing it. Of these, the older men show the most inclination for it, probably because they have the most leisure, or are not disposed to exert themselves unnecessarily.

The game is played with counters and a board, the "ubọ-okwe ".[3] This is furnished with two rows of holes set parallel one with the other, the number varying from six to twenty per side. The boards are often cleverly carved; some of them being black and polished with long usage. These are treasured as heirlooms. The players may be two, three or four, the opponents facing each other on opposite sides of the board. It is impossible without taking up too much space to write full directions for playing the game. Briefly, the procedure is as follows : Working always from left to right on the board the counters are distributed thus :

5 counters in each of the first seven holes on both sides.
1 counter in each of the next two holes on both sides.
5 counters in the tenth hole on both sides.
1 counter in the eleventh hole on both sides.

The challenger always concedes first move.

Player No. 1 immediately appropriates (lit. " eats ") all the counters in holes 8, 9, 10 and 11, as a sort of nucleus for his working capital.

No. 2 likewise appropriates a number, but in his case leaves the single counter in hole 11, that is, No. 1 is one counter to the good from the start.

Players can begin where they like on the board, but must take all save one of the counters from the hole selected, and these must be distributed singly along the row of holes until they are exhausted. The object is so to place the counters that the last one drops into a hole in which the opponent has one or three counters. If a player can do this, he " eats " the one or three, in other words, he appropriates them. The object is to force one's opponent to move out his counters in such a way that he cannot save himself from the one and three traps. As soon as a player wishes, he can replace his playing counters by redistributing his own working capital. To do this, he must drop the counters singly, one in each hole and, if a surplus remains after passing down all the holes of the board, then the process is repeated until all the " eaten " counters are once more in the game. It is astonishing how quickly a capable player can force his opponent into distributing his counters so as to bring about the existence of holes containing one or three. A clever player calculates numbers and spaces at an extremely rapid rate. A weak opponent is apt to lose his original counters in an incredibly short time, which is either very humbling, or exasperating, according to temperament. A white man usually has no chance against a good native player.

The game often leads to excessive gambling, some men accumulating large debts in this way. Resort is had to theft

RECREATIONS

and other undesirable methods of raising funds to clear the debts. Occasionally, cases come into special prominence; there may be quarrels and other disturbances arising out of the incident and, then, the chiefs prohibit the game for a season.

A simple form of the game is played with a board having six holes a side. The players place four counters in each hole. In turn, they start by clearing one hole completely, moving always to the right and transferring the counters singly. Again, the object is to trap your opponent in such a manner that, when you drop your counter into one or more of his holes, it makes the number either two or three. In each case where this is effected, you appropriate all in that hole. But the appropriation only goes back to the last hole containing two or three; the player cannot "jump" over holes containing more, or over a blank, e.g. the player might manage to arrange to leave the right numbers in a series of three or four holes and still have one or two counters left in his hand, these falling into blanks or holes with wrong numbers. In such case he gains none; it is an unprofitable round. The game progresses round and round until the counters have been worked off the board; the number held by each competitor is counted, and the loser pays the difference between what he holds and his original bank to the winner; in other words, he redeems his lost cowries.

The game of "okwe" has the merit that skill is essential to success; there is not the same expression of the gambling spirit as in games of pure chance.

The following is a brief account of the way "Pitch and Toss" ("Igba-ita") is played in the Ibo country, one of the fastest ways of winning and losing money ever devised by man. It demands smart alertness and exceptional eyesight to become an expert at the game.

The medium used is cowries. The shells used in the interior are of a small variety and the backs of many are broken through. This latter characteristic needs to be noted, because it adds greatly to the difficulty in counting, both upper and under sides of the shells appearing somewhat alike when the position of the shells have to be observed in a flash.

The number of players may be from two to a dozen or more. They squat round in a circle, each man placing a heap of cowries before him to serve as a bank. A start is made by the one who challenges first; afterwards, the privilege of challenging passes round from left to right, though a man may "pass" his chance if he wish. The banker is not changed, however,

WOOD-WORKERS' ART.
Left: MODEL OF A WOMAN USED AS A SPECIAL FETISH.
Centre: ROYAL DRUMS OF PALACE AT UBULUKU.
Right: CORNER POST OF GRAND STAND AT THE PLAYGROUND AT AGULERI.

RECREATIONS

for every round. He may carry on until his bank is depleted or, if he win, until he chooses to retire—with the consent of the other players.

The challenger takes twelve (in some districts four only) cowries in his hand. He raises his hand and calls to the others to speculate on the throw. Each player may stake what he likes, six, twelve or more shells. Immediately the calls cease, the challenger gives a peculiar twist to his hand from back to front, causing the shells to spread as they fall. Quick as lightning, the players note the positions and either forfeit their stakes or collect their gains. The play becomes exceedingly fast, and soon a cloud of dust encircles each group of gamblers. I have watched players at this game, and it has always been quite beyond me to note the positions of the fall; the cowries have been counted and snatched up again long before I could begin to count.

The rules of the game are these :

The challenger (banker) wins if all twelve fall alike, that is, with either tops or bottoms lying the same way.

If six fall one way and six the other way.

The only other variation which can secure a win is eleven one way and the remaining one the other, whether eleven tops upward and one bottom upward or *vice versa*.

Any other combination means loss to the challenger, with the exception of seven and five, which is regarded as a " dud " throw.

A turn up of four and eight displaces the challenger and he must retire. Should the combination be favourable, the challenger collects all the stakes and adds to his pile; on the contrary, if the throw be unfavourable, he must pay the equivalent to the number staked by each player. It is permissible for one player to call on behalf of three. After play, the winner either takes from all three, or pays to all three as if they had called individually.

Some, of course, quickly lose their little piles of shells and then immediately begin to borrow until all resources are depleted. Not infrequently, the challenger breaks the bank. As a rule, however, he is sportsman enough to retire before that happens and gives place to another in order that he may have a chance to win. It is not considered good form for one man to have too much of the play.

A lot of gambling is done in this crude way. As stated, it is an exceedingly fast game and, withal, rather a grimy one. At some markets it is a regular institution, half a dozen or more groups being busily engaged at the edge of the market square.

RECREATIONS

As some players retire, others take their places. Some men become greatly addicted to the game and lose all sense of control. Men have been known to gamble away their money, their property, and even their children at the game of " Igba ita ".[4] And the loser must pay, whatever it may involve. The winner will receive the full support of chiefs and people should any attempt be made to evade payment to the full amount due. When a particularly bad case arises, though making the loser pay to the uttermost, the chiefs will put a ban on the game for a time. If any opinion on the subject of gambling is sought, it is generally to the effect that " gambling is a bad thing, indeed, except for the one who wins ! "

Another type of recreation, innocent, yet oft-times clever, may be mentioned. I allude to the forming of figures by the aid of a piece of cord. Girls are particularly adept at string games and the figures vary from the familiar " cat's cradle " to the most complicated combinations. It may be an old man with a long beard, or a cow's head with short or long horns, and a whole variety of other figures. It is bewildering to watch the fingers making twists and loops, and even a big toe may be brought into action. After an intricate series of movements, and when the whole appears to be nothing more than a tangled skein of string, calmly the girl makes one final move and the pattern reveals itself as if it were the simplest operation possible.

Over the whole Ibo country nowadays, athletics are fast gaining popularity, especially football, tennis and, to a lesser extent, cricket (owing to the cost of preparing pitches). They are played not only by schoolboys ; clubs are springing up in all the chief centres, the African copying and vying with the European in his enthusiasm. Regular habits of recreation are being taught and encouraged, and an outlet provided for superfluous energy by means of games and sports which, formerly, found expression in tribal war and other undesirable activities. The ball and racket are being substituted for the gun and matchet. This is all to the good, both for the individual and the community at large. Much can be done to develop self-control, independence and friendliness (especially between members of different tribes, for generations at enmity one with another) by means of athletics and the inculcation of the spirit of sound sportsmanship.

NOTES TO CHAPTER XXVI

[1] Cf. the custom among the Fang. " Men and women sometimes—not often—dance simultaneously, but never in couples, nor is there any physical contact between them."—" *Fetish Folk of West Africa* ", p. 143.

RECREATIONS

[2] The " Warri " of Yoruba-land ; the " Morabaraba " of Basutoland ; the " Tsoro " of Gazaland.

[3] A six-a-side double row of kitchen patty tins serves very well, with beans as counters !

[4] " Igba-ita " = gambling as met with under old conditions before changes brought about by contact with foreigners. The new term is " Igba-ego ", which indicates gambling with modern money (coins).

IBO " PITCH AND TOSS " (" IGBA-ITA ")
A banker's winning throw.

CHAPTER XXVII

MUSIC

THE IBO IS NATURALLY gifted with a sense of rhythm. Whether his musical talents have evolved from that, or vice versa, I make no attempt to discuss. Like his religion and worship, his ideas of music do not coincide with those of the European, at least, they did not until the European reverted to type and produced some of the " modern " music ! The music, and the instruments wherewith it is made, must be ancient, for it is only recently that foreign influence has filtered into the country. With the exception of the drums, native instruments are likely to disappear; they are being discarded in favour of the foreign article all along the line. This is, perhaps, no more than might be expected seeing that they are about as crude and primitive as it is possible to find.

To the uninitiated, the main objective of the native seems to be to create noise rather than melody. In this he has succeeded, although not all his instruments are equally strident. As indicated in the previous chapter, he can produce rhythm from his limited outfit and for dancing displays his music is fairly suitable. Orchestral (sic) music begins in a similar manner to performances in England, that is, with tuning in. Unless harmony is first established, the instrumentalists refuse to play. Once it is established, then each performer applies himself whole-heartedly to his task: hence the volume of sound. Sounds produced by striking predominate over other forms of music. There are a few wind and string instruments, one or two of which are interesting and, perhaps, they are the prototypes of modern ones now developed almost beyond recognition.

The Ibos have one instrument, if it is not a misnomer to term it an instrument, which no foreigner would ever connect with music at first sight and, probably, not even after handling. Further, it is one of the instruments to which women and girls are particularly partial. It is known as the " udu ". The second instrument used by girls is nothing more elaborate or musical than a pair of wooden clappers resembling as near as possible a pair of stout butter-patters. They are called

MUSIC

" nkpo-nkpo " or " aja " and, almost invariably, are used as an accompaniment to " udu " music.

The " udu " is made of clay, moulded and baked similarly to other pottery. At first sight, it appears to be an ordinary water-pot. Closer inspection reveals the fact that it has an outlet hole on the shoulder as well as the inlet hole at the top of the somewhat prolonged neck. The scheme of decoration is different also, the majority of water-pots being plain while the " udu " is scored with neatly scribed lines. (*Vide* p. 328.)

The foreigner left to his own thoughts would never dream that any sounds, let alone music, could be extracted from such an unpromising instrument. Yet, from the " udu ", the girls produce curious sounds which are not unpleasant, perhaps better described as rhythm rather than music. The performer sits upon a stool or mat and balances the " udu " on her lap, gripping it sufficiently tightly between her knees to keep it in position. Raising her hands, she brings the palm of one sharply down on the inlet hole at the top. The second palm follows the first, striking over the hole on the shoulder of the pot. The notes and intervals are according to the particular syncopation required for the song or dance. Two dull booming sounds result which can be varied slightly in volume by the force and style of striking. The notes are fuller and less harsh, otherwise they are not unlike those produced by a bass drum lightly beaten. Between the thudding over the holes, the girl, at appropriate intervals, slaps the side of the pot and so introduces a staccato accompaniment. The rhythmic sounds are excellent for dancing purposes.

The regular season for using " udu " (" su udu ") is during the time the young brides-elect are passing through the preliminary stages to marriage. Songs and recitatives, sometimes quite long narrations, are chanted to the accompanying notes of the " udu ". It seems a simple business to plump one's hands over two holes in a water-pot, whereas, it really calls for some skill. Three or four girls in full swing quickly demonstrate the speed and dexterity with which they perform. They bring out much more from these pots than would, normally, be expected and the rhythm is extraordinarily good. The music is of a haunting character and, at first, inspiring, but, after a time, to the foreigner it becomes very monotonous, and as wearisome as an unmerciful saxophone.

Another primitive instrument is the " ugene "—a kind of whistle. It is made of baked clay, in shape round, and about the size of a billiard ball. A substitute is occasionally used, cut from a piece of " ukpadi " wood. This has two holes ; one at the top which serves as the mouthpiece, the other at the front for measuring and varying the piped notes. I first met with it during a minor war where it was used for signalling purposes.[1] The notes, which are produced by blowing through the upper hole, piccolo fashion, are shrill and piercing. The alarm was sounded and messages communicated by means of these little instruments by the men on outpost duty, perched in trees.

The custom of transmitting signals by sounds is a common one and is not confined to these whistles. The chiefs entitled to carry ivory horns send out messages by powerful blasts of " dot-and-dash " notes. The horns are blown flute-wise, and the note can be varied in length, and higher or lower in tone. The chiefs are experts in the art of trumpeting on the horns, and use them for communicating quite long messages. More often, they perform upon them purely for display, especially in assemblies. Half a dozen chiefs, emulating one another, are capable of making a great noise ! A satisfactory result depends on the proper use of the lips rather than blowing with force.

Other methods of spreading information are practised, notably by the beating of drums, of which more will be said later, and by the common method of whistling with the lips. Men can communicate with one another quite freely by this method when completely out of speaking range. I, myself, have been " whistled " through a strange town, my passage being announced by one man to another as I passed along the bush path, the signallers remaining out of sight. Unless the stranger has sharp ears, he will pay no heed to the whistling. He will be under the impression that the notes emanate from birds. Boys make whistles from grass stems or the hollow stalks of freshly cut pawpaw leaves. With these they are able to imitate bugle calls.

Besides these, I know of only one other wind instrument, the " ọja ", a reed some six inches in length furnished with three holes for fingering, one in front, one at the back for the thumb, and the bottom outlet. It is always used in assemblies of men, especially when a big piece of work is in progress. The instrumentalist blows vigorously through the pipe ; the tones being shrill and piercing. It is supposed to instil energy into the workers. It undoubtedly does have an inspiring effect, for natives do exert themselves under its influence. On the western side of the Niger, the " akpele " is used instead of the " ọja ". The purposes of both are similar, but, in addition, the " akpele " serves as a trumpet in war. I am well acquainted

MUSIC

with the one who blew the signals on the "akpele" in 1904 at the time of the Ekumeku Rising.

Tom-toms, for the most part, are cylinders of wood. The big tom-toms ("ikolo") are not intended to be instruments of music; rather they are used for spreading information, for ceremonial purposes, and at sacrificial festivals. Meetings are called by their use, and various announcements proclaimed.[2] The beating of an "ikolo" can be heard up to a distance of five miles and other villages are able to pick up the message and pass it on to those dwelling in the regions beyond. An "ikolo" is in great request when a man proceeds to the highest titular degree. On completion of all the business connected with the taking of the "Ọzọ" title, the fact is communicated by beating the tom-tom. The smaller tom-toms ("ufie" or "ekwe") may be of similar pattern, or they may be wooden cylinders with skin stretched over one end, the most prized, and now rather rare, being those covered with human skin. In the old days, it was not uncommon for human victims to be flayed alive and their skins converted into drum-heads. The "ekwe" (drum) is also used as an instrument in band music.

Some of the drums are of smaller pattern. They are distinguished from the "ekwe" and are technically known as "ufie". The "ufie" is generally found in the royal palace and not in the hands of commoners. It is the king's prerogative to own and to have the sole right to use one. Its sound is somewhat different from the ordinary "ekwe" and its note is immediately recognised by the native though, maybe, the foreigner is unaware of any difference. Some of these are cylinders standing upright (nearly three feet) on legs with skin stretched over the top. Steady application is necessary in order to become a qualified performer on these. The performer must know his instrument thoroughly, and be able to gauge the differences in sound to be extracted from the whole top surface of the drum. Often two drums are used simultaneously and the hands cross and recross after the manner of a cavalry drummer. Similarly, variation of note is produced by the performer on the all-wood drums. Each square inch around the slotted opening in the cylinder has its own depth of note and these notes are further supplemented by fingering. An instance of one curious form of drumming may be mentioned. The drum was oblong in shape with a skin covering at one end. The drummer sat straddled upon the dumb end. He played his instrument with the fingers of both hands and fitted in the bass accompaniment with his right heel. He certainly extracted a full measure of music from his instru-

MUSIC

ment! Hence, although to the European tom-toms are apt to become monotonous and wearisome, yet it must be allowed that the native exponent exhibits great skill in beating his tattoo upon it. To the native, indeed, the beating of the drum is always significant; something is conveyed to his mind which is incomprehensible to the European. What we need to recognise is the very great importance of the drum in every function.

Many of the " ikolos " are of huge size, particularly those which form part of the municipal regalia, and some have romantic histories attached to them. There is one such at a town called " Umu-Nze ". In the centre of the market there is a gigantic tom-tom. The dimensions are: length of actual drum cylinder, 5 ft. 8 in., extended ornamental ends, each 2 ft. 3 in.; length over all, 10 ft. 2 in.; height, 8 ft. 5 in.; breadth (diameter) 7 ft. 10 in.

It is hewn from a single block of " ojji " wood, and shows distinct signs of age and use. Local tradition affirms that this tom-tom was the work of a man from the town of Amawbia. He had earned a great reputation as a drum-maker and his services were therefore sought by the Umu-Nze people. He was promised a handsome fee on condition that he produced a larger drum than any possessed by neighbouring towns. He undertook the task, the tom-tom duly materialised, and was an object of supreme pride to the people. Then arose a disturbing thought, " What if a rival town contracted with the maker for a yet bigger drum? " This would be disastrous; the pride of " Umu-Nze " would be brought low, their fame short-lived. The possible humiliation was altogether too great to contemplate and drastic steps had to be taken to prevent such a debacle. Hence, it came about, that the maker of the wonderful tom-tom was paid his price and allowed to depart, well satisfied with his handiwork and its reward. His satisfaction was short-lived, for he had hardly got clear of the town when he was waylaid, led back to the market-place and, then and there, sacrificed, his own blood being shed to dedicate that which his hand had produced. All town tom-toms are consecrated and, consequently, regarded as sacred things, and it was customary to sprinkle the blood of a human sacrifice upon them before they were ceremonially beaten.

The " ubọ " is an instrument which cannot be compared with any foreign one with which I am acquainted. It is composed of very thin pieces of soft wood (" okwe ") and in shape resembles an oblong box. It is from five to fifteen inches long, from four to six inches wide, and from one to two inches deep.

MUSIC

Thus far, it is similar in principle to a violin, but in lieu of strings thin strips of " offolọ " or bamboo are used. " Offolọ ", as used here, means the hard outer skin of the frond of a palm. These are lashed to the sound-box between two fixed bridges. (*Vide* p. 365.) The loose ends are cut to different lengths and separated widely enough to permit freedom in fingering. The instrument is held in both hands, with the tail-piece pointing away from the musician, and the thumbs are used for manipulating the strips of wood. The thumbs press cleanly on the strips, and are then slipped sharply backward, the result being a twanging sound, the notes varying according to the different lengths of the six or eight strips. Occasionally, loosely threaded cowrie shells are attached to the tail end of the " ubọ ", which are shaken to add an accompaniment. The music is not unpleasant, though there is little life in it, the cane strips producing dull notes. One notices young men leisurely parading the streets strumming these instruments. They are not in demand at assemblies; indeed, they could not be heard; the " ubọ " is eminently a solo instrument.

Probably the most interesting of the Ibo instruments is the " ubọ-akwala ", a primitive guitar—or is it the original of the banjo? It has a triangular-shaped body formed by sewing together three pieces of soft wood with fibre. To the underpart from four to eight pliable canes of different lengths are securely lashed, all of them extending well beyond the head of the instrument. They are then bent upwards and the strings are attached to the ends, crossed over the bridge, and tied to the tail-piece. The strings (" omi " or " akwala ") are pieces of fibre taken from the base of the palm tree, rubbed down to the required fineness. The instrument is held like the " ubọ ", though the method of playing is different, the thumbs lightly twanging the strings, the left and right working an equal number of them. It has rather a sweet sound, not unlike light staccato notes from a violin. The instrument is tuned by bending the canes and passing the strings one or more times round them until the desired pitch is secured. The musician must learn all tunes by ear, or compose his own, which he frequently does. The " ubọ-akwala " is the favourite instrument for accompanying songs and chants and is particularly favoured by strolling singers at night.

Ibo boys make music of a kind on a bow (" une "). It resembles an ordinary bow; a piece of stick bent and strung across with a thin strip of bark skinned from a green palm frond. It is usually about two feet in length. The left hand

MUSIC

holds one end, while the other is placed between the lips. With the right hand, taps are made with a short stick on the taut string, the performer at the same time working his lips after the manner of a devotee of the jew's-harp. The result is a series of dull twangy notes and that is all that can be said of it and for it.

After all, instrumental music among the Ibos, in common with all peoples, is limited to those who have special gifts. The other folk may have no such ability, or insufficient inclination to learn the art of playing. This does not mean that they are devoid of musical instinct; most have a fair stock of this and manifest it when listening by swaying the body or humming the refrain. More particularly is it in evidence when singing; indeed, the singing appeals more to the cultivated ear than the instrumental music. Some of it is characteristic of the now well-known "spirituals", though there seem to be few instances of what may legitimately be termed songs. The words are not "set" or fixed, whereas the tunes are. There is always a leader for a company of singers. He (or she) alone sings the refrain, the remainder sing the chorus only. Hence, music and poetry are linked together inasmuch as the leader has to invent his theme as the song proceeds. Some leaders are exceptionally clever, and are able to carry on for quite a long time by making use of past history, and of any unusual incidents. It may be said with truth that the Ibo soloist corresponds closely with the minstrel of mediæval Europe.[3]

The most usual form of singing is by means of couplets, that is, the leader sings his part and the others take up the chorus. There are a few four-lined songs ("abu") and for these the natural voice is used. In the majority of cases, a falsetto voice is substituted for the natural. This is rather peculiar. In the mass, it is effective and not unpleasant. The objectionable part comes when, after a bout of singing, men talk in this falsetto voice. Some men, indeed, become addicted to the habit; they converse in a highly pitched key which is distinctly irritating to the ears of a foreigner.

Except on special occasions, the choral societies sing late at night at the time when the moon is low. When the moon shines with power, dancing supersedes all other forms of entertainment. Usually, it is too dark for most of the chorus to distinguish the figure of the leader, and they can take no visible directions from him. This does not militate against a good performance, because every member of the party knows his part to the minutest detail. There is a clear volume of

MUSIC

sound, the whole company singing in perfect unison. To listen to a party of singers on a still night, as they pass along the bush paths, is a gratifying experience. The voices rise and fall as the men approach and recede. The strident, and often raucous, notes of individual singers are mellowed when they are grouped in the mass. The general effect is novel and pleasing. It should be noted that the Ibo has a more diverse scale than that of the European. He uses quarter tones in addition to the customary full and half tones.[4]

It is quite worth while for the foreigner to learn some of the native chants, at any rate to know the tunes. When labourers are tired, and work is inclined to drag, it is useful to start a refrain. This is particularly the case in certain circumstances, such, for example, as when travelling by canoe. Perhaps, the paddlers are weary after hours of pulling and are inclined to lag. One starts to hum a well-known chorus suitable for the type of work in hand. The effect is often surprising, as well as exhilarating. One of the crew picks up the time and smacks his paddle on the water in unison with the rhythm. Soon his fellows join him, and almost unconsciously the canoe is being gaily propelled on its way. For the time being, weariness is forgotten; the lilt of the song instilling fresh spirit and strength into the crew.

What is the future for Ibo music whether instrumental or vocal? It is unwise to prophesy. There seems to be little doubt but that the instruments, with the exception of some of the drums, will disappear. The chants, songs and choruses may fare better. These are days when gramophones and records are being imported in ever-increasing quantities,[5] and the modern and foreign form of concert is now coming largely into favour. With their inherent instinct for music, the young Ibo people quickly master the latest ditty. They are also adepts at making some sort of music from the instruments they are able to purchase. Many of the villages now boast a band composed of fifes, cornets and other instruments. Little, if any, attempt has been made to bring into service any of the native tunes. On the surface this seems regrettable, but it must always be remembered that many of them are associated with undesirable words and topics which render them unsuitable for church or other general public use. Many of the Ibos are gifted with musical talent and will repay instruction, as in the case of other West Africans.

In the past, it has been customary to translate English hymns into the native dialect and sing these to their associated tunes. The natives sing these lustily, but one wonders what meaning

MUSIC

they convey. All too often, the result is a massive volume of sound and that is all that can be truthfully reported. It is only to be expected that the native cannot, in the early stages of transition, sing the foreign hymns, however good the translations may be, with the same spirit of abandonment with which he sings his own chants. Moreover, the translations are often imperfect. Frequently, the words have to be modified by clipping or omission in order to fit in the right number of syllables. At the same time, it must be stated that there is a vastly increased amount of singing, and a much wider range and use of instruments than was the case in former days. The musical instinct is being developed under new conditions and, in due time, some good exponents of singing and playing will be forthcoming. It is just as well that some description of the instruments and the singing customs of the primitive Ibos should be placed on record before they are entirely overwhelmed by the inrush of new conceptions of music.

The changes are inevitable, but they produce a feeling of some regret. The old type of music is crude and noisy, but it is definitely vital and soul-stirring. It penetrates deeply, and stirs the pulses of the native in a way which no modern instrument will or can do. On occasions, it has almost a sinister power which casts a spell over an assembly which must be *felt*, since no words will adequately describe the sensations. Passions are roused, abnormal strength is instilled, men and women acting as they never would under ordinary conditions. The effect of some of these primitive forms of music on the Ibo can be compared with that of the bagpipes on the typical Scotsman and the drums on an Orangeman, but in an even more pronounced fashion. In the case of the Ibo, the result goes beyond a mere quickening of the pulses; the end is often an outburst of passionate abandonment.

NOTES TO CHAPTER XXVII

[1] The Rev. J. C. Taylor, in 1858, describing a skirmish at Onitsha says: " The spies on the tops of the trees, with their piped instruments, congratulated any man when he fired and killed another. The people of Onitsha drove away their enemies and killed four men" (cf. p. 383).—" *Niger Expedition* ", p. 334.

[2] " The Kru pilot, Glasgow, was in Captain Allen's cabin one day, answering some queries relating to the river. Suddenly he became totally abstracted and remained for awhile in an attitude of listening. On being taxed with inattention, he said: ' You no hear my son speak? ' As we had heard no voice he was asked how he knew it. He said, ' Drum speak me, tell me come up on deck.' This seemed very singular, so Captain Allen desired him to remain below and privately sent messages to the

MUSIC

performer in the boat alongside, who executed them by a variety of taps on his wooden drum; and these Glasgow interpreted in a way that left no doubt of his having understood perfectly all that the 'drum spoke'. He also said that they could communicate by this means at very great distances by the 'war-drum' which is kept in every village to give and repeat these signals."—" *Expedition to the Niger, 1841* ", Vol. II, p. 308.

[3] " There are professional singers whose position is somewhat analogous to that of minstrels several centuries ago in Europe—the monotony of the solo, which is a dramatic recitative, is broken by a somewhat regular and frequent choral response."—" *Fetish Folk of West Africa* ", p. 77.

[4] Milligan states that " the melody of African music is usually derived from tone-systems that are unlike either our major or minor scales. They have their pentatonic scale, that is, a major scale without the fourth and seventh notes, thus avoiding the use of semitones."—" *Fetish Folk of West Africa* ", pp. 79–80.

[5] Musical instruments to a value of over £12,500 were imported into Nigeria in 1934. *Vide* " *Trade Report* ", pp. 146–7.

The Ubọ, (p. 361).
Bamboo strips on wooden box, played with the thumbs.

CHAPTER XXVIII

DAY & NIGHT CLUBS

THERE ARE CERTAIN clubs which have, in some measure, elements of secret societies. At times, they were a little troublesome, though, on the whole, they did little material damage to property. They inspired fear, but as practically every man was a member, it was the women and children who suffered intimidation. There are no secret societies addicted to committing outrages after the manner of the Human Leopard Society of Sierra Leone, or the Ogboni of the Yorubas. The Ibo Societies' affinity with these was limited to the emphasis placed on secrecy; they were never guilty of the atrocities perpetrated by the Sierra Leone and Yoruba miscreants.

The secrets of the societies were rigorously guarded. In former days, a member proved guilty of exposing the practices of the society was punished drastically. The manner of "making maw" (spirit) "maw-napu-apu" = wandering spirit, was known only by initiates, and to reveal its procedure was to court a dreadful death, a stake being driven vertically through the body, a cruel form of impalement.

The Ibo believes that intercourse with the spirit world presents no great difficulty, and it is practised as a common custom, though, nowadays, it has rather degenerated into a form of play-acting. A manifestation of re-embodied spirits can take place at any time, with a more pronounced display on festal occasions. It is not connected with religious beliefs or ceremonies unless it can be said that the appearances concluding Second Burial (Maw-afia, *vide* p. 294) can be reckoned to have a religious significance. Rather, it is a return of deceased friends in the form of re-embodied spirits to their former surroundings, especially at festivals, when they are disposed to share in the celebrations.

The "making of maw", as it is termed, is entirely a man's affair; women are not allowed to participate; indeed, a woman is prohibited from seeing a "maw". Should one do so unwittingly, she will be severely chastised and, in former days, might suffer the extreme penalty.[1] As a man advances in years, he generally ceases to take an active part in the ceremonies ; he leaves the business to the younger men. A member may arrange for a display whensoever he is disposed. He can act alone with but one or two young acolytes. This, however, is not usual ; a member rarely acts alone. On occasions, groups of " maws " appear and make a gala-day of the entertainment. If it is desired that a number shall appear simultaneously this can easily be arranged. One of the young men visits the club-house and communicates his intentions to others by blowing signals on an " igwe " (p. 368). This is known as " itipu-maw " (calling out of the spirit).

In bygone days, " maw " exercised power over life and death. Even to the present day, an infringement of the laws of " maw " is punished with heavy fines. It is an institution bound up inextricably with the life of the old generation of Ibos. The idea of " maw " at Onitsha originates with the Igarra people. In the more southern parts of the country, the " maw " has not such a hold on the community.

The amount of " make-up " possessed by the club is the determining factor which governs the number of the re-embodied spirits who shall sally forth in public. The dress of one selected to impersonate a spirit is so fitted that no particle of the human skin is visible to the spectator. Some fit the body similarly to tights, while others have kilts, and legs and arms only are closely cased. The pants are of cloth grimed with dirt ; occasionally, they are stained with dyes. Again, other costumes are of a stockinet material highly adorned with rings and patches in bright colours, red being the most prominent. The cloth encasing the hands and feet generally overlaps and the loose (empty) ends flap about like elongated socks and mittens. The " maw " is able to discern his way by means of two slits in the cloth which serve as peepholes. A similar small slit admits a small quantity of air for breathing purposes. Some " maws " wear voluminous skirts of " ufelle " (" agwo "), the midribs of " ngwo " palm leaves, from twelve to fifteen inches in length. They are called " egwugwu ", a term which suggests fear. Other " maws ", e.g. the " ejelle-egwu ", have their heads and shoulders enveloped in mantles of " ufelle ". The most common, perhaps, are the " maws " who impersonate deceased virgins (" agbo-maw "). The men attire themselves in a tightly fitting multi-coloured dress, with appropriate trimmings, (!) in order to impersonate girls at the time they are passing through the " nkpu " ceremonies preparatory to marriage. Why there is this tendency to represent young women, with no corresponding impersonation of young men, is not explained; it probably arises from the prominence attached to the female sex in animistic thought.

Sometimes, the face covering is joined to the dress, as a part of the whole, but more often a mask is used. It is usually made of a soft wood, and is always carved in one piece from a solid block. (*Vide* p. 323.) Most are clumsy affairs, made to slip over the head. A few are face masks only; others have faces attached to crown pieces. Those which caricature wild beasts are very heavy, and the same is also true of many of the "agbọ-maw" masks. Masks of this type are a burden to bear; they are dead weights borne by the top of the head. The "agbọ-maw" masks generally have regular features with a curious resemblance to Egyptian carvings and drawings. These have always *white* faces, the idea being to emphasise the resurrection principle. (*Vide* p. 138.) The masks which typify wild beasts are grotesque, inventions of vivid imagination. The impersonators who use these must, of necessity, be strong, otherwise they could not endure the weight on the head and, at the same time, be half-suffocated. Instead of being "spirit" they are extra solid figures!

In order to make the apparition appear the more inhuman, an "igwe" is inserted in the mouth wherewith to disguise the natural voice. Instead of plain speaking, squeaky words issue forth. Only with difficulty can the words be distinguished. The "igwe" is a small section of reed, with a spider's web fixed in the tube by means of raw rubber juice. This instrument is never used for any purpose other than for "making maw". The nearest impression of the sound produced is that made from speaking through a comb encased in tissue-paper.

When the impersonators have donned their grotesque costumes, they, in company with their lay assistants, issue from the club-house. There are usually more assistants than there are "maws", though not always so. They have no distinguishing dress. Their business is to attend to the "maws" and to clear a path before them. This they do by arming themselves with switches and laying about them vigorously, whether there is anything to strike or not. If they do happen to hit a person, they do not stop to look round to observe the effect. As a matter of fact, they do not strike many people, because, at the first sight or sound of an approaching "maw", the women and children rush into hiding. It is discreet to leave men unscathed as they are familiar with the business and might retaliate on an over-zealous lay assistant. The "maw" himself may rush hither and thither as impulse moves him; the assistants career about practically the whole time the "maw" is on

AGBQ-MAW.

RE-EMBODIED SPIRITS. MALE IMPERSONATIONS REPRESENTING GIRLS PASSING THROUGH "NKPU," WITH AN ATTENDANT. (PAGES 223-367.)

DAY & NIGHT CLUBS

parade. They assert their authority by the use of their switches; the " maw " relies on his power to inspire awe and fear. Between them, they make the weaker folk suffer if so be they lay hands on them.

The " maw " has little respect for persons or property. He considers himself at liberty to enter any compound or hut. His visit is not altogether welcomed, for he is apt to be truculent and will not depart until he has been mollified with gifts. An occasional visit would not matter much, but, in the dry season, when there is much free time, the visits of " maws " are too frequent and too often are of the character of an inquisition.

In past days, a " maw " generally kept in the background whenever a European was in the neighbourhood, possibly because of fear of exposure. If a meeting could not be avoided, he seemed to think that a European ought to react similarly to the women-folk, for there is no doubt that many " maws " thought that, in some mysterious manner, they were privileged beings owing to their alleged associations with the underworld. Endowed with the sanctity of " spirit " and, in virtue thereof, inviolate, they claimed the rights of " onye-nwe-obodo " = " lord or master of the country ".[2] In the old days they were cheeky and, at times, little short of insolent. Perhaps, they might retort that we did not play the game; our unmoved attitude was contrary to the rules!

The original unadulterated custom has wellnigh vanished from the countryside. In most parts, it has become little more than a holiday pastime and the serious side has no longer a part in it. Even the attitude towards women and children has changed. Nowadays, they mingle freely and openly among the spectators at a " maw " display. The inherent sense of fear, however, dissipates slowly. The belief that these apparitions were really visitors from the unseen world is so tenacious and so deeply ingrained, that it will be some time before all fear will be lost. This is not surprising in a country steeped in animistic belief, for some of the " maws " are such fearsome-looking objects that anyone might be momentarily disturbed.

So far this chapter has been concerned with " maws " that operate by day. Those known as " night-maws " are in another category; they differ considerably from the " day-maws ". They are regarded with greater seriousness, and the regulations are much more rigorously enforced. One of the most prominent of the night societies is that known as the " Ayakka ". The activities of this society are carried through on the darkest nights in contrast to those which meet only when the moon is bright. Moreover, the " Ayakka " operates during a part of the year only, namely, from early January till the end of March. These are the dry-season months when bush fires burn furiously. The idea seems to hold that the fires are responsible for quickening the ancestral spirits ; their rest is disturbed. The " Ayakka " are alleged to be these resurrected and wandering spirits.

The spirits (" Ayakka ") start their activities about midnight. Suddenly, a peculiar cry pierces the air—a stranger might be deceived into thinking that it was the cry of a night bird. That impression would be quickly dispelled, because the note is repeated at short intervals, but, more especially, from the fact that answering cries respond from all the surrounding neighbourhood. Creeping stealthily through the bush, the members scatter themselves over a wide circle about the village. When the leader is ready, he sounds the signal on the " odegilligilli ". The unearthly sounds, rising and falling in the stillness of the night, strike terror into the hearts of the uninitiated. When properly handled, the " odegilligilli " produces an uncanny moaning effect. This curious implement (or instrument) is a thin slat of wood, about twelve inches long by from two to three inches in width : the edges of the slat are notched. A cord is attached to one end. Allowing it to swing loosely at the end of a yard of cord, the operator whirls the slat around his head. The serrated wood cleaving the air produces the sound ; it is like a miniature aeroplane propeller. The volume of noise is modulated by the speed and force with which the " odegilligilli " is swung.[3]

The sounding of the " odegilligilli " is the signal for the scattered members to work their way towards the rallying centre. The sounds being repeated at intervals, together with the " cooees " of the leader, serve as direction indicators, and gradually the men converge and gather round him. When all is ready, the company moves off towards the village Stragglers are picked up along the way until, eventually, the procession may constitute a large body of men. As they march, they chant in the peculiar falsetto voice previously noticed (p. 362), the soloist singing the refrain and the whole company responding in chorus.

If, by any chance, the crowd stumbles upon a man who is not an initiated member of the Society, he will be maltreated and made to suffer for his foolish indiscretion. He should secrete himself, for he could not fail to know that the " Ayakka " were approaching. A man so caught is soundly beaten and thrown into the bush. This is the procedure according to the

Society's regulations, but it is the law rather than the practice ; it is not likely that an uninitiated person would be abroad when the " Ayakka " is on the march.

Another rule stipulates that no fire, or other form of light, may be visible in a house or compound. Failure to comply with this regulation was followed with severe penalties, including the destruction of the house.

Members are warned to refrain from making any sound likely to betray the human element. They must not laugh audibly : even to cough is an offence. Mystery must be maintained throughout the ceremonies, and nothing must be allowed to jeopardise that prime factor. A laugh, a cough, or other normal sound might endanger the secrets of the Society and destroy the belief that the visitors were from the nether world.

The first part of the " Ayakka " season is devoted to the observance of the ceremonies of the individual wards or villages of the town. This occasionally leads to friction for, if two companies should select the same night to parade, and happen to meet, fierce fighting ensues, neither party being prepared to give right of way to the other. When all the villages have completed their individual celebrations, they combine together for the winding up of the season's activities.

Some mention should be made of the operations of the " Ayakka " after the entry of the procession into a village. The first incident is to visit the house of one of the brethren (" umunna "), or that of one whose mother hails from the brethren's quarter, or to the house of a daughter of the " Ayakka's umunna ". This is important to note as it indicates that the members cannot make demands for gifts from unrelated folk. From their own kith and kin they expect offerings. These must be handed over by the head of the house in person ; they cannot be presented by the agency of a third party. The " Ayakka " spokesman relates a story to the effect that he and his followers are visitors from a far-distant country. The fact that they have found their way during the dark hours is explained by stating that darkness is no bar to spirits. The master of the house is fully alive to the situation and loses no time in bringing gifts wherewith to propitiate his strange and probably unwelcome visitors. It would be extremely imprudent to cross the " Ayakka ". To do so would bring retribution upon himself and his household. Hence, as a premium to secure the safety of his property, his person and his family, he hastens to satisfy the demands imposed upon him. The " Ayakka " representative is not identified, he and his fellows keep well concealed. Only a hand is felt; it is thrust from the darkness and snatches the gift. Meanwhile, the head of the house prays that his offering may prove acceptable and that the " spirits " may leave him in peace and return to their own habitation.[4]

The programme is repeated throughout the time the " Ayakka " are parading the village. Then, the night being well advanced, the signal is given for withdrawal. The procession wends its way back to the spot where they originally assembled. On arrival there, they scatter once more and, one by one, the men steal away to their homes. It is incumbent that each should be within doors by the first streak of dawn. There is little reluctance in complying with this rule, since the majority of the members are fatigued with the exertions of the night. There has been much walking and running under difficult conditions; also great strain on vocal chords, to say nothing of nervous tension. Hence, the prospect of rest and sleep is welcomed.

The mention of the word " initiation " indicates that there are certain rites and ceremonies to be fulfilled before a youth is admitted to the ranks of the " Ayakka " Society. The age of discretion is rather early among the Ibos and a boy becomes eligible for initiation round about his tenth year. The rite is referred to as " iba-na-maw ", that is " the entering into spirit ". Arrangements for the rite are managed by the older men of the family: they inform the lad that it is time for him to gain experience, and to assume the privileges that are attached to membership of the " Ayakka ". The lad's father opens negotiations by offerings of palm wine to the " umunna ", (male relatives); they being members of the Society. On the night chosen for his son to enter into " maw ", he brings gifts of soup (relish) and yams.

The common practice is for several youths to be initiated at the same time. This mutual arrangement saves trouble and expense. The candidates are ordered to retire into a room and wait there until everything is in order for the ceremony. In due time, they are conducted outside where, they are told, the " maw " will come to test them. They are bidden to lie flat and, at all costs, keep their faces to the ground; on no account must they look about them. While so lying, the " maw " steps over each of them. Next, they are ordered to roll themselves over and over back to the room—(instead of rising to their feet and walking). When once more settled in the chamber, a piece of bone, preferably the tooth of a goat, is handed to each lad with instructions to bite it. They are informed that these bones are the teeth of the " maw ". This part of the proceedings is known as " ọlukpulu-maw ", lit. " eating dirt off the teeth of the spirit ".

The element of mystery deepens, and the lads are rather frightened, and huddle together in a corner for mutual comfort. A little time elapses, and then the " maw " enters the room and goes through a mock performance of excising certain organs from the body of each. These are his special appurtenances wherewith to provide his evening meal. As the " maw " completes this symbolical operation, the members of the Society urge the candidates to offer them gifts, promising that, if they do so, they will intercede on their behalf. They are assured that it is the only way whereby merciful treatment can be secured. If there be any symptom of reluctance in producing gifts, the lads are told that their friends will refrain from using their influence with the " maw ", and they will be obliged to fend for themselves. They are made to understand that, having been borne down into the underworld, they will be forced to remain there. Also, that in order to reach the house of the spirits, they must pass *via* the hole of an " agbisi " (a tiny insect) and, after that, they will be required to cross a very wide river with no more than a thread to serve as a bridge. To negotiate this dangerous crossing safely, the help of friends is necessary, and this help can be given only on condition that worthy payments are forthcoming. Unless the members are satisfied, the candidates must make the venture by virtue of their own personal efforts.

The gifts are distributed between the officiating members. They, being satisfied, prepare to serve supper, and the boys are invited to share the meal. The invitation is little more than an act of courtesy, for the boys are too agitated to settle down to enjoy the food. They are not, by any means, in a festive mood, whereas their mentors are thoroughly enjoying themselves and quickly consume the provisions. After supper, there is a respite. Strict silence is enjoined. The apartment is dark, most are tired, the members are replete with food, hence, the whole party is soon soundly asleep. When the novices are wakened, they receive profuse congratulations. They are informed that their gifts proved satisfactory, and that their friends had fulfilled their promises. They had been so successful in their intercessions, that the " maw " had acquiesced to their pleadings. He had escorted them to and from the underworld while they were asleep. They had passed through the many unknown perils of the journey without being aware of the hazards. They had come through the adventure unscathed and so had every reason to be thankful on their own account, and grateful to their intercessors.

The awakening takes place as day begins to dawn. The fathers and other old men, bearing certain leaves in their hands, come to ask for the release of the newly initiated members. The leaves serve as sponges wherewith to remove the earth-stains contracted during the journey to and from the nether regions. These stains are symbolically washed away. The cleansing concludes the actual rites. The boys are now ready to return to their homes to which the " maw " himself conducts each lad separately. It is not entirely an act of grace ; the " maw " has an ulterior motive. This ostensibly generous act is undertaken in order that he may collect a gift from the anxious mother who gladly offers a contribution as a token of thanksgiving for the safe return of her son. He has been called upon to pass through dangers the nature of which she can only imagine, as women have no knowledge of the secrets of the Society.

On emerging from the night's ordeal, the youth is, forthwith an accredited member of the " Maw Society ". He is, however, but a novice, and knows nothing of its secrets or of its procedure. There is a further ceremony to be observed known as " ikpu ani " (lit. to dive underground, the word used in initiating the candidate into the secrets and mysteries of the Maw). The novice himself must make the arrangements for this. He visits each member of the " umunna " and hands to him a present. When all the " umunna " have been thus favoured, they consent and arrange for the ceremony to be performed. All being in order, the novice is invited to enter the " okwule ", a dark inner room which serves as the club's storehouse. In this secret room are stored the " awo̱lo̱ ", that is, the " make-up " materials used in " making-maw ". This word " awo̱lo̱ " technically applies to the dress and mask used when a man is impersonating a spirit ; its underlying idea is that of naturally putting on or off as, for example, a snake casting its skin.

The lad is bidden to lie down face downwards and wait. After a short interval, the " maw " arrives. His first act is to administer a few lively strokes with a stick on the back of the stranger. Having relieved his feelings of anger caused by this intrusion, and also given the boy a salutary taste of his power, one of two things follows : The " maw " may straightway throw off his dress and thus reveal his human form, or one of the members openly inserts an " igwe " into his mouth, and illustrates the way the peculiar sounds are produced by the

" maw " when he is abroad. Either one or both these things may be done. Whichever is adopted, there is no further mystery attached to the business. What had, hitherto, been accepted in all faith to be a re-embodied spirit proves to be no more than a man, probably a kinsman, masquerading as such.

Then follows the administration of the oaths whereby the novice is sworn to maintain absolute silence in respect of all he sees and hears and learns of the activities of the " maw ". With impressive words, he is warned that the penalty awaiting him, should he reveal the secrets of the Society, is torture and death. While this is the rule, there appears to be no record of the penalty having ever been exacted. There was probably never any reason or need to apply the rule. Apart from the threat of retribution, there was the fact that the youth, having experienced the chagrin of being duped himself, he, in his turn, would find great entertainment in sharing in the fun of gulling the non-initiated folk of the village.

If, on some pretext, or by accident, a man who is not a member of the " Ayakka " gains admittance to the club-house wherein the " awolo " is stored, and he be discovered in the act, he is liable to severe penalties. Unless he can pay substantial bribes as compensation, he will receive drastic treatment, possibly forfeit his life and property. Similar punishment is inflicted on a non-member who presumes to place an " igwe " in his mouth. As previously noted (p. 368), this item of the " awolo " is jealously restricted to the sole use of the " maw " ; it is forbidden to use it on any occasion except when the " maw " is making a public appearance. For an outsider to violate this rule is a flagrant offence.

Should a woman by chance happen to trespass in this way, that is, to catch sight of an " igwe " or the " awolo ", she is condemned to pay a heavy fine and is, forthwith, initiated as a member. This seems contrary to the regulations as they concern women ; apparently it is a case where necessity compels.

No one may molest or fight with a " maw ". In former days, the penalty of such an insult was death, not only for himself, but for all his relatives also. At the present day, it is not uncommon for " maws " to prosecute an offender in a Native Court and claim compensation for an infringement of his privileges while masquerading in public.

NOTES TO CHAPTER XXVIII

[1] This corresponds to the " egungun " of the Yorubas who follow almost identical methods. Johnson states that " the mysteries connected with it are held sacred and inviolable and, although little boys of five or six years are often initiated, yet no woman may know these mysteries on pain of death. The women believe (or rather feign to believe) that the Egunguns come from the spirit world. An Egungun is the executor of women accused of witchcraft and of those proved guilty of such crimes as murder, incendiarism, &c."—" *History of the Yorubas* ", p. 29.

" It also corresponds to the ' Dodos ' of Northern Nigeria."—" *Northern Tribes of Nigeria* ", Vol. II, p. 19.

[2] " It is considered a crime to touch an Egungun in public, and disrespectful to pass him by with the head uncovered. Even a boy Egungun is considered worthy of being honoured by his (supposed) surviving parents."—" *History of the Yorubas* ", p. 30.

[3] The " Bull-Roarer " of the Kafirs. The " Oro " of the Yorubas.

[4] " These (Egungun) festivals are lucky times for the men for, on these occasions, the women are made to spend largely to feast ' deceased relatives ', while the food is consumed by the men. The number of fowls and goats killed at such times is simply prodigious."—" *History of the Yorubas* ", p. 30.

CHAPTER XXIX

DISTURBERS OF THE PEACE

PRIOR TO THE pacification of the country under British Administration, there were constant outbreaks of fighting between the different villages. This has sometimes been referred to as " Intertribal Warfare ", but that term is hardly the correct one, nor is it justifiable ; it exaggerates the petty fighting that used to take place in the Ibo country. It never amounted to one tribe warring against another in order to vanquish and virtually destroy it. I have found no evidence of campaigns such as those which were undertaken in the neighbouring Yoruba country. There were skirmishes ; they were almost a pastime ! Not much blood was shed at most of them. Only when mercenaries were employed was any serious havoc wrought. There seems to have been little confederation, by the aid of which tribe engaged in war with tribe, unless we reckon that of the Esa people dwelling in the district north of Abakaliki. These people were beginning to combine for aggressive purposes when a check was put upon their activities by the advent of the Government.

Other than this budding confederation, there was practically no cohesion among the people. Though of the same stock, speaking the same language, and with similar customs and practices, the villages remained separate from one another. They not only kept themselves more or less isolated ; there was always a varying amount of rivalry and jealousy between them. These evils prevailed to such an extent that it was never safe to wander far afield ; to do so was almost certain to lead to disaster. The friction frequently led to desultory fighting, especially in the dry season. Peace was constantly being broken and often but a very slight pretext was sufficient to start a minor conflict between rival villages. The baleful effect of these skirmishes was not so much the physical suffering inflicted ; more serious was the dislocation of trade. All communications were suspended during the time operations were in progress, except that the " adas " (daughters) of a village were usually allowed to pass unmolested if they wished to visit their homefolk. The disruption of trade did not really amount to much in the old days and was scarcely worth consideration. Under the new conditions, such interruptions would be an intolerable nuisance. Happily they have ceased to exist, and intercourse between the villages to-day is unfettered and free from risk of attack.

When battles took place between neighbouring towns, the rule was to decapitate all captives and display their heads as trophies. It is alleged that, in former days, when the Onitshas went forth to battle, the women followed the men in order to bring in the dead and wounded and thus prevent them being taken by the enemy and, at the same time, leaving the soldiers free from any anxiety on this account.[1]

These petty fights were not confined to affrays between one town and another. Quarrels often arose between quarters of the same town and, instead of attempting to settle the trouble by arbitration, the people fought. This, of course, is only what other folk do, even civilised nations. Civil war stood, however, on a higher level than that conducted against a strange enemy. It was governed by certain regulations, one of which was that firearms were barred. There was no restriction against manual weapons, including cutlasses, but there was no shooting; the fighting was man to man. It was open to the warriors to protect themselves and many did so by wearing helmets, breast and back coverings; also they carried shields. The helmets were composed of large dried koko-yam leaves (" akasi-oyibo "), or the bark of " achi " wood. They completely covered the head, but afforded no protection for the face. The breast and back coverings were either a primitive sort of doublet, or flat pieces of woven koko-yam leaves suspended back and front by means of shoulder-straps. The shields were, for the most part, plaited palm leaves (*igu*); occasionally one was of dried rawhide. The cutlass (matchet) in common use for farming and domestic purposes served as a sword. The quality of the metal is not of a high standard, nevertheless, when well honed on a stone, it is a formidable weapon. A well-worn cutlass may have a fairly sharp point and be effective in thrusting; new ones have a blunt curved end. Finesse was not a strong feature; a lusty straightforward blow answered the purpose of these fighters.

There was never as much havoc wrought as the noise and turmoil on a day of battle seemed to warrant. There was more shouting and gesticulating than actual fighting. As the contest advanced, a number would receive cuts and bruises, some of them nasty gashes. It was quite likely that one or two would be fatally wounded. In such case, the party which had

DISTURBERS OF THE PEACE

lost a comrade generally retired to mourn their loss. The other party, meeting with no further resistance, continued to hurl threats and jeers for a time and then returned home to exult over their victory.

Whenever quarrels broke out between towns, or sections of a town, no action was begun without preliminary swearing of oaths. They were ultimately settled by the same procedure, the oaths, as a rule, being as binding as the oaths of enmity.

Another rule was that women and children must not be killed in war; they might be taken as captives, but not wantonly slaughtered.

This was the ordinary practice in civil conflict. Occasionally, events followed a different course, the outcome of stronger animosity or bitter jealousy. In such circumstances, the regulation in respect of the use of firearms was sometimes disregarded. An instance of this may be quoted. In 1903, serious differences arose between several quarters of the town of Awka and a single quarter owing to its alleged infringements and appropriation of proprietary blacksmiths' rights. The dispute developed into warfare and the larger body surrounded and laid siege to the offending quarter. There were frequent attacks, but the assailants never succeeded in penetrating the lines of the besieged. The latter made uncommonly good use of the cover afforded by the dense bush around the village, and sniped a number of the attackers from platforms fixed high up in the big trees. During this campaign there was no restraint from using guns, and several men were killed outright or died from wounds. The struggle went on for many months, the besieged holding their own against all attacks. The end was eventually brought about by Government mediation.

Another reason for referring to this episode is to note the way in which preparations were made for an attack in force. When this had been planned a noted " dibia " (priest) was sought from another town and engaged to assist the attacking party. He undertook to provide charms and medicines whereby he affirmed that success would certainly attend their efforts. Three days were occupied in offering sacrifices and in dispensing and applying medicine. This had to be smeared on the bodies of the warriors. What the ingredients were I am unable to state other than that chalk formed a very appreciable part. As the concoction dried, the men were whitened from head to feet. The men believed implicitly in its efficacy and seemed to forget the fact that the chalk made them much more conspicuous as targets for the enemy's bullets. More probably they ignored this fact, because they were encouraged to believe that the application of the medicine would cause the slugs fired at them to miss their mark or, should they strike, they would fall harmlessly to the ground. Needless to say, their faith was not rewarded ; the medicine utterly failed to respond to its reputation. More were shot, and more died, as a result of that particular engagement, than on any other occasion. Even so, the men were not convinced of its uselessness ; they were only disappointed. It was obvious to them that they had been outdone by the enemy, magically as well as materially. Their medicine was more powerful !

The fragments of broken iron and brass used as slugs were responsible for terrible wounds, particularly those which entered the body. They were rough-edged and difficult to extract ; also no qualified aid was available. The surgical knowledge of the natives was practically nil : they could render but little help, and the men wounded in the chest and abdomen either bled to death or died from exhaustion. In one case the slug had penetrated into the chest. The native surgeon decided that the logical way to extract it was to open a hole in the man's back in order to allow it to complete its journey through the body. The hole was made, but the man died before the slug was induced to move !

Out of evil sometimes good may come. Up to the time of this civil war foreigners were not welcomed in that district. Our presence was resented. To a certain extent this was plainly obvious, though the opposition did not assume an aggressive form. At a later date, we discovered that our tenure had been much more precarious than we had realised. This war made a great difference. Resentment changed to appreciation, the result of efforts made on behalf of the wounded. Our knowledge and equipment were very limited, nevertheless the rendering of " First Aid " treatment brought relief and healing to a number of disabled men. In order to treat them we were called to the compounds. Suspicion and prejudice gradually gave place to a better spirit and acquaintances were made which ripened into friendship. This increased with the passing years and remains unbroken till the present day, after more than thirty years.

Organisation, as the word is commonly understood, has no place in Ibo warfare. There was generally a director (" odogu ") of operations whose position was acknowledged, but whose orders were mostly wasted on the men. They followed their own inclinations, each man acting individually. There was no attempt to follow a prescribed order. Men ran hither and thither, fired their guns indiscriminately, or ran away according to circumstances. They degenerated into an excited mob of separate units without cohesion or control; a rabble rather than an army.

Chiefs seldom shared in the fighting; they went into retreat in a secluded spot to discuss the situation and to offer sacrifices to woo success. In a safe place, they waited for reports from the battle-front. When the fight was over, they returned to their people. If their forces had met with defeat, they were forlorn and depressed. If victory had been vouchsafed, they shared in the rejoicing, and claimed that the good fortune was a sure proof that their intercessions with the gods had met with approval.

Apart from the commander, there was one man who acted as leader, somewhat equivalent to a standard-bearer. He was recognised by his carrying a small sheaf of young palm leaves (" omu ") in his mouth. (*Vide* p. 409.) The leaves signified that he was " holy ". So long as he had association with war " medicine ", it was incumbent upon him to abstain from sexual intercourse. Should he offend in this respect, the " medicine " would be " spoiled " and he, himself, would be slain. And not only he, but *all* the men taking part must refrain from sexual relationships; such an act at such a time was abomination, utterly unholy. War is not pleasure, and to mix with women is foolish and will be tempting fate. Should a man be so indiscreet and offend by committing the act, he had to seek the " Eze-aja-ana " (the king (priest)) who sacrifices to the land to remove the pollution. A sheep, alive or dead, had to be offered to expiate his sin. Until that was done, he was forbidden to take any further share in the war; nor, until he was cleansed, could he climb a palm tree to collect wine.

Men who performed heroic deeds, or became famed for their prowess in battle, were accorded great honour. To such was granted the right to wear the wing feathers of an eagle.[2] The plumes corresponded to the medals and decorations of modern days, only that it was one feather for each man killed, only the D.S.O.'s received a plume! They were displayed on all possible occasions and they entitled the owner to special privileges, including a title when being saluted. At his death, he was honoured with a funeral befitting a brave old soldier. He had won renown in battle and his fame should herald his entry into the realm of the spirit world.

So far the fighting described has been connected with the comparatively small affrays between village and village. There were occasions when it was a really serious affair. This

DISTURBERS OF THE PEACE

occurred when a town sought the assistance of mercenaries to aid them in their campaign against another town. These professional soldiers were always ready to raid whenever opportunity presented itself. They never declined an invitation to render service when called upon. In the more southerly districts on the eastern side of the Niger, the most famous were the Abams, Adas and the Abikiris. These were fearless fighters; the very mention of their names was sufficient to inspire fear. They inflicted great damage to life and property wherever they went.

On the western side, the Ekumeku was the most formidable confederation in the country lying between Asaba and Benin. Some account of the society may be given here, inasmuch as war was one of its principal functions, otherwise it would be more accurately described as a secret society. It is rather difficult to state what is the precise meaning of the word " Ekumeku ". During the 1904 rising, the members of the confederacy were named the " Silent Ones ". That rendering assumed that the word was a corruption of Ekwumekwu, " Don't speak." It has also been interpreted as meaning " a breathing " or " blowing ". Probably the idea is similar to that of the wind which " bloweth where it listeth ; thou canst not tell whence it cometh, nor whither it goeth ". So it was with the Ekumeku ; they went here, there and everywhere, swiftly and silently. Their gatherings and exploits were always carried out on dark nights. No country could be better adapted for their operations than the forest districts of the Asaba hinterland.

The King of Iselle-Ukwu was the accredited head of the whole society, but members could, and did, act independently of him. A description of him by an actual member of the Ekumeku reads quaintly. It clearly illustrates the awe with which he was held by the rank and file. " He is the greatest man ever seen in the world and second only to the King of Benin. And his wives will be more than fifty." When I called upon him in 1900, it was maintained that his harem contained some two hundred wives ; it required a good-sized village to house them and their children. A report was circulated later to the effect that, having wearied of some of them, and become impatient owing to their constant quarrels, he had divorced over fifty of them (cf. p. 237). " And he died in his bed ", a natural death which, apparently, was quite contrary to expectation.

For a period, the society was wont to remain quiescent ; its members disbanded and pursued the ordinary avocations

DISTURBERS OF THE PEACE

of normal citizens. The oath of allegiance was not lifelong; it was repeated with every revival of activity. These outbreaks were not governed by any fixed rule; they were quite sporadic. When the spirit moved a member, in any district, he would communicate with eight or ten others and they met together and conferred in a secluded spot in the forest. They laid their guns cross-wise in a pile on the ground and, over these, clasped hands and took a solemn oath of loyalty and secrecy. The oath stipulated that a member revealing the watchwords or plans of the society should be shot, the executioner to be chosen by the leader of the band of which the traitor was a member. After the preliminary meeting, the members forthwith took steps to augment their forces. They knew, of course, all their old comrades and every likely freshman and, gradually, the band increased in numbers until they were sufficiently numerous to begin operations. The whole of these proceedings were carried through with the utmost secrecy under cover of darkness; nothing whatever could be done by daylight. The requisite number having been recruited, they proceeded to waylay travellers and market women and entered upon a course of systematic pillage, inspiring such fear that none dared report his losses openly.

It was a safe and quick method of acquiring property, hence, within three months of the original gathering, practically every able-bodied man in the locality was an active member of the society. Their activities were still carried out during the hours of darkness, wild, wet, and dark nights being particularly favoured for their nefarious purposes. Should the men of any town refuse to join in the movement, the Ekumeku made it its particular business to persecute its inhabitants.

Before any really serious expedition was undertaken, the raiders had recourse to the inevitable " medicine ". They whitened themselves with chalk and, by this means, were able to recognise fellow-members in the darkness and avoid fighting with them. When on the war-path, the company marched in procession, the leader bearing the calabash containing the " medicine " which was to protect the party from the guns of the enemy. In the centre were the buglers, those who sounded the call on the " akpele ". This is a long cucumber-shaped calabash with both ends cut off and a blow-hole provided in the middle. With it a series of notes and calls were blown; it served as a bugle. (*Vide* p. 358.)

The force worked its way towards the town selected for attack and fell upon it suddenly, drove out the inhabitants and took possession. The invaders quickly made their position secure and laid hands on all the foodstuffs they could discover, cows, goats, yams and other commodities; following this up by a systematic looting of the town at their leisure. They manifested no inclination to depart until supplies showed signs of exhaustion; sometimes they settled down and their occupation extended over a month.

The wives of the members of the Ekumeku society enjoyed certain privileges; they came under the protection of the society and were free from molestation when passing to and from market.

When the time was considered opportune, the "Ndi-Ekumeku" abandoned all pretence of secrecy and proceeded to rob and plunder in open daylight. Each member provided his own equipment which consisted of two bottles (calabashes) of powder, his gun and cutlass, and they forgathered at the appointed rendezvous. The king of the town selected for the gathering sat in the place of honour, supported on each side by the chiefs from all the towns represented sitting on their royal stools. Together, they acted as a council of war and drew up the programme for future operations. At the close of the deliberations, the young braves ("ikolobia") had their turn and rushed about, firing guns, whilst the buglers surpassed themselves; in fact, the whole assembly resolved itself into a chaotic military parade before the natives of the town. The men yelled out challenges and, by gesture, demonstrated the kind of treatment that awaited any who should dare to defy them. After these manœuvres, the king presented two slaves, one of each sex, to those who had condescended to honour his town with their company. The rendezvous was regularly changed; the general programme was followed with but little variation.

The Abams, Adas and Abikiris followed quite different methods. They did not act spontaneously as did the "Ndi-Ekumeku". They were more or less organised and always prepared for active service, whenever it was made worth their while. They were a source of terror to the countryside, for it was not known when an attack might be suddenly launched on a village. They were feared by old and young alike, the old, because they knew what to expect from these raiders; to the young it was mental fear. The elders took advantage and frightened the children with the threat that the Abams would "come and eat them". When other methods failed this threat succeeded in restraining the boisterous spirits of the little ones.

These mercenary bands were under the control of the Aros,

DISTURBERS OF THE PEACE

and all arrangements had to be negotiated through them. A town desirous of receiving assistance in a campaign applied to the Aro agents for a band of these professional fighting men. For their services a price had to be paid prior to operations being undertaken. Besides this money payment in advance, the condition was laid down that the heads of all the slain should be reckoned as their special perquisites. These Abams did not use firearms, they relied solely on their cutlasses, their reputation and their sudden onslaughts. By the use of these bands, the Aros gained complete control of the country. Companies of Aros emigrated from their home at Aro-Chuku and formed settlements in different parts of the Ibo country. These ousted the Ibo landlords and assumed ownership of large tracts of land. It was a prosperous enterprise. Moreover, they increased their wealth by slave dealing. As long as they were able to maintain control over these marauding bands, the Aros were the dominating power in the country lying between Awka in the north and Aro-Chuku in the south. Their agents visited Calabar, Bonny and other ports, in order to purchase guns and ammunition. These were for their own use, not for the Abams and Adas. By means of their own superior equipment, the Aros were able to keep in subjection the companies of raiders and the Ibos whom they conquered.

Early in the present century, the Aros were themselves brought into subjection. They were deprived of their powers and there appears to be no prospect of their regaining them. It meant a great loss of prestige and also of property. Their incomes, blocked at the source, dwindled, and they became poor instead of being rich. They have had to turn to other methods of a more legitimate character in order to earn their livelihood. They will never again dominate the southern Ibo country as they did prior to British control.

Apart from the fighting hitherto described, petty wars were undertaken for the sake of prospective booty. On the western side, all movable property was appropriated by the raiders. All adults and children seized were doomed to slavery which meant that, either they would become slaves in the ordinary sense of that word, or they would augment the supply of victims for human sacrifices. There is no evidence, as far as I am aware, that cannibalism was ever practised in this part of the Ibo country. With danger of sudden onslaughts always hovering over their heads, the people were accustomed to storing their yams in secluded places in the forest in the hope that they might escape the notice of the marauders. The objective of the Abams and their confederates, the Adas and

Abikiris, was to secure as many human heads as possible, these being the trophies most coveted. Victims taken alive were destined to become slaves. They might, as a result, be retained for work, or be bought for sacrificial purposes or, again, they might provide the means of a feast, the people in the eastern districts being addicted to the practice of eating human flesh.[3]

Living, as they did, with the menace of attack constantly in their minds, it was natural that the men of the village should take precautions to make their homes as secure as circumstances permitted. Hence, there were outer defences. Deep trenches were dug around some towns. In the wet season, these became moats, but, for most of the year, they were devoid of water. During the intervals of peace, bridges spanned the trenches. These were light and somewhat precarious, being no more than split sections of palm trees. These possessed the advantage of being quickly removed at the first sign of an advancing foe. A body of stout-hearted defenders made the crossing of a trench a stern and grim business. It was not difficult, perhaps, to get into them; it was a very different thing to climb the opposite steep bank while the defenders sturdily thrust at the attackers from above. There was nothing, however, approaching the mighty wall that encompasses Benin with its great depth and width, an almost impregnable defence against old-fashioned weapons.

These flimsy bridges were not free from mishap in times of peace. Some were so slender that they were scarcely equal to supporting the weight of a man. On one occasion, a man appeared at my quarters in a fainting condition. He was crossing a light gangway and, in the act, it snapped in sunder beneath him. One end was wrenched from the bank, the other remained firmly embedded. As the unfortunate man fell, his arm caught on the jagged end of the fixed piece of timber. The flesh was pierced to the bone and turned back to the top of his shoulder. Happily, we were able to dress the lacerated flesh and the wound healed with no more inconvenience than a long horse-shoe-shaped scar.

Another method of defence was provided by the construction of earthworks ("ekpe"). This name is derived from the manner in which the walls were built. (*Vide* p. 313.)[4] These "ekpe" were raised a short distance beyond the village boundaries. The undergrowth was cleared for the purpose, thus giving an open view of an invading force. They consisted of embankments some forty to fifty yards in length. The trench made by scooping out the earth, of which the "ekpe" were built, provided additional shelter for the defenders. The lower part of the wall was from four to six feet thick. It was tapered from the bottom to the top which attained to a height of between four and five feet. No bullet from a flint-lock gun could pierce the thickness of earth, hence the bodies of the men manning the trench behind were well protected. Nor was there much danger from snipers since a man was able to make an observation and drop back behind the crest of the wall much quicker than one of the enemy could take aim and fire his antiquated gun. There were often a series of these earthworks so that, if driven from one line, the defenders could retreat to the next one behind them and continue the struggle.

The final line of defence was the thick belt of trees and undergrowth surrounding the village (p. 116). The paths were mere foot-tracks abounding in twists and turns. The boles of large cotton trees furnished excellent cover. Some of these were loopholed and commanded the pathways. The paths, themselves, also had their defences. These consisted of pits ("ọbu"), dug at intervals on both sides of the track. It was unsafe to stray from the path lest one stumbled into one of these pits and fell on the pointed stake (or stakes) standing upright in the bottom of the hole. If the enemy traversed the path, he was exposed to the concealed marksmen. He naturally tried to steal through the thicket and, in doing that, he was in danger of being impaled in a pit.

Nowadays, travellers pass along well-made roads. In certain areas, attention is attracted to high towers standing in the midst of some compounds. Many of these stand some thirty feet above ground-level. Some are round, others are square built, the former being well-turned structures. The walls are of puddled clay laid in courses much more substantial than those used in ordinary house building. Thus, they not only stand the weather well, they are, in addition, sufficiently strong to withstand assault. They are provided with an upper storey which is reached by mounting a ladder standing inside the tower. There are no proper windows, a few narrow apertures, mere slits, let in a little light: these also serve as loopholes. The owner uses this upper chamber as a room wherein to store his treasures. He may also use it as a bedroom. Should he have cause for suspicion, when he retires, he hoists the ladder clear of reach from the ground floor. In normal times, it is the owner's strong room. When raiders are in the vicinity, it becomes his castle and his last line of defence.

William Cole, writing in 1859,[5] gives an account of the confirming of peace after war: "The two head-men engaged purchase conjointly an albino. He is brought forward between them. The head-men, placing one hand upon his shoulders, seize his hands in theirs and drag him forward declaiming aloud that war is over and, should either of them (the chiefs) have cause to fight again, it must be as allies, or not at all. Should this vow be broken, the family of the offender is to be seized and is liable to be sold into slavery. Upon this they swear by the albino's blood ; an attendant quickly advances, and strikes off the head of the victim, whilst the chiefs uphold the body."

NOTES TO CHAPTER XXIX

[1] *Vide " Niger Expedition ",* p. 428.

[2] " No man is allowed to wear, or even possess one (eagle plume), who has not killed his man, or a leopard, both of which are considered as of equal value. It matters not how you have killed your victim, so that you have a skull to produce."—" *Life on the Niger ",* p. 11.

[3] Warneck states that, among the features of Animistic Heathenism, " captives are tortured to death with incredible cruelty ; nay with voluptuous joy ".—" *Living Forces of the Gospel ",* p. 123.

[4] Egwe (p. 313) = dry earth wall. Ekpe = dry earth wall with a trench behind it made for defensive purposes.

[5] " *Life on the Niger ",* p. 13. For the procedure when trouble arises between Ibo villages see p. 409 dealing with the use of young palm leaves.

CHAPTER XXX

YAMS [1]

BEFORE GIVING AN account of the important place that Yam occupies in the life of the Ibo, the legend of its origin may be noticed.

The story runs that, in the olden time, there was nothing to eat, so " Eze Nri " (King of Nri) considered what should be done to remedy the defect. He took the drastic course of killing his eldest son, cutting the body into small pieces and burying them. His daughter shared a similar fate. Strange to say, five months later, yam tendrils (" ome ji ") were observed to be growing at the very places where the dismembered parts of the son's body had been planted. In similar fashion " edde " (koko-yam) began to grow where the remains of the daughter had been buried. In the sixth month, the " Eze Nri " dug up fine large yams from his son's grave and " edde " from the place where he had buried his daughter. He cooked both and found them sweet.

At this time, the King was unable to rest or sleep during the day. On one occasion, one of the children of the village came along seeking fire. " Eze Nri " gave a piece of cooked yam to the child who ate it, went home, and promptly fell asleep. The child's people were surprised and, when he awoke, asked him to relate what had happened. He replied that he did not know what it was that " Eze Nri " had given him to eat. So the process was repeated, and it happened again as at the first instance. Then the people asked for yam and " edde ". The King demanded a great price and then handed out a supply, at the same time giving instructions how to plant. From that time yams and " edde " spread throughout the country.

The above is the legend as related at Nri. In general, the origin of yam is traced to wild species found in the " bush ". Through the generations they have been collected and, by cultivation, improved until they are as we have them to-day. A more probable explanation of its presence is that it was introduced by the Portuguese during the slave-trading days.

Yam is the Ibo's favourite food. It stands to him as the potato does to the typical Irishman. A shortage of the yam

YAMS

supply is a cause of genuine distress, for no substitute gives the same sense of satisfaction. This partiality for it, and the time and labour necessary for its production, are the reasons why some account should be given here. At one time, its cultivation was the most serious occupation of the native. Conditions have changed of recent years and the more sophisticated people are not now so entirely dependent upon it as their fathers were.

There are many varieties of the tuber; they differ in size, appearance and flavour. The same soil does not suit the growing of all varieties. Native farmers plant several kinds when testing the qualifications of a fresh plot of ground. They argue that one or two out of the four or five varieties with which they experiment will surely bring good results and will serve as a guide to them in subsequent planting. On the other hand, the style of planting varies very little, the type of country and soil being the governing factors. There are a fair number of kinds, probably twenty at the lowest estimate, and the farmer knows in a general way the type of soil likely to prove suitable for each of them.

As there is practically no dressing for the land, owing to the entire absence of horses and but few cattle, the plots are worked out after three or four years of cultivation. Fresh sites have to be chosen, and the old plots left to lie fallow for a few years to give them the chance to regain their natural fertility. In most parts of the country, the necessity to change presents no great difficulty. In other parts, and especially Southern Ibo, the problem is much more acute, with the result that the land is exhausted, and the yams deteriorate in size and quality, many being so small that they are scarcely worth the time and labour expended to produce them. In some areas, as at Isu (Udi Division), should a feather be observed falling from a flying " udene " (vulture), the owner of the ground upon which it falls will refrain from planting on the plot, nor will he take wine and fruit from the palms and other trees. Should a dog or other beast touch the feather, it is killed and the carcase cast away.

The first thing to be done on a new site is to clear the undergrowth. It is cut, allowed to dry, and then fired. Small trees are felled to just above ground-level, the larger ones are heavily lopped to eliminate shade from overhanging branches. The roots are left undisturbed, partly to avoid the burden of grubbing, but, chiefly, because it is more important to conserve the soil during the wet season. Unless the soil is held together by these roots, it would disintegrate by the wash of water from the tropical downpours, and speedily be reduced to unproductive desert conditions. The trees are not killed by this drastic treatment; during the ensuing months they put forth fresh growth. On the higher ground, the soil is earthed up into circular mounds from twelve to eighteen inches in diameter; where it is boggy, it is formed into beds equal to about a cube yard of earth. The seed planted is selected for its suitability to the type of soil as far as can be calculated. A single seed yam is inserted in the centre of the mound. Whole seed yams may be used, and are preferable, or sections cut from larger roots, care being exercised to make sure that each section has a sprouting " eye ".

The code of laws that formerly operated in connection with yam planting was a very stringent one. Infringement of the laws led to serious results, not infrequently to bloodshed. It was a capital offence to rob a farm of its yams whether they were newly set seed or the mature roots. In spite of the danger attendant upon the deed, farms were sometimes raided. There was always a big element of risk. The thief might be detected in the midst of his nefarious task by a watchful farmer and that meant serious fighting. Both fought relentlessly, the thief to win freedom, the farmer as he strove to protect his property. Many farmers erect little booths on their farms where they encamp during the first weeks of the season and, again, at a later date as harvest time approaches. It is not a rare occurrence to be wakened in the early morning by the cries of those whose farms have been robbed. The thieves are very expert, and act quickly and surely when they raid a farm to steal seed yams. It has become more common since the introduction of British Criminal Law, because there is not the fear of such heavy reprisals as those which existed under old native law and custom.

A feature to be noticed is the remarkable way in which natives are able to recognise seed yams which they have handled. On one occasion, a young fellow planted his farm and then went away for a few days. It was but a small plot near the village, not the usual outlying farm. While he was absent, a woman appeared bearing a basket of seed yams. She lodged a complaint to the effect that her farm had been robbed and that she had traced the tracks of the thief who turned out to be the lad in question. An inquiry was held. The woman could produce no witness to support her allegations, whereas the lad advanced two or three. The opinion was unanimous that the seed produced had been planted by a man, they had been cut into sections in a manner that no woman would have divided them! That was a crucial point. How this was detected with such unerring certainty and unanimity was a mystery to a mere foreigner. Next, a man came forward and declared that he recognised certain of the yams as those he had, himself, given to the lad. That, again, was a mystery, yet he was emphatic that they were the identical yams he had given. The evidence was completely conclusive and, instead of the woman receiving sympathy, she was forthwith pronounced to be a thief. Had she not been protected, she would have been dealt with summarily and heaven alone knows what her fate would have been. As it was, she escaped lightly. She was ordered to replant the plot, and to pay a sum of money to the boy for attempting to bring him into disrepute on the allegation that he was a yam thief.

The first tornado of the season is the signal for great activity. For a short period nearly everybody works with intense zeal in the fields, beginning at daylight and plodding on without rest till noon. A month of steady work brings the yam plot into good order, and the majority of the men-folk do not suffer from over-exertion during the next five or six months.

After sticking the young yam plants, the soil around the roots must be earthed up and, during the early torrential downpours, this work must be repeated. Weeds flourish, and constant labour is required to check their growth. This is mostly done by the women, who use small semicircular hoes—a bow-shaped piece of iron with a handle at each end worked in the same manner as a spokeshave.[2]

When the operations in the field are at an end, a regular time of feasting follows, beginning with the " Iwa-ji " (breaking of the new yam). Betweenwhiles, the men are engaged in tying the yams, one by one, to open upright frames in such a manner that wind and sun may have free access to them. Yams rot very quickly if left lying on the ground. The yamstack (" ọba ") stands in a secluded part of the compound, and is penned off with a stout fence and the entrance locked. No one may enter without the knowledge and sanction of the owner. He, himself, usually deals out the daily supplies for the household, and woe to anyone found loitering in close proximity to an " ọba ", or caught in the act of robbing one.

Yams will not thrive unless properly tended. Not only must they be kept free from weeds; they must also be supported by sticks. The tendrils run to several feet in length and will deteriorate unless they can climb. When the plant is young and vigorous, the tendrils are inclined to run up the sticks too quickly. They have to be unwound by hand and set back to lower levels. To some extent this is because the sticks are not long enough. At full growth, a well-tended yam farm has the appearance of a hop-field when it is about half-way through the season and the foliage has not become too dense. A man, here and there, will plant a few yams in his compound and give them special attention. For these, extra long poles, up to twelve feet in height, are provided. Very often strings are stretched from the roots of the plant up to the branches of tall trees and the tendrils climb up the strings. When in full leaf, these specimen plants are very graceful and pretty, while the roots are usually of great size and weight.

The yams known by the names " Adaka ", " Awudu " and " Aga " come into season first. They also produce very large tubers, some measuring as much as two feet in length, or more, by from five to seven inches in diameter. These early varieties are grown in marshy localities where the annual floods leave a heavy deposit of alluvial soil. If a stream run alongside the farm, the owner can assist nature by watering the plants in the early days after planting. By the time the plants are well set, the rains begin to fall and there is no need for watering ! Under these favourable conditions, the yams make vigorous growth. There is, however, a drawback ; they have to be lifted a few weeks before they are mature, since, by the time they are fit to dig, the flood waters are rising and the yams must be removed before the ground is covered. As they are not dry and ripe, they are unsuitable for storage purposes. They are of much better flavour (to Europeans !) than the dry yams, and more appetising in appearance when cooked. The flesh is white and floury instead of being stodgy and dingy looking.

When these " water " yams come into the market they meet with a ready sale. The stock remaining from the previous season's crop is wellnigh exhausted, and those that are still on the " ọba " frame are hard outside, discoloured inside, and unsavoury to the palate. A change to fresh yams is welcome, but due care must be taken, because a too free indulgence in eating unripe yam will lead to stomach disorders. A safer way is to mix old and young together when preparing the " nni-ji " ; the balls of pounded yam for the evening meal. The main crop of yams grown on higher dry soils is not harvested till later in the year, round about the end of October and November. These are left to dry thoroughly before being dug up, otherwise they would not store satisfactorily.

Until the last few years, it might be legitimately affirmed that the life of the people was bound up with the yam supply.

YAMS

For generations it was *the* staple food of the country. Large tracts of land were devoted to its cultivation and, to ensure good crops, fairly fertile soil is required. It will be seen that there is a close connection between the staple food and land disputes : the land lies fallow between the seasons, but as soon as the farmers renew operations there will surely be land troubles. It is worse where the soil is naturally poor, or has been impoverished by unremitting planting ; then good land is a precious possession, the rights of which are jealously guarded.

From an agricultural point of view, the yam is a very extravagant vegetable to grow. Each tuber requires a full square yard of land which, in itself, is a big demand. For seven or eight months of the year, regular attention must be given to its care, absorbing much time and labour. If wages had to be paid, it is doubtful whether a yam farm would pay its way, let alone yield a profit. The normal Ibo farmer, however, is never embarrassed by a wages roll ; the farm is a family concern, wages do not enter into the calculations, nor does time count to the native.

The means of propagation may be noticed. Certain kinds of yam produce two of its kind ; other kinds do not. In the case of the former, two yams are dug up at harvest, one of full size, the second a diminutive one. This smaller one is set apart as seed for the following season. Other seed yams are raised by two methods. From August onwards, the yam stack is almost depleted. To augment the family food supply, new yams are dug up as required. They are not fully ripe, but are advanced enough for eating. When they are lifted at this premature stage, the tendrils are carefully separated from the roots and the butt ends planted. There is sufficient time remaining before the wet season ceases, and there is enough sap left in the tendrils for a small seed yam to form. The second method is to slice stock-sized yams into small sections and raise seed from them.

Under old Ibo conditions, the marketing of yams was not a very serious business as most folk had their own supply. The general practice was (and is) for each family to plant its farm and raise crops sufficient to meet its needs. If desired, or necessary, it could manage to live independently of food from outside sources. Here and there, this practice does not apply as, for instance, at Awka, where the men have little time for farm work and little inclination to engage in it. They have a profession which is more lucrative and attractive than farming. They purchase their yams from neighbouring towns, entering

YAMS

into arrangements with the growers which are of the nature of unwritten agreements whereby supplies are more or less guaranteed. Great changes, which are fundamental in character, are following rapidly one upon another since the country was first brought under British protection. The yam market has been considerably disturbed. The swelling numbers of non-farming immigrants has created a demand which is, in many places, in excess of the supply. The price of yams rose steadily for a number of years, because of this increased demand. The producer was tempted to part with some of his limited household stock in order to profit by the good prices. To compensate for this, the family must eat much more maize, koko-yam and, especially, cassava. The cultivation of cassava has spread extensively during the last twenty-five years.

In cosmopolitan centres, at railway depots, and other places, bread is now baked and sold in great quantities daily, where, formerly, a chunk of roasted yam would have formed the subsidiary meal. For parties also, it constitutes the chief item on the menu. There does not seem to be much prospect of the yam supply being adequate to meet the needs of the country under the changed conditions. Apart from the immigrants, the manner of work and life is, to-day, so completely different from what it was a generation ago. So many thousands are, in these days, employed in non-agricultural pursuits who do not, and cannot, produce food for themselves. The old type of farmer is not inclined to swerve far from the conservative practices of his forefathers. He continues to grow yams with only his household in mind.[3] He may sell some of his stock, either as a special concession, or because he is pressed for money. A few of the younger and more alert men, who can still find means of securing cheap labour, are extending their operations and selling their crops. There is an element of danger in what appears to be a very commendable effort. Owing to the lack of manure, there is the prospect of the land being overworked and thus, to become so impoverished, that the yield may deteriorate in quality and also be reduced in quantity. As the country is in process of development, more and more foreigners arrive, European and African, to fill the various posts in the Government and Commercial services. Around these gather locally born natives until, literally, there are thousands employed in occupations where they are entirely dependent on the market for their food.

One further point should not be overlooked. It has been stated earlier that the production of yam is an " extravagant " business owing to the extensive amount of ground required

YAMS

for the cultivation of a single root. In addition to this handicap, it has the disadvantage of being rather deficient in its nutritive properties. A man expects to eat a large quantity *per diem* and, thus, even a small household will consume a considerable number in a week. In the case of " Adaka ", " Awudu " and " Aga ", the number is much less, as they are of great size. On the other hand, they are only in season for a brief period. If the supply be inadequate, a man speaks of himself as being in a state of hunger, and he invariably answers any inquiry concerning his health by " Very well, only for hunger ". (This has another meaning. It is really an idiomatic way of saying that " one is well ".) A person must needs eat a very generous allowance of yam to sustain his physical powers. He must compensate for the deficiency in nutriment by consuming an extra large quantity!

The establishment of peace conditions, the introduction of Medical and Sanitary Science, and the labours in connection with Child Welfare and Mother Craft, lead one to expect an increase in the population. It may not prove embarrassing to the country inasmuch as the increase may not be too great. Some of the enlightened people are beginning to realise that vast numbers of children are not necessarily the sign of wealth as they once were. A few well-educated children in regular employment are now considered a better speculation than a mass of young people who can earn little, but who eat heartily. Still, with the improved conditions, the expansion of trade, and the introduction of new occupations, there are many more to feed. These will have to depend very considerably on imported food, the chief items being bread, biscuits, dried and tinned fish and rice. This is inevitable, partly because of the insufficiency of locally grown products, but quite as much for economic reasons, the foreign commodities being cheaper than the home-grown supplies, particularly at certain seasons of the year when yam is at a prohibitive price, a single root fetching as much as sixpence in the open market. On the eastern side of the Niger, the conditions are much worse than on the western, the soil being less productive, while the demand is much greater owing to the larger population and the presence of many more foreigners.

In order to secure a good crop of yams, the soil must lie earthed up around the plants continuously. It is more incumbent because the heavy rains wash it down repeatedly and the work must be done again and again. This fact points to the improbability of reforms in methods being welcomed by the farmers. Ploughing would not answer, even were it possible.

With no draught animals available, the plough could not be adopted for general use; it might find its place in maize growing, if motor driven. But to use a plough would necessitate the grubbing up of roots and that would be fatal. The roots serve to conserve the soil; once they are removed, the heavy rains quickly convert the soil into sand and desert conditions result. The good soil is washed away and the land becomes unproductive. I have brought specimens of soil from different localities to England for analysis by expert agriculturists and they have expressed surprise that any crops could be induced to grow in them. The remedy suggested was the planting and digging in of buckwheat and white mustard, but it can hardly be expected that the simple, and often poor, native could afford to adopt these measures. Moreover, he has not the patience to experiment with these methods; he wants an immediate return for his labour. As yet, he thinks of his own needs and wants to enjoy the profit himself; he is not concerned with posterity. The Local Authorities, however, are doing their utmost to inculcate the principle of rotation of crops in order to benefit the farmer. Artificial manures are also prohibitive in price. Further, the employment of these requires some protection of the plots under cultivation, otherwise the dressing is washed away as the result of two or three heavy rainfalls.

On the face of things, it seems highly improbable that the primitive hoe will be quickly displaced for yam-farming purposes. There is no question that the implement is peculiarly suitable and very effective in the hands of the native.

The future of agriculture in the section of Southern Nigeria under review provides scope for thought. It may follow a line of development by which certain crops will gain favour at the expense of others. Produce, for which there is a good foreign market, such as palm oil, maize and cocoa may prove more profitable to the agriculturist than yam growing. Certain it is that the old methods have gone for ever; they could not continue under British Administration. The old chiefs and wealthy men relied on their slaves for the cultivation of their farms. No wages were paid to these. They were granted the privilege of working for their own private interests every fourth day, but they were no expense to their masters. In those days, a rich man's farming operations were limited only by the acreage at his disposal and the number of his slaves. The slave days are over, and the large farms cultivated by them have largely ceased to be.

Finally, one doubts whether the foreigner can teach the

native much in respect of yam growing. With palm-oil cultivation and the production of other crops, there will be definite success as a result of instruction. The great problem is to instil patience, and to secure stable market prices for produce. Granted that agriculture can be made a paying proposition, there will be no cause to reiterate the cry " back to the land " among the Ibo people ; they will certainly work if encouraged by a fair prospect of a reasonable return for their labour, time and expense. Failing this prospect, the young and enterprising men will seek a form of employment that offers a more lucrative return. The Ibo loves the land, and will work on it, providing he can be sure that he will be able to maintain and educate his family from the proceeds of his labours. In other words, we see the same causes at work in the Ibo country as those which lead to the drift away from the land in England.

NOTES TO CHAPTER XXX

[1] *Dioscoreacae.* The Black Bryony (Tamus Communis) is the only variety found in England.

[2] " The men do all the building, and when a new garden is to be made the men cut down the trees . . . the regular work is done by the women." —" *Fetish Folk of West Africa* ", p. 126.

" Men clear the ground for the farms because women are not strong enough ; they hunt because women are not able to do so ; they fight their enemies to prevent them carrying off their wives and children and it is at this time, I suppose, that the division of labour takes place."— " *Tailed Headhunters of Nigeria* ", p. 199.

[3] This is as it was nearly 100 years ago. Crowther states (1858) that " the Ibos cultivate the land but, as everyone cultivates only what will do for his own wants, provisions become very dear before a new crop comes in . . . one must starve at Onitsha, or pay an enormous sum in cowries for a trifle at the time of want ".—" *Niger Expedition* ", p. 435.

CHAPTER XXXI
OIL & WINE

THE VISITOR TO the Ibo country cannot fail to notice the immense number of palm trees. There are several species, the most profuse being the oil-palms. All the palm trees have their particular value, because of the fruit they produce, or the wood, or both. They supply food and drink, also materials for house-building. Quantities of all these are in daily use, especially the food and drink, while the surplus is sold to commercial companies as raw produce.

This is not an academic treatise; rather it is an attempt to show the benefits which the palms confer upon the native. They almost seem to have been created to meet his needs, for there is no tree which, in itself, has so many uses since every part is of value, timber, leaves, sap and fruit. The account given here concerns those palm trees that are in constant demand for one purpose or another.

The most abundant, and the best for all round value and use, is the oil-palm (*Eloesis guineensis*). This tree is monœcious; the male flower grows above the female. It is found all over the Ibo country, though it grows more freely in some parts than in others. As a rule, it is not so profuse in the wide open spaces whereas, in the vicinity of villages it flourishes luxuriantly.

Left to himself, the native accepts the oil-palm as a gift from the gods. He makes no effort to improve on nature's handiwork; he does not attempt to conserve it, nor take the trouble to cultivate it. It just grows, and he is content with the benefits he derives from it. The reason for this is that he knows nothing of the science of arboriculture. This deficiency is now being tackled by the energetic efforts of the Agricultural Department of the Government. Selected seed is being distributed, and plantations are being laid out in a scientific manner. Local growers are being encouraged to adopt the new methods, and cultivated plantations are increasing in number.

To a certain extent the native realises how much he is indebted to the palm trees. He never wilfully destroys one, yet he is apathetic in that he rarely exerts himself to save one from destruction, neither does he trouble to plant seeds. Hitherto, he argues, there has never been any reason why he should plant seeing that they grow in rich abundance without assistance on man's part. They all grow from self-sown seed. Myriads of seedlings spring up annually of which thousands come to an untimely end. They are trodden down, dug into the farms, or burnt by the fires which rage towards the close of the dry season. The reason why the finest palms are found in the villages is because they escape the ordeal by fire when very young, and have the benefit of the compound refuse about their roots. The seeds are scattered unintentionally. Some fall from the bunches of nuts as they are carried home. Very often the nuts are stripped from the heads in the farms. This relieves the bearers of the burden of carrying dead weight of useless substance; they carry the nuts only and not the massive heads on which they cluster. It also means that, in the process of stripping, and in the course of carrying, many nuts are left lying on the ground. Also, parrots and other birds add their quota of dropped seeds. The ripe seeds germinate freely, with the result that oil-palms are found in every region.

No attention whatever is bestowed on young trees until they are well established. A tree begins to bear fruit as soon as the crown is mature. It usually appears when the crown is a foot or two above ground-level. The nuts form in clusters which hang in large pendulous bunches attached closely to the trees just below the fronds. At a distance they resemble a mass of mussel shells, black and polished. At a later stage, they turn red and yellow which indicate that they are ripe and ready for ingathering.

At Nachi (Udi Division), when a man dies all his palm trees are stripped of green. The treatment may cause the trees to die. Usually, however, it survives the ordeal and puts forth a fresh cluster of fronds.

Although the native does not plant oil-palms yet, with the exception of those growing in the forest, which are any man's property, every palm is claimed by some man or woman. The claim of ownership is honoured to the extent that the trees can be sold and, when land is bought, the standing oil-palms go with it. On the contrary, this rule does not apply to cocoanut palms. A man may purchase a plot of land; in doing so he understands that cocoanut trees are not included in the conveyance. These remain the property of the purveyor; they cannot be felled nor the nuts removed. They cannot, in any way, be interfered with except with the ex-

WARRIORS.

FIGHTING MEN OF THE OLD TYPE WITH THEIR ANCIENT FLINTLOCK GUNS AND THEIR PATRONAL FETISHES. THE MAN ON THE LEFT IS WEARING A HELMET OF WOVEN MATERIAL. (PAGE 378.)

pressed sanction of the original owner or his successors. The new owner may settle down permanently on the plot, he may build his house upon it, or farm it, but his occupation of the land does not confer proprietary rights over the cocoanut palms. He must allow the original owner free access at all times, either to gather the fruit or to fell the trees.

The fronds ("igu") are in great demand for various purposes. Lopping begins as soon as these are of serviceable size. Many are cut before the tree is mature. The outer circles are cut away, leaving a small cluster of undeveloped fronds standing upright (instead of inclining gracefully) on the crown of the tree. These are used for protecting walls and, in the farming season, when the goats are generally penned, for fodder. One has the feeling that the trees must suffer greatly from the drastic lopping, whereas they do not seem to be seriously affected. It is possible that the tree is benefited by the heavy pruning.

The palm tree presents a picturesque appearance. The feathery green swaying leaves stand forth as a crest above the mottled trunk. This is grey in colour, pocked with splashes of deep black. It is studded with holes and rough excrescences. These holes provide rooting space for ferns and other parasitic plants. The grey, black and green blend harmoniously and, altogether, make a pleasing picture. The holes and excrescences are mainly the result of the severe lopping of the fronds, and the many tappings for palm wine. The crown of the tree is a large bulbous growth. From it the fronds spring, and the head of fruit bulges its way through them where they join the tree.

The stem of the tree can scarcely be termed "timber"; it is really a compact mass of fibre. Walking-sticks manufactured from the wood, well smoothed down and oiled, are handsome examples of a beautiful grain. For two or three feet above the ground, the trunk consists of a tangled collection of strong fibres. This fibrous growth is the salvation of the tree. Without its supple aid, the tree could not withstand the blasts of the frequent tornadoes. The elasticity of the roots allows for the swaying of the tree as the wind strikes it. The knotted mass of natural cordage is capable of withstanding an immense strain. Often the trees remain standing, whereas the lofty crowns are snapped off by the sudden gusts of wind. Many of the trees growing outside the villages appear to be in danger of complete destruction when the annual fires rage about them. In the crowns, a considerable quantity of debris collects during the year, blown by the wind, and becoming entangled between the thorny stems of the fronds. When the fires burn, this is often ignited by sparks and blown tufts of burning grass, and the rubbish burns furiously until it is consumed. All the leaves are burned, and the head of the tree becomes a black smouldering mass. Strangely enough, the tree apparently suffers no permanent injury ; in a very short time it puts forth fresh green shoots and looks healthier than ever. The natives assert that the trees are improved by this fiery ordeal : it acts as a sort of spring-cleaning by destroying the weeds and other refuse which might, eventually, smother the tree.

The colour of the nuts shows when they are ready for gathering. This is easily discernible from the ground. When ripe they are usually cut down, this being preferable to waiting until they rot off the stalks. Many nuts are wasted if they are allowed to fall as they become detached one by one. Men are employed to climb the trees in order to sever the complete bunch from the crown of the tree. There are two common methods followed by these men, one requiring a single climbing rope, the other two. For the former method, some stout live creeper-canes are plaited into a rope from eight to ten feet in length. The central part is heavily sheathed with grass carefully bound on, thus increasing the diameter to three or four inches. This precaution is taken to prevent chafing the rope itself and, further, which is equally important, the extra size enables the climber to slide the rope more readily up and down the rough surface of the trunk ; the larger it is the less liable it is to jam in a notch. When about to climb, the man encircles himself and the trunk with his rope and firmly joins the two ends. Slipping his matchet into his girdle, or carrying it between his chin and shoulder, he grasps the rope firmly with both hands, throwing his whole weight back upon it. Then, assuming an angle of about $45°$, he proceeds to walk up the trunk, throwing the rope higher as he ascends by jerking it upwards about two feet at a time. To execute the movement, he presses his feet firmly against the tree and keeps his legs rigid. He then pulls himself forward with his hands and, for a second, releases the strain on the rope, at the same time sliding it up the trunk before he, again, drops back into the reclining position. Although each act is separate and distinct, yet so rapidly is the whole carried out that it appears to be but one movement. The top of the tree is reached in a very short time, and there the climber maintains his position by stiffening his legs and pressing backwards on the rope. He thus has the free use of his hands, and he proceeds to cut nuts or branches, working round the crown of the palm until his task is accomplished.

OIL & WINE

The double rope method is quite different. It is more intricate and it also looks more dangerous. The two ropes have looped ends and are about five feet in length. The climber casts one rope round the tree, threads one loop through the other and pulls it just taut enough to prevent it from slipping. He then passes his left leg through the dangling loop as far as the middle of the thigh. The second rope is treated likewise, but is placed some eighteen inches lower than the first and, instead of the right leg being passed through, the sole of the foot is inserted (as in a stirrup) and pressed upon the loop. Whilst climbing up and down, the weight is changed alternately from one rope to the other, each being slipped higher or lower in turn. It is obvious that greater balancing power is demanded for this second method. The man must assume a more or less upright position, always pressing backward with his foot and leg to keep the loops from slipping. He is also necessarily brought closer to the trunk of the tree and, consequently, the scope for arm play is more restricted.

Occasionally, the rope breaks or slips, or the climber misses his grip, and the result is always horribly painful, if not fatal. The man makes a desperate effort to throw his arms round the tree; he may save himself from an actual fall and yet be unable to check his descent before he has slipped a considerable way down the trunk. The rough jagged excrescences tear the climber's flesh in a particularly agonising manner. He may lose his hold altogether and fall to the ground, which is still more disastrous. When a man slips down a palm tree, he receives a series of gashes covering the whole front of his body, legs and arms.

At Agukwu (Nri), contrary to practically universal custom, women may, if they wish, climb palm trees, only they must do so by sheer climbing; they are forbidden the use of a rope. Further, they are permitted to cut fronds only; they may not touch the nuts. Even so, the permission is restricted to women who have no husbands.

Occasionally, it is tabu for a woman to touch a palm tree with her foot. Should she do so, either purposely or accidentally, she is expelled from the town.

The natives derive many benefits from the oil-palm, in fact, very little is wasted or lost. Its timber is not often used for posts in house-building, but it is much in demand, when split into suitable sizes, for wall-plates and rafters. It has not sufficient substance to resist the termites (white ants). That is not exceptional, for there is very little wood that will withstand the ravages of these insatiable little pests. The fibres are put to a variety of uses and are an excellent substitute for cord or string. They are stout or finely drawn according to the purpose for which they are wanted, including strings for musical instruments such as the "ubo-akwala". The leaves (fronds) are very good for protecting the clay walls which surround the compounds. They are laid lengthwise, one on top of another, along the crest of the walls, being held in position by supporting stays fixed in the clay. They serve to throw off the water during the rainy season and preserve the walls from being washed down. Quantities of leaves are used as fodder for goats. Finally, the midriffs of the leaves, "bones" as they are aptly called by the people, are bound up into compact little bundles which make very efficient besom brooms.

These uses are common to all the oil-palms; for wine and fruit the value of the trees varies considerably. The natives have distinguishing names for most varieties of which the following are quoted as examples. Three of them are styled "ojukwu", "okpoloko" and "osukwu". The first (ojukwu) does not produce heavy crops of nuts. The oil from them is bright red in colour and is highly esteemed. Some yield oil in rich abundance and these are styled "osukwu". Some trees produce nuts of very fine appearance, but they have not much flesh, the kernel being large in proportion. These are called "okpoloko". A tree that is exceptionally prolific in its yield of nuts is given a courtesy title such as "nne-nkwu" (mother of palms) in acknowledgement of its unusual productive properties.

Mention ought to be made of one other oil-palm since it figures rather prominently in the lives of the people, more particularly, the men-folk. It is known as "oke-nkwu" (the male palm). It does not bear fruit as the common trees; instead a cluster of flowers grows on the crown. These soon wither, but remain suspended on the tree for a fair length of time. From the "oke-nkwu" a wine of stronger potency is drawn, spoken of as "up-wine". This is obtained by tapping the head of the tree immediately below the cluster of flowers.

The women are responsible for extracting the oil from the nuts. In cases where the bunches are brought home complete, they are laid aside for a few days in order to dry the stalks. Once these are dry, the nuts can be easily plucked off the large bulbous head ("ogbe-akwu"). After stripping, the nuts are pounded to a mushy state in a wooden mortar. This is a hollowed-out section of a hardwood tree fixed immovably upright in the ground, and is about two feet in depth and a foot or more in diameter. In the more southern parts of the Ibo country, a log is laid flat on the ground and scooped out. It is nearly as long and as broad as a small punt. The mortars, as a rule, are owned by the heads of families and are generally placed close to the entrance to the compound. The nuts are pounded until all the flesh is separated from the kernels. It is strenuous labour and often the young men will render assistance in this operation. The sticky mass is then carried to the waterside. A hole is dug and filled with water into which the pulp is thrown. The women stir the mass continuously and, gradually, the kernels and fibrous matter are disintegrated. The oil rises slowly to the surface and is skimmed off into large earthen pots.

The people of Onitsha and those dwelling on the western side of the Niger, practise a different method of extracting oil. The nuts are first boiled in massive iron pots. After that, they are pounded, and the oil squeezed out of the pulp by hand. The residue may be boiled a second time and the last remnants of oil retrieved. This strict attention to economy is, however, not often followed. The residue is not cast away, it is used as fuel. The ashes ("ngu") are carefully collected and form one of the chief ingredients in the manufacture of soap. Some are dissolved in water and compounded into medicine. Others are cooked with beans or breadfruit.

Fresh oil is used for food. It is easy to manipulate in its liquid state. Normally, it does not take long for raw oil to harden to the consistency of butter. The natives retain as much as they need for household uses, for relish, lamp oil, soap and other purposes, and sell the surplus. Immense quantities are exported to Europe for the manufacture of soap, candles and other commodities.[1]

After drying, the nuts are shelled and the kernels are sold to the commercial firms for export. The intrinsic value of the kernel is increased if, in the process of stripping off its shell, care be taken to preserve it intact. If the kernels are much broken they are not so readily marketed. The women retain small quantities for domestic and other purposes. A fine oil is extracted from these by placing them over a slow-burning fire. The oil obtained in this way is used for anointing the skin and as brilliantine for the hair. Raw kernels are not actually a foodstuff; they are eaten as cheese is eaten with bread, a kernel being chewed as a juicy morsel to relieve the dryness of corn or cassava meal. The nuts generally have one undivided kernel. Odd ones will have kernels that divide naturally into two and, very occasionally, into three, sections. A person who happens to crack a nut which contains a divisible kernel will not part with it; it will either be eaten forthwith, or deposited in a safe place. No one else will share a kernel of this description; it is unlucky to do so. Failure to observe this rule will lead to the man or woman becoming the father or mother of twins, a risk to be avoided like the plague. Multiple kernels are, as a matter of fact, more often preserved for medicinal purposes; they are seldom eaten.

The trees are tapped in order to extract the sap commonly called " palm wine ". A sharp wedge is driven into the trunk just below the crown. Under this incision a calabash is hung, and the two are connected with a reed (" ami ") or a leaf which serves the purpose of a funnel to conduct the wine into the pot. It is usual to visit the trees twice a day, morning and evening, more particularly the latter. The number of trees tapped varies greatly according to the locality, the season and the circumstances of the time. Naturally, more wine is on demand during festivals, weddings and similar joyful occasions. Some trees are left untouched for long periods; some owners do not bother to collect wine from their trees.

The wine itself is not uniform in pungency or flavour; it fluctuates according to the qualities of the tree. It used to be alleged, with some truth, that the natives were so addicted to the wine that they had not sufficient patience to wait for the supplies obtained by the slow process of tapping. Instead, they felled palm trees for the sake of a quick supply. This practice prevailed only in certain parts on the western side of the Niger and, even there, it was not a regular custom. Such a foolish deed would only be perpetrated for some special reason where haste was essential. It does not appear to have been done much, if at all, on the eastern side.

By far the greatest quantities of wine are extracted from the " ngwọ " palm (*Raphia Vinifera*). This species flourishes most luxuriously in marshy country, though it grows also in drier areas. The fruit is of no known value or use. The leaves make excellent thatching material when converted into " bamboo mats ". The fronds, stripped of their leaves, are very serviceable for rafters and laths, in house-building. Huge quantities of wine are drawn from the " ngwọ " thickets. The wine is grey in colour and has a resemblance to old English ginger-beer. It is a refreshing and pleasant beverage; the most fanatic teetotaller may drink it without suffering from qualms of conscience. Either because it is prohibited under law of tabu by the village priest, as is sometimes the case, or for some other reason, some natives will not partake of it. Old men frankly despise it as being fit only for women

OIL & WINE

and children. There is not sufficient tang about it for their taste. So much has to be drunk, and the time is so long before they begin to feel merry and bright!

The wine from the oil-palm is much more potent; it is also different in flavour. Because of its extra strength, it is preferred by the men. If a man indulge his appetite too freely, the effects will certainly be as apparent as with more familiar forms of alcohol. This " nkwu-enu " (" up-wine ") is claimed to have medicinal as well as stimulating properties. Quite probably the latter has been confused with the former! Fermentation sets in quickly and, in due course, it is more comparable to vinegar than wine. When it reaches this stage, it is not, in the opinion of one European, a delectable drink. The old Ibo does not share that opinion, yet, even he, perforce, will make a wry face. If, by chance, some be left unconsumed it is not wasted, it is poured into the new stock to stiffen it and give it added bouquet.

It must not be assumed that, because there is an abundance of natural wine needing only to be collected that, therefore, there must be much drunkenness. It is not so; there is much less of this than might reasonably be expected. It is only on special occasions that there is heavy drinking; it is not a daily habit with the average Ibo any more than is the case elsewhere.

Where supplies are taken to market, the collectors dilute their stocks pretty liberally with water. This practice applies more particularly to large towns which have to depend upon outside sources for their supplies. In the interior villages, the temptation to adulterate the wine is practically nil; it is not worth while, seeing that abundant supplies are at the door. In many villages palm wine is much easier to obtain than water.

Among the élite in the business centres, where the sophisticated and superior young men congregate, palm wine is being superseded by foreign drinks. On the contrary, in the countryside, the consumption of palm wine is on the increase, and the demand for foreign liquors appears to be diminishing.

There is another species of palm which flourishes freely in certain localities, generally where the soil is inclined to be poor and stony. The native name is " Ubili ". The foliage is very graceful, each frond springing up on a long stem and then opening out fanwise. The divisions of the leaves are webbed for about half their length and then separate into individual spikes. The fruit is not unlike a small flattened cocoanut in appearance and has a very hard kernel. It is occasionally eaten by the natives, though it is not a popular article of diet. The chief value of this tree lies in the wood which is eagerly sought for house-building purposes, the posts, wall-plates and any part coming in contact with the clay walls, being of " ubili " whenever possible. The leaves are cleverly plaited into fans, baskets, mats and the like.

Finally, there is the cocoanut which is widely distributed over the country. We have already noted that every cocoanut palm is the property of the family who planted it, wherever it may stand. The slender, graceful trunk often develops a leaning tendency in contrast with the more stocky oil-palm. It grows to a great height and the blossom springing from the crown is a pronounced feature. The fruit is in season all the year round. The timber of this palm is also in great request for building purposes. A great many nuts are cut down whilst the kernel is in the creamy stage ; these are gathered for the sake of the refreshing liquid they contain. The quantity of milk yielded by some of the fresh green nuts is extraordinary. They must be used without long delay as the unripe nuts spoil quickly. The ordinary nuts are eaten, not exactly as a food-stuff ; rather they are chewed as something pleasant to the palate. In famine time, they are eaten as a relish with dry corn. The eating of cocoanut is also one of the signs of mourning. In one town of my acquaintance, the cocoanut is tabu in every form and no native will touch it. It is the more remarkable, inasmuch as there are no water springs thereabouts, and the natives are forced to rely for water largely on the limited and impure supplies stored in catchpits.

The natives extract oil from the ripe cocoanuts chiefly for the purpose of anointing their bodies.

When nuts are required, the boys readily climb the trees, clasping the trunk with their hands, doubling their bodies, and then walking up on their feet. The tallest trees are climbed in this manner without the slightest hesitation or fear.

Before leaving the subject of palms, reference must be made to the use of the very young palm leaves (before they have opened out and are pale yellow in colour, not having been exposed and so become green), for they have a very significant place in the life of the Ibo. These young palm leaves are known as " omu ".

They are in constant demand for religious purposes ; they have a place in almost all sacrifices ; they advertise sorrow and signify victory, such leaves being worn for four days by a conqueror. When preparing small sacrifices (offerings), a young palm frond is taken and a piece about eighteen inches

OIL & WINE

in length is cut off from the top. The leaves are plaited on both sides of the frond, thus producing a small mat equivalent to a dish or plate. On this mat platter the gifts are deposited, kola nut and other small offerings, as noted in the chapter on sacrifices (II).

When seeking forgiveness of sins, the offerings are so placed; also, when returning thanks for favours received. In time of war, these " omu " are used in connection with the sacrifices devoted to the particular deity whose assistance is desired, chiefly the head and entrails of a fowl being deposited in the leafy dish.

" Omu " are also associated with the ceremonies performed to ensure the spoiling of the enemy's medicine. The leader in battle grips a young palm leaf between his teeth, an action which proclaims him " holy ". (*Vide* p. 381.)

When trouble arises between villages, the carrying of " omu " indicates that the bearers are seeking a settlement of the differences. In some places, the " omu " are tied round the neck; this signifies that the parties are honest and sincere in their desires to reach agreement. Should, however, peace measures fail and conflict ensue, the wearers have this means of recognising one another as fellow-townsmen.

Young palm leaves have their part to play both before and after burial. (*Vide* pp. 275 and 410.)

Sometimes dancers are noticed with young palm leaves thrust into their belts. Usually, this is when dancing is associated with mourning, particularly during " Second Burial " ceremonies. The " omu " advertises the fact that the dancer is fortified with appropriate medicine. Fear of this will cause other folk to treat him with fitting respect.

" Omu " which have been used on special occasions are preserved, and are hung near the fireplace in the house (" obi ") of the headman of the compound. Sometimes, the remnants are retained for as long as five or six years (at least so it is declared and, from those I have seen, I have no reason to disbelieve the statement). When a member of the " otu " company (*vide* p. 194) dies, or, for some very particular reason, these old leaves will be brought forward for further use.

" Omu " are also used in the dance called " Abia ". This dance only takes place when a titled man has died, and is restricted to men who have won renown in war.

When drinking palm wine called " Ite ike ", e.g. at the " Udonka " shrine at Agulu, the " omu " are tied round the pot containing the wine. Only men who nave killed others in battle are permitted to partake of this.

To cover palm wine with "omu" signifies that the wine is not common; it is "holy", sanctified for the king's use. Likewise, wine that is being carried to one of the chief idols, as at "Ekke, Nibo" must be so covered, inasmuch as it is "holy".

When a girl is ready to go to her husband he, the husband, will provide palm wine for consumption at his father-in-law's house. The whole family to the nth cousin gather together for the occasion. One big pot (among many others) is adorned with "omu" tied round the neck. This wine is designated "Nkwu omu maw", that is "sacred wine". It is of the quality known as "Nkwu enu" (up-wine). Only titled men may partake of it.

"Omu" serves also as a protective agent. When threaded on string and stretched round a plot of land, it proclaims that that piece of land is about to be put under cultivation, or that it is an area, or even a tree, reserved by the Maw Society, or it is surrounding an "alusi" (shrine). Transgression, in the form of breaking the "omu" placed around such an enclosed area, or ignoring its presence, is punished by the Maw Society. In modern days, a motor-lorry bearing a corpse will be strung round lavishly with "omu" to indicate to all on the road that a corpse is being carried. Everything on the road will give way to the passage of the lorry, because of "omu" associations, and as a mark of respect to the dead. See also p. 275 for use of "omu" preparatory to the digging of a grave.

At the other extreme, "omu" tied to the wrists are the signs of victory, the "laurel" of the triumphant conqueror.

NOTE TO CHAPTER XXXI

[1] "In 1934, which was by no means a 'peak' year, 289,447 tons of palm oil were exported from Nigeria valued at £1,590,646 and 112,773 tons of palm kernels valued at £885,400."—"*Nigeria Trade Report, 1934*", p. 73.

CHAPTER XXXII

SOME SIMILARITIES BETWEEN THE ISRAELITES & THE IBOS

WHILE PRESENTING the following notes on some similarities between the Israelites and the Ibos, I am quite conscious that they do not exhaust the subject; further investigation may prove interesting and of some comparative value.

Over twenty years ago, I wrote: "To any contemplating residence in the Ibo country, particularly those likely to be associated with native affairs, I would recommend a careful study of Levitical Law. In many ways the affinity between Native Law and the Mosaic System is remarkable."

It seems to me that, before we embark upon the discussion of the subject, we should arrive at some fairly definite conclusion as a basis for argument. In the process, we get back, ultimately, to the question, "Are we justified in believing that, in the beginning, man was monotheistic?" I am quite aware of the theory that man has passed through many stages since the time when he was but little in advance of the other animals of the universe, and that through the course of the ages his powers developed; thought and conscience evolved and, after a prolonged struggle, a sense of the spiritual. As the ages rolled on, this sense of the spiritual became more pronounced until man began "to feel after God if haply he might find Him". This theory finds support from the fact that the phenomena are universal. All primitive races whose religious ideas have been studied show them to be possessed of deeply seated beliefs in the supernatural. This is the case even among the so-called lowest types. This only in passing: I am not contending for or against this theory at the moment.

There is not only the belief in the supernatural; there are also practices which are found in all primitive peoples which prove the universal prevalence of sacrifice in varying degree, from the crudest to the more advanced type: from the examples which are little more than an expression of instinctive feeling to those of more elaborate character, offered for definite and specific purposes. Incidentally, the sacrifices of the Ibos come mainly under this latter category. Whence comes this instinct of feeling after some power outside the human self; this inherent belief in the supernatural? There is a variety of causes. Perhaps, the main cause is *fear*. Primitive man felt himself surrounded by forces over which he had no control: forces which, on occasions, demonstrated to him in no uncertain manner his own puny insignificance. The rising of the sun in his strength; his apparent falling into space; above all, the storm and the tempest, the shrieking of the tornado, the flashing of the lightning, the rolling of the thunder; all these, and many others instilled fear into his mind. He realised his helplessness; he could only take note of the result of the forces of nature and bow in submission. It was all beyond his understanding and it drew from him an urge to try, in some way, to appease these outside forces; in other words, to propitiate the mighty spirits who, at intervals, gave expression to their wrath. So, then, out of the fear of the unseen, which was yet none the less real to the primitive man, there developed the sense of the supernatural and, in different ways, methods of approach in order to appease or propitiate these devastating forces.

One is tempted to carry on this theme through its subsequent stages showing how life became bound up with prohibitions; tabus on food, freedom of movement, the normal affairs of life, birth and death and, indeed, in every department of man's existence.

One further point must not be omitted and that is, that after *fear* came a *desire* to pray and worship. Deep calling unto deep in trying to find companionship and the search after a way of forgiveness and eternal life. I must check myself otherwise I shall be plunging into the fascinating study of Tree Worship, the Earth Mother, and other forms of native worship whereas, the subject is " Similarities between the Israelites and the Ibos ".

We turn to the contrary view, namely that man, at the beginning, had a knowledge of his Creator and, later, fell away from his allegiance to God. That God did not place man upon the earth and leave him entirely to his own resources is clear from Genesis vi. 3 : " My spirit shall not always strive with man." Here we have the implication that, with the life of man, came also the gift of the Spirit, ever striving to lead him by the right way and to maintain his relationship with God. The self-will of man broke that contact with God and that was the beginning of a new order. This was a disaster not at all surprising. To the best of us it is often difficult to maintain an abstract faith; it is much easier to accept only what we can see, handle or understand.

It was far more difficult for early man. As far as we know, the original revelation of God was kept alive by Adam and some of those who followed him, but man gradually fell away and the knowledge of God became dimmed.

We must remember that primitive men had nothing but oral methods to preserve their records, and memory is a fickle jade. And so it was not long (comparatively) before men, while still retaining the name and belief in God, added something else. They began with natural objects and felt, in doing so, that they were not dishonouring Him. I quote from Dr. Nassau: " They could not see God; in their expression of their wants in prayer they were speaking into vague space and heard no audible response. The strain on simple unassisted faith was heavy. The senses asked for something on which they could lean. Very reasonable, therefore, it was, in speaking to the Great Invisible, to associate closely with His name the great natural objects in which His character was revealed or illustrated. The sun, shining in his strength giving life, the sky from which spake the thunder, the mountain and the great waters. All these illustrating some of Jehovah's attributes: His power, goodness, infinity, without impropriety associated themselves in man's thought of God, were named along with His name, and were looked upon with some of the same reverence which was accorded to Him. In all this there was no conscious departure from the one living and true God." [1]

There is abundant evidence to support this view. Almost without exception, throughout the tribes and nations, there is behind all else a belief in a Supreme Being. In some cases, the belief may be extremely vague; in others, it is much more distinct. Livingstone said, " There is no need to speak of the existence of God, or of a future life, even among the lowest tribes, for these are generally accepted truths among them."

In his account of Battak Heathenism, John Warneck, the great authority on the subject, states that the only explanation is in " assuming that there is in the popular consciousness the remains of a purer idea of God, alongside and above the recognition of a plurality of gods. Belief in God has been reduced by nature worship. The host of spirits, born of fear, thrust themselves between God and Man, and left behind that faded image of God, which still throws a faint shadow on the feelings of the people, but not on its thought, which is therefore so full of contradictions. Without that assumption, we are in the

SIMILARITIES BETWEEN ISRAELITES & IBOS

presence of an enigma. Whence comes the idea of a Supreme Deity exalted above all, which is no longer understood by the heathen of to-day, and which has become a mere phrase on their lips. It cannot have been distilled from the motley jumble of the worship of gods and of nature, for it exists alongside it. In all the religions of the Indian Archipelago (and probably also of Africa) we meet with the idea of God as a dimly felt highest court of appeal, enthroned above all the gods that are known and named. He is not worshipped : He is scarcely even feared. . . . The realities of animistic heathenism are polytheism and worship of spirits, nevertheless, though much obscured, the original has not been entirely defaced." [2] Though supreme, God's supremacy is no longer exclusive, but simply comparative. He is not denied : He becomes one of many gods.

First, then, man has a knowledge of God. Later, he seeks something tangible and makes an image to represent God, but still he is not an idolator. The next stage is when he begins to substitute and worship beings other than God, and he proceeds to become a polytheist and an idolator. Finally, God is little more than a name, a being definitely acknowledged, but enshrouded in a multitude of other beliefs. And, throughout it all, the spiritual life remains uppermost until everything has in some way or another a spiritual significance or implication and the animist is the resulting product.[3]

In my opinion, such a belief is the only explanation that will satisfactorily account for so many similarities between the Ibos and the people of the Old Testament. The primary fact upon which to start comparisons is this original revelation of God to man. What is the second step ? I offer the suggestion which, perhaps, may prove more than an abstract idea, that the Ibo people, like their Yoruba neighbours, at some remote time either actually lived near, or had very close association with, the Semitic Races. The successive waves of invasion from the North-East of Asia down through Egypt pressed these people to the South-West. As wave after wave came, they were borne onwards until, finally, the Ibos came to rest where we find them to-day and, throughout the ages, they have retained ideas and customs handed down from generation to generation.

It must have been noticed by all who have resided in this country that, occasionally, we meet light-coloured and even red folk. Also, that, every now and then, features are Egyptian in type. Then, again, in their drawings and carvings and their " maw " masks the type of face is eastern, not negro. This by the way ; other indications may appear to other students.

SIMILARITIES BETWEEN ISRAELITES & IBOS

And now we come to the proper consideration of the subject, the Similarities between the Israelites and the Ibos. My first point is language. There are one or two peculiarities of idiom in Ibo similar to some found in Hebrew. The chief parallel is found in the repetition of words to express a single idea and, perhaps, to add emphasis. The practice of reduplicating verbs, or adding their cognate nouns is characteristic of Ibo—e.g. ọ galu aga = he passed ; ọ jelu ije = he went. As a rule, the addition makes little or no appreciable difference to the meaning. There are many verbs which are rarely used without reduplication or with their derived noun, either attached, or in close proximity, e.g. we have such terms as " to murmur a murmur " = " ọ natamu ntamu ", or, as we have in the Litany, " those who have erred " = " ndi jefielu ejefie ", and " those who are deceived " = " ndi alaputalu alaputa ". I do not attach any particular significance to these resemblances to the Hebrew idiom ; they are quoted only as a matter of interest.

My next point is in connection with land and with this we are more familiar. In the Ibo country, the word " communal " is frequently heard and it has, usually, reference to land. I am inclined to think that this word is used in all sincerity, but emphasis needs to be restrained. One doubts whether land is communal in the strict sense of the term. There are town and village boundaries which rather correspond to the borough boundaries in England. On the other hand, I cannot locate any " commons " or " heaths ". Inside those boundaries, it is open to question whether there is any parcel or plot of land which is not definitely and absolutely claimed by some individual owner, or by representative heads of families. What is obvious is that, if a man trespass on his neighbour's land, there is speedily a full-fledged dispute. In other words, " Thou shalt not remove thy neighbour's landmark " (Deut. xix. 14).

This, again, may not be an important resemblance to Levitical Law, but it may be quoted.

Then we have the " Lex Talionis " = the law of retaliation. Deuteronomy xix. 21 : " Life shall go for life, eye for eye, tooth for tooth, hand for hand, foot for foot." The demand of " life for life " is a predominant feature in Ibo custom [4] and instance after instance can be quoted. One example is given on p. 126.

Deuteronomy xxii states that " the woman shall not wear that which pertaineth unto a man ". This is a very strict law among the Ibos and very strong feeling used to be aroused at such an indiscretion. I well remember the disrespectful remarks made by the people when an official's wife began to travel round in land-worker's kit. There was great indignation and it was distinctly displeasing to the people; also, it was just as well that the lady did not hear all that was said. Nor did her husband escape criticism. It is tabu for a woman to wear an ogodo as a man, "Onye walu ogodo." (*Vide* p. 348.) A small girl might do so in ignorance. Even such an one at Awka was exiled to Agukwu (Nri) and either sold, or taken as a wife by an Agukwu man; she could not return home.

Then we have the Law of Sanctuary. We are told that Moses set apart three cities on each side of the Jordan " that the slayer might flee thither, which should kill his neighbour unawares, and hated him not in time past" (Deut. iv. 41, 42; xix). The escape to a city of refuge gave opportunity to investigate the circumstances and thus avoid the shedding of innocent blood. With the Ibos also, the benefits of sanctuary are recognised. For a fuller exposition of this custom see Chapter XVII where the "Osu" system is described in detail. A man or woman, labouring under the impression that he or she was in danger, could flee to the deity and claim its protection. In return for the benefits of sanctuary, such an one forfeited his or her liberty and became an "osu", in other words, the property (slave) of the deity.

In the case of unequivocal murder, the Ibo practice is almost identical with Levitical procedure. Deuteronomy xix. 21 tells us, "Thine eye shall not pity the murderer," and Leviticus xxiv. 17 states, "He that killeth any man shall surely be put to death." Capital punishment is not usually carried out directly; that is, there is no official executioner. It is left to the condemned to undertake his own punishment. The common practice is either to indicate that a rope will assist him to expiate his crime, or blatantly present him with one. This is usually sufficient; if it is not, then he is dealt with summarily. Generally it suffices, and the culprit is found hanging next morning. In some towns, there are trees set apart for the purpose. One can be seen, for instance, in the Nkwo market at Awba. The houses and property of the whole family of the murderer are destroyed. It may be, of course, that the criminal runs away and manages to find sanctuary. In such case, when feeling has died down, say after about three years, he may possibly be permitted to return. He will be called upon to fulfil ceremonies of purification and offer acceptable sacrifices and then he is allowed to rehabilitate himself in the town. (*Vide* Chap. XVIII.)

ON THE WAY TO MARKET.

THE TRADE OF THE COUNTRY IS LARGELY IN THE HANDS OF THE WOMEN. TO BE PREVENTED FROM ATTENDING MARKET IS A GREAT DEPRIVATION.

SIMILARITIES BETWEEN ISRAELITES & IBOS

Coming to more intimate practices, we find a number of similarities which are associated with life. Beginning with the infant, we have Circumcision. This rite is normally carried out on the eighth day after birth as in the case of the Israelites. (*Vide* p. 176.)

Among the Israelites, the rite was never practised on female children. On the other hand, the Ibos carry on a practice which has come down to them through the generations. And it may well be of Eastern origin. Burton, in his " *Wanderings in West Africa* ", states that the Jews themselves adopted the custom from the Egyptians, and it is quite feasible that the Ibos learned from the same original source. Both for male and female, the Ibos, while retaining the rite, have quite lost the reasons for its practice and to all questions reply : " that it has always been done and we follow the custom of our forefathers ". Beyond that they cannot go although some try to manufacture reasons.

After childbirth, the mother must pass through a period of seclusion the climax of which is the ceremony of purification. For the Israelitish woman, the days of seclusion for a male child were thirty-three and for a daughter sixty-six days, after which she brought a lamb of the first year for a burnt offering, and a young pigeon or a turtle dove for a sin-offering. If unable to provide a lamb, then two turtle doves or two young pigeons sufficed. With these, the priest made an atonement for her and she was cleansed (Lev. xii).

The Ibo woman remains in seclusion for twenty-eight days, whether for boy or girl. She must forbear to enter the house until the period of her seclusion is ended ; instead, she uses a shelter placed at the side.

There are corresponding laws in respect of the menstruation of women (Lev. xv. 19 *seq.*). During the time of her period, the Ibo woman must dwell apart ; she is forbidden to enter her husband's house until after her ceremonial cleansing. The woman moves to a neighbour's compound and abides in a corner near the entrance.

In certain other respects, laws concerning Ibo women have an extraordinary resemblance to those which applied to Israelitish women (Lev. xv. 19 *seq.*). After the time of seclusion, with accompanying specific prohibitions, there follows the ceremonial purification. This is performed by the chief woman of the family with the aid of a chicken, young palm leaves (ọmu) and immature palm kernels.

The degrees of affinity in the matter of marriage are even more strictly adhered to, or, rather, they are more meticulous

SIMILARITIES BETWEEN ISRAELITES & IBOS

than those set forth in the Levitical code (Lev. xviii. 6), except in the case of inheritance. Such exceptions are by right of succession, not by marriage.

In the matter of adultery with another man's wife, the Levitical Law ordained death to both man and woman (Lev. xx. 10; Deut. xxii. 22). Old Ibo law gave sanction to the same procedure. I remember hearing of a case where the offenders were tied back to back, placed upright in a pit and buried alive. Or, again, the husband, perhaps unable to deal with the adulterer, might put his wife to death. (*Vide* p. 233.)

The punishment meted out under Israelitish Law to the man found guilty of spoiling a betrothed girl against her consent was death, but if the offence was against an unbetrothed girl, he was called upon to pay the father fifty shekels of silver (Deut. xxv *seq*.). Among the Ibos the capital punishment was never inflicted; a stipulated fine had to be paid. The misbehaviour is invariably confessed at the ceremony known as " Isa ifi " and, under fear of death, the name of the offending man is pronounced and the matter settled by payment of a fine. If reconciliation be not made, the offending man will not be allowed to pass through the compound of the woman's family. Should he attempt to do so, the aggrieved family will fall upon him and maltreat him.

Levitical Law condemned to death the witch and the wizard (Lev. xx. 27). Such were to be regarded as abominations and not to be allowed in Israel (Deut. xvii. 10–11). The Ibos have no love towards such people, especially in respect of witches (" amosu "), and used not to hesitate to ill-treat, drive away, or even kill them. This, of course, only tallies with the prevalent custom in England up to comparatively recent times, and the fear of witches is by no means extinct in parts of Europe to this day, and there is the same tendency to penalise the witch rather than the wizard.

It is time for me to turn to the religious side of life. Here we have a fairly wide field and it will not be difficult to find some interesting comparisons. I am deliberately omitting folk stories and legends; they come under another category. I seek rather to concentrate on similarities by comparing the actual practices of Israelites and Ibos.

Just briefly I mention " Tree Worship ". In the long history of the Hebrew nation prior to the return from the Exile, there is mention of groves and the prophets of the grove. That, of course, is connected with the days when the Israelites fell away into idolatry, especially during the times of the Kings. But, apart from idolatry, trees were held in special respect. In

SIMILARITIES BETWEEN ISRAELITES & IBOS

Deuteronomy xx. 19, the Israelites were commanded that, in making war against a city, they should not destroy the trees thereof: " thou mayest eat of them, but shall not cut them down (for the tree of the field is man's life) ". Now, " Tree worship ", its history and all it signifies, and the place it has taken for generations untold, is too big a subject for consideration here; it would provide material for a whole discourse. Woods and groves are natural temples, and so we find them in the Old Testament in connection with the worship of Astarte. Likewise, in the old Druidic worship in England, and in other lands. Throughout the Ibo country, there are similar groves and also individual trees. In England, the last remnant of tree worship is the Maypole. It is not so very long back, as history goes, since Stubbs in his book the *Anatomie of Abuses* describes the bringing in of the Maypole as " this stinkyng ydol ".[5] Here, in Iboland, we have something similar to the Maypole or to the " Jack-in-the-Green ", and for a like purpose, namely, to bring good fortune upon house and byre during the ensuing year. With just this reference, I must pass on to the subject of sacrifices. Chapter II is devoted to this in a general way; the resemblances to Jewish sacrifices have not been noted there.

As with the Israelites, so with the Ibos, there are distinct classes of sacrifices, more particularly those with and those without the shedding of blood. Again, it might be argued, that sacrifice is an almost universal practice among primitive peoples and that no marked significance can be attached to the Ibo customs. Still, our business is to trace similarities between the Israelitish and Ibo sacrifices.

The manual of the Hebrew sacrifices is found in Leviticus i–v. The Ibo, unfortunately, has no such handy reference; we are left to collect the information piecemeal.

First, the meat and drink offering. The Hebrew word " Minchah " rather indicates an offering made to secure or retain good-will. It really has the nature of a " present " in order to obtain favour, as the gift from Jacob to Esau described in Genesis xxxii. 13–18. So, too, the Ibo, in past days, invariably made similar offerings or presents to strangers on arrival. It was a regular ceremonial proceeding, and goods were always carried by travellers wherewith to make suitable return gifts.

It is rather difficult to disintegrate the various forms of sacrifice as so much is inextricably bound up together in the religious rites and ceremonies of the Ibos. I will allude to certain:

The *Iwa-ji*. A harvest thanksgiving corresponding to the

Feast of Tabernacles (Deut. xvi. 13). Likewise, " Ife-ji-oku ", also a thanksgiving for harvest. Reference has already been made to these in Chapter II.

In the matter of sin and trespass offerings we are on clearer ground. There is an inherent belief among the Ibos that the " blood is the life ", for it is the life of all flesh ; the blood of it is for the life thereof" (Lev. xvii. 14 ; Deut. xii. 23), and, further, the Ibo holds as strongly as the Jew that " without shedding of blood there is no remission (Heb. ix. 22). It is the only way known by which forgiveness of sin can be sought (cf. Lev. iv. 20). Among the Ibos, we find the underlying principle in all such sacrifices is that it is the blood alone which avails, the carcase is nothing ; it can be eaten or cast away, according to the nature and purpose of the sacrifice. As an instance of the Ibo's deep-seated belief that the blood is the life, let me relate an experience. I happened to be walking alone one morning and came upon two old men engaged in making a sacrifice. I will state the details briefly and leave out the non-essentials. The priest received a fowl from the suppliant, cut its throat and drained the blood into a small wooden bowl. He then took from the man a stick and smeared the blood upon it. The stick was about an inch in diameter ; a foot in length. The centre part had received so many coatings of blood that there was now an egg-shaped blob some three inches in diameter. When the ceremony was over, I asked the reason for it, and the old suppliant looked up pathetically and replied, " We are seeking life." The sacrifice had been repeated regularly for years, and the mass of congealed blood on the stick was the record of the offerings made ; life offered for life.

A full account of the " scape-goat " in Ibo sacrifice has been given on p. 60.

One of the most remarkable and definite instances of correspondence with Levitical procedure is connected with the rites for the presentation and redemption of the first-born son. The regulations in respect of the presentation of the first-born son among the Israelites are set forth in various passages of Exodus, Deuteronomy, &c., and the redemption is likewise commanded. We have it in the case of Our Lord (Luke 11. 22–3). " They brought Him to Jerusalem, to present Him to the Lord (as it is written in the Law of the Lord ' Every male that openeth the womb shall be called holy to the Lord ')."

Now this custom of presenting the first-born son used to exist, if it does not still, at Achi. The parents brought the babe to the sacred grove and there deposited it as the rightful property

SIMILARITIES BETWEEN ISRAELITES & IBOS

of the deity. It was left, that is, presented or devoted to the god ; in other words, abandoned to its fate. The action may have been prompted by fear, or it may have been the fulfilling of an ancient tradition that only the best gift would be acceptable to the god. The interest lies in subsequent procedure. On the birth of a second son, he also was brought and presented to the god but, in this instance, the father followed with a ram (sheep or goat) and the beast was substituted, and thus redemption was wrought for the son.

By Levitical custom, " If any man strive, and hurt a woman with child, so that her fruit depart from her, . . . he shall be surely punished, . . . and if any mischief follow, then thou shalt give life for life " (Gen. xxi. 22–3). Ibo practice is very similar. Compensation is demanded in respect of two lives. (*Vide* p. 259.)

" If a thief be found breaking up, and be smitten that he die, there shall be no blood shed for him " (Exod. xxii. 2). The Ibo considers it perfectly justifiable to kill or maim a thief caught in the act. In one case brought to the hospital, a suspected thief had been maltreated badly, the chief torture being two nails driven into his skull and flattened down so firmly that the bone had to be chiselled away before the nails could be levered up sufficiently to withdraw them. In some cases, the thief was killed off-hand and usually decapitated.

" If a man deliver unto his neighbour . . . any beast to keep, and it die, or be hurt, or driven away, no man seeing it, . . . or it be stolen from him, he shall make restitution unto the owner thereof " (Exod. xxii. 10–12). A similar law applies when an Ibo man places goods into the care of a neighbour. Restitution for any losses must always be made. Likewise, any offspring must be shared equally between the parties concerned.

" Thou shalt rise up before the hoary head, and honour the face of the old man " (Lev. xix. 32). Among the Ibos reverence for old age was a very marked feature. Education and contact with civilisation have weakened this ancient and honourable custom, which is much to be regretted.

Trial by ordeal arising from a spirit of jealousy, as set forth in Numbers v. 14 and following verses, has its counterpart in Ibo custom, though more commonly used in connection with witchcraft charges and accusations of poisoning.

Inhibitions and tabus with respect to food and drink imposed on individuals have some resemblance to the prohibitions which separated the Nazarites from the rest of the people of the community (Num. vi).

SIMILARITIES BETWEEN ISRAELITES & IBOS

In the matter of Inheritance, it is decreed in Numbers xxxvi. 7 that property shall not be removed from tribe to tribe ; for every one of the children of Israel shall keep himself to the inheritance of the tribe of his fathers. This question was raised in connection with the procedure where there was no male relative to inherit. This is Ibo law in principle. Property cannot be alienated from the family. A woman is married *into* the family and becomes a member of it hence, property is not transferable to another clan through inheritance. (*Vide* p. 268.)

The presumptuous and stubborn man according to Israelitish Law was to be put to death (Deut. xvii. 12). Likewise, the stubborn and rebellious son who refused obedience to father and mother was liable to be stoned with stones that he die (Deut. xxi. 18–21). The ancient Ibo method of dealing with similar unsatisfactory characters also resulted in violent ends for the culprits. (*Vide* p. 261.)

From Deuteronomy xxiv. 7 we learn that it was forbidden for an Israelite to steal or sell one of his brethren. It is so with the Ibos. A member of the clan may be held in pawn, but he cannot be sold to strangers. (*Vide* p. 255.)

Among the Israelites, a childless widow automatically became the wife of the deceased husband's brother (Deut. xxv. 5), and this is the law of the Ibos in essence. Actually, widows are inherited as part of a deceased man's property ; certainly a man would be expected to perform a husband's part on behalf of the widow of his deceased brother.

I anticipate that others, and especially my Ibo friends, will discover yet more comparisons and resemblances between Israelitish Law and ancient Ibo custom. It may not be of much significance, and prove no more than coincidence, but it is, nevertheless, an interesting subject.

Writing of Southern Guinea the Rev. J. Leighton Wilson states : " The traces of Judaism here are not less numerous than in other parts of Africa. Circumcision, bloody sacrifices, demoniacal possession, the observance of new moons, mourning for the dead, purifications, and other observances of like character are practised throughout the whole country " (" *Western Africa, 1856* ", p. 399) and this might with all truth be written of old Ibo life and custom.

Students desirous of further information on the subject should consult " *Hebrewisms in West Africa* ", by Joseph J. Williams, S.J. (George Allen & Unwin).

SIMILARITIES BETWEEN ISRAELITES & IBOS

NOTES TO CHAPTER XXXII

[1] "*Fetishism in West Africa*", p. 44.
[2] "*The Living Forces of the Gospel*", p. 35.
[3] Cf. "*Fetishism in West Africa*", p. 75.
[4] "The law of *Life* for *Life* among the Ibos is very strong, and is more to be dreaded than any other. Should any person, by accident or grudge, kill any of another family, life must go for life—there is no way of escape ; if the murderer or manslaughterer himself does not suffer for it, someone else in his family must ; and, again, if the person killed be a great person, and the manslaughterer be an inferior, this inferior person will not be accepted for the payment of the superior ; but some person of equal worth in the family must be delivered in his stead. Should this not be complied with now, the injured family keep quiet, and a watch is kept, it may be for years, and at an unguarded hour, when it appeared all things were forgotten and past, one of the injured family aims a deadly shot at a person of worth, equal with his slaughtered relative."—"*Niger Expedition*", p. 430.

An instance is quoted by the Rev. J. C. Taylor : "The people of Ogidi sent a man to Obori, in the room of a man they had killed some time ago, which had created the unhappy fightings which have incessantly occurred. Poor fellow ! he was killed to atone for the crimes of others. After he was killed they took the body home to bury it."—*Ibid.*, p. 353.

[5] "*The Golden Bough*", p. 123.

CHAPTER XXXIII

FIRESIDE STORIES

THE IBOS, IN COMMON with other West African tribes, have a great fondness for fairy tales. They have a big stock of legends and folklore. The examples recorded below lack one essential quality ; they can only be read, whereas they ought to be heard. On paper, expression and gesture are lost, and these are just the elements that make the stories live. The Ibo is a good story-teller, with a faculty of putting reality into fables. He uses as illustrations animals and birds in such a way that they seem to be endowed with human powers. He can conjure up an atmosphere, and carry his audience with him, and thus provide a thrilling entertainment. Some are good mimics and add to the enjoyment by emulating the sounds of the animals and birds they impersonate. A compilation of fables would provide entertaining reading and a large volume could easily be filled. To quote a few examples.

OLIJI AND HER THREE SUITORS

A rich man had a very beautiful daughter. His great love for her, and the fact that he was wealthy, led him to adopt the unusual practice first, of allowing her to choose a husband for herself and, secondly, that no bride-price should be demanded from the accepted suitor. Needless to say, many men aspired to become the husband of such a desirable maiden.

To all she returned an unfavourable answer until, one day, three men appeared who resembled each other very closely ; they were equally handsome and suitable. Hence, she was puzzled and felt unable to decide. She was prepared to accept one, but which one ?

To solve the problem, her father sought counsel of Ujakwu, a wise man. He advised that Oliji should accept the man who brought her the most wonderful gift.

So the men sailed to a distant country in search of a treasure that would win the coveted bride. After long journeying, one of them entered a shop and saw a box on which was written, " It carries you wheresoever you desire to go in a moment of

BURDENSOME, BUT HIGHLY PRIZED.

GIRLS WHO GLADLY CONFORM TO THE FASHION OF WEARING "NJA"—BRASS SPIRAL LEG RINGS. THEY ARE WORN PRIOR TO MARRIAGE. (PAGE 206.)

FIRESIDE STORIES

time." The man bought the box and, thereupon, told the other two that, now, they might all return home. To this pointed suggestion, the two were unwilling to agree, and threatened to kill the purchaser of the box unless he continued to accompany them in the prosecution of their quest.

In due time, the second man discovered and bought a mirror on which was inscribed, " Look in this and you will be able to see everything." The two who had succeeded sought to return home straightway, but the third man insisted on all three continuing the search. Eventually, he was rewarded and purchased a bottle of medicine which was guaranteed to restore the dead to life. Having completed their purchases, they considered the next step to be taken. The one who had bought the mirror determined to test the truth of its reputation. He gazed into the glass and, to his great amazement, discovered that the bride, for whom all three were competing, had recently died.

Thereupon, all entered the box and were immediately transported to the home of Oliji. Here they learned that she had been dead for some hours and that the corpse was already " dressed " for burial. The man who had secured the bottle of medicine hastened to test its properties. He anointed the hands and head of Oliji with the joyful result that she was restored to life.

Now arose a great discussion among the men. Which one of the three had brought back the most wonderful gift ? The owner of the mirror claimed that he was the right man to marry Oliji since, without his mirror, they would not have known that she was dead, and would still be in a distant country, and still be ignorant of the catastrophe.

The owner of the box was of the opinion that he was the right man. He said to the man with the mirror, " Yes, it is true that your glass revealed the fact that Oliji was dead, but what good would that knowledge have been unless my box had brought us here before she was buried ? Therefore, as possessor of the magic box, I am the one to marry her."

When the turn of the third man came he said, " Undoubtedly, what you both say is true, but it was my medicine that restored Oliji to life. It would have been of no avail our knowing she was dead, unless my medicine had proved successful."

As each was able to put forward a substantial claim for the hand of Oliji, the controversy seemed to be no nearer settlement. In his dilemma, Oliji's father again consulted Ujakwu, the wise man. His counsel was that the girl should be blindfolded and the man whom she touched should be accepted as her suitor. This advice was followed, and the owner of the medicine had the good fortune to become the husband of Oliji.

THE TORTOISE AND THE CRICKET

It came to pass that Tortoise was called upon to mourn the death of his father-in-law. The custom of the country was that a son-in-law must shed tears at the funeral ceremonies. The penalty of abstaining from tears was the forfeiture of his wife.

Now Tortoise, owing to his inability to shed tears, was in great distress at the thought of being deprived of his wife. All the other animals sympathised deeply and expressed their readiness to assist by any plan Tortoise might devise. The difficulty was that, though they might weep, not one could act as proxy for Tortoise. After much anxiety a cricket (Abuzu) came to the rescue.

An arrangement was made whereby the cricket should be hidden in the bag of Tortoise, while he should insert a soaked sponge under his hat. On arrival at the scene of bereavement, the assembled company looked eagerly for signs of mourning on the part of Tortoise. Acting upon pre-arranged signals between Tortoise and Cricket, the latter began to chirp :

> " Ga, tuga, tuga,
>   Ngalatu ;
> Ga, tuga, tuga,
>   Ngalatu ;
> Mbe je be ọgọ-ya
>   Ngalatu ;
> N'anya mili agbarọ-ya
>   Ngalatu ;
> Ga, tuga, tuga
>   Ngalatu."

The fifth and seventh lines translated are :
" Tortoise went to the home of his father-in-law ; he could not weep."

The other lines are onomatopœic, merely indicating the chirruping sounds of the cricket.

As Cricket raised his voice, Tortoise laid his hands upon his head as though torn with grief, while artfully pressing upon the sponge and thus causing drops of water to course down his cheeks. The spectators were astonished and marvelled that Tortoise, who had never been known to weep hitherto, was now showing such evident tokens of sorrow. He was led indoors to partake of refreshment. While eating as much as he wished himself, he offered no share to Cricket. Cricket resented the greediness of Tortoise and, being annoyed, bored a hole through the bottom of the bag and flew away.

When the meal was finished, Tortoise was called upon to weep again, and the multitude of animals stood by waiting for him to lead off as chief mourner. Unsuspectingly, Tortoise made signs for Cricket to begin his part, but, alas, no sounds were forthcoming. Tortoise was completely at a loss for he was helpless. He was declared to be a fraud and forced to suffer the loss of his wife. Greediness had led to his undoing. Had he been generously minded, and shared the food with Cricket, he would have retained his wife and been saved from chagrin and disappointment.

THE TORTOISE AND THE BEETLE

Why the Tortoise is in his present form

The Tortoise and the Beetle (" Nte " or " Tente ") were friends. Together they conspired to make a snare for catching other beasts. With this intention, they sought from a doctor a medicine which would attract their prey. After fulfilling their request, the doctor informed the pair that they must visit their trap daily with the exception of Ekke Day. Why they were to refrain on this particular day he did not tell them.

The tortoise, being cunning and crafty, made it a practice to visit the trap on the forbidden day, whereas the beetle accompanied him only on the other three days of the (Ibo) week.

On a certain Ekke Day, the tortoise went alone to the trap. To his amazement he found that, instead of a beast, a fairy had been caught. When he saw it was a fairy (ifilifi = a round object without limbs) he turned to run away, but the fairy said, " If you do not carry me home with you ' imii la anyai la ' " which, being translated, is " be round as I am ". The tortoise was hypnotised, and could not resist the spell placed upon him. He, therefore, carried off the " ifilifi ". On his way home, he called upon the beetle who, however, refused to come out to him.

When the tortoise arrived home he placed " ifilifi " on the ground with the intention of leaving her outside. Realising this, " ifilifi " cried out, " Take me inside for, if you do not, you shall be round." So " ifilifi " was taken into the house. When the tortoise wanted to eat, he climbed up into a space between the ceiling and the roof. As he was eating, a piece of yam fell down and betrayed him to "ifilifi", whereupon, he was bidden to yield up the food. This the tortoise found very disconcerting, and was puzzled what to do. He decided to set fire to his house and, in this way, destroy the fairy. He removed his goods by night, shut tight the door, and fired the house.

When morning came, the tortoise went to see what had happened and rejoiced to find that "ifilifi" had perished in the flames. The dead body was dripping with fat, hence tortoise deemed that it must be good to eat. He put forth his finger to touch the juicy morsel. Immediately he placed his finger in his mouth he was transformed into a round shape. In vain he cried to be restored to his former condition, but the fairy was dead, and could no longer exercise her gifts. The tortoise in his despair could only roll away. He then sought the aid of a carpenter and asked him to make openings in his shell in order that his legs might be freed.

Because of his disobedience and greediness the tortoise, whose limbs originally were similar to those of other animals, had to be content with just sufficient freedom to enable him to crawl.

WHY EVERY PERSON HAS THE REFLECTION OF ANOTHER MAN IN THE PUPIL OF HIS EYE

There was once a wicked couple, a man and wife, who were cannibals. When a child was born to them, they devoured it. Then came a time when another child was born. He was not an ordinary infant, for he stood and walked from the hour of his birth. The parents were not impressed by this extraordinary feat and, acting in accordance with previous custom, struck the boy on the head with a club preparatory to eating him. The result was not the same as hitherto inasmuch as the child showed no sign of injury. He told them that he would be known as "Ama-nne-ama-nna", (not acknowledging mother or father ; otherwise "Mischievous"). His parents, thereupon, seized an axe and a matchet wherewith to kill him. He started to run away and, as he was being chased, he cried aloud. The road immediately divided into two. His parents turned to the left and went astray, while he followed the right and escaped to the house of a farmer.

The farmer was very wealthy and his "ọba" was well stocked with yams. The lad entered the farmer's service as a house-boy. One day the farmer instructed the lad to roast some yams while he, himself, went away to work. On his return, he found that the boy had set fire to the yamstack. He, forthwith, seized his matchet in order to kill him for his mischievous act. The boy raced away to save his life and ran on until he came to a shrine.

The god who dwelt there made him one of his servants. He was engaged to take care of the stones with which, so the god said, he made men and women. He commanded the boy to wash the stones daily with hot and cold water respectively. Being of a mischievous nature, the boy reversed the order. The god became angry and sought to take the lad's life and, again, he was forced to flee. The god pursued him until the boy cried out in fear praying that the road would divide. On this occasion, however, there was no response to his appeal for aid. In his distress, the boy rushed to a palm tree. He climbed it and, as he reached the top, missed his hold and fell into a suspended palm-wine calabash.

The god called upon the owner of the calabash to remove it and drink the wine, in order that he might catch the boy when it was empty. While the man was drinking the wine, the boy sprang out of the calabash and entered his eye. Every effort to extract the boy was in vain. The god made gestures for the boy to come out while the boy beckoned the god to enter. So the boy is to be seen in every man's eye responding to the movements of the man gazing at him.

WHY THE RABBIT'S TAIL IS WHITE

A tortoise made friends with a rabbit and persuaded him to burrow a large hole in order to trap a leopard. When it was prepared, the tortoise went to a leopard and told him that he knew where a rabbit dwelt and it would be easy for them to catch it. The leopard agreed and followed the tortoise. The tortoise had already instructed the rabbit to have ropes in readiness with which to tie the leopard and had arranged the programme of operations.

On arrival at the hole, the tortoise first thrust in his hand. He brought out a few hairs and made the excuse that his arm was not long enough to take a firm grip of the rabbit. He said to the leopard, "Put in your hand." The leopard did so, and the rabbit immediately bound it with the rope. The tortoise said: "Try again with your other hand." The leopard did as he was advised only to have that hand seized and bound. The tortoise then urged him to thrust in his feet to assist him to free his hands. These also the rabbit tied with ropes. The tortoise then said, " Put in your head and bite the rabbit with your strong teeth and kill him." As soon as the leopard did this, a rope was passed around his neck and he was completely helpless. The tortoise and the rabbit then proceeded to kill the leopard.

The meat was taken to the tortoise's house to be cooked, and the old rabbit and her five young ones were invited to share the feast. While the meat was cooking, the old rabbit left the house for a short time whereupon, the tortoise seized the opportunity to betray the little ones. He ordered them to replenish the fire. Then he told each one in turn to lift the lid of the pot in order to see if the meat was cooking properly. As each one peeped into the pot, the tortoise gave it a push so that, in turn, they all fell into the boiling water.

Presently, the old mother rabbit returned ignorant of all that had happened during her absence. The tortoise told her to look to the fire. She did this, and then lifted the cover of the pot to see whether the meat was cooked. The tortoise, who was waiting for the opportunity, gave her a push and she, too, fell into the boiling water. But the water did not kill the rabbits ; only the youngest died from being suffocated by pressure from those above it.

In due time, the tortoise reckoned that the meal was ready and raised the lid of the pot. Immediately, the old rabbit and four of the young ones leaped out. They had managed to keep themselves above the water with the exception of their tails. These had been scalded and this is the reason why the tails of rabbits are white.

This is not the end of the story. As the rabbit sprang out of the pot, she flicked her tail and sprayed the boiling water on the eyes of the tortoise causing him to be blind. As he groped about, he missed the food and the rabbits ate it. He cried, " Anum, nwunyem, weta ndudu, weta ara garagham anya = Anum (female tortoise) my wife, bring a pin, bring a lance to open my eyes." His wife did as she was bidden, but only succeeded in making a little opening. This is the reason why the eyes of the tortoise are so small.

WHY THERE ARE TWO KINDS OF FROGS

A frog went to visit his father-in-law. He took with him a number of his companions. At the time it was very cold and soon all were shivering. His companions could not bear the cold and hopped into the fireplace to warm themselves. They urged the frog to join them, but he refused and remained where he was with the result that the cold caused his body to swell and to be covered with lumps (? gooseflesh).

By the time it was due for them to depart, the frog had become stiff with cold and could scarcely move at all. Moreover, his appearance had changed so much that his companions were ashamed to own him and they refused further association with him. This is the reason why there are two kinds of frogs, those that have clear skins and are always sunning themselves, and are able to jump nimbly, and those which are slow of movement and have rough spotted skins.

GOD AND THE TWO BROTHERS

There were two brothers and to each god gave a goat for safe keeping. One day, while the younger brother was cooking, the goat annoyed him by its continued bleating. In anger, the boy threw a palm-nut at the goat. It struck the goat with such force that it dropped down dead. Thereupon, the boy cried sorrowfully and carried the carcase to the owner. In answer to those who inquired how the goat had died he replied :

" Nkpulu-aku-o Kpalanuma !
Nkpulu-aku-o Kpalanuma !
Ya tigbu ewu Chukwu Kpalanuma !
Ewu Chukwu adachapu Kpalanuma !
Kamneje Kpalanuma !
Oliem isi m'neje Kpalanuma !
Nkpulu-aku-o Kpalanuma ! "

" O Palm-Nut, Kpalanuma !
Has killed god's goat, Kpalanuma.
And god's goat has died, Kpalanuma.
Let me depart, Kpalanuma.
If I die I must go, Kpalanuma.
If I live I must go, Kpalanuma.
O Palm-Nut, Kpalanuma ! "

The boy came to god's house and reported what had happened. God received him kindly and graciously forgave him. Food was prepared, and god placed two kinds before him, one choice (white) and the other inferior (black). The boy was told to choose the one he preferred. He chose the second and more unsavoury dish saying, " It is not right for me to eat the better and leave the worse for you."

When bedtime came, god brought two mats, a ragged worn one and a fine new one. Again, god told the lad to choose. For the same reason that he had chosen the poorer food so, now, he chose the old worn bed.

In the morning, god placed two boxes before him and invited him to take either the large or the small one. The boy accepted the latter. Then god permitted him to return to his home, at the same time giving him strict instructions that on no account must he open the box until all doors and windows had been securely closed.

The boy fulfilled these commands and, to his great surprise, discovered that the box contained all manner of riches so that he found himself to be a wealthy man. Filled with joy, he went to his elder brother with a present. At the sight of his brother's good fortune, however, the elder brother became filled with jealousy and rejected the proffered gift. Instead, he decided to imitate his brother's actions in the hope that he would likewise become wealthy.

So, the next day, he took a stick and killed the goat committed to his charge. He proceeded to carry the carcase to the house of god repeating, as he went along the road, the words sung by his brother, but substituting " stick " for " palm-nut ". The same gracious treatment was granted to him by god as that given to his younger brother. To him also was given the free choice of food. Unlike his brother, he chose the better. When nightfall came, the two mats were brought forth and, again, the youth chose the better for himself. Finally, when god placed two boxes before him, he took the larger one, because he coveted greater riches than those bestowed upon his brother.

He received a similar command to close all the doors and windows of his house before opening the box. On arrival, he opened the box only to find that he had brought home all manner of diseases. The result was that he died soon after his return.

The moral of the story is that he who loses his life shall save it and he who seeks to save his life shall lose it.

WHY THE SHELL OF THE TORTOISE HAS DIVISIONS

Among others, the tortoise was invited to attend a meeting to be held at the top of a big tree. The tortoise was puzzled how to reach the appointed place. As a possible way to solve the problem of transport, he appealed to the birds to lend him some feathers whereby he might fly to the top of the tree. So each bird gave him a feather and, with these, he contrived wings.

At the meeting, pride overtook him, and he strutted about boasting of his fine feathers. The birds were disgusted with his behaviour, and relieved him of the feathers they had loaned to him. When the business was concluded, all the birds flew away, leaving the tortoise marooned at the top of the tree. He cried loudly for help. In response to his cry, his wife appeared at the foot of the tree, but she could do nothing to help him in his predicament.

Seeing no other means of descending, he allowed himself to fall with the result that his shell was shattered to pieces. About that time, an ant was passing that way and the tortoise appealed to it for assistance. The ant set to work and fitted the broken pieces together to the great joy of the tortoise. He gave the ant a palm tree as a reward and the two became very great friends.

One day when the ant was collecting nuts from the tree, the tortoise, armed with a matchet, laid wait for him and, with a blow, divided him in sunder. He then exercised his knowledge of surgery and joined the two parts together again, at the same time remarking that each had conferred a similar benefit on one another and mutual service had put them on equal terms.

This is why the shell of the tortoise is serrated, and why the ant is in two parts linked together.

WHY MONKEYS ARE GOOD JUMPERS

In the olden days, the fruit of a certain tree was enjoyed by all the animals and birds generally. At the head of the animals was the tortoise. He called a meeting to discover who was really the owner of the tree. Meanwhile, neither bird nor beast was to touch the fruit. One day, however, a monkey, being very hungry, took of the forbidden fruit. When the tortoise was made aware that the fruit had been stolen, he called another meeting to discover the culprit. All declared that they were innocent of the charge. Not being satisfied with their denial, he called upon each to swear an oath and to undergo trial by ordeal. Each was to swear and then throw himself down from the tree. If he were innocent, no harm would befall him; if guilty, then he would perish.

So they assembled and proceeded with the trial. As each prepared to fall he said, " Let me fall and die if I am guilty of stealing the fruit." All the birds and beasts passed safely through the ordeal until it came to the turn for the monkey to swear and fall. He, the guilty one, changed the words and said, " Let me jump from tree to tree if I have stolen the fruit." He immediately became an expert jumper and has remained so ever since.

FIRESIDE STORIES

THE GREAT FAMINE

A great famine fell upon the land and all the animals suffered severely. In order to obtain relief, the tortoise, which was the head of the animals, called a meeting to discuss the situation. It was known as " the meeting of the dead and of the living ". The tortoise reminded them that their forefathers used to worship a certain tree called " Akpu ". Because of their disregard for him, the god had sent famine to punish them. The only way to remedy matters was to revive this service. He stated that he had seen in a dream, and had been confirmed in his opinion by means of charms, that they must, again, make sacrifice to " Akpu " even as their ancestors had done. All agreed that the advice was sound and a day was appointed for the service. " Oye " Day, fourteen days distant, was fixed for the ceremony. They were to prepare as they were able and to cook as much food as possible, and bring fowls for sacrifice.

On the day appointed, the animals appeared with their offerings. They placed the food at the foot of the tree. Then, the tortoise came forward, killed the fowls, and sprinkled the blood upon " Akpu ". When all was nearly ready, the tortoise ran to his house and took an " ekpilli " and an " uyọlọ ". With these he went back quietly and managed to secrete himself in a hole of the tree. Presently he shook the rattle (" ekpilli ") and made music on the " uyọlọ ". On hearing the sounds coming from the inside of the tree, the animals became quiet, and listened for any message that " Akpu " wished to make known to them. They heard words which startled them :

" Olili nni ọdi ndu ọnwu
Onye elili nni ọdi ndu ọnwu
Onye lie nni ọdi ndu ọnwu."

As soon as they grasped the meaning of this speech, the animals fled in consternation, for the words were to the effect that whoever ate of the food would die. The god had spoken, and their fear was greater than ever.

When darkness fell, the tortoise and his family collected the food, ate until they were replete and stored the remainder. While the rest of the animals continued in want, the tortoise and his dependants had no shortage.

In due time, the supply was exhausted, and the tortoise planned to repeat his tactics. He called another meeting of the animals and urged them once more to bring their sacrificial offerings, encouraging them by saying that, perhaps, on this occasion, " Akpu " would relent and send a favourable answer to their petitions. They fell in with the suggestion only to meet with a similar fright and loss of the food they had provided. Again, the tortoise and his family reaped the benefit by means of his cunning deceit.

Later, he persuaded the animals a third time, but, on this occasion, a monkey climbed a tree and kept watch in order to observe what really happened to the food. Presently, he saw the tortoise and his people come to gather it and, thus, they were caught in the very act of appropriating the food to their own use and benefit.

The monkey reported his discovery to the other animals. They decided that the tortoise should be killed as a punishment for his deceitful conduct. A friend sent a message to inform him of the fate awaiting him. In consequence, he remained quietly at home, planning what he should do to avert the threatened catastrophe. Finally, he decided to smear his body with oil and camwood dye to signify that he was suffering from sickness. Then he took his " ubọ-akwala " (stringed instrument, p. 361) and began to play.

" Ubọm ubọ ọgazi anutamgoli
Ubọ ọgazi anutamgoli."

When the animals heard the music, they were carried away by the sweetness of it ; they forgot the purpose for which they had met and, instead of killing the tortoise, they gave themselves over to dancing. As he played, he sang, and the animals were gratified to hear themselves mentioned in the songs with promises of honours to come. The monkey tried to bring them back to their purpose, but the animals paid no heed to his appeals.

Eventually, the tortoise became fatigued. With his fingernails, he cut the strings of his instrument and the music forthwith ceased. The animals wanted more of it, and asked him where they could purchase a new set of strings. He replied that new strings could only be bought at a place far distant. Thereupon, the hawk boasted of his flying powers and said that, even if it meant soaring up to the sky he would go and fetch some strings. The tortoise replied that this would not avail. The rabbit said that, even if it meant descending to the deepest part of the earth, he would burrow down until he reached the place where strings were to be obtained. One after another, the animals professed their willingness to strain every nerve to secure strings according to their strength and abilities.

FIRESIDE STORIES

The tortoise was highly gratified, because he now saw a way to rid himself of his enemy, the monkey. He told the animals that the strings must be extracted from the monkey; the sinews of this beast made the finest strings for his instrument. Thereupon, the animals set out to hunt the monkey. He sprang into a tree, the animals tried to follow and many of them fell down and were killed. Finally, the monkey climbed into an " ukọ " tree, the wood of which is so hard that the tree cannot be felled. So the monkey escaped, and the tortoise avoided the punishment he so richly deserved. So we have the proverb that " when a monkey is chased, it climbs an ' ukọ ' tree ", meaning that, " in time of danger, one seeks a safe place ", otherwise " any port in a storm ".

PROVERBS

Besides the wealth of folklore in the form of fables and legends, the Ibo has a generous store of proverbs which are continually brought into use. They are so profuse that often it is impossible to understand the full meaning of a conversation without knowing some of the more common ones. Frequently, a question is asked to which no direct answer is given; instead a proverb is quoted. It is always very apt to the occasion, but quite confusing to a person not acquainted with either the words or their interpretation. The following are a few examples of proverbs in common use among the Ibo people with whom I am acquainted.

Ọku rua nwata nke izizi ọ malu ife = The child which has first been burnt by the fire knows a thing = Once bit, twice shy. People learn from adversity.

Onye aghughọ nwuru ; onye aghughọ enie ya = The cunning man dies ; the cunning man buries him, or, The deceitful man dies, the deceitful man buries him.

Onye gwalu ọchinti na agha esu ? = Who told the deaf that the war had started ?

Atua inu nkilika nkata, onye talu aru aghọlu = When you speak a parable of an old basket, the one who is not in good health understands it = If the cap fits, wear it.

Ajọ ozi ananu ọsisọ = Bad news is heard quickly.

Mbekwu si na ọlu ikpo di nma, (ma olili ya adirọ nma) = The tortoise says that to labour in company is good (but to feed all is another question) = Many hands make light work.

Agwọ ta nwata nkita nke iboa ọ zelu ya = When a snake

FIRESIDE STORIES

bites a puppy twice he (the puppy) will shun it = Once bit, twice shy.

Ọnwu amarọ dike = Death does not recognise strength.

Adegbu dibia makana onye ọ nazọ nwulu = The doctor is never killed because his patient dies.

Netinye ego n'akpa, makana adamama = Put money in the bag, because one never knows (what may happen). Equivalent to our " Put by for a rainy day ".

Ncha gbọ, ncha agbọ, echukọm iyi akwa ? = Whether soap washes or does not, am I going to wash clothes ? An expressive way of saying " I don't care ".

Ikengam kwu ọtọ tata = My god is standing up straight to-day. Life is very good = prosperous.

Aka nni kwọ aka ekpe ; aka ekpe akwọ aka nni ; fa nabọ di ọcha = The right hand washes the left ; the left hand washes the right, that both may be clean. It is natural and right to help one another.

Onye nagbacharọ okpu ofufu ameli ife = He who does not wipe away sweat shall not eat.

Ọ ka onye ka chi ya = He who is greater than one is also greater than one's own god.

Ofu nne namu ma ofu chi adi eke = One mother brings forth children, but they are not created by one god, that is, children of the same parents have different characteristics.

Chi onye adi n'izu ma ọnwu egbune ya = If one's own god is not in the meeting death will not kill him.

Ebe onye dalu ka chi ya kwatulu ya = Where one falls, there his own god pushes him down.

Akpanye nwa nkita n'aru ọ taka akwa = When you play with a puppy he tears your clothes. This has a similar meaning to " Familiarity breeds contempt ". It is used when an adult is treated unceremoniously by children or servants.

Niri kam za unọ bu ọchuchu = Arise, that I may sweep the house is driving (the visitor) away. This is equivalent to " Your company is no longer acceptable ".

Onye lue n'ani anebe nti ọ belu nke ya tinye = When one reaches a land where men cut off the ears, he cuts off his own. Cf. " When in Rome do as Rome does."

Asusu onye adadia ntulu = One's own language is never hard.

Ebe onye bi k'ọ nawachi = It is the place one lives in that he repairs. " Charity begins at home."

Enenia nwa ite ọgbọnyua ọku = A small despised pot will boil over and put out the fire. A man may appear insignificant and yet be overflowing with energy and ability.

FIRESIDE STORIES

Okelekwu amanuma ta akpa dibia ; ma dibia amanuma bu okelekwu ǫnu = Let not the rat wilfully tear the doctor's bag ; and let not the doctor wilfully curse the rat. The idea is, a child may take certain liberties with his elders, but let him not go too far lest he bring punishment upon himself. Likewise, let not the elder trifle with the child lest the child turn against him and curse him.

Adeji ife anagba na nti agba n'anya = We do not wash our eye with that with which we wash our ear. Precious things are not to be trifled with.

Akpa ǫfu ananya n'obi = New brooms sweep clean.

Kabia, kabia nalu awǫ epuna ǫdu = Wait, wait, hindered frog from having a tail. Procrastination is the thief of time. Never put off till to-morrow what ought to be done to-day.

K'ǫdi nǫfu = Let it be so ; that is enough. A useful and convenient expression when one wishes to bring an argument to a conclusion. It also serves the appropriate purpose of applying " *Finis* " to this volume.

BIBLIOGRAPHICAL NOTE TO THE 1966 EDITION

By JOHN RALPH WILLIS

George T. Basden's *Niger Ibos* remains a fundamental study of many aspects of Ibo life and culture. The fruit of thirty-five years' residence among the Ibo, the book is unique in that its author's account of ancient customs and traditions reflects his access to things ordinarily forbidden the stranger.[1] In view of the profound changes which have been and are taking place within the fabric of Ibo society, it seems certain that scholars will long be indebted to Dr. Basden for his recording of a way of life which might otherwise have been lost to posterity.

For this second edition it has been thought beneficial to bring the reader up to date with the wide range of research conducted among the Ibo[2] since Basden's time. Those who would require a more detailed list of works on specialized subjects should consult Daryll Forde and G. I. Jones, *The Ibo and Ibibio-Speaking Peoples of South-eastern Nigeria* (Ethnographic Survey of Africa, International African Institute, London, 1950, pp. 9-67) and Simon Ottenberg's supplement to this survey in

---

[1] See *Journal of the African Society*, July, 1938, p. *394*.
[2] It should be borne in mind that the Ibo did not formerly constitute a unified political group and that among the main groupings there exist differences in social organization, political structure, and religious belief. They can, however, be looked upon as one people insofar as they share a common heritage and geographical location and speak a number of related dialects. They are situated generally in South-eastern Nigeria in the provinces of Onitsha, Owerri, Rivers, Ogoja, Benin, and Warri and have been grouped into five main divisions: (1) Northern or *Onitsha* Ibo (a—Western or *Nri-Awka*; b—Eastern or *Elugu*; c—*Onitsha* Town); (2) Southern or *Owerri* Ibo (a—*Isu-Ama*; b—*Oratta-Ikwerri*; c—*Ohuhu-Ngwa*; d—*Isu-Item*); (3) Western Ibo (a—Northern *Ika*; b—Southern *Ika* or *Kwale*; c—Riverain); (4) Eastern or Cross River Ibo (a—*Ada (Edda)*; b—*Abam-Ohaffia*; c—*Aro*); and (5) North-Eastern Ibo, called *Ogu Uku*. See Daryll Forde and G. I. Jones, *The Ibo and Ibibio-Speaking Peoples of South-Eastern Nigeria*, p. 10.

BIBLIOGRAPHICAL NOTE

African Studies (14, 2, 1955, pp. 63-85). For the reader's convenience, this bibliography has been divided topically into seven sections: (I) *General Studies;* (II) *History, Literature, Arts & Crafts;* (III) *Social Organization and Political Structure;* (IV) *Education and Community Development;* (V) *Religion;* (VI) *Economy;* and (VII) *Ecology* and *Social Change.*

I GENERAL STUDIES

"Akwa: Town of Smiths," *Nigeria*, 61, 1959, pp. 136-156. *Akwa* lies between *Onitsha* and *Enugu.* Many illustrations.

Basden, G. T., *Among the Ibos of Nigeria*, 1921. (New impression, Frank Cass & Co. Ltd.)

Dike, K. Onwuka, *Trade and Politics in the Niger Delta* 1830-1885, 1956.

Forde, Daryll and Jones, G. I., *The Ibo and Ibibio-Speaking Peoples of Southeastern Nigeria*, 1950. The standard short work on the subject.

Green, Margaret, *Igbo Village Affairs.* (2nd edition, 1964, Frank Cass & Co. Ltd., contains new preface by the author commenting on changes which have occurred since its first publication.) Work is chiefly with reference to the Village of *Umueke Abgaja* in the *Isu-Ama* group of Southern Ibo. See also review by G. I. Jones cited in III *Social Organization and Political Structure.*

Jones, G. I., *The Trading States of the Oil Rivers*, 1963. Subtitled "A Study of Political Development in Eastern Nigeria."

Leith-Ross, S., *African Conversation Piece* (A Picture of Ibo Life), 1944.

Leith-Ross, S., *African Women*, 1939 (reprint, 1965).

Meek, C. K., *Law and Authority in a Nigerian Tribe: A Study in Indirect Rule.* (2nd impression, 1950.) Contains chapters on Ibo history, Environment, Religion, Social and Political Structure, Titles, Kinship, Age-Grades, Law and Administration, Law of Marriage, Birth and Training of Children, Death and Inheritance.

Murdock, George Peter, *Africa Its Peoples and Their Culture History*, 1959. See Chapter 31.

Nzekwu, J. O., "Onitsha," *Nigeria*, 50, 1956, pp. 200-233. Sketches *Onitsha* history from traditional accounts.

Ottenberg, Simon, "The Development of Local Government in a Nigerian Township," *Anthropologica*, n.s. 4, 1, 1962, pp. 121-161.

Ottenberg, Simon, "The Present State of Ibo Studies," *Journal of the Historical Society of Nigeria*, volume 2, no. 2, December 1961, pp. 211-230. Reviews the major forms of research and the publications on the Ibo since World War II and makes recommendations for types of research projects that would be of value in the future. Bibliography.

Talbot, P. Amaury, *The Peoples of Southern Nigeria*, 4 vols., 1926. Contains mine of information on various tribes of Southern Nigeria, including the Ibo. Volume I History; Volumes II and III Ethnology; and Volume IV Languages and Statistics. Study evolved out of 1921 Census.

BIBLIOGRAPHICAL NOTE

Talbot, P. Amaury, *The Tribes of the Niger Delta*, 1932.

Wood, A. H. St. John, "Nigeria: Fifty Years of Political Development Among the Ibos" in *From Tribal Rule to Modern Government*. (13th Conference of the Rhodes-Livingstone Institute for Social Research, 1959, pp. 121-136.)

II HISTORY, LITERATURE, ARTS AND CRAFTS

Achebe, Chinua, *Things Fall Apart*, 1958. A novel about the Ibo.

Azikiwe, Nnamdi, "Fragments of Onitsha History," *The Journal of Negro History*, 15, 1930, pp. 474-97. An early study by the first President of Nigeria, himself an Ibo.

Boston, J. S., "Notes on Contact Between the Igala and the Ibo," *Journal of the Historical Society of Nigeria*, Volume 2, No. 1, December 1960, pp. 52-58. Summarizes evidence from traditional and written historical sources about the relationship of some of the Ibo-speaking peoples with their neighbours, the Igala, who live north of Ibo territory between the left bank of the Niger and the country of the Idoma peoples.

Chadwick, E. R., "An Ibo Village Art Gallery," *Nigerian Field*, 4, 4, October 1935, pp. 175-183.

Ewo, Dixon Ogaranya, *History and Customs of Ogbaland*, 1952.

Field, J. M. O., "Bronze Castings found at Igbo, Southern Nigeria," *Man*, 40, 1, January 1940, pp. 1-6. First report on castings found at Igbo, Awka Division. See recent articles by Shaw (cited below) who followed up Field's study.

Ike, A., *The Origin of the Ibos*, 1951, 44 pp. Attempts to establish Hebrew origins of Ibo by use of historical material from the Bible and cultural data.

Kalu, Eke, "An Ibo Autobiography," *Nigerian Field*, 7, 4, October 1938, pp. 158-170.

Murray, K. C., "Ogbom" (Ibo Carvings), *Nigerian Field*, 10, October 1941, pp. 127-131.

"Nri Traditions," *Nigeria*, 54, 1957, pp. 273-288. Ibo clan which author claims has tended more than other Ibo clans to keep its life based on ancient traditions.

Nzekwu, J. O., "Ofala Festival," *Nigeria*, 61, 1959, pp. 104-122. The *Onitsha* festival of the year, climaxing the New Yam Festival, the traditional annual, thanksgiving celebration.

Nzekwu, Onuora, "Ibo Dancing," *Nigeria Magazine*, 73, June 1962, pp. 35-43. Author claims dancing remains the most developed and most important art form of the Ibo as well as their most important pastime.

Shaw, Thurstan, "Excavations at Igobu-Ukwu, Eastern Nigeria: An Interim Report," *Man*, 60, 210, November 1960, pp. 161-164. Follow up to Field's report in which author estimates dates of castings discovered to be 17th century. Findings seemed to represent sacred vessels and regalia of a former day as kept in storage between ceremonies. Burial uncovered appeared to be that of actual former *Eze Nri* (Priest-king). See also Shaw's articles in *West African Review*, 31, 197, pp. 30-37, and *Journal Historical Society of Nigeria*, Vol. 2, No. 1, pp. 162-165.

BIBLIOGRAPHICAL NOTE
III SOCIAL ORGANISATION AND POLITICAL STRUCTURE

Ardener, Edwin W., " Lineage and Locality Among the Mba-Ise Ibo," *Africa*, 29, 2, April 1959, pp. 113-133. Discusses inter-relationships between lineage, territorial organization, and other kinds of groupings of an exceptionally dense population (186,300 people confined to 167 sq. miles), in *Owerri* Division.

Ardener, Edwin W., " The Kinship Terminology of a Group of Southern Ibo," *Africa*, 24, 2, April 1954, pp. 85-99. Evolved out of 2½ year study of administrative unit of *Mba-Ise*.

Brown, Paula, " Patterns of Authority in West Africa," *Africa*, 21, 4, October 1951, pp. 261-278. Concerns eight West African societies, including the Ibo, analyzing authority exercised by persons holding certain positions in kinship groups, associations, and states, as well as total pattern of authority in societies having certain combinations of these groups.

Chinwuba Obi, S. N., *The Ibo Law of Property*, 1963. Study by a Nigerian lawyer of the Ibo customary law relating to property.

Chubb, L. T., *Ibo Land Tenure*, 115 pp., 1961 (first published by Gaskiya Corporation 1947, this second issue is by Ibadan University Press). Result of 1945 recommendation by committee headed by Lord Hailey to investigate land tenure in Africa. Author urged wider participation of experts in fields of anthropology and agriculture in coping with problems of land tenure in six localities.

Esenwa, F. A., " Marriage Customs in Asaba Division," *Nigerian Field*, 13, 2, October 1948, pp. 71-81.

Green, Margaret, *Land Tenure in an Ibo Village* (London School of Economics Monographs on Social Anthropology, No. 6), 1941.

Harris, Jack, " Some Aspects of Slavery in South-eastern Nigeria," *Journal of Negro History*, 27, 1, January 1942, pp. 37-54.

Horton, W. R. G., " The Ohu System of Slavery in a Northern Ibo Village Group," *Africa*, 24, 1954, pp. 311-335. Discusses role of *Nike* (village group to immediate north-east of Enugu, capital of Eastern Provinces of Nigeria) who tradition held to be principal slave-traders in northern Iboland before advent of British administration.

Jeffreys, M. D. W., " Dual Organization in Africa," *African Studies*, 5, 2, June 1946, pp. 82-105.

Jones, G. I., " Dual Organization in Ibo Social Structure," *Africa*, 19, 2, April 1949, pp. 150-156. Review article of Margaret Green's *Igbo Village Affairs*.

Jones, G. I., " Ibo Age Organization with Special Reference to the Cross River and North-eastern Ibo," *Journal of the Royal Anthropological Institute*, 92, 2, July-December 1962, pp. 191-211.

Jones, G. I., " Ibo Land Tenure," *Africa*, 19, 4, October 1949, pp. 309-323. Remarks limited to Northern, Southern, and Cross-River Ibo. Concerns land tenure in relation to social structure and processes of change in population density, soil-types, and other socio-ecological conditions.

Meek, C. K., " Ibo Law " (in Essays to C. G. Seligman), 1934.

Meek, C. K., *Report on Social and Political Organization in the Owerri Division*, 1933.

BIBLIOGRAPHICAL NOTE

Ottenberg, Simon, " Double Descent in an Ibo Village-group." (*Selected Papers of the 5th International Congress of Anthropological & Ethnological Sciences, Philadelphia*, 1-9 September 1956, ed. by A. F. L. Wallace, pp. 473-481.)

Rowling, C. W., *Notes on Land Tenure in Benin, Kuruku, Ishan and Asaba Divisions of Benin Province*, 1948.

Spörndli, J. I., " Marriage Customs Among the Ibos," *Anthropos*, 37-40, 1-3, 1942–1945, pp. 113-121. Explains marriage customs of Ibo in terms of their religious nature, economy, and culture.

Thomas, Northcote W., *Anthropological Report on the Ibo-speaking Peoples*, 6 vols., 1913–1914. For a critique of Part IV: Law and Custom of the Ibo of the Asaba District, Southern Nigeria, see Hartland, E. S., " Ibo-Speaking Peoples of Southern Nigeria," *Journal of the African Society*, 14, 1915, pp. 271-277. Part I of Thomas's Report is Law and Custom of the Ibo of the Awka Neighbourhood, Southern Nigeria.

Wieschhoff, H. A., " Divorce Laws and Practices in Modern Ibo Culture," *Journal of Negro History*, 26, 3, July 1941, pp. 299-324.

Wieschhoff, H. A., " Social Significance of Names Among the Ibo of Nigeria," *American Anthropologist*, 43, April 1941, pp. 212-222. Naming customs and interpretation and social significance of names, European influences.

IV EDUCATION AND COMMUNITY DEVELOPMENT

Chadwick, E. R., " Communal Development in Udi Division," *Oversea Education*, 19, 2, January 1948, pp. 627-644. Discusses problems and political effects of mass education in *Udi*, a Division of *Onitsha* Province.

Chadwick, E. R., " Mass Education in Udi Division," *African Affairs*, 47, 186, January 1948, pp. 31-41. Concerns self-help project among local inhabitants in reading and writing.

Ottenberg, Simon, " Improvement Associations Among the Afikpo Ibo," *Africa*, 25, 1, January 1955, pp. 1-28. *Afikpo* are Eastern Ibo who reside between the headquarters of *Afikpo* Division, *Ogoja* Province, South-eastern Nigeria and the Cross River to the east. Covers economic, educational, political and social improvement activities directly related to changing cultural conditions.

Ottenberg, Simon, " The Development of Village ' Meetings ' among the Afikpo People," pp. 186-205 (a publication of the *Annual Conference Sociology Section*, March 1953, West African Institute of Social and Economic Research, University College, Ibadan). Discusses village ' improvement ' unions among the *Afikpo*.

V RELIGION

Boston, John, "*Alosi* Shrines in Udi Division," *Nigeria*, 61, 1959, pp. 157-165. The *Alosi* are spirits which are said to occupy forests and rivers lying on fringes of cultivated land. " They are regarded as the spiritual owners of tracts which they occupy, and their shrines are prominent landmarks within their territory, such as large trees, stones, or shady pools."

Correia, R. P. J. Alves, " L'animisme Ibo et les divinités de la Nigéria," *Anthropos*, 16-17, 1921–1922, pp. 360-366. Includes sections on L'idée de Dieu. Produit d'importation: Les dieux Divinités universelles; Divinités locales; and Nature des divinités conçues par l'Ibo.

BIBLIOGRAPHICAL NOTE

Correia, R. P. J. Alves, " Le Sens moral chez les Ibos de la Nigéria," *Anthropos*, 18-19, 1923-1924, pp. 880-889. Topics covered are La justice; L'Amour, La Vérité; Tempérance, Pudeur nigérienne; and Obéissance a la loi du pays et discipline.

Correia, R. P. J. Alves, " Vocables religieux et philosophiques des peuples Ibos," *Bibliothecha Africana*, 1, 1925, pp. 104-113.

Horton, W. R. G., " God, Man, and the Land in a Northern Ibo Village-group," *Africa*, 26, 1, January 1956, pp. 17-28. Explains Ibo conceptions of the deity. Study conducted among the *Nike*.

Jeffreys, M. D. W., " Ikenga: the Ibo Ram-headed God," *African Studies*, 13, 1, March 1954, pp. 25-40. Discusses religious cult associated with good fortune, success, and the ability and strength of the right arm. Mentions other instances of the Ram-headed god, including the ancient Egyptian rite from whence the author asserts is derived the ram-god cults of the rest of Africa.

Jeffreys, M. D. W., " The Divine Umundri King," *Africa*, 8, 3, July 1935, pp. 346-354. Describes coronation-ceremony of two divine kings who are the spiritual heads of the *Umundri* Ibo of *Onitsha* Province.

Jeffreys, M. D. W., " The Umundri Tradition of Origin," *African Studies*, 15, 3, September 1956, pp. 119-131. Result of survey begun in 1930 under auspices of Nigerian government to uncover magico-religious beliefs of Ibo in the environs of *Awka* Division.

Leith-Ross, S., " Notes on the Osu System Among the Ibo of Owerri Province, Nigeria," *Africa*, 10, 1937, pp. 206-220. The *Osu* group in this province traditionally held task of offering sacrifices on behalf of their masters and of tending the shrines of the *jujus* (i.e., spirit-like deities).

Noon, John A., "A Preliminary Examination of the Death Concepts of the Ibo," *American Anthropologist*, 44, October-December 1944, pp. 638-654. The author used an Ibo informant for his investigations.

O'Donnell, W. E., " Religion and Morality Among the Ibo of Southern Nigeria," *Primitive Man*, 4, 4, 1931, pp. 54-60.

Ottenberg, Simon, " Ibo Oracles and Intergroup Relations," *Southwestern Journal of Anthropology*, 14, 3, Autumn 1958, pp. 295-317. Based on research conducted on *Afikpo* Village Group. Author traces origin and expansion of organizations associated with oracles which he claims derive from the European and American slave trade along Eastern coast of Nigeria between about 1650 and 1850. Study is concerned with how oracles organizations functioned to provide a degree of integration of these Ibo groups.

Thomas, Northcote W., " Some Ibo Burial Customs," *Journal of the Royal Anthropological Institute*, 1917, pp. 160-213.

VI ECONOMY

Ardener, Shirley G., " The Social and Economic Significance of the Contribution Club Among a Section of the Southern Ibo," pp. 128-142. A publication of the *Annual Conference, Sociology Section, March 1953*, University College, Ibadan. (West African Institute of Social and Economic Research, University College, Ibadan.)

BIBLIOGRAPHICAL NOTE

Forde, Daryll, and Scott, Richenda (edited by Margery Perham), *The Native Economies of Nigeria*, 1946. Part II, Chapter 3 deals with the Southern Ibo community of the *Ozuitem* Ibo of Bende. Topics discussed are Land rights; Farm labour and Food Supplies; Oil-Palm and Other Production for Exchange. Other parts of chapter concern Ibo Economy in a Congested Area: Migrant Wage Labour, Accumulation of Currency, and Levies of Consumption.

Hair, P. E. H., " Enugu: an Industrial and Urban Community in East Nigeria, 1914-1953," pp. 143-167. A publication of the *Annual Conference, Sociology Section, March* 1953, University College, Ibadan. (West African Institute of Social and Economic Research, University College, Ibadan.)

Harris, Jack, " Papers on the Economic Aspect of Life among the Ozuitem Ibo," *Africa*, 14, 1, January 1943, pp. 12-23. Mainly concerned with agriculture and the division of labour between the sexes in crop cultivation.

Harris, Jack, " Some Aspects of the Economics of Sixteen Ibo Individuals," *Africa*, 14, 6, April 1944, pp. 302-335. Study of annual monetary incomes and expenditures of sixteen Ibos living in community of *Ozuitem*.

Jones, G. I., " Agriculture and Ibo Village Planning," *Farm and Forest*, 6, 1, 1945, pp. 9-15.

VII ECOLOGY AND SOCIAL CHANGE

Jones, G. I., " Ecology and Social Structure Among the North-eastern Ibo," *Africa*, 31, 2, April 1961, pp. 117-134. Attempt to show how effects of new environment modified features of the social structure of the *Ezza, Ikwo, Izi*, and *Ngbo* tribes.

Ottenberg, Simon, " Ibo Receptivity to Change," in *Continuity and Change in African Cultures* (ed. Bascom, W. R., & Herskovits, M. J., 1958, pp. 130-143). Author asserts " Ibo probably most receptive to culture change and most willing to accept Western ways of any large group in Nigeria."

Ottenberg, Phoebe, " The Changing Economic Position of Women Among the Afikpo Ibo," in *Continuity and Change in African Cultures* (ed. Bascom, W. R., & Herskovits, M. J., 1958, pp. 205-223). One of several studies conducted among Ibo women after the *Aba* riots of December 1929 in which women attacked administrative authorities. Riots are said to have revealed how ill-suited Indirect Rule was for the Ibo.

John Ralph Willis

London, 1965

A MAP OF
SOUTHERN NIGERIA

MAP OF

Drawn by

Boundaries of

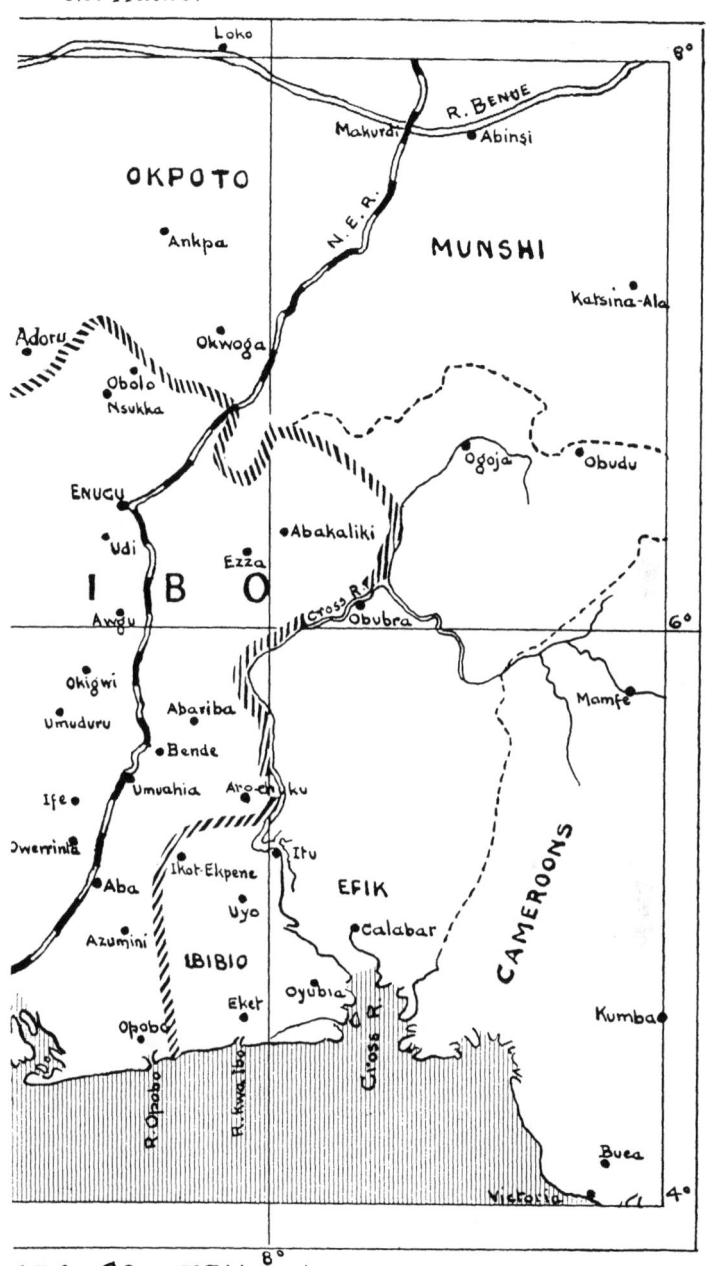

S. NIGERIA
the Author

IBO COUNTRY hatched

INDEX

Aboh, 111, 113, 114, 121, 294
Abutshi, 114
Adornment, bodily, 197, 199, 204, 205
Adultery, 60, 66, 233, 234, 418
Affinity, laws of, 215, 417
Age-grades, 194, 223
Agriculture, 192, 208, 238, 265, 300
Aggry beads, 198, 202
"*Albert*", s.s., 112
Albinos, 124, 388
"*Alburkah*", s.s., 111
Anklets and bracelets, 137, 139, 198, 207, 222, 319
Ancestral spirits (*see* Okpensi, Glossary), 57, 167, 266, 281
Animism, 35, 37, 214, 280
Ante-natal customs, 168
Archery, 343
Asaba, 114, 115, 276, 294
— mats, 326
Athletics, 354
Attendance, School, 190, 209
Awka blacksmiths, 77, 192, 195, 205, 312, 318, 379

Babies, treatment of, 172
Baikie, Dr. W. B., 112
Bamboo mats, 315, 316
Banking, 340
Battak heathenism, 413
Battles, 195, 244, 377
Beads, 198, 222
Beds, 154
Beecroft, Consul, 112

Being, the Supreme, 36, 37, 46, 59, 283, 413
Beliefs, religious, 266
Bende, 115
Benin, 121, 131, 225, 321, 382, 386
Betrothal, 216, 217, 218, 220
Bigamy, 235
Birth customs, 167, 172
Blacksmiths, 192, 195, 205, 318
Body painting, 222, 329
Bonny, 115
Bows and arrows, 342
Brass rods, 337
Breaking " Ju-ju ", 61
Bride price, 216, 218, 223, 227, 232, 240, 268
British Government, 131, 133, 143, 145, 192, 243, 249, 257, 264, 298, 379, 385
Building and decorating, 312, 316
Burial rites, 269, 289
Burton, Sir Richard, 417
Buxton, Sir T. F., 111

Camwood stain, 103, 223, 271, 273, 276, 284, 330
Cannibalism, 126, 129, 195
Capital crime, 259, 391
— punishment, 259, 262, 416
Carpentry, 322
Carrier problem, 129
Carving, 316
Charms, 48, 51, 55
Chiefs, 131, 133, 381

451

INDEX

Child stealing, 243
Childbirth, 167, 172
— seclusion after, 172, 175
Children, 180, 188, 209, 245, 248, 282
— dedication of, 175
Cicatrisation, 192, 222, 224, 331
Circumcision, 176, 213, 417
Clay eating, 171
— puddling, 195, 312
Climate, 118
Cloth, native, 325
Clubs, day and night, 366
— women's, 209, 225, 335
Cocoanut palms, 117, 314, 400, 408
Compounds, 151, 154
Cooking, 155, 156
Cotton spinning, 325
Courtship, *see* Marriage
Cowrie shells, 337
Craw-craw, 180, 193
Crowther, Archdeacon D. C., 69
Currency, 336

Dancing, 342, 343
Death ceremonies, 269
Dedication of children, 175
Deities, 246, 249
Dentistry, 198
Devil, the, 36, 37, 276
Discipline, lack of, 189, 200
Divination, 51, 76, 86, 91, 251
Divorce, 228, 235, 239
Domestic slavery, 258
Dowry, 216, 218, 223, 227, 232, 240, 268
Drums, 173, 295, 336, 345, 358, 359
"Dug-out" canoes, 113, 120, 303, 350

Earth goddess, 98, 99, 107, 412

Elms, Sister Mary, 185, 186
Engagements, 214, 216, 218
Etiquette, 161
Evil doers, 261, 296, 422
Exchange, 337

Fables, 424
Farming, 148, 255, 265, 300, 390
Festivals, 67
Fetishes, 45, 48
Fishing, methods, 302
Fishing-nets, 302
Flora, 113, 117, 147
Folklore, 424
Food problems, 337, 396
Furniture, 153, 199
Future life, 36, 143, 282

Gall-bladder, 157
Gambling, 351, 353
Games, 342, 350, 354
Gibson, Miss, 35

Hair-dressing, 208, 210, 222, 224
Handiwork, women's, 392
Harlotry, 103, 239
Harmattan, 118
Herodotus, 110, 176
Hoe, native, 301, 321
Household utensils, 155
Houses, 244, 265, 312, 316
Human sacrifices, 60, 72, 126, 252, 292, 385
Hunting, 117, 306
Huts, 151, 154, 196, 312

Ibn Batuta, 110
Ibo Country, 110, 115, 119
— People, 110, 121
— Week, 151, 334
Igarra People, 281, 294, 367
Ijaw People, 113

INDEX

Implements, 301, 318
Indigo stain, 284, 330
Infant mortality, 180, 190, 200, 236
Infanticide, 180, 181, 220, 259, 262, 290
Inheritance, 208, 215, 239, 264, 268, 422
Initiatory rites, 89, 134, 213
Innocency, 214
Insect pests, 119
Insignia, chief's, 135, 136, 139
Intoxicants, 125, 129, 197
Iroko tree, 114, 148
Israelites, 56, 214, 411

Jekri People, 113
Joliba, River, 110

Kafir customs, 182
Kernels, palm, 405
Kidd, Dudley, 182
Kidnapping, 243, 244
Kingsley, Mary, 338
Koko yam (edde), 68, 149, 208, 378, 379
Kola nuts, 161, 165
— tenancy, 264

Laird, Mr. John, 112
Laird, Mr. Macgregor, 111, 112
Laird's Port, 114
Land tenure, 57, 264, 394, 415
Lander, the brothers, 111
Language, 115, 198, 243, 415
Leg rings, 206, 207, 223, 338
Leo Africanus, 110
Leopard-killer, 308
— traps, 308
Lepers, 58, 241, 276
Levitical Law, 411
Lex Talionis, 415
Liquor Traffic Commission, 340

" Little Dries ", 118
Livingstone, Dr. David, 413
Long " Ju-ju ", 78, 250
Looms, 326
Love, 214

Manatee, 305
Mangroves, 113, 120
Manillas, 199, 337, 338, 341
Manners, 161
Manslaughter, 259
Manslayer, 309
Marital relations, 151, 226, 230
Marketing, 204, 334
Markets, 150, 151, 247, 249, 334
Marriage, 176, 203, 207, 213, 221, 256, 331
— annulment of, 241
— ordinance, 234, 239
Masks, 323, 368, 414
Matrilineal succession, 268
Mats, 326
— palm-leaf, 315, 316
Maw (night), 366, 369
Maw-Afia, 366
May-Pole, 419
Mbari houses, 98
Meek, Mr. C., 177
Menstruation, 61, 62, 68, 104, 205, 214, 223, 232, 417
Messages, transmitting, 273, 358
Metamorphosis, 286
Miscarriage, 170, 171, 173
Miscegenation, 215, 234
Moats, 386
Mourning, 270, 278, 289
Mud-treading, 196
Murder, 359, 416
Music, 356, 363

Naming of children, 174, 175
Nassau, Rev. Dr., 413

INDEX

Necklaces, 171, 207, 279, 291
Niger, River, 110, 113
Night maws (spirits), 366, 369
Nri, town of, 115, 251, 262, 403, 416
— priests of, 59, 115, 182, 192, 210, 291

Oaths, 57, 61, 379, 383
Obi Ossai, 114
Objects of worship, 246
Oil, extraction of palm, 337, 398, 399, 404
Okosi, King Samuel, 70
Oldfield, Dr., 215, 258
Oldham, Dr., 35
Onitsha, 69, 70, 113, 114, 121, 126, 131, 204, 207, 220, 243, 277, 286, 290, 294, 308, 367, 405
Ophiolatry, 41
Oracles, 76, 250
Ordeal, trial by, 259, 421
Ornaments, 197, 199, 204, 205

Painting the body, 222, 329
Palm kernels, 405
Palm-leaf mats, 315, 316
Palm-leaves, 69, 90, 148, 153, 275, 314, 381, 408 *seq.*, 417
Palm oil, 337, 338, 399, 404
Palm wine, 125, 196, 221, 289, 399, 406
Palms, 117, 125, 265, 399, 401
— cocoanut, 117, 314, 400, 408
— Ubili, 314, 407
Park, Mungo, 110
Pastimes, 342
Pawning, 244, 253

Peace ceremonies, 94, 387, 409
Personal adornment, 197, 199, 204
Pestle and mortar, 155
Pests, insect, 119
Phallic worship, 168
Pitch and Toss, 352, 355
Pitfalls, 387
"*Pleiad*", s.s., 112
Pollutions, 60, 61, 182, 192, 266, 271, 381
Polygamy, 228, 229
Population, 117, 180, 231, 236
Pottery, 328
Priests, 54 &c.
Property, personal, 267
— women's, 208, 240
Proverbs, 436
Puberty, 176, 213
Public meeting ground, 48, 150, 155, 190
Pupils (school), 190, 209
Pythons, 43, 107, 108, 157

Quarters of Towns, 150
Queen of the Market, 210, 335
Quorra, River, 110

Rabba, Agulu, 84
Rainfall, 115, 120
Rank (social), 131, 133
Rape, 418
Recreations, 342
Reincarnation, 175, 285, 286
Religion, 33, 35, 151, 208
Religious beliefs, 266
Royal Niger Company, 113, 114

Sacred waters, 40, 41, 184
Sacrifices, 54, 55, 56, 59, 60, 61, 246, 265, 411, 419

INDEX

Sacrifices, human, 60, 72, 126, 252, 292, 385
— Black, 61
— White, 61
Sacrificial system, 54
Salutations, 161, 163
Sanctuary, 247, 249, 297, 416
Sanitation, 149
Scapegoat, 60, 420
Scarification, 192, 224, 225, 331
Schön, Rev. J. F., 111
School attendance, 190, 209
Seabrook, W., 128, 177
Seasons, 118
Second Burial, 181, 199, 269, 276, 280, 283, 289, 409
Secret societies, 89, 366
Shrines, 151, 152, 247
Sickness, 50, 60, 63, 269
Singing, 362
Sin-offering, 59, &c.
Slaves, 143, 192, 248, 275, 385, 397
Slave-trade, 111, 115, 243, 249, 252
Small-pox, 50, 58, 148, 276
Snakes, 43, 107, 108, 157
Society, 121, 192, 228
Songs, 362
Spinning, 325
Spirits, departed, 283, 296
— evil, 59, 61, 183, 413
Sports, 342, 350, 354
"*Soudan*", s.s., 112
Soul, 266, 278, 281
String games, 354
Suicide, 58, 60, 270, 276
Supreme Being, 36, 37, 46, 59, 283, 413
Swimming, 342, 349

Tattooing, 331
Taylor, Rev. J., 69
Teeth, 184

Temperature, 118, 120
Thatching, 315
Titles, 130, 133-5, 143, 193
Tom-toms, 78, 97, 157, 336, 359
Tornadoes, 118, 315
Totemism, 199
Trade, 334
Tree worship, 412, 418
Tremearne, A. J., 299
Trespass offerings, 73
Trial by Ordeal, 259, 421
Tribal marks, 331
Twins, 60, 61, 181, 262, 406

Ubili palms, 314, 327, 407
Umbilical cord, 173, 183
United Africa Company, 113, 114
Usury, 253, 258

Vegetation, 113, 117, 147
Visiting, 131, 161

War, 195, 244, 377
Warneck, John, 214, 413
Water god, 92, 100, 107, 184
Water supply, 149, 159, 203
Waters, sacred, 40, 41
Weaning, 188
Weather, 118
Weaving, 325
Week, Ibo, 151, 334
White sacrifices, 61
Widows, 270, 278, 290, 422
"*Wilberforce*", s.s., 112
Williams, Joseph J., 422
Wilson, Rev. J. L., 422
Witch-wizard, 418
Wives, status of, 140, 194, 229, 268, 384
Women, property of, 208, 240
Women's committees, 209, 225, 335

INDEX

Women's handicrafts, 392
Woodworkers, 322
Worship, 35
— objects of, 246
Wrestling, 47, 347

Yams, 70, 123, 149, 155, 300, 337, 389
Yam stealing, 302
Yaws, 180, 193
Young, Rev. T. Cullen, 35